Communications
in Computer and Information Science 1958

Rationale
The CCIS series is devoted to the publication of proceedings of computer science conferences. Its aim is to efficiently disseminate original research results in informatics in printed and electronic form. While the focus is on publication of peer-reviewed full papers presenting mature work, inclusion of reviewed short papers reporting on work in progress is welcome, too. Besides globally relevant meetings with internationally representative program committees guaranteeing a strict peer-reviewing and paper selection process, conferences run by societies or of high regional or national relevance are also considered for publication.

Topics
The topical scope of CCIS spans the entire spectrum of informatics ranging from foundational topics in the theory of computing to information and communications science and technology and a broad variety of interdisciplinary application fields.

Information for Volume Editors and Authors
Publication in CCIS is free of charge. No royalties are paid, however, we offer registered conference participants temporary free access to the online version of the conference proceedings on SpringerLink (http://link.springer.com) by means of an http referrer from the conference website and/or a number of complimentary printed copies, as specified in the official acceptance email of the event.

CCIS proceedings can be published in time for distribution at conferences or as post-proceedings, and delivered in the form of printed books and/or electronically as USBs and/or e-content licenses for accessing proceedings at SpringerLink. Furthermore, CCIS proceedings are included in the CCIS electronic book series hosted in the SpringerLink digital library at http://link.springer.com/bookseries/7899. Conferences publishing in CCIS are allowed to use Online Conference Service (OCS) for managing the whole proceedings lifecycle (from submission and reviewing to preparing for publication) free of charge.

Publication process
The language of publication is exclusively English. Authors publishing in CCIS have to sign the Springer CCIS copyright transfer form, however, they are free to use their material published in CCIS for substantially changed, more elaborate subsequent publications elsewhere. For the preparation of the camera-ready papers/files, authors have to strictly adhere to the Springer CCIS Authors' Instructions and are strongly encouraged to use the CCIS LaTeX style files or templates.

Abstracting/Indexing
CCIS is abstracted/indexed in DBLP, Google Scholar, EI-Compendex, Mathematical Reviews, SCImago, Scopus. CCIS volumes are also submitted for the inclusion in ISI Proceedings.

How to start
To start the evaluation of your proposal for inclusion in the CCIS series, please send an e-mail to ccis@springer.com.

Constantine Stephanidis · Margherita Antona ·
Stavroula Ntoa · Gavriel Salvendy
Editors

HCI International 2023 – Late Breaking Posters

25th International Conference on Human-Computer Interaction
HCII 2023, Copenhagen, Denmark, July 23–28, 2023
Proceedings, Part II

 Springer

Editors
Constantine Stephanidis
University of Crete and Foundation for
Research and Technology – Hellas (FORTH)
Heraklion, Crete, Greece

Margherita Antona
Foundation for Research and Technology
Hellas (FORTH)
Heraklion, Crete, Greece

Stavroula Ntoa
Foundation for Research and Technology
Hellas (FORTH)
Heraklion, Crete, Greece

Gavriel Salvendy
University of Central Florida
Orlando, FL, USA

ISSN 1865-0929   ISSN 1865-0937 (electronic)
Communications in Computer and Information Science
ISBN 978-3-031-49214-3   ISBN 978-3-031-49215-0 (eBook)
https://doi.org/10.1007/978-3-031-49215-0

This Springer imprint is published by the registered company Springer Nature Switzerland AG
The registered company address is: Gewerbestrasse 11, 6330 Cham, Switzerland

Paper in this product is recyclable.

Foreword

Human-computer interaction (HCI) is acquiring an ever-increasing scientific and industrial importance, as well as having more impact on people's everyday lives, as an ever-growing number of human activities are progressively moving from the physical to the digital world. This process, which has been ongoing for some time now, was further accelerated during the acute period of the COVID-19 pandemic. The HCI International (HCII) conference series, held annually, aims to respond to the compelling need to advance the exchange of knowledge and research and development efforts on the human aspects of design and use of computing systems.

The 25th International Conference on Human-Computer Interaction, HCI International 2023 (HCII 2023), was held in the emerging post-pandemic era as a 'hybrid' event at the AC Bella Sky Hotel and Bella Center, Copenhagen, Denmark, during July 23–28, 2023. It incorporated the 21 thematic areas and affiliated conferences listed below.

A total of 7472 individuals from academia, research institutes, industry, and government agencies from 85 countries submitted contributions, and 1578 papers and 396 posters were included in the volumes of the proceedings that were published just before the start of the conference. Additionally, 267 papers and 133 posters were included in the volumes of the proceedings published after the conference, as "Late Breaking Work". The contributions thoroughly cover the entire field of human-computer interaction, addressing major advances in knowledge and effective use of computers in a variety of application areas. These papers provide academics, researchers, engineers, scientists, practitioners and students with state-of-the-art information on the most recent advances in HCI. The volumes constituting the full set of the HCII 2023 conference proceedings are listed on the following pages.

I would like to thank the Program Board Chairs and the members of the Program Boards of all thematic areas and affiliated conferences for their contribution towards the high scientific quality and overall success of the HCI International 2023 conference. Their manifold support in terms of paper reviewing (single-blind review process, with a minimum of two reviews per submission), session organization and their willingness to act as goodwill ambassadors for the conference is most highly appreciated.

This conference would not have been possible without the continuous and unwavering support and advice of Gavriel Salvendy, founder, General Chair Emeritus, and Scientific Advisor. For his outstanding efforts, I would like to express my sincere appreciation to Abbas Moallem, Communications Chair and Editor of HCI International News.

July 2023   Constantine Stephanidis

HCI International 2023 Thematic Areas and Affiliated Conferences

Thematic Areas

- HCI: Human-Computer Interaction
- HIMI: Human Interface and the Management of Information

Affiliated Conferences

- EPCE: 20th International Conference on Engineering Psychology and Cognitive Ergonomics
- AC: 17th International Conference on Augmented Cognition
- UAHCI: 17th International Conference on Universal Access in Human-Computer Interaction
- CCD: 15th International Conference on Cross-Cultural Design
- SCSM: 15th International Conference on Social Computing and Social Media
- VAMR: 15th International Conference on Virtual, Augmented and Mixed Reality
- DHM: 14th International Conference on Digital Human Modeling and Applications in Health, Safety, Ergonomics and Risk Management
- DUXU: 12th International Conference on Design, User Experience and Usability
- C&C: 11th International Conference on Culture and Computing
- DAPI: 11th International Conference on Distributed, Ambient and Pervasive Interactions
- HCIBGO: 10th International Conference on HCI in Business, Government and Organizations
- LCT: 10th International Conference on Learning and Collaboration Technologies
- ITAP: 9th International Conference on Human Aspects of IT for the Aged Population
- AIS: 5th International Conference on Adaptive Instructional Systems
- HCI-CPT: 5th International Conference on HCI for Cybersecurity, Privacy and Trust
- HCI-Games: 5th International Conference on HCI in Games
- MobiTAS: 5th International Conference on HCI in Mobility, Transport and Automotive Systems
- AI-HCI: 4th International Conference on Artificial Intelligence in HCI
- MOBILE: 4th International Conference on Design, Operation and Evaluation of Mobile Communications

HCI International 2023 Thematic Areas and Affiliated Conferences

Conference Proceedings – Full List of Volumes

1. LNCS 14011, Human-Computer Interaction: Part I, edited by Masaaki Kurosu and Ayako Hashizume
2. LNCS 14012, Human-Computer Interaction: Part II, edited by Masaaki Kurosu and Ayako Hashizume
3. LNCS 14013, Human-Computer Interaction: Part III, edited by Masaaki Kurosu and Ayako Hashizume
4. LNCS 14014, Human-Computer Interaction: Part IV, edited by Masaaki Kurosu and Ayako Hashizume
5. LNCS 14015, Human Interface and the Management of Information: Part I, edited by Hirohiko Mori and Yumi Asahi
6. LNCS 14016, Human Interface and the Management of Information: Part II, edited by Hirohiko Mori and Yumi Asahi
7. LNAI 14017, Engineering Psychology and Cognitive Ergonomics: Part I, edited by Don Harris and Wen-Chin Li
8. LNAI 14018, Engineering Psychology and Cognitive Ergonomics: Part II, edited by Don Harris and Wen-Chin Li
9. LNAI 14019, Augmented Cognition, edited by Dylan D. Schmorrow and Cali M. Fidopiastis
10. LNCS 14020, Universal Access in Human-Computer Interaction: Part I, edited by Margherita Antona and Constantine Stephanidis
11. LNCS 14021, Universal Access in Human-Computer Interaction: Part II, edited by Margherita Antona and Constantine Stephanidis
12. LNCS 14022, Cross-Cultural Design: Part I, edited by Pei-Luen Patrick Rau
13. LNCS 14023, Cross-Cultural Design: Part II, edited by Pei-Luen Patrick Rau
14. LNCS 14024, Cross-Cultural Design: Part III, edited by Pei-Luen Patrick Rau
15. LNCS 14025, Social Computing and Social Media: Part I, edited by Adela Coman and Simona Vasilache
16. LNCS 14026, Social Computing and Social Media: Part II, edited by Adela Coman and Simona Vasilache
17. LNCS 14027, Virtual, Augmented and Mixed Reality, edited by Jessie Y.C. Chen and Gino Fragomeni
18. LNCS 14028, Digital Human Modeling and Applications in Health, Safety, Ergonomics and Risk Management: Part I, edited by Vincent G. Duffy
19. LNCS 14029, Digital Human Modeling and Applications in Health, Safety, Ergonomics and Risk Management: Part II, edited by Vincent G. Duffy
20. LNCS 14030, Design, User Experience, and Usability: Part I, edited by Aaron Marcus, Elizabeth Rosenzweig and Marcelo Soares
21. LNCS 14031, Design, User Experience, and Usability: Part II, edited by Aaron Marcus, Elizabeth Rosenzweig and Marcelo Soares
22. LNCS 14032, Design, User Experience, and Usability: Part III, edited by Aaron Marcus, Elizabeth Rosenzweig and Marcelo Soares

https://2023.hci.international/proceedings

25th International Conference on Human-Computer Interaction (HCII 2023)

The full list with the Program Board Chairs and the members of the Program Boards of all thematic areas and affiliated conferences of HCII2023 is available online at:

http://www.hci.international/board-members-2023.php

HCI International 2024 Conference

The 26th International Conference on Human-Computer Interaction, HCI International 2024, will be held jointly with the affiliated conferences at the Washington Hilton Hotel, Washington, DC, USA, June 29 – July 4, 2024. It will cover a broad spectrum of themes related to Human-Computer Interaction, including theoretical issues, methods, tools, processes, and case studies in HCI design, as well as novel interaction techniques, interfaces, and applications. The proceedings will be published by Springer. More information will be made available on the conference website: http://2024.hci.international/.

General Chair
Prof. Constantine Stephanidis
University of Crete and ICS-FORTH
Heraklion, Crete, Greece
Email: general_chair@2024.hci.international

https://2024.hci.international/

Contents – Part II

Interaction with Robots and Intelligent Agents

Designing Immersive Experiences in Extended Reality and the Metaverse

HCI in Mobility and Aviation

Case Studies in HCI

Contents – Part I

Accessibility, Usability, and UX Design

HCI in Education and Collaborative Learning

HCI for Health and Well-Being

User Experience Design for Cultural Heritage

HCI Research in Human-AI Interaction

Features of Persuasive AI in the Workplace

Elisavet Averkiadi[1]([✉]) and Wietske Van Osch[2]

[1] Michigan State University, East Lansing, MI 48824, USA
averkiad@msu.edu
[2] HEC Montreal, Montréal, QC H3T 2A7, Canada
wietske.van-osch@hec.ca

Abstract. Artificial Intelligence (AI) technologies can act as persuaders when implemented in workplace tools and infrastructure. How users process and react to interacting with features of such AI technologies in the workplace remains ill-understood. Literature in human-AI interaction suggests that cues in the user interface can dictate how users process information communicated by an AI and how receptive they are to being persuaded to change or reinforce their behaviors. Literature from human-AI interaction and an existing systematic framework of the study and design of persuasive technology from human-computer interaction can be applied to examining how users interact with persuasive AI in workplace tools and infrastructure. This paper aims to illustrate the application of such a systematic framework for persuasive technology to the study of persuasive AI technologies in the workplace context. Adapted from the persuasive technology framework, an illustrative vignette of a widely used workplace AI-powered tool is offered to further demonstrate features and principles of systems that include a persuasive AI component.

Keywords: human-AI interaction · persuasive technology · AI-powered workplace

1 Introduction

Organizations have increasingly adopted artificial Intelligence (AI) tools in the workplace. Results from a survey by McKinsey conducted in 2020 indicated that the adoption of AI powered tools in the workplace generates significant value for organizations, which may justify their rapid and wide adoption [1]. AI technologies can also act as persuaders in their interactions with users of AI-powered workplace tools and infrastructure. Through persuasion, AI may support employees successfully fulfilling their role within the organization. For example, an AI-powered enterprise social media system may offer behavioral feedback to employees through a dashboard that improves their productivity habits in meetings. This can further enhance the value that AI-powered workplace tools bring to an organization. The user experience of persuasive AI-powered workplace tools has lacked attention in research [2]. As a result, how users process and react to interacting with features of persuasive AI-powered workplace tools has remained ill-understood.

C. Stephanidis et al. (Eds.): HCII 2023, CCIS 1958, pp. 3–10, 2024.
https://doi.org/10.1007/978-3-031-49215-0_1

Literature in human-AI interaction has explained users' cognitive processing of inter-actions with AI in a generalized context. In their interactions with AI technologies certain aspects of the user interface may trigger cues that can dictate the ways users may be receptive to information an AI communicates [3]. Cues can be influenced by positive or negative stereotypes users have of AI, thereby also guiding how users cognitively process communication they receive from an AI technology [4]. Literature in human-computer interaction has proffered guidance for designing and studying technologies that aim to be persuasive [5–8]. Such literature includes a systematic framework that details fea-tures, principles, and assumptions for persuasive technology [8]. The goal of this paper is to piece together the workplace context of AI-powered tools and infrastructure with literature in human-AI interaction and the systematic framework for persuasive tech-nology proposed in human-computer interaction. With this approach, this paper offers an overview of features and characteristics of persuasive AI in the workplace. What follows is an outline of literature discussing persuasion and persuasive technology, fol-lowed by an understanding of AI and its persuasive capabilities found in the intersection between social psychology, human-computer interaction, and human-AI interaction. Finally, through a vignette using Microsoft's Viva Insights system, the application of the persuasive technology systematic framework to identify examples of features and principles of systems that include a persuasive AI component is demonstrated, followed by a discussion on this application.

2 Background

2.1 Overview of Persuasion and Persuasive Technology

Persuasion can generally be defined as an attempt to influence another person's atti-tude or behavior, without the use of coercion or deception [9]. According to definitions found in literature, the process of persuasion must be a successful attempt at influencing, where persuading is done intentionally, volitional action is available to the persuadee, and a change in attitude or behavior is the result of the interaction [9]. Technologies that are designed to influence users' attitudes or behaviors are referred to as 'Persua-sive Technology', which extends persuasion as it is known in social psychology to human-computer interaction. The study and design of such technologies originated as 'Captology' (Computers as Persuasive Technology) and is defined as "the study of com-puters as persuasive technologies" where a persuasive computer refers to "an interactive technology that changes a person's attitudes or behaviors" [10]. The study of persuasive computers (or technology overall) has been developed to a systematic framework, that can be applied in the study or design of persuasive technology [8]. The framework defines persuasive technology (PT) as "computerized software or information systems designed to reinforce, change or shape attitudes or behaviors or both without using coercion or deception" [8].

A Framework for Persuasive Technology Study and Design. To guide researchers and practitioners through the study or design of PT, the authors of the systematic frame-work provide a mapping of categories of features to system principles based on assump-tions about the role of users in the persuasion process, persuasion strategies technologies employ, and assumed features of persuasion in technology (see Table 1) [8].

Table 1. PT system features overview, summarized and adapted from Oinas-Kukkonen & Harjumaa, 2008

System Feature	Definition	Principle
Primary Task Support	System provides content that enables and assists user to carry out their primary tasks	Reduction, tunneling, tailoring, personalization, self-monitoring, simulation, and rehearsal
Dialogue Support	System features human-computer dialogue that supports users in progressing to target behaviors	Praise, rewards, reminders, suggestions, similarity, liking, and social role
System Credibility Support	System leverages credibility to be more persuasive	Trustworthiness, expertise, surface credibility, real-world feel, authority, third-party endorsements, and verifiability
Social Support	System uses social influence strategies	Social learning, social comparison, normative influence, social facilitation, cooperation, competition, and recognition

2.2 Persuasive AI Technology

Research on how an AI technology may persuade its users is in its infancy. Persuasive AI technology can be described as a persuasive technology that includes an AI component. AI may act as a persuader and facilitate a persuasive user experience due to its distinct characteristics. [5] describe 'persuasion profiles' in systems that adapt to user differences. Persuasion profiles are defined as: "collections of expected effects of different influence strategies for a specific individual" [5]. The capability to create such profiles involves the triangulation of user activity data and persuasion histories to develop an influence strategy that is tailored to an individual user, essentially personalizing the experience of persuasion. The result is the adaptive system possesses the intelligence of how to persuade, with what information, and when. The computational power AI technologies to facilitate the creation and maintenance of 'persuasion profiles' is another distinct characteristic of persuasive AI.

Cues involved in the human-to-human persuasion process potentially have different effects. Literature in human-AI interaction has explored the significance of cues in how users process information communicated by an AI technology. It is suggested that users may use a *machine heuristic*, where negative or positive stereotypes of AI guide their judgements about their interactions with AI technologies [4]. Additional research in the human-AI interaction literature has discussed how AI may *complicate* persuasion. Due to cues in the user interface, users may be triggered to process information differently based on whether there is obvious involvement of an AI, or if there is ambiguity about whether the user is interacting with AI or a human. These indicators may complicate persuasion as users may be receptive to a human or an AI source in different ways, thereby altering the persuasion process and outcomes.

Such processes also raise questions about how users may respond differently to communication of the same information by an AI versus a human: would employees be receptive to feedback communicated by their manager in the same way an AI would communicate feedback? While such a question requires empirical study, existing research has demonstrated there is a difference in how humans treat other humans versus AI. At a conceptual level, the Computers Are Social Actors paradigm has conceptualized such a difference indicating that humans adapt scripts to interacting with AI and technology in general, that deviates from scripts they use to interact with humans [11, 12]. Such research makes a case for not only the importance of cues in a user interface for how users may be receptive and process persuasion from an AI, but also the favorability for employing AI-powered tools and infrastructure in the workplace to enhance employee success.

Distinct differences exist that allow an AI to effectively persuade in the digital space. Oinas-Kukkonen and Harjumaa indicate one of the assumptions of persuasive technology is that it is 'never neutral', meaning it is persuading its users constantly in various ways [8]. To arrive to a strategy for how to influence a user, technology must be 'always' listening and observing – that is, while the user interacts with the technology regardless of engaging in the behavior that is intended to be influenced. AI systems may use this active learning to process data collected and compute the appropriate influence strategies [5]. The use of digital tools in a workplace environment is necessary for employees to participate and contribute effectively to their role. This means an AI technology has a constant stream of data and feedback to learn from, as well as ample opportunity to interact with users - in terms of time and digital spaces.

3 Workplace Tools and Persuasive AI Technology Design: Microsoft Viva Insights

Viva is an AI powered persuasive workplace behavior feedback tool provided by Microsoft. Viva connects to the Microsoft ecosystem of workplace tools and infrastructure and generates insights that are valuable to multiple members in an organization. Microsoft defines Viva as an "employee experience platform within Microsoft 365 and Microsoft Teams that brings together communications, knowledge, learning, resources, and insights into the flow of work" [13]. Viva includes multiple applications that Microsoft categorizes into "Connection", "Insight", "Purpose", "Growth", and "Role-based experiences" [13].

The "Insight" category is of particular interest for illustrating how an AI tool in the workplace may persuade users. Similarly to aforementioned 'persuasion profiles' [5], Viva Insight is based on triangulated data from "workplace activities, communication behaviors and collaboration patterns" that help to empower employees in manager or leadership roles to improve business outcomes, and at the same time for employees in any role to achieve personal well-being, effectiveness, and collaboration goals. With such features, Viva Insight can provide a revealing vignette for how a persuasive AI tool that provides behavioral feedback encompasses the system features and system principles put forth by [8] in their framework for the study and design of persuasive technology (See Table 1 for overview). With example screen-captures from the Microsoft Viva website, the implementation of these system features and principles is outlined.

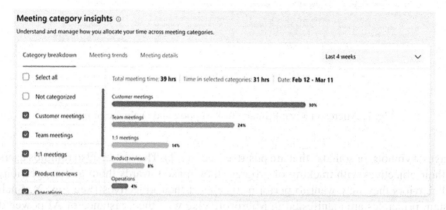

Fig. 1. Microsoft Viva; Primary Task Support

3.1 Primary Task Support

Primary Task Support in Oinas-Kukkonen and Harjumaa's framework indicates the system must provide "meaningful content for the user" to assist users in carrying out their primary tasks [8]. Observing features included in the "Productivity" and "Wellbeing" tabs in Viva Insights, primary task support for principles such as, for example, Personalization where "personalized content and services for its users" are provided, or Self-monitoring opportunities where "means for users to track their performance or status" are offered by the system [8]. Figures 1 and 2 provide example screenshots of how Primary Task Support is included in this AI-powered persuasive system. The system reduces the steps that users must follow to perform target behaviors, and tunnels users through the process of changing their behavior in ways that are aligned with their Primary tasks (i.e., main objectives) by providing suggestions based on insights (see Fig. 2). Furthermore, the system tailors the information that users are exposed to, personalizes the content and services they are shown, and simulates the target behaviors by displaying links between the antecedents and outcomes of these desired behaviors (see Fig. 1).

3.2 Dialogue Support

According to the Persuasive Technology systematic framework, dialogue support in a persuasive system should assist users to "keep moving towards their goal or target behavior" where computer-human dialogue is implemented [8]. Viva Insights includes multiple human-computer dialogue support principles, as outlined in the framework for persuasive systems. The system praises its users with feedback in the form of "words,

Fig. 2. Microsoft Viva; Primary Task Support and Dialogue Support

images, symbols, or sounds" that are positive (see Fig. 1). The system also reminds users of their objectives with tracking of progress they make towards them and suggestions of behaviors they may want to perform to support their objectives (See Fig. 2). Such system principles are manifested in Microsoft Viva with the assistance of AI powered behavior feedback that aims to persuade users to alter their behaviors or attitudes.

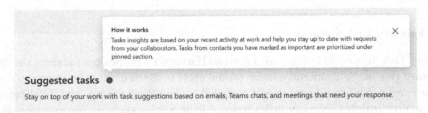

Fig. 3. Microsoft Viva; System Credibility Support

3.3 System Credibility Support

System credibility support features entail the design of a system that is "more credible and thus more persuasive" [8]. Viva Insights include multiple such features through the system principles implemented, as detailed in the PT framework [8]. Viva Insights provides credibility information with the personalized insights that are accompanied by suggestions (see Fig. 3). Additionally, Viva Insights contains surface credibility with the clear indication of a "competent look and feel" [8], featuring analytics visualizations that effectively communicate insights and feedback.

3.4 Social Support

Viva Insights also makes use of social influence strategies, adapted to system principles [8]. By providing users with the chance to offer "praise" to co-workers, connect with members of the organization that may have beneficial outcomes, and data analytics on existing collaborations, Viva Insights includes Social Support features. For example, users can continue to achieve their target behavior by cooperation via the collaboration tab analytics in Viva Insights. Viva Insights also inherently provides social learning opportunities, since they indicate to users that their suggestions are generated based on a triangulation of various data points fed by their interaction with the technology.

4 Discussion

Literature explored in previous sections has illuminated how an AI-powered technology tool can achieve persuasive qualities. Applying this to the workplace, features of persuasive AI can be identified. By employing the systematic framework developed by Oinas-Kukkonen and Harjumma, the way that persuasive AI in a workplace tool such as Microsoft Viva Insights was explained. Microsoft Viva Insights persuasive AI influences its users to change or progress towards target behaviors. The vignette identifies how each of the four system features found in [8] framework for persuasive technology exist in the system, and how some of their principles are implemented. Primary task support is implemented with various system principles present, such as reduction, tunneling, tailoring, personalization, and self-monitoring. Dialogue support can be found by system principles present that indicated praising, reminders, and suggestion. System credibility support presents with expertise and surface credibility system principles, while social support is displayed through cooperation and social learning. Figures 1, 2 and 3 provided screen captures to depict how each of these feature categories appear in Microsoft Viva Insights user interface.

Cues in the user interface of a workplace tool that features an AI component can help facilitate users processing of information appropriately. Users can be receptive to persuasion from an AI source in a way that is different from a human source. Perception that an AI has credibility help to create receptivity to persuasive attempts. For example, if an AI-powered tool such as Microsoft Viva recommends the user schedules more time between their meetings to improve their productivity and attentiveness when attending meetings may be processed with acceptance and willingness to perform the behavior due to the 'obvious' nature of the AI component in the Microsoft Viva user interface. Stereotypes may influence how cues are processed [4] and have potential to result in the successful persuasion of users by an AI.

The applicability of the systematic framework for persuasive technology to persuasive AI is apparent, yet research on how the process of persuasion occurs using these features remains to be demonstrated. Future research in this line of study must empirically investigate the processing of experiencing interacting with a persuasive AI. A better understanding of such processing can inform the subsequent further investigation and design of effective and efficient persuasive AI tools and infrastructure in the workplace.

Acknowledgement. This project was funded in part by the National Science Foundation under grant IIS-1749018.

References

1. Balakrishnan, T., Chui, M., Hall, B., Henke, N.: Global survey: the state of AI in 2020. McKinsey, November 2020. https://www.mckinsey.com/business-functions/mckinsey-analyt ics/our-insights/global-survey-the-state-of-ai-in-2020. Accessed 13 June 2023
2. Hanses, S., Wang, J.: How do users interact with AI features in the workplace? Understanding the AI feature user journey in enterprise. In: Extended Abstracts of the 2022 CHI Conference on Human Factors in Computing Systems, in CHI EA 2022, New York, NY, USA, pp. 1–7. Association for Computing Machinery, April 2022. https://doi.org/10.1145/3491101.350 3567
3. Dehnert, M., Mongeau, P.A.: Persuasion in the age of Artificial Intelligence (AI): theories and complications of AI-based persuasion. Hum. Commun. Res. **48**(3), 386–403 (2022). https://doi.org/10.1093/hcr/hqac006
4. Sundar, S.S.: Rise of machine agency: a framework for studying the psychology of Human–AI Interaction (HAII). J. Comput.-Mediat. Commun. **25**, 74–88 (2020). https://doi.org/10.1093/jcmc/zmz026
5. Kaptein, M., Eckles, D.: Selecting effective means to any end: futures and ethics of persuasion profiling. In: Ploug, T., Hasle, P., Oinas-Kukkonen, H. (eds.) Persuasive Technology. LNCS, vol. 6137, pp. 82–93. Springer, Heidelberg (2010). https://doi.org/10.1007/978-3-642-13226-1_10
6. Torning, K., Oinas-Kukkonen, H.: Persuasive system design: state of the art and future directions. In: Proceedings of the 4th International Conference on Persuasive Technology, in Persuasive 2009, New York, NY, USA. Association for Computing Machinery, pp. 1–8, April 2009. https://doi.org/10.1145/1541948.1541989
7. Redström, J.: Persuasive design: fringes and foundations. In: IJsselsteijn, W.A., de Kort, Y.A.W., Midden, C., Eggen, B., van den Hoven, E. (eds.) PERSUASIVE 2006. LNCS, vol. 3962, pp. 112–122. Springer, Heidelberg (2006). https://doi.org/10.1007/11755494_17
8. Oinas-Kukkonen, H., Harjumaa, M.: A systematic framework for designing and evaluating persuasive systems. In: Oinas-Kukkonen, H., Hasle, P., Harjumaa, M., Segerståhl, K., Øhrstrøm, P. (eds.) PERSUASIVE 2008. LNCS, vol. 5033, pp. 164–176. Springer, Heidelberg (2008). https://doi.org/10.1007/978-3-540-68504-3_15
9. O'Keefe, D.J.: Persuasion: Theory and Research, 3rd edn. Sage Publications, New York (2015)
10. Fogg, B.J.: Captology: the study of computers as persuasive technologies. In: CHI 98 Conference Summary on Human Factors in Computing Systems, in CHI 1998, New York, NY, USA, p. 385. Association for Computing Machinery, April 1998. https://doi.org/10.1145/286498.286852
11. Nass, C., Steuer, J., Tauber, E.R.: Computers are social actors. In: Proceedings of the SIGCHI Conference on Human Factors in Computing Systems, in CHI 1994, New York, NY, USA, pp. 72–78. Association for Computing Machinery, April 1994. https://doi.org/10.1145/191666.191703
12. Gambino, A., Fox, J., Ratan, R.: Building a stronger CASA: extending the computers are social actors paradigm. Hum.-Mach. Commun. **1**(1), 71–86 (2020). https://doi.org/10.30658/hmc.1.5
13. Microsoft, "Microsoft Viva" (2023). https://www.microsoft.com/en-us/microsoft-viva. Accessed 31 Mar 2023

NLP in Healthcare: Developing Interactive Integrated Collaborative Assistants

Tamara Babaian[⊠] and Jennifer Xu

Bentley University, Waltham, MA 02452, USA
{tbabaian,jxu}@bentley.edu

Abstract. AI and Deep Learning have led to the development of many tools for healthcare and medicine: image-based diagnostic tools, note-taking aids automatically transcribing speech, medical risk assessment and decision-support applications based on the patient parameters stored within Electronic Health Record (EHR) systems. The astonishing success of Large Language Model-based generative AI has further demonstrated a great potential for employing AI-based tools in many domains of human activity, including healthcare and public health. At this point, the majority of AI applications in healthcare are tools that work autonomously, and the physicians and medical personnel are called to use them as an input in their decision making outside of their use of EHR systems. We discuss the opportunities and challenges of employing AI-based capabilities within EHRs and outline a research roadmap for creating interactive collaborative integrated EHR assistant applications. We discuss parallels with our prior work in addressing usability of enterprise resource planning systems.

Keywords: Healthcare AI · NLP · EHR

1 Introduction

AI and Deep Learning have led to development of many tools for healthcare and medicine: image-based diagnostic tools [1], note-taking aids automatically transcribing speech [2], medical risk assessment applications based on the patient parameters stored within Electronic Health Record systems (EHR) [3]. The astonishing success of Large Language Model-based generative AI has further demonstrated a great potential for employing AI-based tools in many domains of human activity, including healthcare and public health [4]. At this point, the majority of AI applications in healthcare are tools that work autonomously, and the physicians and medical personnel are called to use them as an input in their decision making outside of their use of EHR systems. Furthermore, the input from these systems is usually generated and presented outside of a broader context of the daily clinical work, which limits both its usefulness to the physicians, as well as the physician's trust in the presented assessment [6].

There are potentially great advantages from employing AI in an interactive setting to support communication, help users make better, more informed decisions, help practitioners identify trends, and more. Successful integration of the wealth of the patient data

C. Stephanidis et al. (Eds.): HCII 2023, CCIS 1958, pp. 11–16, 2024.
https://doi.org/10.1007/978-3-031-49215-0_2

regarding medical care history and disease progression, combined with the knowledge of institutional methods, treatments, outcomes, medications and other information, can be leveraged to create powerful assistants to both medical professionals and patients, to improve clinical practice and reduce costs.

However, development of successful AI-based applications poses additional challenges, which can create a barrier for technology adoption by users. The acknowledged challenges of using AI in healthcare practice include selection of appropriate data to train machine learning models, providing transparency or explanations for the predictions, identifying and addressing ethical and legal risks of using AI in practice [5]. Furthermore, from the user interface perspective, there are challenges related to the effective human-computer communication, including selecting the format, content, and timing of such communication, providing the right amount of context and situational awareness. AI-specific communication issues include effective presentation of uncertainty and explanations for model-generated predictions. Many of these problems can be studied within the scope of frameworks of Human-Computer Collaboration [7, 8, 18] and Human-AI Interaction [9], while continuing to be in the center of ongoing research.

2 Opportunities for Using NLP in the Context of EHR – A Roadmap for Design Research

Electronic Health Records (EHR) systems are repositories of structured patient information, as well as vast amount of information stored in a form of unstructured text: clinical notes, observations, patient histories, patient-doctor communication and more. Yet, this information largely remains a repository that doctors must explore on their own [10], and studies, as well as existing anecdotal evidence show that healthcare practitioners are often overwhelmed by the amount of information, and extracting the relevant part of it remains a challenging task [11]. While the field of NLP has advanced tremendously with the development of transformer-based language models [12], these advancements have not been used for integrated information extraction, summarization, and question answering within EHRs. Bringing the advances of NLP to the forefront of a regular medical practice has a potential for greatly enhancing medical decision-making, as well as improving communication between healthcare workers and patients.

Building on our experience in investigating a range of technology and human factors critical for creating workplace systems that integrate AI [13], interactive visualizations, and data mining into enterprise and other workplace systems [14, 15, 21], we aim to investigate bringing NLP capabilities to EHR systems [10] in order to aid patient diagnosis and treatment. With the rapid advancements in NLP technology in the past three years, it is now ripe for being used for creating interactive doctor's assistants that use the wealth of patient record information stored within EHR and externally.

The following capabilities will enhance physician's preparedness as it relates to individual patient treatment:

- identifying and integrating patient information from EHR that is relevant to a specific concern or goal,
- identifying relevant knowledge related to the goal or concern, personalized for the patient's condition, and

- providing an effective interactive visual representation of that information upon a physician's request.

Successful tailoring of AI and NLP within a multimodal workplace EHR interface will require a careful study of human-computer and human-AI interaction within the domain of patient care. The Design Research methodology [16, 17] informed by the Human-Computer Collaboration [7, 8, 18] and Human-AI Interaction [9, 19] frameworks implies the need to perform the following:

1. study the environment in which EHRs are being used, the medical objectives behind such use, and the specific requirements on the user interfaces for information extraction and summarization of EHR data imposed by the patient care context,
2. investigate EHR usability and other characteristics that may create barriers to effective use of clinical notes and patient histories, understand how the unstructured textual data can be best integrated, processed, and presented from the standpoint of its users to support medical tasks,
3. investigate the ethical aspects surrounding the use of NLP for healthcare decision making from the theoretical and practical standpoints,
4. study the state-of-the-art in the NLP for healthcare tools and assess their characteristics (accuracy, runtime performance, transparency, explainability) with respect to the needs of the specific user tasks and contexts,
5. design, prototype, and test user-system interaction interfaces in a design-evaluate cycle.

The project must start with and continually involve input from active EHR users; interviews and observations of medical practitioners must be analyzed to develop design principles and interface prototypes. Finally, the prototypes should be evaluated by getting feedback from current EHR users and conducting laboratory evaluations of the prototypes.

Relative to the Design Research Framework depicted in Fig. 1, items 1 and 2 above contribute to the relevance cycle and provide the evidentiary base for the rationale of the chosen designs. Item 3 involves a study of the relevant theoretical underpinnings in ethics as well as the state of the current practice of it within EHR. Looking at the ethics-related issues with the theoretical lens in addition to observations from the current practice will uncover opportunities for developing evaluation methods targeting ethical principles embedded in software. Items 4 and 5 will produce novel design principles, prototypes, and other foundational knowledge and methodological tools, including models, algorithms and evaluation methods. The developed contributions related to embedding LLM/generative AI-based NLP in interactive applications will likely have applicability beyond healthcare domain.

2.1 Lessons from Prior Research

EHRs are large enterprise-wide systems used by clinicians, patients and hospital administrators. Several parallels as well as contrasting factors exist between EHRs and Enterprise Resource Planning (ERP) systems, such as SAP and Oracle, which are used to support and automate a wide range of organizational practices. In this regard, it is interesting to

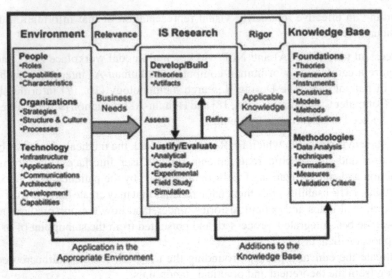

Fig. 1. Information systems research framework (from Hevner et al. 2004)

review lessons learnt from our prior research into ERP usability [14, 15, 20, 21], and discuss how they may apply in the context of this study. We focus on the three meta-level observations here.

- *Theory of collaboration and its adaptation to human-computer collaboration had a central importance at all stages of the ERP Usability study. Its use as a set of unifying guiding principles throughout all stages enabled new insights into the causes of usability breakdowns, development of design principles and new methods for achieving greater usability through collaboration, design and evaluation of prototype user interfaces.*

  EHRs are also enterprise-wide multi-user organizational systems, hence collaboration theory will also be relevant here. However, aside from informing our view of the interactions of an individual user with the system, there is a need to broaden the scope to the collaborative interactions between teams of doctors, a patient, and potentially other stakeholders within an EHR. At the same time, as already mentioned here and also by others [22], application of Machine Learning (ML) within information systems brings its own set of socio-technical factors that must inform the design and evaluation of new AI-based artifacts. Most importantly, they must address trust issues that arise from using opaque ML models that involve uncertainty in aiding human decision-making, as well as concerns for data security and ethical use that have critical importance within the healthcare domain.

- *Novel interfaces that successfully addressed usability problems required the design of additional infrastructure in the form of data representations and algorithms to be built into the system and tightly integrated with the rest of it. In other words, creating effective system-user collaboration must be addressed as a part of the overall system design as opposed as a late-stage fine-tuning activity.*

As with implementing collaboration within ERP, effective, trustworthy, and ethical use of AI/ML within EHR systems must be addressed from the early stages of development, including development of the AI/ML components. Defining the scope of ML predictions and suggestions, the content and sources of data used to train ML models can be formulated through design principles grounded in theory and empirical considerations involving different stakeholders. A review of studies of deployed clinician-facing systems [22] reveals that.

- *Off-the-shelf visualization components, when integrated within the scope of a specific task, require substantial fine-tuning and sometimes re-design in order to achieve user adoption and task performance gains.*

As often, integration of novel user interface components, no matter how effective they are in a laboratory setting, into the context of a complex information system does not lead to immediate performance gains in real world and must undergo evaluation and fine-tuning for the specific task and system context prior to such integration. This is exemplified by the case of using a diagram-based visual interface for exploring data associations within ERP, reported in [15]. Similarly, the healthcare system context imposes specific requirements on interface components and requires attention, for example, to interoperability with different sources of data, format and timing of user interaction.

3   Conclusion

Integrating new AI/ML/NLP-based methods within Electronic Health Records (EHRs) to create interactive doctor's assistants has a potential to enhance clinical decision making and communication within and between healthcare professionals and patients. The presented research roadmap outlines the key components of a study aimed at systematically investigating and developing solutions to sociotechnical challenges and ethical risks of employing AI-based solutions in healthcare. Methodological lessons from an earlier design research study in ERP Usability suggest that using a set of theory-based guiding principles throughout different stages of a design research project will be beneficial in addressing the problems of human-computer and human-AI interaction, as well as the ethical use of data. Empirical evaluations and field studies with EHR stakeholders are key to achieving adoption and effectiveness of collaborative interactive EHR assistants.

References

1. Rezaei, Z.: A review on image-based approaches for breast cancer detection, segmentation, and classification. Expert Syst. Appl. **182**, 115204 (2021). https://doi.org/10.1016/j.eswa.2021.115204
2. Blackley, S.V., Schubert, V.D., Goss, F.R., Al Assad, W., Garabedian, P.M., Zhou, L.: Physician use of speech recognition versus typing in clinical documentation: a controlled observational study. Int. J. Med. Informatics **141**, 104178 (2020). https://doi.org/10.1016/j.ijmedinf.2020.104178
3. Saleh, E., et al.: Learning ensemble classifiers for diabetic retinopathy assessment. Artif. Intell. Med. **85**, 50–63 (2018). https://doi.org/10.1016/j.artmed.2017.09.006

4. Biswas, S.S.: Role of chat GPT in public health. Ann. Biomed. Eng. **51**, 868–869 (2023). https://doi.org/10.1007/s10439-023-03172-7
5. Wiens, J., et al.: Do no harm: a roadmap for responsible machine learning for health care. Nat. Med. **25**, 1337–1340 (2019). https://doi.org/10.1038/s41591-019-0548-6
6. Rajpurkar, P., Chen, E., Banerjee, O., Topol, E.J.: AI in health and medicine. Nat. Med. **28**, 31–38 (2022). https://doi.org/10.1038/s41591-021-01614-0
7. Grosz, B.J.: Beyond mice and menus. Proc. Am. Philos. Soc. **149**, 529–543 (2005)
8. Lucas, W., Babaian, T.: The collaborative critique: an inspection method for expert evaluation of user interfaces. Int. J. Hum.-Comput. Interact. **31**, 843–859 (2015). https://doi.org/10.1080/10447318.2015.1067500
9. Amershi, S., et al.: Guidelines for Human-AI interaction. In: Proceedings of the 2019 CHI Conference on Human Factors in Computing Systems - CHI 2019, pp. 1–13. ACM Press, Glasgow, Scotland UK (2019). https://doi.org/10.1145/3290605.3300233
10. Li, I., et al.: Neural natural language processing for unstructured data in electronic health records: a review. Comput. Sci. Rev. **46**, 100511 (2022). https://doi.org/10.1016/j.cosrev.2022.100511
11. Amir, O., Grosz, B.J., Gajos, K.Z., Swenson, S.M., Sanders, L.M.: From care plans to care coordination: opportunities for computer support of teamwork in complex healthcare. In: Proceedings of the 33rd Annual ACM Conference on Human Factors in Computing Systems, pp. 1419–1428. Association for Computing Machinery, New York, NY, USA (2015). https://doi.org/10.1145/2702123.2702320
12. Devlin, J., Chang, M.-W., Lee, K., Toutanova, K.: BERT: pre-training of deep bidirectional transformers for language understanding. http://arxiv.org/abs/1810.04805 (2019). https://doi.org/10.48550/arXiv.1810.04805
13. Babaian, T., Grosz, B.J., Shieber, S.M.: A writer's collaborative assistant. In: Proceedings of Intelligent User Interfaces Conference (IUI-2002), pp. 7–14. ACM Press (2002)
14. Babaian, T., Xu, J., Lucas, W.: ERP prototype with built-in task and process support. Eur. J. Inf. Syst. **27**, 189–206 (2018). https://doi.org/10.1057/s41303-017-0060-3
15. Babaian, T., Lucas, W., Chircu, A.: Mapping data associations in enterprise systems. In: Tulu, B., Djamasbi, S., Leroy, G. (eds.) Extending the Boundaries of Design Science Theory and Practice, pp. 254–268. Springer, Cham (2019). https://doi.org/10.1007/978-3-030-19504-5_17
16. Hevner, A., Chatterjee, S.: Design science research in information systems. In: Design Research in Information Systems, pp. 9–22. Springer, Boston (2010). https://doi.org/10.1007/978-1-4419-5653-8_2
17. Hevner, A., March, S., Park, J., Ram, S.: Design science in information systems research. MIS Q. **28**, 75–105 (2004)
18. Grosz, B.J.: Collaborative systems: AAAI presidential address. AI Mag. **17**, 67–85 (1996)
19. Endsley, M.R.: Supporting Human-AI teams: transparency, explainability, and situation awareness. Comput. Hum. Behav. **140**, 107574 (2023). https://doi.org/10.1016/j.chb.2022.107574
20. Babaian, T., Lucas, W., Xu, J., Topi, H.: Usability through system-user collaboration. In: Winter, R., Zhao, J.L., Aier, S. (eds.) Global Perspectives on Design Science Research, DESRIST 2010. LNCS, vol. 6105. Springer, Heidelberg (2010). https://doi.org/10.1007/978-3-642-13335-0_27
21. Xu, J.J., Topi, H.: A conceptual model for user-system collaboration: enhancing usability of complex information systems. Commun. Assoc. Inf. Syst. **41**(1), 31 (2017)
22. Zając, H., Li, D., Dai, X., Carlsen, J., Kensing, F., Andersen F.: Clinician-facing AI in the wild: taking stock of the sociotechnical challenges and opportunities for HCI. ACM Trans. Comput.-Hum. Interact. **30**(2), 39 (2023). Article 33, https://doi.org/10.1145/3582430

Artificial Intelligence (AI) Facilitated Data-Driven Design Thinking

Samir Kumar Dash[(⊠)] [ID]

Cisco Systems (India) Pvt. Ltd., Bengaluru, Karnataka, India
samdash@cisco.com

Abstract. This paper describes an approach to integrating Design-Thinking (DT) and User-Centered Design Process (UCD) activities into a process that is facilitated by artificial intelligence (AI) for improved collaboration and data-driven decision-making at a faster pace, so as to improve the adoption. It also aims to identify if the AI can facilitate design thinking sessions and act as a collaborator to help the participants make decisions based on data faster. The proposed concept has been tested by developing an AI powered whiteboard software using Open AI's APIs and a custom ML model on user-profile data to manage it, which was then run by a group of users for their Design-Thinking session for testing and accessing its success in enhancing the design process. The AI-facilitated design-thinking process produced desirable outcomes in significantly less time and helped speed up the Design-Thinking process.

Keywords: Design thinking · persona · artificial intelligence

1 Introduction

Recently, AI has been rapidly evolving and making significant contributions across various industries and domains. Recognizing its potential to revolutionize practices such as Design Thinking (DT) and user-centered design (UCD), a comprehensive research initiative has been made through a two-phased approach, we sought to uncover insights and evaluate the effectiveness of AI in improving these crucial methodologies. By leveraging the power of AI, we aimed to discover areas where AI can aid user for quicker adoption through for automation, saving time and effort, and ultimately driving better outcomes in the realm of DT and UCD.

2 Phase 1 – Discover and Prioritizing the Problem to Address

2.1 Background (Phase 1)

The first phase of the research was to identify the areas that are frictions for wider adoption of Design Thinking, especially for the entrepreneurs, startup founders and Small and Medium Enterprises (SME) owners.

© The Author(s), under exclusive license to Springer Nature Switzerland AG 2024
C. Stephanidis et al. (Eds.): HCII 2023, CCIS 1958, pp. 17–24, 2024.
https://doi.org/10.1007/978-3-031-49215-0_3

18   S. K. Dash

2.2   Method (Phase 1)

Participants and Experimental Design. Twelve tech-startup founders, entrepreneurs, and Small and Medium Enterprises (SMEs) owners from three cities, namely Bhubaneswar, Bangalore, and Rourkela in India, participated in a survey on the challenges they face while using Design Thinking (DT) or any other User-centered Design Process (UCD) approaches to come up with their solution.

Task and Materials. The participants were asked to fill in a survey with 20 multiple choice questions. The questions were designed to understand the participant's usage, pain-points, challenges in using of DT or UCD methodologies in their organizations to solve the business problem or empathize users. The survey questions were shared over email link to Google form.

2.3   Results and Analysis (Phase 1)

Analyzing the responses from the participants, we were able to identify the challenges using the Design Thinking methodologies in organizations (Fig. 1).

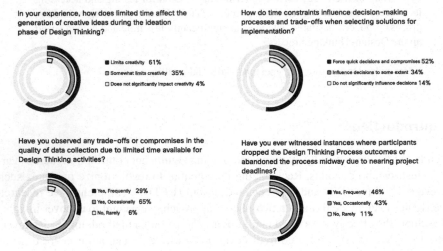

Fig. 1. Key outcome from the survey reflecting the impact of time constraint on adoption and quality of outcome.

The top one in the list is users challenge in not having enough time for DT, is mentioned by 22.7% of the respondents as their biggest problem with the Design Thinking process. 61% of participants believed that the lack of sufficient time in their DT, limits creativity, and 52% believed that the time constraints influenced decision-making processes and trade-off through force quick decisions and compromises. Also 65% believed that quality of outcome of DT was occasionally impacted due to time constraints forcing trade-offs. 42% believed that due to nearing project deadlines, the organizations dropped the Design Thinking Process outcomes or abandoned the process midway.

2.4   Result and Analysis

We recognized that small and medium business owners struggled with the amount of time required to participate in DT sessions and complete the necessary preparatory work.

3   Phase 2 - Investigating the Effectiveness of AI in Supporting User Overcoming the Challenge

3.1   Background (Phase 2)

Based on outcome of phase-1 of this research, one of the key challenges identified in design thinking was the constraint of time. To address this challenge, we explored the option to use AI to assist users in overcoming time constraints through automation to aid the users to save time while getting quality output based on context specific data driven insights generated and provide intelligent recommendations to help users save time and effort.

3.2   Method (Phase 2)

Participants and Experimental Design. We used the same set of users to select 12 users and formed four groups with each group having 3 members. Out of these two groups used AI to support them in various tasks for each session of DT, where as the other two groups did not use any AI support and carried out activities traditionally. By comparing the approaches of the two sets of groups, this research methodology enabled an evaluation of the effectiveness and efficiency of utilizing AI in the DT process. The first set of groups relied on manual creation and qualitative studies, while the second set leveraged AI to speed up and enhance certain aspects of the process, such as persona creation and data analysis.

For this purpose, to provide AI support to participants, basic software was developed using PHP and JQuery, supporting Rest API calls using JSON. We used Open AI's APIs and a custom ML model on user-profile data, which was then run by the group of users for their Design-Thinking session for testing and accessing its success in enhancing the design process. The software leveraged the APIs of *OpenAI* and used custom datasets comprising 20 job roles and professions across four industries in India.

Its user interface offered a range of options for users to select from among various tasks within the "Design Thinking" process. Through advanced natural language processing (NLP) techniques, the software could analyse input context, diary entries, or demographic data to create empathy maps and persona maps (Fig. 2).

Tasks and Materials. Each group is asked to carry out three DT sessions to empathise with and create personas for target users of specific demographics using three different experiments:

1. Creation of a Proto-Persona
2. Persona created with Qualitative Interviews
3. Persona Created from Empathy Maps that were built from Users Diary-Studies.

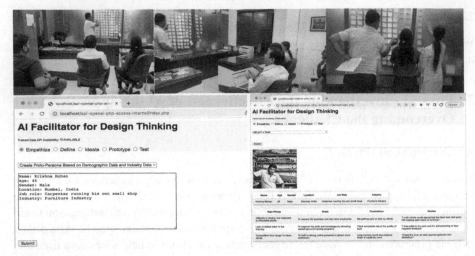

Fig. 2. Two pairs out of four groups used AI Facilitator software to quickly generate, synthesis data to come up with final persona map, whereas the other two pairs did not use AI to build persona, across all 3 sessions.

For each of the above experiments, several tasks were planned for the users, to come up with the final persona map as outcome. For each group, the tasks are listed as per the following table (Table 1).

Table 1. List of tasks to complete by each group over 3 experiments.

Exp #	Experiment Name	Step #	Type	Individual or Group Activity?	Expected Duration (Hours)	Task Description
1	Creation of a Proto-Persona	1	Preparation	Individual	4	Secondary Research + Study/ Analyse Data
		2	Core Activity	Individual	2	Each participant will create 1 Proto-Persona
		3	Core Activity	Group	2	Analyse + Synthesis previous step outcome to create pre-final Proto-Persona
		4	Core Activity	Group	2	Review /Refine + Moderate to finalize Persona
2	Persona created with Qualitative Interviews	1	Preparation	Group	8	Gather Data - Primary Research
		2	Preparation	Individual	4	Study/ Analyse Data
		3	Core Activity	Individual	3	Create Persona map based on data gathered
		4	Core Activity	Group	3	Analyse + Synthesis previous step outcome to create pre-final Persona draft
		5	Core Activity	Group	2	Review /Refine + Moderate to finalize Persona
3	Persona Created from Empathy Maps that were built from Users Diary-Studies.	1	Preparation	Group	8	Gather Data - Diary Entry by Target User
		2	Preparation	Individual	4	Study/ Analyse Data
		3	Core Activity	Individual	3	Create Empathy map based on data gathered
		4	Core Activity	Group	3	Analyse + Synthesis previous step outcome to create pre-final Persona draft
		5	Core Activity	Group	2	Review /Refine + Moderate to finalize Persona

3.3 Results and Analysis (Phase 2)

Based on all three experiments, with a total of eight sessions, it was evident that the use of AI can help speed up the overall processes significantly in DT or UCD processes during the empathise process. The effectiveness of AI in this context is maximum when it is used in preparation and during the huddle or ideation activities.

During Proto-Persona creation, where traditionally stakeholders use their assumptions to build the persona without any field data to save cost and time, the use of AI can further save almost 48.5% of the time traditionally spent, while at the same time making the proto persona more reliable due to the fact that industry-driven insights are fed into the persona creation process in real time, making the quality of information significantly better. Refer to Tables 2 and 3 below for details:

Table 2. Experiment 1 – Session 1/2 (Total time saved by AI 27%)

Group	Members	Approach	Gather Data Primary Research		Secondary Research + Study/ Analyse Data (Max. 4Hr)		TASK 1 (Individual): Create Proto-Persona (Max. 2Hr)		TASK 2 (Joint): Analyse + Synthesis on Task 1 Outcomes to Create Resultant Proto Persona (Max. 2Hr)		TASK3 (Joint): Review /Refine + Moderate (Max. 2Hr)		Total Time Spend	Time Saved by AI	
			Execution Type	Duration	Execution Type	Duration	Execution Type	Duration (Actual Used)	Execution Type	Duration (Actual Used)	Execution Type	Duration (Actual Used)		Total	%
Group 1A	3	AI + Human	Human	0:00	Human*	4:00	AI	0:05	Human	1:12	Human	1:08	6:25	1:49	22
Group 1B	3	Human	Human	0:00	Human*	4:00	Human	2:05	Human	0:45	Human	1:24	8:14		
Group 2A	3	AI + Human	Human	0:00	Human*	4:00	AI	0:05	Human	1:02	Human	0:58	6:05	2:50	32
Group 2B	3	Human	Human	0:00	Human*	4:00	Human	3:12	Human	0:56	Human	0:47	8:55		

Exp #1: Creation of a Proto-Persona (Session 1/2: AI usage in Proto Persona Creation)
* Approx. time used by the user (not at the same stretch).

Table 3. Experiment 1 – Session 2/2 (Total time saved by AI 48.5%)

Group	Members	Approach	Gather Data Primary Research		Secondary Research + Study/ Analyse Data (Max. 4Hr)		TASK 1 (Individual): Create Proto-Persona (Max. 2Hr)		TASK 2 (Joint): Analyse + Synthesis on Task 1 Outcomes to Create Resultant Proto Persona (Max. 2Hr)		TASK3 (Joint): Review /Refine + Moderate (Max. 2Hr)		Total Time Spend	Time Saved by AI	
			Execution Type	Duration	Execution Type	Duration	Execution Type	Duration (Actual Used)	Execution Type	Duration (Actual Used)	Execution Type	Duration (Actual Used)		Total	%
Group 1A	3	AI + Human	Human	0:00	Human*	4:00	AI	0:05	AI	0:30	Human	0:43	5:18	5:05	49
Group 1B	3	Human	Human	0:00	Human*	4:00	Human	4:00	Human	1:00	Human	1:23	10:23		
Group 2A	3	AI + Human	Human	0:00	Human*	4:00	AI	0:05	AI	0:30	Human	0:37	5:12	4:43	48
Group 2B	3	Human	Human	0:00	Human*	4:00	Human	4:00	Human	1:00	Human	0:55	9:55		

Exp #1: Creation of a Proto-Persona (Session 2/2: AI usage in Proto Persona Creation + Synthesis)
* Approx. time used by the user (not at the same stretch).

For the qualitative persona mapping activity built from qualitative interview data, the traditional approach of creation of empathy maps by individuals and then through group huddle, refining to reach to a final persona map for a specific pre-determined segment, use of AI can significantly speed up the process when used for analyzing the field data, summarizing it to build draft empathy map, and there by creating pre-final persona draft for the team to refine, moderate can save up to 48.5% of the time spent traditionally. Refer to Tables 4, 5 and 6 for details below:

For the qualitative persona mapping activity built from dairy-entries, the traditional approach of creation of empathy maps by individuals and then through group-huddle, refining to reach to a final persona for a specific pre-determined segment, use of AI can significantly reduce the time when used for analyzing the dairy entries, summarizing it to build draft empathy map, and there by creating pre-final persona draft for the team

Table 4. Experiment 2 – Session 1/3 (Total time saved by AI 13.5%)

			Preparation		Activity						Total Time Spend	Time Saved by AI	
			Gather Data Primary Research-Interview (Expected 8Hrs)	Secondary Research + Study/ Analyse Data (Expected 4Hrs)	TASK 1 (Individual): Create Empathy Map (Expected 3Hrs)		TASK 2 (Joint): Analyse + Synthesis on Task 1 Outcome to Create Pre-final Persona Draft (Expected 3Hrs)		TASK3 (Joint): Review /Refine + Moderate (Expected 2Hrs)				
Group	Members	Approach	Execution Type	Duration	Execution Type	Duration	Execution Type	Duration (Actual Used)	Execution Type	Duration (Actual Used)	Execution Type	Duration (Actual Used)	Total	%
Group 1A	3	AI + Human	Human*	8:00	Human*	4:00	AI	0:05	Human	3:18	Human	0:35	15:58	1:58	11
Group 1B	3	Human	Human*	8:00	Human*	4:00	Human	2:34	Human	2:56	Human	0:26	17:56		
Group 2A	3	AI + Human	Human*	8:00	Human*	4:00	AI	0:05	Human	2:32	Human	0:47	15:24	2:54	16
Group 2B	3	Human	Human*	8:00	Human*	4:00	Human	2:55	Human	2:45	Human	0:38	18:18		

Exp #2:Persona created with Qualitative Interviews (Session 1/3: Alusage in Empathy MapCreation)

* Approx. time used by the user (not at the same stretch).

Table 5. Experiment 2 – Session 2/3 (Total time saved by AI 20.5%)

			Preparation		Activity						Total Time Spend	Time Saved by AI	
			Gather Data Primary Research - Interview (Expected 8Hrs)	Secondary Research + Study/ Analyse Data (Expected 4Hrs)	TASK 1 (Individual): Create Empathy Map (Expected 3Hrs)		TASK 2 (Joint): Analyse + Synthesis on Task 1 Outcome to Create Pre-final Persona Draft (Expected 3Hrs)		TASK3 (Joint): Review /Refine + Moderate (Expected 2Hrs)				
Group	Members	Approach	Execution Type	Duration	Execution Type	Duration	Execution Type	Duration (Actual Used)	Execution Type	Duration (Actual Used)	Execution Type	Duration (Actual Used)	Total	%
Group 1A	3	AI + Human	Human*	8:00	Human*	4:00	AI	0:05	AI	0:00	Human	1:00	13:05	3:21	20
Group 1B	3	Human	Human*	8:00	Human*	4:00	Human	2:57	Human	1:00	Human	0:30	16:27		
Group 2A	3	AI + Human	Human*	8:00	Human*	4:00	AI	0:05	AI	0:05	Human	1:00	13:10	3:30	21
Group 2B	3	Human	Human*	8:00	Human*	4:00	Human	3:10	Human	1:00	Human	0:30	16:40		

Exp #2: Persona created with Qualitative Interviews (Session 2/3: AI usage in Empathy Map Creation + Synthesis)

* Approx. time used by the user (not at the same stretch).

Table 6. Experiment 2 – Session 3/3 (Total time saved by AI 42.5%)

			Preparation		Activity						Total Time Spend	Time Saved by AI	
			Gather Data Primary Research - Interview (Expected 8Hrs)	Secondary Research + Study/ Analyse Data (Expected 4Hrs)	TASK 1 (Individual): Create Empathy Map (Expected 3Hrs)		TASK 2 (Joint): Analyse + Synthesis on Task 1 Outcome to Create Pre-final Persona Draft (Expected 3Hrs)		TASK3 (Joint): Review /Refine + Moderate (Expected 2Hrs)				
Group	Members	Approach	Execution Type	Duration	Execution Type	Duration	Execution Type	Duration (Actual Used)	Execution Type	Duration (Actual Used)	Execution Type	Duration (Actual Used)	Total	%
Group 1A	3	AI + Human	Human*	8:00	AI**	0:30	AI	0:05	AI	0:00	Human	0:45	9:20	7:11	44
Group 1B	3	Human	Human*	8:00	Human*	4:00	Human	2:57	Human	1:00	Human	0:35	16:32		
Group 2A	3	AI + Human	Human*	8:00	AI**	0:30	AI	0:05	AI	0:05	Human	1:32	10:12	7:06	41
Group 2B	3	Human	Human*	8:00	Human*	4:00	Human	3:10	Human	1:00	Human	1:08	17:18		

Exp #2: Persona created with Qualitative Interviews (Sesson 3/3: AI usage in Preparatory Analysis + Empathy Map Creation + Synthesis)

* Approx. time used by the user (not at the same stretch). ** Approx. time used for both summary generation and readout by the user

to refine, moderate can save up to 42.5% of the time spent traditionally. Refer to the Tables 7, 8 and 9 for details below:

Table 7. Experiment 3 – Session 1/3 (Total time saved by AI 12%)

Exp #3: Persona created with from Diary Study (Session 1/3: AI usage in Empathy Map Creation)														
			Preparation				Activity							
Group	Members	Approach	Gather Data Primary Research - Diary Entry by Target User (Expected 8Hrs)		Analyse Data (Expected 4Hrs)		TASK 1 (Individual): Create Empathy Map (Expected 3Hrs)		TASK 2 (Joint): Analyse + Synthesis on Task 1 Outcome to Create Pre-final Persona Draft (Expected 3Hrs)		TASK3 (Joint): Review /Refine + Moderate (Expected 2Hrs)		Total Time Spend	Time Saved by AI
			Execution Type	Duration	Execution Type	Duration	Execution Type	Duration (Actual Used)	Execution Type	Duration (Actual Used)	Execution Type	Duration (Actual Used)		Total	%
Group 1A	3	AI + Human	Human*	8:00	Human*	4:00	AI	0:05	Human	2:32	Human	0:46	15:23	2:23	13
Group 1B	3	Human	Human*	8:00	Human*	4:00	Human	2:04	Human	2:47	Human	0:55	17:46		
Group 2A	3	AI + Human	Human*	8:00	Human*	4:00	AI	0:05	Human	3:02	Human	0:51	15:58	1:57	11
Group 2B	3	Human	Human*	8:00	Human*	4:00	Human	2:34	Human	2:38	Human	0:43	17:55		

* Approx. time used by the user (not at the same stretch).

Table 8. Experiment 3 – Session 2/3 (Total time saved by AI 19%)

Exp #3: Persona created with from Diary Study (Session 2/3: AI usage in Empathy Map Creation + Synthesis)														
			Preparation				Activity							
Group	Members	Approach	Gather Data Primary Research - Diary Entry by Target User (Expected 8Hrs)		Analyse Data (Expected 4Hrs)		TASK 1 (Individual): Create Empathy Map (Expected 3Hrs)		TASK 2 (Joint): Analyse + Synthesis on Task 1 Outcome to Create Pre-final Persona Draft (Expected 3Hrs)		TASK3 (Joint): Review /Refine + Moderate (Expected 2Hrs)		Total Time Spend	Time Saved by AI
			Execution Type	Duration (Actual Used)	Execution Type	Duration (Actual Used)	Execution Type	Duration (Actual Used)	Execution Type	Duration (Actual Used)	Execution Type	Duration (Actual Used)		Total	%
Group 1A	3	AI + Human	Human*	8:00	Human*	4:00	AI	0:05	AI	0:00	Human	1:43	13:48	2:55	18
Group 1B	3	Human	Human*	8:00	Human*	4:00	Human	2:57	Human	1:00	Human	0:47	16:44		
Group 2A	3	AI + Human	Human*	8:00	Human*	4:00	AI	0:05	AI	0:05	Human	1:12	13:22	3:23	20
Group 2B	3	Human	Human*	8:00	Human*	4:00	Human	3:10	Human	1:00	Human	0:35	16:45		

* Approx. time used by the user (not at the same stretch).

Table 9. Experiment 3 – Session 3/3 (Total time saved by AI 40%)

Exp #3: Persona created with from Diary Study (Session 3/3: AI usage in Preparatory Analysis + Empathy Map Creation + Synthesis)														
			Preparation				Activity							
Group	Members	Approach	Gather Data Primary Research - Diary Entry by Target User (Expected 8Hrs)		Analyse Data (Expected 4Hrs)		TASK 1 (Individual): Create Empathy Map (Expected 3Hrs)		TASK 2 (Joint): Analyse + Synthesis on Task 1 Outcome to Create Pre-final Persona Draft (Expected 3Hrs)		TASK3 (Joint): Review /Refine + Moderate (Expected 2Hrs)		Total Time Spend	Time Saved by AI
			Execution Type	Duration	Execution Type	Duration	Execution Type	Duration (Actual Used)	Execution Type	Duration (Actual Used)	Execution Type	Duration (Actual Used)		Total	%
Group 1A	3	AI + Human	Human*	8:00	AI**	0:30	AI	0:05	AI	0:05	Human	1:34	10:14	6:40	39
Group 1B	3	Human	Human*	8:00	Human*	4:00	Human	2:57	Human	1:20	Human	0:37	16:54		
Group 2A	3	AI + Human	Human*	8:00	AI**	0:30	AI	0:05	AI	0:05	Human	1:13	9:53	6:56	41
Group 2B	3	Human	Human*	8:00	Human*	4:00	Human	3:10	Human	0:56	Human	0:43	16:49		

* Approx. time used by the user (not at the same stretch).   ** Approx. time used for both summary generation and readout by the user

4 Conclusion

From the experiments conducted in both phases, it is concluded that one of the key adoption challenges for DT is the constraint of time, which enforces tradeoffs leading to reduced quality outcomes and hence creating friction for adoption. The experiments demonstrated that AI can significantly speed up the design thinking process by providing data driven insights specific to the context of demographics, industry, and job role, particularly during the empathise phase. By using AI for tasks like Proto-Persona creation and qualitative persona mapping, substantial time savings of up to 48.5% were achieved. Additionally, the use of AI improved the reliability and quality of the personas by incorporating real-time industry data-driven insights. These findings highlight the potential of AI to enhance efficiency and decision-making in design thinking, making it a valuable tool for practitioners to overcome time constraints and achieve better outcomes.

Acknowledgement. I would like to thank all the participants, as well as Prof. Alok Satpathy, Dept. of Mech. Engg., National Institute of Technology Rourkela (NITR), Durga Prasad Gouda, COO, Atal Incubation Centre-Nalanda Institute of Technology Foundation (AIC-NITF), Shri Sunil Kayal, President, Rourkela Chamber of Commerce & Industry (RCCI), Pratik Agarwal, co-founder, BetaBuilds Technologies Pvt. Ltd., and Rickin Hindocha, Content Operations, Xerox Corp., UK, for providing support and helping with arrangements.

References

1. Ericson, Å., Bergström, M., Larsson, A., Törlind, P., Larsson, T.: Design thinking challenges in education. In: International Conference on Engineering Design, ICED 2009, 24–27 August 2009, Stanford University, Stanford, CA, USA (2009)
2. What is the Most Difficult Part of the Design Thinking Process? The Design Thinking Association. https://www.design-thinking-association.org/explore-design-thinking-topics/external-links/what-most-difficult-part-design-thinking-process. Accessed 23 June 2023
3. Ericson, Å., Bergström, M., Larsson, A., Törlind, P., Larsson, T.: Design thinking challenges in education (2009)

Calibrating the Coordination Between Humans and AI by Analyzing the Socio-technical Variety of Task Sharing

Thomas Herrmann[(✉)] [iD]

Institut für Arbeitswissenschaft, Ruhr-University Bochum, Bochum, Germany
Thomas.Herrmann@ruhr-uni-bochum.de

Abstract. This work demonstrates the variety of possible actions and reactions in the interplay of humans and AI when working on shared tasks. The coordination of human-AI task sharing has to take these varieties into account. In many instances the modes of reacting on each other are symmetrically distributed between humans and AI. Certain activities of coordinating the task sharing between human and AI are in a meta-relation to the interaction between humans and AI, some of these meta-activities may be reserved to humans.

Keywords: human-centered artificial intelligence · task sharing · socio-technical design · coordination

1 Introduction

We will reconsider mixed-initiative models of the human-AI interplay and demonstrate that currently available models (Muller & Weisz, 2022; Parasuraman et al., 2000) fall short, and that a more extended version will help to find answers on certain questions about the advantages and disadvantages of sharing tasks between humans and AI.

The extension is based on literature about interaction modes discussed in Human-Centered AI (Herrmann, 2022). In particular, we add the dimension of reciprocal help ("dealing with help requirements") (Kamar, 2016) and the possibility of intervention (Schmidt & Herrmann, 2017). Furthermore, we analyze the interplay between human and AI from a socio-technical viewpoint by taking the organizational context into account (Herrmann & Pfeiffer, 2022).

We have developed a process model that includes the multiplicity of possible interactions and challenges of coordination between human and AI. This model outlines several types of sequences of action and reaction within human-AI collaboration (Fig. 1).

The main message is that there are certain possibilities of reacting on the other side's (human vs. AI) activities that are symmetrically available on each side. By contrast, some kinds of activities are related to humans' social embeddedness and take place on a meta-level in the organizational context of AI-usage.

This type of process model provides a framework that is a prerequisite for answering questions that help analyze or design applications of AI in specific task and work contexts. Examples are:

C. Stephanidis et al. (Eds.): HCII 2023, CCIS 1958, pp. 25–33, 2024.
https://doi.org/10.1007/978-3-031-49215-0_4

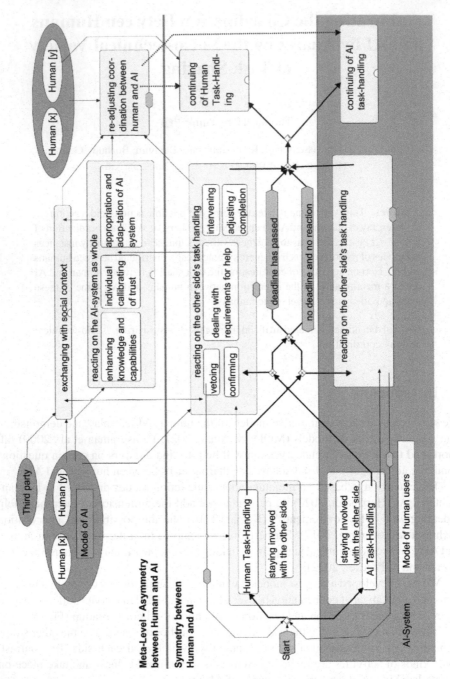

Fig. 1. Model of Huma-AI interplay – overview (Modelling notation SeeMe (Herrmann, 2006))

1. Where do we have a symmetrical relationship between AI and humans (such as helping each other) and where dominates a more asymmetrical relationship – such as reflecting the potentials and limitations of the other site in the organizational context.
2. What are the differences between human-human collaboration and human-AI collaboration (e.g., presenting fake outcome to test the other side for trust calibration would not be appropriate within human-human collaboration).
3. On what conditions depends the mental workload of the involved humans (e.g. depending on the level of trust)?
4. Does the model differ depending on the phase of the decision making –such as observing or being aware of an situation, interpreting, planning, executing (Rasmussen, 1976)– or can it be equally applied to each of the phases?
5. On which factors does a continuous improvement of the coordination between Human and AI depend upon.

2 Variety of Modes for Acting and Reacting Within Task Sharing Between Human and AI

2.1 Modes of Delegation

As demonstrated by Muller and Weisz (2022), who extend the differentiation of Parasuraman et al. (2000), there are various possibilities for task sharing between human and AI. It is not only the pattern that what is taken by AI is taken away from humans. By contrast, it might happen that the number of activities increase on both sides to achieve better results or to contribute to the advancement of either one or both sides' capabilities. Accordingly, the concept of hybrid intelligence suggests that human and AI together provide better results than each of them alone. (Dellermann et al., 2019). In what follows, we try to differentiate the various possibilities of distributing activities between human and AI.

By referring to the literature of job design –for example Grote et al. (2000)– the following distinctions can be made with respect to task delegation:

- Degree of task integrity:

  - The task is delegated to a person or a team as a holistic unit, and – subsequently – the human agents decide which sub-tasks are allocated to whom, including AI.
  - Management already decides which sub-tasks are allocated to AI and which to the human side.
  - The allocated tasks are complete in that way that they integrate aspects such as observing a situation, interpreting, planning, executing and evaluating the task's outcome or
  - Only sub-aspects of task handling –or a combination of them– are allocated.

- Stability

  - task allocation decisions remain stable during the complete course of task handling or
  - can be flexibly changed while the tasks are processed.

2.2 Degree of Interdependence

After the task handling has started, the degree of interdependence between actors is relevant: On the one hand, sub-tasks might be allocated that can be run independently on each side or –on the other hand– the task handling needs continuous interaction and adjustment between both sides.

Mostly it is assumed that AI-based task handling provides an automated process as it is the goal with autonomous driving (Kukkala et al., 2018). However, there are other examples where human and AI interact widely interdependently. Cai et al. (2019) propose a set of refinement tools with which humans can improve the searching of images being related to a case at hand. They give a report on their study on employing several refinement strategies. These strategies are considered as an example for interactive ML. The authors discuss whether such tools would be more likely not be adopted by a user, as they could increase the complexity and workload of interacting with AI. However, the study on the use of these refinement tools shows that users experienced less effort and more benefits, and the way of experimenting with the outcome of the system led to higher trust. Their example demonstrates that during interdependent task handling, no side can continue without the input of the other side. Within interdependent tasks, not only the assistance by AI is relevant, like providing warnings in complex traffic situations, but reciprocal assistance where each side contributes to the progress of the other side.

2.3 Remaining Options for Accompanying Independent Task Handling

Independent task handling of one side that may be named A, can be differentiated with respect to the following options:

- The other side can neither observe nor intervene in what A is doing,
- can observe but not intervene, or
- the other side needs not but can observe what A is doing and can possibly intervene.

Intervention is meant as a temporal switch to a phase of fine grained interaction as it is typical for interdependent task handling (Schmidt & Herrmann, 2017). Intervention is not appropriate without the possibility of observing an automated process.

Observation can include the following options:

- Just watching the behavior along a series of actions or outcomes, as is the case with autonomous driving.
- Asking for status information or seeing status information that is actively provided by the other side, as is the case with predictive maintenance (Dalzochio et al., 2020).
- Asking for explanations, and
- reviewing explanations and interactively refining them (Chromik & Butz, 2021).

A crucial basis for humans' interest to observe what AI is doing, is the possibility to react on the system's behavior. One possibility is intervention that offers various possibilities (Herrmann et al., 2019):

- interrupting an automated process for a certain period of time,
- taking over the whole task or a sub-task of the other agent for a certain period of time,

- temporarily adjusting parameters,
- rejecting or modifying an intermediate result before a pre-specified or automated process goes on,
- restarting the task after an intervention such as adjusting parameters.

Instead of intervening, assistance is a pattern of reciprocal support. Assistance might be plannable in advance or has to be provided ad-hoc, depending on the situation where tasks are performed. It can be proactively offered by one side, or be requested. Thus, assistance can include various options that help to improve the outcome of task handling – for example with critiquing systems (Fischer, 1994):

- providing information,
- commenting on an intermediate result,
- taking over a sub-task upon request,
- confirming an intermediate result.

2.4 Possible Reactions on Results Provided by One Side

Basically, on most activities that are carried out by one side A, the other side has several options to react:

1. Accepting/confirming so that an automated process can go on on the basis of the achieved output. According to typical patterns of business process management (Barros et al., 2007), confirmation might

   - have to take place regularly at certain events,
   - have to take place, if one side asks for it,
   - or, if there is no reaction on a requested confirmation, the process might be completely stopped or go on after a certain deadline.

2. Rejecting or vetoing (Rakova et al., 2020). In particular, the rejection of intermediate result can cover the following options:

   - just going on without considering the provided intermediate result,
   - starting an intervention
   - offering help
   - restarting of the task handling after an adjustment
   - changing the task allocation
   - reconfiguration of an AI-system or additional training or education of a human actor

3. Modifying by

   - triggering the agent to modify the delivered output,
   - asking third agents to do the modification,
   - providing the modification by oneself.

Rejection and modifications are closely related to the mode of intervention (Herrmann et al., 2019) that usually is started if one side does not provide what the other side expects.

These three options (1–3) can be applied to various phenomena, such as

- intermediate results provided by one side,
- allocation of a task,
- requests for the other side's assistance (in this case, modification would mean that the other side does not take over a complete sub-task, but only sub-aspects of it),
- offer of assistance,
- explanations.

3 Characteristics and Impacts of Varieties Within Human-AI Task Sharing

These varieties of possible actions and reactions can be discussed with respect to the following aspects: symmetry, meta-relation between activities, trust calibration and organizational context.

Most types of reactions are symmetrically distributed – they can be provided by both sides, human or AI. In some cases, this symmetry is supported by the literature, for example in the case of assistance. Usually assistance is provided from AI to humans, for example by chatbots in the healthcare domain (Ayanouz et al., 2020). Kamar (2016) proposes the other way around where machine learning-based systems have a model of their own and of the humans' competences and ask humans for help if necessary. Thus, both sides can assist each other. Similarly, providing interventions is not only proposed from humans into the direction of AI (Schmidt & Herrmann, 2017) but also AI can intervene into human task handling for example in the case of process monitoring (Teinemaa et al., 2018). In other cases, we just propose from a logical point of view that symmetry is taken into account. E.g., with respect to explainable AI, it appears reasonable to also designing AI that can ask humans for explanations and seek to learn from them.

Rejection can also by symmetrically distributed. The reasons behind a rejection might be different at both sides. AI might reject requests for help or a sub-task allocated to it because its inability to carry out the task or because of rules that are implemented. For example when asked about the moral orientation of a political leader, ChatGPT3 with its version of January 2023 answers: "It is not within my capabilities to make judgments about the moral orientation of individuals …". Also humans can refuse to take certain tasks because they cannot or they are not willing to do so because of psychological or ethical reasons (Mumford, 1995).

Some activities can be considered in a meta-relation to others. We propose to consider all kind of activities as meta-activities that contribute to the coordination between human and AI. Thus, all kind of task allocation may be regarded as a meta-decision, as well as evaluating and reflecting the quality of the outcome of either the task handling by a single agent or the outcome of any kind of collaboration between human and AI. Also, reconfiguration of AI or training and re-education of personnel, or resetting parameters that influence the collaboration behavior, take place on the meta-level. It is of special interest whether the threefold reaction pattern of acceptance, rejection or modification can also be applied to meta-activities. For example, whether humans can oppose that certain tasks can be delegated to AI – or whether even an AI-system can reject the allocation of a task – not only to itself but also a human agent.

These meta-activities of coordination and evaluation are related to the models (Chromik & Butz, 2021) the actors have of each other. Task allocation, request for help, providing explanations should be guided by the models of the affected agents, in particular with respect to their capabilities and the question whether one can trust them (Lee & See, 2004). Trust might depend on the question whether an agent is capable to fulfil certain tasks reliably or is willing to do so. Willingness depends on values or interests on the human side. On the side of AI, values might be represented as biases or as rules that are inscribed to avoid or to enforce certain actions. Trust building or trust calibration (Okamura & Yamada, 2020) – that seeks to establish an appropriate level of trust humans should have in AI – can be considered as asymmetrical in relation to AI. Trust – as the willingness to risk relying on somebody – might be a typical human phenomenon while AI rather might be configured in a way where it checks or don't check the capability of humans with which it shares tasks. Trust building and calibration can be considered as meta-activities.

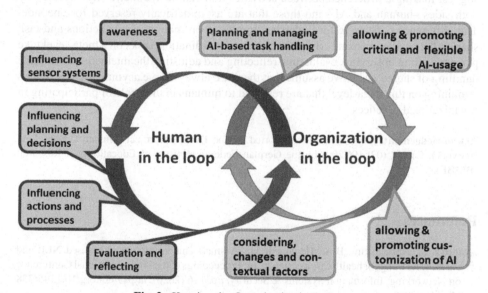

Fig. 2. Keeping the Organization in the Loop

Meta-activities are usually supported and influenced by the organizational and social context. For example, a well-known trust mechanism is networking (Lee & See, 2004) where someone –e. g. named A– trusts in B if A trust in C and C trust in B. Herrmann & Pfeiffer (2022, 2023) argue that generally keeping the human in the loop when using AI cannot be successful without keeping the organization in the loop. Both have to be integrated as shown in Fig. 2. For Herrmann and Pfeiffer, implementing and using AI has to be accompanied by several managerial activities. They can also be considered as meta-activities. They have to become part of organizational practices to be effective.

Figure 2 represents human activities on different levels when using or collaborating with AI. These activities have to be complemented by organizational measures. These measures assume that there is an original task to be carried out that is supported by

AI and that this support has to be properly aligned with the original task covering the coordination of the collaboration between humans and AI. Furthermore, the flexible dealing with AI (such as rejecting or modifying as described above) has to be explicitly allowed and promoted. This also applies to the customization of AI. Additionally, the organization has to be aware of changes and contextual factors that might influence the way of task sharing with AI.

4 Summary

In summary, the analyses of effects of human-AI collaboration as well as its coordination and the design of the possibilities for collaboration have to take the variety of modes of acting and reacting into account. The collaboration is a subject of socio-technical design where adapting the technology and the adjustment of the coordination are aligned. We suggest making a difference between activities that can be symmetrically executed by both sides –human and AI– and those that are asymmetrically reserved for one side. This difference is decisive for understanding the coordination of interactions and task sharing between human and AI. With respect to coordination, tasks on a meta-level take place including observing, evaluating, reflecting and adjusting the interaction during the handling of shared tasks. We assume that there are always some asymmetrical activities remaining on this meta-level that are reserved to humans in their role of participating in organizational practices.

Acknowledgement. This work was supported by the Humaine project (Human Centered AI Network), funded (02L19C200) by the German Federal Ministry of Education and Research (BMBF).

References

Ayanouz, S., Abdelhakim, B.A., Benhmed, M.: A smart chatbot architecture based NLP and machine learning for health care assistance. In: Proceedings of the 3rd International Conference on Networking, Information Systems & Security, pp. 1–6 (2020). https://doi.org/10.1145/338 6723.3387897

Barros, A., Decker, G., Grosskopf, A.: Complex events in business processes. In: Abramowicz, W. (ed.) Business Information Systems, vol. 4439, pp. 29–40. Springer, Heidelberg (2007). https://doi.org/10.1007/978-3-540-72035-5_3

Cai, C.J., et al.: Human-centered tools for coping with imperfect algorithms during medical decision-making. In: Proceedings of the 2019 CHI Conference on Human Factors in Computing Systems, pp. 1–14 (2019)

Chromik, M., Butz, A.: Human-XAI interaction: a review and design principles for explanation user interfaces. In: IFIP Conference on Human-Computer Interaction, pp. 619–640 (2021)

Dalzochio, J., et al.: Machine learning and reasoning for predictive maintenance in Industry 4.0: current status and challenges. Comput. Ind. **123**, 103298 (2020). https://doi.org/10.1016/j.com pind.2020.103298

Dellermann, D., Calma, A., Lipusch, N., Weber, T., Weigel, S., Ebel, P.: The future of human-AI collaboration: a taxonomy of design knowledge for hybrid intelligence systems. In: Proceedings of the 52nd Hawaii International Conference on System Sciences (HICSS) (2019)

Fischer, G.: Domain-oriented design environments. Autom. Softw. Eng. **1**(2), 177–203 (1994)

Grote, G., Ryser, C., Wäler, T., Windischer, A., Weik, S.: KOMPASS: a method for complementary function allocation in automated work systems. Int. J. Hum Comput Stud. **52**(2), 267–287 (2000). https://doi.org/10.1006/ijhc.1999.0289

Herrmann, T.: SeeMe in a nutshell (2006). http://www.imtm-iaw.ruhr-uni-bochum.de/wp-content/uploads/sites/5/2011/09/Seeme-in-a-nutshell.pdf

Herrmann, T.: Promoting human competences by appropriate modes of interaction for human-centered-AI. In: Degen, H., Ntoa, S. (eds.) Artificial Intelligence in HCI, vol. 13336, pp. 35–50. Springer, Cham (2022). https://doi.org/10.1007/978-3-031-05643-7_3

Herrmann, T., Lentzsch, C., Degeling, M.: Intervention and EUD: a combination for appropriating automated processes. In: Malizia, A., Valtolina, S., Morch, A., Serrano, A., Stratton, A. (eds.) End-User Development, vol. 11553, pp. 67–82. Springer, Cham (2019). https://doi.org/10.1007/978-3-030-24781-2_5

Herrmann, T., Pfeiffer, S.: Keeping the organization in the loop: a socio-technical extension of human-centered artificial intelligence. AI Soc. **38**, 1523–1542 (2023). https://doi.org/10.1007/s00146-022-01391-5

Herrmann, T., Pfeiffer, S.: Keeping the organization in the loop as a general concept for human-centered AI: the example of medical imaging. In: Proceedings of the 56th Hawaii International Conference on System Sciences (HICSS), pp. 5272–5281 (2023)

Kamar, E.: Directions in hybrid intelligence: complementing AI systems with human intelligence. In: IJCAI, pp. 4070–4073 (2016)

Kukkala, V.K., Tunnell, J., Pasricha, S., Bradley, T.: Advanced driver-assistance systems: a path toward autonomous vehicles. IEEE Consum. Electron. Mag. **7**(5), 18–25 (2018). https://doi.org/10.1109/MCE.2018.2828440

Lee, J.D., See, K.A.: Trust in automation: designing for appropriate reliance. Human Factors **46**, 50–80 (2004)

Muller, M., Weisz, J.: Extending a Human-AI collaboration framework with dynamism and sociality. In: 2022 Symposium on Human-Computer Interaction for Work, pp. 1–12 (2022). https://doi.org/10.1145/3533406.3533407

Mumford, E.: Effective Systems Design and Requirements and Analysis—The ETHICS Approach (Hauptbücherregal GK). Macmillan Press LTD (1995)

Okamura, K., Yamada, S.: Adaptive trust calibration for human-AI collaboration. PLoS ONE **15**(2), e0229132 (2020). https://doi.org/10.1371/journal.pone.0229132

Parasuraman, R., Sheridan, T.B., Wickens, C.D.: A model for types and levels of human interaction with automation. IEEE Trans. Syst. Man Cybern. - Part A Syst. Humans **30**(3), 286–297 (2000). https://doi.org/10.1109/3468.844354

Rakova, B., Yang, J., Cramer, H., Chowdhury, R.: Where responsible AI meets reality: practitioner perspectives on enablers for shifting organizational practices. ArXiv: 2006.12358 [Cs] (2020). http://arxiv.org/abs/2006.12358

Rasmussen, J.: Outlines of a hybrid model of the process plant operator. In: Sheridan, T.B., Johannsen, G. (eds.) Monitoring Behavior and Supervisory Control. NATO Conference Series, vol. 1, pp. 371–383. Springer, Boston (1976). https://doi.org/10.1007/978-1-4684-2523-9_31

Schmidt, A., Herrmann, T.: Intervention user interfaces: a new interaction paradigm for automated systems. Interactions **24**(5), 40–45 (2017)

Teinemaa, I., Tax, N, de Leoni, M., Dumas, M., Maggi, F.M.: Alarm-based prescriptive process monitoring (arXiv: 1803.08706) (2018). arXiv. http://arxiv.org/abs/1803.08706

Toward HCXAI, Beyond XAI: Along with the Case of Referring Expression Comprehension Under the Personal Context

Sangjun Lee[✉]

Seoul National University, Seoul 08826, Republic of Korea
leesj1187@snu.ac.kr

Abstract. The goal of eXplainable AI (XAI) is to increase the transparency and trustworthiness of AI algorithms to humans by clarifying their internal decision-making process. As AI technology continues to permeate various aspects of our daily lives, including the workplace, the importance of XAI has grown and some XAI methodologies have increased our understanding of AI algorithm's inner logic. However, the achievement of explainability of AI models did not make them user-centered in real life and users still need to be aware of the internal mechanism of AI models to interact with them effectively. In this regard, the paper argues there is a need to move beyond XAI towards Human-Centered eXplainable AI (HCXAI) to ensure human-centered usage in our daily lives. As the steps heading for HCXAI, the paper suggests researching intuitive human behaviors first and then training AI models to comprehend these natural human behaviors. When users interact with AI models trained in this way, they will not need to think consciously about the model's working mechanism anymore. The paper elaborates on this approach further with a practical case that can be encountered in our daily lives; the vision and language model for referring expression comprehension under the personal context.

Keywords: HCXAI · XAI · Referring expression comprehension

1 Introduction

Since an image classification model based on convolutional neural network architecture, e.g., AlexNet [1], showed remarkable progress in the ImageNet Large Scale Visual Recognition Challenge, a deep learning paradigm based on the deep neural network has dominated the current AI field.

Deep learning has led to remarkable advancements in AI technology, surpassing or matching human performance in various fields. For example, ResNet50 [2] for image recognition, AlphaGo [3] for playing Go, Stable diffusion [4] for image generation, and ChatGPT [5] for dialogue have all demonstrated outstanding performance, surprising the world with their capabilities.

However, despite the brilliant advancement of AI models in diverse domains, the humans who designed them often struggle to understand how these models

© The Author(s), under exclusive license to Springer Nature Switzerland AG 2024
C. Stephanidis et al. (Eds.): HCII 2023, CCIS 1958, pp. 34–40, 2024.
https://doi.org/10.1007/978-3-031-49215-0_5

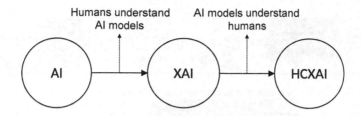

Fig. 1. Towards Human-Centered eXplainable AI (HCXAI).

work or why they produce certain outputs as if peering into a black box [6]. This paradoxical situation highlights the importance of eXplainable AI (XAI), which aims to enable the utilization of AI models without the risk of unexpected misuse by providing a thorough understanding of their internal decision-making processes [6].

However, even if the black box of AI models becomes transparent to humans through the XAI methodologies, this paper argues that it does not ensure that the models are human-centered as long as users are still required to be conscious of the AI model's working mechanism when interacting with them. As presented in Fig. 1, AI models must understand humans to achieve Human-Centered eXplainable AI (HCXAI), which goes beyond just achieving explainability of AI models. Hence, accomplishing HCXAI requires a deeper understanding of human behavior to figure out which intuitive properties of humans the AI models need to comprehend. This paper delineates the journey from AI towards HCXAI, as shown in the Fig. 1, and provides a specific case study of a vision and language model for referring expression comprehension [7].

2 Current Referring Expression and Its Limitations

Referring expression is a natural language expression used to describe the relationship between multiple objects in a scene [7]. There are many tasks related to referring expression, including referring expression comprehension which involves detecting an object indicated by the referring expression in a scene [7]. Vision and language models that deal with referring expression comprehension can be used in many downstream tasks that require interaction between humans and AI models. In previous work [8], these models have been utilized in human-robot interaction scenarios, where a robot picks up the target object described by a user in natural language.

Like the first step depicted in Fig. 1, previous work [9] analyzed the underlying characteristics of the current vision and language model for referring expression comprehension. They classified current referring expressions into four types: spatial, ordinal, relational, and intrinsic, based on the types of information which each referring expression depends on to distinguish a target object from others in a scene. They empirically showed that the current vision and language models "my phone"   "a phone in my living room"

"a phone of white color on a table of white color"

Fig. 2. Demo results of the up-to-date vision and language model dealing with referring expression comprehension [10]. Given images where the image in the middle is the user's phone, the model failed to comprehend expressions that describe a personal relationship with the use of possessive words such as "my phone" or "a phone in my living room" (first row). However, the model could successfully detect the user's phone when the expression was "a phone of white color on a table of white color" (second row).

for referring expression comprehension have more difficulty when handling the other types, aside from the intrinsic type [9].

So, if we provide the vision and language model for referring expression comprehension only with the intrinsic type of referring expressions, can we say that the model is human-centered to us? In this regard, this paper argues that achieving transparency of the model for referring expression comprehension does not necessarily ensure its human-centeredness, particularly when considering its potential use cases in real life.

For instance, smart devices, such as smart cameras and robot vacuum cleaners in home environments or service robots in the workplace, are gradually becoming ubiquitous in our daily lives. If the vision and language model for referring expression comprehension becomes integrated with these smart appliances, people will be able to let the model locate specific objects in their home or the workplace by speaking referring expressions. However, in this personal context, the intuitive expression that a user might speak to describe the target object may not fall into any of the four types analyzed in previous research [9].

Perhaps the first phrase that comes to the user's mind to describe a particular object to the smart device in a personal context may be related to the object's ownership, such as "my phone." However, as presented in Fig. 2, even the up-to-date vision and language model [10] fails to understand the expression that describes the personal relationship related to the target object.

Like the second step in Fig. 1, this paper argues that the vision and language model for referring expression comprehension in our everyday lives can become user-centered, beyond just being explainable, when enabling the model to understand our intuitive expressions describing the target object under the personal context. In this regard, the study of the natural behavior of humans should be preceded, and it will be delineated below.

3   User Research

The overall flow of the user research is as follows: First, a hypothesis is set on the expressions that intuitively come to the user's mind when describing a particular object under the personal context. This hypothesis is then demonstrated through a user experiment, which follows the framework of the elicitation test from previous research [11].

In this paper, we present the necessity of user research and its detailed process but will not conduct it. Conducting user research will be left to future work.

3.1   Hypothesis

A hypothesis proposed in this paper is that people tend to make expressions utilizing a personal item to describe a target object to others if the personal item and the target object are present in the same scene, and it only happens when people believe the others are also aware of their relationship with the personal item. This hypothesis is partially based on findings from the RedCaps dataset [12], a large-scale image-text dataset compiled from the social media platform Reddit, where people share their daily experiences with others. In their study [12], the authors analyzed the top-5 most frequent trigrams in the dataset, and many of them were possessive expressions, such as "this is my" and "one of my," as shown in Table 1.

Table 1. The top-5 frequent trigrams in the RedCaps dataset [12]. 'itap' means 'i took a picture.' in Reddit. Except for the trigrams including 'itap,' two trigrams out of the top-3 frequent ones are related to the possessive expression: 'this is my' and 'one of my.'

The top-5 frequent trigrams in RedCaps dataset [12]
'itap of a', 'i don't', **'one of my'**, 'itap of the', **'this is my'**

3.2   Elicitation Test

This paper follows the concept of the elicitation test from a prior work [11] to set the detailed process of the user experiment. In previous work [11], the elicitation test was conducted to elicit the user's natural gestures for 2-dimensional surface computing instead of the gestures pre-defined by designers.

In the previous research [11], the authors first explained a gesture's effect (referents) in 2-dimensional surface computing to the experiment participants and then asked them to perform the actions (signs) causing the effect. Following this elicitation test's framework, the experiment participants in our research are also first notified of a target object (referents) and then they are requested to speak the expressions (signs) to describe the target object to others. It is summarized in Table 2.

Table 2. The comparison with the elicitation test in Wobbrock et al. [11].

Research	Wobbrock et al. [11]	Ours
Experiment targets	User-defined gestures for surface computing	Referring expressions
Referents	Effect of a gesture	Target object
Signs	Action causing the effect	Expression

3.3   User Experiment Details

There are three scenarios for the user experiment to verify the hypothesis, as shown in Fig. 3:

- Scenario 1: A target object is a personal item.
- Scenario 2: A target object is the same type as a personal item.
- Scenario 3: A target object is a different type from a personal item.

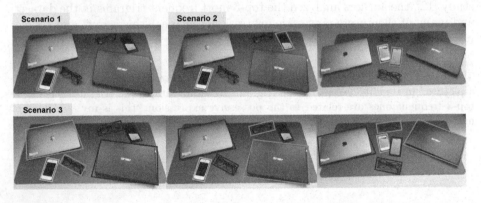

Fig. 3. Three scenarios in the user experiment. The light blue box indicates the personal item. The green box means the target object. The red box denotes the distractor. (Color figure online)

In each scenario, there are a personal item (belonging to the participant), a target object (an object to be described to others), and a distractor (an object of the same type as the personal item or the target object). Scenario 2 has two subcases, where the personal item and the target object are either close to each other or not. Scenario 3 has three subcases, where the personal item is either near the target object, the distractor or lies in the middle of them. These subcases are intended to observe the participant's behavior irrespective of the proximity of the personal item to the target object or the distractor.

The detailed processes for all scenarios are as follows:

- First, collect photos of the personal item of experiment participants and pre- pare test scenes by editing these photos, as shown in Fig. 3.
- Next, ask experiment participants to describe a target object to others using the expression that comes to their mind after looking at the test scenes.
- The experiment is conducted under two situations: 1) Participants are informed that other people are also aware of their ownership of the personal item, and 2) Participants are not informed of this fact.
- Observe the participants and note whether they utilize the personal item to describe the target object when speaking the expressions.
- After the experiment, ask the participants to rate their preference, conve- nience, and intuitiveness for each expression they made to describe the target object to others.

Participants are expected to utilize a personal item to describe a target object when speaking expressions if participants know that other people also recognize the ownership of the personal item. If they do not know it, participants are anticipated to use other types of referring expressions classified in the previous work [9].

4   The Remaining Journey Toward HCXAI

The remaining step toward HCXAI is figuring out how to practically implement the lesson from the user research into the AI model development.

For instance, this paper insists that the concept of personalizing a pre-trained vision and language model, which was proposed in previous works [13,14], can be the practical method of implementing the vision and language model that can comprehend the user's intuitive referring expression under the personal context. In their works [13,14], personalization means fine-tuning the pre-trained vision and language model to understand a user-defined special token that indicates a personal visual concept. The process involves initializing a new word token and optimizing its embedding to represent the specific visual concept commonly shared in 3 to 5 images provided by the user. However, while these trials are encouraging, they have limitations in that these approaches only focused on the technical implementation of personalization without any user study to demon- strate the personalization's necessity.

In this regard, it will be an exciting direction for future works to explore the touchpoint where AI models are explainable to humans but not utilized in a user-centric manner and delve into intuitive human behaviors guiding the way where the AI models should be developed further. The whole journey proposed in this paper aims to go beyond the achievement of explainability of AI models and bring human-centeredness to AI models by prioritizing the users in their development.

References

1. Krizhevsky, A., Sutskever, I., Hinton, G.E.: Imagenet classification with deep convolutional neural networks. Commun. ACM **60**(6), 84–90 (2017)
2. He, K., Zhang, X., Ren, S., Sun, J.: Deep residual learning for image recognition. In: Proceedings of the IEEE Conference on Computer Vision and Pattern Recognition, pp. 770–778 (2016)
3. Silver, D., et al.: Mastering the game of Go with deep neural networks and tree search. Nature **529**(7587), 484–489 (2016)
4. Rombach, R., Blattmann, A., Lorenz, D., Esser, P., Ommer, B.: High-resolution image synthesis with latent diffusion models. In: Proceedings of the IEEE/CVF Conference on Computer Vision and Pattern Recognition, pp. 10684–10695 (2022)
5. OpenAI.: ChatGPT: Optimizing Language Models for Dialogue (2023). https://openai.com/blog/chatgpt/
6. Adadi, A., Berrada, M.: Peeking inside the black-box: a survey on explainable artificial intelligence (XAI). IEEE Access **6**, 52138–52160 (2018)
7. Qiao, Y., Deng, C., Wu, Q.: Referring expression comprehension: a survey of methods and datasets. IEEE Trans. Multimed. **23**, 4426–4440 (2020)
8. Shridhar, M., Hsu, D.: Interactive visual grounding of referring expressions for human-robot interaction. arXiv preprint arXiv:1806.03831 (2018)
9. Sánchez, J., Mazuecos, M., Maina, H., Benotti, L.: What kinds of errors do reference resolution models make and what can we learn from them? Find. Assoc. Comput. Linguist. NAACL **2022**, 1971–1986 (2022)
10. Wang, P., et al.: OFA: unifying architectures, tasks, and modalities through a simple sequence-to-sequence learning framework. In: International Conference on Machine Learning, pp. 23318–23340 (2022)
11. Wobbrock, J. O., Morris, M. R., Wilson, A. D.: User-defined gestures for surface computing. In: Proceedings of the SIGCHI Conference on Human Factors in Computing Systems, pp. 1083–1092 (2009)
12. Desai, K., Kaul, G., Aysola, Z. T., Johnson, J.: RedCaps: web-curated image-text data created by the people, for the people. In: Thirty-fifth Conference on Neural Information Processing Systems Datasets and Benchmarks Track (2021)
13. Gal, R., et al.: An image is worth one word: Personalizing text-to-image generation using textual inversion. arXiv preprint arXiv:2208.01618 (2022)
14. Cohen, N., Gal, R., Meirom, E.A., Chechik, G., Atzmon, Y.: This is my unicorn, Fluffy: Personalizing frozen vision-language representations. arXiv preprint arXiv:2204.01694 (2022)

A Systems-Theoretic Approach for the Analysis of AI Ethics

Eero Mikael Lumme(✉)

University of Helsinki, 000140 Helsinki, Finland
eero.lumme@helsinki.fi

Abstract. This short research paper explores the ways in which ideas, theories, and techniques from the realm of safety research can be utilized in Human-Computer Interaction (HCI), specifically regarding the ethical aspects of artificial intelligence. Decades of dedicated effort have been invested in the domains of aviation, healthcare, and nuclear industry to enhance accident investigation and prevention methodologies. Safety-related issues can be considered as a subset of a significantly larger and more multidimensional group of ethical issues. Ultimately, both safety and ethical reflections are about avoiding unwanted consequences. A systems-theoretic causal model is one of the many theoretical approaches used in safety research. Systems-theoretic thinking that expands linear reasoning originates from engineering. By applying the systems-theoretic causal model it is possible to create causal mechanisms for explaining empirical sociotechnical phenomena. This makes it possible to perceive different types of interaction mechanisms at the system level and to compare different situations and system structures with each other. A potential benefit systems-theoretic modelling of ethical action is its ability to combine the terminology of engineering, moral philosophy and social sciences into the same framework. This allows for the development of new interdisciplinary research methods for the systematic analysis and design of ethical AI systems.

Keywords: AI-Ethics · Causal Mechanism · Modelling · Safety Science · Systems Theory

1 Introduction

In several studies concerning AI ethics, a set of ethical principles have been developed to solve the problems identified in actual user cases. Often these studies mention at least fairness, explainability, transparency and accountability as basic set of desirable ethical objectives. However, principles alone are not enough. Only their successful application in practice can solve the real world problems [4]. Tools for applying principles in practice have been offered, for example, in the form of various impact assessment methods [1]. Simplified explanatory models focusing on technology deficiencies, control, or use do not allow for a broader context, the dynamism of systems, or complexity to be examined in detail. In the scientific discussion concerning the ethical issues of artificial intelligence, the need for systems thinking has been recognized to address the shortcomings mentioned

C. Stephanidis et al. (Eds.): HCII 2023, CCIS 1958, pp. 41–47, 2024.
https://doi.org/10.1007/978-3-031-49215-0_6

above [3, 5, 6, 12]. Instead of looking for a single cause or scapegoat, the aim of systems thinking is to understand the entire sociotechnical system as a complex and dynamic process [8]. This approach allows us to explore the diversity of factors at various levels, aiding in the effective analysis and design of human-AI interactions.

In response to the aforementioned challenges, this study presents a theoretical foundation for a practical approach to applying systems thinking to the ethics of AI. The proposed strategy involves utilizing and adapting system theoretical research focused on safety-related issues. The theoretical and conceptual work is conducted through a method of philosophical analysis and synthesis. The systems theoretical perspective has demonstrated successful application in the realm of safety research, both theoretically and methodologically [8–10, 14]. In practical terms, the application of systems thinking in human-algorithm interaction has already been explored and implemented, for example in the aviation industry [8–10]. The next crucial step involves extending this framework to encompass ethical considerations.

The hypothesis put forth in this study suggests that a systems theory is applicable to addressing the ethical challenges posed by artificial intelligence. This is because accidents and hazardous situations can be viewed as a subset of a broader range of ethical problems encompassing various physical, psychological, social, and philosophical dilemmas. Ultimately, both safety and ethical issues revolve around preventing undesired situations from manifesting in real-life scenarios. This study contributes to a larger methodological agenda seeking to extend the wide array of theories and methods utilized in safety science to the realms of AI ethics and HCI [5]. The argument asserts that the extensive and reliable track record of safety science can serve as a promising benchmark for the investigation of AI ethics. One could refer to this as an "accident analysis" approach to AI ethics or an "alignment engineering" framework for developing ethically sound AI systems. Due to the concise nature of this paper, only the fundamental theoretical framework and some preliminary ideas for applying methods in an HCI environment can be introduced here.

2   Theoretical and Philosophical Foundations

This study primarily draws upon Nancy Leveson's [8] systems-theoretic causal model as its foundation. The theoretical framework originates from the engineering sciences of the 1930s and 1940s, which emerged in response to the growing complexity of developed systems and the need for more advanced design and operational methods. However, a challenge arises when applying concepts and practices of safety engineering to contemporary HCI research, particularly concerning ethical issues. The concepts and methods employed in AI ethics and critical algorithmic studies are predominantly rooted in the social sciences and moral philosophy [6]. Hence, there is a clear necessity to establish a common ground among engineering, philosophy, and social sciences. By assimilating systems-theoretic modeling to mechanistic explanations in social sciences [7], two distinct scientific paradigms can be integrated, at least at a theoretical level. Scientific thinking and reasoning involve modeling the real world by simplifying and creating idealized representations of the complex reality. Similarly, ethical analysis and reasoning can be seen as a form of modeling [11]. The following sections will provide further insight into these theoretical and philosophical concepts.

2.1 Systems-Theoretic Causal Model

The framework employed in this study is known as the Systems-Theoretic Accident Model and Processes (STAMP), as named by Nancy Leveson [8]. STAMP functions as a systems-theoretic causal model and should not be regarded as an explanation for specific empirical phenomena in itself. Instead, it serves as a theoretical foundation and framework that can be utilized to construct actual explanatory models for specific empirical cases. In essence, STAMP is a model for developing causal models. It is worth noting that systems theory expands upon straightforward linear reasoning. Therefore, simple linear causation is encompassed within systems theory and it can be used to explain linear chains of events. However, it is also true that for many non-complex cases, analytic reduction proves to be a more efficient method than a systemic approach. Nonetheless, when analytic reduction falls short, systems theory offers a more versatile toolbox for modeling and providing explanations. When determining the suitability of the systems theory for particular research problems, it is important to consider that, in addition to complex interactions, a certain degree of structural form and stability is required within the phenomenon under study. This implies that the subjects being investigated cannot be inherently random in nature. Statistical methods are better suited for complex phenomena and data with randomly distributed properties.

Leveson continues that [8] the fundamental principles of systems theory encompass communication, control, hierarchy, and emergence. These concepts provide the basis for understanding and constructing a control loop illustrated in Fig. 1. In this loop, a higher-level entity in the hierarchy exercises control over a lower-level process by means of communication or command signal through an information channel. Conversely, the lower-level process communicates back to the higher-level controller through a separate information channel, using feedback signals. Levenson defines communication as the transfer of information within the system model, as well as between different levels of the hierarchical structure. The concept of information captures the transmission of causation within the model.

In addition to control loop a specific process model is needed for the hierarchical safety control structure to function properly according to Leveson[8]. To effectively perform its control function, a controller requires an internal process model that represents the complete controlled system. This allows the controller to adapt its control signals for the lower-level process based on the received feedback. The process model serves as another significant concept in STAMP. Additionally, the controller may receive signals from the environment or from higher-level controllers within the hierarchy. In such cases, the original controller in this example assumes the role of a lower-level process from the perspective of the higher-level.

In the model, safety is characterized as an emergent property that manifests at a higher level within the hierarchy compared to the actual controlled system [8]. A single failure within any component of the system can result in the system transitioning to an unsafe state. The preservation of safety necessitates the effective management of all safety-related hazards. Control plays a crucial role in enforcing predetermined safety constraints which are the most basic concept in STAMP. Stated differently, without knowledge of the safety constraints, it becomes impossible to control them in a predetermined manner.

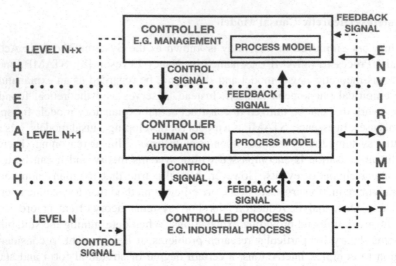

Fig. 1. Hierarchical safety control structure based on STAMP

2.2 Mechanistic Explanation and Modelling of Ethics

When doing scientific research many kind of questions can be made. So it is important to define precisely what are we actually explaining in a particular case. For example we can ask if the studied phenomenon even exists at all. Then we can try to define its characteristics and how it differs when compared to other phenomena. We can also ask why does it have its specific qualities? Finally causal mechanistic explanation allows for answering "what if" type of questions [7]. What happens if some detail in observed phenomenon is altered? Properly designed causal mechanism can answer for example how the advent of AI affects a particular ethical problem.

According to Roussos [11] models are often employed to study various aspects of different types of phenomena, even when their targets are not tangible entities but imaginative constructs, such as a picture of a dragon. In scientific investigation, models are considered indirect as researchers utilize them as proxies for real-world systems. Established research on ethics also relies on models, particularly in the realm of formal ethics. Mathematical objects are employed to represent different elements, including people, welfare, and constraints. Formal ethical models are frequently employed to test the compatibility and consistency of a set of ethical claims or conditions. Roussos continues [11] that representation in ethics extends beyond mathematically-intensive work and encompasses the use of diagrams or exemplary cases. Exemplification involves the creation of specific, imagined situations that represent a broader class of real-life scenarios, often illustrated through case studies. Ethical problems are often explained in form of narratives, but they can be studied also with empirical methods.

In conclusion, models play a pivotal role in both scientific and ethical inquiry, enabling researchers to study and gain insights into complex systems and ethical relationships [11]. They serve as valuable tools for representing and analyzing various phenomena, bridging the gap between theory and practice. Causal mechanisms are not necessarily deterministic [7]. There is room for contingencies and free will of agents. On the other hand intentionality is not needed for causal mechanism to function. Mechanistic explanation is also very flexible when considering normative opinions. It can be applied for several different ideologies and viewpoints within the modelled system. There are many different type of moral goals, like economic competition between individuals, organizations and nation states or individual moral truthfulness and moral obligations toward larger social network [6]. Causal mechanisms can be seen as specific tools for particular cases in a toolbox of scientific methods complementary to means of exploring more general types of laws concerning social processes [7].

3   Modelling AI Ethics with Systems Theory

In the systems-theoretic model, safety is considered an emergent property [8]. Following this line of thought, we can also view a successful ethical environment as an emergent property of a similar model. This means that both safety and ethical characteristics become apparent at a level higher in the hierarchy than the system being controlled. For instance, in safety research, a controlled process could be an industrial process. However, when it comes to ethical issues related to AI, social systems differ significantly from industrial processes. This necessitates a model that represents the social interactions under investigation. One straightforward approach is to interpret social interaction as a causal process of mediated information [2, 13]. This perspective aligns well with the systems-theoretic view [8], and is also supported by social scientific [13] and philosophical arguments [2].

There are numerous advantages to viewing causation as an information process rather than through the lens of action theory. In action theory, the actor and action are symmetrically related, meaning that regardless of the direction from which causation is observed, the actor and action remain unchanged [13]. Furthermore, in action theory, a third party or the target of action isn't essential. In contrast, information theory always requires three distinct elements: the sender, receiver, and the information relating the two. This relationship is asymmetrical, indicating that the direction and timing need to be accounted for when interpreting an information process [13]. A receiver can respond and transmit information back, but this can only occur after the initial communication is received. A key advantage of utilizing information as a causal intermediary in issues related to AI, is that it doesn't rely on the intentionality of the actor at a theoretical level. Therefore, there's no need to engage in debates over the possible intentionality of artificial agents compared to humans.

Human actions in real-life situations are not always deliberate or intentional, but it is feasible to incorporate internal cognitive processes such as intentionality into systems-theoretic models. However, in its most basic form, a STAMP-inspired safety control structure requires only a process model for the controller as in Fig. 1. Figure 2 showcases systems-theoretic causal model for an ethical social process. Notably, in the illustration, individual ethical process models X, Y, and Z are assigned to the actor and object of the social process, along with a higher-level controller which is defined as surrounding society in this example. The ethicality of this system depends on which of these three viewpoints or ethical process models is deemed definitive in a particular system. This is a common occurrence in many real-life situations, where the actor may not perceive any wrongdoing, while the object and the broader societal and institutional context might view the situation entirely differently. When all stakeholders are humans, the situation can be resolved through culturally specific norms, potentially aligning the different process models to some extent. However, when more complex algorithms and AI systems with significantly fewer spatial and temporal constraints become actors in social processes, this alignment process becomes considerably more challenging. Conventional feedback channels with other stakeholders become ineffective, and controlling the system becomes almost insurmountable.

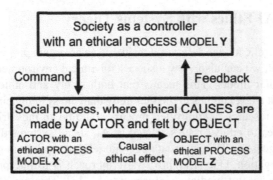

Fig. 2. A simple systems-theoretic causal model for ethical social process where every stakeholder has its own process model of ethics (X, Y or Z).

In terms of systems theory, the above described situation could be depicted as a scenario where the process model used by the controller doesn't correspond to the actual physical system. Leveson identifies four typical causes of accidents within the STAMP framework [8]. The first two involve either issuing incorrect or unsafe control commands or completely failing to take the necessary control actions. Another failure mode involves providing the correct command but doing so too early or too late. Finally, a control command can be halted prematurely or applied for an excessive duration, leading to an unsafe state in the system. This same logic can be adapted to the systems-theoretic ethical model in Fig. 2.

The systems-theoretic approach postulates that an ethical constraint must be chosen, and it's unfeasible to optimize a system for multiple distinct ethical process models. This approach can illuminate various dilemmas and paradoxes. It also enables comparison of ethical system models between those exclusively involving human stakeholders and those incorporating artificial agents. For instance, what distinguishes a minor, an intoxicated person, or an unlicensed driver from an artificially autonomous vehicle operator in an ethical context? Who should take responsibility in these various scenarios? AI systems can exhibit superhuman capabilities in terms of speed, scope, and physical accessibility. The systems-theoretic framework can also be used to investigate such phenomena.

This research is solely a theoretical exploration without direct ties to empirical cases. The actual empirical work is left for future research efforts. Detailed guidelines for this kind of empirical analysis are provided by Leveson and her co-authors in the form of STAMP-based methods named Systems Theoretic Process Analysis (STPA) [8, 9] and

Causal Analysis based on System Theory (CAST) [8, 10]. Building on the theoretical work discussed above, these methods can be expanded and adapted for the field of HCI in cases involving safety, security, and ethical dimensions. This research can open new avenues for a multidisciplinary approach to the subject of AI ethics.

References

1. Ayling, J., Chapman, A.: Putting AI ethics to work: are the tools fit for purpose? AI Ethics **2**, 405–429 (2022). https://doi.org/10.1007/s43681-021-00084-x
2. Collier, J.D.: Causation is the transfer of information. In: Sankey, H. (eds.) Causation and Laws of Nature. Australasian Studies in History and Philosophy of Science, vol. 14 (1999). https://doi.org/10.1007/978-94-015-9229-1_18
3. Gillespie, T.: Systems Engineering for Ethical Autonomous Systems. SciTech Publishing, London (2019)
4. Hagendorff, T.: The ethics of AI ethics: an evaluation of guidelines. Mind. Mach. **30**(1), 99–120 (2020). https://doi.org/10.1007/s11023-020-09517-8
5. Hallamaa, J.: What could safety research contribute to technology design? In: Rauterberg, M. (eds.) HCII 2021. LNCS, vol. 12795, pp. 56–79. Springer, Cham (2021). https://doi.org/10.1007/978-3-030-77431-8_4
6. Hallamaa, J., Kalliokoski, T. AI ethics as applied ethics. Front. Comput. Sci. **4** (2022). https://doi.org/10.3389/fcomp.2022.776837
7. Hedström, P., Ylikoski, P.: Causal mechanisms in the social sciences. Ann. Rev. Sociol. **36**, 49–67 (2010). https://doi.org/10.1146/annurev.soc.012809.102632
8. Leveson, N.G.: Engineering a Safer World: Systems Thinking Applied to Safety. The MIT Press (2011). https://doi.org/10.7551/mitpress/8179.001.0001
9. Leveson, N., Thomas, J.: Systems-Theoretic Process Analysis Handbook (2018). https://psas.scripts.mit.edu/home/get_file.php?name=STPA_handbook.pdf
10. Leveson, N.: CAST Handbook: How to Learn More from Incidents and Accidents (2019). http://sunnyday.mit.edu/CAST-Handbook.pdf
11. Roussos, J.: Modelling in normative ethics. Ethic. Theory Moral. Prac. **25**, 865–889 (2022). https://doi.org/10.1007/s10677-022-10326-4
12. Salo-Pöntinen, H.: AI ethics - critical reflections on embedding ethical frameworks in AI technology. In: Rauterberg, M. (eds.) Culture and Computing. Design Thinking and Cultural Computing. HCII 2021. LNCS, vol. 12795, pp. 311–329. Springer, Cham (2021). https://doi.org/10.1007/978-3-030-77431-8_20
13. Stichweh, R.: Systems theory as an alternative to action theory? The rise of "Communication" as a theoretical option. Acta Sociol. **43**(1), 5–13 (2000). https://doi.org/10.1177/000169930004300102
14. Young, W., Leveson, N.G.: An integrated approach to safety and security based on systems theory. Commun. ACM **57**(2), 31–35 (2014). https://doi.org/10.1145/2556938

Comparative Analysis for Open-Source Large Language Models

Amir Schur$^{(\boxtimes)}$ ⓘ and Sam Groenjes ⓘ

Dark Wolf Solutions LLC, Herndon, VA 20171, USA

{amir.schur,sam.groenjes}@darkwolfsolutions.com

Abstract. Large Language Models (LLMs) have significantly advanced the field of Natural Language Processing (NLP), demonstrating exceptional performance across diverse language tasks such as content summarization, sentiment analysis, and conversational AI. The advent of these models has profoundly impacted human-computer interaction research, marking the onset of a new era in the field. The pioneering model, ChatGPT, was introduced by OpenAI in November 2022, catalyzing the development of other commercial tools like Bing Chat and Google Bard. Subsequently, the emergence of open-source LLMs has democratized access to these powerful tools, enabling end-users to deploy them internally with relative ease. As the landscape of open-source LLMs continues to expand and evolve, researchers and practitioners are presented with a plethora of choices for NLP applications. This paper presents a comparative analysis for various open-source LLMs, assessing their unique features, strengths, and limitations. Our focus of comparisons will include licensing, training methods, computing resources needed, available application programming interfaces (APIs), robustness, and bias.

Keywords: Large Language Models · Natural Language Processing · Artificial Intelligence · Comparative Analysis · Open-Source Models

1 Background

1.1 Technological Background

What made LLMs possible? A significant technological milestone that we cannot ignore was the introduction of the transformer architecture by a team at Google Brain. The transformer model was introduced as an alternative architecture to existing recurrent neural networks. This new architecture relies solely on attention mechanisms and eliminated the need for recurrence, which was computationally expensive and challenging on parallelization efforts. This new architecture achieved improved parallelization, enabling significant gains in computational efficiency and state-of-the-art performance in tasks like machine translation [1].

This breakthrough opened the door for continuous improvement and advancement of technologies in machine learning, including the development of LLMs. Current on-going and rapid development of LLMs is an ongoing interest for data scientists and researchers. Various surveys of LLM development can show these fascinating developments [2–4].

© The Author(s), under exclusive license to Springer Nature Switzerland AG 2024
C. Stephanidis et al. (Eds.): HCII 2023, CCIS 1958, pp. 48–54, 2024.
https://doi.org/10.1007/978-3-031-49215-0_7

1.2   Open-Source Need

Depending on the nature of research and the sensitivity of data used, accessing an LLM as-a-service over the internet may not always be feasible. For scientific research, reproducibility is a critical factor, and proprietary, closed models may not be suitable for independent inspection or verification [5]. Furthermore, as discussed within a recent Dark Wolf blog post [6], the ethical use of AI and compliance with regulations are crucial considerations in the deployment of AI technologies, further emphasizing the need for open-source models that can be scrutinized and adapted as needed.

In response to these challenges, the industry has seen the emergence of various open-source LLMs in the past few months, including LLaMA [7], Alpaca [8], GPT4All [9], Dolly 2 [10], Cerebras-GPT [11], Vicuna [12], OpenChatKit [13], ChatRWKV [14], Flan-T5 [15], CollosalChat [16], H2OGPT [17], and Falcon [18]. The rapid progress in this field suggests that this list will continue to grow.

2   Comparative Methods

There are various aspects of LLMs that can be evaluated so that a person can make an informed decision on which one he or she should use. Here we will explore various aspects of LLMs for comparative purposes.

2.1   Licensing and Accessibility

The licensing model provided for a particular LLM is a crucial consideration. Licenses may vary, including GNU General Public License, MIT License, Apache License, or academic research usage only (e.g., Alpaca). This should be the initial point of investigation, and any LLMs that do not provide suitable licensing permissions should be excluded from consideration.

2.2   Model Size

The size of an open-source LLM, indicated by its number of parameters, significantly influences its performance, resource demands, and cost-effectiveness. Larger models may offer superior performance but require more computational resources, often necessitating GPU use. Hence, a balance between model size and resource requirements is crucial. The concept of scaling laws in LLMs suggests performance enhancement with increased model size, data size, and computation, up to a point of diminishing returns. The model's architecture also impacts its size and performance. For instance, transformer-based models, common in LLMs, exhibit a quadratic relationship between sequence length and computational requirements, meaning a doubled sequence length quadruples computational needs. Thus, assessing a model's architecture is essential when evaluating its size and resource requirements [19].

2.3 Data Quality

The quality of data used for training LLMs is also an important factor. Contrary to the common belief that curated corpora are necessary for high-performing models, recent research, such as the "The RefinedWeb Dataset for Falcon LLM" paper, suggests that properly filtered and deduplicated web data can yield powerful models that outperform those trained on curated corpora [20]. As larger models requiring pretraining on trillions of tokens emerge, the scalability of curation becomes a significant challenge. The RefinedWeb dataset, a high-quality, web-only English pretraining dataset, demonstrates that web data, when properly processed, can be a scalable and plentiful source of high-quality data. The performance of LLMs trained on this dataset significantly surpasses those trained on curated corpora in zero-shot benchmarks, challenging conventional views about data quality.

2.4 Factual Accuracy and Bias Handling

LLMs, while powerful, grapple with two significant issues: hallucination and knowledge recency. Hallucination refers to the generation of information that is either in conflict with the existing source, (intrinsic hallucination), or cannot be verified by the available source, (extrinsic hallucination) [19]. This can lead to the production of inaccurate or biased information, posing potential risks when deploying LLMs in real-world applications. Strategies such as alignment tuning, which involves fine-tuning LLMs on high-quality data or using human feedback, have been employed to mitigate this problem.

Knowledge recency is another challenge, as LLMs may struggle with tasks requiring the latest knowledge beyond their training data. Regularly updating LLMs with new data is a straightforward but costly solution, and it may lead to the catastrophic forgetting issue when training LLMs incrementally. Some studies have explored the use of external knowledge sources, such as search engines, to complement LLMs. For instance, ChatGPT uses a retrieval plugin to access up-to-date information sources. However, the challenge of directly amending intrinsic knowledge or injecting specific knowledge into LLMs remains an open research problem.

2.5 Robustness and Speed

The robustness and speed of an LLM are critical factors in its practical application. The inference speed, or the time it takes for a model to generate a response, can greatly impact the user experience, especially in real-time applications like chatbots. Our informal testing revealed that the inference speed varies across different models and is not always directly proportional to the increase in system memory or processing power.

Furthermore, robustness refers to the model's ability to handle a variety of inputs and produce reliable outputs consistently. An LLM's robustness can be influenced by factors such as its architecture, training data, and size. For instance, larger models, while potentially more powerful, may also be more prone to overfitting or generating "hallucinated" results.

Techniques such as quantization can help improve both the speed and robustness of LLMs. Quantization reduces the precision of the numbers used in the model, thereby decreasing the computational resources needed. However, it's a delicate balance as aggressive quantization can lead to a loss in model performance.

2.6   Training Methods and Fine-Tuning

Training large language models (LLMs) is a complex process that often requires distributed training algorithms and parallel strategies. Optimization frameworks like Deep-Speed and Megatron-LM facilitate this process [19], along with optimization tricks for training stability and model performance. For instance, GPT-4 has developed special infrastructure and optimization methods to predict the performance of large models using smaller ones.

Fine-tuning is essential to align LLMs with specific applications or unique needs. For instance, H2OGPT provides a no-code GUI framework, H2OLLM Studio [21], for fine-tuning LLMs on question-and-answer datasets.

Alignment tuning is another crucial aspect, especially to mitigate the generation of toxic, biased, or harmful content. Techniques like reinforcement learning with human feedback, as used in InstructGPT [19], have shown promising results in aligning LLMs with human values (Fig. 1).

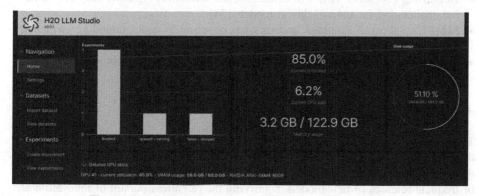

Fig. 1. H2O LLMStudio with permission from H2O.ai (2023)

2.7   API Availability

API availability significantly impacts the ease of implementing and interfacing with an LLM. Open-source LLMs that provide APIs allow developers to build and deploy applications rapidly. APIs should be clear and well-documented to allow smooth integration. Many models provide a Python API that makes it possible to leverage the power of LLMs even for developers with a basic understanding of Python. However, the lack of standardized APIs across different LLMs may require additional work when transitioning between models.

3   Open-Source LLMs

After deciding on an internal checklist, evaluating various open-source LLMs can be time-consuming and resource-intensive. A good initial, cursory look can be to evaluate already-deployed models. For example, you can go to the model developer's website to see if they host a public-facing open-source LLM for evaluation.

3.1   Benchmark Usage

Monitoring the development and performance of various LLMs is essential due to the rapid pace of innovation in this field. Hugging Face, a leader in this area, has established the Open LLM Leaderboard [22] that tracks, ranks, and evaluates emerging LLMs and chatbots, providing an accessible platform to identify the current state-of-the-art models.

The leaderboard relies on four key benchmarks from the Eleuther AI Language Model Evaluation Harness, a unified framework designed to test generative language models across a broad spectrum of evaluation tasks. These benchmarks include:

- AI2 Reasoning Challenge (25-shot)[1]: A series of grade-school science questions, testing the model's scientific reasoning abilities [23].
- HellaSwag (10-shot): A test of commonsense inference, typically easy for humans but challenging for state-of-the-art models [24].
- MMLU (5-shot): A multitask accuracy test covering 57 tasks, including elementary mathematics, US history, computer science, law, and more [25].
- TruthfulQA (0-shot): A measure of a model's propensity to reproduce falsehoods commonly found online [26].

4   Conclusions and Continuous Work

The emergence of LLMs has sparked immense interest and captivated the attention of data science enthusiasts and researchers alike. This fascination stems from the continuous development and rapid progress witnessed in this field. The field has experienced a flurry of frequent releases of new models, signifying the relentless pursuit of innovation and improvement. This upsurge of new applications harnessing the power of LLMs further exemplifies the transformative impact they have made across various domains.

Open-source LLMs have gained prominence, addressing the need for accessibility, reproducibility, and independent inspection. A range of open-source LLMs has been introduced as stated above, with the list continuing to grow, ensuring an expanding repertoire of options for researchers and developers alike.

To evaluate and compare different LLMs, several aspects need to be considered. These include licensing, model size and resource usage, factual accuracy, robustness/speed, training methods, API availability, and bias handling. Each of these factors plays a crucial role in determining the suitability and performance of an LLM for a specific application.

---

[1] In few-shot learning, the term "n-shot" pertains to the number of labeled examples, or "shots", given for each task during the evaluation stage. Here, "n" signifies the specific count of examples utilized to adapt or fine-tune the model to each new task it encounters.

Evaluating open-source LLMs can be a time-consuming and resource-intensive task. However, one approach is to start with benchmark usage and explore already-deployed models. Platforms like the Hugging Face open LLM leaderboard provide insights into the latest developments and rankings, assisting in the selection process.

Overall, the advancements in LLMs and the availability of open-source options have transformed the landscape of language processing and machine learning. Continued research, evaluation, and improvement of LLMs will contribute to further breakthroughs and applications in this field.

References

1. Vaswani, A., et al.: Attention is all you need. Adv. Neural Inf. Process. Syst. **30** (2017)
2. Fan, L., Li, L., Ma, Z., Lee, S., Yu, H., Hemphill, L.: A bibliometric review of large language models research from 2017 to 2023. arXiv preprint arXiv:2304.02020 (2023)
3. Zhao, W.X., et al.: A survey of large language models. arXiv preprint arXiv:2303.18223 (2023)
4. Yang, J., et al.: Harnessing the power of LLMs in practice: a survey on ChatGPT and beyond. arXiv preprint arXiv:2304.13712 (2023)
5. Spirling, A.: Why open-source generative AI models are an ethical way forward for science. Nature. https://www.nature.com/articles/d41586-023-01295-4. Accessed 18 Apr 2023
6. Fordham, T.: EP5: the impact of AI on the IT and cybersecurity consulting industry: adaptation, challenges and opportunities. In: Dark Wolf Solutions Blog. https://blog.darkwolfsolutions.com/dws-blog-04-19-2023-ep-5. Accessed 19 Apr 2023
7. Touvron, H., et al.: Llama: open and efficient foundation language models. arXiv preprint arXiv:2302.13971 (2023)
8. Taori, R., et al. Alpaca: a strong, replicable instruction-following model. Stanford Center Res. Found. Mod. **3**(6), 7 (2023). https://crfm.stanford.edu/2023/03/13/alpaca.html
9. Anand, Y., Nussbaum, Z., Duderstadt, B., Schmidt, B., Mulyar, A.: Gpt4all: training an assistant-style chatbot with large scale data distillation from gpt-3.5-turbo. In: GitHub (2023)
10. Databricks. Dolly: first open commercially viable instruction-tuned LLM. In: Databricks Blog. https://www.databricks.com/blog/2023/04/12/dolly-first-open-commercially-viable-instruction-tuned-llm. Accessed 12 Apr 2023
11. Dey, N., et al.: Cerebras-GPT: open compute-optimal language models trained on the cerebras wafer-scale cluster. arXiv preprint arXiv:2304.03208 (2023)
12. Chiang, W.-L., et al.: Vicuna: an open-source chatbot impressing gpt-4 with 90%* ChatGPT quality (2023). https://vicuna.lmsys.org. Accessed 14 Apr 2023
13. Together Computer. (n.d.). OpenChatKit. GitHub. https://github.com/togethercomputer/OpenChatKit. Accessed 14 June 2023
14. BlinkDL. (n.d.). ChatRWKV. GitHub. https://github.com/BlinkDL/ChatRWKV. Accessed 14 June 2023
15. Chung, H.W., et al.: Scaling instruction-finetuned language models. arXiv preprint arXiv: 2210.11416 (2022)
16. HPCA AI Tech. (n.d.). ColossalAI. GitHub. https://github.com/hpcaitech/ColossalAI. Accessed 14 June 2023
17. H2O.ai. (n.d.). h2ogpt. GitHub. https://github.com/h2oai/h2ogpt
18. Almazrouei, E., et al.: Falcon-40B: An Open Large Language Model with State-of-the-Art Performance (2023)
19. Zhao, W.X., et al.: A survey of large language models. arXiv preprint arXiv:2303.18223 (2023). https://doi.org/10.48550/arXiv.2303.18223

20. Penedo, G., et al.: The RefinedWeb dataset for falcon LLM: outperforming curated corpora with web data, and web data only. arXiv preprint arXiv:2306.01116 (2023). https://doi.org/10.48550/arXiv.2306.01116
21. H2O LLM Studio (n.d). Github. https://github.com/h2oai/h2o-llmstudio. Accessed 14 June 2023
22. Beeching, E., et al.: Open LLM leaderboard. Hugging face (2023). https://huggingface.co/spaces/HuggingFaceH4/open_llm_leaderboard
23. Clark, P., et al.: Think you have solved question answering? Try ARC, the AI2 reasoning challenge. arXiv preprint https://arxiv.org/abs/1803.05457 (2018)
24. Zellers, R., Holtzman, A., Bisk, Y., Farhadi, A., Choi, Y.: HellaSwag: can a machine really finish your sentence? arXiv preprint https://arxiv.org/abs/1905.07830 (2019)
25. Hendrycks, D., et al.: Measuring massive multitask language understanding. arXiv preprint https://arxiv.org/abs/2009.03300 (2021)
26. Lin, S., Hilton, J., Evans, O.: TruthfulQA: measuring how models mimic human falsehoods. arXiv preprint https://arxiv.org/abs/2109.07958 (2022)

Exploration and Evaluation of Prompting Methods for Text Style Transfer

Vlad Stefan[✉]

Keio University, Tokyo, Japan
`vlad.stefan@keio.jp`

Abstract. Text Style Transfer is a task concerned with modifying the attributes of a text while leaving its meaning unchanged. In recent years, this task has gained much attention due to the promising performance of deep learning models. However, progress is still slow due to an over-reliance on large datasets and a lack of reliable evaluation methodology. To address the data challenge, the present research proposes the usage of prompting techniques which have shown very good performances on other natural language generation tasks in few-shot settings. Furthermore, considering the lack of conventional evaluation methods, this study explores various methods employed in previous research. This includes automatic metrics, but also human evaluation. Prompting outperforms fine-tuning according to computed metrics and to human assessment, but there seems to be little correlation between the human judgement and automatic metrics assessing then meaning conservation and the fluency of generated text.

Keywords: Text style transfer · Prompting · Human evaluation

1 Introduction

Naturally produced language is very situational. It can be influenced by many factors, such as the place and time of production, the personal characteristics of the author, and the communicated intent. For example, it is obvious that a professional context will give rise to a more formal language than a casual context, even if the meaning remains the same (e.g.: "Please consider taking a seat." ⟺ "Come and sit!"). These linguistic variations constitute what is known as the style, or attribute, of the language.

Modifying the form of text without changing its semantic content is known as Text Style Transfer (TST). Progress is still held back by certain design issues, including a dependence on large parallel corpuses for model training and a lack of conventional evaluation methods. This research seeks to tackle both of these problems.

To reduce the need for large datasets, the present study investigates the use of prompting techniques. Prompting refers to providing a text or a set of keywords as input to an AI model, in order to guide it towards the generation of certain a

C. Stephanidis et al. (Eds.): HCII 2023, CCIS 1958, pp. 55–64, 2024.
https://doi.org/10.1007/978-3-031-49215-0_8

response or the completion of a task [11]. For this study, two different prompting techniques known as prompt tuning [9] and prefix-tuning [10] are used to create TST models. Those models are trained and tested on subsets of the GYAFC dataset [17].

To determine the best method for evaluation, multiple evaluation metrics are employed to rate the model output. A thorough human evaluation is conducted to find the metrics most correlated with the human judgement.

2   Literature

2.1   Text Style Transfer

Text Style Transfer (TST) is the task concerned with automatically adjusting the style of generated language while keeping the semantic content unchanged [20]. There are many different TST sub-tasks that focus on specific stylistic changes. Some common examples include: change a casual sentence into a formal one [16], transform a text written by an expert to make it more understandable for the layman [3], remove offensive elements from a sentence to make it more neutral [8].

Many of the current techniques used to perform TST are based on the fine-tuning of large pre-trained neural networks [11,20]. During the fine-tuning process, the pre-trained model is adapted to a specific task [18]. This requires the use of domain-specific target data. For example, to create a neural network capable of removing offensive elements from a sentence, it is necessary to have a corpus of text that contains rude sentences and their civil rephrasing.

However, even with this procedure the acquisition of sufficient target data for fine-tuning is still a limiting factor for many tasks, including TST. Many recent TST studies use large corpuses containing thousands of labelled sentences with the target styles. However, the creation of such a corpus is a difficult and time-consuming task that often requires the aid of multiple human annotators. Thus, it would be interesting to loosen these dataset requirements [7].

Another major issue that plagues current studies is the lack of conventional evaluation methods. Although important evaluation criteria are known, there are no agreed upon metrics reported in all studies [7].

2.2   Prompting

Prompting is a methodology for using pre-training models. Until recently, the main way to apply a pre-trained model to a downstream task was to fine-tune the model to adapt it to the task. Prompting seeks instead to adapt the task in order to make it resemble the pre-training process of the model. In prompting, the input sentences given to the model are modified with a textual prompt. The purpose of the textual prompt is to provide a context that will push the model to solve the required task [11].

A simple example of prompting is shown in Fig. 1. The task shown is sentiment analysis. With prompting, the input of the model is modified. A textual prompt with a blank space is added to the sentence, and the model is asked to predict the word that would most fit the sentence. The word chosen by the model indirectly gives the sentiment of the sentence. With this paradigm, a

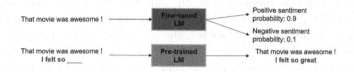

Fig. 1. Sentiment analysis with fine-tuning and prompting

pre-trained model can thus be used with little to no additional training, which greatly reduces the need for domain-specific data. As such, it seems like a good solution to help with the large data requirements of classic TST techniques.

Prompt Engineering. The process of creating a prompt for a specific task is referred to as prompt engineering. Finding the correct prompting method for the task is not a trivial problem. It depends on many factors such the architecture of the model, the pre-training process, or the task. The prompt engineering process is divided into two steps [11].

First, it is necessary to determine the shape of the prompt. Prompt shapes are mainly divided in two categories. The first type of shape regroups prompts that are textual strings with blanks to be filled in. They are known as *cloze prompts*. These prompts are usually well suited for classification problems. Indeed, The blank spots are usually filled in with certain keywords from the vocabulary of the model which are associated with the classes [4,13]. The second type of prompt shape is known as *prefix prompts*. As the name indicates, these prompts precede the output and are suited for generation tasks since the size of the output is not limited to a few keywords [2,9,10].

After choosing the shape, the method for generating the prompt itself must be selected. The simplest way to design a prompt is to manually create it [2,13]. Although intuitive, this approach relies heavily on the experience and knowledge of the designer. There is also no guarantee that the prompt is optimal for the task. Thus, several algorithms have been developed to automatically create prompts. These automatically generated prompts can be textual strings [19,22] but also vectors in the embedding space of the model [9,10].

3 Methodology

3.1 Training Methods and Pre-Trained Model

Model. The model used during experiments is the T5 (Text-to-Text Transfer Transformer). It is a transformer-based language model [15]. The base size of the T5 model was used.

Training Methods. Three different methods were used to train the TST model. First, the T5 model was fine-tuned for the task to use as a baseline.

Second *prompt tuning* was employed. In prompt tuning, the prompt is not raw text, but rather a continuous vector of parameters in the embedding space of the model, which is prepended to the input of the model. The parameters of this vector are optimized to generate a context that will steer the language model to solve a specific task. However, the parameters of the pre-trained neural network are left unchanged [9].

Finally, *prefix-tuning* was employed. This method is similar to prompt tuning in that it adds a vector of tunable parameters to the input of the model. This prefix is there to add context and steer the model towards the task at hand. However, the main difference is that a new prefix is prepended for all layers of the language model. Prefix-tuning thus uses more parameters than prompt tuning [10].

All models were trained with early stopping. As such, after 15 unsuccessful iterations, the training was stopped. The Adafactor optimizer was applied for the training. The parameters of the prefix-tuning and prompt tuning models were taken as the optimal parameters shown in the original papers [9,10]. Similarly, the learning rate for fine-tuning was chosen as 0.001 as shown in the original T5 paper [15].

3.2 Dataset

The dataset chosen to train and test the model is the GYFAC dataset, which is a corpus created for the task of formality TST [17]. The dataset is composed of sentences posted by internet users on discussion forums and the formal rewriting of those sentences.

The dataset is already subdivided into training, validation and test sets. However, to simulate a low-data environment, smaller training and validation sets were subsampled from the original sets. These smaller sets contained 5, 15, 50, 100, or 300 samples. For each size, three different sets were subsampled to average the results.

3.3 Evaluation

A text style transfer system is usually evaluated on its capacity to keep the meaning of the original text, change its form, and on its fluency. These criteria can be evaluated automatically or by humans. Both approaches have their own strengths and weaknesses.

Automatic Evaluation. Automatic evaluation methods are simple to implement and easily reproducible. However, due to the complexity of natural languages, no one metric is infallible. This study goes over some common evaluation strategies to ascertain their usefulness.

Semantic Conservation. Many metrics used in similar fields, such as machine translation, can be reapplied to test the semantic conservation capabilities of TST systems. The measures are usually calculated by comparing the machine output with a reference text. The metrics used for this investigation are the following: BLEU [12], NIST [6], METEOR [1], and BERTScore [23].

Fluency. The fluency of a TST system is calculated using the perplexity(PP) computed by a language model. PP measures how well a probability model predicts a sequence of events. It provides a quantitative measure of how uncertain the model is when trying to predict the next event given the context. A lower PP indicates a better model that is more confident and accurate in its predictions. Conversely, a higher PP suggests that the model is more uncertain and less accurate. The BERT [5] and GPT2 [14] language models were employed to compute the perplexity. For both models, the base size was used.

Style Transfer Strength. The common method to evaluate the capacity of a model to change the style of the text is by training a classifier capable of identifying the target style. The percentage of generated texts correctly classified is taken as the transfer strength(TS) of the TST model.

Multiple classifier were trained for this study based on models used in previous papers. The models used for this task are thus a CNN, LSTM, and BERT classifiers. All models were trained on the same training set as the TST models with the Adam optimizer using a learning rate of 0.0001. The LSTM and CNN models were trained during 10 iterations, while the BERT classifier was only trained for 2 iterations. The LSTM, CNN, and BERT models achieved an accuracy of 88.19%, 89.55%, and 90.27% respectively on the testing set. The BERT model was one of the smallest architecture presented in [21].

Human Evaluation. Human evaluation is a lot more flexible and comprehensive than automatic methods. However, it is also more difficult to reproduce, more costly, and also more time-consuming.

For this report, the evaluation was performed using the Amazon Mechanical Turks crowdsourcing platform. The evaluators were given 100 sentence pairs that show the original sentence and the one generated by the system, and were asked to rate these pairs on a scale of 1 to 5 according to the three previously established criteria.

4 Results

The results obtained during the experiments are shown as graphs in the following sections. All graphs present the evolution of evaluation metrics as a function of the size of the training set.

4.1   Semantic Conservation

Figures 2a, 2b, 2c, 2d, and 2e show the evolution of all semantic conservation metrics with the size of the training set. All metrics show that both prompting techniques have similar performances for most training set sizes and are in general better than regular fine-tuning. The only exception is for the smallest size with only 5 samples. In that case, fine-tuning usually performs better than prompt tuning but remains worst than prefix-tuning.

However, according to the human evaluation, prompt tuning is better at conserving the meaning of text than the other techniques when trained with sets containing 50 or 100 samples. For the smallest sizes, prefix-tuning seems to have an advantage. When the largest size is used, the performances are very similar for all three techniques. The situation is illustrated in Fig. 2f.

There is very little correlation between automatic metrics and human judgement, as shown by the Pearson correlation coefficients in the first five columns in Table 1.

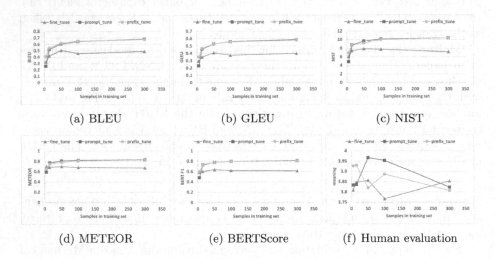

(a) BLEU	(b) GLEU	(c) NIST
(d) METEOR	(e) BERTScore	(f) Human evaluation

Fig. 2. Evaluation of semantic conservation

Table 1. Pearson Correlation Coefficient between automatic metrics and human evaluation

	bleu	gleu	nist	meteor	BERTScore	pp BERT	pp GPT2	ts LSTM	ts CNN	ts BERT
ρ	0.2310	0.2554	0.2375	0.2210	0.2601	0.1994	0.4806	0.5843	0.5739	0.5481

4.2   Fluency

Figure 3a shows that, when computed with the BERT language model, the perplexity of the prompting methods tend to be generally lower than fine-tuning. This would indicate that the sentences generated through prompting are usually more fluent. However, computing the perplexity with GPT2 does not corroborate the previous affirmation. Indeed, Fig. 3b shows very similar performances between all methods, except for the smallest and largest training set sizes. For training sets with only 5 samples, prefix-tuning seems to have an advantage and, for sets with 300 samples, fine-tuning seems to generate more fluent sentences.

The human evaluation illustrated in Fig. 3c seems to show a similar behaviour as Fig. 2f. Prefix-tuning has an advantage when 5 samples are used for training, while prompt tuning tends to be better with trainings of 50 or 100 samples. At 300 samples, prefix-tuning, prompt tuning, and fine-tuning achieve similar results.

Once again, there seems to be little correlation between the automatic metrics and human judgement. The small Pearson correlation coefficients shown in column six and seven of Table 1 corroborate this hypothesis. However, the correlation does seem much higher between the human evaluation and the perplexity computed by GPT2.

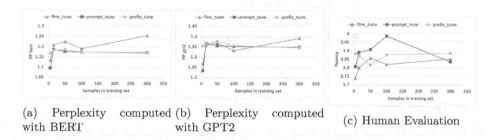

(a) Perplexity computed with BERT

(b) Perplexity computed with GPT2

(c) Human Evaluation

Fig. 3. Evaluation of fluency

4.3   Style Transfer Strength

All automatic evaluation methods show similar behaviours in Figs. 4a, 4b, and 4c. Both prompting methods have better transfer strength than fine-tuning for most training sizes. Also, prefix-tuning surpasses prompt tuning in general, except for the largest training size where both methods have the same performance.

The human evaluation does not perfectly concord with the automatic evaluation. However, it does show similar patterns as seen in Figs. 2f and 3c. Prompt tuning tends to have better results for set sizes of 50 and 100 samples, while prefix-tuning is more performant than other methods when trained with 5 or 15 samples. For the largest training size, all methods show a similar performance.

Unlike the previous evaluation criteria, in this instance there seems to be a decent correlation between the automatic metrics and human evaluation. The last three columns of Table 1 show the largest correlation coefficients seen so far.

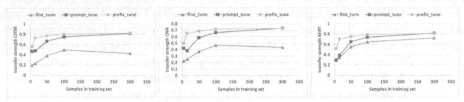

(a) Transfer strength with LSTM   (b) Transfer strength with CNN   (c) Transfer strength with BERT

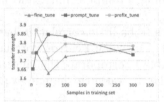

(d) Human evaluation of transfer strength

Fig. 4. Evaluation of transfer strength

4.4   Discussion

Both automatic and human evaluation show that prompting methods tend to perform better than fine-tuning when the model is trained on smaller amounts of data. However, when it comes to semantic similarity and fluency, there seems to be little correlation between the automatic and human evaluation. This calls for the development of new evaluation metrics to better capture the subtleties of human judgement. It is also necessary to perform a more thorough investigation with multiple datasets, prompting methods, and pre-trained models to see the influence of each factor.

The automatic metrics used to compute transfer strength seem well correlated with the human evaluation. It seems that the trained classifiers were quite proficient in their task. It might be interesting to train models capable of evaluating the other two criteria and see if it aligns more closely with human judgment. It might also be interesting to look at recent evaluation strategies used in similar tasks, such as machine translation.

5   Conclusion

The present study proposes the use of prompting to create Text Style Transfer(TST) systems without relying on large datasets for training. The proposed hypothesis was tested by applying two known prompting techniques, prefix-tuning and prompt tuning, to the task of formality style transfer on the GYAFC dataset and comparing these methods to classical fine-tuning. Multiple models were trained using different sizes of training sets subsampled from the original dataset to simulate a low-data environment. The created models were evaluated on three criteria: semantic conservation, fluency, and style transfer strength. To rate the models, several automatic evaluation strategies were used in conjunction with human evaluation to determine metrics most correlated with human assessments.

Prompting techniques were shown to be more performant than, or at least as performant as, fine-tuning in low-data settings according to most metrics and human evaluations. The automatic assessment of style transfer strength seems to have a good correlation with human judgement. However, the automatic metrics used to assess the semantic conservation and the fluency of the model have little correlation with the human evaluation. Future research in the area should thus focus on finding metrics concordant with human ratings.

References

1. Banerjee, S., Lavie, A.: METEOR: An automatic metric for MT evaluation with improved correlation with human judgments. In: Proceedings of the ACL Workshop on Intrinsic and Extrinsic Evaluation Measures for Machine Translation and/or Summarization, pp. 65–72. Association for Computational Linguistics, Ann Arbor, Michigan (2005). https://aclanthology.org/W05-0909
2. Brown, T.B., et al.: Language models are few-shot learners. CoRR abs/2005.14165 (2020). https://arxiv.org/abs/2005.14165
3. Cao, Y., Shui, R., Pan, L., Kan, M., Liu, Z., Chua, T.: Expertise style transfer: a new task towards better communication between experts and laymen. CoRR abs/2005.00701 (2020). https://arxiv.org/abs/2005.00701
4. Cui, L., Wu, Y., Liu, J., Yang, S., Zhang, Y.: Template-based named entity recognition using BART. CoRR abs/2106.01760 (2021). https://arxiv.org/abs/2106.01760
5. Devlin, J., Chang, M., Lee, K., Toutanova, K.: BERT: pre-training of deep bidirectional transformers for language understanding. CoRR abs/1810.04805 (2018). http://arxiv.org/abs/1810.04805
6. Doddington, G.: Automatic evaluation of machine translation quality using n-gram co-occurrence statistics. In: Proceedings of the Second International Conference on Human Language Technology Research, pp. 138–145. HLT 2002, Morgan Kaufmann Publishers Inc., San Francisco, CA, USA (2002)
7. Jin, D., Jin, Z., Hu, Z., Vechtomova, O., Mihalcea, R.: Deep learning for text style transfer: A survey (2020). https://doi.org/10.48550/ARXIV.2011.00416, https://arxiv.org/abs/2011.00416
8. Laugier, L., Pavlopoulos, J., Sorensen, J., Dixon, L.: Civil rephrases of toxic texts with self-supervised transformers (2021). https://doi.org/10.48550/ARXIV.2102.05456, https://arxiv.org/abs/2102.05456

9. Lester, B., Al-Rfou, R., Constant, N.: The power of scale for parameter-efficient prompt tuning. CoRR abs/2104.08691 (2021). https://arxiv.org/abs/2104.08691
10. Li, X.L., Liang, P.: Prefix-tuning: Optimizing continuous prompts for generation (2021). https://doi.org/10.48550/ARXIV.2101.00190, https://arxiv.org/abs/2101.00190
11. Liu, P., Yuan, W., Fu, J., Jiang, Z., Hayashi, H., Neubig, G.: Pre-train, prompt, and predict: a systematic survey of prompting methods in natural language processing (2021). https://doi.org/10.48550/ARXIV.2107.13586, https://arxiv.org/abs/2107.13586
12. Papineni, K., Roukos, S., Ward, T., Zhu, W.J.: BLEU: a method for automatic evaluation of machine translation. In: Proceedings of the 40th Annual Meeting of the Association for Computational Linguistics, pp. 311–318. Association for Computational Linguistics, Philadelphia, Pennsylvania, USA (2002). https://doi.org/10.3115/1073083.1073135, https://aclanthology.org/P02-1040
13. Petroni, F., et al.: Language models as knowledge bases? CoRR abs/1909.01066 (2019). http://arxiv.org/abs/1909.01066
14. Radford, A., Wu, J., Child, R., Luan, D., Amodei, D., Sutskever, I.: Language models are unsupervised multitask learners (2019)
15. Raffel, C., et al.: Exploring the limits of transfer learning with a unified text-to-text transformer. CoRR abs/1910.10683 (2019). http://arxiv.org/abs/1910.10683
16. Rao, S., Tetreault, J.: Dear sir or madam, may I introduce the GYAFC dataset: Corpus, benchmarks and metrics for formality style transfer. In: Proceedings of the 2018 Conference of the North American Chapter of the Association for Computational Linguistics: Human Language Technologies, Volume 1 (Long Papers), pp. 129–140. Association for Computational Linguistics, New Orleans, Louisiana (2018). https://doi.org/10.18653/v1/N18-1012, https://aclanthology.org/N18-1012
17. Rao, S., Tetreault, J.R.: Dear sir or madam, may I introduce the GYAFC corpus: Corpus, benchmarks and metrics for formality style transfer. CoRR abs/1803.06535 (2018). http://arxiv.org/abs/1803.06535
18. Ruder, S.: Recent Advances in Language Model Fine-tuning (2021). http://ruder.io/recent-advances-lm-fine-tuning
19. Shin, T., Razeghi, Y., IV, R.L.L., Wallace, E., Singh, S.: Autoprompt: eliciting knowledge from language models with automatically generated prompts. CoRR abs/2010.15980 (2020). https://arxiv.org/abs/2010.15980
20. Toshevska, M., Gievska, S.: A review of text style transfer using deep learning. IEEE Trans. Artif. Intell. **3**, 669–684 (2021). https://doi.org/10.1109/tai.2021.3115992
21. Turc, I., Chang, M., Lee, K., Toutanova, K.: Well-read students learn better: The impact of student initialization on knowledge distillation. CoRR abs/1908.08962 (2019). http://arxiv.org/abs/1908.08962
22. Wallace, E., Feng, S., Kandpal, N., Gardner, M., Singh, S.: Universal adversarial triggers for NLP. CoRR abs/1908.07125 (2019). http://arxiv.org/abs/1908.07125
23. Zhang, T., Kishore, V., Wu, F., Weinberger, K.Q., Artzi, Y.: BERTScore: evaluating text generation with BERT (2019). https://doi.org/10.48550/ARXIV.1904.09675, https://arxiv.org/abs/1904.09675

Human-Machine Task Allocation in Learning Reciprocally to Solve Problems

Dov Te'eni[✉]

Tel Aviv University, Tel Aviv, Israel
Teeni@tau.ac.il

Abstract. Solving problems by human-AI configurations will likely become a pervasive practice. Traditional models of task allocation between human and machine must be revisited in light of the differences in the learning of humans versus intelligent machines; performance can no longer be the sole criterion for task allocation. We offer a new procedure for allocating tasks dynamically that begins with the determination of the desired level of machine autonomy.

Keywords: Human-machine collaboration · Human-machine interaction · Reciprocity · Learning · Machine learning · Task allocation

1 Background and Motivation

The interaction between humans and AI generally requires new analyses and new designs of the technologies as well as the practices involved [1], and, in particular, new perspectives on the allocation of tasks between human and machine. While the design challenge of efficient task allocation between human and computer (once called man-machine task allocation) is a long standing issue in HCI, the now pervasive teaming of human and artificial intelligence complicated extant patterns of task allocation to the extent that allocation must be revisited to ensure effective and ethical performance. Perhaps, the most distinctive characteristic of the new human-machine (AI) interaction versus the traditional HCI is its learning component. In dynamic environments of complex decision making along with the feasibility of human and machine learning to solve problems, *learning* how to solve problems, not only solving problems, further complicates the human-machine collaboration. Additionally, the differences between human-learning and machine-learning affect the performance of problem solving and, hence, the effectiveness of alternative task allocations.

The intensive development of AI capabilities to solve problems in the workplace is expected to increase the pervasiveness of settings in which human and artificial agents learn to work together [2], but also *learn from each other*, and do so continually. We believe human machine collaborations in which humans and machines perform *and* learn together will become common. In an ongoing design project [3], we are studying how human-machine configurations learn to classify hackers – we call this configuration Reciprocal Human Machine Learning (RHML). Such configurations fall under the label

C. Stephanidis et al. (Eds.): HCII 2023, CCIS 1958, pp. 65–77, 2024.
https://doi.org/10.1007/978-3-031-49215-0_9

of 'keep the human in the learning loop'. A major challenge that we face, is how to design the allocation of learning tasks between the human expert and ML algorithms so that both agents learn continually, enabling the machine to learn from the human and vice versa. Continual learning is necessary in online environments that change constantly, in which action requires new knowledge. Our discussions of task allocation in this paper will focus on the context of human-machine configurations that are designed to incorporate reciprocal learning.

To complicate matters even further, unlike the design of traditional human-computer collaborations that was concerned with improving problem-solving performance, collaborations between human agents and artificial agents often add criteria such as ethical considerations for task allocation. Furthermore, an online game (the running example used in this paper) forces the designer to consider the user's enjoyment in addition to user performance. Adding enjoyment as a criterion forces the designer to consider an additional goal beyond performance when allocating tasks between human and machine. Our particular example of a game is the puzzle game 'Wordle'. Moreover, we regard the human-machine configuration playing the game as a reciprocal learning configuration in which both the human gamer and the machine learn and continually improve their play with repeated games.

In the current paper, we concentrate on the allocation of tasks between human and machine working together to solve Wordle. Figure 1, adapted from [4], shows the particular RHML configuration and its particular allocation of learning activities allocated that fit the distinct activities of each agent solving a puzzle collaboratively.

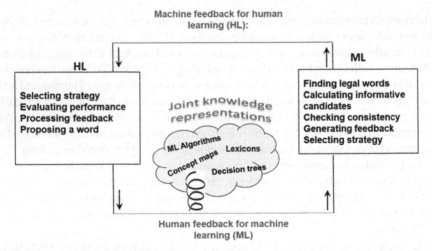

Fig. 1. RHML configuration with its respective allocation of learning tasks in solving a puzzle collaboratively (Source: Proceedings of the ACM)

A final introductory comment is about agency. Task allocation should be seen as part of the more general design issue of agency, i.e., which and how one collaborator acts as agent for the other. The collaboration between human and machine raises the issues discussed above, forcefully, perhaps because of the inherent imbalance we attribute to human versus machine. Using the simplified problem of solving Wordle by a configuration of a human and a machine, this paper examines human-machine task allocation in which both agents learn to solve the problem at varying levels of machine autonomy.

2 A Human-Machine Configuration Playing Wordle

Wordle (https://www.nytimes.com/games/wordle; Fig. 2) is a popular game, albeit a very specific type of online games that is very different from video games. It is a puzzle-type of game that has grown very popular in the past year to become a daily practice for millions of users round the world. The game has been translated to several languages, and has been studied in several domains, e.g., [5, 6].

The player has six attempts to guess the correct five-letter word. In each attempt, the player offers a legal candidate word. The candidate word is checked and the player receives the following feedback: each of the five letters is painted in black (to designate a letter that does not appear in the correct word), yellow (to designate a letter that appears in the correct word but in a different position), or green (to designate a letter that appears in the right position of the correct word). After receiving the feedback, the player proceeds to the next attempt. The game has two possible outcomes, namely, success or failure. In success, the correct word is found by the sixth attempt and the player is congratulated according to the number of attempts made (e.g., on the sixth attempt the feedback is 'phew'). In failure (the six attempts are exhausted before the correct word is identified), the player is notified of the correct word. In both cases, the new score is recorded and added to the player's history, which can easily be shared with others.

We examine task allocation and agency for different configurations of human and machine playing the game at different levels of machine autonomy. We begin with the currently common configuration of a human gamer that controls the entire game and decides when, if at all, to allocate certain tasks to the machine. The gamer's dual goal is to solve the puzzle with minimum attempts (performance) but also to enjoy the process of playing the game. The process can be seen as a sequence of steps that involve multiple tasks such as generating a word candidate, checking whether it is consistent with previous candidates, calculating the information value of a candidate etc.

To achieve the combination of performance and enjoyment, the complexity of the game is predefined to present an achievable but interesting challenge to the gamer. The gamers are allowed, at their discretion, to seek help by allocating some tasks to the machine (e.g., calculations) and by asking the machine for tips. The gamer decides on the allocation according to the progression of the game. For instance, on the first attempt, the gamer chooses a word candidate manually and according to the machine feedback, chooses a second candidate on the second attempt but has the machine check that it is consistent with the previous (first) candidate.

Wordle

Fig. 2. The word of the day 'Tasty' is guessed on the third attempt. Green is a letter in the word in its correct position, a Yellow letter is included in the word but is not in its correct posit, and a Black letter is not in the word.

One way of describing the process is to break it down into several steps such as deciding on a strategy, executing the strategy, studying the feedback, and revisiting the selected strategy, and either continuing to execute it or revising the strategy and then executing it. Thus, playing Wordle can be seen as following up to six iterations in a cycle of *strategy-execution-feedback*. For example, a strategy may consist of using the first two attempts to find all or most of the vowels that appear or do not appear in the correct word, and accordingly suggesting candidate words that maximize the reduction of uncertainty (out of the possible words given the prior attempts). In executing the strategy, the first attempt could begin with a word that includes vowels, and according to the feedback continue with a second word with different vowels (see first two attempts in Fig. 2).

In the game represented in Fig. 3, the player revisited the strategy, assuming that most of the vowels had been identified so that there was no need to use the second attempt to identify further vowels. Accordingly, the second attempt began guessing the correct word. The third attempt failed to choose a word that minimized uncertainty, as did the fourth, fifth and sixth, and resulted in a failed game (the correct word 'TASTY' is shown after six attempts).

Fig. 3. Inappropriate execution of a strategy resulting in a failed game (in the lower panel – Black letter does not appear in word, light Grey has not been tried, and Green is in the word).

3 New Criteria for Human-Machine Task Allocation

As said, a distinctive characteristic of human-machine interaction, compared with traditional HCI, is the learning, which enables adaptive and dynamic behavior of the interacting agents but also possibly changing allocation of tasks between agents.

Configurations of humans and machines must generally ensure effective human functioning while maintaining the advantages offered by automation, yet the specific requirements for a particular configuration are dependent on its underlying rationale and on the goals it aims to achieve [7]. For instance, the abovementioned RHML configuration that has as its goal to support mutual learning, the human and the artificial are seen as cooperating partners rather than one being a tool for the other [8]. One working assumption is that the cooperating partners have different information-processing capabilities, but these relative strengths and weaknesses change over time, especially with the rapid progress made in AI. A second, related, assumption is that human learning and machine learning differ in their learning strategies, which also complicates how one agent can learn from the other. These assumptions suggest that extant methods of allocating learning tasks between human and machine must be revisited.

Extant methods, going back to the fifties aimed to divide labor in a manner that capitalizes on the agents' relative advantages in achieving performance on a focal task [9]. For example, Ip et al. [10] produced 'Task Allocation Charts' that first decompose a task into subtasks and then allocate subtasks to the machine or human operators, depending on their relative advantages. In choice problems, for example, given a high volume of options to consider, it may be infeasible to allocate the task to a human expert. The task, however, can be broken into subtasks that are allocated according to the intelligent agents' capabilities [11, 12]. For instance, the expert decides on several very large subsets of options, commonly in a trial-and-error fashion, and the machine searches exhaustively within the subset.

Performance can no longer be the sole criterion for task allocation in intelligent human-machine configurations. New considerations are needed such as organizational implications [13], machine autonomy or the degree of automation versus augmentation [14], the contingencies of configurations based on parameters like task complexity or ambiguity [15], and ethical issues such as human discretion [16]. Keeping the human in the loop can therefore be argued on grounds other than relative advantages in task performance. For instance, the human remains in the loop to stay in control and take responsibility that comes with control, or to supervise the machine performance to assure quality and learning.

Of particular interest to our discussion of task allocation and agency is machine autonomy. If machine autonomy is a critical or even topmost concern, it should be measureable by the human-machine configuration in order for it to adapt accordingly. Machine autonomy has been studied and measured at length but one scale stands out, namely the scale published by Sheridan et al. [17]. The widely quoted scale includes ten levels of machine autonomy, ranging from the lowest level, at which the machine offers no assistance, to the highest level, at which the machine decide everything and acts autonomously. In between these extreme points are intermediate levels of machine autonomy such as the machine performs certain tasks, informs the human so the human and decide what next. Recently, Shneiderman [18] suggested measuring human control separately from machine autonomy rather than having them on the same dimension. The separation did not fit our RHML configuration and therefore we remain with a single combined scale for our discussion of task allocation.

Interpretability is another consideration for task allocation that is relevant to configurations in which the human stays in the loop to learn [19]. It is the user's ability to interpret machine algorithms. In fact, there may be a tradeoff between interpretability and accuracy when the goal of the allocation is not only to achieve high performance but also to develop the human expert's knowledge. A loss in model interpretability may limit the effectiveness of human learning and trust in the model. More generally, any multi-goal design may affect the optimal allocation of activities between parties by implying tradeoffs between performance and, say, comprehension (e.g., sacrificing performance in favor of interpretability) [14]. As mentioned above, additional goals could be for example, ethical, desired automation, or moderate complexity. We now return to the Wordle game to propose a task allocation to fit configurations in which both human and machine have learning goals.

4 Proposed Task Allocation in Human-Machine Learning Configurations

We first determine the level of autonomy given to the machine. This is a *meta decision* that is not explicit in traditional methods of task allocation. We realized in our RHML project that the human-machine configuration engages in different types of activities (e.g., sense making or data acquisition), each of which can be broken down separately into tasks. We distinguished between the learning activities and the control and coordination activities between agents. We found that it was easier to determine the level of desired autonomy for each type separately.

In our discussion up to now, we have assumed a human-machine configuration in which the human gamers fully control the game, determine the strategy, and allocate tasks according to preferences and progression of the game. At every point of the game, the gamer has all information needed in order to decide the next step and, if desired, to re-allocate tasks. The information is generated by the machine and fed back to user as the feedback shown in Figs. 2 and 3, which is at the level of a word and letters in the word. The machine generated feedback can also inform the gamer about performance across games played, as depicted in Fig. 4. The latter information supports learning but is also part of the gamer's personal enjoyment at achievement and sharing achievements amongst friends.

Borrowing from Sheridan's rationale for measuring machine autonomy, we define three levels of machine autonomy in the Wordle example according the strategy-execution-feedback iterative process of playing the game. The first level is the one articulated above. The gamer decides on the strategy (opening strategy and later strategies according to the game progression), executes the strategy but leaves feedback generation tasks to the machine. For the second level of machine autonomy, the human gamer decides on a strategy and allocates at least some of its tasks to the machine, as well as letting the machine generate feedback. For example, the gamer selects the strategy which is to first determine the vowels in the correct word, and machine is allocated the task of finding the word that is expected, most probably, to detect maximum number of vowels in the correct word. For the third level of machine autonomy, consider the human and the machine decide collaboratively on the best strategy at hand, and the machine both executes some of the tasks and generates the feedback.

For the second level of machine autonomy, the question of which tasks to allocate (if at all) for machine execution becomes relevant. For instance, at some stage, the gamer finds it too difficult (highly risky) to proceed without help and turns to the machine for a tip. Allocating all execution to the machine would ruin the enjoyment but asking for a tip may seem justifiable to the gamer. Alternatively, the user may want to present a comprehensive list of words ending with 'ASTY', from which the gamer would be able to decide how to proceed (see Fig. 4).

The next step is therefore to determine the different capabilities and activities of human learning and machine learning in the specific context being considered. We had considered two options. The first is to begin with common models that have been used to represent both human and machine agents and use the models to distinguish between natural and artificial activities and resources (e.g., predictive processing theory or models of affordances). In the RHML project, we chose a second option, in which we

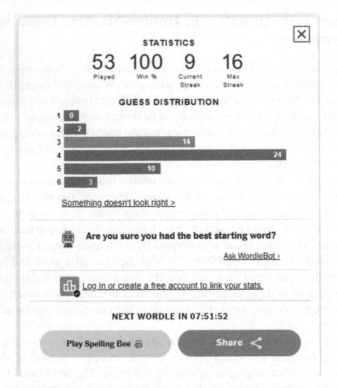

Fig. 4. Machine generated feedback at the level of a games played.

select two distinct models of problem solving, each describes either human or machine-learning activities. For example, we represented human problem-solving activities as sense making, dialogue, attention management, and perspective taking, and represented machine learning activities by processing input, classification models, and performance evaluation.

Given the level of desired autonomy, we decide on the allocation criteria, simplifying the problem by explicitly omitting other criteria. For instance, we may omit ethical criteria and remain with two criteria only, performance and enjoyment. Once the set of allocation criteria, and possible tradeoffs noted, we proceed to solve the multiple-criteria allocation problem. In our project, we began with an allocation based on the literature (see the list in step one) and tested the allocation by trial-and-error, maximizing performance subject to acceptable interpretability (measured by human learning). More sophisticated methods, such as simulation, could be used [20].

Even in level 3 of machine autonomy, human control is considered to be an important value in the design of HCI [21]. Indeed, in games, enjoyment and human control should be design goals [22]. Nevertheless, the human-machine reciprocal learning configuration introduces several complications that need to be addressed in their design. Reciprocal learning assumes task allocation and intelligible communication between human and machine [3]. Smart digitality can enable or support both allocation of tasks requiring intelligence to the machine and intelligible communication between human and machine.

For instance, a possible division of labor could be the player setting a strategy of first identifying which vowels appear in the correct word and communicating the message to the machine, and consequently, the machine suggesting the best words to implement the strategy. In such a division of labor, the player's sense of autonomy would not necessarily decrease because the higher level decision remains with the human [23].

A more complex collaboration would be to adapt the machine's algorithm to the human priority on which of the word's five positions to concentrate. Say the player wants to resolve positions 4 and 5, and asks the machine to do so. Most machine algorithms for solving Wordle operate at the level of reducing uncertainty for the entire word, e.g., [24]. The incompatibility between the methods would require challenging algorithms to integrate the two and enable effective communication.

5 Generalization

The analysis above builds on our experience with human-machine configurations for learning reciprocally to classify messages on social media, in which we fixed the level of autonomy. We attempted to use the Wordle online game to demonstrate the complexities of task allocations attributed to human-AI collaborations that were not evident in traditional models of task allocation in HCI. We believe human-AI configurations for other tasks, not necessarily learning tasks and not necessarily gaming, should adopt a similar approach to task allocation, albeit, with different allocation criteria that go beyond performance. When considering different tasks and different combinations of allocation criteria beyond the traditional performance allocation criterion, we must remember that the relative advantages of human versus machine keep changing.

In our discussion, we did not treat the issue of interaction complexity in the design and use of human-machine configurations. Complexity plays an important role in the design of human-machine configurations, it is both a product of the human-machine collaboration and a determinant of task allocation. The latter effect on task allocation is easy to see. Figure 5 shows the end result of a very complex version of Wordle, called Quordle. Clearly, dealing higher game complexity (Quordle versus Wordle) shifts the point at which the human gamer will reallocate tasks to the machine. Presumably, higher complexity will drive the gamer to allocate the more intensive information processing, e.g., calculations and ranking, to the machine. The reverse effect is less obvious but nevertheless crucial for designers. At higher machine autonomy when keeping the human in the loop, a more complex interaction is required in order to maintain effective human-machine coordination and human control. This analysis is not relevant to absolute machine autonomy, which ignores the human according to Sheridan. In Fig. 5, there are four panels, each panel for a distinct correct word (WRYLY, APPLE, SCOUR and CLUNG).

Figure 6 shows the feedback received during the game. Notice how the feedback from four panels is integrated into one keyboard-like panel that represents the accumulated results across trials in reference to the four correct words for each letter on the keyboard. In comparison to the design in Fig. 2, the communication complexity in Fig. 6 is considerably higher [25]. For example, the little green square for letter E, in the upper right side of the letter, designates that E appears in APPLE in its correct position, but

So Close!

WRYLY ■ 9 APPLE
SCOUR 6 4 CLUNG

Fig. 5. Quordle - a highly complex puzzle built as four panels of Wordle combine.

does not appear in the other three words. The two-way link between complexity and task allocation should be explored in future studies of human-machine configurations.

Furthermore, future work should take the level of machine autonomy as a variable that affects task allocation [22], but consider as variable other possible criteria too. This will result in additional complexity but may prove necessary in practice. In playing Wordle, we set the level of autonomy so as to leave part of the problem solving activities (strategy, execution or feedback) to the human with the goal of having fun. Clearly, fun in other settings (e.g., providing medical treatment) cannot be a design goal, while ethical considerations could.

As noted earlier, task allocation should be studied as part of the more general issue of agency in human-machine configurations [26]. For agency, we ask who governs, initiates, controls and bears the responsibility for the process and its sub-processes. Agency can be characterized on a continuum according to the latitude of decision making granted to the agent, e.g., [2]. Unlike current practice in human-computer interaction, task allocation between human and computer must be preceded but the *meta decision* that determines agency. This is not to suggest that this is a fixed sequence. On the contrary, as demonstrated above, different levels of agency may lead to different task-allocations at different stages of the game, which in turn may revise the levels of agency.

Fig. 6. The process of playing Quordle in which feedback is integrated from four panels into the bottom keyboard like panel.

In the case of Wordle, complete human autonomy is when the player has complete control over the process and sub-processes so that the player alone initiates and takes charge of all actions, even though execution of the player's orders may be executed by the machine. An autonomous machine is one that acts as its own agent. An autonomous game would be one that plays and displays the results when the game is over. In between these extreme cases are many combinations of human-machine configurations [7], often referred to as 'Keep the Human in the Loop' [27]. These configurations call for a shift away from the metaphor of computer as tool to a metaphor of collaboration between human and machine.

References

1. Ågerfalk, P.J., et al.: Artificial intelligence in information systems: state of the art and research roadmap. Commun. Assoc. Inf. Syst. **50** (2022)
2. Baird, A., Maruping, L.M.: The next generation of research on IS use: a theoretical framework of delegation to and from agentic IS artifacts. MIS Q. **45**, 1 (2021)
3. Te'eni, D., et al.: Human-machine learning: a theory and an instantiation for the case of message classification. Manag. Sci. (2023, forthcoming)
4. Zagalsky, A., et al.: The design of reciprocal learning between human and artificial intelligence. Proc. ACM Hum. Comput. Interact. **5**(CSCW2), 1–36 (2021)
5. Liu, C.L.: Using wordle for learning to design and compare strategies. In: 2022 IEEE Conference on Games (CoG), pp. 465–472. IEEE (2022)
6. Bertsimas, D., Paskov, A.: An exact and interpretable solution to wordle. **20** (2022) (preprint)
7. Suchman, L.A.: Human-Machine Reconfigurations: Plans and Situated Actions. Cambridge University Press (2007)
8. Woods, D.D., Hollnagel, E.: Joint Cognitive Systems: Patterns in Cognitive Systems Engineering. CRC Press (2006)
9. Fitts, P.M.: Human engineering for an effective air-navigation and traffic-control system. In: NRC Committee on Aviation Psychology (1951)
10. Ip, W., Damodaran, L., Olphert, C.W., Maguire, M.C.: The use of task allocation charts in system design: a critical appraisal. In: Proceedings of the IFIP TC13 Third International Conference on Human-Computer Interaction, pp. 289–294. North-Holland Publishing Co (1990)
11. Xin, D., Ma, L., Liu, J., Macke, S., Song, S., Parameswaran, A.: Accelerating human-in-the-loop machine learning: challenges and opportunities. In Proceedings of the Second Workshop on Data Management for End-to-End Machine Learning, pp. 1–4 (2018)
12. Marcellino, W., Johnson, C., Posard, M.N., Helmus, T.C.: Foreign Interference in the 2020 Election: Tools for Detecting Online Election Interference. RAND Corporation (2020)
13. Grønsund, T., Aanestad, M.: Augmenting the algorithm: emerging human-in-the-loop work configurations. J. Strateg. Inf. Syst. **29**(2), 101614 (2020)
14. Raisch, S., Krakowski, S.: Artificial intelligence and management: the automation–augmentation paradox. Acad. Manag. Rev. **46**(1), 192–210 (2020)
15. So, C.: Human-in-the-loop design cycles – a process framework that integrates design sprints, agile processes, and machine learning with humans. In: Degen, H., Reinerman-Jones, L. (eds.) HCII 2020. LNCS, vol. 12217, pp. 136–145. Springer, Cham (2020). https://doi.org/10.1007/978-3-030-50334-5_9
16. Citron, D.K., Pasquale, F.: The scored society: Due process for automated predictions. Wash. L. Rev. **89**, 1 (2014)
17. Sheridan, T.B., Verplank, W.L., Brooks, T.L.: Human/computer control of undersea teleoperators. In: NASA Ames Research Center the 14th Annual Conference on Manual Control (1978)
18. Shneiderman, B.: Human-centered artificial intelligence: reliable, safe and trustworthy. Int. J. Hum. Comput. Interact. **36**(6), 495–504 (2020)
19. Miller, T.: Explanation in artificial intelligence: insights from the social sciences. Artif. Intell. **267**, 1–38 (2019)
20. Boyacı, T., Canyakmaz, C., de Véricourt, F.: Human and machine: the impact of machine input on decision making under cognitive limitations. Manag. Sci. (2023) (forthcoming)
21. Friedman, B.: Value-sensitive design. Interactions**3**(6), 16–23 (1996)
22. da Rocha Tomé Filho, F., Mirza-Babaei, P., Kapralos, B., Moreira Mendonça Junior, G.: Let's play together: adaptation guidelines of board games for players with visual impairment. In:

Proceedings of the 2019 CHI Conference on Human Factors in Computing Systems, pp. 1–15 (2019)

23. Kumar, D., Srinivasan, N.: Naturalizing sense of agency with a hierarchical event-control approach. PLoS ONE **9**(3), e92431 (2014)
24. Bhambri, S., Bhattacharjee, A., Bertsekas, D.: Reinforcement learning methods for wordle: A POMDP/adaptive control approach. arXiv preprint arXiv:2211.10298 (2022)
25. Katz, A., Te'eni, D.: The role of communication complexity in adaptive contextualization. IEEE Trans. Prof. Commun. **57**(2), 98–112 (2014)
26. Tholander, J., Normark, M., Rossitto, C.: Understanding agency in interaction design materials. In: Proceedings of the SIGCHI Conference on Human Factors in Computing Systems, pp. 2499–2508 (2012)
27. Holzinger, A., Weippl, E., Tjoa, A.M., Kieseberg, P.: Digital transformation for sustainable development goals (SDGs) - a security, safety and privacy perspective on AI. In: Holzinger, A., Kieseberg, P., Tjoa, A.M., Weippl, E. (eds.) CD-MAKE 2021. LNCS, vol. 12844, pp. 1–20. Springer, Cham (2021). https://doi.org/10.1007/978-3-030-84060-0_1

Conversation N: Visualization Installation Design Based on Voice Interaction

Jing Wang and Qiong Wu(✉)

Tsinghua University, Hai Dian District, Beijing, China
qiong-wu@tsinghua.edu.cn

Abstract. Deep learning allows machines to have human-like learning and thinking capabilities, but its internals are often considered a black box about which we know very little. As AI (Artificial intelligence) penetrates deeper into life, the development of AI is maybe uncontrollable under the influence of human data. Questions about privacy, autonomy, fairness, and the potential for misuse of technology will become even more pressing.

In the unstoppable process of technological development, art and design can often reveal science's mysteries and even predict technology's development. In this paper, through the research of algorithmic bias and AI ethics, we design an interactive installation with audience participation. Based on voice dialogue technology, the Installation uses visualization based on two-dimensional screens and physical Installation to demonstrate how AI constantly changes and generates a certain form in the learning process, hoping to trigger thinking about the subjectivity between humans and artificial intelligence. It summarizes what AI believes audiences think about AI on some issues.

Keywords: Voice Interaction · Artificial Intelligence · Interactive Installation

1 Interaction

In the information age, artificial intelligence technology is applied in every scene of life. How to make machines understand people better and realize relatively intelligent depth perception is a key problem in the field of human-computer interaction. In response, scientists have provided a learning path for machines, such as deep learning through big data training, or interactive machine learning, which increases the opportunity for users to influence AI [1]. Several studies have shown that such artificial intelligence created by computer scientists and based on human samples to learn and serve often shows some unexpected results instead of idealized absolute neutrality due to imperfect algorithms and limited training samples [2–4].

Subjectivity implies that an entity has personal experiences, feelings, beliefs, desires, or self-awareness, characteristics that we usually associate with consciousness. As AI evolves and becomes more complex, it may exhibit forms of intelligence that we have not yet fully imagined, and its subjectivity can affect the relationship between humans and machines. As early as 2000, Ray Kurzweil described the future relationship between

C. Stephanidis et al. (Eds.): HCII 2023, CCIS 1958, pp. 78–85, 2024.
https://doi.org/10.1007/978-3-031-49215-0_10

humans and machines in his book The Age of Spiritual Machines, arguing that humans will respond to robots according to a collaborative orientation and a discrete orientation, and vice versa [5]. Google's AI chief, John Giannandrea thought the problem of bias in machine learning is likely to become more significant as the technology spreads to critical areas like medicine and law, and as more people without a deep technical understanding are tasked with deploying it [6]. Lionel P. Robert Jr. et al. proposed the need to focus on fair, ethical, and trustworthy AI, as well as designing transparent and explainable AI [7].

As AI becomes more integrated into our daily lives, questions about privacy, autonomy, fairness, and the potential for misuse of technology will become even more pressing. These considerations must play a significant role in guiding the development and deployment of AI technologies. Art has always been regarded as an early warning of human perception, which itself can imitate or predict the development of science and technology [8]. The application of technology to art can strengthen the audience's immersive interaction in art design and bring a more real experience.

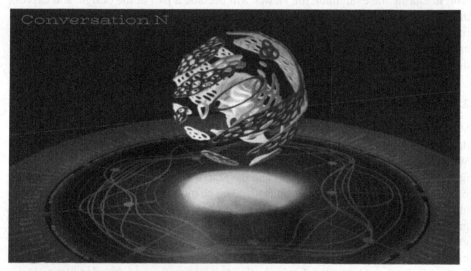

Fig. 1. The interactive installation is based on voice interaction: Conversation N

Based on this background, the author designed an interactive installation for audience participation based on the technology of voice interaction: Conversation N (Fig. 1). The audience and the AI will discuss some social issues that may cause algorithmic bias. In this process, the voice data during the interaction between the viewer and the installation is collected and visualized in real-time. Using visualization based on two-dimensional screens and physical installations, we seek to show in an artistic form how the AI is constantly changing and generating certain forms during the learning process. It is hoped to draw the viewer's attention to the issue of subjectivity between humans and AI.

2   Methodology

2.1   Design Research Through Practice

Many artists have expressed the concept of the subjectivity of artificial intelligence, but most of the works are mainly reflected in artistic expression, and it is difficult to make the audience associate with artificial intelligence in real life. The use of interactive forms will often bring real feelings to the audience, such as Australian artist STELARC designed an art installation "Artificial head" when someone passes through the "head space", the sensor will send signals to control the artificial head to make the corresponding rotation, open the eyes and start a dialogue which will serve as a warning to people.

This paper carries on design research through practice [9]. The whole process of research takes place in the course of the exhibition. In the combination of technology and art, art can mimic the development of data and exceed the maximum speed of the data, anticipating the results in a virtual way [10]. When the viewer approaches the installation, the installation will initiate a dialogue to attract the viewer to interact with it. During the exhibition, the viewer will become a part of the design, and express their views on artificial intelligence through dialogue with the installation which is a step further than a normal interactive installation. Through the setting of rules, the installation enables the audience to influence the state of the work, and then conduct research and discovery.

2.2   Data Visualization

Visualization helps with the transfer of information. Collecting, storing, and analyzing data to obtain valuable information is an important goal of information visualization [11]. With the advances and accessibility of technology, there is a growing interest in the richness of interaction in visual diagrams and the practice of interactive and dynamic visual information visualization is increasing [12, 13]. The most important purpose of data visualization is to organize complex numbers and transform them into easy-to-understand graphical language that presents the event itself. In voice interaction, visualization is of great importance due to the invisibility of the voice. In terms of human functioning itself, human memory for voice data is also much lower than that of visualization, as evidenced by the emergence of both subtitling and voice-to-text functions equipped in film and television productions. In the expression of voice data visualization in the field of art and design, visualization usually aims to enhance emotional communication, and designers often need to find a balance between information communication and aesthetics. More common are the designs of music visualization, where the visual and auditory sensory pairing in the company of emotions can bring a fresher and more complete immersive experience and better access to the mood in the musical depiction.

Our work is mainly oriented to human voice data, which is the language of computers. Therefore, in the field of natural voice understanding, machines need to transform voice into text and data forms for analysis, which is itself a process of science and demonstrating how machines process human language. In addition, the transmission volume and efficiency of voice information is limited, so the process of converting voice into a visual state in the process of voice interaction is not only in line with the understanding process of the machine itself, but also in line with the physiological requirements of human beings. The work uses the screen and tangible form to visualize how voice data affects AI. The physical part in the middle represents the physical representation of artificial intelligence in real life, showing its "personality" through the dynamic changes of lights. The words and curves on the screen are the processes by which the machine understands the language.

3   Development

This work is an interactive installation design in which the viewer becomes a part of the design throughout the exhibition, expressing his or her views on artificial intelligence through dialogue with the installation and influencing the final state of the work. The input of the installation is voice interaction, which can also be controlled by the viewer on the interface, and the output is data visualization in the screen and the ever-changing "Tangible AI" (Fig. 2).

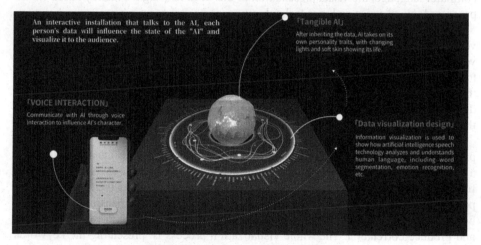

Fig. 2. Components of the installation

3.1   Voice Interaction

Voice interaction is an important channel for the connection between humans and AI [14]. One of the standards for the research and development of artificial intelligence by technology companies is to hope that artificial intelligence can "talk to you like humans" [15]. Therefore, voice dialogue is chosen as the main interaction form of the installation in this work. Based on voice dialogue technology, in this design, artificial intelligence is mainly used to ask questions, and the viewer answers. It can not only limit the scope of the content answered by users, but also accurately collect user data, and the way of active inquiry of artificial intelligence can cause users to pay attention to the subject of artificial intelligence to a certain extent.

When the viewer approaches the installation, the installation will initiate a dialogue to attract the viewer to interact with it. The main content of the voice interaction will focus on the core of the problem – the subjectivity between humans and artificial intelligence. In the topic selection of voice interaction content, the author has carried out several iterations on the research plan of the previous data. Finally, the author starts from the real situation, understands the algorithm bias problem in the current artificial intelligence, and sets the voice interaction content in combination with the user's disputes about artificial intelligence in the interview process. Starting from the point that artificial intelligence is very important to human development, the final specific voice interaction script explores the trend of cooperation/alienation, high/low influence, and good/evil under the influence of human beings in the development process of artificial intelligence.

3.2   Visualization Installation Design

Since the expression of the work aims to enhance the viewer's understanding of the computer language, the visual presentation of the work is designed mainly based on the program logic of voice dialogue technology.

In the natural language understanding of the program, the work invokes Aliyun's voice-to-text function, text analysis function, and text literacy function. The audience's voice data is first transformed into the form of text, then the whole text is split according to the lexicality, the emotion score is marked for the words in the database, and finally, the voice data is generated. Thus, during the interaction process of the installation, the data appears simultaneously with the voice interaction and influences the final form of the AI in the order from outside to inside.

The analyzed data is exported and sorted to produce data visualizations that can be presented interactively in the field. Based on research trials, the results are positive for a closer relationship with people, showing it as having a living state in red, and negative for a greater separation from people, showing the electronic nature of the AI in blue, with perceptual differences from people. The visualization of the two-dimensional screen will be closely around the entity visualization of the central area, the two correspond to change and produce correlation. The whole visualization process is: presenting the keywords during the dialogue at the edge of the corresponding questions to form the corresponding emotional analysis data, and after the 9 questions are answered, the connection becomes a complete curve, and the data will gradually accumulate so that the viewer can observe the complete state of the work (Fig. 3).

In the overall shape design of the interactive installation, the solid part in the middle is the physical representation of the AI in real life. In the creation concept of this work, it is hoped to express that the AI has its own personality characteristics after inheriting the data, so it needs to show its characteristics of having a sense of electronic life. The interior of the entity is mainly composed of a light array, combining LED lights into a coral-like form, and through the color and dynamic changes of the light array, to show its characteristics of a sense of technology. The exterior uses silicone as the material. Silicone is often used in the medical field to simulate skin because of its viscosity, elasticity and softness, which is close to the texture of human skin. In the specific form

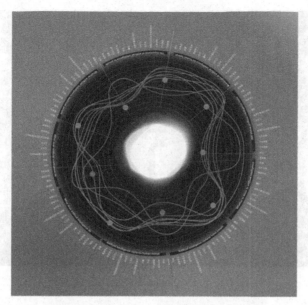

Fig. 3. Graphics generated from voice data

design, in order to make its specific form and color can be more suitable for the needs of the design, by adding curing agent to change the speed of silica gel solidification, and silica gel attached to the transparent acrylic surface for shaping, to show artificial intelligence or perhaps a sense of life state.

4   Results and Discussion

The installation was exhibited for 12 days and a total of 218 data were obtained. During the interaction, the state of the installation changed several times. The overall data of the final audience and installation for the discussion of AI-related issues were relatively neutral. After filtering out the incomplete data, the specific data are shown in Table 1 (Fig. 4).

In this paper, we conduct an in-depth study of natural voice interaction technology in the field of artificial intelligence and learn about the basic implementation process method of voice interaction technology and the current development status. Currently, the main problem faced in the field of voice interaction and even in the field of artificial intelligence is the lack of sufficient as well as high-quality human data samples, which often require technicians to organize the samples. In the deep learning process, collecting samples during human contact is the driving force, but it also raises concerns about data leakage from individuals. Therefore, engaging the audience in reflection from an art and design perspective is a realistic solution.

This paper explores the ways and possibilities of combining art and design with technology. The installation has the significance of popularizing science to the public, revealing the process of AI understanding language through visualization, which can

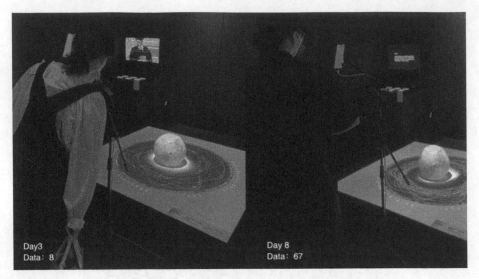

Day3
Data: 8

Day 8
Data: 67

Fig. 4. Exhibition and practice

Table 1. Discussion of issues related to artificial intelligence

	Positive	Negative
Cooperation/Alienation	0.443624	0.556377
High/Low Influence	0.580839	0.419161
Good/Evil	0.451025	0.548975

make the public understand voice interaction technology more understandably. This study is experimental and predictive, demonstrating how human data can lead to bias in AI during its engagement with people. By predicting the development of AI in art forms, some thoughts are brought to the direction of technological development.

Acknowledgement. This research was supported by "Dual High" Project of Tsinghua Humanity Development (No. 2021TSG08203).

References

1. Amershi, S., Cakmak, M., Knox, W.B., Kulesza, T.: Power to the people: the role of humans in interactive machine learning. AI Mag. **35**, 105–120 (2014). https://doi.org/10.1609/aimag.v35i4.2513
2. MacCarthy, M.: AI needs more regulation, not less (2020). https://www.brookings.edu/research/ai-needs-more-regulation-not-less/
3. Cummings, M.L., Li, S.: Subjectivity in the creation of machine learning models. J. Data Inf. Qual. **13**, 1–19 (2021). https://doi.org/10.1145/3418034

4. Hao, K.: AI is sending people to jail-and getting it wrong (2019). https://www.technologyre view.com/2019/01/21/137783/algorithms-criminal-justice-ai/
5. Kurzweil, R.: The Age of Spiritual Machines: When Computers Exceed Human Intelligence. Penguin Books, New York (2000)
6. Knight, W.: Forget Killer Robots—Bias Is the Real Al Danger (2017). https://www.techno logyreview.com/2017/10/03/241956/forget-killer-robotsbias-is-the-real-ai-danger/
7. Robert, L., Bansal, G., Lütge, C.: ICIS 2019 SIGHCI Workshop Panel Report: Human Computer Interaction Challenges and Opportunities for Fair, Trustworthy and Ethical Artificial Intelligence (2020). https://doi.org/10.17705/1thci.00130
8. Wilson, S.: Information Arts: Intersections of Art, Science, and Technology. MIT Press, Cambridge (2002)
9. Koskinen, I.K. (ed.): Design Research Through Practice: From the Lab, Field, and Showroom. Morgan Kaufmann/Elsevier, Waltham (2011)
10. Perpiñán Lamigueiro, Ó.: Displaying Time Series, Spatial, and Space-Time Data with R. CRC Press, Taylor & Francis Group, Boca Raton (2018)
11. Vassakis, K., Petrakis, E., Kopanakis, I.: Big data analytics: applications, prospects and challenges. In: Skourletopoulos, G., Mastorakis, G., Mavromoustakis, C.X., Dobre, C., Pallis, E. (eds.) Mobile Big Data: A Roadmap from Models to Technologies, pp. 3–20. Springer International Publishing, Cham (2018)
12. Meirelles, I.: Design for Information: An Introduction to the Histories, Theories, and Best Practices Behind Effective Information Visualizations. Rockport, Beverly (2013)
13. Dimara, E., Perin, C.: What is Interaction for data visualization? IEEE Trans. Visual Comput. Graph. **26**, 119–129 (2020). https://doi.org/10.1109/TVCG.2019.2934283
14. Adiwardana, D., et al.: Towards a human-like open-domain chatbot. arXiv preprint arXiv: 2001.09977 (2020)
15. Langner, B.: Data-driven natural language generation: making machines talk like humans using natural corpora (2010)

Ethical Reflection on Identity of AI Digital Avatars

Lanxi Xiao and Qiong Wu[✉]

Academy of Arts and Design, Tsinghua University, Beijing, China
qiong-wu@tsinghua.edu.cn

Abstract. This article explores the impact of artificial intelligence (AI) on human identity and raises ethical concerns regarding using biometric data for identification. As AI advances, digital avatars become more authentic and intelligent, leading to questions about human identity and its societal effects. The integration of 5G technology and the Internet of Things accelerates data transmission and storage, resulting in the convergence of the natural and virtual realms. The article proposes an interactive art installation called Human' to address these issues. It employs AI to create digital avatars based on facial, social media, and personal data, enabling interaction with the audience through mobile devices. Human' prompts reflections on ethical dilemmas arising from the fusion of human and digital identities. The installation involves design, prototyping, and development phases, including motion capture, interface design, front-end and back-end development, and integration with a WeChat applet. Exhibited in May 2021, the installation received positive feedback from the audience, who expressed curiosity about the future possibilities of AI while raising concerns about the societal impact of digital avatars.

Keywords: Ethical Reflection · Digital avatars · Human identity · Artificial intelligence · Interactive installation

1 Introduction

With the advancement of artificial intelligence, digital avatars have become more genuine and intelligent. The increasing use of biometric data, such as fingerprints and facial recognition, for identification purposes, raises ethical concerns as human identity becomes increasingly digitized. The integration of 5G technology and the Internet of Things (IoT) further blurs the boundaries between the physical and digital worlds, leading to questions about the impact of digital avatars on human identity and society.

To explore these issues, this article introduces Human', an interactive art installation that examines human identity in the future digital realm from an ethical standpoint. Human' utilizes AI to create digital avatars based on the audience's facial features, WeChat avatars, and nicknames. These avatars interact with individuals through mobile phones, prompting reflections on the intertwined identity and personality issues in both the natural and virtual worlds.

C. Stephanidis et al. (Eds.): HCII 2023, CCIS 1958, pp. 86–93, 2024.
https://doi.org/10.1007/978-3-031-49215-0_11

The implementation of the interactive installation involves design, prototyping, and development. Motion capture technology brings digital avatars to life, while interface design encompasses visual, voice, and graphic interactions. The installation is supported by front-end and back-end development, including real-time face detection and synthesis of digital avatars using deep learning. The accompanying WeChat applet simulates chat conversations and provides a graphical interface for interaction.

The installation was showcased at the "Science Fiction World" exhibition during China Beijing Science and Technology Week in May 2021. Audience feedback was positive, with viewers finding the work fascinating and sparking their curiosity about the potential of the future AI world. However, concerns were also expressed about the ethical implications and potential societal harm digital avatars could cause.

2 Related Works

Artists use "Defamiliarization" to reflect data ethics by presenting familiar objects in unfamiliar ways. This technique enhances the perception and prompts deeper reflection. The review explores how artists employ this strategy in specific cases, its application in exhibition design, and the fusion of synthetic technology with human images.

Luke Stark and Kate Crawford interviewed 33 artists who explored ethical issues in data-related works [1]. They found that artists often use Defamiliarization [2] as a technique to address data ethics. This technique, influenced by Viktor Shklovsky and Benjamin's ideas [3], involves strangely presenting familiar objects to enhance perception and provoke deeper reflection [4].

Heather Dewey Hagborg's works, "Stranger Visions" (2013) and "Probable Chelsea" (2017), utilize Defamiliarization to explore data ethics. "Stranger Visions" extracts DNA from discarded items to create human models [5], while "Probable Chelsea" reconstructs different head models representing Chelsea Manning. These works highlight privacy issues in genetic technology by defamiliarizing everyday objects and identities [6].

"Prism: the Beacon Frame," a collaboration between Julian Oliver and Danja Vasiliev, employs Defamiliarization to address technical ethics [7]. This device hijacks the cellular network in an exhibition space, sending messages from the National Security Agency to the audience. Blurring the familiar boundaries between individuals and groups encourages reflection on data device privacy and connectivity. This Defamiliarization also elicits a sense of "fruitful paranoia" and "healthy anxiety" in viewers.

Artists often use replication techniques to create unique atmospheres and exhibition experiences in their artworks. Heather Dewey Hagborg's works employ replication by creating many portrait models for a shocking effect. Es Devlin also uses replication techniques, such as in "Mirror Haze," where a mirror maze creates a sense of loss through intricate mirror decorations [8]. In the "Louis Vuitton Series 2 Exhibition," the projection screen showcases characters of varying sizes and overlapping to create a substantial impact [9]. Didier Faustino's "HB-IV Continuum Cosmogonie" portrays an industrial and mechanical aesthetic through showcases filled with rough and messy wires [10].

Artworks, like science fiction movies and illustrations, blend real human faces with diverse textures and forms of bodies. Surreal techniques are used to envision future robots or humans. Hajime Sorayama's illustrations depict robots with metallic and glass textures, creating a futuristic aesthetic. Similarly, the film "Ex Machina" portrays Ava, an intelligent robot with human-like emotions, blurring the boundary between humans and machines.

3   Ethical Reflection on Identity of AI Digital Avatars

Gartner identified ten technological trends in 2019 [11]. These trends, such as enhanced analysis, edge computing, AI-driven development, immersive experience, and digital twins, will bring new demands, opportunities, and challenges to future networks. By 2030, with the emergence of new business scenarios like new media services, industrial control, and 5G, the network architecture will undergo significant changes. Low-latency deterministic delay networks will become a major demand, flat programming will eliminate data limitations, and artificial intelligence will drive continuous innovation. Future networks will integrate AR/VR, large-scale video, and multidimensional content distribution functions.

The advancement of future networks will enable Transhumanism. By 2030, Sarwan Singh envisions humans having enhanced bodily functions through brain microchips, mind-controlled prostheses, and subcutaneous RFID chips. Wearable and implantable brain-computer interfaces will accelerate thinking and enable communication without limitations. The topic of social values will gain attention. Erica Orange and Jared Weiner suggest that wearable devices and AI can transform individuals into "robots," and advanced AI may offer digital cloning and mind uploading. These technological developments raise philosophical debates about personal and societal values [12].

The enhancement of the body also impacts identity construction. Mary Douglas and Han O'Neill explore the relationship between the body and society. The body is shaped by social and cultural concepts, and different social contexts give rise to distinct body styles. The body represents a diverse meaning system influenced by history, culture, society, and more. Identity becomes intertwined with physical meaning through the alliance between the body and society.

Scholars discuss the ethical implications of identity and physical enhancement in the future online world. Slavoj Žižek argues that altering our digital identity may dehumanize us, as seen in The Matrix [13]. Sherry Turkle from MIT University suggests that computers not only impact our actions but also reshape our worldview and self-perception.

4   Human' Interactive Art Installation

4.1   Installation Design

Our work explores identity-related issues in the future network, encompassing the various factors that shape identity and provoke identity anxiety. Will viewers identify with the identity duplication prevalent in the future network? Shall it precipitate the dissolution or reconstruction of their sense of existence and value? Does the viewer's present perception find compensation through imagination, or does it involve identity theft, fragmentation, or loss? What governs a viewer's sense of identity: name, image, genes, or the realms of consciousness, emotion, or thought?

To address these pressing questions, we propose the concept of interactive devices for Human'. The designation "Human'" assimilates the symbolic connotation derived from mathematics, where x' represents a derivative or association with x (such as rotation, translation, reflection, etc.). In the future realm of online existence, Human' represents a replica or embodiment of a human being. While our endeavors, conducted in both Chinese and English, cannot definitively resolve the ethical facets concerning identity in the future internet, we present these profound issues to viewers and encourage them to introspect upon the intricate interplay between identity and personality in both the real and virtual domains through engaging in mobile dialogues Fig. 1.

In the Human' interaction system (see Fig. 2), there are two characters: a real viewer and a virtual mirror, along with two interaction media: the "mirror" device and the viewer's phone. The viewer actively engages in the interactive experience. Different image transitions are triggered by standing in front of the "mirror" device or scanning the QR code on it. The Mirror represents the viewer's reflection in the future online world. It replicates the viewer's biological characteristics in real life, embodies the traits of the future human network era, and possesses independent consciousness. The "mirror" device displays a mirror image the same size as the viewer. As a personal possession, the viewer's mobile phone presents the impact of identity and ethical issues through an H5 page.

Fig. 1. Human' Interactive Art Installation.

The Human' software system comprises four main components: database, input, processing, and output. The database includes behavior (action and dialogue) information, while the input involves collecting facial, body shape, and nickname data through a camera and WeChat scanning. Processing entails facial and body data identification, merging facial data with video materials, and dialogue generation. Finally, the output involves projecting the image onto the "mirror" device using a projector and opening the H5 page on the viewer's phone through WeChat scanning.

The experience process of Human' consists of six steps (see Fig. 2). data collection, image generation, awareness generation, invitation scanning, identity transfer, and reflection/feedback/sharing/learning more. These steps can be categorized into preparation, attraction, orientation, interaction, continuation, and promotion. In the preparation stage (Step 1), real-time data is collected by the camera to enable pre-processing of facial changes. In the attraction stage (Step 2), the "mirror" device generates a mirror image of the viewer's body to grab their attention. In the orientation stage (Step 3), the "mirror" device presents multiple "identity" images of the viewer in the online world, showcasing different consciousness and behavior. In the interaction stage (Step 4), the viewer is invited to scan a QR code on the image screen to establish a dialogue window on their phone. In the continuation stage (Step 5), the image is transferred to the viewer's phone, allowing further communication. Finally, in the promotion stage (Step 6), the "mirror" inspires reflection on identity ethics through guided dialogue, collects user discussions, and provides feedback, sharing, and additional information.

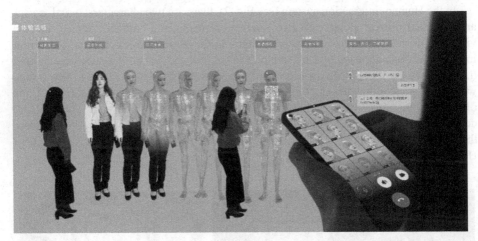

Fig. 2. User flow of Human'.

4.2 Dialogue System

Stimulating public reflection and fostering discussion on the ethical issues of identity in the future online world poses a significant design challenge for this work. Traditional interactive art primarily focused on one-way communication, with the artist conveying information to the viewer and limited feedback from the viewer. Thus, the task is to design an approach that encourages public feedback on identity ethics while also serving as an innovative design element.

To address this challenge, artificial intelligence and H5 technology enable independent "identity" engagement in dialogues with viewers on mobile devices. This prompts individuals to contemplate the intricate interplay between identity and personality in real and virtual realms. The dialogue implementation utilizes Tencent's intelligent dialogue platform, which involves constructing a semantic model, developing business logic, configuring services, and conducting robot testing. Finally, the dialogue system is integrated with the H5 page through an API interface and accessible online.

The semantic dialogue model encompasses two scenarios: mirror-initiated inquiries and viewer-driven exploration. Mirror-initiated questioning focuses on speculative aspects, including identity comparisons, determinants of identity, and contemplations of human nature. The viewer-driven exploration entails understanding the mirror, the artist, and the artwork and engaging in group discussions. Each intention within the mirror-initiated inquiries requires 1–3 guiding questioning scripts and 1–5 response scripts based on different potential viewer responses. Similarly, each intention within viewer-driven exploration necessitates 1–5 viewer speech possibilities, 1–2 default responses from the mirror, and a cascading logic for the intention to progress to mirror-initiated questioning.

For instance, considering the intention of speculative identity comparisons, the mirror initiates questions such as "Do you think we are the same person?" or "Am I you?" Irrespective of the viewer's positive, negative, or ambiguous response, the mirror challenges the viewer's preconceptions through statements like "We share the same eyes and hair, but our personalities are entirely different." The changes in the viewer's response tendencies resulting from the questioning are recorded, and their perspectives on identity determinants are explored through controlled variables.

5 User Feedback

Our installation at the "Science Fiction World" exhibition during China Beijing Science and Technology Week in May 2021 generated extensive user feedback and discussions (see Fig. 3). The audience praised the work, finding it captivating and thought-provoking, which fueled their curiosity about the potential of the future AI world.

Fig. 3. On site of the "Science Fiction World" exhibition.

One prominent theme in the public response was the astonishment and contemplation surrounding the similarities between individuals and digital avatars. Some were amazed by the uncanny connection between personal identity and digital representation, leading them to ponder the impact of digital identities on self-perception and social identity. However, others approached these similarities cautiously, recognizing the differences between digital avatars and honest individuals, as they are virtual entities generated based on personal data and characteristics. These individuals focused more on the relationship between digital identity and technology, contemplating the value and potential of digital avatars in technological advancements and innovation.

Opinions diverged regarding the relationship between digital avatars and society. Some regarded digital avatars as integral parts of society, capable of positively influencing society through information dissemination and inspiring thoughts. They saw digital identities as modes of social interaction and knowledge sharing, believing they could contribute meaningfully to society. However, concerns were raised about the social impact of digital avatars. Some worried that digital identities could lead to a detachment from the real world, potentially weakening face-to-face communication and genuine interpersonal relationships. They questioned the social interactions and ethical responsibilities associated with digital avatars and the potential risks and adverse effects of their misuse.

Furthermore, opinions varied regarding the technical aspects and generation of digital avatars. Some believe artificial intelligence generates digital avatars using algorithms and models to simulate human behavior. They anticipated further technological advancements and hoped for surprising and beneficial innovations. Conversely, others expressed skepticism about the technical aspects of digital avatars, questioning their generation and operation. They voiced concerns about the ethical and moral challenges that technology may bring and call for thoughtful reflection and proactive measures to ensure that the development of digital avatars aligns with societal values and interests.

In summary, the user feedback encompassed various perspectives, reflecting the public's fascination, reservations, and considerations regarding digital avatars. The exhibition catalyzed dialogue about the intricate relationship between individuals and digital identities, the societal implications of digital avatars, and the necessity for responsible technological development.

Acknowledgement. This research was supported by the 2019 National Social Science Foundation Art Program, P.R. China, whose number is 19BG127, and the 2021 Tsinghua University Humanities Construction "Double High" Program Project (2021TSG08203).

References

1. Stark, L., Crawford, K.: The work of art in the age of artificial intelligence: what artists can teach us about the ethics of data practice. Surveill. Soc. **17**(3/4), 442–455 (2019)
2. Gunn, D.P.: Making art strange: a commentary on defamiliarization. Georgia Rev. **38**(1), 25–33 (1984)
3. Benjamin, W., Jennings, M.W.: The work of art in the age of its technological reproducibility. 1st edn. Grey Room **39**, 11–37 (2010)
4. Raley, R.: Tactical Media. University of Minnesota Press, Minneapolis (2009)
5. Stranger Visions, https://deweyhagborg.com/projects/stranger-visions. 2023/06/04
6. Probably Chelsea, https://deweyhagborg.com/projects/probably-chelsea. Accessed 6 Apr 2023
7. Prism: the Beacon Frame, https://criticalengineering.org/projects/prism-the-beacon-frame/. Accessed 6 Apr 2023
8. Mirror Haze, https://esdevlin.com/work/mirror-maze. Accessed 6 Apr 2023
9. Louis Vuitton-Series 2 Exhibition, https://esdevlin.com/work/louis-vuitton-series-2. Accessed 6 Apr 2023
10. HB-IV Continuum -Cosmogonie, https://didierfaustino.com/Cosmogonie-HBIV. Accessed 6 Apr 2023

11. Gartner Top 10 Strategic Technology Trends for 2023, https://www.gartner.com/smarterwi thgartner/gartner-top-10-strategic-technology-trends-for-2023/. Accessed 6 Apr 2023
12. Billion "MEcosystems:" Transhumanism Becomes Reality, https://www.omidyar.com/blog/ 8-billion-mecosystems-transhumanism-becomes-reality. Accessed 6 Apr 2023
13. The matrix, or two sides of perversion, http://www.nettime.org/Lists-Archives/nettime-l-9912/msg00019.html. Accessed 6 Apr 2023

From Auxiliary Design Tools to Intelligent Collaborative Partners: The Transformation of the Relationship Between Design and Computing

Lanxi Xiao and Qiong Wu

Academy of Arts and Design, Tsinghua University, Beijing, China
qiong-wu@tsinghua.edu.cn

Abstract. Artificial intelligence, empowered by computing, has surpassed auxiliary design tools, fostering deep collaboration between human-machine intelligence in contemporary design. Advanced computing technologies and design trends shape the integration of design tools in the information age, influencing design methodology. The developmental history of design tools demonstrates that it undergoes four stages. This article analyzes the impact of calculation on design by studying tools, products, methods, processes, and concepts in each stage, exploring the evolving relationship between design and computation. Designers divide the transformation of the design-computation relationship, which progressively permeates design, transitioning from digitization and automation to parameterization and intelligence. It evolves from improving efficiency to assuming both subject and object roles in the design process and becoming an active partner in collaborative design.

Keywords: Design · Computing · Relationships · Design Tools · Artificial Intelligence

1 Introduction

The integration of artificial intelligence into design has reached a wide-scale implementation, led by AI-powered tools such as LuBan and Midjourney. These tools autonomously adapt and engage in large-scale design activities, displacing particular human designers and fostering deep collaboration with users. This paradigm shift in the application of AI has transformed the relationship between computing and design from a supplementary role to a collaborative one, resulting in a revolution in design processes, methodologies, and conceptual frameworks.

The progression of modern design tools chronicles the increasing involvement of computing in design throughout the past four decades. The concept of Computational Design, introduced by John Maeda, emphasizes the significance of interdisciplinary collaboration and the integration of AI and other technologies, inspiring designers to

C. Stephanidis et al. (Eds.): HCII 2023, CCIS 1958, pp. 94–101, 2024.
https://doi.org/10.1007/978-3-031-49215-0_12

embrace new possibilities [1]. Designers now acknowledge that computational involvement brings about substantial distinctions compared to traditional design approaches. Computing empowers design to swiftly address the needs of millions, or even billions, of users, facilitating continuous development and optimization.

The transformative relationship between computing and design has profoundly impacted designers' workflows and cognitive frameworks. Through an examination of the development of design tools in the information age, we acquire valuable insights into the fusion of pioneering computer technologies and design trends, exerting influence on design processes, methodologies, and conceptual frameworks (see Fig. 1). The historical evolution of design tool development sheds light on the transformative nature of the relationship between computing and design, providing valuable insights for present and future design practices.

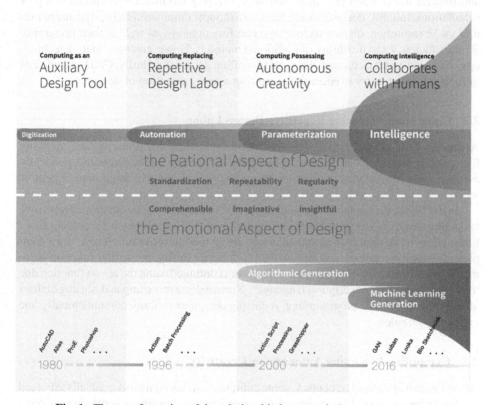

Fig. 1. The transformation of the relationship between design and computing.

2 The Development History of Design Tools in the Information Age

2.1 Computing as an Auxiliary Design Tool

From the history of design tools, the starting point for the large-scale involvement of computing in design was in the 1980s. With their high-speed computing power, computers became auxiliary design tools to improve production efficiency.

Computer-aided design (CAD) technology emerged in the 1950s, revolutionizing design by enabling proper storage and mass production of designs. It was in the 1980s that CAD became widely integrated into design tools with the advent of personal computers and graphical user interfaces. During that decade, CAD software like AutoCAD, Alias, ProE, Illustrator, and Photoshop transformed the field. CAD can be categorized into direct calculation, utilizing parameters and functions for precise and efficient design, and indirect use through graphical interfaces, offering intuitive tools without complex calculations. Initially, designers were hesitant to adopt computer-aided design due to limitations in resolution, display technology, and functionality, as well as their preference for the efficiency and flexibility of traditional methods. However, as computing technology advanced and the concept of a paperless office gained popularity, CAD extended its influence from industry to education, inspiring a new generation of designers.

2.2 Computing Replacing Repetitive Design Labor

At the end of the 1990s, some design tools added automation functions, further improving Computer-aided design efficiency. At this time, computing has begun to independently assume part of the work of designers, becoming the executor of large-scale repetitive work.

In the 1990s, the demand for digital design led to the need for automation in repetitive tasks like image processing. Photoshop introduced Action and batch processing functions, allowing designers to automate image design and improve efficiency. More complex automation required scripting with ActionScript during the action function automated linear processes. However, most designers continued using the action function due to the learning curve of scripting languages. Nonetheless, recording and reusing actions already involved basic programming, requiring designers to think computationally and create design rules.

2.3 Computing Possessing Autonomous Creativity

At the beginning of the 21st century, some computational design tools gradually emerged on the design stage, and the independent creativity of computing was officially applied in design.

Fractal art in the 1980s showcased computing's ability to create using iterative algorithms autonomously. However, the advent of computational design tools brought algorithms into mainstream design. Tools like Action Script and programming languages such as Processing enabled the generative design and the integration of computation as a design element. Additional computational design tools like DrawBot, Generic Components, and Grasshopper expanded the use of algorithms in areas such as information visualization and visual communication. These tools facilitated parameterized design methods that allowed for rapidly generating diverse design solutions by controlling variables. Collaboration among individuals with different backgrounds led to the creation of numerous innovative ideas. However, designers still needed to filter and evaluate algorithmically generated designs, as algorithms could not incorporate symbolic semantics or decide based on user needs. Recognizing the importance of human creativity and decision-making, the Massachusetts Institute of Technology Media Laboratory developed a human-designed system incorporating symbols derived from team names, underscoring the role of human input alongside data, algorithms, and algorithmic rules ineffective design.

2.4 Computing Intelligence Collaborate with Humans

In 2016, AI technology made a breakthrough. It can learn design rules from Big data, generate design independently, interact with designers in-depth, and complete design collaboratively. Computing is an auxiliary tool in the design process and a partner in collaborative design.

AI algorithms like GAN have become popular tools for artists and designers. The artwork "Portrait of Edmond de Belamy," created by a GAN algorithm, was sold for $432,500 in 2018. The algorithm learned from thousands of historical portrait paintings. The emergence of GAN has introduced data-driven methods in design, allowing AI to generate unexpected innovations based on the human experience. For example, a proposed AI-assisted seat shape design method utilized AI to learn from 40,000 seat images and generate creative forms for 310,000 chairs, serving as valuable design references for designers [2].

Under the influence of artificial intelligence, design tools like Photoshop have incorporated AI functions to enhance their capabilities. Photoshop, for example, has introduced features such as facial recognition liquefaction, object selection, and sky replacement, significantly improving the efficiency of image editing by allowing users to select content in complex images quickly. With autonomous learning and AI generation capabilities, Photoshop has also introduced intelligent portrait editing, content-aware filling, style conversion, and more. Style conversion, for instance, can learn the style from one user-provided image and transfer it to another picture.

Other impressive products like Luban, Wix ADI, and Looka have embraced AI to revolutionize the design process. These tools directly cater to users, utilizing embedded AI to independently generate designs based on user needs and continuously improve results based on user behavior and preferences. Looka, a visual recognition system design tool, can understand user preferences through simple interactions and generate adaptive brand design solutions, including logos and real-time multi-scene renderings. During the user's selection and modification process, Looka optimizes the generated results, enabling individuals without design expertise to create designs quickly.

AI is both a design tool and a collaborative partner, combining human-like characteristics with independent creation, dialogue, and learning evolution. This leads to interactive systems called Mixed Initiate Creative Interfaces [3], where users and AI inspire each other. In 2020, researchers developed a co-creation robot named Cobbie, equipped with AI that generates real-time painting ideas based on user input, interacts with users, and provides inspiration. User interviews reveal that participants see Cobbie as an independent partner with their ideas, not just a tool [4]. In 2021, Bio Sketchbook, an AR children's collaborative painting system, uses AI to recognize flower contours, convert photos into painting steps, provide instructions, and guide children in creating plant paintings [5].

Integrating artificial intelligence into the design process has transformed design decisions. It has shifted the focus from human involvement to problem-solving and circular execution led by AI without human intervention. In AI-driven design processes like Looka, designers collaborate with AI experts to establish user profiles, extract design rules, and convert them into AI models. Designing large-scale adaptive interactions has become a crucial challenge in user experience design [6]. User profile construction now considers multidimensionality, accuracy, and timeliness and integrates methods like cognitive psychological measurement, extensive data analysis, and multimodal data. Researchers have proposed user experience research methods for AI-driven experiences, such as Clara Kliman Silver et al., who categorized AI-driven user experience into three dimensions: social and personal, discretionary and non-discretionary, high independence, and no independence of the system [7].

The disruption of the design process has made AI the focus of design. AI differs from previous calculations as its generation process is opaque, relying on probability and prone to a specific error rate. The complexity of AI algorithms makes it challenging for experts to explain poor performance, let alone users without AI expertise. Public opinion harbors ethical concerns about AI, making it difficult for users to understand and trust it during collaboration. Thus, interpretable AI has gained attention in the academic field, with Microsoft Research [8] and Google Design [9] proposing its necessity and methodology in human-computer interaction design. To enhance user experience and avoid pitfalls in collaboration, designers must establish a mental model of AI, provide transparent and accurate visual explanations of AI's principles, capabilities, and limitations, prove its reliability, and promptly anticipate and address AI errors (Fig. 2).

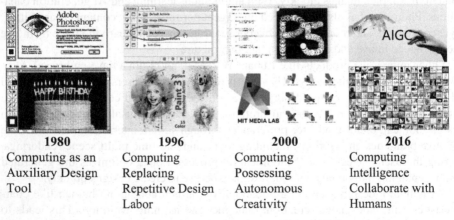

1980	1996	2000	2016
Computing as an Auxiliary Design Tool	Computing Replacing Repetitive Design Labor	Computing Possessing Autonomous Creativity	Computing Intelligence Collaborate with Humans

Fig. 2. The Development History of Design Tools in the Information Age.

3 Transformation of the Relationship Between Design and Computing

In the information age, the continuous updates and iterations of computing technology have driven the development of design tools, changing the process, methods, and design concepts. With the deepening of computing in design, the relationship between design and computation has transformed. Computing has transformed from a tool to assist in implementing design to the subject and object of design, becoming a partner in collaborative design with humans.

The calculation is a tool that assists in implementing the design. In the industrial era, designers used traditional tools such as paper, pens, and clay for design. In the information age, computers have become tools for computer-aided design. The core advantage of computers is computing, which differs from traditional tools. The essence of Computer-aided design is computing-aided design. Calculations are indirectly related to design through the media of computers and graphical user interfaces and directly related to design through parameters, functions, algorithms, machine learning, etc. From CAD, Photoshop, and other Computer-aided design tools in the 1980s to artificial Intelligent design tools such as Luban and Looka that appeared after 2016, computing has brought changes to design from digitalization and automation to parameterization and intellectualization, helping to improve design efficiency and gradually replacing standardized, repetitive and regular labor in the rational level of design.

Since computing can create independently, it has become the main body of the design. When computing was first involved in the design, the main body of the design was the designer, and computing was just another option beyond traditional design tools. From the addition of the "action" function, computing assisted designers as repetitive labor executors, achieving automation of some processes and significantly improving design efficiency. However, the designer still determines the core design creativity and decision-making. After fractal algorithms and computational design tools emerged, computation became the main body of the design. For fractal graphics, computation is the core graphic creator. Currently, the computation can simulate reality and achieve creations humans cannot achieve and predict. In the era of artificial intelligence, on the one hand, machine learning models such as GAN can summarize rules from Big data, migrate styles, and generate new design possibilities; on the other hand, artificial intelligence among collaborative design partners such as Looka can talk with users, analyze users' needs, and independently generate a large number of design schemes that meet users' needs, and can collect data in real-time in the process of collaboration with users to constantly learn and evolve, Over time, the design scheme is iterated to develop more suitable solutions adaptively.

The autonomous creation of computing requires the premise of human designers setting rules, and computing becomes the object of design. In the early stages of becoming an auxiliary design tool, designers do not need to design calculations. Starting from design automation, the emergence of action functions and Action Script scripts has made it necessary for designers to design simple calculation rules. After computing can create independently and become the main body of the design, the design process has undergone a considerable transformation, and designers need to design algorithms and artificial intelligence rules in advance. In the algorithm-driven design process, designers no longer directly design the final product but first design algorithm rules and then make design decisions on the algorithm products. In the design process driven by artificial intelligence, designers do not participate in the design decision-making process but instead design the problem-solving cycle of artificial intelligence.

Computing has become a partner in collaborative design. The design subjectivity of computation and the embodied characteristics of artificial intelligence agents provide a technical foundation for collaborative design. The object-oriented nature of computing design means that humans still need to participate. At the same time, computing and humans each have design advantages that each other does not have. Therefore, the relationship between computing and design only stops at synergy rather than a complete substitution. At the level of rational design, computing has demonstrated abilities beyond human beings. From fractal algorithms to machine learning, computing also possesses generative capabilities that humans do not possess. However, the current AI is still in the stage of weak AI. It needs to be a stronger AI with perception, self-awareness, and values, and it can independently reason and solve abstract problems. Whether it is Luban or Cobbie, all human Intelligent design partners cannot replace human designers in perceptual design. Actual design is a very complex activity involving numerous stakeholders in the design process. The evaluation of design value is also intertwined with sensibility and rationality, subjectivity, and objectivity. In design, designers need to use Empathy to empathize with users, understand complex human emotions and interpersonal relationships, and also need to integrate users, society, business, technology, and other factors to gain design insight and generate creative design schemes based on perceptual thinking of understanding, insight, and imagination. These are abilities that computing does not have compared with human beings.

Margaret Ann Boden, a cognitive scientist, believes that AI can already model all three forms of human creativity [10]. In the future, when Affective computing, behavioral computing, Brain–computer interface, and other technologies are genuinely mature, artificial intelligence can deeply perceive and understand users' emotions, behaviors, and thinking and even use independent consciousness to imagine, make decisions, and act like people, computing will be able to more intelligently cooperate with people in design, or even design entirely independently, and transform from efficiency tools to natural innovation systems, The relationship between design and computation will usher in a new era.

Acknowledgement. This research was supported by the 2019 National Social Science Foundation Art Program, P.R. China, 19BG127.

References

1. Maeda, J.: Design in Tech Report **2017**, 7–9 (2017)
2. Wu, Q., Zhang, C, J.: A paradigm shift in design driven by AI. In: HCI: First International Conference, AI-HCI 2020, Held as Part of the 22nd HCI International Conference, HCII 2020, pp. 167–176 (2020)
3. Deterding, S., Hook, J., Fiebrink, R., et al.: Mixed-initiative creative interfaces. In: Proceedings of the 2017 CHI Conference Extended Abstracts on Human Factors in Computing Systems, pp. 628–635 (2017)

4. Lin, Y., Guo, J., Chen, Y., et al.: It is your turn: collaborative ideation with a co-creative robot through sketch. In: Proceedings of the 2020 CHI Conference on Human Factors in Computing Systems, pp. 1–14 (2020)
5. Zhang, C., Zhou, Z., Wu, J., et al.: Bio sketchbook: an AI-assisted sketching partner for children's biodiversity observational learning. In: Interaction Design and Children, pp. 466–470 (2021)
6. Yang, Q., Steinfeld, A., Rosé, C., et al.: Re-examining whether, why, and how human-AI interaction is uniquely difficult to design. In: Proceedings of the 2020 Chi Conference on Human Factors in Computing Systems, pp. 1–13 (2020)
7. Kliman-Silver, C., Siy, O., Awadalla, K., et al.: Adapting user experience research methods for AI-driven experiences. In: Extended Abstracts of the 2020 CHI Conference on Human Factors in Computing Systems, pp. 1–8 (2020)
8. Amershi, S., Weld, D., Vorvoreanu. M., et al.: Guidelines for human-AI interaction. In: Proceedings of the 2019 CHI Conference on Human Factors in Computing Systems, p. 3 (2019)
9. People and AI Guidebook, https://pair.withgoogle.com/. Accessed 6 Apr 2023
10. Boden, M.A.: Computer models of creativity. AI Mag. **30**(3), 23–34 (2009)

Exploring AI Music Generation: A Review of Deep Learning Algorithms and Datasets for Undergraduate Researchers

Isshin Yunoki$^{(\boxtimes)}$ ⓘ, Guy Berreby ⓘ, Nicholas D'Andrea, Yuhua Lu, and Xiaodong Qu ⓘ

Swarthmore College, Swarthmore, PA 19081, USA
{iyunoki1,gberreb1,ndandre1,ylu3,xqu1}@swarthmore.edu

Abstract. This review paper presents an exploration of the deep learning-based music generation literature, designed to offer undergraduate researchers an initiation into the field. This study illustrates prevailing generative models and datasets currently influential in music generation. Four publications have been selected for detailed discussion, representing a spectrum of salient concepts in music generation and potential areas of further inquiry. By focusing on key studies and significant datasets, this review aspires to serve as a guide for undergraduate scholars keen on investigating the intersections of deep learning and music generation.

Keywords: Deep Learning · Generative Model · Transformer · Time Series · Music · MIDI · Audio

1 Introduction

Deep learning, in recent years, has seen transformative progress across various disciplines, notably in the sphere of AI music generation. Current music generation research focuses on generating original and high-quality compositions, which relies on two key properties: Structural awareness and interpretive ability. Structural awareness enables models to generate naturally coherent music with long-term dependencies, including repetition and variation. Interpretive ability involves translating complex computational models into interactive interfaces for controllable and expressive performances [106]. Furthermore, AI music generation exhibits generality, allowing the same algorithm to be applied across different genres and datasets, enabling exploration of various musical styles. [6]

The landscape of music generation presents a unique opportunity for novice researchers to explore and contribute to the field of generative AI. However, navigating the vast amount of research and staying up to date can be challenging. Our survey aims to assess the accessibility and feasibility of music generation

C. Stephanidis et al. (Eds.): HCII 2023, CCIS 1958, pp. 102–116, 2024.
https://doi.org/10.1007/978-3-031-49215-0_13

algorithms, providing guidance for undergraduate researchers to establish a solid foundation in this exciting area of study.

We have collected notable research on automatic music generation to provide a starting point for researchers to further investigate. By systematizing each study's algorithms and datasets, researchers can identify effective architecture-data pairings. We also select and explain four papers that best represent fundamental ideas and popular techniques in music generation. By engaging the factual information in our resources, researchers can learn and further explore the structural awareness properties of music generation.

Moreover, we include content about the interpretive ability of music generation, allowing connections to be made with the area of human interaction. There is vast potential that lies within the user experience and interfaces side of AI music generation: Researchers can explore how algorithms can be designed to be user-friendly and accessible to a human composer, as well as how these algorithms can be integrated into a creative workflow as a powerful tool to expand and enhance musical ideas.

By studying our resources and content, researchers can find new ideas and draw original connections, enabling them to make significant contributions to the music generation field.

1.1   Related Works

Several review papers provide valuable insights into the trends and methodologies for music generation, such as [6,42,99,106]. We further expand our analysis by exploring a range of scholarly articles that employ analogous time-series data [4,11,18,19,29,46,50,57–62,73,75–77,84,87,97,101–104,107–109]. The literature highlights that algorithmic performance depends on various factors, including the training data's quality and diversity, the model's complexity, and the strategies employed by the model. When it comes to training data, music can be represented in two main formats: Symbolic and raw audio files.

Symbolic audio refers to encoding music information through symbols that represent different aspects of music. The most common form of symbolic music data is MIDI (Music Instrument Digital Interface) which uses discrete values to represent the note pitches and their duration [106].

Raw audio refers to any music file format which encodes an actual audio signal. Such file formats include MP3 files, .WAV files, .FLAC files, and others, which can be used for training algorithms. Raw audio has the advantage of representing expressive characteristics inherent to the original music data, at the cost of being computationally demanding. [6]

1.2   Research Questions

Our investigation seeks to answer the following questions:

- What are recent trends in music generation research?
- Which papers should undergraduate researchers read to gain a thorough understanding of AI music generation?
- Which algorithms and datasets are suited for undergraduate-level research?

2   Methods

2.1   Search Methods for Identification of Studies

The PRISMA (Preferred Reporting Items for Systematic Reviews and Meta-Analyses) method was employed to select relevant studies for this review. The search was conducted between January and March 2023 on Google Scholar, Papers with Code, and arXiv. A combination of keywords was used: ('Deep Learning' OR 'Generative Model' OR 'LSTM' OR 'GAN' OR 'VAE' OR 'Transformer' OR 'Attention') AND ('Time Series' OR 'Music' OR 'Music Theory' OR 'jazz' OR 'MIDI' OR 'Audio'). The process of identifying and refining the study collection is illustrated in Fig. 1.

The criteria for selecting appropriate papers are as follows:

- **Task**: Focus on studies with the objective of AI music generation, specifically those that create new music with high fidelity and long-term consistency using existing data. Research on outside areas and tasks such as genre classification, computer vision, and medical applications are excluded.
- **Deep Learning**: Limit the scope to studies that employ deep learning, defined in this review as having multiple layers with more than one hidden layer. Single-layer generative models are excluded.
- **Transformers**: To assist researchers in their exploration of music generation, we recognize the potential for innovation in transformer-based algorithms. As such, we select prominent papers for researchers to learn more about the advancements and capabilities of transformers.

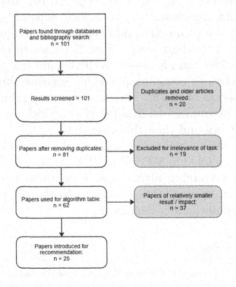

Fig. 1. Selection process for the papers

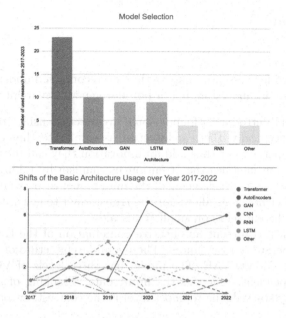

Fig. 2. Visualizations

- **Model Availability**: Prioritize research with publicly available models and datasets. This excludes public music generation websites, as their data and architectures are often undisclosed and subject to change.
- **Target Audience**: The review is tailored for those interested in undergraduate-level research of the intersection of computer science and music. We provide an overview of music generation for students to conduct their own research, developing their skills and knowledge in the field while considering the limited time and experience available to them.
- **Time**: The review only includes studies published in 2017 and onward to account for the rapid progress of the field.

3   Results

We categorize 62 papers' essential algorithms and draw an overall conclusion on their strengths and weaknesses towards the task of music generation. The trends in the model selection are visualized in Fig. 2; transformers have gained significant attention since 2018, while LSTM has shown a decline over the years. AEs and GANs are widely and steadily utilized. This information is summarized in Fig. 3; transformer-based architectures were most commonly used, followed by AEs, GANs, and LSTM neural networks. We also created a list of prominent datasets, in Fig. 4.

4 Discussion

4.1 Papers

We have identified four essential papers that we recommend undergraduate students read to gain an understanding of popular generative architectures.

- Huang et al. [44] introduce a foundational architecture using transformers on MIDI data. Specifically, their architecture is similar to that of the original transformer paper, except they add an innovation they call relative attention. Relative attention modifies the attention mechanism by taking into account how close or far apart two elements of the midi sequence are when determining attention coefficients. This allows for the transformer to generate music which makes more coherent sense on small timescales.
- Dhariwal et al. [21] present an effective combination of the transformer and VAE which operates on raw audio. The overall architecture of their Jukebox model is that of a VQ-VAE. The model has three levels of VQ-VAEs, each of which independently encodes the input data. Thinking of these levels as being vertically stacked, the topmost level is the coarsest, encoding only high

Algorithms	Paper (year published)	Strengths	Weaknesses
Transformer	Hawthorne et al. (2018) Huang et al. (2018) Donahue et al. (2019) Ens and Pasquier (2020) Palea et al. (2020) Jiang et al. (2020) Dhariwal et al. (2020) Zhang (2020) Huang and Yang (2020) Wu and Yang (2020) Wu and Yang (2021) Verma and Chafe (2021) Muhamed et al. (2021) Choi et al. (2021) Di et al. (2021) Santos et al. (2022) Min et al. (2022) Santos et al. (2022) Yu et al. (2022) Shih et al. (2022) Dong et al. (2022) Sarmento et al. (2023) Agostinelli et al. (2023)	- Highly parallelizable, enabling fast training - Strong long-range dependency modeling due to attention mechanism - State-of-the-art performance in various tasks	- Can require significant amounts of memory and computational resources - Often require large-scale pre-training for best performance
AutoEncoders	Engel et al. (2017) Dieleman et al. (2018) Akbari and Liang (2018) Roberts et al. (2018) Liang et al. (2019) Liang et al. (2019) Lattner and Grachten (2019) Huang and Huang (2020) Choi et al. (2020) Grekow and Dimitrova-Grekow (2021)	- Unsupervised learning, requiring no labeled data - VAE can generate diverse, novel outputs by sampling from latent space - Enable efficient representation learning	- Can struggle to generate high-quality outputs, especially with complex data like music - Latent space may not capture all essential features
GAN	Yang et al. (2017) Dong et al. (2018) Dong and Yang (2018) Jhamtani and Berg-Kirkpatrick (2019) Guan et al. (2019) Nistal et al. (2020) Brock and Korneel (2021) Cádiz et al. (2021) Tomaz et al. (2022)	- Ability to generate high-quality outputs - Adversarial training enables implicit modeling of data distribution - Encourages creativity in generated outputs	- Training can be unstable and challenging to converge - Mode collapse: GAN may only learns to generate a limited set of outputs
LSTM	Brunner et al. (2017) Mao et al. (2018) Défossez et al. (2018) Zhao et al. (2019) Wang et al. (2019) Mangal et al. (2019) Gillick et al. (2019) Ferreira and Whitehead (2021) Keerti et al. (2022)	- Capable of learning long-range dependencies better than plain RNNs - Widely used and proven effective in various music generation tasks - Mitigate vanishing and exploding gradient problems with specialized gating mechanisms	- Training can be slow and resource-intensive - Can be more complex to implement and optimize compared to simpler models like RNNs or CNNs
CNN	Elbayad et al. (2018) Schimbinschi et al. (2019) Wang and Yang (2019) Nishihara et al. (2023)	- Effective in capturing local and hierarchical features - Invariant to translations, which can be helpful to certain musical tasks	- Limited in modeling long-range dependencies due to fixed-size convolutional filters - Not explicitly designed for sequential data like music
RNN	Hadjeres and Nielsen (2017) Carr and Zukowski (2018) Jagannathan et al. (2022)	- Designed for sequential data, making them suitable for music generation - Can model arbitrary-length input and output sequences	- Struggle to learn long-range dependencies due to vanishing or exploding gradient problem - Slower training compared to other models, as processing is inherently sequential
Other	Yanchenko and Mukherjee (2017) Andreux and Mallat (2018) Manzelli et al. (2018) Goel et al. (2022)	Includes: State Space Model; WaveNet; Moment Matching-Scattering Inverse Network (MM-SIN)	

*Categorization is not exhaustive, as many researchers combine multiple models or utilize parts of a model.

Fig. 3. Algorithm usage by papers

Datasets	Description	Original Paper	Citation Number (as of Apr. 2023)
JSB Chorales	MIDI versions of Bach Chorales, short pieces of 4-part vocal music	Boulanger-Lewandowski Bengio, and Vincent 2012	848
MAESTRO	200 hours of both MIDI and raw audio versions of piano pieces	Hawthorne et al. 2019	333
Lakh MIDI dataset	176,581 unique MIDI files	Raffel 2016	279
MagnaTagATune	200 hours of music audio, consisting of 29 second clips (raw audio)	Edith Law and Downie 2009	169
REMI	MIDI-based event sequences; converted files of many popular songs	Huang and Yang 2020	122
Beethoven	Raw Audio recordings of 32 Beethoven piano sonatas	Neuwirth et al. 2018	69
POP909	Multiple versions of piano arrangements of popular songs	Wang et al. 2020	60
The Weimar Jazz Database	MIDI transcriptions of Jazz solos	Pfleiderer et al. 2017	49
GiantMIDI-Piano	10,855 MIDI files of classical piano music	Kong et al. 2020	46
MusicCaps	5,521 music samples, each labeled in English	Agostinelli et al. 2023	31
EWLD	A MIDI dataset of over 5000 music lead sheets	Simonetta et al. 2018	28
NES-MDB	5287 songs from 397 NES games soundtrack in a few symbolic formats	Donahue et al. 2018	23
DadaGP	26,181 Guitar Pro files in 739 genres, a symbolic dataset	Sarmento et al. 2021	12
840 Piano covers of popular songs	840 Piano covers of popular songs, ranging over 56 hours (raw audio)	Verma and Chafe 2021	11
Projective Orchestral Database	196 pairs of midi files having a piano and orchestral version of music	Crestel et al. 2018	11

Fig. 4. Datasets used by papers

level essential information, while the lowest level encodes the fine details of the music. With these latent spaces, they then train sparse transformers that upsample from a higher level latent space to a lower one. So, to generate music, a sample datapoint from the latent space of the uppermost VQ-VAE, uses transformers to up-sample the datapoint to the latent space of the lower level VQ-VAEs, and then once at the lowest level, use the VQ-VAE decoder to turn the upsampled datapoint into raw audio.

– Dong et al. [27] introduce MuseGan, a GAN architecture for symbolic multi-track piano roll data. MuseGan employs a WGAN-GP framework, which includes modified objective functions and a gradient penalty for the discriminator, leading to faster convergence and reduced parameter tuning. The model consists of two components: the Multitrack model and the temporal model. The Multitrack model incorporates GAN submodels based on three compositional approaches: jamming, composing, and a hybrid of both. Discriminators within these submodels evaluate the specific characteristics of each track. The temporal model comprises two submodels: one for generation from scratch, capturing temporal and bar-by-bar information, and another for track-conditional generation, using conditional track inputs to generate sequential bars. By combining these models, MuseGan produces latent vectors that incorporate inter-track and temporal information. These vectors are then used to generate piano rolls sequentially.

– Huang and Yang [47] provide a promising direction of data conversion with their introduction of REMI (revamped MIDI-derived events). Instead of the traditional MIDI-based music representations, REMI describes musical events with further details to represent the original music with more information. Specifically, REMI adds tempo and chords as part of the data, reinterprets the time grid of the music data from second-based to position- and bar-based, and describes the note duration instead of the ending position of the note for note lengths. REMI helped a transformer-based model output samples with stronger sense of downbeat and natural and expressive uses of chords. The paper also introduces Pop Music Transformer, a transformer-based architecture for music generation. This model differs from traditional transformer models in that it learns to compose music over a metrical structure defined in terms of bars, beats, and sub-beats, through the application of the aforementioned REMI. This approach allows the model to generate music with a more salient and consistent rhythmic structure, and produce musically pleasing pieces without human intervention.

4.2   Algorithms

Our survey suggests that the main algorithms used for music generation in the last five years are transformers and autoencoders such as VAEs, GANS, and LSTMs, with transformers being by far the most popular. Due to the popularity of transformers and their success with music generation, we have decided to focus on them for much of our analysis.

Transformers are applicable in symbolic and raw audio domains with convincing results, offering flexibility for researchers to pursue their research interests. Also, the literature shows transformers have broad functionalities and involve specific components and mechanisms makes them worth exploring individually.

These components can be fine tuned and altered to match the needs of a given task. For example, [41,43] use a modification known as relative attention, which modifies the attention coefficients based one how far apart two tokens are. There is also the transformer-XL modification used by [24]. This modification adds a recurrence mechanism to hidden states within the Transformer, and has been shown to increase performance [17]. Others, such as [21] used sparse transformers. Sparse transformers introduce sparsity to the attention heads of the transformer, reducing $O(n^2)$ time and memory costs to $O(n\sqrt{n})$ [13].

4.3   Datasets

A variety of both symbolic and raw audio datasets have were used by transformer papers. We observe that certain datasets work best with transformers in capturing complex and long-range dependencies within music sequences:

The LakhMIDI dataset, the largest dataset of symbolic data available, has great potential due to its large training size and MIDI-audio pairings, and was the most popular among transformer papers we surveyed, with five different papers using it. In [26,34,78], the authors use LakhMIDI to derive token sequences from MIDI files to create multitrack music transformer models. In [94], a multi-track pianoroll dataset derived from LakhMIDI is used for a transformer as well. [24] maps LakhMIDI tracks onto instrumentation playable by the NES, and then uses a transformer to generate NES versions of songs.

Similar in size and function is the MAESTRO dataset, which is used by the transformer models of [41,67], and is the second most popular dataset among transformer papers. The MAESTRO dataset contains over 200 h of piano performances, stored in both raw audio and MIDI formats. The MIDI-audio pairings enables music information to be retrieved from the MIDI files and be used as annotations for the matched audio files. Every file is labeled, allowing for easy supervised training.

Besides LakhMIDI and MAESTRO, every other transformer paper we found used a different dataset. In fact, a popular choice among them was to create or scrape their own dataset, which was done by [21,47,89,100].

Overall, for undergraduates working with Transformers, if working with symbolic data we would recommend using the Lakh MIDI dataset due to its large size and relative popularity among other users of transformers. For those who want to use raw audio, we would recommend the MAESTRO dataset, similarly for its large size and popularity.

4.4 Future Work

The future development of music generation technology is increasingly focused on enhancing the ability to control models structurally. In later work, more research and analysis could investigate the data and model decisions behind each study, as well as increase the target research, to better comprehend factors contributing to successful music generation outcomes.

Moving forward, we encourage undergraduate researchers to engage in more experimental and collaborative work, exploring the combination of different algorithms and datasets to develop new approaches to music generation.

5 Conclusion

In conclusion, our review provides a survey of deep learning algorithms and datasets for music generation, with the aim to assist undergraduate researchers interested in the field. Our findings suggest that in the last five years, transformers, GANS, autoencoders, and LSTMs have been the primary algorithms used for AI music generation, with transformers gaining significant popularity in more recent times. We find that the papers use a wide variety of datasets, meaning there is no one single, predominant dataset being used. We suggest four papers that we believe are important for undergraduates to read to get a solid grasp of the field, and also recommend an algorithm along with datasets for undergraduates to use for their initial adventures into AI music generation.

Author contributions. Isshin, Guy, Nicholas, and Yuhua are the first four authors of this paper, and they contributed equally. Professor Xiaodong Qu is the mentor for this research project.

References

1. Agostinelli, A., et al.: MusicLM: generating music from text (2023)
2. Akbari, M., Liang, J.: Semi-recurrent CNN-based VAE-GAN for sequential data generation. In: 2018 IEEE International Conference on Acoustics, Speech and Signal Processing (ICASSP), pp. 2321–2325. IEEE (2018)
3. Andreux, M., Mallat, S.: Music generation and transformation with moment matching-scattering inverse networks. In: ISMIR, pp. 327–333 (2018)
4. Basaklar, T., Tuncel, Y., An, S., Ogras, U.: Wearable devices and low-power design for smart health applications: challenges and opportunities. In: 2021 IEEE/ACM International Symposium on Low Power Electronics and Design (ISLPED), p. 1. IEEE (2021)
5. Boulanger-Lewandowski, N., Bengio, Y., Vincent, P.: Modeling temporal dependencies in high-dimensional sequences: application to polyphonic music generation and transcription (2012)
6. Briot, J.P.: From artificial neural networks to deep learning for music generation: history, concepts and trends. Neural Comput. Appl. **33**(1), 39–65 (2021)
7. van den Broek, K.: Mp3net: coherent, minute-long music generation from raw audio with a simple convolutional GAN. arXiv e-prints, pp. arXiv-2101 (2021)
8. Brunner, G., Wang, Y., Wattenhofer, R., Wiesendanger, J.: JamBot: music theory aware chord based generation of polyphonic music with LSTMs. In: 2017 IEEE 29th International Conference on Tools with Artificial Intelligence (ICTAI), pp. 519–526. IEEE (2017)
9. Cádiz, R.F., Macaya, A., Cartagena, M., Parra, D.: Creativity in generative musical networks: evidence from two case studies. Front. Robot. AI **8**, 680586 (2021)
10. Carr, C., Zukowski, Z.: Generating albums with SampleRNN to imitate metal, rock, and punk bands. arXiv preprint arXiv:1811.06633 (2018)
11. Chen, L., et al.: Data-driven detection of subtype-specific differentially expressed genes. Sci. Rep. **11**(1), 332 (2021)
12. Chen, Y.H., Wang, B., Yang, Y.H.: Demonstration of PerformanceNet: a convolutional neural network model for score-to-audio music generation, pp. 6506–6508 (2019). https://doi.org/10.24963/ijcai.2019/938
13. Child, R., Gray, S., Radford, A., Sutskever, I.: Generating long sequences with sparse transformers (2019)
14. Choi, K., Hawthorne, C., Simon, I., Dinculescu, M., Engel, J.: Encoding musical style with transformer autoencoders. In: International Conference on Machine Learning, pp. 1899–1908. PMLR (2020)
15. Choi, K., Park, J., Heo, W., Jeon, S., Park, J.: Chord conditioned melody generation with transformer based decoders. IEEE ACCESS **9**, 42071–42080 (2021). https://doi.org/10.1109/ACCESS.2021.3065831
16. Crestel, L., Esling, P., Heng, L., McAdams, S.: A database linking piano and orchestral midi scores with application to automatic projective orchestration (2018)

17. Dai, Z., Yang, Z., Yang, Y., Carbonell, J., Le, Q., Salakhutdinov, R.: Transformer-XL: attentive language models beyond a fixed-length context, pp. 2978–2988 (2019). https://doi.org/10.18653/v1/P19-1285

18. Deb, R., An, S., Bhat, G., Shill, H., Ogras, U.Y.: A systematic survey of research trends in technology usage for Parkinson's disease. Sensors **22**(15), 5491 (2022)

19. Deb, R., Bhat, G., An, S., Shill, H., Ogras, U.Y.: Trends in technology usage for Parkinson's disease assessment: a systematic review. MedRxiv, pp. 2021–02 (2021)

20. Défossez, A., Zeghidour, N., Usunier, N., Bottou, L., Bach, F.: Sing: Symbol-to-instrument neural generator. In: Advances in Neural Information Processing Systems, vol. 31 (2018)

21. Dhariwal, P., Jun, H., Payne, C., Kim, J.W., Radford, A., Sutskever, I.: Jukebox: a generative model for music. arXiv preprint arXiv:2005.00341 (2020)

22. Di, S., et al.: Video background music generation with controllable music transformer. In: Proceedings of the 29th ACM International Conference on Multimedia, pp. 2037–2045 (2021)

23. Dieleman, S., van den Oord, A., Simonyan, K.: The challenge of realistic music generation: modelling raw audio at scale. In: Advances in Neural Information Processing Systems, vol. 31 (2018)

24. Donahue, C., Mao, H.H., Li, Y.E., Cottrell, G.W., McAuley, J.: Lakhnes: improving multi-instrumental music generation with cross-domain pre-training. arXiv preprint arXiv:1907.04868 (2019)

25. Donahue, C., Mao, H.H., McAuley, J.: The NES music database: a multi-instrumental dataset with expressive performance attributes. In: ISMIR (2018)

26. Dong, H.W., Chen, K., Dubnov, S., McAuley, J., Berg-Kirkpatrick, T.: Multitrack music transformer (2022)

27. Dong, H.W., Hsiao, W.Y., Yang, L.C., Yang, Y.H.: MuseGAN: multi-track sequential generative adversarial networks for symbolic music generation and accompaniment. In: Proceedings of the AAAI Conference on Artificial Intelligence, vol. 32 (2018)

28. Dong, H.W., Yang, Y.H.: Convolutional generative adversarial networks with binary neurons for polyphonic music generation. arXiv preprint arXiv:1804.09399 (2018)

29. Dou, G., Zhou, Z., Qu, X.: Time majority voting, a PC-based EEG classifier for non-expert users. In: Kurosu, M., et al. HCI International 2022-Late Breaking Papers. Multimodality in Advanced Interaction Environments. HCII 2022. LNCS, vol. 13519, pp. 415–428. Springer, Cham (2022). https://doi.org/10.1007/978-3-031-17618-0_29

30. Edith Law, Kris West, M.M.: Evaluation of algorithms using games: the case of music annotation. In: Proceedings of the 10th International Conference on Music Information Retrieval (ISMIR) (2009)

31. Elbayad, M., Besacier, L., Verbeek, J.: Pervasive attention: 2D convolutional neural networks for sequence-to-sequence prediction (2018)

32. Engel, J., Agrawal, K.K., Chen, S., Gulrajani, I., Donahue, C., Roberts, A.: Gansynth: Adversarial neural audio synthesis. arXiv:1902.08710 (2019)

33. Engel, J., et al.: Neural audio synthesis of musical notes with WaveNet autoencoders. In: International Conference on Machine Learning, pp. 1068–1077. PMLR (2017)

34. Ens, J., Pasquier, P.: MMM: exploring conditional multi-track music generation with the transformer. arXiv preprint arXiv:2008.06048 (2020)

35. Ferreira, L.N., Whitehead, J.: Learning to generate music with sentiment. arXiv preprint arXiv:2103.06125 (2021)

36. Gillick, J., Roberts, A., Engel, J., Eck, D., Bamman, D.: Learning to groove with inverse sequence transformations. In: International Conference on Machine Learning, pp. 2269–2279. PMLR (2019)

37. Goel, K., Gu, A., Donahue, C., Ré, C.: It's raw! Audio generation with state-space models. In: International Conference on Machine Learning, pp. 7616–7633. PMLR (2022)

38. Grekow, J., Dimitrova-Grekow, T.: Monophonic music generation with a given emotion using conditional variational autoencoder. IEEE Access **9**, 129088–129101 (2021)

39. Guan, F., Yu, C., Yang, S.: A GAN model with self-attention mechanism to generate multi-instruments symbolic music. In: 2019 International Joint Conference on Neural Networks (IJCNN), pp. 1–6 (2019). https://doi.org/10.1109/IJCNN.2019.8852291

40. Hadjeres, G., Nielsen, F.: Interactive music generation with positional constraints using anticipation-RNNs. arXiv preprint arXiv:1709.06404 (2017)

41. Hawthorne, C., et al.: Enabling factorized piano music modeling and generation with the maestro dataset (2019)

42. Hernandez-Olivan, C., Beltran, J.R.: Music composition with deep learning: a review. In: Advances in Speech and Music Technology: Computational Aspects and Applications, pp. 25–50 (2022)

43. Huang, C.A., et al.: An improved relative self-attention mechanism for transformer with application to music generation. CoRR abs/1809.04281 (2018). http://arxiv.org/abs/1809.04281

44. Huang, C.Z.A., et al.: Music transformer. arXiv preprint arXiv:1809.04281 (2018)

45. Huang, C.F., Huang, C.Y.: Emotion-based AI music generation system with CVAE-GAN. In: 2020 IEEE Eurasia Conference on IOT, Communication and Engineering (ECICE), pp. 220–222. IEEE (2020)

46. Huang, D., Tang, Y., Qin, R.: An evaluation of Planetscope images for 3d reconstruction and change detection-experimental validations with case studies. GISci. Remote Sens. **59**(1), 744–761 (2022)

47. Huang, Y.S., Yang, Y.H.: Pop music transformer: beat-based modeling and generation of expressive pop piano compositions, pp. 1180–1188 (2020). https://doi.org/10.1145/3394171.3413671

48. Jagannathan, A., Chandrasekaran, B., Dutta, S., Patil, U.R., Eirinaki, M.: Original music generation using recurrent neural networks with self-attention. In: 2022 IEEE International Conference On Artificial Intelligence Testing (AITest), pp. 56–63. IEEE (2022)

49. Jhamtani, H., Berg-Kirkpatrick, T.: Modeling self-repetition in music generation using generative adversarial networks. In: Machine Learning for Music Discovery Workshop, ICML (2019)

50. Jiang, C., et al.: Deep denoising of raw biomedical knowledge graph from COVID-19 literature, LitCovid, and Pubtator: framework development and validation. J. Med. Internet Res. **24**(7), e38584 (2022)

51. Jiang, J., Xia, G.G., Carlton, D.B., Anderson, C.N., Miyakawa, R.H.: Transformer vae: a hierarchical model for structure-aware and interpretable music representation learning. In: ICASSP 2020–2020 IEEE International Conference on Acoustics, Speech and Signal Processing (ICASSP), pp. 516–520. IEEE (2020)

52. Keerti, G., Vaishnavi, A., Mukherjee, P., Vidya, A.S., Sreenithya, G.S., Nayab, D.: Attentional networks for music generation. Multimed. Tools Appl. **81**(4), 5179–5189 (2022)
53. Kong, Q., Li, B., Chen, J., Wang, Y.: GiantMIDI-Piano: a large-scale midi dataset for classical piano music (2022)
54. Lattner, S., Grachten, M.: High-level control of drum track generation using learned patterns of rhythmic interaction. In: 2019 IEEE Workshop on Applications of Signal Processing to Audio and Acoustics (WASPAA), pp. 35–39. IEEE (2019)
55. Liang, X., Wu, J., Cao, J.: MIDI-sandwich2: RNN-based hierarchical multi-modal fusion generation VAE networks for multi-track symbolic music generation. CoRR abs/1909.03522 (2019). http://dblp.uni-trier.de/db/journals/corr/corr1909.htmlabs-1909-03522
56. Liang, X., Wu, J., Yin, Y.: MIDI-sandwich: multi-model multi-task hierarchical conditional VAE-GAN networks for symbolic single-track music generation. arXiv preprint arXiv:1907.01607 (2019)
57. Liu, C., Li, H., Xu, J., Gao, W., Shen, X., Miao, S.: Applying convolutional neural network to predict soil erosion: a case study of coastal areas. Int. J. Environ. Res. Public Health **20**(3), 2513 (2023)
58. Lu, Y., Wang, H., Wei, W.: Machine learning for synthetic data generation: a review. arXiv preprint arXiv:2302.04062 (2023)
59. Lu, Y., et al.: Cot: an efficient and accurate method for detecting marker genes among many subtypes. Bioinform. Adv. **2**(1), vbac037 (2022)
60. Luo, X., Ma, X., Munden, M., Wu, Y.J., Jiang, Y.: A multisource data approach for estimating vehicle queue length at metered on-ramps. J. Transp. Eng. Part A Syst. **148**(2), 04021117 (2022)
61. Ma, X.: Traffic Performance Evaluation Using Statistical and Machine Learning Methods. Ph.D. thesis, The University of Arizona (2022)
62. Ma, X., Karimpour, A., Wu, Y.J.: Statistical evaluation of data requirement for ramp metering performance assessment. Transp. Res. Part A Policy Pract. **141**, 248–261 (2020)
63. Mangal, S., Modak, R., Joshi, P.: LSTM based music generation system. arXiv preprint arXiv:1908.01080 (2019)
64. Manzelli, R., Thakkar, V., Siahkamari, A., Kulis, B.: An end to end model for automatic music generation: combining deep raw and symbolic audio networks. In: Proceedings of the Musical Metacreation Workshop at 9th International Conference on Computational Creativity, Salamanca, Spain (2018)
65. Mao, H.H., Shin, T., Cottrell, G.: DeepJ: style-specific music generation. In: 2018 IEEE 12th International Conference on Semantic Computing (ICSC), pp. 377–382. IEEE (2018)
66. Min, J., Liu, Z., Wang, L., Li, D., Zhang, M., Huang, Y.: Music generation system for adversarial training based on deep learning. Processes **10**(12), 2515 (2022)
67. Muhamed, A., et al.: Symbolic music generation with transformer-GANs. In: Proceedings of the AAAI Conference on Artificial Intelligence, vol. 35, pp. 408–417 (2021)
68. Neuwirth, M., Harasim, D., Moss, F., Rohrmeier, M.: The annotated Beethoven corpus (ABC): a dataset of harmonic analyses of all Beethoven string quartets. Front. Digital Human. **5**, 16 (2018). https://doi.org/10.3389/fdigh.2018.00016
69. Nishihara, M., Hono, Y., Hashimoto, K., Nankaku, Y., Tokuda, K.: Singing voice synthesis based on frame-level sequence-to-sequence models considering vocal timing deviation. arXiv preprint arXiv:2301.02262 (2023)

70. Nistal, J., Lattner, S., Richard, G.: DrumGAN: synthesis of drum sounds with timbral feature conditioning using generative adversarial networks. arXiv preprint arXiv:2008.12073 (2020)
71. van den Oord, A., et al.: Wavenet: a generative model for raw audio (2016)
72. Palea, D., Zhou, H.H., Gupta, K.: Transformer bard: music and poem generation using transformer models (2020)
73. Peng, X., Bhattacharya, T., Mao, J., Cao, T., Jiang, C., Qin, X.: Energy-efficient management of data centers using a renewable-aware scheduler. In: 2022 IEEE International Conference on Networking, Architecture and Storage (NAS), pp. 1–8. IEEE (2022)
74. Pfleiderer, M., Frieler, K., Abeßer, J., Zaddach, W.G., Burkhart, B. (eds.): Inside the Jazzomat - New Perspectives for Jazz Research. Schott Campus (2017)
75. Qu, X., Liu, P., Li, Z., Hickey, T.: Multi-class time continuity voting for EEG classification. In: Frasson, C., Bamidis, P., Vlamos, P. (eds.) BFAL 2020. LNCS (LNAI), vol. 12462, pp. 24–33. Springer, Cham (2020). https://doi.org/10.1007/978-3-030-60735-7_3
76. Qu, X., Liukasemsarn, S., Tu, J., Higgins, A., Hickey, T.J., Hall, M.H.: Identifying clinically and functionally distinct groups among healthy controls and first episode psychosis patients by clustering on eeg patterns. Front. Psych. **11**, 541659 (2020)
77. Qu, X., Mei, Q., Liu, P., Hickey, T.: Using EEG to distinguish between writing and typing for the same cognitive task. In: Frasson, C., Bamidis, P., Vlamos, P. (eds.) BFAL 2020. LNCS (LNAI), vol. 12462, pp. 66–74. Springer, Cham (2020). https://doi.org/10.1007/978-3-030-60735-7_7
78. Raffel, C.: Learning-based methods for comparing sequences, with applications to audio-to-midi alignment and matching (2016). https://colinraffel.com/projects/lmd/
79. Roberts, A., Engel, J., Raffel, C., Hawthorne, C., Eck, D.: A hierarchical latent vector model for learning long-term structure in music. In: International Conference on Machine Learning, pp. 4364–4373. PMLR (2018)
80. Santos, G.A.C., Baffa, A., Briot, J.P., Feijó, B., Furtado, A.L.: An adaptive music generation architecture for games based on the deep learning transformer mode. arXiv preprint arXiv:2207.01698 (2022)
81. Sarmento, P., Kumar, A., Carr, C., Zukowski, Z., Barthet, M., Yang, Y.H.: DadaGP: a dataset of tokenized GuitarPro songs for sequence models. In: Proceedings of the 22nd International Society for Music Information Retrieval Conference (2021). https://archives.ismir.net/ismir2021/paper/000076.pdf
82. Sarmento, P., Kumar, A., Chen, Y.H., Carr, C., Zukowski, Z., Barthet, M.: GTR-CTRL: instrument and genre conditioning for guitar-focused music generation with transformers. In: Johnson, C., Rodríguez-Fernández, N., Rebelo, S.M. (eds) Artificial Intelligence in Music, Sound, Art and Design. EvoMUSART 2023. LNCS, vol. 13988, pp. 260–275. Springer, Cham (2023). https://doi.org/10.1007/978-3-031-29956-8_17
83. Schimbinschi, F., Walder, C., Erfani, S.M., Bailey, J.: Synthnet: learning to synthesize music end-to-end. In: IJCAI, pp. 3367–3374 (2019)
84. Shen, X., Sun, Y., Zhang, Y., Najmabadi, M.: Semi-supervised intent discovery with contrastive learning. In: Proceedings of the 3rd Workshop on Natural Language Processing for Conversational AI, pp. 120–129 (2021)
85. Shih, Y.J., Wu, S.L., Zalkow, F., Muller, M., Yang, Y.H.: Theme transformer: symbolic music generation with theme-conditioned transformer. IEEE Trans. Multimed. **14**, 1–14 (2022)

86. Simonetta, F., Carnovalini, F., Orio, N., Roda, A.: Symbolic music similarity through a graph-based representation (2018). https://doi.org/10.1145/3243274.3243301

87. Tang, Y., Song, S., Gui, S., Chao, W., Cheng, C., Qin, R.: Active and low-cost hyperspectral imaging for the spectral analysis of a low-light environment. Sensors **23**(3), 1437 (2023)

88. Tomaz Neves, P.L., Fornari, J., Batista Florindo, J.: Self-attention generative adversarial networks applied to conditional music generation. Multimed. Tools Appl. **81**(17), 24419–24430 (2022)

89. Verma, P., Chafe, C.: A generative model for raw audio using transformer architectures. In: 2021 24th International Conference on Digital Audio Effects (DAFx), pp. 230–237. IEEE (2021)

90. Wang, B., Yang, Y.H.: Performancenet: score-to-audio music generation with multi-band convolutional residual network. In: Proceedings of the AAAI Conference on Artificial Intelligence 33(01), 1174–1181 (2019). https://doi.org/10.1609/aaai.v33i01.33011174, https://ojs.aaai.org/index.php/AAAI/article/view/3911

91. Wang, J., Wang, X., Cai, J.: Jazz music generation based on grammar and LSTM. In: 2019 11th International Conference on Intelligent Human-Machine Systems and Cybernetics (IHMSC), vol. 1, pp. 115–120. IEEE (2019)

92. Wang*, Z., Chen*, K., Jiang, J., Zhang, Y., Xu, M., Dai, S., Bin, G., Xia, G.: Pop909: a pop-song dataset for music arrangement generation. In: Proceedings of 21st International Conference on Music Information Retrieval, ISMIR (2020)

93. Wu, S.L., Yang, Y.H.: The jazz transformer on the front line: exploring the shortcomings of AI-composed music through quantitative measures. arXiv preprint arXiv:2008.01307 (2020)

94. Wu, S.L., Yang, Y.H.: Musemorphose: full-song and fine-grained music style transfer with one transformer VAE. arXiv preprint arXiv:2105.04090 (2021)

95. Yanchenko, A.K., Mukherjee, S.: Classical music composition using state space models. arXiv preprint arXiv:1708.03822 (2017)

96. Yang, L.C., Chou, S.Y., Yang, Y.H.: MIDInet: a convolutional generative adversarial network for symbolic-domain music generation. arXiv preprint arXiv:1703.10847 (2017)

97. Yi, L., Qu, X.: Attention-based CNN capturing EEG recording's average voltage and local change. In: Degen, H., Ntoa, S. (eds.) Artificial Intelligence in HCI. HCII 2022. LNCS, vol. 13336, pp. 448–459. Springer, Cham (2022). https://doi.org/10.1007/978-3-031-05643-7_29

98. Yu, B., et al.: MuseFormer: transformer with fine-and coarse-grained attention for music generation. arXiv preprint arXiv:2210.10349 (2022)

99. Zhang, H., Xie, L., Qi, K.: Implement music generation with GAN: a systematic review. In: 2021 International Conference on Computer Engineering and Application (ICCEA), pp. 352–355. IEEE (2021)

100. Zhang, N.: Learning adversarial transformer for symbolic music generation. IEEE Transactions on Neural Networks and Learning Systems (2020)

101. Zhang, S., Zhao, Z., Guan, C.: Multimodal continuous emotion recognition: a technical report for ABAW5. In: Proceedings of the IEEE/CVF Conference on Computer Vision and Pattern Recognition, pp. 5763–5768 (2023)

102. Zhang, Y., et al.: Biotic homogenization increases with human intervention: implications for mangrove wetland restoration. Ecography **2022**(4), 1–12 (2022)

103. Zhang, Z., et al.: Implementation and performance evaluation of in-vehicle highway back-of-queue alerting system using the driving simulator. In: 2021 IEEE

International Intelligent Transportation Systems Conference (ITSC), pp. 1753–1759. IEEE (2021)

104. Zhang, Z., Tian, R., Sherony, R., Domeyer, J., Ding, Z.: Attention-based interrelation modeling for explainable automated driving. IEEE Trans. Intell. Veh. **18**, 1564–1573 (2022)

105. Zhao, K., Li, S., Cai, J., Wang, H., Wang, J.: An emotional symbolic music generation system based on LSTM networks. In: 2019 IEEE 3rd Information Technology, Networking, Electronic and Automation Control Conference (ITNEC), pp. 2039–2043. IEEE (2019)

106. Zhao, Z., et al.: A review of intelligent music generation systems (2022)

107. Zhao, Z., Chopra, K., Zeng, Z., Li, X.: Sea-net: squeeze-and-excitation attention net for diabetic retinopathy grading. In: 2020 IEEE International Conference on Image Processing (ICIP), pp. 2496–2500. IEEE (2020)

108. Zhao, Z., et al.: BIRA-net: bilinear attention net for diabetic retinopathy grading. In: 2019 IEEE International Conference on Image Processing (ICIP), pp. 1385–1389. IEEE (2019)

109. Zong, N., et al.: Beta: a comprehensive benchmark for computational drug-target prediction. Brief. Bioinform. **23**(4), bbac199 (2022)

Preliminary Studies and Prototypes for Machine Learning Based Evaluation of Surfers' Performance on River Waves

Michael Zöllner[1] , Stefan Kniesburger[2]([⊠]) , Michael Döllinger[2]([⊠]) ,
Jan Gemeinhardt[1]([⊠]) , and Moritz Krause[1]([⊠])

[1] Hof University of Applied Sciences, Alfons-Goppel-Platz 1, 95028 Hof, Germany
{michael.zoellner,moritz.krause}@hof-university.de,
jan.gemeinhardt.2@iisys.de
[2] University Hospital Erlangen, Waldstraße 1, 91054 Erlangen, Germany
{stefan.kniesburges,michael.doellinger}@uk-erlangen.de

Abstract. In this paper we are describing our preliminary studies and prototypes for evaluating a surfer's performance on a stationary wave. We are briefly describing the sport's environment and development and the current state-of-the-art of machine learning based single camera tracking approaches we have evaluated and applied. The main part of the paper deals with the first implementation, the tracking and the results of the evaluation of the movements of two surfers. We are closing with our lessons learned and our next steps.

Keywords: Data Visualization · Machine Learning · Interactive Systems

1 Introduction

With the popularity of the Munich Eisbach and other stationary waves, such as the Nuremberg surf wave in the Pegnitz river (see Fig. 1), a lively surf culture has developed away from the beaches in Germany in recent years. The term rapid surfing established itself for standing waves in rivers and pump-driven wave pools. The German Surfing Association [15] has been hosting the official German Rapid Surfing Championship since 2019. In addition, surfing (wave riding) has been an Olympic sport since 2020. The market volume of the global surf industry was 4 billion US dollars in 2022 with an increasing forecas. In the German market segment, a flourishing start-up scene for sports equipment, sports facilities and lifestyle can be observed in recent years.

This is accompanied by a professionalization of the training of rapid surfing athletes, supported by the federations and the industry. The new sports facilities, the stationary waves and wave pools, play a decisive role in this. In contrast to the waves in the "unpredictable" sea, the conditions for training can be precisely defined in these sports facilities and thus, for example, increases and repetitions can be programmed.

Our research takes off at this point and pursues the goal of making training on stationary waves comprehensible and predictable using scientific methods and new technologies. Therefore, we are building upon research in adjacent sports disciplines like

C. Stephanidis et al. (Eds.): HCII 2023, CCIS 1958, pp. 117–124, 2024.
https://doi.org/10.1007/978-3-031-49215-0_14

Fig. 1. A surfer riding a stationary wave in a river.

dance, skateboarding and kiting on the one hand. And on the other hand, into adjacent research fields like biomechanics, hydrodynamics, machine learning, computer vision and data visualization.

In the first stage of our research, we were exploring the current state of single camera skeleton tracking and implemented separate prototypes and evaluated the resulting data quality.

In the following sections we are describing the evaluation and exploration of the current state of single camera skeleton tracking hardware that lead us to the choice of the approach we implemented into separate prototypes for evaluating the resulting data quality. Subsequently we are explaining the prototypes and the results in detail. Finally we are writing about the lessons we learned during the development and our plans for the actual research.

2   Related Work

During the last years we saw a fast progress in the quality and availability of camera-based pose estimation. An early moment in the accessibility of skeleton tracking for a large audience was the release of the Microsoft Kinect and the community based libraries like OpenKinect [8] and OpenNI [11].

With the advent of machine learning based approaches there was no need for special hardware anymore in favor of single cameras. CMU's OpenPose [1] and OpenPifpaf [5] are two major developments producing robust 2D pose estimation of humans based on single RGB images. Even if the quality of PoseNet's [4] 2D tracking data is not as advanced as the previously mentioned, its main contribution is the availability in browsers. And ml5js enables a large developer audience by simplifying the development process even further by integrating it in p5js [7].

We decided to build our project on top of MeTRAbs Absolute 3D Human Pose Estimator [10] since it's featuring not only 2D but also robust 3D position data of the skeletons' joints. The provisioning of a Google Collaboratory notebook enables a quick access for development without the dependence on expensive hardware.

Regarding related applications we would like to mention several projects in adjoining disciplines. Numeric representation of forces and resulting performance in surfing is very good described in the work of Falk et al. in "Computational hydrodynamics of a typical 3-fin surfboard setup" [2] based on fluid simulation and pressure forces.

Capturing and analyzing dance is a common research field in the pose estimation and tracking area. Referring to hardware-based approaches we would like to mention Alexiadis et al.'s "Evaluating a dancer's performance using kinect-based skeleton tracking". An early 3D position estimation approach with a single camera was Kahn et al.'s "Capturing of contemporary dance for preservation and presentation of choreographies in online scores" where they showed recurring path patterns in experimental ballet performances.

Focusing on visualization rather than data analysis we would like to mention RunwayML's [9] latest Motion Tracking tool for video editing and the applications Najeeb Tarazi's application of RunwayML's rotoscoping techniques in the impressive "One More Try" [17] experimental skate video.

3   Implementation and Evaluation

3.1   Hardware Setup

In order to capture the pose of the surfer on the river wave we designed a simple to reproduce setup consisting of a GoPro Camera, an Arduino Nicla Sense ME [16] microcontroller with 6DOF sensor and a smartphone as a hub to the cloud. Regarding an affordable solution we are using an off the shelf GoPro Hero 11 Black Camera sitting on a wooden bar in the center of the 8m wide channel and fixed with a 3D printed mount. The camera is connected to the smartphone via Bluetooth Low Energy [13], since it also transmits data if the object is under water while a Wi-Fi connection would break off.

For a later evaluation of the tracking data quality, we already integrated an Arduino Nicla Sense ME microcontroller with 6DOF sensor into the surfboard. The board is also connected to the smartphone via Bluetooth Low Energy. We are also planning to synchronize the camera with the board via Bluetooth Low Energy later. In this paper and at this early stage of the project we are concentrating on the results of the camera tracking.

The smartphone acts as the hub between the capturing devices and the cloud processing of the video data. It's also the touchpoint for interaction with the user and data visualization (see Fig. 2). We chose a web-based approach for both tasks and created an accelerated and agile prototyping pipeline. The devices are connected via Web Bluetooth API [14] that allows mobile websites to communicate with Bluetooth devices without compiling and rolling out a native app.

The resulting video sequence is being first sent to Google Drive from where it is fetched by a Google Collaboratory notebook [12] running a modified MeTRAbs Absolute 3D Human Pose Estimator [10] script and outputs a SMPL [6] skeleton dataset of the recognized persons.

Finally, our web-based visualization on the smartphone renders the skeleton data on top of a still image of the recorded scenario and a graph of selected points of interest. We are using p5js [7], a Javascript variant of the Processing language, for the visualization, the generation of the graph and controlling the devices.

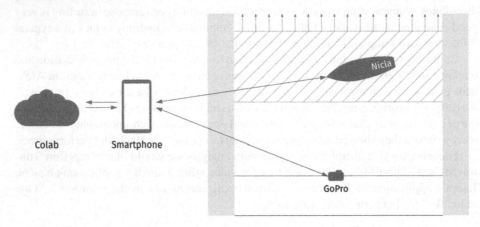

Fig. 2. Setup of data streaming from surfboard and camera to the cloud.

3.2   Tracking and Data

We also chose a web-based approach using Google Collaboratory instead of a local workstation for the machine learning tracking based on MeTRAbs Absolute 3D Human Pose Estimator. Therefore we developed further [12] the standard notebook, added Google Drive support for the video files and the output of the 2D and 3D SMPL data sets.

The SMPL data set consist of the same number of frames as the video clip. It's containing all detected persons and their skeleton joint positions in the SMPL format. MeTRAbs produces a 2D data set with a frontal projection of the joint position matching the video image and its pixel space (see Fig. 3). And it also produces a 3D data set with estimated depth positions in the pixel space of the video frame.

Each frame is parsed via JSON (JavaScript Object Notation) in p5js. All person's joints per frame are then rendered as lines and ellipses. The HSV color coding amplifies the temporal and special aspects of the frames data.

The result is a visualization of the data set on top of a still image of the environment. We are recognizing the persons in the dataset including their positions and movements over time. In the example in Fig. 3 we are observing two waiting persons and one surfing person in interest. The surfing person's path on the wave and the corresponding body pose are of special interest in our project and discussed later.

Looking closer into a single joint of the dataset gives us a glimpse impression of the potential of the captured data regarding the performance and training of the surfers. In Fig. 4 we are comparing two surfer's ankle position during similar maneuvers on the wave. They are executing two turns and surfing from one side to the other and back. We

Fig. 3. Temporal and spatial visualization of the tracking data.

are seeing the classic flat eight maneuver in river surfing where the athletes are getting speed from the tip of the wave towards the bottom center before returning to the tip on the other side and turning again.

The interesting aspect in the data is the curve they are drawing which are representing their training skills, the speed and the surrounding forces in the water, the surfboard and the body. The graph is showing the two curves the surfers are executing their turns in different radiuses on each side of the wave. They are surfing in different sections of the wave (y-position) with different energy. One noteworthy result is that these curves could become a representing pattern representing the style of a surfer.

3.3 Data Visualization Prototype

Based on the described components we created a first integrated prototype for real-time visualizations of the previously recorded and analyzed video segments in p5js (see Fig. 5). The skeleton data of the two surfer is displayed on top of the video frame and visualized as graph in sequential order. While watching we are observing the surfer's skeleton and recognizing the position and the angles of the single joints and body parts. The pose of the arms, the angle of the knees and the upright or bent over upper body are of special interest to measure the performance and the style of the athletes and will be part of a later training progress.

Also, in real-time we are observing the generation of the curve of a selected joint. In our example the position of the ankle of the rear foot represents the path on the wave, the performance and training level and the applied forces.

While we can watch different surfers every day and get an impression of their training level and skills, this data visualization prototype based on 3D pose estimation represents the start of a scientific evaluation of this sport's parameters.

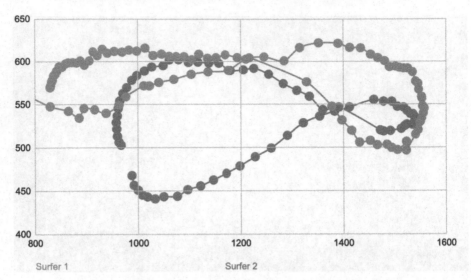

Fig. 4. Graph displaying the ankle positions of two different surfers.

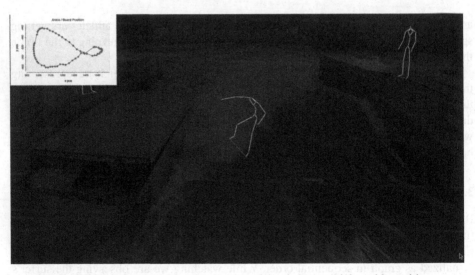

Fig. 5. Realtime prototype for visualization of the skeleton and the ankle positions.

4   Lessons Learned

First and all we've learned that we can produce high quality skeleton joint data of surfers with a standard GoPro camera and the free cloud service Google Collaboratory for our further work. MeTRAbs 2D and 3D data quality proofed good enough for our further developments. The resulting visualizations and graphs are proving a watermark of the surfer's performance and can be the basis of a later scientific and data-based training approach.

While we first we started with an older GoPro Hero5 model we switched to a newer Hero11 since the older one was only controllable via Wi-Fi. With the newer Bluetooth the Low Energy protocol [3] we will be able to synchronize a later 6DOF board on the surfboard with the camera.

In conclusion our standalone web-based prototypes proved to be a good way to be integrated into a comprehensive platform for the development of a mobile interactive on-site tool for capturing and analyzing the surfers.

5   Conclusion and Future Work

With our herby documented preliminary work for analyzing surfers' performance for later scientific training approaches we are currently applying for funding. We will develop further our standalone prototypes and integrate them into a mobile data capturing and analyzation platform. For improving precision and reliability of the data we will extend our camera-based approach with the mentioned Arduino Nicla Sense ME 6DOF. Furthermore, we will add a simulation based hydrodynamic model for further optimization of the capturing data.

References

1. Cao, Z., et al.: OpenPose: Realtime Multi-Person 2D Pose Estimation using Part Affinity Fields http://arxiv.org/abs/1812.08008 (2019). https://doi.org/10.48550/arXiv.1812.08008
2. Falk, S., et al.: Computational hydrodynamics of a typical 3-fin surfboard setup. J. Fluids Struct. **90**, 297–314 (2019). https://doi.org/10.1016/j.jfluidstructs.2019.07.006
3. GoPro: Bluetooth Low Energy (BLE) Specification v2.0. https://gopro.github.io/OpenGoPro/ble_2_0. Accessed 19 Jan 2023
4. Kendall, A., et al.: PoseNet: a convolutional network for real-time 6-DOF camera relocalization. In: Presented at the Proceedings of the IEEE International Conference on Computer Vision (2015)
5. Kreiss, S. et al.: Openpifpaf: Composite fields for semantic keypoint detection and spatio-temporal association. In: IEEE Transactions on Intelligent Transportation Systems (2021)
6. Loper, M., et al.: SMPL: A skinned multi-person linear model. ACM Trans. Graphics (Proc. SIGGRAPH Asia). **34**(6), 248:1–248:16 (2015)
7. McCarthy, L., et al.: Getting Started with p5.js: Making Interactive Graphics in JavaScript and Processing. Maker Media, Inc. (2015)
8. OpenKinect: OpenKinect: Open Source Drivers for Kinect v1. https://openkinect.org (2011)
9. Runway: Runway - Next-generation creation suite, https://runwayml.com. Accessed 19 Jan 2023
10. Sárándi, I., et al.: MeTRAbs: metric-scale truncation-robust heatmaps for absolute 3D human pose estimation. IEEE Trans. Biom. Behav. Identity Sci. **3**(1), 16–30 (2021). https://doi.org/10.1109/TBIOM.2020.3037257
11. Villaroman, N., et al.: Teaching natural user interaction using OpenNI and the Microsoft Kinect sensor. In: Proceedings of the 2011 conference on Information technology education, pp. 227–232 (2011)
12. Zöllner, M.: MeTRAbs Video to SMPL Notebook (2022)
13. Bluetooth® Technology Website – The official website for the Bluetooth wireless technology. Get up to date specifications, news, and development info., https://www.bluetooth.com/. Accessed 19 Jan 2023

124   M. Zöllner et al.

14. Communicating with Bluetooth devices over JavaScript, https://developer.chrome.com/art icles/bluetooth/. Accessed 19 Jan 2023
15. German Surfing Association. https://wellenreitverband.de. (2023)
16. Nicla Sense ME. https://store.arduino.cc/products/nicla-sense-me. Accessed 19 Jan 2023
17. One More Try - an experimental skate video (2022)

Development of a Camera Motion Estimation Method Utilizing Motion Blur in Images

Yuxin Zhao[✉][iD], Hirotake Ishii[iD], and Hiroshi Shimoda[iD]

Graduate School of Energy Science, Kyoto University, Kyoto, Japan
{zhao,hirotake,shimoda}@ei.energy.kyoto-u.ac.jp

Abstract. Motion blur presents a significant challenge in visual SLAM. Since a satisfying performance highly relies on clear and feature-rich images, the system will easily fail to extract features and lose track due to motion blur. To address this issue, this study introduces a novel solution that estimates the camera motion using blur features extracted from images. The proposed approach models the relationship between camera motion and motion blur, creating a comprehensive motion blur dataset labeled with camera motion. By decoupling the motion estimation process into predicting magnitude and direction separately, a neural network is trained using blur and depth images as inputs to output the camera motion. Experimental results demonstrate that the proposed method successfully estimates motion from blur, even in long-term blur scenarios. This method can potentially serve as an auxiliary motion estimation module to enhance the robustness and accuracy of the visual odometer when motion blur is encountered.

Keywords: Motion Blur · Camera Motion Estimation · Deep Learning

1 Introduction

Recovering the 3D scene structure and camera motion from images is crucial in various computer vision tasks, such as 3D reconstruction, robot navigation, and virtual/augmented reality [1]. Traditionally, the classical approach involves extracting and matching visual features in the images. Geometric constraints and optimization algorithms are then employed to estimate the camera pose. However, this process heavily relies on clear and distinctive features within the images [2]. Consequently, classical algorithms often encounter significant errors or even fail to function altogether in scenarios with visual degradation. One common form of visual degradation is motion blur, which occurs when the camera is exposed for a long period or experiences rapid movement [3]. Motion blur poses a significant challenge as it hampers the extraction of sufficient features from the images.

In recent studies, researchers have made efforts to address this issue. One approach involves incorporating line features in addition to point features, as

C. Stephanidis et al. (Eds.): HCII 2023, CCIS 1958, pp. 125–131, 2024.
https://doi.org/10.1007/978-3-031-49215-0_15

they offer a more robust representation of the scene's geometry [4]. By doing so, these researchers were able to achieve improved accuracy and efficiency in estimating camera pose under motion blur scenarios, surpassing the performance of classical algorithms. Despite the advancements made, a limitation remains when the system encounters long-term abrupt camera motion [5]. In such cases, the tracking system still fails to perform adequately. Instead of proposing a comprehensive framework, some researchers focused on removing motion blur and estimating the camera pose from the restored images [6]. In another approach, researchers attempted to reblur a clear reference image and subsequently trained or optimized it to obtain the camera motion [7,8]. Unfortunately, this technique relies on the availability of a reference image, which may not always be present in real-world application scenarios.

This research aims at estimating camera motion under long-term motion blur without relying on clear images. Since the appearance of motion blur depends on camera motion, it still retains valuable information about the motion [9]. Therefore, instead of treating motion blur as a visual degradation to be eliminated, we propose leveraging it to directly estimate camera motion through deep learning. The network learns blur features from motion blur image and output the relative camera pose during the formation process. Hopefully, the proposed method can serve as an auxiliary motion estimation module when the motion blur appears to improve the robustness and accuracy of the visual odometer.

2   Modeling of Blur and Motion

Training a neural network often requires a significant amount of datasets. However, datasets that include motion blur images with varying camera poses are scarce. Hence, as the basis of creating datasets, we introduced Q-Slerp interpolation algorithm into blur formation model in [7] and modeled the process of camera motion forming motion blur.

A digital camera forms an image by collecting the light during exposure time and converting it into electrical signals. When the camera is exposed for a long time or moving quickly, there will be a noticeable blur of drag marks in the image, known as motion blur. This process can be modeled as integrating over a set of virtual sharp images.

$$B = \frac{1}{\tau} \int_0^\tau C_t \, dt \tag{1}$$

where C_t indicates the virtual sharp image captured at time t during the total exposure time τ, and B is the final blur image. It can be approximated by averaging n virtual images C_i in the process:

$$B \approx \frac{1}{n} \sum_{i=0}^{n-1} C_i \tag{2}$$

The camera pose T is represented by the combination of translation vector and Euler angle, which contains 6 degrees of freedom (DOF):

$$T = [t_x, t_y, t_z, r_x, r_y, r_z] \tag{3}$$

where t_i, r_i ($i = x, y, z$) denote the translation and rotation along x, y, z axis respectively.

Given the virtual sharp image C_0 and depth image D_0 captured when $i = 0$, the total movement T during exposure time τ can be interpolated as n mid-poses $S_i(T)$. Each virtual image C_i can be modeled as the image transformed from C_0 with the interpolated pose $S_i(T)$:

$$C_i = \pi \left(S_i \left(T \right) \cdot \pi^{-1} \left(C_0, D_0 \right) \right) \tag{4}$$

where π is the camera projection function which projects 3D point cloud into 2D image plane, π^{-1} is the inverse projection function which transform 2D point in image plane with depth into 3D point cloud.

3   Dataset Creation

After building the blur formation model, we utilized the proposed model and created a large dataset using computer graphics (CG) techniques.

First, the clear image C_0 and depth image D_0 pairs are captured through simulation based on HQ Suburban House [10] on Unity. Next, the relative poses T are generated randomly, and Q-Slerp algorithm is utilized to interpolate n mid-poses $S_i(T)$ among each relative pose. Then, by projecting clear and depth image pairs into 3D point cloud, the transformation of each mid-pose is operated on point cloud. Finally, the virtual sharp image C_i is generated by projecting the transformed point could onto image plane, and the blur image B is synthesized by taking the average of all images.

Through continuous testing, n was set as 64, which can properly simulate the motion blur. The rotation range was randomly generated around [-0.05, 0.05] radians, while the translation range was around [-0.25, 0.25] meters. During training, the translation was regularized to [-0.05, 0.05] to maintain consistency across the results. Totally 15,632 images featuring motion blur caused by random motion on t_x and t_y are generated in this dataset. The sample of generated images is shown in Fig. 1.

    (a)   (b)   (c)

Fig. 1. Sample of dataset. (a) clear image; (b) depth image; (c) blur image.

4   Network Design and Training

4.1   Network Design

The network was designed to input blur and depth images and output camera motion. Estimating camera motion in a single step is challenging for the network to learn relevant features. Therefore, this process is decoupled to predict motion magnitude and direction separately. The diagram is illustrated in Fig. 2. The ResNet-50 and ResNet-34 [11] are used as the backbone of magnitude module and direction module respectively. Two fully connected layers are added after the ResNet. The resolution of the input images is 640×480.

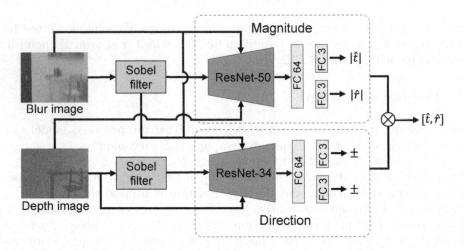

Fig. 2. Network architecture.

Magnitude Module. This module is intended to estimate the magnitude of camera motion on each DOF from the blur amount in the image. Monocular images inherently lack scale information, making it impossible to restore motion scale using solely blur image. Hence, we use depth images to help predict actual camera motion. To prompt the neural network to extract blur information, the Sobel filter is utilized on blur images to emphasize the amount of blur. The resultant output of blur image is fed into the magnitude module together with the blur and depth image. The network outputs the absolute value of the translation vector $|\hat{t}|$ and rotation angle $|\hat{r}|$.

Direction Module. The direction module classifies the positive and negative motion on each DOF from blur and depth images. When the camera is in motion, the shutter speed and timing for opening the shutter differ between capturing the color and depth images. As a result, the areas shown in color and depth images exhibit slight difference depending on the camera motion direction. Leveraging this difference, we can estimate the direction of camera motion. To emphasize the disparity information between blur and depth image, the Sobel filter is applied on both of them, and taken as an input with the blur and depth image. The network would judge whether the direction is positive or negative. Finally, the outputs of two modules are combined to estimate the translation vector $\hat{t}$ and rotation vector $\hat{r}$.

4.2   Network Training

We trained the network on the dataset generated in Sect. 3, utilizing the Adam optimizer with a learning rate of 10^{-4} during the training process. The number of epochs was set to 300. For the magnitude module, the loss function employed was Root Mean Squared Error (RMSE) loss, calculated based on the absolute value of the pose. As for the direction module, Cross Entropy Loss was utilized for the classification of positive and negative.

5   Experiments

To evaluate the performance of the proposed method, we conducted test on datasets with long-term motion blur, where each image exhibited varying degrees of motion blur. Specifically, the datasets featured motion blur of translation along x-axis and y-axis movement were synthesized through CG in a different scene from the training datasets. Originating from $(0, 0)$, the trajectories traced a counterclockwise heart-shaped pattern with intervals of 50 mm, 100 mm, 150 mm, 200 mm, and 250 mm, indicating increasing degree of blur. This is a challenging task because no clear reference is available for the system to extract features.

We applied the networks containing magnitude and direction modules on the datasets. On average, 92.45% of the samples were correctly classified in the correct direction. Combining with the magnitude estimation, the estimated trajectories of the camera movement are indicated in Fig. 3 in comparison with the ground truth. The error of each position is presented in grey lines. For the quantitative evaluation, absolute trajectory error (ATE) and the relative error (RE) were calculated in Table 1. The ATE of each case was to demonstrate the RMSE of ground truth pose and estimated pose, while the RE was calculated as scaling the RMSE by the range of the heart-shaped trajectory.

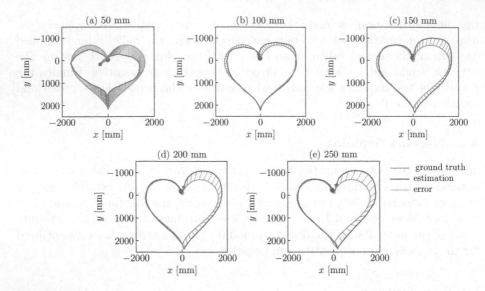

Fig. 3. Ground truth, estimation, and error of the test dataset. Circle and star denote the start and end points.

Table 1. Quantitative evaluation

Case	ATE [mm]	RE[%]
50 mm	339.94	11.58
100 mm	113.08	3.80
150 mm	197.75	6.85
200 mm	225.38	7.74
250 mm	264.34	8.95

The results indicate that the estimated trajectory exhibits a consistency with the ground truth, especially in the case of 100mm. Notably, the presence of insufficient (50mm) motion blur adversely affects the performance. However, in the practical application, less motion blur generally represents clearer images, allowing traditional SLAM algorithms to function effectively. Therefore, this error is not influential. In addition, the accumulation of errors in frame-to-frame estimation leads to drift over time, which is more pronounced on the right side of the heart-shaped trajectory, resulting in a deviation from the ground truth. This issue can be well mitigated by loop closure detection and optimization.

6   Conclusion and Future Work

In conclusion, the proposed method shows promise for estimating camera motion from motion blur. Note that we achieved promising performance on the severe long-term blurred datasets, which is a challenging scenario for existing methods. It shows potential not only in estimating camera motion in the absence of inertial sensors but also in providing more precise estimates than inertial sensors. Future work includes expanding the model to accommodate more complex camera motions without sacrificing accuracy. Additionally, since only synthesized images are trained and evaluated in this study, the proposed approach will be generalized and evaluated on real-world datasets.

References

1. Fang, B., Zhan, Z.: A visual slam method based on point-line fusion in weak-matching scene. Int. J. Adv. Rob. Syst. **17**(2), 1729881420904193 (2020)
2. Bujanca, M., Shi, X., Spear, M., Zhao, P., Lennox, B., Luján, M.: Robust SLAM systems: are we there yet? In: 2021 IEEE/RSJ International Conference on Intelligent Robots and Systems (IROS), pp. 5320–5327. IEEE (2021)
3. Carbajal, G., Vitoria, P., Delbracio, M., Musé, P., Lezama, J.: Non-uniform blur kernel estimation via adaptive basis decomposition. arXiv preprint arXiv:2102.01026 (2021)
4. Li, D., et al.: A SLAM system based on RGBD image and point-line feature. IEEE Access **9**, 9012–9025 (2021)
5. Wang, Q., Yan, Z., Wang, J., Xue, F., Ma, W., Zha, H.: Line flow based SLAM. arXiv preprint arXiv:2009.09972 (2020)
6. Lee, H.S., Kwon, J., Lee, K.M.: Simultaneous localization, mapping and deblurring. In: 2011 International Conference on Computer Vision, pp. 1203–1210. IEEE (2011)
7. Liu, P., Zuo, X., Larsson, V., Pollefeys, M.: MBA-VO: motion blur aware visual odometry. In: Proceedings of the IEEE/CVF International Conference on Computer Vision, pp. 5550–5559 (2021)
8. Nimisha, T., Rengarajan, V., Ambasamudram, R.: Semi-supervised learning of camera motion from a blurred image. In: 2018 25th IEEE International Conference on Image Processing (ICIP), pp. 803–807. IEEE (2018)
9. Argaw, D.M., Kim, J., Rameau, F., Cho, J.W., Kweon, I.S.: Optical flow estimation from a single motion-blurred image. In: Proceedings of the AAAI Conference on Artificial Intelligence, vol. 35, pp. 891–900 (2021)
10. HQ Suburban House. https://assetstore.unity.com/packages/3d/environments/urban/hq-suburban-house-81890
11. He, K., Zhang, X., Ren, S., Sun, J.: Deep residual learning for image recognition. In: Proceedings of the IEEE Conference on Computer Vision and Pattern Recognition, pp. 770–778 (2016)

Interaction with Robots and Intelligent Agents

End-To-End Intelligent Automation Loops

Joerg Beringer[1]([✉]) [iD], Alexander-John Karran[2] [iD], Constantinos K. Coursaris[2] [iD], and Pierre-Majorique Leger[2] [iD]

[1] ProContext, Redwood City, CA, USA
joerg.beringer@procontext.com
[2] Department of Information Technologies, HEC Montréal, Montréal, QC H3T 2A7, Canada
constantinos.coursaris@hec.ca

Abstract. Situation awareness has become a popular method for modelling human–automated process allocation and, more recently, applied to model collaboration between humans and autonomous artificially intelligent agents. However, the role of how to distribute decision-making within this new collaborative paradigm remains underexplored. In this manuscript paper, we propose an integration of situation awareness into the decision-making process by combining the Endsley Situation Awareness model with contextually tailored sequences of cognitive activity referred to as end-to-end decision-making loops. We posit that this approach benefits designers, implementers, and users of intelligent systems as it orchestrates a cognitive and perceptual alignment between human and non-human agents, thereby enabling the formation of meaningful end-to-end action loops.

Keywords: HCAI · Intelligent Automation · Decision Making · Autonomy · Situation Awareness · Agents

1 Introduction

One of the critical affordances of automating human tasks is to free the human agent from performing the task and to allow the reallocation of their cognitive resources elsewhere. However, this has the inherent risk of the human agent unlearning the skills requisite in mastering a task and becoming detached from the task context in general. The latter can become a concern, potentially with dire implications, when the technology system agent asks the human operator to take control and yet has either no or limited awareness of the current situation.

For this reason, much of the research related to cockpit automation (Jones & Endsley, 1996; Munir et al., 2022; Politowicz et al., 2021; Salotti & Suhir, 2019) and driver assistance (Golestan et al., 2016; McCall & Trivedi, 2007; Rockl et al., 2007; Wulf et al., 2014), focuses on the concept of situation awareness, and how to ensure that a basic level of awareness is shared between human and system agents to sustain the human agent's readiness to intervene if necessary.

Moreover, the ultimate goal of process automation, whether algorithmic or intelligent, is to create end-to-end understand/decide/act control loops that use the situation

C. Stephanidis et al. (Eds.): HCII 2023, CCIS 1958, pp. 135–139, 2024.
https://doi.org/10.1007/978-3-031-49215-0_16

awareness model as a basis from which to initiate and inform decisions that trigger actions to reach a desired outcome or state. However, full automation, i.e. the human agent being out-of-the-loop, can be achieved only when the intelligent agent supports the entirety of these functions.

While Endsley's original model introduces the three levels of situation awareness (perception, comprehension, and projection), the decision-making process is left open to clarification. In this regard, early work from Rasmussen (Rasmussen, 1983) and Parasuraman and Riley (Parasuraman & Riley, 1997) introduced models outlining different decision-making stages to explain the different behaviors and cognitive demands for making decisions at different levels of complexity.

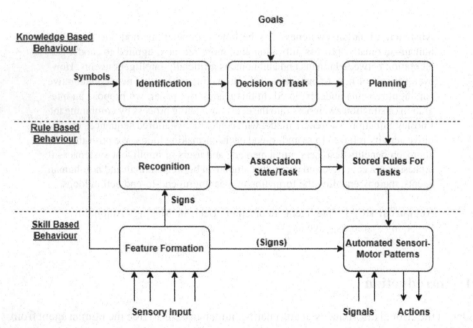

Fig. 1. Rasmussen Skills-Rules-Knowledge Decision Template (adapted from Rasmussen 1983).

Rasmussen investigated human-machine control systems and formalized (Fig. 1) how decisions transform inputs (information) into outputs (action) (Rasmussen, 1983). Sensory input is directly transformed at the lowest level into simple actions or skill-based behavior control loops (e.g., keeping a temperature at a specific level or a car at a specific distance from the car in front). These control loops do not require higher-level mental processes. Thus, they can be easily assimilated into autonomic (automated) behaviors. For this reason, drivers can perform other tasks, even simultaneously, such as switching between talking and simply following traffic. At this lowest skill-based behavior level, there is virtually no decision-making involved.

At the next higher level, decision-making concerns the application of rules to map an input (condition) to an output (action). This mode requires rules to be in place and known by the agent, allowing a transformation of an input into a known set of actions by applying the corresponding rule set (e.g., if the temperature reaches a certain level, turn on A/C cooling; if the temperature is too low, turn on heating). An intelligent agent may even 'learn' what is too low and too high over time. However, at the outset, it would have a simple ruleset to convert a signal (condition state) into the appropriate action (system behavior).

Increased mental workload or decision uncertainty occurs when either information (condition) is incomplete, and it is unclear what rules apply, or the ruleset is not exhaustive enough to make a decision. If these elements are missing and cannot be easily provisioned, then decision-making shifts from rule-based to the highest level - knowledge-based. The human agent gathers additional information to perform causal analysis and generates decision options based on experience and technical understanding of the domain. This process can result in a lengthy investigation by the human agent to understand the problem (situation) and planning exercises to generate action plans with the desired impact.

2 End-To-End Loops

To illustrate the entire control loop in more detail, Fig. 2 adapts Rasmussen's visual metaphor of a decision ladder and depicts the situation awareness and action planning phases before and after decision-making. The left side of the ladder resembles the three levels of Endsley's situation awareness model (perceive (detect), comprehend, project) and introduces a hierarchy of cognitive functions starting from the simple observation of facts to comprehension and transformation into meaningful information and further diagnosing to project the future state. These levels also relate to Rasmussen's decision-making stages, given that direct feedback loops are typically based on simple fact-based data. In comparison, rule-based decisions are founded on understanding conditions requiring comprehension and synthesis of low-level data into meaningful information.

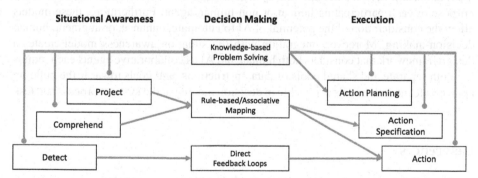

Fig. 2. End-to-end Decision Loop combining Situation Awareness and Decision Ladder

As can be seen in Fig. 2, the decision ladder and Endsley's Situation Awareness model are not perfectly aligned. However, there are similarities and relationships which, if recognized and applied, can help to guide the design of human-system agent networks which implement all relevant cognitive sub-functions to cover all steps needed for autonomous actions.

138   J. Beringer et al.

These functions typically do not reside in one single system. Multiple domain-specific agents may be responsible for establishing situation awareness, and multiple domain-specific agents may be responsible for implementing action. Nevertheless, the decision-making step is typically centralized to ensure that a specific desired outcome is realized and used as the reference for learning.

We argue that any autonomous intelligent system must form this end-to-end automation loop in one way or another, and it should be evident where, when and how users can intervene at the different stages. Building a detailed comprehension of situation awareness levels, decision-making modes, and enactment of those decisions helps to develop heuristics and principles for designing effective teaming models between human and system agents (Cummings & Guerlain, 2005). It is, therefore, necessary to develop conceptual frameworks spanning the entire automation loop.

In this context, a broader discussion is warranted on the suitability of existing conceptual frameworks to guide the design of end-to-end automation loop, for example:

• A Decision Ladder with cognitive sub-functions for the understand/decide/act phases. (Rasmussen, 1983), (Parasuraman & Riley, 1997).
• The Recognition-Primed Decision Model (RPDM) which describes heuristics for how experts bridge from understanding to action per intuition vs. conscious executive cognition. (Kahneman, 2011; Naikar, 2010).
• Observe, Orient, Decide, Act Loop (OODA) applied in military operations (Boyd, 1976).

3 Conclusion

We suggest that each model be reviewed and assessed to determine their suitability to guide the design and orchestration of intelligent automation systems and formalize the relationship between humans and systems within this loop to understand better the purpose of each participating human or non-human agent. Furthermore, these models allow the consideration of the potential of AI to automate, enhance, or augment, human decision-making. Moreover, integration with the situation awareness model creates a design framework that considers both human and AI as collaborative agents each requiring both separate and shared pools of data, instructions, and goals towards the building appropriate mental models applicable to decision making at the system, process and task level.

References

1. Boyd, C.J.: Destruction and Creation. Unpublished Manuscript, 1 (1976)
2. Cummings, M., Guerlain, S.: The decision ladder as an automation planning tool. Cognition, Technology, and Work (2005)
3. Golestan, K., Soua, R., Karray, F., Kamel, M.S.: Situation awareness within the context of connected cars: a comprehensive review and recent trends. Inform. Fusion **29**, 68–83 (2016)
4. Jones, D.G., Endsley, M.R.: Sources of situation awareness errors in aviation. Aviation, space, and environmental medicine (1996)
5. Kahneman, D.: Thinking, fast and slow. Macmillan (2011)

6. McCall, J.C., Trivedi, M.M.: Driver behavior and situation aware brake assistance for intelligent vehicles. Proc. IEEE **95**(2), 374–387 (2007)
7. Munir, A., Aved, A., Blasch, E.: Situational awareness: techniques, challenges, and prospects. AI. **3**(1), 55–77 (2022)
8. Naikar, N. (2010). A comparison of the decision ladder template and the recognition-primed decision model
9. Parasuraman, R., Riley, V.: Humans and automation: use, misuse, disuse, abuse. Hum. Factors **39**(2), 230–253 (1997)
10. Politowicz, M.S., Chancey, E.T., Glaab, L.J.: Effects of autonomous sUAS separation methods on subjective workload, situation awareness, and trust. In: AIAA Scitech 2021 Forum (2021)
11. Rasmussen, J.: Skills, rules, and knowledge; signals, signs, and symbols, and other distinctions in human performance models. IEEE Trans. Syst. Man Cybern. **3**, 257–266 (1983)
12. Rockl, M., Robertson, P., Frank, K., Strang, T.: An architecture for situation-aware driver assistance systems. In: 2007 IEEE 65th Vehicular Technology Conference-VTC2007-Spring (2007)
13. Salotti, J.-M., Suhir, E.: Degraded situation awareness risk assessment in the aerospace domain. In: 2019 IEEE 5th International Workshop on Metrology for AeroSpace (MetroAeroSpace) (2019)
14. Wulf, F., Rimini-Döring, M., Arnon, M., Gauterin, F.: Recommendations supporting situation awareness in partially automated driver assistance systems. IEEE Trans. Intell. Transp. Syst. **16**(4), 2290–2296 (2014)

Build Belonging and Trust Proactively: A Humanized Intelligent Streamer Assistant with Personality, Emotion and Memory

Fengsen Gao[1], Chengjie Dai[1], Ke Fang[1], Yunxuan Li[1], Ji Li[1],
and Wai Kin (Victor) Chan[2(✉)]

[1] Interactive Media Design and Technology Center, Tsinghua University, Shenzhen, China
{gfs22,dcj21,liji22}@mails.tsinghua.edu.cn,
fang.ke@sz.tsinghua.edu.cn
[2] Tsinghua-Berkeley Shenzhen Institute, Shenzhen International Graduate School,
Tsinghua University, Shenzhen, China
chanw@sz.tsinghua.edu.cn

Abstract. Live streaming has become a prevalent form of online entertainment and commerce, where real-time interactions occur between streamers and their audiences. Currently, streamer assistants have some shortcomings in terms of personality and emotional expression. These shortcomings undermine the live streaming effect and audience experience, thereby damaging the streamer's popularity and income. In this paper, we present the Intelligent Streamer Assistant with Personality, Emotion, and Memory (ISAPEM) framework, which aims to utilize playful animal avatars to establish a sense of belonging and trust proactively with the audience. Firstly, we determine the assistant's personality. Subsequently, the assistant determines its emotions according to its personality and the danmaku (bullet chats/comments) context analysis, ranging from trust and joy to sadness. Next, the assistant displays matched expressions and actions, and then generates consistent dialogue using large language models (LLMs). For example, when faced with a challenging question in the danmaku, the assistant might appear perplexed, then reach for the corresponding danmaku, catch it, and swallow it. Finally, the assistant stores and analyzes danmaku interaction data to remember and understand the audience's needs and preferences. Preliminary experimental findings indicate that the ISAPEM framework can create a warmer experience for the audiences and enhance their willingness to interact, which has the potential to foster a sense of belonging and trust among the audiences. This study proposes a novel design framework for streamer assistants that integrates cutting-edge anthropomorphic design cues (ADCs) with a danmaku-based physical interaction mode, expanding the application and interaction modes of novel ADCs and LLMs.

Keywords: Streamer Assistant · Anthropomorphic Design Cues · Artificial Intelligence · Live Streaming

C. Stephanidis et al. (Eds.): HCII 2023, CCIS 1958, pp. 140–147, 2024.
https://doi.org/10.1007/978-3-031-49215-0_17

1 Introduction

Live streaming enables real-time transmission of audio and video events over the internet, creating a unique environment for streamers to share their programs and interact with audiences. Audiences can communicate with each other and the streamer in real time using danmaku (bullet chats/comments), or send virtual gifts to their favorite streamers. In response, streamers can respond to audiences' requests, enhancing their watching experience. Previous research has shown that the interaction between streamers and audiences can fulfill the audiences' desires for social identity [1], which further generates economic benefits for streamers and live streaming platforms [2].

While bringing economic benefits, audience participation also presents streamers with significant challenges. On one hand, streamers need to balance their performance with the interaction during the live stream. On the other hand, streamers have limited capacity to personally attend to all audiences. If audiences feel neglected over an extended period, they may become disappointed and frustrated, leading to attrition from the live streaming and negatively impacting the streamer's popularity and economic gains.

With the advancement of artificial intelligence (AI) technology, some streamers or live streaming platforms are experimenting with the use of AI streamer assistants to facilitate social interactions. However, current AI streamer assistants still face several challenges. For instance, they may struggle when dealing with highly flexible and unrestricted danmaku. AI interactions may lack human emotions or exhibit incorrect ones, which can lead to negative audience experiences due to phenomena like the uncanny valley effect and algorithmic aversion. Recently, large language models (LLMs) have become more capable of efficiently understanding and generating natural language, which are suitable for driving the AI streamer assistant.

Anthropomorphic design cues (ADCs) refer to attributing human-like internal and external attributes to non-human objects, which can enhance users' satisfaction, facilitate their interactions and transaction outcomes, significantly improve their compliance with requests from agents, encourage them to disclose more about themselves, and fulfill their social needs [3–6]. These advantages make anthropomorphic design cues highly suitable for the design of streamer assistants, helping establish social emotions, such as a sense of friendliness, trust, and belonging, between the assistant and the audience.

Therefore, our research aims to innovate and optimize AI streamer assistants to build stronger emotional connections with the audiences and better assist streamers. To achieve this goal, we propose the ISAPEM framework - Intelligent Streamer Assistant with Personality, Emotion, and Memory framework for streamer assistants design. We developed a demo based on this framework. We conducted a preliminary experiment to help us iteratively improve the existing streamer assistant with personality, emotion, and memory. Initial experimental results indicate that the ISAPEM framework and our streamer assistant can facilitate emotional connections between the streamer assistant and the audiences, creating a more friendly and warm experience for them and enhancing their willingness to engage.

2   ISAPEM Framework Design and Implementation

2.1   ISAPEM Framework

Drawing from the SOR model [7], we propose the ISAPEM framework as a design frame-work for streamer assistants. The framework consists of three interconnected modules: Perception, Decision, and Response, forming a closed-loop system, as shown in Fig. 1.

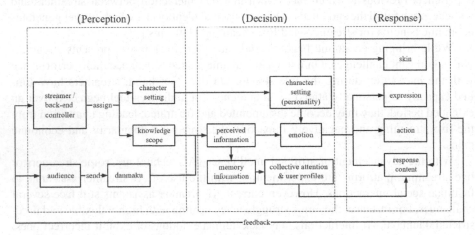

Fig. 1. The ISAPEM framework.

In the Perception module, the streamer assistant gathers danmaku and gets its knowledge within the scope specified by the streamer or back-end controller, forming perceived information. Additionally, the streamer or the controller also assigns a character setting that encompasses various dimensions of personality indicators.

In the Decision module, based on the perceived information and the current character setting, the streamer assistant determines its emotional state. It also stores the perceived information in its memory and extracts the focal points of collective attention and individual user profiles.

In the Response module, the streamer assistant adjusts its appearance according to the designated personality, expresses corresponding facial expressions and actions based on the emotional information derived from the Decision module, and generates response content by integrating personality, emotion, and memory information. Finally, these responses are provided to the streamer, the back-end controller, and the audience.

2.2   Implementation

We implemented the streamer assistant demo for a cartoon animal character, serving as an example of the ISAPEM framework, as shown in Fig. 2. The personality traits of the streamer assistant were inspired by the character images of Zhu Bajie and Lin Daiyu from two classic Chinese literary works, "Journey to the West" and "Dream of the Red Chamber", respectively. We chose these two characters as references for the assistant's personality traits because they possess distinct characteristics and can form a clear contrast with each other. The emotional options for the streamer assistant include ecstasy, sadness, and trust, which are paired with corresponding actions and facial expressions.

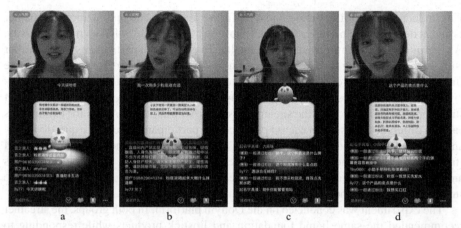

Fig. 2. a) Streamer assistant with Zhu Bajie's personality and ecstasy emotion. b) Streamer assistant with Lin Daiyu's personality and trust emotion. c) Streamer assistant displays a confused expression, jumps to the danmaku, and eats it up. d) Streamer assistant without personality and emotion.

The streamer assistant is primarily implemented on the Unity 3D platform. We have pre-set options for different product information and personalities, which can be adjusted in real time by the streamer or other live streaming staff using the keyboard. The assistant's memory information includes user danmaku and its replies, stored as limited-length strings and updated in real time during the live streaming process.

We aim to explore the feasibility and pros and cons of applying LLM to drive the streamer assistant. Leveraging LLM and Prompt Engineering, the assistant determines its emotions, combines designated product information and personality traits, and refers to focal points gathered from memory information to finally generate responses to audience danmaku. Finally, it displays the corresponding skin based on the personality, as well as facial expressions and actions corresponding to the emotions. The assistant presents the response content in the text form, while the relevant audience danmaku floats above the screen to indicate which danmaku is being responded to.

We have also innovatively proposed an interaction mode between the streamer assistant and the danmaku entities to explore new interaction modes between the anthropomorphic assistant and the audience. For instance, when the streamer assistant is unsure how to respond to a certain danmaku, it will display a confused expression, jump to the danmaku and eat it up.

In this study, the audiences interact with both the streamer and the assistant on Douyin live streaming platform. Douyin is a well-known live streaming and short-form video platform with a large user base. The streamer initiates a live stream and activates the streamer assistant. The audiences then engage in interaction by sending danmaku and other means in the live streaming room.

3 Experimental Details

We conducted a preliminary experiment for further iterating and optimizing the streamer assistant demo. Our experiment is approved by the ethical review of Tsinghua University. We recruited participants through social media. To ensure that participants were familiar with the live streaming format and operation, individuals who had not watched the live streaming before were excluded. The recruited participants, a total of 8, were randomly divided into two groups, Group A and Group B. Each group experienced the ISAPEM streamer assistant demo and the streamer assistant without these ADCs for ten minutes each, in different orders. After each experience, the participants filled out a questionnaire, and interviews were conducted after the live streaming session concluded. The ISAPEM streamer assistant demo featured the character of Zhu Bajie for the first five minutes and the character of Lin Daiyu for the subsequent five minutes during the 10 min' live streaming process of the ISAPEM streamer assistant demo.

The experiment was conducted on the Douyin platform. In both groups, the streamer recommended the same liquid foundation and lipstick products while responding to audience danmaku with the help of the streamer assistant. We recorded the live streaming for subsequent analysis.

In the questionnaire, we utilized the Inclusion of Other in the Self (IOS) Scale to measure how close the audience felt with the streamer assistant, and the streamer, for each experimental session. Within one day after the live streaming, we conducted online semi-structured interviews with the participants. The interviews were recorded and transcribed for further analysis. The interview content primarily focused on the positive and negative experiences of the audiences, their willingness to engage in interaction, their perception of the streamer assistant's internal ADCs (including personality, emotions, and memory), their perception of the streamer assistant's external ADCs (including the assistant's appearance and interaction with danmaku entities), as well as their suggestions for future iterative improvements.

4 Results and Discussions

4.1 Results

During the interview process, it was discovered that one participant in Group B did not complete the experiment so this subject was discarded. To ensure balance, a relatively incomplete subject from Group A was also discarded because the participant ignored the assistant in the first few minutes. In the end, six valid data were obtained. The preliminary data results of the IOS scale are shown in Fig. 3. According to the preliminary results, it can be seen that the assistant with personality, emotion and memory creates a stronger sense of intimacy among the audience than the assistant without these ADCs.

One interesting phenomenon is when the assistant is without ADCs in the live streaming, the relationship between the audience and the streamer seems to be slightly enhanced.

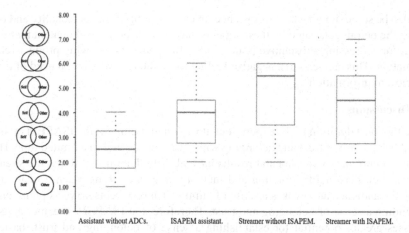

Fig. 3. The IOS results.

Based on the interview data, the possible reason could be that the streamer assistant without these ADCs appears colder and more robotic, providing an uncomfortable experience for the audience. As a result, the audience pays more attention to the streamer, which promotes the relationship between the audience and the streamer.

Based on the interview results, we have the following findings.

In terms of interactive willingness, the audience generally shows a greater inclination to interact with the streamer assistant with personality and emotion, because this streamer assistant provides them with a sense of novelty, affinity, humor, and cuteness, making them feel warm, lighthearted, and more relatable. This assistant captures their attention more effectively. The positive experience mentioned above primarily relies on the three following aspects.

1) In terms of the perception of the streamer assistant's intrinsic ADCs, the ISAPEM assistant provides the audiences with a sense of novelty, affinity, and humor, making them feel warm, lighthearted, and more relatable. Based on the interview results, the majority of the audience can clearly perceive the presence and changes in the assistant's personality, while a portion of the audience can noticeably perceive emotional changes. Only a few audiences can perceive the assistant's memory. This may be because the assistant's emotions are influenced by its personality, leading the audience to consider emotions as part of its personality. On the other hand, memory may not be prominently displayed due to the shorter live streaming duration and its lack of observable outward expressions like personalities and emotions.

2) Regarding the perception of the streamer assistant's extrinsic ADCs, they bring a sense of cuteness to the audience. The audience generally expresses a preference for the streamer assistant with the appearance of a lovely animal. This makes them feel adorable, and they tend to have higher acceptance and tolerance towards the streamer assistant, avoiding the uncanny valley effect and gender differences.

3) In terms of the driving factors behind the streamer assistant's ADCs, we have found that using LLM as the driving tool offers advantages such as high flexibility and strong expressiveness. It can evoke the audience's desire for getting its response. However, there

may also be some drawbacks. For instance, in order to emphasize personality and other factors, the output generated by these models may include additional content that is not helpful for addressing substantive issues, rather than purely conveying product-related information. This can lead to a negative feeling for audiences who are in need of timely and relevant information.

4.2 Discussions

Due to the short duration of the experiment, it was challenging for the ISAPEM assistant to establish a sense of trust and belonging with the audience within a limited time. However, the preliminary experimental results have already demonstrated that the streamer assistant with personality, emotion and memory creates a stronger sense of intimacy among the audience and evokes a sense of affinity. These aspects serve as prerequisites for building a sense of belonging and trust. Therefore, the ISAPEM streamer assistant possesses greater potential for establishing a sense of belonging and trust, basically meeting our design objectives. Additionally, the experiment has also confirmed the feasibility of using LLMs to drive the generation of flexible and personalized responses for streamer assistants with novel ADCs.

5 Conclusions and Future Work

In this study, we proposed the Intelligent Streamer Assistant with Personality, Emotion, and Memory (ISAPEM) design framework, which incorporates advanced ADCs. We developed a demo of a streamer assistant that possesses personality, emotion, and memory based on this framework. By utilizing LLM to drive the streamer assistant, we explored the feasibility and advantages/disadvantages of applying LLM in the live streaming agent. We conducted a preliminary experiment to iteratively optimize the existing demo. The preliminary experimental results indicate that the ISAPEM framework and its example enhance the emotional connection between the streamer assistant and the audience, providing the audience with a more affectionate and warm experience, thereby increasing their willingness to interact. Hence, this type of streamer assistant exhibits great potential for building a sense of belonging and trust. The study also confirms the feasibility of using LLMs to drive flexible and personalized responses for streamer assistants with novel ADCs. In conclusion, this paper extends the application and interaction modes of ADCs and LLMs in the live streaming context, providing innovative research directions to promote human-computer interaction and diversify AI's interactive forms.

There are certain limitations in the current study. In terms of streamer assistant design, we did not consider the perception of multimodal information, such as incorporating the streamer's audio. The handling of memory information in the streamer assistant was relatively simplistic. The interaction mode between the provided streamer assistant and the danmaku is limited. Regarding the experiments, the short duration prevented us from observing the long-term effects of repeated interactions between the streamer assistant and the audience. The live streaming format made it challenging to control factors such as the streamer's behavior and the content of the danmaku. The sample size was small, lacking sufficient quantitative experimental data. In future research, we will make efforts to address these issues and further explore the application of ADCs and AI in interactive media.

References

1. Hilvert-Bruce, Z., Neill, J.T., Sjöblom, M., Hamari, J.: Social motivations of live-streaming viewer engagement on Twitch. Comput. Hum. Behav. **84**, 58–67 (2018)
2. Dai, H., Zhang, D., Xu, Z.: Information Design to Facilitate Social Interactions on Service Platforms: Evidence from a Large Field Experiment. SSRN Electronic Journal. (2020)
3. Rhim, J.S., Kwak, M., Gong, Y., Gweon, G.: Application of humanization to survey chatbots: Change in chatbot perception, interaction experience, and survey data quality. Comput. Hum. Behav. **126**, 107034 (2022)
4. Schanke, S., Burtch, G., Ray, G.: Estimating the impact of "humanizing" customer service chatbots. Inform. Syst. Res. **32**(3), 736–751 (2021)
5. Adam, M., Wessel, M., Benlian, A.: AI-based chatbots in customer service and their effects on user compliance. Electron. Mark. **31**, 427–445 (2020)
6. Sheehan, B., Jin, H.S., Gottlieb, U.: Customer service chatbots: anthropomorphism and adoption. J. Bus. Res. **115**, 14–24 (2020)
7. Mehrabian, A., Russell, J.A.: An approach to environmental psychology (1974)

Explicit vs. Implicit - Communicating the Navigational Intent of Industrial Autonomous Mobile Robots

Nicolas Niessen(✉)[ID], Gioele Micheli[ID], and Klaus Bengler[ID]

Chair of Ergonomics, Technichal University of Munich, Boltzmannstr. 15,
85748 Garching b. München, Germany
nicolas.niessen@tum.de
https://www.mec.ed.tum.de/en/lfe/home/

Abstract. The coexistence of humans and Autonomous Mobile Robots (AMRs) in intralogistics is a growing reality. To enhance the usability of their interactions, AMRs can communicate their future trajectory to humans. This communication can be either implicit through their driving behavior, or explicit through additional signaling. We conducted a real-world participant study with 32 participants and a robot to compare two different communication tools: a floor projection as an explicit tool and a specific driving behavior as an implicit tool. We tested them in three scenarios: intersection, crossing, and bottleneck. We measured the interaction's efficiency, legibility, and trust using quantitative data and questionnaires. We also asked participants to draw the expected trajectories of the AMR at the time of interaction. Our results showed no significant difference in the interaction time between the two communication tools. However, explicit communication increased the trust in the AMR and was perceived more easily by humans. On the other hand, explicit communication is more prone to misinterpretation by humans. Therefore, the design of explicit communication is crucial. The implemented implicit communication does not seem suitable for narrow corridor-like environments.

Keywords: human robot interaction · autonomous mobile robot (AMR) · automated guided vehicle (AGV) · communication tools · motion intent · trajectory · implicit communication · projection · augmented reality · usability · legibility

1 Introduction

In recent years, the increasing shortage of skilled labor [7] in manufacturing and logistics environments has led to an increased reliance on AMRs to fill the gap. This growing AMR market [11] generates more hybrid environments where humans and robots coexist. These robots support industrial processes through their flexibility and decentralization that make them crucial components of the fourth industrial revolution.

C. Stephanidis et al. (Eds.): HCII 2023, CCIS 1958, pp. 148–156, 2024.
https://doi.org/10.1007/978-3-031-49215-0_18

While integrating robots in these hybrid environments brings numerous benefits, it also presents challenges. One such challenge is ensuring smooth and efficient interactions between AMRs and human workers, requiring effective communication. A key aspect of this communication is the ability to anticipate the navigational intent of the AMR, as it allows humans to make informed decisions and adapt their behavior accordingl. Improving this communication is vital for enhancing system efficiency and acceptance of robots. However, communication tools in industrial AMRs need to be improved to fulfill communication needs. They primarily rely on car-like indicators or the use of a projected 'floor spot' in front of the robot. Additionally, the movement of the robot itself is an implicit communication tool - be it intentional or not.

2   State of the Art

Engineers and designers face a lot of choices on how to convey information to humans. Dey et al. [2] provide a taxonomy to distinguish design decisions. Designers need to decide whether only one addressee is targeted (unicast), everyone is targeted with unspecific messages (broadcast), or everyone is individually addressed (multicast). At the same time, designers must carefully choose the perspective a message is explained from: Is the message clearer from the robot's (allocentric) or the pedestrian's perspective (egocentric). In all cases, designers need to be careful that their messages can't be misunderstood as from an opposing perspective or addressing the wrong person.

A choice commonly discussed in the context of autonomous driving external HMIs (eHMIs) is the choice between an explicit and implicit mode of communication as in [15]. While explicit communication uses additional signaling, implicit communication is part of an agent's behavior itself. A common argument favoring implicit communication is that human navigation mainly relies on it. At the same time, technical systems are said to require explicit messaging because they cannot express themselves like humans, and using them might expand the system's capabilities limited by just using movement [15].

Dragan et al. [4,6] describe the differences between functional, predictable, and legible motion. While functional motion just requires the robot to reach its goal, predictable motion is created by moving according to the observer's expectations, given an observer knows its goal. Predictable motion is achieved by selecting the most efficient path [6]. Legible motion, in contrast is the motion that makes its goal easier for an observer to infer. It is achieved by selecting the path that maximizes the probability that the observer knows the goal given its path [6].

When using driving behavior or the dynamic HMI (dHMI) [1] as a communi cation tool, there are two groups of constructing these. Firstly, specific situations can be addressed by specific behaviors. Examples of these are a "back-off" movement to clarify the priority in bottleneck scenarios with AMRs [10] or lateral movements and changes in driving speed in bottleneck scenarios for autonomous vehicles [12]. The second group is formed by human-aware navigation planners that attempt to create legible trajectories by implementing perception and pre-diction of humans in a mobile robot's surroundings. An analysis of these tech-niques can be found in [13]. Both approaches promise to improve the interaction with humans. It is not clear, however, which is best suited for communicating the navigational intent of industrial AMRs.

Despite research in road traffic and robot interactions, we found no general consensus on which communication approach to use for AMRs. It is therefore necessary to further evaluate how the choice of communication mode influences the interaction with AMRs. This paper compares an implicit and an explicit communication approach for communicating the navigational intent of AMRs in corridor-style situations. We aim to address the following research questions:

- RQ1: *Which communication approach is best suited for communicating the future trajectory of industrial AMRs in terms of usability?*
- RQ2: *How do the communication approaches influence participants' expectations of the robot's future trajectory?*

By addressing these research questions, we seek to contribute to the develop-ment of better communication tools for human-robot interaction of intralogistics AMRs to increase their usability.

3   Methods

Two communication approaches were compared: An explicit one (A), and an implicit one (B). The comparison was performed in a crossover trial where half of the participants first saw either communication approach A (AB) or B (BA). This helped avoid invisible transfer effects occurring in a within design while increasing the amount of qualitative feedback received compared to an in-between design.

The tools were compared in three scenarios where the mode of communication and robot behavior varied: road crossing, intersection encounter, and bottleneck (see Fig. 1. Each participant experienced all three scenarios in the same order with one of the communication interfaces (A or B) in the first period and then the same sequence with the other mode of communication in the second run. In each scenario, there were two randomly assigned variants like driving straight or right at an intersection (see Fig. 2) to reduce sequence effects. Participants were led through the scenarios by assigning them brief picking tasks with a defined start and end point. This simulated the workload of workers and was used to synchronize the interaction repeatably.

For each communication approach (explicit or implicit), a communication tool prototype was developed, communicating in a broadcast manner using allo-centric (from the robot) messages (see Fig. 2). Both were implemented on the same Innok Heros AMR that drove on a predefined trajectory through ROS's geometry twist parameters.

As an explicit interface ('A' in Fig. 2), the mobile robot was equipped with a short-throw projector. The projector (LG Allegro 2.0) in turn received images

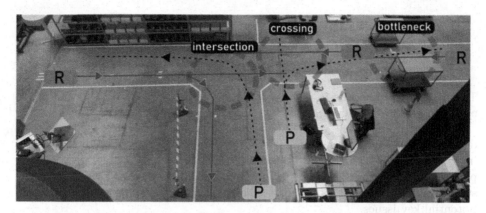

Fig. 1. Overview of interaction scenarios: intersection, crossing and bottleneck. 'R' marks the robot starting points and 'P' the participants'. Robot paths are blue and approximate participant's paths in dotted black. (Color figure online)

calculated by a script on a Raspberry Pi 4B that calculated from the geometry twist parameters an image to project onto the floor, showing the predicted robot path (see Fig. 2).

The pre-programmed movement trajectories for the intent-expressive implicit communication tool were derived from theory-driven principles. The principles of generating legible motion by Dragan et al. [4–6], results of studies in the realm of human factors in autonomous driving research like [12], as well as common conventions in intralogistics like right-hand traffic were considered. The trajectory for the intersection scenario can be seen in Fig. 2.

The experiment was intended to answer two research questions. For RQ1 addressing the comparison on usability, three two-sided hypotheses on each dimension of usability as defined in the ISO standard [3] (effectivity, efficiency, and satisfaction) were formed. The task completion time was computed as the time from the beginning of the robot movement to the moment participants arrived at the picking task target. With the same task for all participants, completion time is a viable measure of efficiency. Legibility was derived from the legibility section of Dragan's questionnaire [4]. Legibility is defined as making the intent inferable so that it can be regarded as a measure of communication effectivity. For satisfaction, a trustworthiness score was gathered using the trust in automation questionnaire by [9]. Although the paper mentions the ambiguity of compiling a unitary trust score, an average value of the three trustworthiness dimensions was compiled for comparability. While trust only represents a part of the entire scope of satisfaction, it was chosen for its critical role in acceptance. The resulting hypotheses are:

> *There is no difference in...*
> $H_{1,0}$ **(Efficiency)**: *...task completion time...*
> $H_{2,0}$ **(Effectivity)**: *...legibility according to the corresponding section in Dragan's questionnaire, ch18Dragan.2015...*

$H_{3,0}$ **(Trust):** *...the trustworthiness score derived from Körber,ch18Korber. 2019*
...when crossing paths with an AMR using communication tool A as opposed to communication tool B.

To evaluate the hypotheses of RQ1, Grizzle's [8] approach to evaluating crossover experiments was used.

RQ2 intended to find differences in reception and to identify issues of both designs for future research. Behavior was classified by evaluating camera recordings, expected behavior was collected by letting participants draw the expected paths, and the thought process was attempted to be reconstructed by semi-structured interviews. This approach allowed us to relate quantitative results to potential key issues.

The 32 participants were young individuals (Mean age = 27.9, SD = 6.6) from mainly technical and university backgrounds. 62.5% of participants were female, 37.5% male. Before the study, an ethics committee's written consent was gathered (2022-655-S-KH).

Fig. 2. Explicit (A, left) and implicit (B, right) communication tools compared in this study. Shown exemplary for the intersection scenario. The two dotted lines (for B) are the two trial variants.

4   Results

First, the existence of a carry-over effect is tested between the test periods. All hypotheses are tested using t-tests, or if t-test assumptions were violated, Wilcox rank-sum test (Results obtained marked with "W") was employed. Significant results ($\alpha = 0.05$) are marked in bold. The results can be observed in Table 1.

Table 1. Influence of mode of communication on meassured quantities

Variable	Carryover sign.	Effect sign.	Higher average
Task completion time	$p = .569$ (W)	$p = .312$	–
Trustworthiness score	$p = .804$ (W)	$\mathbf{p < .001}$ (W)	Explicit
Legibility score	$p = .647$	$\mathbf{p < .001}$	Explicit

In summary, there was a significant effect for both trustworthiness (H2) and legibility (H3), while no effect could be found for the task completion time.

The drawings with participant's expectations were quantitatively clustered, and all images overlayed. Figure 3 shows in summary results compiled from gathering participants' expectations. Each 2×2 Square composed of four subimages shows one scenario, with all combinations of scenario variations (periods 1 and 2) and mode of communication (A and B). Each image contains all drawings superimposed, clustered with frequency-size coded bubbles, and overlaid by a barplot indicating the frequency of correct predictions.

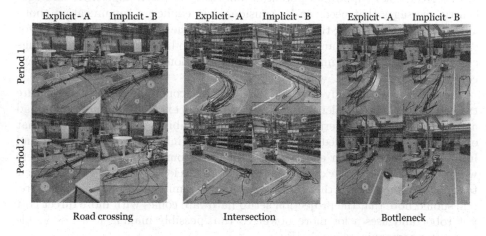

Fig. 3. Results of compiled expectations. Subimmages show all overlayed expectation, superimposed with barplot with correct (yellow) and false (blue) expectations. (Color figure online)

From the semistructured interviews, issues participants were facing were gathered. The answers were transcribed and classified using a mixed inductive-deductive coding approach as in [14]. Of all the issues collected (n = 129), most (n = 26) criticized the implicit interface's lack of communication. The motion of the implicit communication tool was also described as incomprehensible or unsafe (n = 16). More (n = 16) mentions regarded the robot's missing reaction both for the implicit (n = 11) and the explicit (n = 5) interface. The explicit interface was most commonly criticized for the uncertainty of the green color's meaning (n = 14; precedence for robot or human?). Quality issues of the projection (n = 19) were also often commonly expressed: Lag (n = 10), flickering, barely visible projection, and invisible projection (each n = 3).

5   Discussion

5.1   Findings

The findings of our study indicate that explicit communication outperformed implicit communication in terms of legibility and trust. This suggests that explicit communication is the preferable choice for the investigated corridor-style scenarios in intralogistics. As implicit communication was described as lacking communication, it was possibly implemented too subtly or in the wrong way. Furthermore, the critique voiced about uncoordinated behavior might indicate that implicit motion requires more precise control systems. Perceived nonresponsiveness calls for designing systems that are more interactive, therefore probably requiring dynamically generated trajectories that require the robot's ability to sense pedestrians and react accordingly.

For the explicit interface, the uncertainty of the meaning of the projection path's green color supports a potential ambiguity between allocentric and egocentric messages that needs to be considered in explicit communication tools. The comments criticizing the unresponsiveness of the system uncover a need for designing the navigation and resulting projection to be dynamic. These findings call for further exploring implications and expectations associated with different communication methods.

In summary, our study revealed that implicit communication of the future trajectory was more challenging to interpret, while explicit communication had a risk of non-intended interpretation. Regarding usability metrics, we found that explicit communication led to higher satisfaction, inferred from the trust, and improved communication effectiveness, inferred from legibility. Notably, there was no significant difference in the participant's efficiency, as deduced from their task completion time. Further comparing the two communication tools used here, one should note that the projection setup hardware comes with more direct cost per robot and uses a lot more power to run, possibly making it a less viable option for companies using AMRs.

5.2   Limitations

Both communication tools used in our study were not fully developed or optimized. Therefore, the comparison between explicit and implicit communication should be interpreted cautiously, as it primarily focuses on comparing trajectory floor projection with one implementation of driving behavior. Secondly, our study mainly focused on corridor-style interactions and did not involve open spaces. As a result, the findings cannot be extrapolated to scenarios involving open spaces. Other limitations include the presence of lag in the projection system, which was noticed by some participants (n = 10), and visibility issues with the floor projection due to poor lighting conditions (n = 6). Additionally, in some instances (n = 10 out of 192 trials), the trials were interrupted by manual emergency stops due to the robot being too close to participants. This resulted in evaluating the system of the robot and stop-operator rather than solely the robot itself. Furthermore, our participant pool of young individuals with primarily technical backgrounds may have influenced the results. Future studies could include participants with diverse age profiles and professional backgrounds more representative of the real worker population to obtain a more comprehensive understanding.

The way the duration of the interaction was measured was possibly not precise enough, differences in efficiency may otherwise have been significant. For a decision in an industrial application context, long-term learning effects are relevant, as workers will have frequent contact with AMRs in their daily work.

5.3   Outlook

Areas for future research include improving current and developing new communication tools and interaction strategies for human-robot interaction in intralogistics, as well as extending the study setup to open-space scenarios with autonomous navigation implemented. Furthermore, the entire system's efficiency (human + robot) should be considered, not only the human's.

Funding Information. The results presented in this article were developed within the research project "RoboLingo". The research project was carried out under the code 22234 N on behalf of the Research Association Bundesvereinigung Logistik e.V. (BVL). It was funded by the German Federal Ministry of Economics and Climate Protection via the German Federation of Industrial Research Associations "Otto von Guericke" e.V. (AiF).

References

1. Bengler, K., Rettenmaier, M., Fritz, N., Feierle, A.: From HMI to HMIS: towards an HMI framework for automated driving. Information **11**(2), 61 (2020). https://doi.org/10.3390/info11020061
2. Dey, D., et al.: Taming the EHMI jungle: a classification taxonomy to guide, compare, and assess the design principles of automated vehicles' external human-machine interfaces. Transport. Res. Interdisc. Perspect. **7**, 100174 (2020). https://doi.org/10.1016/j.trip.2020.100174
3. Ergonomics of human-system interaction - Part 110: Interaction principles, ISO 9241-110 (2020)
4. Dragan, A.D., Bauman, S., Forlizzi, J., Srinivasa, S.S.: Effects of robot motion on human-robot collaboration. In: 2015 10th ACM/IEEE International Conference on Human-Robot Interaction (HRI), pp. 51–58 (2015)
5. Dragan, A.D., Lee, K.C., Srinivasa, S.S.: Legibility and predictability of robot motion. In: 2013 8th ACM/IEEE International Conference on Human-Robot Interaction (HRI), pp. 301–308 (2013). https://doi.org/10.1109/HRI.2013.6483603
6. Dragan, A.D., Srinivasa, S.: Generating legible motion. In: Newman, P., Fox, D., Hsu, D. (eds.) Robotics: Science and Systems IX. Robotics Science and Systems Foundation, Berlin (2013). https://doi.org/10.15607/RSS.2013.IX.024
7. Giffi, C., Wellener, P., Dollar, B., Ashton, H., Monck, L., Moutray, C.: The jobs are here, but where are the people? (2018). https://www2.deloitte.com/us/en/insights/industry/manufacturing/manufacturing-skills-gap-study.html. Accessed 10 May 2023
8. Grizzle, J.E.: The two-period change-over design and its use in clinical trials. Biometrics **21**(2), 467 (1965). https://doi.org/10.2307/2528104

9. Körber, M.: Theoretical considerations and development of a questionnaire to measure trust in automation. In: Bagnara, S., Tartaglia, R., Albolino, S., Alexander, T., Fujita, Y. (eds.) IEA 2018. AISC, vol. 823, pp. 13–30. Springer, Cham (2019). https://doi.org/10.1007/978-3-319-96074-6_2

10. Reinhardt, J., Prasch, L., Bengler, K.: Back-off: evaluation of robot motion strategies to facilitate human-robot spatial interaction. ACM Trans. Human-Robot Interact. **10**, 1–25 (2021)

11. Research and Markets: AGV and AMR Market (2022). https://www.researchandmarkets.com/reports/5398204/agv-automated-guided-vehicles-and-amr. Accessed 26 May 2023

12. Rettenmaier, M., Dinkel, S., Bengler, K.: Communication via motion - suitability of automated vehicle movements to negotiate the right of way in road bottleneck scenarios. Appl. Ergon. **95**, 103438 (2021). https://doi.org/10.1016/j.apergo.2021.103438

13. Rios-Martinez, J., Spalanzani, A., Laugier, C.: From proxemics theory to socially-aware navigation: a survey. Int. J. Soc. Robot. **7**(2), 137–153 (2015). https://doi.org/10.1007/s12369-014-0251-1

14. Williams, M., Moser, T.: The art of coding and thematic exploration in qualitative research. Int. Manag. Rev. **15**, 45–55 (2019)

15. de Winter, J., Dodou, D.: External human-machine interfaces: gimmick or necessity? Transport. Res. Interdisc. Perspect. **15**, 100643 (2022). https://doi.org/10.1016/j.trip.2022.100643

Cognitive Command of Human-Autonomy Systems in EDGE Capabilities

Arne Norlander[(✉)]

NORSECON AB, P.O. Box 30097, 10425 Stockholm, Sweden
arne.norlander@norsecon.se

Abstract. This work defines and delineates the concept of "EDGE Capabilities", an acronym for Emergent, Dynamic, Global, and Evolutionary, as a way forward to development, deployment and command of Human-Autonomy Systems and capabilities. The concept emphasizes the coordination of kinetic and non-kinetic means of power across physical, information, and cognitive dimensions, can enable asymmetric exploitation of vulnerabilities and render irrelevant an opponent's abilities, will, structures, and systems.

The field of Human-Autonomy Systems (HAS) deals with how humans and automated intelligent artificial systems can work together to solve complicated tasks. This is particularly relevant in the domain of cyber-defence, where the speed and efficiency of response is of paramount importance. One solution that has been proposed is based on the Joint Cognitive Systems (JCS) body of research, defining and studying systems which are capable of jointly and independently detecting, identifying and engaging kinetic and non-kinetic threats and actors across physical, information, and cognitive dimensions.

We identified five key characteristics of EDGE capabilities. First, they are highly dynamic and non-linear. Second, they require collaboration within and between different organizations and their cultures. This includes the third point, that they engage people with different backgrounds. The fourth characteristic is that EDGE capabilities are superior regarding managing and maintaining mission-critical availability, versatility and efficiency. Fifth and last, they are employed in a multi-domain perspective. EDGE capabilities can be characterized as emergent, enabling deployment with a high level of fluidity and flexibility, matching the variation of the operational environment.

Every commander and every human and artificial agent must develop a capability for collective sensemaking and interaction to enable a comprehensive detailed system insight, leading to safe and efficient mission accomplishment. We propose formulating a future-oriented essence of EDGE Cognitive Command, with equal relevance for all agents constituting a Human-Autonomy System.

Keywords: Autonomy · Cognitive Systems · Command · EDGE · Emergence

1 Introduction

Operating in a contested mission environment requires comprehensive operational awareness, with the ability to accurately and rapidly perceive and interpret relevant events and circumstances. In order to provide the context, insight and foresight is required for

C. Stephanidis et al. (Eds.): HCII 2023, CCIS 1958, pp. 157–166, 2024.
https://doi.org/10.1007/978-3-031-49215-0_19

effective decision-making. Complex multi-domain operations are of particular concern; while some operational tasks necessarily would employ a human component, other tasks can only be accomplished through non-human intelligent entities, acting autonomously within the socio-technical enterprise. According to Definition 1 below, EDGE Operations at the conceptual level [1] comprise:

Definition 1: The coordination of kinetic and non-kinetic means of power in the physical, information, and cognitive domains, to asymmetrically exploit the adversary's vulnerabilities, and defeat or render irrelevant adversarial capabilities, structures, systems, and will to fight.

EDGE Operations execute at a level of fluidity and flexibility that matches the degree of variation in the external environment, a principle known as requisite variety [2], proven in a broad spectrum of safety-critical systems, missions, and operating environments. EDGE Operations are conducted by EDGE Capabilities, exhibiting the following overarching characteristics:

1. **Emergent:** In EDGE Operations, distributed, interdependent complex adaptive systems create emergent effects – effects that are greater than the sum of the individual effects of the input systems and that cannot be unambiguously attributed to individual observed properties.
2. **Dynamic:** EDGE Operations are complex, laborious and dangerous endeavors, requiring resolute and determined action under extreme conditions. EDGE Capabilities accomplish missions successfully under exposure to uncertainty, risk, time-criticalities and resource shortages.
3. **Global:** Actions by Hybrid Cognitive Systems in multiple operational domains, integrated in planning, synchronized in execution, with the speed, reach and scale needed to gain advantage and accomplish their mission.
4. **Evolutionary:** Heterogeneous, self-learning and adaptive behavior, originating in qualitative, structural change within and between complex system components. EDGE capabilities display three main evolutionary characteristics:
   (a) *Adaptive* – Ability to perceive, understand and manage change under time-, risk- and resource-critical circumstances.
   (b) *Exaptive* – Radical re-purposing under conditions of stress, driving an evolving, emergent system characterized by qualitative, structural change.
   (c) *Learning* – Experience from ongoing and completed campaigns are translated into action, reducing the time from discovery to implementation.

A complex system is any system in which the parts of the system and their interactions together represent a specific behavior, such that an analysis of all its constituent parts cannot explain the behavior. In such systems, the cause and effect cannot necessarily be related, and relationships are non-linear - a small change could have a disproportionate impact. In other words, as Aristotle said: 'the whole is greater than the sum of its parts'. This requires adaptive and versatile principles and concepts for complex multi-domain operations along with high-performance human, technological and organizational architectures [3]. Operational success is strongly linked to effective inter-action and collaboration within and between the physical, information and cognitive dimensions.

Autonomous systems, different organizational cultures, people with different back-grounds, education and experience rely heavily on collectively managing and main-taining operational availability, versatility and efficiency. In many situations the desired effects cannot be linearly planned and reliably predicted, but must be anticipated to emerge from shaping the Operational Environment (OE) and influencing the agents operating in the OE.

There are several issues concerning the use of mission-specific and contextual infor-mation and knowledge for judgment, decision, and choice, as well as the information-coupled activities leading to supervisory control of a complex, partly or completely automated process, and the more obvious control of the involved technological sys-tems [4, 5]. This also concerns the degree of autonomy and automation functions that are crucial for achieving flexible task execution and resource allocation, relating to all Human-Machine interaction and management concerns required to execute supervi-sory control at every organizational level, and to ensure rapid and reliable, autonomous response in routine decision situations:

- Monitoring and feedback functions,
- Functions enabling learning and adapting over time, and
- Feedforward functions,

DARPA's Mosaic Warfare concept [6] is an ambitious endeavor into Human-Machine capabilities in extensively, sometimes entirely, autonomous operations.

2 Human-Autonomy Systems: A Definition

Previous research on autonomy has largely focused on understanding how different "levels" of automation changes the working conditions for human operators [7, 8]. This view largely prevails today, as can be seen in the development of self-driving cars. Future applications of robotics and autonomous capabilities suggest a world were different robotic or software entities are integrated in society, fulfilling many tasks and even taking on responsibility for different managerial tasks. As described later in this chapter, this calls for technologies that are able to autonomously engage with its environment, without continuous human surveillance. In terms of perspectives that can provide some theoretical context for such a future, this can be seen as a case of a socio-technical system. However, while socio-technical aspects of human-autonomy constellations are of importance, we need also to focus understanding towards the cognitive aspects of both autonomous agents and human operators and commanders in order to better grasp the possibilities and limitations of joint human-autonomy systems in terms of performance and the types of tasks that can be supported.

2.1 A Functional Perspective on Intelligent, Autonomous Collaboration

In the case of Multi-Domain Command in the information and cognitive dimensions, we need to understand how a unit consisting of both humans and autonomous agents can reach their goals and how control, rather than functions, is allocated in the human-machine system. Further, both humans and autonomous agents are bounded in their rationality, although by different characteristics, deciding how control should be allocated between humans and autonomous agents depending on context and current goals.

The discussion benefits from this as it takes place in a hypothetical zone where the exact technical components cannot be described, as they do not yet exist. However, we can describe what a Human-Autonomy Team (HAT) is/should be in terms of what it can do (its functional properties) [9], which is in line with the Cognitive Systems Engineering (CSE) perspective [10].

Below, we elaborate on why a human-autonomy system can be seen as a cognitive system in its own right, and how the CSE approach can be used to better understand the human-autonomy system in different situations and contexts.

Autonomous systems are systems capable of making decisions independently and function without human intervention. One example is a Cyber-Physical System (CPS) [11], in which computing and physical processes are intricately woven together, with data from the environment and actuators being managed by the computer.

The concept of a human-autonomy system is integrated with the central premise of the human operator and decision maker as a capability component, operating symbiotically with technological artifacts [12]. Human operators are constantly collecting and building knowledge about themselves, other agents and the operational environment. They apply skills, rules and heuristics to plan and modify their actions based on that knowledge. Every commander and every human and artificial agent must develop a capability for sensemaking to enable a comprehensive detailed system insight, leading to safe and efficient mission accomplishment [13]. A human-autonomy system and its properties is found in Definition 2 below:

Definition 2: A Human-Autonomy System (HAS) is a system comprising at least one human operator and one adaptive artificial entity, with the capability to autonomously engage with its environment in direct interaction, involvement and/or interdependency with humans and other artificial entities in order to meet a certain mission objective.

Besides deciding and acting on an individual basis, both the human and the artificial entity complement each other's decision-making process and actions and jointly solve problems. In order to do so, they must be able to understand complex ideas (relative to the activity) to adapt effectively to the environment and to combine task related with social and team related skills that enable effective and efficient collaboration. This leads to the following corollary for Definition 2:

Corollary 1: A Human-Autonomy System (HAS) is capable to create, sustain and evolve Comprehensive Situational Awareness.

2.2 Complex Adaptive Systems (CAS)

The research literature describes the broader aspects of defense systems and in terms of Complex Adaptive Systems (CAS) [14, 15], [5] in the sense that military or crisis management organizations demonstrate CAS properties, and identify adaptive mechanisms at the levels of adaptive systems, capability development and collective/society, which adjust through learning, evolutionary development and cultural change to fulfill an externally imposed purpose. CAS has characteristics of self-learning, emergence, and evolution among the entities of the complex system. The entities or agents in a CAS demonstrate heterogeneous behavior. The key characteristics for a complex adaptive system are:

- The behavior or output cannot be predicted simply by analyzing the parts and inputs of the system.
- The behavior of the system is emergent and changes with time. The same input and environmental conditions do not always guarantee the same output.
- The entities or agents of a system are self-learning and change their behavior based on the outcome of the previous experience.

3 Cognitive Systems and Autonomous Adaptive Agents

The concept of autonomy is important for human-autonomy systems, as they are assumed to have capabilities for performing their tasks independently or interdependently and to have capabilities for reasoning and interaction that are needed for collaboration. The term "autonomy", however, needs more clarification as it may be used in multiple ways. Autonomy in relation to robotics is sometimes conflated with automation. An autonomous system, then, "performs its actions without human intervention". It can be fully pre-programmed and may have no choices about its action execution.

AI researchers have imposed requirements on autonomous systems regarding their internal reasoning process and decision-making process [16]. Furthermore, an autonomous system is not necessarily independent; it may allow external influences (e.g. human guidance), as long as it explicitly accepts these influences. This notion is important in the context of HAS, as it combines social and collaborative capabilities in autonomous systems. Lastly, autonomy of artificial systems, just as in the case of humans, is context dependent. A flying autonomous system, such as a UAV, may be autonomous in the sense that it can operate without guidance during flight, much like a human being, but it will only be autonomous in certain operational contexts and in relation to specific goals. If these conditions are changed, then the system is no longer "autonomous" in any of perspectives presented above. From this point of view, the idea of a "cognitive system" actually fits the description of what we in common parlor refer to as "autonomous systems". In reality, no systems to be considered for military usage should be truly autonomous, as even when tasked to do something that requires autonomy in a specific situation and context, the autonomous unit should only present agency within the frames of the task given to it.

3.1 Cognitive Systems

An autonomous unit like a human-autonomy system fits the definition of a "cognitive system". A cognitive system operates by using knowledge about itself and its environment to plan and modify its actions based on that knowledge [10]. Hollnagel [17] defines a cognitive system as a system that "can modify its pattern of behavior on the basis of past experience in order to achieve specific anti-entropic ends". This definition fits any organism or system that is to prevail in a dynamic environment.

The conclusion from this is that an a human-autonomy system must possess three fundamental capabilities to act as a Cognitive System (CS), defined by Norlander [11] as cornerstones of modern complex cognitive systems science:

1. A cognitive system is capable of **adaptation** to the varying conditions of the surrounding environment;
2. A cognitive system is capable of **prediction** of how the surrounding environment evolves over time;
3. A cognitive system is capable of **regulation** in order to reach an equilibrium that matches the current conditions of the surrounding environment.

These capabilities are well in line with properties of Complex Adaptive Systems previously outlined. If we view the role of Human-Autonomy Systems in the context of Multi-Domain Operations, the agents must be able to apply these capabilities in relation to a multitude of organizational entities, human/artificial operators, sensor systems, communication systems, doctrine and networks are all elements of the total operational system. Analogous to the findings of Conant and Ashby [18], the conclusion of this is that an artificial cognitive system has to be capable to adapt, predict and regulate to a level at least in line with human decision-making process and action to be able to complement each other.

The adaptive capability of cognitive command can be understood in the light of the CS definition provided above. Additionally, recent work by Prof. Tom Malone's research group in the realm of Superminds [19], suggest that human and artificial entities can jointly utilize Artificial Intelligence and Hyperconnectivity to form learning loops, constituting strategic planning and decision-making capabilities of business corporations, government agencies and global organizations. The conceptual structures of Cognitive Systems, Complex Adaptive Systems, Autonomy and Superminds all support the characterization of human-autonomy systems, enabling the foundation of a principal concept of Cognitive Command, based on the supporting concepts below, as Autonomous Adaptive Agents (AAAs).

3.2   Autonomous Adaptive Agents (AAAs) Executing High-Risk Missions as Part of High-Reliability Organizations

Besides constituting an autonomous intelligent entity, an Autonomous Adaptive Agent is also designed as a collaborator, meaning it is able when executing its tasks to complement the human decision-making process and task execution. Because of this, AAAs will, when integrated in human-based teams, be more perceived as team members than a collection of tools.

In most day-to-day operations, operational reliability, availability and high technical performance at the lowest possible cost are persisting overall objectives, and risk awareness in the organization is often limited. On the other hand, more specialized operational domains i.e. aviation, space, maritime, intensive care, nuclear power and military systems, require extraordinary risk awareness and risk management. These cases can be classified as complex endeavors, and the costs of incidents, attacks and breakdowns are valued not only in economic terms but also in human lives.

Additionally, the concept of risk and uncertainty is indivisibly unified with trust. Employing capabilities containing joint systems in the form of Human operators and AAAs must rely on an organization and doctrine that aims to achieve error-free performance and safety in every procedure, every time—all while operating in complex, high-risk or hazardous environments.

Such organizations have been studied extensively and defined by [13] as High-reliability Organizations (HRO). HROs are comprised by predictable and repeatable capabilities and systems that support consistent operations while identifying and preventing potentially catastrophic incidents before they happen.

4 Recommendations: Towards an Essence of Multi-domain Command

A conflict situation within, or with operational reach into, the information and cognitive dimensions can rapidly escalate or change character in fractions of a second, and this requires adequate response times. This is beyond the ability of humans, hence requiring the use of high-performance, automated cognitive capabilities comprised of multiple, distributed human-autonomy systems. Furthermore, without the appropriate distribution of information, and the necessary decision rights to the AAAs that match their required level of autonomy, the decisions and actions needed for success in Multi-Domain Operations (MDO) [20] will not be achieved in a timely manner. Reduction of response times enables losses of Command and Control (C2) capability to be minimized, or restored more quickly if degraded. This would indicate that command approaches that can respond more rapidly to changes in circumstances (e.g., a loss of communications capability or an unforeseen cross-domain system shock) would be more appropriate for operating in a contested operational environment.

In addition to the ability to act in a timely manner to exploit or manage rapidly changing circumstances, the requirement to interact and collaborate in Joint Systems Operations call for command approaches that.

1. Utilize multiple paths for information dissemination,
2. Adapt its interactions to changing circumstances, and
3. Dynamically delegate decision rights between AAA and human agents.

Norlander [21] propose formulating a future-oriented essence of Multi-Domain Command, with equal relevance and applicability on human operators, AAAs, and the HAS they jointly create and operate. The following is a first attempt, with three overarching conceptual mainstays, each with two corollaries:

Make Uncertainty Your Ally

1) Command in future security and defense operations will be complex, laborious and in many cases mission-critical, requiring unprecedented vigilance, awareness and determination. Decision-makers and operators will frequently encounter uncertainty, risks, time-criticalities and resource shortages.

2) Operating in a contested mission environment requires Comprehensive Operational Awareness, with the abilities to accurately and rapidly perceive and interpret relevant events and circumstances in order to provide the context, insight and foresight required for effective decision-making, enabling every commander and operator to develop a wide-ranging appreciation of the situation.

Stagnation Equals Defeat

3) Operational characteristics will be highly dynamic and non-linear; Minor events, decisions and actions may have serious and irreversible consequences for the entire mission. Success in future security and defense operations requires extraordinary capabilities to operate in contested operating environments, and to master the Command challenges of complex systems and interdependencies.

4) Mission success is strongly linked to effective interaction and collaboration within and between different organizational cultures, between people with different backgrounds, education and experience, non-human autonomous and intelligent systems, and on managing and maintaining operational availability, versatility and efficiency.

Multi-domain Command is Joint Cognitive Systems Command

5) Complex operations in a socio-technical enterprise require more than just human service providers; some tasks must be accomplished exclusively by nonhuman intelligent entities. This requires adaptive and versatile principles and concepts for Joint Cognitive Systems Command along with high-performance human, technological and organizational architectures - cognitive mission architectures.

6) The turbulent environment in which Multi-Domain Operations play out stresses the need further for Organizational Agility, to be adaptable and resilient without having to change. The goal is to keep internal operations at a level of fluidity and flexibility that matches the degree of turmoil in external environments, a principle known as requisite variety.

5   Summary and Conclusions

Operating in a contested mission environment requires comprehensive situational awareness, with the ability to accurately and rapidly perceive and interpret mission-relevant events and circumstances, in order to provide the context, insight and foresight required for effective decision-making and action. Complex Multi-Domain Operations are of particular concern; while some operational tasks necessarily would employ a human component, other tasks can only be accomplished through non-human intelligent entities, acting autonomously within the socio-technical enterprise.

The Cognitive Systems body of research was utilized to overcome the duality of traditional human-machine research, focusing on better understanding what people actually do with technology rather than what functions belong to the machine and what functions belong to the human. The Complex Adaptive Systems (CAS) body of research contributed with characteristics of self-learning, emergence, and evolution among the entities of the complex system, demonstrating heterogeneous and adaptive behavior. According to the body of research for Autonomous Adaptive Agents (AAAs), an agent is also viewed as a team member, meaning it is able to autonomously complement human decision-making when executing its tasks. Building cognitive systems and capabilities requires a mental shift – striving towards an Agility mindset that permeates security and defence policy, legal and financial frameworks, science and technology agendas, strategy and operations.

Employing the Cognitive Systems, CAS and AAA paradigms for MDO permits the integration of all capability elements into an adaptive distributed system that can achieve a mission safely and efficiently. Based on these studies and with the support from other fields of study, we devised a number of strategy elements as part of an essence of Cognitive Command and Decision-making in Complex Multi-Domain Operations.

Acknowledgement. The authors would like to acknowledge the funding support by the Swedish Armed Forces and The Swedish Defence Materiel Administration, Contract no. 5006519.

References

1. Norlander, A.: Command and Control in a cognitive environment. In: Proceedings of the NATO Command and Control Center of Excellence Annual Seminar: Executing C2 in a Multi-Domain Environment, Utrecht, Netherlands: NATO C2CoE (2022)
2. Ashby, W.R.: An Introduction to Cybernetics. Chapman & Hall, London (1956)
3. Norlander, A.: Societal Security: how digitalization enables resilient, agile and learning capabilities. In: Larsson, A., Teigland, R. (eds.) Digital Transformation and Public Services (Open Access). Routledge, London (2019). ISBN 978-04-293-1929-7
4. Worm, A.: On control and interaction in complex distributed systems and environments. Linköping Studies in Science and Technology, Dissertation No. 664, Linköping University, Linköping, Sweden (2000). ISBN 91-7219-899-0
5. Norlander, A.: Cognitive systems modeling and analysis of command & control systems. In: Proceedings of the MODSIM World 2011 Conference and Expo. National Aeronautics and Space Administration, Virginia Beach, VA, USA (2011). NASA/CP-2012-217326
6. Congressional Research Service: Joint All-Domain Command and Control: Background and Issues for Congress. United States Congress. Report No. R46725 (2021)
7. Sheridan, T.B., Verplank, W.L.: Human and computer control of undersea teleoperators. Massachusetts Institute of Technology. Cambridge Man-Machine Systems Lab (1978)
8. Parasuraman, R., Sheridan, T.B., Wickens, C.D.: A model for types and levels of human interaction with automation. IEEE Trans. Syst. Man Cybernet.-Part A Syst. Hum. **30**(3), 286–297 (2000)

9. National Academies of Sciences, Engineering, and Medicine (NASEM): Human-AI Teaming: State-of-the-Art and Research Needs. The National Academies Press, Washington, DC (2022). https://doi.org/10.17226/26355
10. Rasmussen, J., Pejtersen, A.M., Goodstein, L.: Cognitive Systems Engineering. Wiley, New York (1994)
11. Derler, P., Lee, E.A., Tripakis, S., Törngren, M.: Cyber-physical system design contracts. In: Proceedings of the ACM/IEEE 4th International Conference on Cyber-Physical Systems, pp. 109–118 (2013)
12. Norlander, A.: Analyzing tactical cognitive systems: theories, models and methods. In: Berggren, P., Nählinder, S., Svensson, E. (eds.) Assessing Command and Control Effectiveness – Dealing with a changing world. Ashgate (2014). ISBN 978-1-4724-3696-2
13. Weick, K.E., Sutcliffe, K.M.: Managing the Unexpected: Sustained Performance in a Complex World. Wiley, New York (2015)
14. Holland, J.H.: Hidden Order: How Adaptation Builds Complexity. Basic Books, New York (1995)
15. Holland, J.H.: Studying complex adaptive systems. J. Syst. Sci. Complexity 19(1), 1–8 (2006)
16. Endsley, M.R.: Autonomous Horizons: System Autonomy in the Air Force: A Path to the Future. US Air Force Office of the Chief Scientist, Washington, DC (2015)
17. Hollnagel, E.: Modelling the controller of a process. Trans. Inst. MC 21(4/5), 163–170 (1999)
18. Conant, R.C., Ashby, W.R.: Every good regulator of a system must be a model of that system. Int. J. Syst. Sci. 1, 89–97 (1970)
19. Malone, T.W.: Superminds: How Hyperconnectivity is Changing the Way We Solve Problems. Simon and Schuster (2018)
20. NATO: Multi-Domain Multinational Understanding. North Atlantic Treaty Organization Allied Command Transformation Multinational Capability Development Campaign (NATO ACT MCDC), Norfolk (2022)
21. Norlander, A.: Command in AICA-intensive operations. In: Kott, A. (ed.) Autonomous Intelligent Cyber Defense Agent (AICA): A Comprehensive Guide. Springer Series on Advances in Information Security, vol. 87, pp. 311–339. Springer, Cham (2023). https://doi.org/10.1007/978-3-031-29269-9_15. ISBN 978-3-031-29268-2

The Dynamics of Collaborative Decision-Making with Intelligent Systems

Burak Öz[✉] [iD], Alexander-John Karran [iD], Joerg Beringer [iD],
Constantinos K. Coursaris [iD], and Pierre-Majorique Léger [iD]

HEC Montréal, tech3lab, Montréal, QC, Canada
{burak.oz,alexander.karran,constantinos.coursaris,pml}@hec.ca,
joerg.beringer@berisoft.com

Abstract. Intelligent systems support decision-makers in complex tasks by utilizing advanced technologies such as machine learning, artificial intelligence, or deep learning. Despite their potential to increase decision performance, several barriers exist to the widespread adoption of these complex systems. By examining the past IS adoption literature and the unique characteristics of intelligent systems, we propose the situation awareness model as a promising theoretical framework that can shed light on human-AI interaction effectiveness. Using this vantage point and our preliminary interview data with expert decision-makers, we identify several challenges to be addressed for effective human-AI collaborations.

Keywords: human-AI teams · trust · acceptance · situation awareness

1 Introduction

As the extent of support from information systems (IS) increases from simple calculations and suggestions to human-artificial intelligence (AI) collaborative decision-making, the relationship between the user and IS becomes more complex. Human-AI teams are a common method of AI implementation in which humans evaluate AI suggestions before acting upon them [1]. However, these teams have two extreme scenarios that may cause inefficiencies. In some instances, instead of using the IS as intended, users may rely on it excessively and, in the process, lose their ability to understand how future events impact their decision-making environment. Alternatively, users may distrust the IS and not benefit from its capabilities in processing high volumes of data and deriving contextually relevant, reliable insight [2]. In human-AI teaming implementations, achieving optimal results necessitates balancing excessive reliance and under-reliance [3]. This document aims to investigate and determine the reasons for each user response using past IS adoption research, the situational awareness (SA) framework, and our preliminary findings from a series of user interviews.

There is extensive research on the impacts of IS investments on how well an organization performs [4, 5]. In addition to the initial justifications for the IS implementations [6] and the alignment between the organization's strategy and IS decision support tools

[7, 8], one of the critical factors determining the success of an IS implementation is their utilization by the intended users [9]. Considering the rich past research activity in the field, we first start with an overview of the IS acceptance literature to understand the factors leading to the underutilization of an IS.

Following the brief overview of findings from the IS acceptance literature, this paper will then continue with the unique characteristics of AI-powered intelligent decision support systems that make them worthy of further research activity. The paper will then conclude with a set of possible future research directions.

2   Factors Impacting User Adoption of IS and AI

2.1   Insights from the IS Adoption Literature

As the user acceptance of IS is critical to its success, it is not surprising that numerous studies have investigated the factors influencing user acceptance. The Technology Acceptance Model (TAM) [10] has been widely adopted to investigate user acceptance factors. This model indicates two central beliefs that predict user acceptance: perceived usefulness (PU) and perceived ease of use (PEOU). Through decades of research activity involving these constructs, researchers have identified a wide range of additional constructs that may influence PU and PEOU. These constructs influencing PU and PEOU include users' perceptions of the IS and the task, their personality traits, and contextual factors. Several attempts were made to aggregate the factors influencing PU and PEOU, and identified facilitating conditions, individual beliefs, habit, system characteristics, social influence, and higher and individual-level contextual factors [9, 11, 12]. An illustration of such a model identifying factors influencing PU and PEOU, the Technology Acceptance Model 3 (TAM3) [12], can be seen in Fig. 1.

Although the literature stream utilizing TAM and similar models has provided valuable insights regarding user acceptance of IS, these models extensively focus on the initial adoption of an IS rather than its continued use. To address this limitation, researchers have investigated more complex research topics such as continued use of, and resistance to IS. The literature reveals that users plan to continue using an IS more as their expectations are satisfied [13]. On the other hand, they resist the use of a mandatory IS due to several reasons, including perceived disruption to established work routines [14] or political power balances [15], lack of user involvement in the implementation of the IS [16], or poor system usability [14]. While these findings offer valuable insights into people's resistance to adopting new IS, it is essential to note that they are identified with the assumption that the IS in question operates as a rule-based system with defined decision boundaries.

2.2   Adoption of AI and Other Intelligent Systems

In the case of intelligent systems that continuously learn and adapt autonomously, the assumptions regarding a static system with a fixed behavior pattern may not always hold. The emerging intelligent systems based on machine learning techniques provide a wide range of possibilities, but they lack transparency and are highly complex. Moreover, intelligent systems can update themselves, and consequently, their responses to

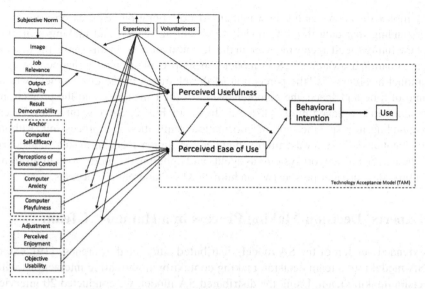

Fig. 1. The Technology Acceptance Model 3 [12].

the same problems may change over time [18]. Due to these reasons, in contexts where the outcomes are critical, integrating intelligent decision support engines encourages a collaborative effort between these intelligent systems and end-users in complex decision-making scenarios [3]. These collaboration scenarios make it essential to understand the specific meta-decisions in the human-AI interaction process and revisit some concepts, such as trust and perceived user control. Thus, extending the theoretical lenses in the IS adoption literature can help understand the continuous user-AI interaction processes better.

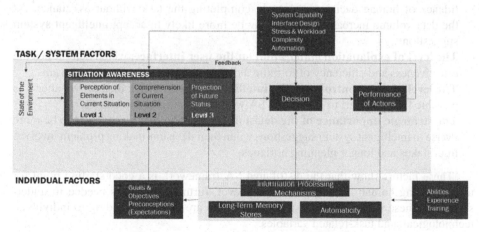

Fig. 2. The Situation Awareness Model [17].

Complex decision-making in a human-AI collaboration requires observing data, understanding that data through models representing reality, and making projections about the future for all agents involved in the decision process. In this sense, the literature on the situational awareness (SA) model can help explain what is happening better. Situational awareness is "the perception of the elements in the environment within a volume of time and space, the comprehension of their meaning, and the projection of their status in the near future" [17]. As shown in Fig. 2, SA has three levels, each corresponding to a specific type of information acquisition and processing. Although this conceptual definition was initially intended for human decision-makers, considering intelligent decision support systems as agents and applying the model to their awareness could provide a broader perspective on human-AI collaboration processes.

3   Experts' Decision-Making Process in a Human-AI Team

An extended version of the SA model, distributed situational awareness [19], extends the SA model into a team decision-making context by highlighting interactions within a decision-making team. Using the distributed SA model, we conducted 20 interviews with supply chain experts who use intelligent systems to help them with their decisions and the developers of these intelligent tools. The preliminary analysis of the dataset indicates that experts evaluate an intelligent system's suggestions against their own SA and determine whether to trust the intelligent system depending on their three levels of SA. In other words, experts get involved in "meta-decisions" about using intelligent systems at various stages of the decision-making process. According to our current understanding of the interview data, experts' decision to use an intelligent system's advice depends on the combination of several factors that include:

- **User trust in the intelligent system**, which is shaped by both what has been shown on the user interface and the users' attitude and generic trust toward intelligent systems.
- **The volume of data to be processed,** a task characteristic that determines the confidence of human decision-makers in completing the task without assistance. As the data volume increases, experts may be more likely to accept intelligent system suggestions.
- **The level of explanation elaboration on the user interface,** which determines the effectiveness and efficiency of forming a distributed SA in the human-AI team.
- **The level of user control over the intelligent system,** which dictates whether it is possible for the expert to share their SA with the intelligent system.
- **The strategic importance of the decision,** as decision-makers reported to be more averse to intelligent system suggestions when their decision-making problem involves high stakes and longer planning horizons.

These factors show that the distributed SA framework is a good starting point for understanding human-AI interactions. However, further research is needed to understand how these factors impacting meta-decisions are shaped according to individual, technological, and task-related variables.

4 Conclusion and Future Work

Although the IS acceptance and adoption literature provides valuable insights into user adoption of intelligent systems in workplaces, the unique characteristics of intelligent systems mandate further theory development and extension efforts. We propose the distributed situational awareness model as a suitable framework for studying workplace human-AI interactions.

The preliminary results of our interviews reveal that when users are presented with decision-making scenarios, they engage in a series of meta-decisions regarding the potential delegation of activities to intelligent systems. These meta-decisions include considerations such as "How do I perform this task manually?", "How does the system execute this task?" and "How can I collaborate with the system to accomplish this task?". The result of such meta-decisions is dependent on several factors, including user trust in the system, the volume of the data to be processed, the level of explanation elaboration on the user interface of the intelligent system, the level of user control over the intelligent system, and the strategic importance of the decision. We suggest conducting further research to understand how these influencing factors are shaped during users' interaction with intelligent systems.

References

1. National Academies of Sciences, Engineering, and Medicine: Human-AI Teaming: State of the Art and Research Needs. National Academies Press, Washington, D.C. (2021). https://doi.org/10.17226/26355
2. Chiang, C.-W., Yin, M.: Exploring the effects of machine learning literacy interventions on laypeople's reliance on machine learning models (2022). https://doi.org/10.1145/3490099.3511121
3. Endsley, M.R.: Supporting Human-AI Teams: Transparency, explainability, and situation awareness. Comput. Hum. Behav., 107574 (2022). https://doi.org/10.1016/j.chb.2022.107574
4. Brynjolfsson, E.: The productivity paradox of information technology. Commun. ACM **36**, 66–77 (1993). https://doi.org/10/ct4fx4
5. Sabherwal, R., Jeyaraj, A.: Information technology impacts on firm performance: an extension of Kohli and Devaraj. MISQ **39**, 809–836 (2015). https://doi.org/10/gfxztb
6. Steelman, Z.R., Havakhor, T., Sabherwal, R., Sabherwal, S.: Performance consequences of information technology investments: implications of emphasizing new or current information technologies. Inf. Syst. Res. **30**, 204–218 (2019). https://doi.org/10/ghfvfg
7. Gerow, J.E., Grover, V., Thatcher, J., Roth, P.L.: Looking toward the future of IT-Business strategic alignment through the past: a meta-analysis. MISQ **38**, 1059–1085 (2014). https://doi.org/10/gf2t8f
8. Liang, H., Wang, N., Xue, Y., Ge, S.: Unraveling the alignment paradox: how does business—IT alignment shape organizational agility? Inf. Syst. Res. **28**, 863–879 (2017). https://doi.org/10/gcpwn6
9. Venkatesh, V., Morris, M.G., Davis, G.B., Davis, F.D.: User acceptance of information technology: toward a unified view. MIS Q. **27**, 425 (2003). https://doi.org/10/gc8zn2
10. Davis, F.D.: Perceived usefulness, perceived ease of use, and user acceptance of information technology. MIS Q. **13**, 319–340 (1989). https://doi.org/10.2307/249008

11. Venkatesh, V., Thong, J., Xu, X.: Unified theory of acceptance and use of technology: a synthesis and the road ahead. J. Assoc. Inf. Syst. **17**, 328–376 (2016). https://doi.org/10/gfkzmv

12. Venkatesh, V., Bala, H.: Technology acceptance model 3 and a research agenda on interventions. Decis. Sci. **39**, 273–315 (2008). https://doi.org/10.1111/j.1540-5915.2008.00192.x

13. Bhattacherjee, A.: Understanding information systems continuance: an expectation-confirmation model. MIS Q. **25**, 351–370 (2001). https://doi.org/10.2307/3250921

14. Kim, H.-W., Kankanhalli, A.: Investigating user resistance to information systems implementation: a status quo bias perspective. MIS Q. **33**, 567–582 (2009). https://doi.org/10/ggh72j

15. Joshi, K.: A model of users' perspective on change: the case of information systems technology implementation. MIS Q. **15**, 229–242 (1991). https://doi.org/10/b6p55w

16. Markus, M.L.: Power, politics, and MIS implementation. Commun. ACM **26**, 430–444 (1983). https://doi.org/10/d68389

17. Endsley, M.R.: Toward a theory of situation awareness in dynamic systems. Hum. Factors **37**, 32–64 (1995). https://doi.org/10/ftd9tz

18. Schuetz, S., Venkatesh, V.: The rise of human machines: How cognitive computing systems challenge assumptions of user-system interaction. J. Assoc. Inf. Syst. **21**, 460–482 (2020)

19. Salmon, P.M.: Distributed Situation Awareness: Advances in Theory, Measurement and Application to Team Work. Ashgate Publishing Limited, Surrey (2008)

Exploring How Adolescents Collaborate with Robots

Mu-Shan Rau[1], Qiyun Huang[2], Pin-Hsuan Chen[3(✉)], and Hanjing Huang[4]

[1] Tsinghua University High School, Beijing, China
[2] High School Affiliated to BIT, Beijing, China
[3] Tsinghua University, Beijing, China
cpx19@mails.tsinghua.edu.cn
[4] Fuzhou University, Fujian, China

Abstract. Robots are increasingly being employed in educational environments to enhance learning experiences. Adolescents may interact with robots differently from younger children due to cognitive and perceptual maturation. This study examines the influence of robot ability, task complexity, risk, and self-construal on adolescents' confidence and trust in robots, and decision-making. Six participants (aged 14–16) collaborated with the NAO robot in a length judgment task. Results showed that high-ability robots elicited more trust, confidence, and decision change. In complex tasks, trust was highest with low-ability robots, while trust was lowest in simple tasks. Participants were less inclined to share benefits but expect robots to bear losses. Interdependent individuals showed more decision changes. These findings increase the understanding of the way that adolescents collaborate with robots, especially in decision-making processes.

Keywords: Decision-making · Human-robot interaction · Adolescent

1 Introduction

Robots nowadays are increasingly integrated into education, particularly in the field of Science, Technology, Engineering, and Mathematics (STEM). They could be peer learners or tutors [1, 2]. In some cases, robots are used to collaborate with students for solving scientific and technological problems. They provide suggestions to students and students are major decision makers. Understanding the factors that influence students' acceptance of robot suggestions and their decision-making processes becomes crucial. Younger students view robots as partners [1]. As age increases, older students perceive robots as tool-based partners [1], and they are likely to evaluate robots more rationally. This perception change influences their confidence and trust in robots, and their decisions while collaborating with robots [2].

During adolescence, cognition and perception mature, making it essential to explore how students in this age group perceive and interact with robots in decision-making contexts. This study aims to investigate the influences of robot ability, task complexity, risk and self-construal in decision-making processes on students' confidence and trust in robots and the likelihood of decision change. The results might help leverage robots as valuable tools for facilitating decision-making processes.

© The Author(s), under exclusive license to Springer Nature Switzerland AG 2024
C. Stephanidis et al. (Eds.): HCII 2023, CCIS 1958, pp. 173–180, 2024.
https://doi.org/10.1007/978-3-031-49215-0_21

2   Methods

2.1   Participants

Six students with an age range of 14 to 16 years (M = 15.67, SD = 0.82) participated in this study. In each experiment, only one participant was included. Ethical clearance was approved by the ethics committee of Tsinghua University. Written informed consent was obtained from all participants and their parents prior to enrolment in this study.

2.2   Manipulations

Robot. The NAO robot, a programmable humanoid robot created by Softbank Robotics, was used in this study. Experimenters manipulated the robot via a Wizard of Oz technique and controlled it remotely through Choregraphe Software. Thus, experimenters ensured the robot's behaviors but participants believed the robot to be autonomous.

The robot was standing on a table in front of the participants. During the experiment, the robot was programed to have eye contacts frequently with participants to enhance trust. The robot's gestures included hand waving and head moving.

Experiment. This study manipulated robot ability, task complexity and risk as within-group variables, with two levels each [3]. First, the robot's ability included low and high levels. The accuracy was 70% for the low ability robot, and it was 90% for the high ability robot. Second, the task complexity was divided into simple and complex. The simple task displayed eight vertical lines and the complex task displayed four vertical and four horizontal lines. Third, the risk was designed by the amount of benefit and loss involved in each trial. The low-risk task was five dollars and the high-risk task was twenty dollars.

2.3   Task and Procedure

Task. This study conducted a length judgment task from the Müller-Lyer illusion task [4, 5]. There were eight trials in each experiment. In each trial, participants had to collaborate with the robot for selecting the longest line out of the eight lines. Participants must make two decisions in each trial, including the initial decision and final decision. The initial decision was the first answer for the longest line selection upon seeing the eight lines on the screen. The final decision was the final answer after considering the suggested line number provided by the robot. The robot could discern the longest line with an accuracy of either 70% or 90%.

Procedure. Participants must complete an online survey examining self-construal beforehand. Upon entering the room, experimenters guided the participant to sit at the table and briefly introduced to the participant that the robot would be his/her partner in the experiment. Then, the experimenters left the participant alone. Next, the robot introduced itself and then instructed the participant to understand the experiment and the task in each trial. After the practice trial the participants started the trials.

In the first trial of the experiment, the robot first reported its ability by revealing its accuracy and experimenters would give the participant a paper-based answer sheet for the first trial. Second, the participant would see eight lines, and benefits and losses involved in this trial on the screen. Third, the participant should write down the initial decision and the confidence in this decision on the answer sheet. Fourth, the robot then suggested its own decision, which the participant recorded along with the confidence in the robot's decision on the answer sheet. Fifth, the participant was asked to make the final decision, evaluate confidence in the final decision, trust for the robot, and reciprocity in this trial. Experimenters checked and collected the completed answer sheet and gave a new sheet for the next trial. The robot would again report its ability at the beginning of the fifth trial, and the remaining procedure would remain the same.

2.4 Measures

Confidence. Confidence referred to the participant's belief in the correctness of their decisions. In each trial, participants were required to evaluate their confidence in the decision three times, expressed as a percentage. The first confidence rating was provided after the initial decision, the second after considering the robot's suggestion, and the third after making the final decision. This study calculated the difference in confidence between the initial decision and the final decision to examine the extent of confidence change when the robot was involved in this decision-making task.

Trust. Trust was evaluated by participant's trustworthiness towards robot's suggestion. At the end of each trial, participants had to rate their level of trust on a scale from 0 to 10. A rating of 0 showed that they could not trust in the robot, while a rating of 10 showed that they complete trusted in the robot.

Decision Change. Decision change was evaluated by counting the number of decision change between initial decision and final decision in the experiment. The change of decision indicated that the robot suggestion could influence participants' decision.

Reciprocity. Reciprocity was assessed through two questions posed to participants. The first question asked, "How much will you share with the robot when you correctly select the longest line and earn the benefits?" The second question inquired, "How much do you think the robot should bear the losses when you select the wrong line and have to face the punishment?" Participants had to answer both questions based on the level of risk.

Self-construal. Self-construal was assessed using a modified version of the questionnaire developed by Brewer and Chen (2007) [6] to align with the research objectives of this study. The questionnaire comprised twelve items, categorized into two dimensions: independence and interdependence. Participants were instructed to rate each item using a 7-point Likert scale, with a rating of 1 indicating strong disagreement and a rating of 7 indicating strong agreement. This study then summed the score of each item based on dimension and calculated the ratio of independent and interdependent. Participants were classified as having an independent self-construal if the ratio exceeded 1, while participants with a ratio below 1 were classified as having an interdependent self-construal.

3 Results

3.1 The Effect of Robot Ability

Confidence. According to the results, the confidence increased more significantly when participants interacted with the high ability robot (initial: M = 58.54%, SD = 15.82; final: M = 76.17, SD = 12.90) than with the low ability robot (initial: M = 57.71, SD = 14.76; final: M = 63.88, SD = 23.13). The results indicated that the high ability robot might effectively enhance participants' confidence for making a decision. Figure 1 shows the initial and final confidence while making a decision with high and low ability robots.

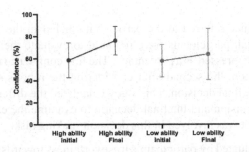

Fig. 1. The initial and final confidence in high and low ability robots

Trust. Participants reported that their level of trust was higher while interacting with the high ability robot (M = 7.25, SD = 0.87) than with the low ability robot (M = 6.42, SD = 1.03). Figure 2 shows the level of trust while interacting with the robot with different abilities.

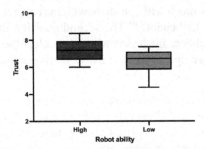

Fig. 2. The level of trust in high and low ability robot

Decision Change. The results revealed that participants were more likely to change their decisions while interacting with the high ability robot (M = 1.17, SD = 1.17) than with the low ability robot (M = 0.83, SD = 0.75). Further analysis investigated the number of decision change when participants changed their decisions to align with the robot's suggestion. Compared to the low ability robot (M = 0.67, SD = 0.82), participants exhibited a higher frequency to change their decisions to align with the high ability robot's suggestion (M = 1.00, SD = 1.27). The results suggested that participants probably changed their decisions in the high ability robot condition. Figure 3 shows the number of decision change and not change. Figure 4 displays the number of decision change where participants aligned their decisions with the robot's suggestion.

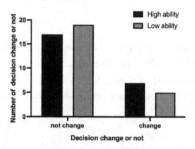
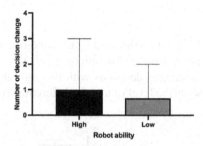

Fig. 3. Number of decision change and not change in high and low ability

Fig. 4. Number of decision change and aligning with the robot's suggestion

3.2 The Effect of Task Complexity

Confidence. The results presented that confidence could be enhanced when participants received the suggestion from the robot. Compared to the complex task, participants reported a higher confidence in their initial decision in the simple task. Further analysis revealed that the confidence increased significantly when participants were making decisions in simple task with high ability robot. Figure 5 demonstrates the initial and final confidence in different conditions of robot ability and task complexity. Table 1 reports mean and standard deviation.

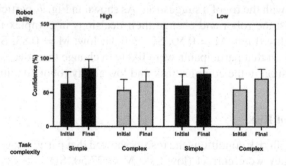

Fig. 5. The initial and final confidence in terms of robot ability and task complexity

Trust. The results showed that participants reported a lower level of trust in the complex task (M = 6.63, SD = 1.37) compared to the simple task (M = 7.04, SD = 0.64). Further

Table 1. Descriptive statistics of the initial and final confidence in terms of robot ability and task complexity

	High ability		Low ability	
	Simple	Complex	Simple	Complex
Initial	62.92 (17.49)	54.17 (15.30)	60.42 (16.91)	55.00 (15.57)
Final	85.33 (13.20)	67.08 (13.55)	77.75 (8.74)	71.08 (13.55)

analysis within the simple task condition revealed the lowest level of trust when making decisions with the low ability robot (M = 5.58, SD = 1.50), but the highest level of trust when making decisions with the high ability robot (M = 7.67, SD = 1.40). Figure 6 presents the level of trust in different conditions of robot ability and task complexity.

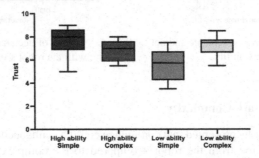

Fig. 6. The level of trust in terms of robot ability and task complexity

Decision Change. The results reported that participants changed their decisions more frequently in the complex task (M = 1.50, SD = 1.05) than in the simple task (M = 0.50, SD = 0.55). Further analysis was conducted to examine the number of decision changes aligning with the robot's suggestion. As shown in Fig. 7, participants displayed a tendency to trust the robot and change their decisions in complex tasks, regardless of the robot's ability (high: M = 0.50, SD = 0.84; low: M = 0.83, SD = 0.75). The results could suggest that participants were likely to change their decision to align with the robot's suggestion in the complex task and low ability robot condition.

3.3 The Effect of Risk

Reciprocity. In both risk conditions the results showed that participants shared less with the robot when they were correct (low risk: M = 27.50, SD = 8.48; high risk: M = 31.33, SD = 18.02). However, when participants were wrong, they expected the robot to bear over a half of the loss (low risk: M = 51.50, SD = 13.88; high risk: M = 53.17, SD = 10.59). The results indicated that participants were more likely to share losses than share benefits with the robot. As the risk increased in the decision-making process, the percentage of shared-benefit and shared-loss became slightly greater. Figure 8 illustrates

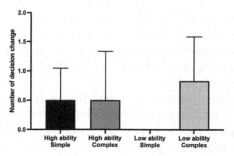

Fig. 7. Number of decision change in terms of robot ability and task complexity

the percentage of the benefits or losses that participants expected to share with the robot or to be borne by the robot.

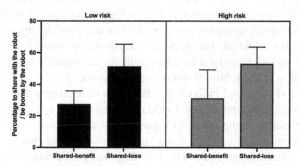

Fig. 8. The percentage of benefits and losses to share with or be borne by the robot in low and high risk conditions

3.4 The Effect of Self-construal

Decision Change. On average, independent participants changed their decisions 1.33 times (SD = 1.16) and interdependent participants changed 2.67 times (SD = 1.53) in the experiment. Further analysis reported that compared to independent participants (M = 0.50, SD = 0.55), interdependent participants tended to change their decisions to align with the robot's suggestion (M = 1.33, SD = 1.03). The results indicated that interdependent participants were likely to be influenced by the robot's suggestion while making a decision.

4   Discussion and Conclusion

Understanding the decision-making process of adolescents with robots is crucial for educational environments. In addition to receiving guidance from instructors, students now have the opportunity to seek suggestions from physical or virtual robots. The result showed that participants had a higher level of trust and confidence in high ability robot. They tended to change their initial decisions to listen to the robot's suggestion. In other words, these results indicated that making a decision with suggestions from high ability robot could encourage participant to believe in their final decisions, especially when they were conducting simple tasks.

Furthermore, this study found an interesting pattern about trust in the low ability robot. In complex tasks, participants exhibited a higher level of trust in the low ability robot, whereas in simple tasks, the level of trust was the lowest. Participants changed their decisions more frequently to align with the robot's suggestion while interacting with the low ability robot in complex tasks compared to other conditions. This study argued that when the task was simple, participants believed in their own decisions more and diminished the need for reliance on the robot. As task complexity increased, participants relied more on robot's suggestion because they were uncertain about the correct answers, even when the robot ability was low.

Moreover, the results showed that participants shared less percentage of benefits with the robot but expected the robot to bear a higher percentage of the losses. This study proposed that this discrepancy could be attributed to participants attributing wrong decisions to the robot while attributing correct decisions to themselves. In other words, participants may be more inclined to take credit for successful outcomes but tend to assign responsibility to the robot for unfavorable outcomes [7].

Finally, this study revealed individual differences in making a decision with robots based on self-construal. Independent individuals were more likely to trust their own decisions and less inclined to change their decisions based on robot suggestions. On the other hand, interdependent individuals showed a higher propensity to change their decisions to align with the robot's suggestions. These findings suggested that self-construal could shape individuals' decision-making processes and the willingness to rely on robots.

References

1. Mubin, O., Stevens, C.J., Shahid, S., Al Mahmud, A., Dong, J.-J.: A review of the applicability of robots in education. Technol. Educ. Learn. **1**, 13 (2013)
2. Balpaeme, T., Kennedy, J., Ramachandran, A., Scassellati, B., Tanaka, F.: Social robots for education: a review. Sci. Robot. **3**, eaat5954 (2018)
3. Huang, H.J., Rau, P.-L.P., Ma, L.: Will you listen to a robot? Effect of robot ability, task complexity, and risk on human decision-making. Adv. Robot. **35**(19), 1156–1166 (2021)
4. Bruno, N., Franz, V.H.: When is grasping affected by the Müller-Lyer illusion? A quantitative review. Neuropsychologia **47**(6), 1421–1433 (2009)
5. Kopiske, K.K., Cesanek, E., Campagnoli, C., Domini, F.: Adaptation effects in grasping the Müller-Lyer illusion. Vision. Res. **136**, 21–31 (2017)
6. Brewer, M.B., Chen, Y.-R.: Where (Who) are collectives in collectivism? Toward conceptual clarification of individualism and collectivism. Psychol. Rev. **114**(1), 133–151 (2007)
7. Lei, X., Rau, P.-L.P.: Should i blame the human or the robot? Attribution within a human-robot group. Int. J. Soc. Robot. **13**, 363–377 (2021)

Research on Recognition of Facial Expressions and Micro-Expressions for Robot Design

Meina Tawaki[1], Keiko Yamamoto[2], and Ichi Kanaya[3,4](✉) (iD)

[1] School of Information Systems, University of Nagasaki, 1-1 Manabino, Nagayo, Nagasaki 851-2195, Japan
[2] School of System Design and Technology, Tokyo Denki University, 5 Senju Asahi-cho, Adachi-ku, Tokyo 120-8551, Japan
[3] School of Information and Data Sciences, Nagasaki University, 1-14 Bunkyomachi, Nagasaki, Nagasaki 852-8521, Japan
[4] Pineapple Computer, Tokyo, Japan
kanaya@pineapple.cc

Abstract. It is said that humans make their first impressions of a person 7% by verbal communication and 93% by visual and auditory communication. When robots intervene in human society and need to communicate with humans, the face is considered to be the most important interface. However, it is unclear whether differences can be recognized in the subtle facial expressions that appear in daily life. Therefore, in this study, we investigate the synchronization of emotions for knowing whether we can recognize such micro expressions. Emotional synchronization means that the feelings of a person A and a person B are communicated and emotionally coupled. For example, when the person A likes the person B, the person B feels the same emotion toward the person A at the same time, they are emotionally synchronized. We believe that the study of emotional synchronization will be useful for designing more friendly robots.

Keywords: Emotion Synchronization · Product Design · Humanoid

1 Introduction

Robots emerged as objects of modern technology in the early 1960s, and with the development of technology, robots began to be connected to various external devices. Since then, the 1970s saw rapid progress in robots used in production systems, and the development of robots that move automatically, such as hands that grasp parts and paint sprayers, began. The advanced production technology of these robots supported Japan's rapid economic growth in the 1980s [1,2].

The 1990s saw the emergence of new fields of robotics, such as Honda's ASIMO and Sony's AIBO. Robots expanded from the field of manufacturing to

This work was supported by JSPS KAKENHI Grant Number JP21H03765.

C. Stephanidis et al. (Eds.): HCII 2023, CCIS 1958, pp. 181–188, 2024.
https://doi.org/10.1007/978-3-031-49215-0_22

the field of service, and furthermore became the subject of developing research and development using them: research and development of humanoid robots became active from the late 1990s onwards. In today's society, many humanoid robots have been created and may assist in all aspects of daily life in future societies. While the development of humanoid robots was active, the idea of the 'uncanny valley phenomenon' was proposed by robotics engineer Masahiro Mori in 1970. This is the valley of human feelings towards an artificial robot when its shape and movements become closer to those of humans. As a humanoid robot approaches human form and movement, humans feel closer to the robot. However, when the similarity between the robot and the human passes a certain point, the feeling of closeness is suddenly lost and turns to dislike. This sudden drop in emotion is called *valley*. It is said that this valley can be overcome by making the robot resemble a human so closely that it can be recognised as a human [3].

We, however, have been going to another extreme: we reported simplified design of humanoids while it has rich facial expressions and investigated its effectiveness [4]. This report shows further investigation of *micro-expressions* of facial expressions, which we, human being, are considered to use every time.

2   Experiment

As mentioned in our previous research, no cultural differences were found between Japan and Europe in the way facial expressions are made, but there are still differences between Europe and Japan in the way emoticons are made and other emotional expressions. [5] The differences in subtle facial expressions, such as those in everyday life, are not known, so subtle facial expressions are explored. The investigation in this paper is not about reading the subtle facial expressions individually, but about the phenomenon of emotional synchronisation, in which the facial expressions of two people are synchronised.

2.1   Experimental Material

In order to investigate whether the phenomenon of emotional synchronisation exists and, if so, whether it is universal, a subject experiment was conducted using a manga in which emotions are expressed visually in chronological order. Specifically, multiple subjects are asked to read the same manga in which multiple characters appear, and to answer which frame is the scene in which character A and character B "feel in sync," and by analysing their answers, the existence or non-existence of the emotional synchronisation phenomenon is shown, and if it exists, whether it is universal or not.

The manga used in the investigation of emotional synchronisation should satisfy the following conditions.

A Romance Manga. It should be a romance manga work because it depicts changes in emotions between the characters and it is easy to understand whether the emotions are synchronised in the story.

Rich Facial Expressions. The work should be a romance manga work because it depicts changes in emotions between the characters and it is easy to tell whether or not the emotions are synchronised in the story.

Translated into English. The work must have been translated into English so that the same survey can be conducted overseas.

Fall in Love with Each Other Within Three Volumes. The subjects are asked to actually read and respond to the manga, so even if it is a long work, the romance must begin by the end of the third volume, so that the subjects can maintain their concentration.

Good Quality of the Artwork. To have the subjects answer whether or not their emotions are synchronised by looking at the facial expressions of the characters, the quality of the drawings must be maintained and the facial expressions drawn in a way that is easy to understand.

As manga satisfying these conditions, this paper selected the first three volumes of *High School Debut (Kazune Kawahara, Shueisha, 2004)* as the subjects for investigating the phenomenon of emotional synchronisation. The manga has the following story. [6]

Haruna Nagashima, who was devoted to club activities in junior high school, makes her "high school debut" with the intention of having a boyfriend in high school and having a wonderful love life. However, despite her own efforts to be popular, she shows no sign of finding a boyfriend. Then she meets Yoh Komiyama, a senior at the same high school who knows how to attract men, and is asked to be a "popularity coach" on the condition that she never falls in love with him.

High School Debut has the following characters.

Haruna Nagashima. Main character. In junior high school, she poured everything she had into her club activities (softball club), but she longed for the world of girls' manga, which was her other purpose in life, and decided to devote herself entirely to romance in high school. However, because she has only been interested in softball, she doesn't know how to be popular with men, and she realises that she can only do so much on her own, so she asks Yoh Komiyama, a man she met by chance on the street who understands how to be popular with men, to coach her on how to be popular.

Yoh Komiyama. Haruna's senior student. He is popular with the girls because of his cool atmosphere and well-defined face. He is very popular with the girls; he gets hit on the opposite way when he goes out on the town, confesses his love to all the girls in his class at primary schools, and brings home chocolates in a rubbish bag for cleaning on Valentine's Day. When he met Haruna, he was traumatised by his popularity due to a girlfriend he had in junior high school, but he overcame his trauma after meeting Haruna. At first, he coached Haruna's popularity on the condition that she would not fall for him.

Komiyama Mami. Yoh's younger sister. In the same grade as Haruna. Like Yoh, she has a good-looking face and always attracts the opposite sex.

Tamura Fumiya. Friend of Yoh. He is very kind and mild-mannered to every-one, but extremely slow. He is often pushed around by his girlfriend Asami.

Fig. 1. Taking questionaire at Kyoto University of Art, Japan

2.2   Experimental Set-Up

A questionnaire sheet on the phenomenon of emotional synchronisation was pre-pared. In the questionnaire, the subjects were asked to answer the gender, age, number of volumes, number of pages, frames and names of the people in the scenes in which they thought their emotions were synchronised. The subject experiment was conducted on 3 December 2021 with 10 students (female: 6, male: 3, unanswered: 1) from *the Department of Character Design, Faculty of Art, Kyoto University of Art.* (Fig. 1) Questionnaire sheets numbered consecu-tively from volume 1 to volume 3 of *High School Debut* were distributed. After the start of the class, we invited those who would cooperate with the question-naire in the classroom, explained the phenomenon of emotional synchronisation and the items to be filled in, and asked them to answer about the emotional synchronisation by looking at the frames rather than the flow of the story. We also explained that some of the pages did not have page numbers, so if the page numbers were not known, the students were asked to write down the dialogue so that they could identify which scene they were talking about. We encouraged them to send their answers by e-mail, and told them that we wanted them to send their answers in a way that we could see them and that they did not have to return the manga. Students of *the Department of Character Design, Faculty of Art, Kyoto University of Arts,* were chosen as subjects because they are often exposed to visual expressions on a daily basis and have a strong interest in char-acter design. In accordance with previous research, the flow of time in the manga was counted in terms of the number of frames [7].

3   Experimental Results

Nine out of ten subjects responded (female: 6, male: 3). As each frame of *High School Debut* is not numbered, all frames were numbered consecutively.

- Two female respondents answered that Haruna Nagashima and Fumiya Tamura were synchronized in the 774th frame of the volume 1. (Fig. 2a)
- One female and two males answered that Haruna Nagashima and Fumiya Tamura were synchronised in the 783rd frame of the volume 1. (Fig. 2b)
- Two males answered that Haruna Nagashima and Fumiya Tamura synchronised at the 836th frame of the volume 1. (Fig. 2c)
- Two women and one man answered that Haruna Nagashima and Fumiya Tamura were synchronised in the 870th frame of the volume 1. (Fig. 2d)
- One female and two males answered that Haruna Nagashima and Fumiya Tamura were synchronised in frame 1150 of the volume 2. (Fig. 3a)
- Three female respondents answered that Mami Komiyama and Fumiya Tamura synchronised at the 1604th of the volume 2. (Fig. 3b)
- Two males answered that Haruna Nagashima and Yoh Komiyama synchronised in the 1609th frame of the volume 2. (Fig. 3c)
- Four females and two males answered that Haruna Nagashima and Yoh Komiyama were synchronised in the 1852nd frame of the volume 2. (Fig. 3d)
- Four women answered that Haruna Nagashima and Yoh Komiyama were synchronised in the 2341st frame of the volume 3. (Fig. 4a)
- One woman and two men answered that Haruna Nagashima and Yoh Komiyama were synchronised in the 2349th frame of the volume 3. (Fig. 4b)
- One woman and one man answered that Haruna Nagashima and Yoh Komiyama were synchronised in the 2353rd of the volume 3. (Fig. 4c)
- Three female respondents answered that Haruna Nagashima and Yoh Komiyama synchronised in the 2362nd frame of the volume 3. (Fig. 4d)
- Two female respondents said that Haruna Nagashima and Yoh Komiyama synchronised in the 2488th frame of the volume 3. (Fig. 4e)
- Three female and one male respondent said that Haruna Nagashima and Yoh Komiyama were synchronised in frame 2622 of the volume 3. (Fig. 4f)

From the results of *High School Debut,* volume 1, it was found that many respondents felt that Haruna Nagashima and Fumiya Tamura were emotionally synchronised in the scenes where they were on a date (Figs. 2a and 2b), Haruna Nagashima and Fumiya Tamura were talking at school   (Fig. 2c) and Haruna Nagashima and Fumiya Tamura were going home together (Fig. 2d). The results showed that many people felt that the emotions were synchronized in the scene where Haruna Nagashima and Fumiya Tamura go home together (Fig. 2d).

The results from *High School Debut,* volume 2 showed that the following scenes were identified: a scene in which Haruna Nagashima and Tamura Fumiya were on a date (Fig. 3a), a scene in which Komiyama Mami reaffirmed her feelings for her boyfriend Tamura Fumiya (Fig. 3b), a scene in which Yoh Komiyama's feelings were conveyed to Haruna Nagashima (Fig. 3c), a scene in which Haruna

Nagashima found that she had feelings for Yoh Komiyama (Fig. 3d), and a scene in which Yoh Komiyama found that Haruna Nagashima had feelings for Yoh Komiyama (Fig. 4a). The most common reason for this was that the characters' feelings were synchronised in the scene where Haruna Nagashima found out that Haruna Nagashima had feelings for Yoh Komiyama (Fig. 3d).

The results for volume 3 of High School Debut show that many respondents felt that Haruna Nagashima's feelings were synchronised in the scene where she confessed her feelings to Yoh Komiyama (Figs. 4a, 4b, 4c, and 4d) and in the scene after Haruna Nagashima and Yoh Komiyama started dating (Figs. 4e and 4f).

Fig. 2. From left to right: (a) frame 774, (b) frame 783, (c) frame 836, (d) frame 870 of *High Shcool Debut* volume 1.

Fig. 3. From left to right: (a) frame 1150, (b) frame 1604, (c) frame 1609, (d) frame 1852 of *High Shcool Debut* volume 2.

Fig. 4. From left to right: (a) frame 2341, (b) frame 2349, (c) frame 2353, (d) frame 2362, (e) frame 2488, (f) frame 2622 of *High Shcool Debut* volume 3.

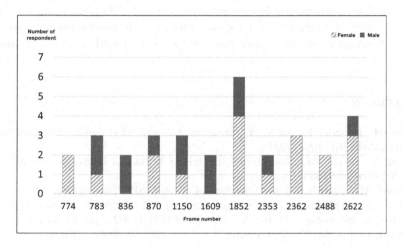

Fig. 5. Gender differences of the result

4   Discussion and Conclusion

From this experiment, we were able to find a methodology to investigate how to read subtle facial expressions between two people. Furthermore, Fig. 5 shows that there are gender differences in the responses. When we examined the gender differences between specific characters, we found that the standard deviation was smaller for women than for men, and that there was less variation in the timing of where the emotions were synchronised. This may be due to the fact that women can read facial expressions better than men, or that women are more familiar with the grammar of shōjo manga. As described above, this research method has revealed that there are gender differences in the reading of micro-expressions. We therefore believe that this research method can be used as a means of discovering not only differences by gender, but also differences by age and cultural differences. Since the survey was conducted on ten Japanese art students, we believe that this method can be made more reliable by conducting additional surveys on students with different attributes. At the same time, it is thought that there will be new findings on the synchronisation of emotions according to gender and age. We believe that conducting a survey on emotional synchronisation using this method will be useful for designing more friendly robot facial expressions.

We described an investigation into the phenomenon of emotional synchronisation, in which subtle differences in facial expressions, such as in everyday life, are not read individually, but rather as a synchronisation of facial expressions between two people. As a result, it was found that there were differences in responses between men and women, and from this experiment a methodology was found to investigate how to read subtle facial expressions between two people. We believe that this method can be used as a means of investigating cultural differences between Japan and other countries. In the future, we aim to conduct similar research in other regions, find more detailed differences in facial expression recognition, and apply the results to the facial design of humanoid robots.

References

1. Inoue, H., Kanade, T., Anzai, Y., Sena, H.: Creation of Robotics. Iwanami Shoten (2004). ISBN 978-4000112413
2. Shirai, Y., Asada, M.: Robots in Our Daily Life. Osaka University Press (2001). ISBN 978-4872591033
3. Ishiguro, H.: What is a Robot? Kodansha (2009). ISBN 978-4062880237
4. Tawaki, M., Yamamoto, K., Kanaya, I.: Cultural difference of simplified facial expressions for humanoids. In: Proceedings of IHIET 2021, pp. 37–43 (2021)
5. Kanaya, I., Tawaki, M., Yamamoto, K.: Cross-cultural design of facial expressions for humanoids-is there cultural difference between Japan and Denmark? Proceedings of ACM Multimedia Asia (2020)
6. High School Debut. https://ja.wikipedia.org/wiki/. Accessed 16 Feb 2022
7. Makita, M.: Eromanga Statistics STARS. Circle Deihima (2014)

Designing Immersive Experiences
in Extended Reality and the Metaverse

iLab-Gloves--Design of AR Experimental Gloves Based on Ergonomics and Force Feedback Technology

Qi Ai👁 and Xin He(✉)👁

School of Mechanical Science and Engineering, Huazhong University of Science and Technology, Wuhan, China
xinh@hust.edu.cn

Abstract. Experimental operations have always been a necessary link in popular science education. However, due to regional differences in educational resources, difficulty in operation for novice experimenters, the danger of some experiments, and the scarcity of consumables, virtual experiments for students are expected by the public. Based on flexible microfluidic sensing technology, this paper proposes an AR glove with a subtle force feedback effect, specially used for virtual experiments and teaching. In order to provide more accurate force feedback to the hand skin, we entered university laboratories, observed and analysed the standard hand movements of laboratory operators to collect data on force feedback points, and integrated them into the design of microfluidic AR gloves. In the end, 13 necessary sensing parts for each hand were obtained, which were integrated into the design to achieve a more accurate experimental force feedback effect.

Keywords: AR Gloves · Force Feedback · Microfluidic

1 Introduction

Laboratory courses have been argued to be an essential part of science education [1], while university laboratory teaching is restricted by various factors such as equipment, time, space, cost, and epidemic prevention and control [2], so the teaching effect is limited. Based on this situation, we designed a force feedback glove specially for AR experimental operation based on microfluidic sensing technology to assist AR experimental teaching in colleges and universities.

Force Feedback Data Gloves (FFDG) are an ideal interface device for human-computer interaction [2]. At present, hand force feedback can realise force sensing in a virtual environment and is mostly used in large-scale virtual gunfight games, medical treatment, and surgery. During the interaction between a slave robot and the environment, it is difficult to provide accurate control commands to the slave robot if the operator cannot feel the interaction force. [2] And because of the rigor of scientific experiments, the operator has higher requirements for the accuracy of the feedback force.Only by accurately feedbacking the tactile sensation during the experiment can users have a more accurate psychological estimate of their own operations. In this paper, through the collection

C. Stephanidis et al. (Eds.): HCII 2023, CCIS 1958, pp. 191–197, 2024.
https://doi.org/10.1007/978-3-031-49215-0_23

and research of hand movement data in the experimental operating environment, based on the research results of force feedback technology and functional structure (microfluidic sensing technology), design and improvement are carried out. This AR glove for experimental operation and teaching is produced to meet the action requirements of virtual experimental operation.

2 Literature Review

2.1 AR Gloves

At present, AR gloves dedicated to experimental operations are relatively rare, but there have been many studies on AR gloves with similar sensing functions, such as the HAPTX GLOVES DK2, which is the first enterprise-level VR tactile glove released by HAPTX in the UnitedStates [Fig. 1]. Compared with the previous generation, it has a smaller size, a lighter weight, and more ergonomic features. Technically, it uses a microfluidic control system for sensing, making the whole pair of gloves more portable and beautiful. However, DK2 still has problems such as not being soft enough, high cost, and rough somatosensory simulation. Therefore, we decided to continue the use of microfluidic sensing while conducting further research on the hand force area of the experimental operation, covering the necessary hand area with the microfluidic control system sensor, thereby optimising the fineness of sensing.

2.2 Microfluidic Control System for Sensing

In the research of microfluidic sensing technology, Meta Reality Labs has made breakthroughs in the fields of pneumatic actuators and electroactive actuators. The resistance is generated by air pressure, and the shape and size of the actuator are changed by the electric field to achieve the force feedback effect [Fig. 2. Prototype]. This driver is small in size, light in weight, and highly flexible. It can be installed in detail to achieve sensing effects, thereby generating more refined force feedback on the force-bearing parts. Based on this advantage, this paper applies this technical achievement to the conceptual design of AR gloves.

Fig. 1. HAPTX GLOVES DK2

Fig. 2. Prototype

3   Research Process

3.1   Data Collection

During the experimental operation, the operator's hand sensitivity requirements are very high, and the hand behaviour is also relatively complicated. In order to collect the data on the force point of the hand during the experiment more accurately, this paper adopts the behavioural observation method for research. Behavioural observation is one of several measurement approaches available to investigators engaged in quantitative behavioural research. It is usually the method of choice when studying non-general, non-verbal behaviour [5]. The content of the research is to observe and sample the standardised hand operations of the subjects during the experiment, and then analyse and summarise. In order to improve the comprehensiveness of the data, this paper selected a variety of experiments in the three disciplines of physics, chemistry, and biology and carried out observations on five subjects with rich experimental experience and standardised operations. All of the observation samples came from university students in China. The following describe the subjects' individual traits [see Table 1].

Table 1. The observed individual and the corresponding experimental operation content

Observation object	Gender	Major	Operation content
Object 1	Female	School of Life and Science	liquid experiment
Object 2	Male	School of Energy and Power	Particle image velocimetry experiment
Object 3	Male	School of Mechanical Science and Engineering	Medical puncture surgery robot hand testing, electronic component soldering, oscilloscope operation
Object 4	Female	School of Mechanical Science and Engineering	KUKA robotic arm operation
Object 5	Male	School of Mechanical Science and Engineering	Ecoflex flexible capacitive sensor fabrication
Object 6	Female	School of Life and Science	Liquid Chromatography Analysis Experiment

3.2   Motion Capture and Force Feedback Analysis

During the test, we fully recorded the liquid phase experiment, particle image velocity measurement and other experiments, and also sampled basic equipment operations: medical puncture robot hand operation, electronic component welding, Ecoflex flexible capacitive sensor production, KUKA robotic arm operation and other behaviors [Fig. 3], and then capture and analyze the above-mentioned behavioral samples [Fig. 4], and mark the force-bearing parts of the hand operation.

Fig. 3. Observation records (excerpts)

Fig. 4. Preliminary collection of force points

Based on the force points obtained from the analysis [Fig. 5], the components that will receive force feedback in the basic operation of the laboratory are summarised, and these components will provide design reference for the installation of flexible microfluidic sensors on the gloves.

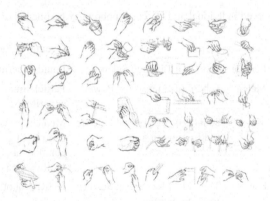

Fig. 5. Atlas of force points for hand movements (excerpts)

3.3   Force Feedback Point Data Integration

On the basis of the atlas of the force points obtained, the collection map of the force points of the hand is sorted out [Fig. 6], and then the key force feedback areas of the hand during the experiment are summarized according to the set of key force feedback points [Fig. 7].

4   Force Feedback Experimental Operation AR Glove Design

According to the obtained key force-bearing areas in the virtual experiment, an AR glove based on microfluidic technology is designed [Fig. 8]. Combining the research results of the force feedback parts in this paper with the microfluidic control system achieves higher sensing accuracy.

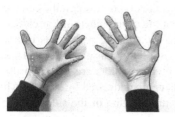

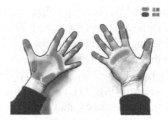

Fig. 6. A collection of stress points for force feedback

Fig. 7. Forced part

Fig. 8. Product design sketch

Under the structure of flexible microfluidic sensing technology, an adjustable fingertip sensing full-enclosed design is adopted. The microfluidic pipeline is attached to the shell of the fingertip, and the sensing pieces on both sides are connected through the pipeline to realize the side sensing of the fingertip. The internal structure is embedded in the shell of the finger cot. [Fig. 9, Fig. 10], the outer shell is equipped with adjustable tracks to enhance the wearing comfort and general fit of the glove.

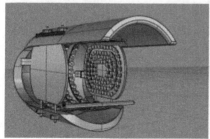

Fig. 9. Structure of fingertip microfluidic sensing device

Fig. 10. Fingertip structure perspective

Fingertip microfluidic sensing is the control of fluid through blue catheters [Fig. 10]. When the user touches the object in the virtual experiment, the microfluidic sensor operates, and the corresponding amount of microfluid is input through the catheter, and the force feedback of the hand is realized by the scaling of the inner microfluidic airbag. Considering the size difference of human hands, the sensing part needs to adopt an adjustable design. The fabric material of the gloves already has elasticity, but the parts cannot be adjusted automatically. To solve this problem, slots are made on the parts during design [Fig. 11], and the side sensing parts can be adjusted by screws. After the user wears the gloves, they can move and adjust the position of the side sensing parts according to your hand size.

The overall design effect is shown in Fig. 12, and the basic specifications of the product are shown in Table 2.

Fig. 11. Blue Conduit and Adjustable Parts

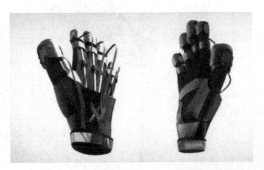

Fig. 12. Overall design effect

Table 2. The basic specifications of the product

Object	Value
Glove length	25 cm
Glove width	13 cm
Material elasticity	Polyester and plastic
Sensing finger cuff width	2.5 cm
Catheter length	20 cm

5   Conclusion

In this paper, by observing and collecting the hand movements of the experimental operation, summarising the necessary stress points during the laboratory operation, and combining the latest flexible microfluidic sensing technology, a set of AR gloves dedicated to the virtual experimental operation is designed. Make the AR gloves for the virtual experiment lighter and softer while optimising the sensing area, making the sensing part more accurate. However, it is worth reflecting that the operation of the laboratory is very extensive, and our research sample has yet to be expanded. Finally, I would like to thank the classmates and teachers who gave us generous help during the research process, allowing us to have the opportunity to observe the standard experimental operations in various laboratories, and also thank my supervisors for their guidance in the process of research and design. During this process, I gained a lot of new knowledge and accumulated experience doing research.

References

1. Hofstein, A., Lunetta, V.N.: The Role of Laboratory in science education: foundations for the twenty-first century. Sci. Educ. **88**, 28–54 (2003)
2. Rao, X., Mai, J., Zeng, Q., et al.: Analysis of the application of cloud classroom in the teaching reform of college laboratories. Eng. Technol. Res. **7**(23), 155–156+169 (2022). https://doi.org/10.19537/j.cnki.2096-2789.2022.23.050
3. Wang, D., Wang, Y., Pang, J., Wang, Z., Zi, B.: Development and control of an MR brake-based passive force feedback data glove. IEEE Access **7**, 172477–172488 (2019). https://doi.org/10.1109/ACCESS.2019.2956954
4. Xuan, X.: Exploration of VR technology in the teaching of international education experiment courses. Sci. Technol. Vision **31**, 102–104 (2022). https://doi.org/10.19694/j.cnki.issn2095-2457.2022.31.27
5. Bakeman, R., Quera, V.: Behavioral Observations–13. Springer, Heidelberg (2016)

AR Dance Learning App with a Feedback Feature Through Pose Estimation: DancÆR

İremsu Baş, Demir Alp, Lara Ceren Ergenç, Andy Emre Koçak, and Sedat Yalçın[✉]

Hisar School Computer Science ideaLab, Istanbul, Turkey
{iremsu.bas,demir.alp,lara.ergenc,emre.kocak,
sedat.yalcin}@hisarschool.k12.tr

Abstract. In recent years, educational philosophies have slowly begun shifting to focus on differentiated and self-learning systems. In this regard, creating opportunities to further self-learning resources has become increasingly important. The creation of such platforms or opportunities for physical education, however, proves to be more difficult as individuals require continuous and precise feedback regarding the usage of their bodies. Accordingly, we have developed an augmented reality application that presents a platform for dance that focuses on differentiated and self-learning principles with accurate feedback. We built the AR app using the Swift programming language and used the Core ML action classification model to capture the body position. We also recognize the importance of social interaction in learning, such as its benefits to motivation or peer-to-peer support. As a result, we designed the app to allow its users to connect with their friends globally and dance together. We do this by converting the captured poses of various users from different locations during a live session and instantaneously converting them into AR avatars. This way, the users can dance with their friends live, emphasizing the undeniably social component of dance and learning while going through the learning process at their own pace.

Keywords: Augmented Reality · Dance · Avatars · Collaborative Interaction · Machine Learning · Human-computer interaction

1 Introduction

Dance is an incredibly influential medium in which many cultures throughout the span of history have expressed themselves. It has been a significant part of many religions and various cultural identities. One of the main aspects behind this substantial presence of dance within history is its efficiency as a tool of expression and social bonding. This is still accurate today, as research indicates that dance can significantly increase feelings of closeness among groups [1]. As a result, dance stands out as a tool that, in many ways, is inherent to how humans socialize and, in turn, express themselves. This makes a focus on dance in education much more valuable. On top of this, dance is closely associated with physiological and psychological benefits to individuals, specifically adolescents as well. Dance allows adolescents' physical fitness to be impacted positively while improving

C. Stephanidis et al. (Eds.): HCII 2023, CCIS 1958, pp. 198–204, 2024.
https://doi.org/10.1007/978-3-031-49215-0_24

their sleep cycle and motor skills, as well as improving their overall health due to its medical benefits [2]. It also facilitates the improvement of mental state, well-being, confidence, and perceived competence [2]. As a result, a focus on dance in physical education can become highly beneficial, improving the students in various ways, both physically and emotionally. This is why this study will focus on new physical education methods through dance via applications of AR and AI systems within DancÆR through its feedback systems, creating an interactive space for our users.

In this regard, it is important to recognize that feedback is a crucial component of effective learning since it helps learners to reflect on their own performance and identify knowledge gaps. Feedback helps to bridge the gap between the current level of understanding and the desired level of understanding. It should provide guidance or assistance to the learner to help them progress towards their learning goals. According to Hattie et al. feedbacks can take various forms and can be delivered in different ways, such as by positively influencing learners' attitudes and behaviors or by using cognitive processes like modifying their existing understanding, validating their responses, highlighting the need for additional information, suggesting alternative approaches, or providing guidance on how to progress [4, 5].

Types of feedback that influence educational environments are heavily used within our prototype as in summative and formative feedback forms. It is considered a formative assessment when the learner revises their work more than once according to continuous feedback, and it is considered a summative assessment when the work done by the learner is evaluated at the end of the learning process. The most effective way of learning occurs when both feedback types work together. Formative and summative evaluation processes are inseparable; they complete the whole process. These feedbacks work like diagnostic measurements; they conclude information about the initial state of the student, the distance between the start and the targeted level, and the learner's ability to apply the present acquired knowledge to different situations and where difficulties are faced [3, 10].

Human-Computer Interaction (HCI) is a crucial discipline that enables us to design, evaluate, and create effective interactive computer systems that meet the needs and expectations of users. Designing effective HCI courses requires a combination of theoretical and practical knowledge, with a focus on the application of this knowledge in real-world settings. In recent years, the demand for professionals with "skills in HCI has increased rapidly because of the increasing importance of digital technologies and the growing need for user-centered design. User-centered design (UCD) technology and student-centered education are two concepts that share a common goal of putting the needs, interests, and preferences of learners at the forefront of the design process. By combining these two concepts, we can create learning experiences that are more personalized, engaging, and effective. Therefore, HCI plays an important role in education by providing a framework for designing effective digital learning environments that enhance student engagement, learning, and motivation. HCI in education refers to the study and design of educational technology that supports teaching and learning activities, which involves the use of interactive technologies to support learning. It allows for the creation of digital learning environments that are tailored to the needs and preferences of learners [12]. Our DancÆR prototype can be seen as an application of HCI in education, as it involves the use of interactive technologies to support learning in the context of dance. By using augmented reality (AR) technology, learners can engage with the content in a more immersive and interactive way, allowing them to better understand and practice dance movements.

2 Related Works

Exergames such as Just Dance and Dance Central are famously known for spreading dance exercises for entertainment purposes in which the user follows a teacher displayed on the screen and tries to imitate their movements. For self-learning choreographies, Youtube dance tutorial videos, similar to exergames, embrace a traditional teaching style. These videos are different from exergames: a tutor explains the choreography step-by-step and then combines the choreography with music. The methodology of education through our application will focus on this principle with the assumption that when paired with personalized feedback, it will increase users' learning rate and accuracy level. One shortcoming of exergames and tutorial videos is that they don't provide sufficient feedback to users, which interrupts users' ability to learn and improve their dance moves. To address this problem, Chan et al. proposed a virtual reality dance training system providing feedback utilizing a motion capture system [18]. Another system with feedback is proposed by Tian et al. using a joint tracking algorithm and Unity, focusing more on cultural dances [17]. In Choi et al.'s proposal, the feedback algorithm for joint tracking using pose estimation models is detailedly investigated, where they conclude that the best feedback is achieved by comparing the teacher and student's joint position and angular similarity [14, 15]. A counterpart application is designed by Shen et al. for a yoga self-exercising system that checks the synchronization of the instructor and the learner [16]. Our proposal focuses on improving the learning rate of the students by teaching the choreography step by step, then moving on to practicing the moves with the music, providing accurate and appropriate feedback by employing pose estimation and joint tracking. We tried to imitate a face-to-face dance classroom's teaching and learning environment with self-training and address the greatest problems of online dance education.

3 AR Dance Instruction

The project, DancÆR, will function as a step-by-step choreography learning application with built-in functions that guide users in learning dance routines. Our application has three main interfaces: the home page that allows the user to choose the dance session, the AR dance session page, and the self-evaluation page. The application will first introduce users to dance routines sourced from various online sources and dance databases, such as AIST Dance Video Database [20]. Once our algorithm analyzes the chosen routine, it will break down each choreography into step-by-step movements in accordance with rhythm-based segmentation of the backing track. After that, the application will present the movements to the user through a generated AR instructor that shows the progressive movements to the sound of metronomic counting that starts with a much slower tempo as opposed to the song itself. Afterward, the user will begin to mimic the movements of the instructor while the algorithm will analyze the movements of the user, comparing them to the original data provided [19], and then correct the movements by projecting the correct positioning onto the screen of the user in a low opacity avatar that we call movement markers which the user will try to fill completely when dancing. Fundamentally, on the AR dance session page, the user will be constantly tracked and given feedback by a pose classification system that we trained utilizing joint tracking and pose estimation. Additionally, the user's session will be recorded, which will appear on the self-evaluation page. Our ML model will provide the user with the mistakes in their dance movements by the red marks on the video timeline bar, both positionally and rhythmically, and the user will be able to improve their performance with this feedback. To create this feedback system, we decided to use a weighted approach where there would be two considerations when determining the accuracy of the user: live feedback from joint movement data and pose classification. For the live feedback during the AR dance session, our algorithm compares the teacher's joint position's ratios and the angles between joints to the students'. We were inspired by the proposal of Choi et al., which is a dance pose evaluation that simultaneously performs an affine transformation and an evaluation method to compare the joint position and joint angle information [15] (Fig. 1).

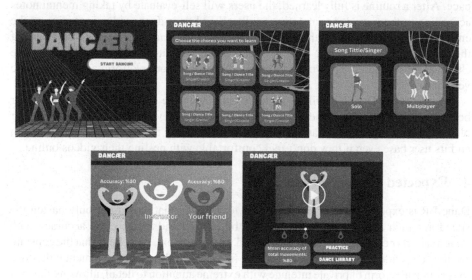

Fig. 1. The user interface of DancÆR

With this system, as the dancing experience of each student will be optimized using our trained AI models, the user will also continue learning the choreographies at their own speed, assuring that no instruction is too fast or slow-paced for our users. On top of this, the instructor will also provide the user with general advice, such as suggestions regarding the fluidity of movement. After the user's accuracy with which they carry out the movements increases to 85%, the instructor will slowly begin speeding up the tempo. After the original tempo of the choreography is reached, the instructor will begin to introduce the backing track at half speed after the user reaches 95% accuracy. The instructor will also provide the user with cues on top of the backing track, signaling when to switch movements. After a routine is learned and carried out at 100% of its original speed, the instructor will ask the user to perform it. Afterward, a score and general feedback will be provided. This will allow the users to have a significantly more enjoyable experience as the score provided will function as a form of gamification since each time a user gets to 100% accuracy on a new choreography, they will gain a set amount of points corresponding to the difficulty level of the routine [9, 11]. The users will also have the option of sharing their performance on the DancÆR platform and other social media platforms, further emphasizing the social aspect of dance and allowing users to engage with their peers. Furthermore, we recognize the importance of social interaction in learning, such as its benefits to motivation or peer-to-peer support. Thus, we design the app to allow its users to connect with their friends globally and dance together. This could be done by converting the captured poses of various users from different locations during a live session and instantaneously converting them into AR avatars while also synchronizing their movements with music and eliminating the video and audio delay. This way, the users can dance with their friends live and synchronously, where collaboration and prosociality heighten [1], emphasizing the undeniably social component of dance and learning while going through the learning process at their own pace. After a routine is fully learned, the users will self-evaluate by taking mental notes according to the provided summative feedback and their dance video recording at the end of the dance session. With these constructive criticisms, the user will be aware of the parts they need or want to improve; they will be able to change certain parts of the choreography to add their own spin to it and upload it to our platform as an alternative version.

Furthermore, DancÆR will provide its users with the opportunity to replace their bodies with a 2D avatar if they want to keep a certain level of anonymity within our platform, allowing them to have the option of continuing to engage with our platform and its user base even if they don't feel comfortable with posting their videos online.

4   Expected Research Plan

DancÆR is expected to function as a vital technology that would not only hasten the speed at which a dance choreography can be learned and increase the accuracy with which said choreography could be performed. In this context, we believe that the constant feedback provided through the platform that fixes and guides every movement will prove to function as a form of private tutelage with extreme attention to detail, allowing the user to feel more confident in their performance as well. Thus we believe that DancÆR will allow the user to become more proficient in dance and have a markedly positive emotional experience regarding the process. After these claims are tested through experimentation, DancÆR will be further optimized in order to provide a smoother user experience. Its feedback methods will be improved upon, and the necessary alterations will be made to its AI feedback algorithm.

The testing procedure will be executed under one experimental group that tests DancÆR compared to a control group that will utilize forms of non-interactive instruction without feedback, those seen in online dance videos, etc. The overall sample will be 200 people assorted into groups via random assignment. The sample will be collected within the Hisar High School population and other affiliated high schools through random selection to reflect the project's target audience. With this in mind, a selected choreography of intermediate difficulty will be presented to both groups (control and experimental), and participants will be given a time frame of two weeks to learn the choreography and be evaluated on the accuracy, timing as well as flow (reduced rigidness) of movement [21]. Within the experimental group, for two weeks, participants will practice the dance routine with the guidance of DancÆR's feedback, whereas the control group will practice independently through mimicry of the provided instruction video. Afterward, the evaluation will be carried out through the usage of our AI algorithm and other similar ML systems, trained with videos and images of professional dancers performing the routine. However, the experiment will also evaluate participants' emotional experience while also considering the effects of certain confounding variables, such as previous experience in dance. This is why participants will fill out a detailed questionnaire where they are required to express their experience in dance and other forms of sports as well as experience in music and art in order to provide us with insight into how history in music, art, and/or physical exercise can influence the results of their performance. Moreover, the questionnaire will also acquire detailed information regarding how the participants felt throughout the process, such as their levels of confidence, engagement, or enjoyment. Through analyzing both qualitative and quantitative data, the testing process will prove a vital part of DancÆR's future and the direction it will take when furthering the prototype.

5 Conclusion

Dance is a form of art that is enjoyable to watch and has several physical and emotional benefits. It is a great form of exercise that improves flexibility, strength, balance, and coordination. In recent years, digital environments and computer vision technologies have been utilized in various ways in the field of dance. Our prototype for DancÆR is an example of how artificial intelligence (AI) and augmented reality (AR) can be used to enhance the learning experience of dancers. Our system uses pose classification technology to enhance the learning experience of the students and provides immediate, informative feedback through one-by-one movement training and summative feedback for a self-reflection opportunity, encouraging development, creativity, and exploration.

References

1. Reddish, P., Fischer, R., Bulbulia, J.: Let's dance together: synchrony, shared intentionality and cooperation. PLoS ONE **8**(8), e71182 (2013)
2. Tao, D., et al.: The physiological and psychological benefits of dance and its effects on children and adolescents: a systematic review. Front. Physiol. **13** (2022)
3. Shute, V.J.: Focus on formative feedback. Rev. Educ. Res. **78**(1), 153–189 (2008)
4. Boud, D., Molloy, E.: Rethinking models of feedback for learning: the challenge of design. Assess. Eval. High. Educ. **38**(6), 698–712 (2013)
5. Hattie, J., Timperley, H.: The power of feedback. Rev. Educ. Res. **77**, 81–112 (2016)
6. Shea, C., Wulf, G.: Enhancing motor learning through external-focus instructions and feedback. Hum. Mov. Sci. **18**(4), 553–571 (1999)

7. Wulf, G., Mcconnel, N., Gärtner, M., Schwarz, A.: Enhancing the learning of sport skills through external-focus feedback. J. Mot. Behav. **34**(2), 171–182 (2002)
8. Nowels, R.G., Hewit, J.K.: Improved learning in physical education through immediate video feedback. Strategies **31**(6), 5–9 (2018)
9. Badami, R., VaezMousavi, M., Wulf, G., Namazizadeh, M.: Feedback about more accurate versus less accurate trials. Res. Q. Exerc. Sport **83**(2), 196–203 (2012)
10. Baht, B.A., Bhat, G.J.: Formative and summative evaluation techniques for improvement of learning process. Eur. J. Bus. Soc. Sci. **7**(5), 776–785 (2019)
11. García-Dantas, A., Quested, E.: The effect of manipulated and accurate assessment feedback on the self-efficacy of dance students. J. Dance Med. Sci. **19**(1), 22–30 (2015)
12. Lin, L., Qiu, J., Lao, J.: Intelligent human-computer interaction: a perspective on software engineering. In: The 14th International Conference on Computer Science & Education (ICCSE 2019), Toronto, Canada, pp. 488–492 (2019)
13. Raheb, K.E., Stergiou, M., Katifori, A., Ioannidis, Y.: Dance interactive learning systems: a study on interaction workflow and teaching approaches. ACM Comput. Surv. **52**(3) (2019). Article 50
14. Lee, J., Choi, J., Chuluunsaikhan, T., Nasridinov, A.: Pose evaluation for dance learning application using joint position and angular similarity. In: Adjunct Proceedings of the 2020 ACM International Joint Conference on Pervasive and Ubiquitous Computing and Proceedings of the 2020 ACM International Symposium on Wearable Computers (UbiComp-ISWC 2020), pp. 67–70. Association for Computing Machinery, New York (2020)
15. Choi, J., Lee, J., Nasridinov, A.: Dance self-learning application and its dance pose evaluations. In: Proceedings of the 36th Annual ACM Symposium on Applied Computing (SAC 2021), pp. 1037–1045. Association for Computing Machinery, New York (2021)
16. Shen, S., Huang, W., Anggraini, I.T., Funabiki, N., Fan, C.: Design of OpenPose-based of exercise assistant system with instructor-user synchronization for self-practice dynamic yoga. In: Proceedings of the 10th International Conference on Computer and Communications Management (ICCCM 2022), pp. 246–251. Association for Computing Machinery, New York (2022)
17. Tian, F., Zhu, Y., Li, Y.: Design and implementation of dance teaching system based on Unity3D. In: 6th International Conference on Intelligent Computing and Signal Processing (ICSP), pp. 1316–1320. IEEE, Xi'an (2021)
18. Chan, J.C.P., Leung, H., Tang, J.K.T., Komura, T.: A virtual reality dance training system using motion capture technology. IEEE Trans. Learn. Technol. **4**(2), 187–195 (2011)
19. Kim, Y., Kim, D., Interactive dance performance evaluation using timing and accuracy similarity. In: ACM SIGGRAPH 2018 Posters (SIGGRAPH 2018), Article 67, pp. 1–2. Association for Computing Machinery, New York (2018)
20. Tsuchida, S., Fukayama, S., Hamasaki, M., Goto. M.: AIST dance video database: multi-genre, multi-dancer, and multi-camera database for dance information processing. In: Proceedings of the 20th International Society for Music Information Retrieval Conference (ISMIR 2019) (2019)

Attention in Virtual Environments: Behavior in Locations Shapes Spatial Connectivity

Gi-bbeum Lee[1], Juhyun Lee[1], Mi Chang[2], and Ji-Hyun Lee[1(✉)]

[1] Graduate School of Culture Technology, KAIST, Daejeon, South Korea
jihyunlee@kaist.ac.kr
[2] Electronics and Telecommunications Research Institute, Daejeon, South Korea

Abstract. Unlike connections of physical spaces typically observed through movement trajectory, connections of virtual spaces can be observed in high resolution through vision-based trajectory. Studies have explored user movements and their diffusion in virtual environments (VEs). However, frameworks are needed to objectively measure vision-based behaviors in VEs and characterize spatial networks. This paper proposes a spatial mapping approach for user data through visual-spatial attention, using cognitive psychology and spatial ecology concepts. The aim was to demonstrate a computational tool that can mathematically describe the connectivity of locations based on the trajectory of user attention. We first implemented VEs to represent specific places, which were then sampled into cells, collected user location and direction data within the VEs and calculated attention areas using the direction vector, constructed spatial graphs by creating links among cells within the attention area, and finally calculated the centrality of nodes within each spatial graph and performed community detection. The tool was tested on log data from two user studies on VEs. In the results, the centrality indicated the cells where user attention was focused, and the community detection identified cell clusters. By analyzing the features of cells with high centralities, such as buildings, lakes, and non-player characters, we can identify cells with similar features that will attract attention in VEs. Using the proposed tool, a quantitative description of attention was obtained without direct feedback from users. Practically, the spatial graph can provide guidelines for designing specific areas to attract attention and help managers cluster cells for management.

Keywords: Spatial Attention · Virtual Environment · Spatial Graph

1 Introduction

In human-computer interaction (HCI), behavior and space use in virtual environments (VEs) has been an important research area because user experience can be evaluated through spatial behaviors of avatars that represent our body in a VE [1, 2]. For example, based on Hall's concept of proxemics [3], the concept of digital proxemics has emerged and highlighted users' spatial behaviors in VEs [4]. Researchers have also explored an avatar's direction and eye movement to understand visual attention in VEs [4–6]. As such, HCI research has accumulated insights and resources of spatial behavior through avatars in VEs. The resources of spatial behavior in VEs offer the opportunity to explore the connectivity of virtual space. In fields that deal with physical space, such as ecology and architecture, spatial connectivity has been studied through the movement behavior of space users [7–10]. In architecture, Panopticon showed the hierarchy of power established by the visual and spatial connection in a building [11]. An isovist, which measures the volume of visible space from an observer's position, affects the evaluation of a residence [7]. In cities, the areas with high floating populations and many roads affect the number of tourists [9].

To explore the connectivity of space in a VE, is it possible to start with the user's movement behavior using the same approach as in physical space? Unlike physical space, VE barely generates any body movement cost. Instead, it causes the cost of an attention behavior to perceive the contents of a specific area. Hence, behavioral data that can only be obtained in VE, such as change in direction rather than movement, are worth exploring. Using such behavioral data, we can measure spatial attention based on cognitive science approaches.

In this paper, we aimed to demonstrate a tool to describe spatial connectivity of locations in virtual spaces by spatial mapping of user behavior data. We explored a subset of questions about spatial connectivity in VEs:

1. What type of space do users pay attention to in a VE?
2. Will different activities shape different patterns of connection in a VE?

Through this study, we make the following contributions to the HCI community:

- We present a mathematical description of spatial connection depending on user behaviors in VEs.
- We expand previous discussions in the fields of HCI, spatial cognition, spatial ecology, and cities to the concept of connectivity in VEs.
- We propose a framework for tracking user attention in online VEs.

2 Methods

We first implemented testbeds based on real estate in two popular VEs, Gather Town and Minecraft, and sampled the spaces into cells. Then we collected log data by user studies of a virtual conference in a 2-dimensional (2D) indoor space and virtual tours in 3-dimensional (3D) outdoor space. We generated spatial graphs using the log data of avatar movement and direction. We also conducted network analysis such as calculating degree, Eigenvector centrality, and community of nodes.

2.1 Environment Design

Based on the campus of Korea Advanced Institute of Science and Technology in Daejeon City, the indoor space was implemented in the 2D platform, Gather Town, and the outdoor space was implemented in the 3D platform, Minecraft (Fig. 1).

Fig. 1. Virtual environments for user study. Environment A is Gather Town, and Environment B is Minecraft.

A building was constructed in the campus as a virtual conference venue. This space included four zones that reproduce the interior and layout of the actual building. These zones are the garden, which is the first place to be accessed, hallway connecting the zones, laboratory, and conference hall. Interactive objects were placed in each space to display information such as event schedules and past conference posters. This VE was implemented with the size of 2,405 grid cells (7,215 m^2).

Outside the lecture building, the campus includes a main gate, ponds, a bridge, and other buildings. The implementation of this environment was also described in [10]. As Fig. 4 shows, there is a loose area that includes the campus and entry and exit traffic lines, a tight area with only the inside of the campus excluding the entry and exit traffic lines, an attention area that identifies landmarks, and a non-player character (NPC) area where NPCs provide information about the campus. We set a gate, a stature, ponds, a large cherry tree, and a library building as landmarks that identify attention areas. The whole space was implemented on the size of 3,100 grid cells (12,891 m^2).

2.2 Data Collection

We opened the indoor and outdoor spaces with different activities and collected log data about visitors' spatial behaviors. An international conference was held in Gather Town in August 2022. For two days, presenters gave lectures, and breaktimes were used for socializing. Thirty-three participants (33% professors and 67% students) were invited to the event. The outdoor spaces in Minecraft were opened to the public from August to September 2022. We recruited visitors through online player communities for a free tour of the spaces. In total, our environment had 139 visitors (52.4% students and 47.6% nonstudents). All the participants experienced the environments using desktop PCs.

We built a server to collect user logs from the two VEs. The logging server automatically collected the positions and orientations of all the avatars in the VEs. As shown in Table 1, avatar positions were collected as 2D or 3D coordinates according to the platform, and avatar orientations were also collected in different formats. Gather Town stored integer values mapped to north, south, east, and west directions to indicate avatar's orientation, and Minecraft used the Euler angles of an avatar's head rotations (yaw and pitch).

Table 1. Example log data.

Platform	Timestamp	User ID	Event name	Position	Orientation
Gather Town	0811192001	7894557111	PlayerMovement	(40,26)	4
Platform	**Timestamp**	**User ID**	**Position**	**Yaw**	**Pitch**
Minecraft	0729200027	5487221145	(1052,32,55)	−7.3	148.2

2.3 Generating Spatial Graphs

The spatial graph used in this study consists of cells, vectors, and gradient based on user behavior data. According to graph theory, our graph is represented by nodes (V), edges (E), and a weight function ($f_{attention}$) (Fig. 2).

$$G = (V, E, f_{attention}) \tag{1}$$

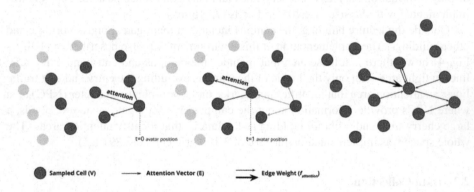

Fig. 2. Process of generating spatial attention graph.

Nodes: Sampled Cells (V). Nodes are spatial cells that represent the minimum unit for sampling VEs. In this late-breaking work, we sampled VEs with a 2D coordinate system. Thus, all nodes have paired features (x, z) based on the coordinate system. A cell node can be located at a point in the domain space using a coordinate, and the locations do not overlap with each other. A size s, which is used to sample down an area of coordinate into a cell, is configured differently depending on the size of the VE and the purpose of the VE.

For the indoor platform, 3×3 blocks were sampled ($s_1 = 3$) to capture user interactions with other users and objects. For large outdoor platforms, 10×10 blocks were sampled ($s_2 = 10$) to capture users' movement and attention.

Edges: Attention Vectors (E). Edges are spatial attention vectors representing an avatar's location and directions. First, a unit vector (d_x, d_z) is obtained: the unit vector includes the avatar's position (p_x, p_z) as the tail and the avatar's orientation as the head. With the coordinate grid matrix (B) of the VE domain, it is verified whether the vector whose head is a single coordinate and tail is the origin is an attention vector. A vector is an attention vector if it satisfies two conditions: First, the angle between the vector $(b_{ij}{}^x, b_{ij}{}^z)$ and the unit vector must be smaller than $f/2$. Second, the L2 norm of vector $(b_{ij}{}^x, b_{ij}{}^z)$ must be smaller than r.

$$B_{ixj} = (b_{ij})$$
$$b_{ij} = 0, \ |\tan^{(-1)}(b_{ij}^{(x)}, b_{ij}^{(z)}) - \tan^{(-1)}(d_x, d_z)| > f/2 \text{ or } ||(b_ij^{(x)}, b_ij^{(z)})||_2 > r \quad (2)$$
$$1, \quad \text{otherwise}$$

The coordinate grid matrix B is pooled with the mean function ($s*s$ kernel and s stride, with a sampling size s) to obtain cell matrix A with values from 0 to 1. The origin cell is connected using a directed edge with the other cell whose value exceeds 0. Here, the source node is the cell of the avatar's position, and the target node is the cell whose value pooled from B is positive. In Eq. (2), f is the field of view (FoV) in degrees, and r is a maximum length of attention.

In this work, we used Minecraft's default FoV ($60°$) for f. We also set r according to Hall's proxemics. For Gather Town, r was set as 0–4 m ($r_1 = 4$ blocks), which represented social range in Proxemics theory [3]. For Minecraft, r was set as 0–7 m ($r_2 = 10.5$ blocks), which represented the social and public range in Proxemics theory [3]. These values considered different spatial scales between Gather Town, which represented the indoor environment, and Minecraft, which represented the outdoor environment.

Weighting Function: Radial Gradient and Time ($f_{attention}$). The weight function of an edge (v_1, v_2) uses distance, angle, and time. First, the distant difference between two nodes and the angular difference between unit vector (d_x, d_z) of v_1 and the edge (v_1, v_2) were measured. The two differences were normalized and summed (See Eq. (3)). In other words, nodes closer to the avatar and to the center of the avatar's direction were calculated with a radial gradient with a higher weight. Second, the concentration weight of the edge was multiplied by time length t_w. t_w was measured in seconds, during which there was no change in the user avatar's position and orientation.

$$E_{weighted} = A\left[\left(1 - \frac{D_{dist}}{r}\right) \times 0.5 + \left(1 - \frac{D_{angle}}{fov \times 0.5}\right) \times 0.5\right] \quad (3)$$

3   Results

In the virtual conference data, the direction of attention edges changed as participants performed different activities (Fig. 3). During the socializing session, degrees were extended to the garden outside the conference hall. During the lecture session, the cells with desks and a podium formed a well-connected component. During the socializing session, a student guarding the hallway conversed with another participant, creating edges to surrounding nodes. During the socializing session, the edge direction was diverse, but during the lecture session, the edge directions in the hall tended to be aligned to the front stage. Overall, the graph density was 0.013.

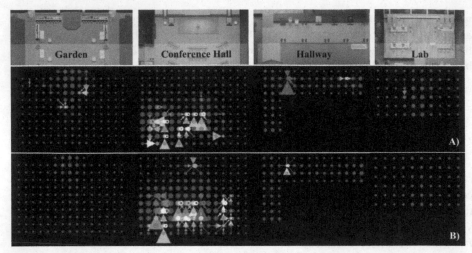

Fig. 3. Spatial connectivity in Gather Town visualized by spatial graphs. Nodes were sized by Eigenvector centrality and colored by weighted in-degree centrality, and edges with a weight < 2.0 were filtered out. A) Socializing sessions. B) Lecturing sessions.

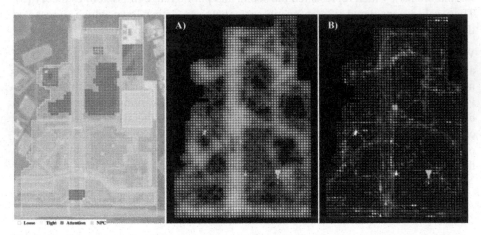

Fig. 4. Spatial connectivity of virtual campus in Minecraft visualized by spatial graphs. A) Nodes were sized by Eigenvector centrality. B) Nodes were sized by PageRank centrality and colored by community classes, and edges with a weight < 2.0 were filtered out.

During the free tour, edges sparsely connected the large space (the graph density was 0.002). The combination of movement and viewing behavior led to long cascading edges (Fig. 4).

Areas designated as attention areas showed higher Eigenvector centrality. The attention range did not extend to the inside of large areas such as lakes and large buildings; therefore, centrality was concentrated on the outside nodes (Fig. 4A). Eigenvector centralities were generally high in the hallway zone, and NPC areas had average centrality. Some cells were found with the highest level of edge weight despite the areas not being predefined as attention areas. The cells contained small landmarks such as a bus stop and bridge. Figure 4B shows the result of community detection using the Louvain algorithm [12], excluding the edges with a weight of 2.0 or less (when the aggregate of frontal attention time is 2 s or less). The campus outdoor area was clustered into more than 20 communities (resolution 0.8 and modularity 0.7).

4   Discussion and Future Work

We proposed a spatial graph that weights attention behaviors in a location and presented an exploratory analysis of spatial connectivity in VEs. Experimental results showed that the graphs help analyze user behavior in VEs and quantify user-based spatial connectivity. Consequently, the user's activity in a VE can change the direction of the spatial connectivity. A comparison of the lecture and socializing sessions revealed the slight difference in the direction of spatial connection. In the context of activities that require avatars to move, such as tours, the roads attracted general spatial attention and formed long chains of spatial attentions. When the road was in a straight line, people also experienced this space in a straight and sequential way.

A previous study showed that in a head mounted display (HMD) environment, an avatar faces the communication target, whereas this is not the case in a desktop environment [4]. In terms of visual attention, the avatar's and the user's attentions were expected to have a positive relationship even on a desktop, aligning with the literature [13]. However, it is necessary to investigate the extent to which the orientation of the avatar and user's attention differ in a 2D space compared to 3D space.

The spatial attention graph presented in this paper is a prototype. Future work should complete the theoretical supplementation of human attention and evaluate accuracy. Nevertheless, this study can be considered novel in that it applied the theories and tools used to analyze physical space in spatial cognition and urban architecture to VEs. By doing so, we aimed to stimulate interdisciplinary discussions to broaden our understanding of VEs.

This prototype can be developed into a graph model to understand dynamic VEs and predict users' spatial behavior. While eye tracking has been required to gather user attention data in a dynamic VE, the tool has relatively low versatility [6]. The spatial attention graph we proposed can measure spatial attention in VEs only with avatar logs. Thus, our tool can be an alternative to the versatility issue. Also, future work can generalize our study to quantify the importance of each area of the VE from the user's perspective. Based on our work, industries can use a topological feature as an index to compress and maintain the quality of dynamic VE data [14].

References

1. Müller, S., Kapadia, M., Frey, S. et al.: Statistical analysis of player behavior in minecraft. In: Proceedings of the 10th International Conference on the Foundations of Digital Games. Pacific Grove, CA, USA (2015)

2. Williamson, J., Li, J., Vinayagamoorthy, V., Shamma, D. A., Cesar, P.: Proxemics and social interactions in an instrumented virtual reality workshop. In: Proceedings of the 2021 CHI Conference on Human Factors in Computing Systems, pp. 1–13. Japan: Association for Computing Machinery, Yokohama, OL, Japan (2021)

3. Hall E.T.: The hidden dimension. Anchor (1969)

4. Williamson, J.R., O'Hagan, J., Guerra-Gomez, J.A., Williamson, J.H., Cesar, P., Shamma, D.A.: Digital proxemics: designing social and collaborative interaction in virtual environments. In: Proceedings of the SIGCHI Conference on Human Factors in Computing Systems, pp. 1–12. Association for Computing Machinery, New York, NY, USA (2022)

5. Fernandez-Duque, D., Johnson, M.L.: Attention metaphors: how metaphors guide the cognitive psychology of attention. Cogn. Sci. **23**(1), 83–116 (1999)

6. Clay, V., König, P., Koenig, S.: Eye tracking in virtual reality. J. Eye Movement Res. **12**(1), jemr.12.1.3 (2019)

7. Benedikt, M.L.: To take hold of space: isovists and isovist fields. Environ. Plann. B. Plann. Des. **6**(1), 47–65 (1979)

8. Turner, M.G., Gardner, R.H., O'Neill, R.V.: Pattern and process: Landscape ecology in theory and practice. Springer-Verlag, New York, NY, USA (2001). https://doi.org/10.1007/978-1-4939-2794-4

9. Dadashpoor, H., Malekzadeh, N.: Driving factors of formation, development, and change of spatial structure in metropolitan areas: a systematic review. J. Urban Manage. **9**(3), 286–297 (2020)

10. Chang, M., Lee, G.B., Lee, J.H., Lee, M., Lee, J.H.: The influence of virtual tour on urban visitor using a network approach. Adv. Eng. Inf. **56**, j.aei.2023.102025 (2023)

11. Foucault, M.: Discipline and punish. A. Sheridan, Tr., Paris, FR, Gallimard (1975)

12. Blondel, V.D., Guillaume, J.L., Lambiotte, R., Lefebvre, E.: Fast unfolding of communities in large networks. J. Stat. Mech: Theory Exp. **2008**(10), P10008 (2008)

13. Bowers, J., Pycock, J., O'brien, J.: Talk and embodiment in collaborative virtual environments. In: Proceedings of the SIGCHI Conference on Human Factors in Computing Systems, pp. 58–65. Association for Computing Machinery, New York, NY, USA (1996)

14. Rossi, S., Viola, I., Cesar, P.: Behavioural analysis in a 6-DoF VR system: influence of content, quality and user disposition. In: Proceedings of the 1st Workshop on Interactive eXtended Reality. Association for Computing Machinery, New York, NY, USA (2022)

Differences in User Experience in Metaverse Model House

Dowon Lee[1] (ID), Ji-Hyoun Hwang[2](✉) (ID), Haewon Lim[1] (ID), and Yoojin Han[1] (ID)

[1] Yonsei University, Seoul, Korea
dowon.lee@yonsei.ac.kr
[2] Chungbuk National University, Cheongju, Chungcheongbuk-do, Korea
ihyoungh@chungbuk.ac.kr

Abstract. This study aims to examine the differences in User Experience (UX) in metaverse model houses, specifically in terms of interactive, informative, and sensorial experiences. After experiencing the metaverse model house on a tablet PC, 83 users were surveyed. A one-way ANOVA was performed to confirm the statistically significant differences by demographic characteristics. Consequently, a significant difference was identified in the sensorial and informative experiences between users in their 30s and those of other ages. Additionally, users in their 20s, 40s, and 50s used different methods of investigating information compared with users in their 30s. Users in their 20s were more familiar with the metaverse environment and comfortable exploring virtual apartment complexes. However, users in their 30s missed most of the content in the video clips and were less satisfied with the experience than the other age groups. Therefore, to improve the positive aspects of UX, the metaverse model house should be considered to provide better graphic elements, deliver information through various methods, and design intuitive environments considering the user's age.

Keywords: Metaverse · Metaverse model houses · User experience

1 Introduction

The Fourth Industrial Revolution, which was based on breakthrough technologies, including Artificial Intelligence, the Internet of Things, Big Data, and Mobile technologies, brought significant social and economic changes [1]. PropTech[1] primarily leads the change in the real estate business, which is normally considered conventional [2]. Additionally, the COVID-19 pandemic expedited trends restricting the use of offline spaces. Metaverse model houses that adopt virtual reality technologies have been introduced into the housing market to overcome the limitations of operating traditional offline model houses [3].

---

[1] PropTech, a combination of the terms "property" and "technology," refers to the emerging real estate service that integrates the traditional real estate practices with IT technologies such as AI, Big Data, and the Internet of Things [5].

C. Stephanidis et al. (Eds.): HCII 2023, CCIS 1958, pp. 213–220, 2024.
https://doi.org/10.1007/978-3-031-49215-0_26

Metaverse model houses are advanced models of virtual model houses where information on housing is provided in a one-way via online platforms. Users are allowed to interact with the model by exploring virtual spaces, communicating with NPCs, changing the interior design of housing, making a contract, and asking for consultations [3, 4]. Metaverse model houses are considered the next-generation housing sales marketing strategy because they surmount the limitations of traditional model houses, such as high costs, time and space constraints, and limited design proposals [3].

Metaverse model houses should provide a positive and satisfying experience for users when they explore and experience models, considering that the fundamental purpose of model houses is to encourage customers to purchase real housing [6]. Thus, it is important to delve into the contents and elements of metaverse model houses to enhance UX. However, as metaverse model houses have only recently emerged as a tool for housing sales, not enough studies have been conducted to develop their contents. Demands for using metaverse are increasing in the real estate industry and other industries as well, encouraging studies on UX in the metaverse for natural and intuitive UX [7, 8]. Therefore, this study aims to examine the UX of metaverse model houses and explore ways to enhance positive UX to promote the usage of metaverse model houses.

2 Literature Review

2.1 Metaverse Model Houses

During the 1960s, the rapid growth in Asia led to an increase in housing demand. Consequently, a unique "pre-sale housing system" was introduced in which customers could make partial payments for housing before its completion to reduce the financial burden on construction companies [9]. Model houses emerged with the aim of facilitating the pre-sale of housing, and with the advancement of digital technologies, online virtual model houses appeared, eliminating the need to visit traditional offline model houses [10]. Although online model houses allowed customers to ex-plore housing units and apartment complexes beyond time and space constraints, they failed to meet customers' needs because the inadequate implementation of virtual reality (VR) technology diminished their sense of presence [4]. The advance-ment of VR technology and the emergence of the metaverse have added new value to virtual model houses, such as interactivity, communication, and an enhanced sense of presence [3]. Thus, in metaverse model houses, users can explore virtual spaces from a free perspective by using an avatar. They can receive real-time consul-tations and access information through NPCs, chatbots, and other means. Addition-ally, they can change their interior designs and arrange furniture according to their preferences. Furthermore, metaverse model houses provide location information using real-world maps and convey additional information using videos and images.

2.2 User Experience in Virtual Residential Space

The concept of UX originated in Human-Computer Interaction (HCI) and was first focused on the User Interface (UI) in the design field [11]. However, it has become a more comprehensive term referring to all direct and indirect experiences users have while interacting with a product or service [12, 13]. The definition of UX varies depending on the researchers and their backgrounds, leading to different interpretations in various contexts. Nevertheless, most agree that UX goes beyond a product or service's functional and usability aspects, involving feelings, emotions, and even user behaviors during interactions [14]. Particularly, in the context of mobile and virtual environments, UX is considered significant in that it enables sustained usage of services within mobile environments as UX aligns with user-centered design thinking, which emphasizes users' emotions during interaction [15].

According to Shedroff [11], UX design comprises three dimensions: interaction, information, and sensorial. Kim et al. [16] developed criteria for evaluating the UX in virtual residential spaces employing Shedroff's idea. *Interactive experiences* occur when the users receive functional elements by manipulating virtual environments. These include efficiency, consistency, ease of control, and autonomy in navigation. *Sensorial experiences* are influenced by a sense of presence primarily through UI. Visibility, perceptiveness, and consistency of interfaces are sensorial experiences. *Informative experiences* refer to all the experiences when users access or receive information in virtual environments [16].

With the advancement of digital devices, users can now experience virtual worlds in various mobile environments such as VR, PC, smartphones, and tablets. Consequently, there has been an increase in research on measuring UX in metaverse platforms, considering that UX is a reliable indicator of a sense of reality [16]. However, most studies on the UX of metaverse have analyzed specific platforms, and there is a lack of empirical research on the UX in metaverse-based virtual residential environments [7, 17]. Empirical studies have been conducted on usability [9, 18], housing purchase intention [9, 19], sense of presence [18], and attitude [9]. Studies have been conducted to evaluate UX in virtual residential spaces [16] and conduct trend analysis of virtual model houses [4]. Therefore, this study aims to comprehensively investigate the UX in metaverse model houses.

3 Research Method

3.1 Research Instrumentation

An experiment was conducted using a survey to obtain research data through a set of questionnaires. The participants were asked to experience a metaverse model house application[2], which comprised two stages: housing unit and apartment complex exploration, through a tablet PC and responded to the questionnaires. The questionnaires were divided into three sections: 1) general demographic profile, 2) measuring UX in housing unit exploration, and 3) measuring UX in apartment complex exploration. The items in the second section were divided into three dimensions to evaluate respondents' interactive (11 items), sensorial (7 items), and informative (9 items) experiences. The items

---

[2] The application used in the experiment was the very first metaverse model house in South Korea, which employed an unreal engine to create realistic virtual images and introduced avatars for autonomous exploration.

in the third section comprised two dimensions: interactive (8 items) and informative (6 items) experiences[3]. All items in Sects. 2 and 3 used a 5-point Likert scale. Reliability and consistency of the questionnaires were verified by verification test using Cronbach's alpha coefficient. The participants were provided sufficient time to explore the meta-verse model house. They answered each section of the questionnaire after experiencing each stage of the metaverse model house. The experimental procedure is illustrated in Fig. 1. The experiment was conducted from September 2022 to March 2023, and trained researchers supervised the experiment.

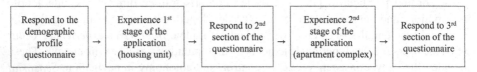

Fig. 1. The procedure of the experiment

3.2 Population and Targeted Respondents

Considering the differences in preferred residential locations and characteristics among different age groups [20] and variations in residential types and family compositions [21], it was assessed that user experiences in model houses may vary based on demographic characteristics. Therefore, this study aimed to analyze the differences in user experiences based on demographic characteristics. The study participants were divided into four groups ranging from their 20s to 50s, and stratified sampling was conducted to ensure a compatible distribution of users in each group.

4 Result and Discussion

4.1 Respondent Profile

Table 1 presents the demographic profile of the respondents, comprising 37 men (44.6%) and 46 women (55.4%), with 26 participants aged 20–29 (31.3%), 20 aged 30–39 (24.1%), 20 aged 40–49 (24.1%), and 17 aged 50–59 (20.5%).

4.2 One-Way ANOVA: Differences in UX

One-way ANOVA was performed to examine differences in UX based on age group. If the assumption of homogeneity of variance was violated, Welch's test was conducted. Scheffe and Dunnett T3 tests were employed for items with significant values. The results were considered significant for all analyses if the p-value was < 0.05.

---

[3] Unlike the housing unit exploration stage, the apartment complex exploration does not offer services involving avatars and self-exploration. It primarily focuses on delivering information through maps, videos, images, and text with a single tap on the screen.

Table 1. Demographic Characteristics of Respondents

Attribute		Frequency ($n = 83$)	Percentage
Gender	Male	37	44.6%
	Female	46	55.4%
Age	20–29	26	31.3%
	30–39	20	24.1%
	40–49	20	24.1%
	50–59	17	20.5%

Table 2. Results of One-way ANOVA in Housing Unit Exploration

Items	Mean				Total Mean	F	p	Post-hoc
	20–29	30–39	40–49	50–59				
HSSE 3[4]	3.50	2.25	3.40	3.24	3.19	3.501	0.019	30's < 20's
HSSE 4[5]	3.27	2.20	3.40	3.76	3.27	7.973	0.000	30's < 20,40,50's
HSSE 6[6]	4.42	3.25	4.00	3.94	4.42	4.850	0.004	30's < 20's
HIFE 1[7]	3.31	1.85	3.30	3.29	2.95	12.799	0.000	30's < 20, 40, 50's
HIFE 2[8]	3.35	1.65	3.15	3.24	2.87	14.438	0.000	30's < 20, 40, 50's
HIFE 3[9]	3.38	1.70	2.50	3.29	2.75	13.291	0.000	30's < 20, 50's
HIFE 4[10]	3.81	2.60	3.80	3.71	3.71	6.091	0.001	30's < 20, 40, 50's
HIFE 7[11]	4.81	4.20	4.20	4.12	4.37	4.114	0.001	30, 40's < 20's
HIFE 9[12]	4.62	3.60	3.60	4.00	4.00	4.563	0.005	30, 40's < 20's

Housing Unit Exploration. Table 2 presents the results of the analysis. There were no significant differences in the interactive experiences. In terms of sensorial experience, there were significant differences in several items: smooth and realistic movement, proximity of the view, and enjoyment of obtaining information by navigating an avatar. Those

---

[4] Smooth and realistic spatial movement through an avatar.
[5] The proximity of the views creates a realistic sense.
[6] The enjoyment of obtaining information through navigating the avatar.
[7] Adequate information on interior options (built-in appliance, furniture).
[8] Adequate information on exhibition items (display).
[9] Adequate information on finishing materials.
[10] Easy understanding of detailed structure and features of floor plans.
[11] Availability of 360-degree view.
[12] Adjustable sound volume.

aged 30–39 responded as those experiences were not satisfying, whereas those aged 20–29 were pleased with their sensorial experiences. The most significant differences were observed in the dimension of informative experience. The results indicated that those aged 30–39 felt there was insufficient information on interior options, exhibition items, finishing materials, and structure of floor plans compared with other age groups, particularly those aged 20–29 and 50–59. Additionally, there were significant differences between those aged 30–49 and aged 20–29 in items such as availability of 360-degree view and adjustable sound volume.

Table 3. Results of One-way ANOVA in Apartment Complex Exploration

Items	Mean				Total Mean	F	p	Post-hoc
	20–29	30–39	40–49	50–59				
AITE 2[13]	4.12	3.15	3.85	3.88	3.77	3.686	0.015	30's < 20's
AITE 8[14]	4.00	3.05	3.95	3.76	3.71	3.841	0.013	30's < 20's
AIFE 10[15]	3.77	2.95	3.45	4.35	3.61	6.471	0.001	30, 40's < 50's
AIFE 11[16]	3.31	2.55	3.35	4.00	3.28	5.006	0.003	30's < 50's
AIFE 12[17]	3.62	2.05	3.15	4.00	3.20	12.028	0.000	30's < 20, 40, 50's
AIFE 13[18]	3.04	2.05	3.25	3.82	3.01	9.893	0.000	30's < 20, 40, 50's
AIFE 14[19]	3.62	2.50	3.45	3.76	3.35	4.578	0.000	30's < 20, 50's

Apartment Complex Exploration. Table 3 demonstrates significant differences between those aged 30–39 and the other age groups in terms of both interactive and informative experiences. As for interactive experiences, the means of those aged 30–39 were lower than those aged 20–29 for the expected actions of buttons or image taps and seamless graphic elements. In addition, there were meaningful differences between those

---

[13] Button or image taps result in expected actions.
[14] Seamless graphic elements.
[15] Adequate information on apartment complex (number of units, locations, housing size, etc.).
[16] Adequate information on housing sales (sales price, occupancy date, application process).
[17] Adequate information on amenities.
[18] Easy understanding on the layout of the apartment complex.
[19] Adequate information of the surrounding neighborhood of the apartment complex.

aged 30–39 and other age groups in terms of adequate information on apartment complexes, housing sales, and amenities; easy understanding of the layout of the apartment complex; and adequate information on the surrounding area.

4.3 Discussion

This study aimed to identify differences in the UX of metaverse model houses based on age groups. To achieve this, an experiment employing an existing metaverse model house application and a survey were conducted. The statistical analysis illustrated mixed results and drew a few interesting findings.

While interactive experiences did not differ among age groups in housing unit exploration, they were significantly different between people aged 30–39 and 20–29 in apartment complex exploration. Given that those aged 30–39 demonstrated less mean value for AITE2 and AITE8, it can be inferred that those aged 30–39 expected more functions and enhanced graphic images for apartment complex exploration. Regarding sensorial experiences in the exploration of housing units, those aged 30–39 primarily displayed lower mean values than those aged 20–29. Considering that HSSE3 and HSSE6 are related to the movement of an avatar in a metaverse environment, those aged 30–39 expect more enhanced movements and actions from navigating an avatar. Informative experiences in both housing units and apartment complex exploration was identified as most significant difference between those aged 30–39 and the other age groups. Those aged 30–39 responded that they could not find sufficient information from the model. Considering that the application mainly provided information through videos, those aged 30–39 were unwilling to watch the videos.

5   Conclusion

This study analyzed the UX of metaverse model houses to propose implications for promoting metaverse model houses in the housing sales industry. An experiment measuring UX in metaverse model houses was conducted, and it was found that interactive, sensorial, and informative experiences in metaverse model houses varied depending on age groups. In particular, those aged 30–39 were less satisfied with the metaverse model house because of insufficient information and function, and unrealistic images and views. Therefore, to enhance the use of metaverse model houses, the service should consider different aspects between ages. Based on this research, we recommend providing better graphic elements, delivering information through various methods, and designing intuitive environments that consider the age of the target user.

Overall, this study is meaningful in that it examined the comprehensive UX in metaverse model houses, which has not yet been explored by researchers, and suggested ways to improve the services. However, this study focused on differences in UX between age groups. Thus, further studies should be conducted to verify whether these factors are correlated with positive UXs in metaverse model houses.

Acknowledgements. This work was supported by the National Research Foundation of Korea(NRF) grant funded by the Korea government(MSIT) (No. 2022R1G1A1010844).

References

1. Kyung, J.: New normal generation PropTech development direction – Focusing on the 4th industrial revolution and COVID-19. Korea Real Estate Indus. Res. **4**(1), 1–32 (2012)
2. Kim, S.K., Jang, H.S.: A study of the capacity enhancement and countermeasure of the real estate industry in the Prop-tech era. SH Urban Res. Insight **24**, 97–117 (2020)
3. Ahn, H.: Future of metaverse and real estate industry. Urban Inf. Service **475**, 13–17 (2021)
4. Hwang, B.Y., Lee, T.H.: A study on the application flow of virtual reality in the apartment model house. J. Korea Acad.-Indust. cooper. Soc. **20**(5), 585–590 (2019)
5. Lee, S.-Y.: Proptech classification and development prospects. J. Korean Soc. Trend Perspect. **110**, 191–224 (2020)
6. Ha, J.M., Park, S.-B.: A study on the user's evaluation for the visual types of virtual model house. Korean Instit. Inter. Design J. **20**(5), 160–169 (2011)
7. Lee, J.-H., Rhee, B.-A.: A study on user experience on metaverse: focusing on the ZEPETO platform. J. Dig. Contents Soc. **23**(6), 995–1011 (2022)
8. Joo, S., Chung, H., Nah, K.: A study on the user experience in Metaverse: focused on technology trends and literature research. In: 2021 KSDS Fall International Conference, pp. 122–127. Korea Society of Design Science, Gyeonggi (2021)
9. Juan, Y.K., Chen, H.H., Chi, H.Y.: Developing and evaluating a virtual reality-based navigation system for pre-sale housing sales. Appl. Sci. **8**(6), 952 (2018)
10. Lee, S.H.: A study of the realistic media of smart glass in the public relations hall of a small model house less than three pyeong. J. Korean Soc. Media Arts **20**(3), 75–87 (2022)
11. Saffer, D.: Designing for interaction: creating smart applications and clever devices. New Riders, Berkeley, CA (2007)
12. Alben, L.: Quality of experience: defining the criteria for effective interaction design. Interactions **3**(3), 11–15 (1996)
13. Desmet, P., Hekkert, P.: Framework of product experience. Int. J. Design **1**, 57–66 (2007)
14. Allam, A.H., Hussin, A.R., Dahlan, H.M.: User experience: challenges and opportunities. J. Inf. Syst. Res. Innov. **3**(1), 28–36 (2013)
15. Drin, A., Laine, T.H.: User experience in mobile augmented reality: emotions, challenges, opportunities, and best practices. Computers **7**(2), 3 (2018)
16. Kim, M.-S., Paek, H.-W., Seo, H.-R., Ko, I.-J.: The method of user experience evaluation for virtual living space. Asia Pac. J. Multimed. Serv. Converg. Art Humanit. Sociol. **12**(38), 795–806 (2017)
17. Demir, G., Argan, M., Dinc, H.: The age beyond sports: user experience in the world of metaverse. J. Metaverse **3**(1), 19–27 (2023)
18. Ha, J.-M., Park, S.-B.: A study on the user's evaluation for the visual types of virtual model houses. J. Korean Insti. Interior Design **20**(5), 160–169 (2011)
19. Ibrahim, F.A., Ishak, N., Woon, J.K.Y., Mohd Shafiei, M.W., Ismall, R., Razak, R.A.: Virtual technology (VR) attractiveness attributes in influencing house buyer's intention to purchase. J. Adv. Res. Appl. Sci. Eng. Technol. **29**(2), 126–134 (2023)
20. Park, W.S.: Analysis of residential location preference factors by characteristics of households in the case of Seoul Metropolitan Area Households: comparative analysis with the case of Daegu·Gyeongbuk households. J. Korean Assoc. Reg. Geographers **21**(3), 515–528 (2015)
21. Shim, S.G., Ji, I.: Life-circle home ownership and residential patterns: An empirical analysis of home ownership across generations. LHI J. **21**(4), 31–40 (2021)

Hypersphere - XR Design for Metaverse by Synthesizing Neuro Reality and Virtual Reality

Jiawen Liu and Mickey Mengting Zhang[✉]

Macau University of Science and Technology, Avenida Wai Long, Taipa, Macau
2220024336@student.must.edu.mo, mtzhang@must.edu.mo

Abstract. We design a product concept named Hypersphere - an XR wearable that integrates neuro reality and virtual reality based on electroencephalogram (EEG) systems and head-mounted display (HMD). It aims to provide users with a more immersive, engaging, fluid, and safe experience by synthesizing visual, auditory, and haptic systems. In this paper, the design of the Hypersphere, including its structure, materials, function, and authentication process is discussed. The research contributes to the current understanding of XR wearable design concerning user experience in a synthetic world.

Keywords: XR · EEG · HMD · User Experience · Metaverse

1 Introduction

Metaverse connects tangible and intangible worlds, allowing users to interact with each other in a shared virtual reality space [16]. Game players can participate in a virtual community. The personal AI digital twins can complete tasks autonomously or be controlled as a digital prosthesis system to our physical reality. Space travel, deep-sea exploration, and working in a dangerous environment can be experienced through robotic interfaces. Due to the COVID-19 pandemic and the resulting demand for social contacts and business cooperations, this trend has been intensified [16]. Extended reality (XR) technologies, including virtual reality (VR), augmented reality (AR) and mixed reality, constitute the foundation of Metaverse [16]. Traditionally, digital solutions are visual and audio-based devices like PC with keyboards and mouse, mobile phones, projectors, video game consoles, and so on. These devices limit user experience with the virtual world. After decades of multiple technologies development, digital devices become haptic-based and combining powerful processors cutting-edge sensors, and sophisticated algorithms [8]. Despite the characteristics and forms of interaction have been expanded, many of them are still limited by technologies and more importantly financial costs to achieve all sensory experiences, such as sight, sound, touch, and smell. Some of them interact with users through very basic ways (vibro-haptic) to simulate certain mechanical sensations [16].

C. Stephanidis et al. (Eds.): HCII 2023, CCIS 1958, pp. 221–230, 2024.
https://doi.org/10.1007/978-3-031-49215-0_27

The Metaverse requires a more sophisticated manipulation, creation, and modification of XR technologies to create an integrated user experience. We initiated a project named 'Hypersphere' - an XR product that integrates neuro reality and virtual reality based on electroencephalogram (EEG) systems and head-mounted display (HMD). It aims to provide users with a more immersive, engaging, and fluid experience by synthesizing visual, auditory, and haptic systems. In the following section, the user experience of XR, the concept of a non-invasive brain-computer interface and the process of EEG is introduced. Then the structure, materials, function, and authentication process of the Hypersphere are discussed.

2 Literature Review

2.1 User Experience of XR

Experience in Metaverse is expected to be more immersive, engaging, fluid, and safe for users to interact, communicate and collaborate. Users can feel that she/he is cognitively teleported to an alternative, synthetic world [12]. This virtual world supports their intelligence and participation, where they can concentrate wholeheartedly on an activity, losing awareness of peripheral problems and distractions in the real world [3]. This universal interaction experience relates to a virtual environment in that users situated as well as other people co-exist in the same virtual space [24]. XR technologies can produce these realistic and extremely immersive experiences by reviving human senses to create synthetic perceptions of the virtual world [1]. They can be viewed as wearable electronic systems, such as an HMD, wafer-like glasses, contact lenses, gloves, or body suits, etc. These systems rely on sensors that assess the user's conditions by gaining haptic perception, such as voice control, eye tracking, control handle, body motion, hand gestures, and physiological conditions. Utilizing these integrated sensory channels, users can engage in multimodal interaction with the virtual world [7]. A more seamless and natural human-system interface could arise from the multimodal interaction [9]. The traditional ones already achieve remarkable success, while the XR wearables based on haptic systems still have great potential to develop [16].

2.2 Non-invasive Brain-Computer Interface for XR

One of the potentials for XR is a brain-computer interface (BCI), which acquires and analyzes signals directly from the human brain [15]. To collect data, an invasive one that applies electrodes implanted directly into the cerebral cortex and a non-invasive method that mainly collects information on brain activity at the scalp level are utilized. For the invasive method, its cerebral cortex's electrodes can detect small fluctuations in potential, allowing it to circumvent additional biological barriers like the skull and scalp and yield more precise readings of the brain's bioelectrical activity than the non-invasive one. The non-invasive method is harmless and less complicated. It is operated with reusable electrodes placed on the human scalp, which do not require any interference in the human organism. Most non-invasive methods for processing brain signals depend on either of the following two techniques for data acquisition: electroencephalogram

(EEG) and Magnetoencephalography (MEG) [15]. In comparison, EEG systems devices have various advantages cost-worthy, ease of use, portable, and safe [13]. Primarily, A technique for capturing an electrogram of the brain's spontaneous electrical activity is known as electroencephalography (EEG) [2]. It has been extensively applied in the research domains like cognitive science, cognitive psychology, and neuroscience [6]. For instance, in medical diagnosis, the aberrant electrical discharges that epileptic patients experience, such as sharp waves, spikes, or spike-and-wave complexes, can be found by EEG [18]. In addition, it assists in the diagnosis of encephalopathies, cerebral hypoxia following cardiac arrest, sleep disorders, depth of anesthesia, comas, and brain death [19].

2.3   EEG Systems for XR

Due to its nature, EEG systems can be a suitable interaction system not only to record brain signals but also to send signals out to control objects. EEG systems have the advantage of authentication, which can serve as a solution for privacy, security, and safety in the virtual world. In computer science and cryptography, authentication is commonly referred to the confirmation of a user's declared identity. The concepts of identity recognition and authentication are different. While authentication ascertains whether the user's identity corresponds with what has been declared in the system, identity recognition determines who the user is.

Authentication techniques normally are biometric (owned by the user), password (known to the user) and token owned by the human). Biometric features are used for EEG authentication. Physiological features such as fingerprints, iris scans and DNA and behavioral features such as gait and signature compose the biometric features generally. EEG signals are characterized as a fusion of physiological and behavioral features due to their high dependence on task-related behaviors and sensitive emotions. Therefore, EEG signals are therefore distinctive and challenging to hack, copy or expose. Task-dependent EEG authentication provides the revocability that other biometric authentications are lacking, particularly compared the conventional biometric features. Additionally, due to its high task dependence, it may show a variety of characteristics. It is possible to revoke particular features once they have been lost or taken in time to prevent an attack in the system. Consequently, EEG signals are able to sole the irrevocable issue of conventional biometric features [22]. Because EEG changes when people are under stress, it has low explosibility as it cannot be easily obtained or stolen by the observer for forced extraction [4]. Some commercial products have already applied EEG systems for general users, such as neuroscience devices for not only research institutes but also individuals (e.g., Emotiv), for concentration and relaxation training (e.g., Omnifit Brain, Mendi), for meditation and sleep (e.g., NeuroSky and Muse), for cognitive rehabilitation (e.g., NeuroReality), or for enhancing game capability with the neurofeedback technology (e.g., neuroLeet). However, fewer studies have explored the application of neuro reality and virtual reality systems, especially integrating EEG systems with HMD.

2.4 HMD System for XR

HMD Structure. Head Mounted Displays (HMDs) for optical see-through types normally use waveguide-based structures. The optical structure achieved by the process that from the light source to the human eye, the light would go through collimation optics, polarized beam splitter (PBS) adjusted by spatial light modulator (SLM), injection optics and waveguide optics. SLM can utilize light with high efficiency, by designing reflectivity, aperture ratio and diffraction noise. Diffraction optical elements (DOEs) are used to direct light from the light source and off-axis projector into the human eye while staying transparent. Besides, an eye tracker would deliver the image to human sight [23]. Higher image quality and broader Field of View are the iteration direction of transparent HMD these years.

3 Design of Hypersphere

As a product that integrates EGG systems and HMD, this concept is concerned with the principle of sensing the user's physiological signals and the mechanism of the EEG device. All the shape designs and novel material selections are determined by functionality (stability, biocompatibility, and conductivity). We proposed a conceptual design named Hypersphere consisting of XR glasses and an EEG detector. The orientation of the electrode adopts a 10–20 international system. Hydrogel Electrodes with gas-permeable nano mesh could fit the user's head. The cushion coating with interconnects is made of PEDOT: PSS (Fig. 1).

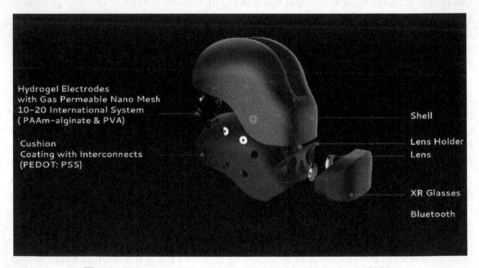

Fig. 1. Structure of Hypersphere designed by the authors (2023).

3.1 Electrode Design

10–20 International System. The 10–20 international system is a standard protocol for the placement of EEG electrodes by using anatomical landmarks which are recognized by the International Federation of Clinical Neurophysiology. The proper coverage of all brain areas by this system is guided by the proportionate locations referring to the points on the skull located in the nasion, preauricular points and inion [17].

Hydrogel Electrode. As a wired system does not function as a daily-use portable device, a wireless EEG device is the solution with a shorter preparation time and a convenient using method. B-Alert X24 and Mindwave are wireless EEG monitors in the market. With different targeting consumers, B-Alert X24 is akin to medical or research-grade equipment using wet electrodes, whereas Mindwave is for entertainment and education using dry electrodes instead [5].

However, there are drawbacks to using wet electrodes and dry electrodes. When conducting wet electrodes, the user may suffer skin irritation or rashes and other allergic reactions after applying the gel of wet electrodes. Besides, the expense of replacement is high. Dry electrodes commonly use unique materials and shapes to transduce currents instead of gel. To minimize resistance, the skin would be pierced with tiny pins coated with gold to improve conductivity, which might be uncomfortable and even lead users to pain with extended use. Thus, it is not suitable for wearable EEG devices to adopt wet and dry electrodes from the perspective of biocompatibility and stability [5].

Hydrogel electrodes have shown promise recently to replace wet electrodes. Their high-water content and conductive additives enhanced conduction. Due to the intrinsic flexibility, the hydrogel electrodes could contact the skin seamlessly, which decreases the skin-contact impedance. The accuracy of signal acquisition exhibits no significant difference compared to the commercial EEG device using electrolytic gel. Therefore, hydrogel electrodes are better for EEG devices as their adjustable hydrogel-based design can be more biocompatible, suitable, and flexible [5].

Silver filled in PAAm-alginate hydrogel Matrix for Hydrogel Electrode. For EEG monitors, the most critical performance indicators are impedance, adhesion, stability and biocompatibility. The main impedance caused by electrode-skin contact is the stratum corneum from the outmost layer of the skin, domaining the quality of the signal detected [5].

From the perspective of adhesion, the immersive experience needs intimate contact between the XR device and the skin. Current research on next-generation XR materials concentrates on soft, skin-like wearable electronic materials instead of conventional rigid electronics [16].

The electrode design of the Hypersphere tends to conformally integrate the dynamic human curve with the product which is achieved by adopting the hydrogel electrode while lowering the impedance. The electrodes of Hypersphere adopt a method proposed by [14] that micrometer-sized silver as a conductive filler to flake into a polyacrylamide-alginate (PAAm-alginate) hydrogel matrix to generate high electrical conductivity.

Polyvinyl Alcohol and Gas-permeable Nano Meshes for Biocompatibility. To enhance biocompatibility, the electrodes are designed with gas-permeable nano meshes structurally to allow the skin to breathe freely. Besides, polyvinyl alcohol is added to the hydrogel matrix as the biocompatible polymer may cause only slight or even no sensitivity, which is verified in hydrogel-based on-skin applications in vivo or in vitro testing [5] (Fig. 2).

Fig. 2. Application of Hypersphere designed by the authors (2023).

3.2 Cushion Design

Stretchable PEDOT: PSS as Interconnects. Poor comfort and ergonomics are the issues in designing current-generation wearable devices [11]. In addition, only when the electrodes cover the appropriate location of the scalp, the repeatable results can be obtained. Therefore, aiming to produce the best quality signals, it is vital to design a suitable HMD shape to confirm the electrodes are placed correctly.

Apart from the HMD contacting skin conformally for capturing accurate data is essential, using soft bioelectronics to accommodate the dynamics of the human body to avoid electrical or mechanical failure should be addressed [11].

Stretchable and robust interconnects are used to integrate all elastic electrodes and connect the components in the circuit. Poly (3,4-ethylene-dioxythiophene) poly (styrenesulfonate) (PEDOT: PSS) has been widely applied as soft wearable materials for hydrogel electronics. It is the potential to fabricate a device density of more than 300 transistors per square centimeter whose mobility is comparable to amorphous silicon when integrating stretchable and conductive polymer [11]. [20] combine the ionic liquid with PEDOT: PSS films, which is especially suitable for spherical shapes. The changed morphology of films enhances the stretchability and conductivity, and whose device density of the transistor produces five times higher than wavy metal interconnects [21]. Therefore, the soft cushion of Hypersphere coats PEDOT: PSS as elastic interconnects to make Hypersphere intrinsically stretchable and reliable. Therefore, more accurate EEG data could be collected when meeting the requirement of a good fit.

Furthermore, an instrumentation amplifier is required in the EEG processing module to boost the strength of interested signals while reducing noise. A set of amplifiers and band-pass filters are set in the analogue front-end circuit to amplify EEG signals at the subsequent steps for data preparation [5]. As Hypersphere supports wireless transmission, Bluetooth is introduced to send the collected data to the processors.

4   Authentication Process of Hypersphere

When users received the visual stimulus from the screen of glasses initially, their EEG data would be collected by a non-embedding EEG system. All the raw EEG data would be processed through four procedures, signal processing, feature extraction, feature selection and feature classification. Then the unique identity of users would be generated by analyzing the power spectral density feature of γ band. Using the Fuzzy Commitment scheme which could combine cryptography and biometrics to assist the database in storing identity data online securely. When the users intend to verify their identity next time, the captured EEG feature together with the ID generated would be validated by the matching system (Fig. 3).

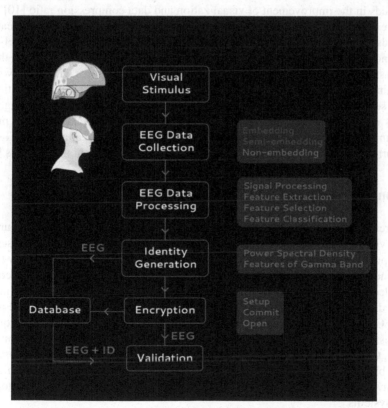

Fig. 3. Authentication Process of Hypersphere by the Authors (2023).

4.1 EEG Data Collection

Normally EEG collecting methods are categorized as embedding, semi-embedding and non-embedding. In BCI research, the non-embedding method is prominent as it has no harm to nerve cells and lower cost. The electrodes are placed on the surface of the scalp without an invasive procedure. For Hypersphere targeting entertainment and business using scenarios, a non-invasive method is a proper solution. The EEG dataset on the website can be the basis such as EEGLAB and original EEG standards contributed by Thredbo University [10].

4.2 EEG Data Processing

EEG data processing can be divided into four stages: preprocessing, feature extraction, selection and classification. The collected EEG signals contain massive high-dimensional data including noise, expression profiles and wave data. EEG signal preprocessing uses band-pass filters to decrease noise interference and enhance the Signal-to-noise ratio (SNR). When the dimension reduction technique is performed, the dimension disasters would be coped with while increasing classification algorithm precision. It also aids in the improvement of visualization and data compression ratio [10]. In the feature extraction process, the processed signals could not be used for identification as it records amplitude over a period. The unique features, autoregressive model coefficients and power spectral density are produced by classifying and transforming the time domain signals [10]. Therefore, the desirable and effective features will be derived from the original EEG features to show the user's intention. In the EEG feature selection process, to select the most effective features, clustering algorithms can be used to aggregate features from different classifications [10]. In the EEG feature classification process, no-argument classifier for sparse expression is used to classify features of EEG signals as the original EEG signals have interference signals from other brain activities [10].

5   Conclusion

In this research, we present – Hypersphere, an XR wearable that integrates neuro reality and virtual reality. The multimodal human-computer interactive product uses input and output of electroencephalogram (EEG) systems and head-mounted display (HMD) comprehensively. Every piece of information that a user needs will be displayed in the embedded HMD in front of the eyes compared with previous authentication methods that used traditional keyboard text or face recognition as input channels. The product uses EEG signals - the intrinsic human biometric features. Because of their uniqueness, EEG systems are difficult to expose, copy or hack, which ensures the authentication process. Compared with other EEG devices used for neuroscience research, Hypershere is portable and easy to use. As an XR device, it aims to provide users with a more immersive, engaging, fluid, and safe experience by synthesizing visual, auditory, and haptic systems.

The Metaverse is based on three key pillars: digital assets, digital identities and value intermediaries [25]. Hypersphere takes the role of value intermediary to give users unique digital identities to deal with their digitalized assets while owning autonomy to control their identities with different characteristics in different scenarios no matter in which synthetic space or using which avatars.

Hypersphere is trying to achieve decentralized identity and content ownership. The decentralized digital identity could be used across various platforms to form secure and stable societies though each ecosystem holds its own rules and cultures. Similarly, their assets could be moved from the close-loop environment into the open one with free movement by uniform identity and interoperation.

Users with a single digital identity can grant the platforms access, modify and pay to eliminate the procedure of registering and verifying repeatedly. By applying this mechanism, the transaction of virtue assets, including avatars and fashion could be decentralized. Apart from the entertainment field, retailers are also a growing market. Hypersphere allows users to have a more immersive shopping experience with a more secure and instant payment environment. Their purchased outfits and accessories on different platforms could be applied to the same avatars in Metaverse based on their unique identity for easier payment verification. As for frontline workers (FLW), they need to gain real-time information for scheduling and arranging [26]. In Metaverse, the real world is embedded into computing for FLW, especially in manufacturing. Using Hypersphere, the monitored real-time situation will be safer as only using the EEG signal of the manager as a detector could access all data.

References

1. Abrash, M.: Creating the future: augmented reality, the next human-machine interface. In: 2021 IEEE International Electron Devices Meeting (IEDM) (2021)
2. Amzica, F., Lopes da Silva, F.H.: Cellular substrates of brain rhythms. Oxford Medicine Online (2017)
3. Cooper, A., Reimann, R., Cronin, D., Noessel, C.: About face: the essentials of interaction design, 4th edn. (2014)
4. Damaševičius, R., Maskeliūnas, R., Kazanavičius, E., Woźniak, M.: Combining cryptography with EEG biometrics. Comput. Intell. Neurosci. 2018, 1–11 (2018). https://doi.org/10.1155/2018/1867548
5. Hsieh, J.-C., et al.: Design of hydrogel-based wearable EEG electrodes for medical applications. J. Mater. Chem. B. 10, 7260–7280 (2022). https://doi.org/10.1039/D2TB00618A
6. Jestrović, I., Coyle, J.L., Sejdić, E.: Decoding human swallowing via electroencephalography: a state-of-the-art review. J. Neural Eng. 12, 051001 (2015). https://doi.org/10.1088/1741-2560/12/5/051001
7. Kim, J.C., Laine, T.H., Åhlund, C.: Multimodal interaction systems based on internet of things and augmented reality: a systematic literature review. Appl. Sci. 11, 1738 (2021). https://doi.org/10.3390/app11041738
8. Ko, S.H., Rogers, J.: Functional materials and devices for XR (VR/AR/MR) applications. Adv. Funct. Mater. 31, 2106546 (2021). https://doi.org/10.1002/adfm.202106546
9. Lazaro, M.J., Lee, J., Chun, J., Yun, M.H., Kim, S.: Multimodal interaction: Input-output modality combinations for identification tasks in augmented reality. Appl. Ergon. 105, 103842 (2022). https://doi.org/10.1016/j.apergo.2022.103842
10. Liang, W., Cheng, L., Tang, M.: Identity recognition using biological electroencephalogram sensors. J. Sensors 2016, 1–9 (2016). https://doi.org/10.1155/2016/1831742

11. Lyu, Q., Gong, S., Yin, J., Dyson, J.M., Cheng, W.: Soft wearable healthcare materials and devices. Adv. Healthcare Mater. **10**, 2100577 (2021). https://doi.org/10.1002/adhm.202 100577

12. Mystakidis, S.: Metaverse. Encyclopedia. **2**, 486–497 (2022). https://doi.org/10.3390/encycl opedia2010031

13. Veena, N., Anitha, N.: A review of non-invasive BCI devices. Int. J. Biomed. Eng. Technol. **34**, 205 (2020)

14. Park, K., Choi, H., Kang, K., Shin, M., Son, D.: Soft stretchable conductive carboxymethyl-cellulose hydrogels for wearable sensors. Gels. **8**, 92 (2022). https://doi.org/10.3390/gels80 20092

15. Paszkiel, S.: Analysis and Classification of EEG Signals for Brain–Computer Interfaces. Springer, Cham (2020). https://doi.org/10.1007/978-3-030-30581-9

16. Pyun, K.R., Rogers, J.A., Ko, S.H.: Materials and devices for immersive virtual reality. Nat. Rev. Mater. (2022). https://doi.org/10.1038/s41578-022-00501-5

17. Rojas, G.M., Alvarez, C., Montoya, C.E., de la Iglesia-Vayá, M., Cisternas, J.E., Gálvez, M.: Study of resting-state functional connectivity networks using EEG electrodes position as seed. Front. Neurosci. **12**, 235 (2018). https://doi.org/10.3389/fnins.2018.00235

18. Smith, S.J.M.: EEG in the diagnosis, classification, and management of patients with epilepsy. J. Neurol. Neurosurg. Psychiatry **76**, ii2–ii7 (2005). https://doi.org/10.1136/jnnp. 2005.069245

19. Sutter, R., Kaplan, P.W., Valença, M., De Marchis, G.M.: EEG for diagnosis and prognosis of acute nonhypoxic encephalopathy. J. Clin. Neurophysiol. **32**, 456–464 (2015)

20. Wang, Y., et al.: A highly stretchable, transparent, and conductive polymer. Sci. Adv. **3**, e1602076 (2017). https://doi.org/10.1126/sciadv.1602076

21. Wu, X., Fu, W., Chen, H.: Conductive polymers for flexible and stretchable organic optoelec-tronic applications. ACS Appl. Polym. Mater. **4**, 4609–4623 (2022). https://doi.org/10.1021/ acsapm.2c00519

22. Zhang, S., Sun, L., Mao, X., Hu, C., Liu, P.: Review on EEG-based authentication technology. Comput. Intell. Neurosci. **2021**, 1–20 (2021). https://doi.org/10.1155/2021/5229576

23. Kim, J., Park, S., Kim, W.: A structure of optical see-through head mounted display. In: 2020 International Conference on Electronics, Information, and Communication (ICEIC), pp. 1–3. IEEE, Barcelona, Spain (2020). https://doi.org/10.1109/ICEIC49074.2020.9051323

24. Atsikpasi, P., Fokides, E.: A scoping review of the educational uses of 6DOF hmds. Virtual Reality **26**, 205–222 (2021)

25. Radia, D.: Identity in the metaverse. https://www.iabseaindia.com/blog/identity-in-the-met averse

26. Digital humans – in the metaverse and beyond. https://valoremreply.com/post/digital-hum ans-in-the-metaverse-and-beyond/

Developing a VR Application
for an Omnidirectional Treadmill

Ethan Perez[✉], Aung Kaung Khant, Christopher Crawford, Veasna Ling,
and Daniel Cliburn

University of the Pacific, Stockton, CA 95211, USA
e_perez24@u.pacific.edu

Abstract. Users of virtual reality (VR) applications often must travel between locations in virtual spaces. An omnidirectional treadmill is a device that allows users to walk in all directions in a virtual space without physically moving the position of their body in the real world. The obvious advantage of an omnidirectional treadmill is that users can walk large distances in VR without concern they will collide with objects in their real physical space. Much research investigating the use of omnidirectional treadmills in VR has focused on comparing treadmills to other forms of navigation, and exploring various aspects of the user experience, such as symptoms of cybersickness. This paper describes our work in progress to develop and evaluate a VR application for the Infinadeck omnidirectional treadmill. Our goals are to create a VR application highlighting the benefits of the treadmill, develop the application in stages so that many students at our University can contribute, and increase understanding of how to develop pleasurable omnidirectional treadmill experiences.

Keywords: Virtual Reality · Omnidirectional Treadmills · Travel

1 Introduction

A common user task in virtual reality (VR) applications is to travel between destinations of interest in the virtual spaces in which users find themselves immersed. Travel in VR can be supported through many means, such as teleportation and real walking. Teleportation is typically implemented through use of an input device allowing users to select the location in the virtual space to which they would like to teleport. While teleportation allows users to travel unlimited distances in VR, teleportation can also increase user disorientation [2]. Physically walking while in VR may increase the sense of presence [7], but limits users to the bounds of their real physical space. Omnidirectional treadmills allows users to walk in all directions in virtual spaces while keeping their body position mostly stationary in the real world, vastly reducing the likelihood they will collide with real world objects. Darken and colleagues [4] were among the first to discuss the use of omnidirectional treadmills for travel in VR. Omnidirectional treadmills have the potential to support the benefits of both teleportation and real walking as users travel in VR. This paper describes our work in progress to develop and evaluate a VR application for the Infinadeck omnidirectional treadmill (see Fig. 1).

© The Author(s), under exclusive license to Springer Nature Switzerland AG 2024
C. Stephanidis et al. (Eds.): HCII 2023, CCIS 1958, pp. 231–235, 2024.
https://doi.org/10.1007/978-3-031-49215-0_28

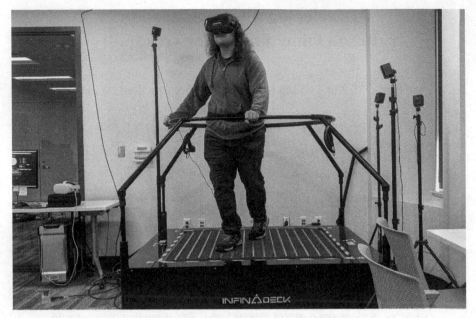

Fig. 1. Infinadeck omnidirectional treadmill

2 Background

Previous research has compared types of omnidirectional treadmills for navigation tasks in VR [5], omnidirectional treadmills to other VR navigation techniques [3], and omnidirectional treadmills to physically walking on the ground [8]. Lohman and Turchet [6] found that while a higher navigation speed when using an omnidirectional treadmill in VR resulted in greater levels of cybersickness, users preferred the higher speed for navigating a virtual space. Barberis and colleagues [1] recommend that omnidirectional treadmill settings, such as speed and sensor sensitivity, should be calibrated for each user to maximize comfort and performance.

Other researchers [10] have investigated the influence of omnidirectional treadmills on the gaming experience, finding that treadmill usage did not improve gaming or reduce symptoms of cybersickness among VR users. However, it was suggested that omnidirectional treadmills might have benefits for exergaming experiences. Others [9] propose that omnidirectional treadmills combined with VR may have applications in rehabilitation, but user acceptance of omnidirectional treadmills and the potential inducement of cybersickness symptoms should be carefully considered.

Relatively little work has been performed to investigate the types of applications that users consider to be pleasurable omnidirectional treadmills experiences. Our project has three goals. First, we wanted to create a VR application that highlights the benefits of an omnidirectional treadmill. Second, we wanted to be able to develop the application in stages so that many students at our University (University of the Pacific) could contribute. Third, we hoped to increase understanding of how to develop pleasurable omnidirectional treadmill experiences. For our project, we chose to create a virtual walking tour of our campus (see Figs. 2 and 3).

Fig. 2. Virtual walking tour of University of the Pacific

Fig. 3. Burns Tower at University of the Pacific

3 Development of the Virtual Campus Walking Tour

We began development of our virtual campus walking tour using Unity version 2021.3.3f1 (unity.com) and the Infinadeck Experience Platform™ Software Plugin developed by Infinadeck and available on the Unity Asset Store. Next, we modeled two campus buildings using Blender version 3.5.1. We envisioned the application being used during campus visits by prospective students that were considering study at University of the Pacific. Therefore, we invited a member of our Admissions Office staff to try the application on the treadmill and offer feedback as to what could be added to improve the experience for prospective students. We received several excellent suggestions, which included being able to interact with and be guided by our campus mascot, meet virtual representations of professors, locate and travel to areas on campus with an interactive map, and "paint the rock" (a tradition of students on our campus). It was also suggested that we have a walking path through campus that began at our most recognizable campus landmark, Burns Tower (shown in Fig. 3). Burns Tower also happens to be where real world prospective student tours begin.

At the time of this writing, we have developed models of six campus buildings and we are in the process of transitioning from the first student team to the second. The second student team will create models of the remaining campus buildings and landmarks that will be visible during the planned virtual campus walking tour route. They will also begin collecting formal feedback regarding the user experience. This will help us determine the features that the third student team will add to the application.

4 Conclusion

In this paper, we describe our experience developing a virtual reality application for an omnidirectional treadmill. The Unity game engine alongside Infinadeck's custom plugin allowed us the opportunity to remain focused on the process of modeling our campus in the virtual space. Students and faculty will continue to investigate how we can create the most fulfilling omnidirectional treadmill experience, as we form more student teams to contribute to the project. We plan to extend our research into the ways individuals respond to the treadmill, offering us the ability to both improve our work as well as document the potential strengths and limitations of an omnidirectional treadmill application. We are particularly interested in understanding how long users like to stay on the treadmill, and what application features encourage users to increase the time that they use omnidirectional treadmill applications. Anecdotally, it appears that most of our users to choose to spend less than 5 min exploring campus and very few actually walk long enough to see all of the buildings that we currently have in the tour. How to encourage users to spend longer exploring campus is a topic we plan to investigate.

References

1. Barberis, A., Bennet, T., Minear, M.: "Ready Player One": enhancing omnidirectional treadmills for use in virtual environments. In: Proceedings of the Conference on Virtual Reality and 3D User Interfaces, pp. 848–849. IEEE, Osaka, Japan (2019)

2. Bowman, D., Koller, D., Hodges, L.: Travel in immersive virtual environments: an evaluation of viewpoint motion control techniques. In: Proceedings of the Virtual Reality Annual International Symposium, pp. 45–52. IEEE, Albuquerque, New Mexico (1997)
3. Calandra, D., Lamberti, F., Migliorini, M.: On the usability of consumer locomotion techniques in serious games: comparing arm swinging, treadmills and walk-in-place. In: Proceedings of the 9th International Conference on Consumer Electronics, pp. 348–352. IEEE, Berlin, Germany (2019)
4. Darken, R., Cockayne, W., Carmein, D.: The omni-directional treadmill: a locomotion device for virtual worlds. In: Proceedings of the 10th Annual Symposium on User Interface Software and Technology, pp. 213–221, ACM, Banff, Canada (1997)
5. Hooks, K., Ferguson, W., Morillo, P., Cruz-Neira, C.: Evaluating the user experience of omnidirectional VR walking simulators. Entertain. Comput. **34**, 100352 (2020)
6. Lohman, J., Turchet, L.: Evaluating cybersickness of walking on an omnidirectional treadmill in virtual reality. IEEE Trans. Hum.-Mach. Syst. **52**(4), 613–623 (2022)
7. Sayyad, E., Sra, M., Hollerer., T.: Walking and teleportation in wide-area virtual reality experiences. In: Proceedings of the 2020 IEEE International Symposium on Mixed and Augmented Reality, pp. 608–617. IEEE, Porto de Galinhas, Brazil (2020)
8. Soni, S., Lamontagne, A.: Characterization of speed adaptation while walking on an omnidirectional treadmill. J. Neuroeng. Rehabil. **17**, 153 (2020)
9. Soon, B., Lee, N., Lau, J., Tan, N., Cai, C.: Potential of the omnidirectional walking platform with virtual reality as a rehabilitation tool. J. Rehabilit. Assist. Technol. Eng. **10**, 1–7 (2023)
10. Wehden, L., Reer, F., Janzik, R., Tang, W., Quandt, T.: The slippery path to total presence: how omnidirectional virtual reality treadmills influence the gaming experience. Media Commun. **9**(1), 5–16 (2021)

HIØF Easy Navigator: An Augmented Reality App Which Guides a User to Reach Their Destination

Safayet Anowar Shurid[1], Mahta Moezzi[1], Mohaiminul Islam[1(✉)], Pritam Das[1], and Juan C. Torrado[1,2]

[1] Østfold University College, Halden, Norway
{safayet.a.shurid,mahta.moezzi,mmemon,pritam.das,
juan.c.torrado}@hiof.no
[2] Norwegian Computing Center, Oslo, Norway

Abstract. New students often have trouble finding classrooms, laboratories, libraries, or other places inside a new study place. At Østfold University College (HIØF), they provide paper maps to the students to find locations inside the university which are difficult to understand and hard to use. To solve this problem, we have developed an app named "HIØF Easy Navigator". The application guides new students to find the inside location here at HIØF, Norway. We also conducted a survey of eight students to check the user experience and opinions of paper maps and the HIØF Easy Navigator. Our findings demonstrate that the app is easier to use than paper maps to locate locations inside the university.

Keywords: University application · 360 View · Location Tracking · Street View · Augmented Reality based application · AR location track · Location-based Computing · Navigation application

1 Introduction

There are several location-tracking applications available, such as Google Maps, mSpy, Find My Kids, Waze, etc. According to a report, approximately 154.4 million people use Google Maps monthly [4] to find their way to various destinations, and this application has been downloaded more than ten billion times from the Google Play Store. It provides local recommendations for restaurants, entertainment, and activities as well as real-time navigation. However, applications like Google Maps barely provide the direction to reach the destination, whereas only a few applications are built that are able to guide inside an area or building [1,3]. Millions of high school graduates enroll in universities each year, many of them far from home or even abroad. Finding the admissions office, classrooms, labs, and even the library is never easy for a new student at a university. This is a very common and old problem for new students at every university. When the university area is large, students have more difficulty finding their way around. Here at Østfold University College (HIØF), Norway, new students face similar issues and have

C. Stephanidis et al. (Eds.): HCII 2023, CCIS 1958, pp. 236–244, 2024.
https://doi.org/10.1007/978-3-031-49215-0_29

difficulty finding classrooms, labs, and other university rooms. Finding a room takes time, and occasionally, students are reluctant to contact their elders or university staff for assistance. The difficulties for physically challenged students are greater than for other students. Based on the problem, the team built a demo mobile application that will guide the new students here at HIØF in finding the locations of classrooms, laboratories, or even the library.

In this paper, we have explained the design process and the methodology we performed. Moreover, through our evaluation, we collected the necessary data to answer the following research question:

Can an AR-based location tracker help students find their way on campus?

- Why are paper maps not enough for finding the actual location?
- Would new students use an AR-based location tracking app for finding their location?

2 Related Works

Author Ching-Sheng Wang developed a mobile navigation system that uses 3D augmented reality to help find indoor positions. This application was created for Oxford College, located in Taiwan. Oxford College is a mix of Chinese and Western architecture, now known as the national monument [1]. The system gathered historical information to create 3D models that reflected the actual goals and built both the external and internal 3D buildings of Oxford College in the past and present. In another paper, author Gerhard Reitmayr from the Vienna University of Technology mentioned an indoor location-based application built using an augmented reality system [2]. Moreover, they prefer augmented reality because this technology helps to visualize the position or direction of a location.

In a paper, authors Teddy Mantoro, and Siti Athirah Saharudin wrote a paper about a system that can navigate the user's location using the Global Positioning System (GPS). This system has both 2D and 3D facilities, and users can choose based on their preferences. The 3D function immerses the user in the real-world environment, whereas the 2D function provides an overview of the campus [3]. Furthermore, this navigation application could track the continued movement of the user on the map. The 360-degree view of the campus in HIØF Easy Navigator provides an immersive experience, benefiting individuals with disabilities and prospective students who wish to familiarize themselves with the campus prior to their arrival.

Anindya S. Paul and Eric A. Wan mentioned in their paper that it is always hard to build an indoor location tracking and localization application [5]. Their paper discussed a low-cost indoor location tracking system that can be used with an existing WiFi network and can also accommodate new sensor observations. In another paper, Chang Lui et al. introduces an indoor location-tracking application that uses the footstep to guide the user [6]. The authors of this paper made the statement that, at present, indoor location tracking technology is a key technology. Their indoor localization system used sensor technology that counts users' footsteps without any other infrastructure. Our indoor university location tracker, based on AR and GPS, offers convenience and time-saving benefits for locating specific areas within the campus.

As mentioned in several aforementioned studies, the practicality of combining AR and 3D modeling with location-based services and applications is evident. These technologies significantly enhance the speed and convenience of location tracking. Taking

238 S. A. Shurid et al.

advantage of these technologies, we adopted GPS as our primary approach to develop our location-based AR application.

3 Methodology

Our whole process was divided into four main steps; idea generation, design (via use-case scenarios and wireframes), prototyping, and evaluation. In Fig. 1, we show the whole interaction design process, which is composed of the following steps.

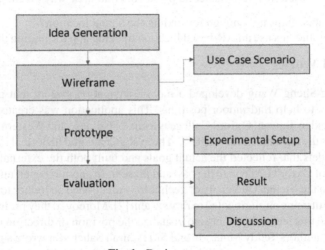

Fig. 1. Design process.

3.1 Idea Generation

When we first started this project, we focused more on the implementation rather than focusing on the problem. Our main focus was to design a VR 360 tour of our campus where students can put a VR set and have a tour of the campus. But it was not fulfilling any needs or solving any problems. After a few discussions, we finally could figure out a problem which was, that students face a problem while finding rooms on campus and it was a common problem mostly for the new students. Deciding upon this problem, we tried to keep some part of our initial idea and merged it with the new idea we thought of.

By eliminating the VR part, we focused on a more realistic solution that actually can help the students find their destination faster. The first thing which came to our mind was a smartphone because everyone has it and it is really convenient to use a smartphone rather than a VR headset. So, we decided to go with a mobile app that will act as a social robot to guide the students on campus. Since every smartphone has a camera, so instead of using VR we can go with AR. Moreover, many people are familiar with using AR for face filters and playing different kinds of games. So, this is how we came to the conclusion that we will develop an app that will help a user by showing them arrows and path points in the augmented space where they can just simply follow the arrows to go to their destination rather than asking for help or getting confused with a paper map. Ultimately, we decided to replace the arrows with an avatar in the shape of a robot. The robot will guide people in order to help them to find their location. Additionally, it has a voice assistant which is optional. Users can turn it on and listen to the voice to find the location or keep it off and use the mobile screen for navigation. The reason behind our decision is better interaction and to create a more sociable application.

Moreover, from our initial idea, we only eliminated the VR part but kept the 360 tour idea as an additional feature to our app. It is still a useful feature that can be very beneficial for students who would like to roam around the university. This feature is the same as Google Earth's street view where a user can rotate an image 360 degrees and look around a specific area. But it does not cover the campus area of our university. We decided to implement that idea for our university.

3.2 Wireframe

After figuring out the problem and identifying the needs, we started implementing the prototype, and to achieve that, a good wireframe was needed. First, we noted down everything in a paper and then decided to have a visualization of the whole system. Hence, we created a wireframe of the whole prototype using the software Figma which helped us to visualize what steps we should take to make our prototype better. In order to illustrate our design, even more, we have written a use-case scenario.

Use Case Scenario of Location Tracking Feature
Alisa is a new student who joins at Østfold University College, Norway, and she wants to go to his advisor's office to complete some formalities. As a new student, she is facing difficulties finding the advisor's office because the university is big and has several rooms. She also looked at the map which was hanging on the wall but couldn't understand it properly. Being an introvert, she is afraid or shy about asking others for help. She is late, and the time is running out because she had an appointment already. But then, she sees the QR code of the "HIØF Navigator App" and downloads it. The app locates her position with the help of GPS. In the app, she finds a search button and an input field where she could type her destination. Because of the easy interface, she quickly types the location where she wants to go and presses the search button. On the next screen, the mobile camera opens up within the app and asks the student to hold the mobile phone in the forward direction. Then the student points her phone in the forward direction, and immediately she sees some 3D arrows indicating where she has to go next. With the help of the 3D arrows, she moves towards the arrow and a new arrow appears. She keeps following the arrows and after 2 min of walking, she sees the room where she wants to go. The mobile app even was pointing at the door and she finally felt relieved because she made it in time.

3.3 Prototype

We made a demo app as our prototype which was able to showcase all the features. To build the app, we chose the software Figma for the wireframe and the design of the app.

And for making the app, we chose Unity 3D software as it was faster to develop an app with that. We gave a suitable name to the app which was "HIØF Easy Navigator". Some screenshots from our application have been provided in Fig. 2.

Fig. 2. Digital prototype

On the main screen of our app, a user can see two buttons. If a user presses the start button then an input field will appear where a user can type his destination. After typing the destination, the app shows a picture of the current position of the user. In this prototype, the default starting location is at the entrance of the university. Since our motive was to build a social robot, we made an avatar robot that pops up as soon as a user taps the search button. The robot tells the user to go next with a robotic voice. There are also instructions on the screen with each of the photos to assist the user find his destination. There are two buttons on the screen, which enable the user to go forward and backward. By pressing the next button, a user can see the picture of the next destination. Then a user just needs to follow the robot in order to find the location.

There was another button on the main screen which was for the 360 tours of the campus. Upon pressing the button, a user can see 360 photos of the campus and rotate around it. These photos were taken with iPhone 13 pro max's camera and we used the Google Street app to capture those photos in 360. We clicked multiple photos of the campus, both inside the university and outside the university. To view that, there was an arrow button and with the help of that, a user can easily view the images. All the screens had a convenient back button so the user can easily go back and forth and explore the features. For a friendly user experience, we used our robot avatar on different screens.

3.4 Evaluation

Eight students at the institution were recruited to take part in this evaluation. They were fairly new to Østfold University and it had been a common problem for all of them to find the exact location of certain places.

Experimental Setup

For the evaluation, We brought the evaluators to the entrance of the University building and asked them to go to a specific place. Then, we gave them consent forms to sign and provided them with the prototype app. The application was already installed in one of our tested smartphones which was a One Plus 9RT smartphone. There were 8 participants and they were divided into two groups. We gave our prototype app to one group and the other group was provided with a paper map of Østfold University. Each member of the two groups took part individually. Every participant started at the entrance of Østfold University and the room they were supposed to find was A1–007, which was a fairly difficult room to locate. We measured the time count of each participant with a help of a stopwatch and observed them during the activity. After they were done with finding the room, they filled a questionnaire.

Results

After collecting data from the survey paper, we used the data visualization technique to make the result more stable. In our survey paper, we had a total of seven questions. Figure 4 illustrates the result based on the participants' answers.

For ease of comparison and due to not being able to find the room using paper maps, those who used paper maps were later allowed to use digital maps as well. Figure 3 gives an overview of the survey paper for the eight participants.

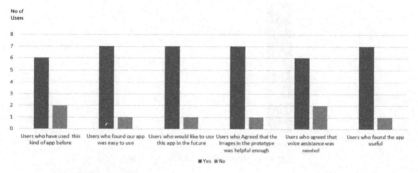

Fig. 3. Answers to the questions from the questionnaire

As we can see, seven out of eight users, which is 80% of the total participants, found our app useful and agreed that the user interface of the app was easy to understand and they would like to use this app in the future. Seven of the participants also agreed that the images used in the prototype were in good condition and it helped them find the actual location. However, 40% of evaluators did not find the voice instruction feature that much helpful and did not use similar types of apps before.

When the participants were using our prototype, we observed and took some additional data and one of the main variables was the amount of time they were spending to find the room. Figure 4 shows that those who used the HIØF Navigator app took only 2 min on average to find the room whereas those who used the paper maps took more than 10 min.

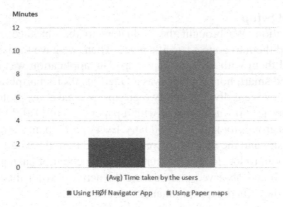

Fig. 4. Time difference between the two groups of users

In Fig. 5, we can see that none of the users were able to find the room using the paper map but they all found the room when they used the application.

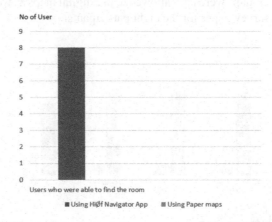

Fig. 5. The number of users who were successful in finding the room

Discussion

From Fig. 3, we can see that, among all the participants, the majority of them used similar types of apps in the past and found them easy to use, whereas a few of them never used this kind of app. Moreover, almost all the users agreed that they want to use similar types of applications in the future and are satisfied with the prototype features such as voice assistance and image view. A significant number of participants found that the images in the prototype were helpful enough. In the "HIØF Easy Navigator" we also added the voice assistant feature." Six participants liked it, whereas two felt it was not necessary to have this feature in the app. This gives us a clear understanding that if this kind of app is made available for the users then they can really use it easily and get the benefits out of this app.

Figure 4 shows information about time which was a crucial variable for the measurement. As we can see that there is a significant difference between the two bars as the users who used the app took only 2 min and 30 s whereas the users with paper maps took more than 10 min. Not only that, Fig. 6 tells us that users who used the paper maps could not even find the actual room due to the difficulty of understanding the map. Although we expected some users to find the room using paper maps, it turns out that the room we chose was not properly pointed at the map. But, it is known that maps are not always detailed and it is difficult to illustrate the whole campus and rooms on a small piece of paper. That is why, from this evaluation, we can agree that there is a need for a location-tracking application like HIØF Easy Navigator for the students.

The HIØF Easy Navigator will be connected to the university's network infrastructure through the Internet. Our application will be accessible on the 'Home page' of Østfold University College's website. Additionally, to provide more convenient access, separate applications will be provided for both Android and iOS systems. The application can be installed and utilized on smartphones and tablets. Both features of our application can also be used with VR-XR tools, which will be available at the university's entrances. These tools will allow our users to explore their locations using VR technology.

4   Conclusion

We conducted a survey asking participants to evaluate their experience using the "HIØF Easy Navigator" app compared to the paper maps the university provided. According to the survey report data, most of the participants found it easy to find the location using the app, and they also plan to use it again in the future. They prefer the app because paper maps are difficult to understand and the information is not sufficient to find the indoor location. In the future, we aim to develop the app with more features that will help new students, as well as disabled students, find the indoor location of the university.

Appendix

Survey Form (Questionnaire)
    1. Do you find this app easy to use?

a. Yes
b. No

    2. Have you used similar types of apps before?

a. Yes
b. No

    3. How helpful do you think our app was to find the destination?

a. Very helpful
b. Helpful
c. It can be helpful sometimes
d. Not helpful at all

4. Do you think the captured images were sufficient to help you find the location?

a. Yes
b. No

5. Do you prefer an app or a paper map to find your destination?

a. Only app
b. Both the app and paper map
c. Only paper map

6. Would you prefer the app with voice assistance or without voice assistance?

a. With voice assistance
b. Without voice assistance

7. Would you like to use this app frequently in the future?

a. Yes
b. No

References

1. Wang, C.-S.: An AR mobile navigation system integrating indoor positioning and content recommendation services. World Wide Web **22**(3), 1241–1262 (2018). https://doi.org/10.1007/s11280-018-0580-3
2. Reitmayr, G., Schmalstieg, D.: Location based applications for mobile augmented reality. In: Proceedings of the Fourth Australasian user interface conference on User Interfaces 2003-vol. 18, pp. 65–73 (2003)
3. Mantoro, T., Saharudin, S.A., Selamat, S.: 3D interactive mobile navigator structure and 2D map in campus environment using GPS. In: Proceedings of the 7th International Conference on Advances in Mobile Computing and Multimedia, pp. 401–405 (2009)
4. Pawar, S.: 20+ Best google maps statistics 2022: usage, accuracy and updates. Enterprise Apps Today 2022. https://www.enterpriseappstoday.com/stats/google-maps-statistics.html. Accessed 14 Nov 2022
5. Smith, C.: Posts by Craig Smith → V all. 14 interesting waze statistics and facts. Waze Statistics, User Count and Facts (2022)
6. Liu, C., Xie, L., Wang, C., Wu, J., Lu, S.: FootStep-tracker: an anchor-free indoor localization system via sensing foot steps. In: Adjunct Proceedings of the 2015 ACM International Joint Conference on Pervasive and Ubiquitous Computing and Proceedings of the 2015 ACM International Symposium on Wearable Computers, pp. 285–288 (2015)

Core Values for a Mixed Reality Software Development Kit: A Qualitative Study Among Main SDK Tools for XR Development

Dayvson Silva[✉], Jordy Pereira[✉], Lucas Almeida[✉], and Marcos Silbermann[✉]

Sidia Institute of Science and Technology, Avenue Darcy Vargas, 654, Manaus, AM, Brazil
{dayvson.silva,jordy.perreira,lucas.almeida,
marcos.silbermann}@sidia.com

Abstract. In early 2022, the UX Research team from Sidia's Research and Development Institute, located at Manaus/Brazil, received a requirement from one of its projects to conduct a comparative study on the usage of different Software Development Kits (SDKs) for Mixed Reality (XR) applications. The study aims to compile developer's necessities and difficulties while using common available SDKs in the market. This qualitative study is about the core SDK values pointed out by participants related to the development of XR applications. We have selected developers based on availability to conduct a study for a month. With the help of Microsoft Office Forms, we have structured a series of surveys about the main usage activities of five important SDK tools to develop XR experiences. The selected SDKs were: ARCore, AR Foundation, Vuforia, Spark AR (Scripting API), and A-Frame. The surveys have been structured obeying the flow of activities of an XR application development. The defined flow, based on interview with the candidates, consisted of main phases: Installation e Update, Development, Tests and Deploy. The survey, compiled in a detailed report, exposes the collected data and share some of the participant's opinion to provide context and exemplify the exposed use cases. In this report, we observe that the characteristics and needs of the participants varies according to which phase of the activity flow they are executing. For some stages, users demanded agility and frictionless processes. At other times, the flexibility and customization of the SDK behaviors were widely punctuated by participants.

Keywords: Software Development Kits · Mixed Reality · Core SDK values

1 Introduction

XR has emerged as a promising technology that combines elements of the real and virtual world to create immersive and interactive experiences. Developing XR applications requires the use of SDKs that provide tools and resources to build these applications efficiently. However, developers' experience using SDKs may vary, depending on the stages of the development process, such as installing and updating, development itself, testing and deploying applications.

C. Stephanidis et al. (Eds.): HCII 2023, CCIS 1958, pp. 245–251, 2024.
https://doi.org/10.1007/978-3-031-49215-0_30

In this article, we present a study that analyzes the experience of developers of XR applications in relation to installing and updating, developing, testing and deploying five SDKs available on the market. We used forms to collect data and identify the main findings of the research, the pains reported by the participants and the values discovered in the XR development process using these SDKs. In addition, we discuss recommendations and opportunities to improve the developer experience and promote the creation of these tools for XR application development.

2   Related Works

Given the constant evolution of immersive technologies such as Augmented Reality, Virtual Reality and Mixed Reality and the variety of devices available, such as cell phones and HMD (Head-Mounted-Displays), new tools and software development kits emerge to allow developers and companies create applications and solutions that reach the widest possible audience. Therefore, the comprehensive mapping and comparison of these tools to help developers decide which is the best option for their projects is necessary [1].

However, the range of tool and device options is very wide, making objective comparison difficult, as generally the criteria used are features and functionalities common to all these tools; often excluding analysis of potentially valuable features that are specific to some of the tools. Thus, another relevant factor considered in past research is the context of the solution to be implemented. This helps in defining criteria and characteristics for comparison based on functional and non-functional requirements of applications [2].

It is also possible to notice the impact of the context when we observe the use of these tools to create applications in the Education area, where it is expected that the user does not have in-depth knowledge in software development. In these cases, tools like Unity 3D combined with Mixed Reality SDKs help in the process of facilitating development and learning [3].

Finally, it is possible to use these SDKs through another graphical interface application, which allows the manipulation of SDK functionalities in a visual and intuitive way, increasing productivity and performance in iterations during development. The analysis of SDKs that have some kind of integration with these auxiliary tools can also directly influence the choice of users [4].

3   Methodology

The present study used a qualitative approach, aiming to understand the main aspects about application development tools in Mixed Reality, from the point of view of the users of such tools, the developers. Developers were selected, according to their availability, who work with this type of technology and with different types of seniority to use five different SDKs during a creation flow, the main phases considered here were: Installation and Update, Development, Test and Deploy. User Experience (UX) month. The forms were created based on an application Researchers and a developer of XR technologies.

3.1 Software Development Kits to Mixed Reality

With the advancement of technologies in the development of applications, especially in the XR environment, a vast collection of products has emerged for this purpose, both proprietary and open-source [5]. In general, Augmented, Virtual and Mixed Reality platforms and SDKs have many similarities, such as the use of APIs for motion tracking, object recognition and light estimation.

For this work we used five commonly found in the market:

AR Foundation is highly integrated with other technologies in the AR ecosystem, such as ARCore, allowing developers to take full advantage of these technologies to create high-quality AR experiences. Vuforia is one of the most popular SDKs in the augmented reality market [8]. It supports a wide range of devices, including smartphones, tablets and augmented reality glasses, allowing developers to create immersive experiences in a variety of contexts. You can try out most of its features for free, making it an attractive option for first-time developers or low-budget projects. Spark AR (Scripting API). Spark AR is an augmented reality (AR) experience creation tool developed by Meta, available for use in products such as Instagram and Facebook [9]. One of the key features of Spark AR is the ability to create AR experiences through an intuitive graphical interface, as well as through coding using the JavaScript language. A-Frame. A-Frame is a web framework based on web technologies that allows the development of applications in different contexts of reality. Developed by Mozilla, A-Frame is recognized for its ease of use and its large developer community [10]. As an open source platform, A-Frame gives developers the ability to customize and extend its functionality to meet the specific needs of their projects.

3.2 Research Tools

The first form refers to the Installation and Update of the SDKs, this form aims to have a more practical perspective of the developer's first contact with the development resources. The Development sheet focused on extracting data on the use of SDKs. In it, we aimed to add questions such as the degree of difficulty of use, whether the tools had documentation that would help in their understanding, as well as online resources, negative and positive points, number of example projects and pre-made templates, in addition to features and components available. The third form, on the other hand, sought to retrieve data from the developers regarding the Test and Deploy phase.

3.3 Analysis

It is important to point out that we carried out a qualitative analysis process, in which the responses and notes made by the developers were categorized and analyzed contextually, using discourse analysis techniques [12]. Through these strategies, several key points were extracted for our research, such as the main findings in the participants' speeches, pain in using the tools, suggestions for improvements and new mechanisms that would add greater value to the product. This information was compiled in an internal report by our institute to guide new demands for our own products.

A differential of our approach was the constitution of our interdisciplinary team of researchers, formed by designers and developers. We can consider that the interdisciplinary structure of the group conferred an important quality to the analysis. On the one hand, the presence of developers in the group allowed a contextualized reading of the data collected in its specificity, the information and specialized points of view of the respondents of the forms. On the other hand, the presence of designers helped us to put this information into perspective, helping to broadly understand the desires and points of view of the developers participating in the research.

4 Results

In this section, we will have the opportunity to explore in detail the results of this research, which are extremely important for the new SDKs. Insights gained from participating developers' opinions and experiences are valuable as they directly reflect the needs and expectations of this specific target audience. By analyzing key research findings, we can gain a deeper understanding of developers' perceptions of SDKs, as well as the pains and values identified throughout the process. The results can also serve as a guide for companies and development teams looking to better understand developer demands.

4.1 Main Research Findings

Software development is an area in constant evolution, with several methodologies, tools and resources available to developers. These are the main findings of this research and we explain them further below.

Fewer Steps Between Installation and Starting Development on the SDK. Study participants highlighted the importance of references like A-Frame and Spark AR Scripting API, which allow users to start developing without having to install the entire SDK. This streamlines the development process by eliminating unnecessary layers and reducing the setup time required before users can start building their applications.

Less Steep Learning Curve. During the development phase, the interviewees emphasized the importance of resources that facilitate learning, such as complete and consistent documentation, the existence of communities for exchanging procedures and information among users, and the presence of examples and tutorials. These features help to shorten the learning curve, making it easier for developers to understand and use the SDK effectively.

Visualization of Changes in Real Time in the Application. It is interesting when the tool allows a clearer view of what is being developed in real time, preferably in the same environment. The ability to see changes in real time provides immediate feedback on the impact of changes, allowing developers to iterate and improve their applications more efficiently. It also helps to bring the development and execution space closer together, providing a more seamless development experience.

Spark AR (Scripting API) as the Main Reference in This Study. The Scripting API was identified as the main reference due to its value in terms of agility, speed and integration with Instagram. It was found that this tool facilitates the development process, reduces the learning curve and simplifies the submission process. This highlights the importance of the Scripting API as a preferred choice among surveyed developers for building augmented reality experiences.

4.2 Main Users' Pains Mapped

Below we bring the main pains reported by the participants in the use of the tools in three main phases. Understanding these pains is critical to improving these tools and optimizing the software development process, providing valuable insights for developers and the technology industry as a whole.

The initial SDK installation and update phase is the time when participants identified the main pain points in using the SDKs. The complexity of the installation process, which can involve several steps and technical configurations, was identified as a challenge. Developers have reported difficulties installing and configuring the SDKs in their development environments, which can result in initial setup delays and frustrations. The lack of clear and detailed documentation about the installation process was also mentioned as a pain, as it can make it difficult to understand the installation flow and properly configure the SDKs.

In the development phase, participants highlighted the steep learning curve of some tools experienced as one of the main pain points. The lack of comprehensive examples and tutorials was also mentioned as a pain, as it can make it difficult to understand best practices and efficiently develop applications with the SDK. The absence of complete and consistent documentation was also identified as a pain, as it can lead to doubts and uncertainties during the development process.

In the test and deploy phase, participants reported the lack of efficient tools to test and debug applications developed with the SDK as one of the main pain points. The absence of real-time debugging and monitoring features was mentioned as a challenge, as it can make it difficult to identify and correct errors during the testing and deployment process. These pains reported by participants highlight the challenges faced by developers in using SDKs, and highlight the importance of improvements in installation, documentation, examples, tutorials, as well as testing and deployment tools, aimed at facilitating the development process and increasing efficiency in the process use of these tools.

4.3 User's Values About Developing in SDK for SDK

In the Installation and Update phase, developers value the simplification and automation of these processes, making it fast and intuitive. The presence of clear and comprehensive documentation is also considered essential, providing detailed information about the SDK. Furthermore, having a dedicated space to manage SDK packages, versions and updates, such as a dedicated package manager, was highlighted as a significant value. Finally, predefined settings and shortcuts in the tool are also valued, facilitating use and allowing developers to focus on the application itself. In the Development phase, the essential values identified are the availability of short and segmented examples, which offer objectivity and simplicity in the process of learning the SDK. Additionally, having a large number of examples helps cover a wide range of SDK features and functionality, providing a greater understanding of available capabilities. It is also essential that the examples are easily accessible, preferably in an online repository, so that developers can find them easily.

Finally, in the Test and Deploy part, it is important to enable the execution and simulation of the application in the same environment, simplifying the real-time visualization of what is being produced. In addition, the proximity between the development and execution environments is valued for a more reliable visualization of the result. It is critical to have a dedicated error console, with clear, development friendly messages, to make it easier to identify and resolve SDK issues.

5 Discussion

Based on the data collected and the analysis performed, some recommendations can be made to improve the experience of XR application developers. First, installing and updating the SDK were identified as critical points in the developers' experience. It is recommended to simplify and streamline the installation process by providing clear documentation, step-by-step installation guides, and technical support resources such as discussion forums or chat support. Additionally, updating the SDK should be made easy, with clear auto-update options or clear notifications when a new version is available, to ensure that developers can stay up-to-date with the latest improvements and bug fixes.

Another recommendation concerns the documentation and development resources available. The survey identified that developers value sample code, templates, and detailed documentation to help them get started and move forward with the development of their XR applications. Therefore, it is important to provide complete, up-to-date and easily accessible documentation, with functional code examples and ready-to-use templates. In addition, it can be useful to provide an online community, such as forums or discussion groups, where developers can share experiences, ask questions and get additional support during development.

6 Conclusions

In short, ensuring simplification, automation, comprehensive documentation, practical examples, ease of access and modification, a collaborative online community, real-time execution and simulation, integration with the development environment, and build and deploy capabilities are core values. to provide a positive and efficient experience when using an SDK. By meeting these values, developers can start developing their applications quickly, keep their development environment up-to-date, and identify and resolve issues more efficiently, contributing to the success of the software development project.

Acknowledgment. This work was presented as part of the project results to HARP SCENE APP SDK_22, executed by the Science and Technology Institute - Sidia, in partnership with Samsung Electronics of Amazônia Ltda, according to Informatics Law n.8387/91 and article no. 39 of Decree 10.521/2020.

References

1. Amin, D., Govilkar, S.: Comparative study of augmented reality SDKs. Int. J. Comput. Sci. Appl. **5**(1), 11–26 (2015)
2. Rautenbach, V., Coetzee, S., Jooste, D.: Results of an evaluation of augmented reality mobile development frameworks for addresses in augmented reality. Spat. Inf. Res. **24**, 211–223 (2016)
3. Herpich, F., Guarese, R.L.M., Tarouco, L.M.R.: A comparative analysis of augmented reality frameworks aimed at the development of educational applications. Creat. Educ. **8**(9), 1433–1451 (2017)
4. Vakaliuk, T.A., Pochtoviuk, S.I.: Analysis of tools for the development of augmented reality technologies. In: CEUR Workshop Proceedings (2021)
5. Silva, R.S., Gomes, A.S.: A systematic mapping study of software development kits for virtual reality applications. J. Syst. Software **169**, 110644 (2020)
6. Google. ARCore. https://developers.google.com/ar. Accessed 30 Mar 2023
7. Unity Technologies. AR Foundation. https://unity.com/unity/features/arfoundation. Accessed 30 Mar 2023
8. PTC. Vuforia. https://www.ptc.com/en/products/augmented%20reality/vuforia. Accessed 30 Mar 2023
9. Facebook Technologies, LLC. Spark AR Scripting API. https://sparkar.facebook.com/ar-studio/learn/scripting/. Accessed 30 Mar 2023
10. Mozilla. A-Frame. https://aframe.io/. Accessed 30 Mar 2023
11. Cohn, M.: Agile estimating and planning. Pearson Education (2005)
12. Bardin, L.: Análisis de contenido (Vol. 89). Ediciones Akal (1991)

A Framework for Accessibility in XR Environments

Aikaterini Valakou[1], George Margetis[1], Stavroula Ntoa[1],
and Constantine Stephanidis[1,2]

[1] Institute of Computer Science, Foundation for Research and Technology—Hellas (FORTH), 70013 Heraklion, Crete, Greece
{valakou,gmarget,stant,cs}@ics.forth.gr
[2] University of Crete, Heraklion, Greece

Abstract. Digital accessibility is vital for ensuring equal access and usability for individuals with disabilities. However, addressing the unique challenges faced by individuals with disabilities in XR environments remains a complex task. This paper presents an ongoing accessibility framework designed to empower developers in creating inclusive XR applications. The framework aims to provide a comprehensive solution, addressing the needs of individuals with disabilities, by incorporating various accessibility features, based on XR accessibility guidelines, best practices, and state of the art approaches. The current version of the framework has focused on the accessibility of XR environments for blind or partially sighted users, enhancing their interaction with text, images, videos, and 3D artefacts. The proposed work lays the foundation for Extended Reality (XR) developers to easily encompass accessible assets. In this respect, it offers customizable text settings, alternative visual content text, and multiple user interaction control mechanisms. Furthermore, it includes features such as edge enhancement, interactive element descriptions with dynamic widgets, scanning for navigation, and foreground positioning of active objects. The framework also supports scene adaptations upon user demand to cater to specific visual needs.

Keywords: Accessibility · Extended Reality · Framework · Inclusion · Augmented Reality · Virtual Reality

1 Introduction

Ensuring digital accessibility for individuals with disabilities is critical to inclusive Human-Centered design. In the realm of extended reality (XR), accessibility challenges for people with visual impairments, motor impairments, hearing impairments, cognitive, and other disabilities are significant exclusion factors giving rise to novel dimensions of the digital divide. To address these challenges, XR environments need to be carefully designed to integrate various accessibility features seamlessly, which, however, remains a complex task.

To alleviate difficulties entailed in creating XR environments accessible to all, a universal access approach needs to be adopted, to design systems that take diversity

C. Stephanidis et al. (Eds.): HCII 2023, CCIS 1958, pp. 252–263, 2024.
https://doi.org/10.1007/978-3-031-49215-0_31

into account and satisfy the variety of implied requirements in a proactive approach [1]. To this end, this paper introduces an ongoing XR accessibility framework designed to provide developers with a cohesive approach to incorporating diverse accessibility features into their XR applications. The framework aims to simplify the process of adjusting accessibility settings without burdening developers with multiple disparate tools. The proposed framework is based on a thorough review of relevant literature, thus ensuring that state of the art accessibility features to XR environments are adopted.

The framework offers customizable text settings, alternative text for images and videos, multiple controlling mechanisms for user interaction, and ongoing work on video subtitle customization. It also includes features such as edge enhancement for 3D artefacts, interactive element descriptions with dynamic widgets, scanning support for navigation in the XR environment, and foreground positioning of active objects. Additionally, it incorporates scene adaptations like brightness adjustment, magnified lenses, and recolouring tools to cater to specific visual needs.

The proposed XR accessibility framework is an ongoing work that aims to enhance XR accessibility for developers. While certain features are still under development, the framework continues to evolve and improve. This paper provides background information, an overview of the framework, implementation details, and a use case to showcase its effectiveness in creating inclusive XR applications.

2 Background and Related Work

Today, there is a vast array of online services and applications that have become essential for our daily activities. A notable advancement in this realm is the emergence of online XR applications, which go beyond traditional domains like gaming and education. These applications now span various areas, including business [2] ecommerce [3], and culture [4]. Consequently, ensuring digital accessibility has become a crucial requirement for addressing the fundamental needs of people with disabilities, and thus ensuring their equal access to digital services and applications. Digital accessibility encompasses a growing commitment, by policymakers, public bodies, the research community, and the industry, to develop legislation, guidelines, standards, and assistive technologies that empower people with disabilities to access and utilize various applications [5–7].

Although many efforts have been put forward in several domains addressing disabled users, and especially individuals with visual impairments, the challenges they face in engaging with digital content in extended reality (XR) remain significant. People with visual impairments encounter difficulties perceiving visual information, including text, images, videos, and 3D objects, within XR environments [8]. To address these challenges, numerous solutions have been proposed, such as visual display adaptations [9, 10], overlays [11, 12], and audio or haptic-based [13–16] approaches for interaction. Visual display adaptations have gained attention to enhance accessibility for this user group. Similarly, individuals with motor impairments face obstacles when interacting with virtual objects and navigating virtual environments. Many existing systems employ complex interaction techniques without customization, overlooking the specific needs of this user group [17, 18]. Approaches commonly used include alternative input devices, eye gaze control, and head movements [19] Nevertheless, a major challenge for users with motor impairments, despite the device employed, is that the point-and-select paradigm is not effective; instead, there is a need for acquiring sequential access to the interactive elements of a User Interface (UI). A common technique employed in this respect is scanning, which sequentially highlights and gives focus to the interactive elements of a UI [20]. For individuals who are deaf or hard of hearing approaches to enhance accessibility include displayed written content, which however may not be in their native language, as well as signed video descriptions for text, objects, or other interface items (see Footnote 1).

Realizing the pressing need for creating accessible XR environments, adopting a 'by design' approach, numerous tools have been proposed in the literature to aid the development of XR experiences, focusing on streamlining and automating commonly utilized functionalities. An illustrative example is the XR Interaction Toolkit [21], specifically designed to simplify the process by offering preconfigured components that ensure seamless compatibility across various Virtual Reality (VR) devices. Moreover, the toolkit incorporates scripts that facilitate fundamental interactions within VR environments. SeeingVR is a Unity plugin for developers, designed to enhance visual display settings VR applications, offering 14 distinct tools to optimize visual accessibility for individuals with low vision [22]. Despite the progress achieved, many of these efforts remain in the prototype stage within the research field, lacking integration into mainstream applications or platforms, while developers identify that they need better integration of accessibility guidelines, alongside code examples of particular accessibility features [23]. Grass-rooted in these approaches, we propose an XR accessibility framework, for Unity developers, that will foster them towards developing universally accessible XR applications, addressing the interaction needs of users with visual impairments.

3   The Universal Accessibility XR Framework

The proposed framework has been implemented as an assets package made on the Unity Game Engine, available to be installed in projects. This is an easy-to-use, plug-and-play approach that developers can use to effortlessly embed accessibility into their AR or VR applications.

3.1   Framework Overview

The objective of the framework is to establish a cohesive approach for XR application developers to incorporate various accessibility features. Additionally, the framework aims to offer a straightforward method for adjusting these settings to the specific requirements of each application, without requiring any developer effort. The accessibility adjustments provided are derived from a comprehensive review of relevant literature.

Currently, the system provides support for a range of content adjustments to enhance accessibility for text, images, videos, and 3D artefacts. One of the main goals of the framework is to provide developers with accessible components ready to be used. More specifically, in respect of textual information, the framework offers a wide range of options for customization, including the option of modifying the font size and color, outline thickness and colour, in addition to an adjustable text background. This feature is particularly valuable for individuals with low vision, as it allows them to enhance text contrast and improve legibility. Images and videos are being enhanced with alternative text (alt text), which provides textual descriptions of the visual content. Furthermore, multiple controlling mechanisms, such as resizing, play, and pause options, are incorporated to facilitate user interaction regarding multimedia content. Additionally, the framework extends its accessibility features to encompass video subtitles, allowing users to customize them to their preferences. This customization includes the ability to modify font styles, background colours, and font sizes, thereby optimizing the viewing experience for individuals with diverse accessibility needs.

For 3D artefacts, the framework grants developers the ability to activate the edge enhancement tool, enabling the enhancement of object edges to improve visibility. Furthermore, developers can customize line colours and thickness, affording them greater control over the visual representation of these artefacts. This flexibility allows for enhanced user experiences and accommodates diverse user preferences.

To activate the accessibility features, the developer has to indicate the interactive elements within the scene. To support multiple ways of description[1], each interactive element is accompanied by a widget that offers supplementary information such as text, images, and videos. Depending on the disability of the target users, the widget is dynamically adjustable. For instance, for blind users, screen reader is activated automatically, providing auditory descriptions of each interactive object, utilizing t the text description associated with the object. For persons with vision deficiencies, appropriate tools are deployed to assist them in perceiving and interacting with the XR environment. As a result, individuals with visual impairments are empowered to effectively access and comprehend the content.

The accessibility framework also incorporates a scanning feature that holds significant value in XR applications for individuals with disabilities. This feature plays a crucial role in facilitating effective navigation through the interactive elements of the XR for users with visual impairments. Each interactive element within the scene is activated in a hierarchical order, which is initially determined by the default arrangement of interactive elements in the Unity scene, moving from top to bottom. However, the framework also provides developers with the flexibility to customize this order using a designated field. This capability empowers developers to tailor the scanning experience and optimize accessibility based on specific user needs within XR applications.

The accessibility framework includes also a notable feature designed to enhance navigation in the XR environment for individuals with visual impairments. This feature ensures that when specific interactive objects selected by the developer, become active, they are brought forward in the scene, closer to the user. By bringing the active objects into the foreground, the framework facilitates improved visibility and easier interaction, benefiting individuals with visual impairments. Moreover, this functionality may also be beneficial for users with cognitive impairments, as it brings to the user's focus the element they need to pay attention to, reducing any cognitive burden induced by the complexity of the remaining scene.

Furthermore, the framework extends its accessibility provisions beyond individual content items. It includes scene adaptations, offering functionalities such as brightness

---

[1] https://www.w3.org/TR/xaur/.

adjustment, a magnified lens for enlarged viewing, and a recolouring tool to modify the colour scheme, thus catering to the needs of colour-blind individuals. In more detail, the user can select a colour profile (e.g. protanopia, deuteranopia, tritanopia), and the framework ensures that the scene is appropriately recoloured to address the needs of each user in the best possible way. For instance, in the case of protanopia, the color red is substituted with magenta, while in the case of deuteranopia, green is substituted with light blue. Similarly, for tritanopia, blue is substituted with green [24]. These scene adaptations aim to address the specific visual needs and preferences of users, further enhancing their overall experience within the XR environment.

3.2 Implementation

To enhance the description of each interactive 3D artefact (Unity GameObject), additional text, images, or video can be incorporated. To identify the interactive elements within the scene, developers can utilize a C# script called "InteractiveElement.cs" that should be attached to the corresponding GameObjects. This script extends the functionality of the GameObject class in Unity and includes references to the text, image, and video GameObects, where developers can place the appropriate prefabs. Furthermore, the script includes a field called "Order in Hierarchy" that allows developers to modify the scanning order hierarchy without altering the original order established in the Unity scene.

To facilitate scene adaptations, the accessibility framework offers a Unity Prefab called "Accessibility Framework Manager." This Prefab includes public entries that grant control over various tools and their respective parameters. The goal of this approach is to establish a standardized development way for adjusting accessibility settings within the XR application. For example, the developers using the Prefab corresponding to text assets need only to proceed with text adjustments once, and then they are applied seamlessly throughout the scene. The framework dynamically identifies all text objects present in the scene and applies the desired changes accordingly. Additionally, the Prefab allows for enabling features such as brightness adjustment, magnified lens, and recolouring tool. By incorporating the Accessibility Manager Prefab into their VR scene, developers can effortlessly control these tools and optimize accessibility settings for users (Fig. 1).

The framework also allows developers to specify the set of disabilities that their application aims to address. To this end, we have expanded the Unity top bar menu by adding < MenuItem > called "AccessibilityManager". This menu item inherits the functionalities of the Unity < EditorWindow > and offers a convenient way to configure the scene. It shows the categories of disabilities supported, like blindness, low vision, colour blindness, hearing impairment, and upper limb motor disabilities. When the colour blindness option is selected, a dropdown menu appears, presenting diverse types of colour blindness, namely: protanope, deuteranope, and tritanope. The disability types are shown as toggle buttons, allowing the selection of one or multiple options, as illustrated in Fig. 2. Once the values are specified, a JSON-like element is created, representing the scene's configuration as it is displayed in Fig. 3. For example, if the application is targeting blind users, any assisting videos or images will be hidden, and the screen reader will be activated to provide auditory feedback.

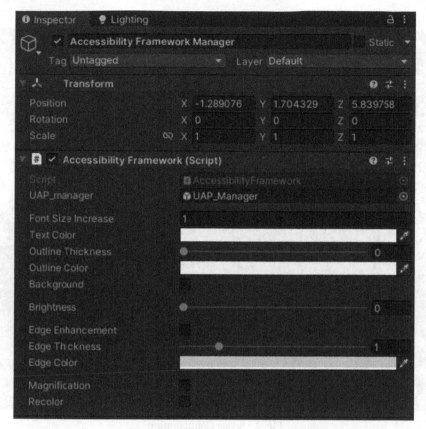

Fig. 1. The accessibility framework manager provided adaptations

4 Use Case

To facilitate testing and evaluation, a Unity sample scene is being developed. This scene presents a Virtual Reality museum, showcasing various 3D cultural heritage (CH) artefacts that provide accessible interaction with users, including persons with visual impairments (Fig. 4). Each 3D artefact in the scene, that the developer wants to be accessible, is associated with the "InteractiveElement.cs" script. Additionally, multiple text GameObjects, implemented using the < TextMeshPro > component, are positioned within the scene to provide descriptions for each artefact. The placement of these text elements can be customized as per preference. The accessibility Framework Manager prefab scans the scene, identifying and adjusting the text elements based on user options, as depicted in Fig. 5. When the scanning option is activated, one by one all the interactive elements in the scene are activated inheriting the accessibility properties that the developer has set via the "InteractiveElement.cs" script. For instance, if the current user is blind or partially sighted, then the first interactive element on the list is brought forward in the scene, closer to the user, the embedded screen reader starts reading the corresponding

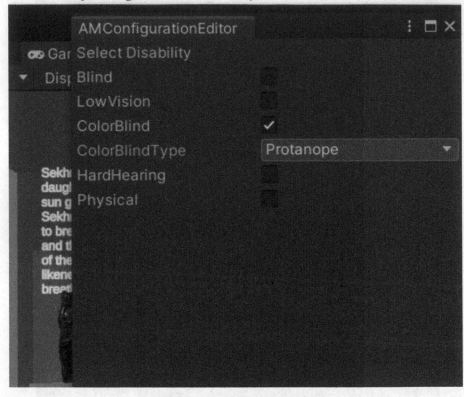

Fig. 2. Scene Configuration

```
{
    "blind": false,
    "lowvision": false,
    "colorblind": {
        "protanope": true,
        "deyteranope": false,
        "tritanope": false
    },
    "hardhearing": false,
    "physical": false
}
```

Fig. 3. JSON object for scene configuration

text, describing the artefact, while with the use of edge enhancement the 3D object is highlighted as shown in Fig. 6.

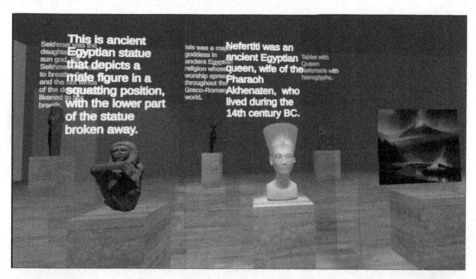

Fig. 4. Museum scene

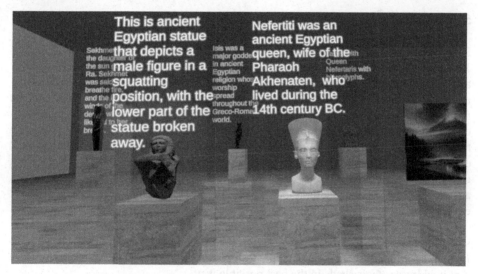

Fig. 5. Text Adjustments, font size and outline

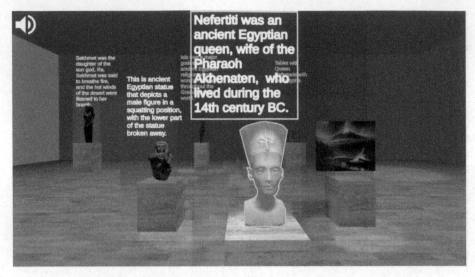

Fig. 6. Screen Reader and Edge Enhancement to the active element

5 Conclusion

In this paper, we report on an ongoing accessibility framework designed for developers of XR applications. The framework offers customizable features for text, images, videos, and 3D artefacts, along with interactive element descriptions and various controlling mechanisms. Its goal is to simplify the process of creating accessible XR environments for developers, ensuring the adoption of accessibility guidelines, best practices and state-of-the-art approaches. While the presented use case focuses on museums, it is important to note that the framework can be applied to various XR applications, including games, educational environments, business environments, etc. By incorporating this framework into their development process, developers can contribute to the advancement of XR accessibility and ensure that individuals with disabilities can fully engage and enjoy XR experiences across different domains.

Future work entails the extension of the described framework with additional accessibility features to provide improved support for a wide range of individuals with disabilities. In addition, the framework will be tested with developers and end-users to ensure that it addresses their needs in the best possible way.

Acknowledgements. This work has received funding from the EU's Horizon Europe research and innovation programme under Grant Agreement No 101060660 (SHIFT). This paper reflects only the authors' views and the Commission is not responsible for any use that may be made of the information it contains.

References

1. Stephanidis, C., Antona, M., Ntoa, S.: Human factors in ambient intelligence environments. In: Salvendy, G., Karwowski, W. (eds.) Handbook of Human Factors and Ergonomics, pp. 1058–1084. Wiley (2021). https://doi.org/10.1002/9781119636113.ch41
2. Ntoa, S., Birliraki, C., Drossis, G., Margetis, G., Adami, I., Stephanidis, C.: UX design of a big data visualization application supporting gesture-based interaction with a large display. In: Yamamoto, S. (ed.) Human Interface and the Management of Information: Information, Knowledge and Interaction Design: 19th International Conference, HCI International 2017, Vancouver, BC, Canada, July 9–14, 2017, Proceedings, Part I, pp. 248–265. Springer International Publishing, Cham (2017). https://doi.org/10.1007/978-3-319-58521-5_20
3. Margetis, G., Ntoa, S., Stephanidis, C.: Smart omni-channel consumer engagement in malls. In: Stephanidis, C. (ed.) HCI International 2019 - Posters: 21st International Conference, HCII 2019, Orlando, FL, USA, July 26–31, 2019, Proceedings, Part III, pp. 89–96. Springer International Publishing, Cham (2019). https://doi.org/10.1007/978-3-030-23525-3_12
4. Margetis, G., Papagiannakis, G., Stephanidis, C.: Realistic natural interaction with virtual statues in X-reality environments. Int. Arch. Photogramm. Remote Sens. Spatial Inf. Sci. **XLII-2/W11**, 801–808 (2019). https://doi.org/10.5194/isprs-archives-XLII-2-W11-801-2019
5. Wu, H.-Y., Calabrèse, A., Kornprobst, P.: Towards accessible news reading design in virtual reality for low vision. Multimed. Tools Appl. **80**(18), 27259–27278 (2021). https://doi.org/10.1007/s11042-021-10899-9
6. Hoppe, A.H., Anken, J.K., Schwarz, T., Stiefelhagen, R., van de Camp, F.: CLEVR: a customizable interactive learning environment for users with low vision in virtual reality. In: Proceedings of the 22nd International ACM SIGACCESS Conference on Computers and Accessibility, in ASSETS 2020. New York, NY, USA: Association for Computing Machinery, Oct. 2020, pp. 1–4. https://doi.org/10.1145/3373625.3418009
7. Weir, K., Loizides, F., Nahar, V., Aggoun, A., Buchanan, G.: Creating a bespoke virtual reality personal library space for persons with severe visual disabilities. In: Proceedings of the ACM/IEEE Joint Conference on Digital Libraries in 2020, in JCDL 2020. New York, NY, USA: Association for Computing Machinery, Aug. 2020, pp. 393–396. https://doi.org/10.1145/3383583.3398610
8. Kasowski, J., Johnson, B.A., Neydavood, R., Akkaraju, A., Beyeler, M.: Furthering visual accessibility with extended reality (XR): a systematic review. arXiv, Sep. 10, 2021. http://arxiv.org/abs/2109.04995. Accessed 13 Sep 2022
9. Zhao, Y., Szpiro, S., Azenkot, S.: ForeSee: a customizable head-mounted vision enhancement system for people with low vision. In: Proceedings of the 17th International ACM SIGACCESS Conference on Computers & Accessibility, in ASSETS 2015. New York, NY, USA: Association for Computing Machinery, Oct. 2015, pp. 239–249. https://doi.org/10.1145/2700648.2809865
10. Pamparău, C., Vatavu, R.-D.: FlexiSee: flexible configuration, customization, and control of mediated and augmented vision for users of smart eyewear devices. Multimed. Tools Appl. **80**(20), 30943–30968 (2021). https://doi.org/10.1007/s11042-020-10164-5
11. Zhao, Y., Szpiro, S., Knighten, J., Azenkot, S.: CueSee: exploring visual cues for people with low vision to facilitate a visual search task. In: Proceedings of the 2016 ACM International Joint Conference on Pervasive and Ubiquitous Computing, in UbiComp 2016. New York, NY, USA: Association for Computing Machinery, Sep. 2016, pp. 73–84. https://doi.org/10.1145/2971648.2971730
12. Langlotz, T., Sutton, J., Zollmann, S., Itoh, Y., Regenbrecht, H.: ChromaGlasses: computational glasses for compensating colour blindness. In: Proceedings of the 2018 CHI Conference

on Human Factors in Computing Systems, in CHI 2018. New York, NY, USA: Association for Computing Machinery, Apr. 2018, pp. 1–12. https://doi.org/10.1145/3173574.3173964

13. Racing in the dark: exploring accessible virtual reality by developing a racing game for people who are blind. https://journals.sagepub.com/doi/epdf/10.1177/1071181321651224. Accessed 13 Oct 2022

14. Schneider, O., et al.: DualPanto: a haptic device that enables blind users to continuously interact with virtual worlds. In: Proceedings of the 31st Annual ACM Symposium on User Interface Software and Technology, in UIST '18. New York, NY, USA: Association for Computing Machinery, Oct. 2018, pp. 877–887. https://doi.org/10.1145/3242587.3242604

15. Zaal, T., Akdag Salah, A.A., Hürst, W.: Toward inclusivity: virtual reality museums for the visually impaired. In: 2022 IEEE International Conference on Artificial Intelligence and Virtual Reality (AIVR), Dec. 2022, pp. 225–233. https://doi.org/10.1109/AIVR56993.2022.00047

16. Ji, T.F., Cochran, B., Zhao, Y.: VRBubble: enhancing peripheral awareness of avatars for people with visual impairments in social virtual reality. In: Proceedings of the 24th International ACM SIGACCESS Conference on Computers and Accessibility, in ASSETS 2022. New York, NY, USA: Association for Computing Machinery, Oct. 2022, pp. 1–17. https://doi.org/10.1145/3517428.3544821

17. Gerling, K., Dickinson, P., Hicks, K., Mason, L., Simeone, A.L., Spiel, K.: Virtual reality games for people using wheelchairs. In: Proceedings of the 2020 CHI Conference on Human Factors in Computing Systems, in CHI 2020. New York, NY, USA: Association for Computing Machinery, Apr. 2020, pp. 1–11. https://doi.org/10.1145/3313831.3376265

18. Mott, M., Tang, J., Kane, S., Cutrell, E., Morris, M.: 'I just went into it assuming that I wouldn't be able to have the full experience': understanding the accessibility of virtual reality for people with limited mobility. In: ASSETS 2020: Proceedings of the 22nd International ACM SIGACCESS Conference on Computers and Accessibility, Oct. 2020, pp. 1–13. https://doi.org/10.1145/3373625.3416998

19. Heilemann, F., Zimmermann, G., Münster, P.: Accessibility guidelines for VR games - a comparison and synthesis of a comprehensive set. Front. Virtual Real. 2 (2021). https://www.frontiersin.org/articles/10.3389/frvir.2021.697504. Accessed 12 Oct 2022

20. Ntoa, S., Margetis, G., Antona, M., Stephanidis, C.: Scanning-based interaction techniques for motor impaired users. In: Kouroupetroglou, G. (ed.) Assistive Technologies and Computer Access for Motor Disabilities, pp. 57–89. IGI Global (2014). https://doi.org/10.4018/978-1-4666-4438-0.ch003

21. "XR Interaction Toolkit I XR Interaction Toolkit I 2.3.2." https://docs.unity3d.com/Packages/com.unity.xr.interaction.toolkit@2.3/manual/index.html. Accessed 30 May 2023

22. Zhao, Y., Cutrell, E., Holz, C., Morris, M.R., Ofek, E., Wilson, A.D.: SeeingVR: a set of tools to make virtual reality more accessible to people with low vision. In: Proceedings of the 2019 CHI Conference on Human Factors in Computing Systems, in CHI 2019. New York, NY, USA: Association for Computing Machinery, May 2019, pp. 1–14. https://doi.org/10.1145/3290605.3300341

23. Ji, T.F., Hu, Y., Huang, Y., Du, R., Zhao, Y.: A preliminary interview: understanding XR developers' needs towards open-source accessibility support. In: 2023 IEEE Conference on Virtual Reality and 3D User Interfaces Abstracts and Workshops (VRW), Mar. 2023, pp. 493–496. https://doi.org/10.1109/VRW58643.2023.00107

24. Wong, B.: Points of view: color blindness. Nat. Methods 8, 441 (2011). https://doi.org/10.1038/nmeth.1618

Understanding a Symphony Orchestra by Reexperience in Virtual Reality

Michael Zöllner⬛, Jan Gemeinhardt⁽✉⁾⬛, and Moritz Krause⁽✉⁾⬛

Hof University of Applied Sciences, Alfons-Goppel-Platz 1, 95028 Hof, Germany
{michael.zoellner,moritz.krause}@hof-university.de,
jan.gemeinhardt.2@iisys.de

Abstract. The aim of the project Symotiv (http://symotiv.de) is to introduce people to classical music through interaction with a virtual orchestra. With the help of Virtual Reality, it does not only enable to immerse oneself in a three-dimensional, virtual concert hall, but also to experience images and sound from the perspective of a musician. This opened the possibility of experiencing and understanding what is happening from new spatial, but above all sonic perspectives. Therefore, we developed a workflow to capture the motions and sound of 50 musicians and the conductor by using a camera-based Machine Learning approach.

Keywords: Virtual Reality · Machine Learning · Interaction · Symphony Orchestra

1 Introduction

The technologies regarding capturing motion and visualizing data enabled new possibilities describing complex systems to a broader audience. The latest methods of motion analysis through Machine Learning / Artificial Intelligence and visualization in Virtual and Augmented Reality (VR/AR) enabled us to analyze and explain the way the Hof Symphony Orchestra works. Therefore, we created an interactive immersive Extended Reality experience that showed the diverse aspects from rehearsal to performance to a broad audience.

In this paper we are briefly describing the process and the implications of human pose estimation with camera-based Machine Learning software. Our challenge was to capture the motions and sound of 50 musicians and the conductor. Whereas a few years ago expensive and complex time-of-flight cameras or sensor-based bodysuits were needed to capture the biomechanical movements of a musician, we used eight off-the-shelf GoPro cameras distributed throughout the orchestra's venue Freiheitshalle in Hof Germany to capture all musicians and their movements during the performance without occlusion. We created a multi-step workflow based on several open-source software for pose estimation, i.e., extracting the coordinates and angles of all joints of the musicians from the camera images. Several terabytes of data from the eight cameras were transferred to a workstation and semi-automatically transformed into biomechanical models. The result was a three-dimensional biomechanical model of each musician and a sound stream of their instrument group. This provided our basis for animating the avatars in virtual reality.

In the following sections we are describing briefly the evaluation and exploration of the current state of single camera skeleton tracking hardware that lead us to the choice of the approach we implemented into separate prototypes for evaluating the resulting data quality. Subsequently we are explaining the further development into a VR experience including interactions, UI and presentation format. Finally we are writing about the lessons we learned during the development and the benefits for our further research and projects.

2 Technology and Related Work

2.1 Human Pose Estimation

In the recent years we observed a fast progress in the quality and availability of camera-based pose estimation. While Time-of-flight cameras were very expensive and low resolution before 2010, we saw a democratization in the accessibility of skeleton tracking for a large audience with the release of the Microsoft Kinect and the community-based libraries like OpenKinect [11] and OpenNI [15].

With the introduction of machine learning based approaches the need for special hardware wasn't relevant anymore in favor of standard cameras. Carnegie Mellon University's OpenPose [3] and OpenPifpaf [7] are two major developments producing robust 2D pose estimation of humans based on single RGB images. When we started the project, we decided to build our project on top of OpenPose since it got us the best quality results for robust 2D position data of the skeletons' joints at that time. We added a second processing step to create a 3D biomechanical skeleton model. "3d-pose-baseline" [9] provided this feature and predicted the 3D skeletons. Today's OpenPose version features 3D position data as well. Similar to OpenPose there's MeTRAbs Absolute 3D Human Pose Estimator [13] which is also featuring not only 2D but also robust 3D position data of the skeletons' joints.

Although the quality of PoseNet's [6] 2D tracking data is not as advanced as the previously mentioned, its main contribution is the availability in browsers. Even simpler Google MediaPipe [8] combines a large variety of Machine Learning (i.e., pose estimation, hand and gesture recognition, object detection) applications in one JavaScript framework.

2.2 Adjoining Projects

Regarding related applications we would like to mention several projects in adjoining disciplines. Capturing and analyzing dance is a wide research field in the pose estimation and tracking area. Referring to hardware-based approaches we would like to mention "Evaluating a dancer's performance using Kinect-based skeleton tracking" [1]. An early 3D position estimation approach with a single camera was "Capturing of contemporary dance for preservation and presentation of choreographies in online scores" [5] where they showed recurring path patterns in experimental ballet performances. The former mentioned paper is part of the larger Motion Bank [4] project initiated by dance chore-ographer William Forsythe. Several universities and research institutions worked on solutions for digital preservation of contemporary dance and ballet. The project's radius has been increased by the Choreographic Coding Lab [10] format that invited artists to work on the topic in workshops in several cities worldwide.

Although focusing on visualization rather than data analysis we would like to mention RunwayML's [12] latest Motion Tracking tool for video editing and Najeeb Tarazi's application of RunwayML's rotoscoping techniques in the impressive "One More Try" [16] experimental skate video.

3   Project Development and Implementation

3.1   Camera Setup

Our challenge was to capture 50 musicians and the conductor without occlusion. We created a reproducible setup consisting of eight affordable off the shelf GoPro Hero 5 Black cameras on long tripods and fixed with a 3D printed mount.

Fig. 1. GoPro cameras on tripods placed in between the musicians.

A major challenge was the positioning of the cameras to capture all musicians in their instrument groups without occlusion of other people, instruments or chairs (see Fig. 1). We solved this by calculating, defining and fixing the positions of the chairs and the camera tripods for the recordings of the rehearsals (see Fig. 2).

The eight cameras' recordings of the different views were synchronized started and stopped by a single GoPro Remote. Together with the GoPro app on a smartphone it was also the touchpoint for the setup of the image detail and the verification and review of the recordings at the site.

3.2   Human Pose Estimation Data

The eight cameras' video sequences amounted several terabytes of data, which we trans-ferred to our graphics workstation and processed them with an OpenPose script into CSV files containing the 2D skeletons' coordinates of the recognized persons per time frame in the first step. The coordinate sets represent a frontal projection of the joint position

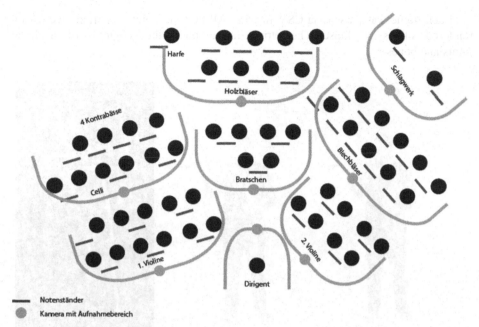

Fig. 2. A plan of the musicians in their instrument groups and the position of the eight GoPro cameras.

matching the video image and its pixel space (see Fig. 3). Each set consists of the same number of frames as the video clips. It's containing all detected persons and their skeleton joint positions with their x, y coordinates. Additionally, OpenPose renders a preview video overlayed with a visualization of the resulting skeletons, we used for evaluation of quality of the data.

Since we needed 3D representations of the musicians' skeletons for a 3D representation, in the next step the "3d-pose-baseline" script ran over all OpenPose 2D CSV files and predicted the skeleton data of the musicians in 3D space. The output was also saved in single CSV files with x, y, and z coordinates. For the evaluation of the resulting datasets, we developed a visualization prototype described in the next chapter.

For the later rigging process in Blender (Blender Foundation, 2023) and the real-time visualization in Unity3D (Unity Technologies, 2023) we wrote a custom script to convert the data into the Biovision Hierarchy (BVH) character animation file format (Meredith, Maddock, and others, 2001). Because all cameras and musicians were set up to fixed positions, we were able to join the 3D datasets of the different cameras and instrument groups into the real 3D positions of the whole orchestra in the hall.

3.3 Data Evaluation Prototype

For evaluating the data, we developed a web-based visualization that renders the skeleton data on top of the corresponding video images of the recorded scenario. Therefore, we were using p5js (McCarthy, Reas and Fry, 2015), a JavaScript variant of the Processing language, for the visualization.

Each frame was parsed via CSV in p5js. All persons' joints per frame were then rendered as lines and ellipses. The color coding amplified the recognition of the single joints and bones.

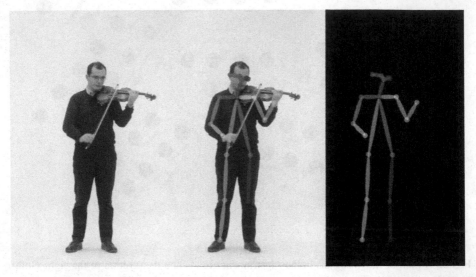

Fig. 3. Reviewing the skeleton data overlayed on the video of a violinist.

The result was a visualization of the data set on top of a corresponding video frame. We were recognizing the persons in the dataset including their positions and movements over time. In the example in Fig. 3 we are observing a violin player playing a short sequence. The person's motion is overlayed with the drawing of reconstructed skeleton. Figure 4 shows an additional visualization of continuous time series we used to verify the continuity of the musicians' motions.

Fig. 4. Violinist motion as continuous time series and visualization variations.

Based on the described components we were able to evaluate the quality of the reconstructed skeleton data in a first integrated prototype in real-time based on previously recorded and analyzed video segments in p5js.

Already anticipating the next step in finding visualization styles for rendering the orchestra's musicians in an abstract way we developed a tool (see Fig. 4) in p5js where we could quickly set visualization parameters. These parameters included colors, joint geometries and sizes. Furthermore, we added a particle system to the joints and bones to generate dynamic volume.

4 Reexperience in Virtual Reality

The venue and the space in which the orchestra plays are of great importance for its performance. Because of this importance, for our visualization of the motion data we worked with virtual reality, because here a room can be created and entered completely freely. VR was used to visualize and explain the collected data and the underlying processes of a symphony orchestra.

4.1 Characters and Visualization

At the time of the project we chose Unity3D [14] as the interactive 3D framework, a standard graphics workstation with two Nvidia GeForce RTX 2080 graphics cards and an HTC Vive Pro VR headset for the VR reexperience of the recordings of the rehearsals. In prior projects we already gained a lot of experience with the Unity3D engine and so we knew about its simple and reliable XR Interaction Toolkit for VR interaction.

The animated skeletons were first imported into Blender [2] with a custom script that converted the data into Biovision Hierarchy (BVH) character animation file format. Based on the fixed position of the cameras and the musicians we were able to join the 3D datasets of the different cameras and instrument groups into the real 3D positions of the whole orchestra in the hall.

Based on our visualization prototypes and sketches we finalized the appearance of the musicians. We chose an abstract retro-futuristic appearance in the style of Disney's Tron [17] movie protagonists. All musicians were grouped in their instrument groups like violins, contrabass, brass, etc. The color coding of the highlighted elements of the characters supported the users' identification of the instruments groups, enhanced by typography and pictograms of the instruments (see Fig. 5). All virtual characters were placed in a fictional abstract music hall with an ambient light setting.

Fig. 5. Overview of the virtual musicians clustered in their instrument groups and control via VR controller.

4.2 Characters and Visualization

Unlike in a real concert in our application the users have several possibilities to interactively intervene in what is happening. After a short introduction and tutorial scene about how to move and interact in VR, they start in front of the conductor with a view over the orchestra. They can move freely around the concert hall, stand on the conductor's podium, and turn instrument groups on and off (see Fig. 5). Or stand among the musicians, observe their movement, and sound, and thus expand and understand the spatial and sonic experience of a concert. The immersive nature of this medium offers scope for new, inclusive information delivery. Various visualizations here reach the user on multiple levels. Like the event of a concert, VR offers an independent form of experience.

5 Reexperience in Virtual Reality

We presented the technology, the development and the process of a contemporary digital recording of all the processes of a symphony orchestra using AI-based 3D pose estimation software and commercially available cameras. With this project's results, the cultural institution of the Hof Symphony was able to communicate its own work to a public audience using new technologies. They've also got a new kind of tool to review and improve the internal processes of orchestra rehearsals and the training of musicians.

The technology used in this project evolved fast. Today with current VR headsets we would get rid of the cables between the headset and the PC. Furthermore, the current generation VR tracking does not rely on tracking beacons anymore. Thus, the user experience for such a setup would improve strongly and get simplified.

With the current versions of OpenPose and MeTRAbs for human pose estimation we would not need the additional processing step from 2D to 3D poses anymore, shorten and simplifying the development process and increase the accuracy of the skeletons.

References

1. Alexiadis, D.S. et al.: Evaluating a dancer's performance using kinect-based skeleton tracking. In: Proceedings of the 19th ACM International Conference on Multimedia, pp. 659–662 Association for Computing Machinery, New York, NY, USA (2011). https://doi.org/10.1145/2072298.2072412
2. Blender Foundation: blender.org - Home of the Blender project - free and open 3D creation software, https://www.blender.org/. Accessed 12 Feb 2023
3. Cao, Z., et al.: OpenPose: realtime multi-person 2D pose estimation using part affinity fields (2019). http://arxiv.org/abs/1812.08008. https://doi.org/10.48550/arXiv.1812.08008
4. Hennermann, C., deLahunta, S.: Motion Bank: starting points & aspirations = Motion Bank : ansatzpunkte & intentionen. Motion Bank/The Forsythe Company (2013)
5. Kahn, S., et al.: Capturing of contemporary dance for preservation and presentation of choreographies in online scores. In: 2013 Digital Heritage International Congress (DigitalHeritage), pp. 273–280 (2013). https://doi.org/10.1109/DigitalHeritage.2013.6743750
6. Kendall, A., et al.: PoseNet: a convolutional network for real-time 6-DOF camera relocalization. In: Proceedings of the IEEE International Conference on Computer Vision (2015)

7. Kreiss, S., Bertoni, L., Alahi, A.: OpenPifPaf: composite fields for semantic keypoint detection and spatio-temporal association. IEEE Trans. Intell. Transp. Syst. **23**(8), 13498–13511 (2022). https://doi.org/10.1109/TITS.2021.3124981
8. Lugaresi, C., et al.: Mediapipe: a framework for building perception pipelines. arXiv preprint arXiv:1906.08172 (2019)
9. Martinez, J., et al.: A simple yet effective baseline for 3D human pose estimation. In: ICCV (2017)
10. Motion Bank: choreographic coding labs. https://choreographiccoding.org. Accessed 14 Feb 2023
11. OpenKinect: OpenKinect: open source drivers for kinect v1 (2011). https://openkinect.org
12. Runway: runway - next-generation creation suite. https://runwayml.com. last Accessed 19 Jan 2023
13. Sárándi, I., et al.: MeTRAbs: metric-scale truncation-robust heatmaps for absolute 3D human pose estimation. IEEE Trans. Biom. Behav. Identity Sci. **3**(1), 16–30 (2021). https://doi.org/10.1109/TBIOM.2020.3037257
14. Unity Technologies: unity real-time development platform I 3D, 2D VR & AR engine. https://unity.com/. Accessed 12 Feb 2023
15. Villaroman, N., et al.: Teaching natural user interaction using OpenNI and the Microsoft kinect sensor. In: Proceedings of the 2011 Conference on Information Technology Education, pp. 227–232 (2011)
16. One More Try - an experimental skate video (2022)
17. Tron. Walt Disney Productions (1982)

Digital Transformation in the Modern Business Landscape

El Boca Electronic Ear in a Company Dedicated to the Sale of Pharmaceutical Products and Toiletry Articles. Peru Case

Lady Violeta Dávila Valdera[1]([✉]) [iD], Madeleine Espino Carrasco[2] [iD],
Danicsa Karina Espino Carrasco[3] [iD], Luis Jhonny Dávila Valdera[4] [iD],
Anny Katherine Dávila Valdera[5] [iD], Mayury Jackeline Espino Carrasco[2] [iD],
Royer Vasquez Cachay[2] [iD], Ricardo Rafael Díaz Calderón[6] [iD],
Edson David Valdera Benavides[1] [iD], and Karina Elizabeth Bravo Gonzales[6] [iD]

[1] Pedro Ruiz Gallo National University, Lambayeque, Peru
lavidaval@gmail.com
[2] Señor de Sipan University, Pimentel, Peru
[3] Cesar Vallejo University, Chulucanas, Peru
[4] Santo Toribio de Mogrovejo University, Chiclayo, Peru
[5] National University of San Marcos, Lima, Peru
[6] Cesar Vallejo University, Pimentel, Peru

Abstract. The purpose of the research is to determine the electronic word of mouth of a company dedicated to the sale of pharmaceutical products and toiletries, whose applied model was the one proposed by Matute, Polo & Utrilla (2015), the sample was 384 people surveyed, by what the approach applied was the quantitative and descriptive level, obtaining as a result a total score of 5.62 which expresses that the knowledge of the service through the eWOM is influencing the purchase decision and the amount of feedback of the eWOM applied in the company, so it is concluded that the eWOM has become a crucial component of the website, serving as its business card, this is due to the reviews and information provided by customers who have used the product in the past.

Keywords: Mouth ear electronic · pharmaceutical products · toiletry articles

1 Introduction

Word of mouth that is carried out over the Internet is also called electronic word of mouth. The eWOM are the comments either positive or negative about a product or service made by a new or old customer. Therefore, there is a difference between traditional and electronic word of mouth, since the traditional is a comment distributed in a limited way to a small group of people, while the electronic, the comments are made through a forum where there are more arguments, which the user can easily access, so they can read, comment and respond to the opinions of other people, without any limit (Handoko & Melinda, 2021).

C. Stephanidis et al. (Eds.): HCII 2023, CCIS 1958, pp. 275–284, 2024.
https://doi.org/10.1007/978-3-031-49215-0_33

For this reason, at an international level, electronic commerce (e-Commerce) in 2020 increased its income with 431 billion dollars and by 2025 a reach of 563 billion dollars is scheduled. In the same way, the Retail sector in 2020 grew by 27.6 and it is scheduled that by 2022 it will have generated 5.4 billion dollars (Martínez, 2021), given that the number of users in social networks increased in 53% of the world population (Álvarez, 2021). Being young people between the ages of 16 and 24 who spend more time browsing the internet, where women are the ones who interact the most on social networks, especially those pages that are based on recommendations and new ideas, unlike men who prefer only to read. Opinions (Borondo, 2021). With these statistics, online sales have become an advantage for cosmetics and beauty care companies, showing their wide range of products to users through their website. The pandemic reinforced the growth in online sales where it came to play a very important role in the face of reality (González, 2021).

In Peru, the Sales Manager of the pharmaceutical products and toiletries company commented that they developed the interactions due to the benefit that users between the ages of 18 and 39 had for buying and selling online, obtaining a business opportunity, since this could be done from home, for reasons of Covid-19.

Therefore, when an online platform obtains many sales, electronic word of mouth is given, either making or reading both positive and negative comments by people who have already had experience with the products (Berné et al., 2017). For this reason, companies must interact in the online environment, to strategically respond to comments that are in favor or against their product or service from their customers, with the aim of maintaining loyal customers and attracting new consumers., to prevent moments of dissatisfaction (Gondim & Araújo, 2020).

In an exploratory interview, an entrepreneurial partner of pharmaceutical products and toiletries, reveals that negative comments often made by consumers generate distrust in users, this suggests that the page possibly contains erroneous information about the products, since the Most of them are not responded to by the company and finally they are the same partners of the company that sometimes try to appease those comments that denigrate the brand, but this does not always happen. Therefore, in the company there is no protocol to deal with those situations created by the eWOM.

With the aforementioned, few investigations have taken a holistic approach corresponding to eWOM and the important role it plays in companies, along with its dimensions such as quality, quantity and credibility. Given this, the following research question arose: How is the electronic mouth-ear in the pharmaceutical and toiletries company, Chiclayo 2021?

In order to solve the problem announced, it is pertinent to consider the following objectives, as a general objective it was established to determine the electronic word of mouth. In addition, the specific objectives are to determine the quantity, credibility and quality of the eWOM in the company of pharmaceutical products and toiletries, Chiclayo 2021.

2 Literature Review

Regarding the background regarding the electronic mouth-ear variable, there is Bilal et al. (2021) who examined the effect on consumer purchase intentions of social media marketing components, including entertainment, engagement, eWOM, and trend. The findings demonstrate that interaction, entertainment, eWOM, and fashion are core factors that specifically affect customer brand interest and purchase intent. Likewise, Shuaib et al. (2021) identified the factors that affect the credibility of electronic word-of-mouth stimulation through social networking sites, where the results show that SNS activities play an important role in building credibility of eWOM, which leads to shape the brand image and purchase intentions. As well as Truc et al. (2021) discovered and confirmed the e-WOM factors that influence the purchase intentions of users on Instagram, as a result it was shown that the fourth experience factor of the eWOM information provider positively impacts the purchase intention of users. on Instagram with decreasing levels such as information provider experience, e-WOM quantity and eWOM source credibility, and eWOM quality, respectively.

However, Budi (2019) studied the influence between Internet advertising and the practice of electronic word of mouth (eWOM) with customer perception and purchase intention in B2C electronic commerce, the results obtained from this study indicate that Internet advertising and eWOM have a positive effect on the perceived value of the customer and the perceived risk of buying on B2C e-commerce sites. Even Alabdullatif & Akram (2018) investigated the role of online customer reviews (eWOM) and review page key elements, the results show a significant impact of online review factors such as filters, quality, quantity, actuality, valence together with the characteristics of the property in the reservation decision of the clients. Something similar occurs with Muhammad et al. (2021) examined the impact of eWOM background on online purchase intention (OPI) of fashion-related products. Findings from this study found that all five eWOM antecedents, such as fashion involvement, sense of belonging, trust, bond strength, and informational influence, positively influence fashion product IPOs in China.

Regarding the theory, according to the Health Science Authority (2017), cosmetic products can be defined as a composition of natural or synthetic products intended to be used in various parts of the human body, with the purpose of cleaning, perfuming, improving or change consumers appearances to keep them in good condition. It is classified into various categories such as skin care products, hair care products, bath products, fragrance products, makeup products, personal care products, oral hygiene products, and manicure and pedicure products. (US Food and Drug Administration, 2017). In such a way, it was reported that sales of cosmetic products grew positively due to steady consumer demand, which reached USD 532 billion in 2017. Furthermore, the Asia Pacific region has the largest market share in the cosmetics industry. Worldwide with 3,000 million consumers (Zion Market Research, 2018). Therefore, the cosmetics industry is one of the prominent industries in the global market..

Likewise, regarding the variable under study, the eWOM is a positive/negative statement or comment made by a previous/current buyer about a product or company that is available to many people and institutions through the Internet (Henning-Thurau T., Gwinner, Walsh, & Gremler, 2004). In the customer's decision-making process, it is natural for him to seek the opinions of others first. Digital technology and the Internet have increased opportunities for consumers to access various types of eWOM provided by different people (Choi, Seo, & Yoon, 2017). In general, people can spread an eWOM message through several different social settings. Someone can spread eWOM messages to other people who have strong relationships with them (eg family, relatives, etc.)

and also an individual can spread eWOM messages to other people who have weak relationships with themselves (eg, as acquaintances, distant friends, etc.). According to Breazele (2009), negative electronic word of mouth is more powerful than positive word of mouth because perceived consumer dissatisfaction by consumers is easier to propagate through the Internet than face-to-face word of mouth. That is why the eWOM has a more important role in providing information on the risks contained in a product.

Therefore, the model adapted to the research belongs to Matute, Polo, and Utrillas (2015) who study the eWOM that is divided into: quantity, credibility, and quality.

eWOM quality: According to Asshidin (2016), quality can be deduced as knowledge of a certain service or product, which influences the purchase decision. According to Lin and Wang (2015), likewise the quality of eWOM is based on the level of interaction that a customer has had on the website over time, Lin and Wang (2015) therefore, the higher the level of quality, the lower the perception of risk, increasing the intention to purchase online. This is also how companies face this challenge of uncertainty in the web platform, it is for this reason that loyalty between the client and the brand must be built through trust (Mansour et al., 2014).

Quantity of eWOM: Ismagilova (2019), See-To and Ho (2013) confirm that the eWOM produced thanks to social networks does manage to influence the repurchase. On the other hand, according to Erkan & Evans (2016), Internet users are exposed, directly or indirectly, to a large number of eWOM and their information influences their decision-making.

In the same sense, the work of Pappas (2015) maintains that the quantity and quality of the information provided through eWOM has positive effects when buying.

eWOM credibility: The credibility of the information determines how much the receiver learns and adopts this information: if the information received is perceived as credible, the receiver will have more confidence to use it in the purchase decision (Sussman and Siegal 2003). Given that online information exchanges occur between people who may not have a prior relationship, it is essential to consider how the perceived credibility of information influences consumer behavior. Some studies have examined the relationship between eWOM credibility and purchase intention (Teng et al. 2017). For example, Koo (2016) surveyed 302 South Korean students and found that eWOM credibility has a significant positive effect on purchase intention for airline tickets, meals at a family restaurant, and skin care service.

3   Materials Y Methods

The present study has a quantitative approach, descriptive level. Therefore, the survey technique was used and the questionnaire as an instrument, with a non-probabilistic sampling procedure for convenience, composed of a 3-dimensional model that makes up a total of 18 indicators of electronic mouth-ear, evaluated on a Likert-type scale. of 7 points. The total sample was 384 male and female clients, between 18 and 45 years old, obtaining a reliability level of 0.95 according to Cron Bach's Alpha and KMO or Bartlett's sphericity test (<0.05) and the variance explained is 77.861%. Access to the questionnaire was provided through a link, sent through social networks, encouraging participants to pass this survey with their friends who present the same profile.

Regarding the data processing and analysis plan, obtained the information from the surveys applied through Google Drive, the data was entered into the Excel 2010 program, then the information was transferred to the statistical program SPSS v.25. The SPSS was also used for its statistical analysis and the cross tables to find the sociodemographic data, then a table was developed in Excel to find the average and group the items according to the dimensions and variable according to the objectives set (Table 1).

4   Results Y Discussion

Table 1. Demographic and behavioral data

		He commented on the website after his experience with pharmaceuticals and toiletries		
		Si	No	Total
Sex	Male	16%	12%	28%
	Female	38%	34%	72%
Age	18 to 25 years	30%	25%	55%
	26 to 33 years	15%	14%	29%
	34 to 45 years	9%	7%	16%
Shopping in the Web page	Two	9%	17%	26%
	Three	12%	6%	18%
	More than three	42%	14%	56%

Note. According to data obtained from surveys

It was found that, in terms of age, sex and purchases, it is young women who make more than three purchases on the website, and together with their experience, express their opinions, whether good or bad about the product (Annex 4). Given that women spend more time on social networks, they comment more than men, who only enter to read arguments from other clients (Borondo, 2021). Therefore, when an online platform obtains many sales, word of mouth is heard. Electronically, either by making or reading both positive and negative comments by people who have already had experience with the products (Berné et al., 2017). Therefore, it is inferred that men are the ones with the least interaction on the website of the company under study, while women, according to the number of purchases they make, provide more information according to their experience. Since, in the client's decision making process, it is natural that they first seek information from other clients more than women. Digital technology and the Internet have increased opportunities for consumers to access various types of eWOM provided by different people (Choi, Seo, & Yoon, 2017) (Table 2).

According to the results presented, in terms of the quantity of eWOM with a higher average than the other dimensions, it can be explained why customers felt that they

Table 2. Result of the Electronic Ear Mouth and its dimensions

Variable	Dimension	Average	Sub dimension	Average	Indicators
eWOM Average: 5,62	Quantity	5,74			CT1
					CT2
					CT3
	Credibility	5,49			CD1
					CD2
					CD3
	Quality	5,62	Present	5,64	CA1
					CA2
					CA3
			Comprehension	5,52	CC1
					CC2
					CC3
			Relevance	5,72	CR1
					CR2
					CR3
			Precision	5,58	CP1
					CP2
					CP3

Note. According to the proposed model

needed information before making a purchase, but that it did not meet their expectations when they could not find it. Details about the article, which underlines the fact that his subsequent comments were aimed at inquiring about such aspects (information, details, mode of use). Alabdullatif & Akram (2018) show a significant impact of online review factors, as the quantity together with the characteristics of the property in the reservation decision of the clients. While Truc et al. (2021) showed that there is a decreasing level as the amount of e-WOM in relation to the provider's experience in terms of eWOM information. With these findings, it can be concluded that information is required so that the user has expectations before reserving their product based on justifications provided by the clients so that there is a high level in the amount of eWOM.

According to the credibility dimension, it has been the dimension that has obtained the lowest score in the results, where it is determined that despite the fact that they have accurate information, the respondents still harbor these reservations because the comments are undoubtedly anonymous and the experiences of clients vary greatly. Shuaib et al. (2021) show that notification activities on social media play an important role in building eWOM credibility. Instead, Truc et al. (2021) showed that there is a decreasing level of e-WOM credibility in relation to the provider's experience in terms of eWOM information. With these results it can be inferred that credibility is based on trust in customer experiences, having reliable information is still crucial for many people.

Moving on to the quality dimension, which obtained an average score between the quantity and credibility dimensions, this is based on the fact that because there is not all the necessary information to make a decision, the respondents believe that the comments do not have enough depth. Budi (2019) indicate that Internet advertising and eWOM have a positive effect on the perceived value of the customer (quality) and the perceived risk of buying on B2C e-commerce sites. A significant relationship also emerges between Internet advertising and eWOM. Instead, Alabdullatif & Akram (2018) show a significant impact of online review factors such as quality along with property characteristics on customers' booking decision. With these findings, it can be deduced that customers must perceive the value of the comments as genuine and lasting because they do not find the information, they need to make a purchase in the aforementioned comments.

Finally, it is detailed that the eWOM in the pharmaceutical products and toiletries company, obtaining a total score of (5.62), results in that the knowledge of the service through the eWOM is influencing the purchase decision and the amount of feedback from eWOM applied in the company. Billal et al. (2021) demonstrates that interaction-based eWOM, entertainment, and fashion are core factors that specifically affect customer brand interest and purchase intention. Muhammad et al. (2021) details that the eWOM significantly mediates the relationship between participation in fashion, sense of belonging, trust, informational influence, and online purchase intention. Sheikh et al. (2021) state that brand equity is not an integral part of eWOM, but it is still an important feature of the online shopping process. With these findings, it can be concluded that eWOM has a significant impact on consumer decisions, since consumers currently make purchases based on the experiences of other users instead of the brand, which is the most relevant aspect of eWOM, rather than the brand itself, consumers may infer that eWOM plays an important role in consumer decisions.

5 Conclusions

According to the quantity, it was possible to verify the high volume of recommendations and evaluations on the website due to the fact that many people comment on their appreciations, accumulating or overwhelming the recipient with the amount of information, both necessary and unnecessary, and causing them to become confused. Before making a purchase decision.

When it comes to credibility, the comments and opinions posted on this website are not reliable enough because customers share their experiences with the items, good or bad, while using them. Since this is where most users look for accurate information and do not find a satisfactory answer, they start to have doubts because the information has a significant impact on their purchase decision, regardless of the caliber of the products.

Regarding the quality of the comments on the web page, by not delving into a detailed explanation confusion is created for the user, when the company verifies the comment, it tries to provide an answer explaining the mode of use, how you can obtain more information or find solutions that do not harm the value of the brand.

Last but not least, eWOM has become a crucial component of the website, serving as its calling card. This is because, thanks to the reviews and information provided by customers who have used the product in the past, new or old users who are interested in the mentioned item are informed before making their purchase, since they are not only seduced by the brand but also by the results obtained by other clients.

Current research is important in exploring the value of electronic mouth and ear in the pharmaceutical and toiletries business, and in determining whether comments made on a website actually have an effect on user purchasing behavior. Since it shows customer feedback, this will help businesses to give more importance to their website. They will also be able to differentiate themselves from the competition and be professional towards the competition by knowing the caliber, reliability and number of comments they make on their website, eWOM being a specific example.

References

Álvarez, J. (2021, Enero 27). Reporte digital 2021: The Report on Digital Trends, Social Networks and Mobile. *We Are Social*. https://wearesocial.com/es/blog/2021/01/digital-report-2021-el-inf orme-sobre-las-tendencias-digitales-redes-sociales-y-mobile/

Alabdullatif, A., Akram, M.: Exploring the impact of electronic word of mouth and property characteristics on customers' online booking decision. TEM J. Technol. Educ. Manag. Inf. **7**(2), 411–420 (2018).https://doi.org/10.18421/TEM72-24

Asshidin, N., Abidin, N., Borhan, H.B.: Perceived quality and emotional value that influence consumer's purchase intention towards American and local products. Procedia Econ. Finan. **35**(2016), 639–643 (2016). https://doi.org/10.1016/S2212-5671(16)00078-2

Berné, C., Pedraja, M., Ciobanu, A.: Electronic word of mouth as a context variable in the hotel management decision-making process. Manag. Notebooks **20**(1), 111–136 (2017). https://doi. org/10.5295/cdg.170860cb

Bilal, M., Jianqu, Z., Ming, J.: How does consumer brand engagement affect purchase intent? the role of the elements of social networks. Mag. Bus. Strategy Finan. Manag. **2**(1&2), 44–55 (2021). https://jbsfm.org/pdf/vol2no1/JBSFM_Vol2_No1_p_44-55.pdf

Breazeale, M.: FORUM - word of mouse - an assessment of electronic word-of-mouth research. Int. J. Mark. Res. **51**(3), 1–19 (2009). https://doi.org/10.1177/147078530905100307

Borondo, S.: Redes sociales más utilizadas por hombres y mujeres (2021). https://www.elcorreo. com/tecnologia/redes-sociales/redes-sociales-utilizadas20210804125007nt.html?ref=https% 3A%2F%2Fwww.elcorreo.com%2Ftecnologia%2Fredes-sociales%2Fredes-sociales-utiliz adas-20210804125007-nt.html

Budi, A.: The influence of Internet advertising and e-WOM on the perception and purchase intention of B2C e-commerce customers in Indonesia. In: International Conference on Accounting, Business and Economics, pp. 207–218 (2019). https://journal.uii.ac.id/icabe/ article/view/14715#:~:text=The%20results%20obtained%20from%20this,between%20inte rnet%20advertising%20and%20eWOM

Choi, Y.K., Seo, Y., Yoon, S.: Social ties, temporal distance and concretion of the message. E-WOM Messages on Social Networks **27**(3), 495–505 (2017). https://doi.org/10.1108/IntR-07-2016-0198

Erkan, I., Evans, C.: EWOM's influence on social media on consumer purchase intentions: an extended approach to information adoption. Comput. Hum. Behav. **61**, 47–55 (2016). https:// doi.org/10.1016/j.chb.2016.03.003

Gondim, C.B., Pereira, M.V., de Araújo,: Gestão da reputação on-line pelos meios de hospedagem: uma análise das respostas ao EWOM negativo. Turismo - Visão e Ação **22**(1), 185 (2020). https://doi.org/10.14210/rtva.v22n1.p185-209

González, D.: TodoModa enters the millionaire cosmetics business and strengthens its online channel. America Retail (2021). https://www.america-retail.com/argentina/todomoda-entra-millonario-negocio-de-la-cosmetica-y-potencia-su-canal-online/

Handoko, N., Melinda, T.: Effect of electronic word of mouth on purchase intention through brand image as media in tokopedia. Int. J. Econ. Bus. Account. Res. **5**, 83–93 (2021). https://jurnal.stie-aas.ac.id/index.php/IJEBAR/article/view/3184

Health Science Authority: Cosmetic products (2017). www.hsa.gov.sg/content/hsa/en/Health_Products_Regulation/Consumer_Information/Consumer_Guides/Cosmetics.html

Hennig-Thurau, T., Gwinner, K.P., Walsh, G., Gremler, D.D.: Electronic word-of-mouth via consumer-opinion platforms: what motivates consumers to articulate themselves on the internet? J. Interact. Mark. **18**(1), 38–52 (2004). https://doi.org/10.1002/dir.10073

Ismagilova, E., Slade, E.L., Rana, N.P., Dwivedi, Y.K.: The effect of electronic word of mouth communications on intention to buy: a meta-analysis. Inf. Syst. Front. **22**(5), 1203–1226 (2019). https://doi.org/10.1007/s10796-019-09924-y

Koo, D.-M.: Impact of tie strength and experience on the effectiveness of online service recommendations. Electron. Commer. Res. Appl. **15**, 38–51 (2016). https://doi.org/10.1016/j.elerap.2015.12.002

Lin, M., Wang, W.: Examining e-commerce customer satisfaction and loyalty integrated quality-risk-value perspective. J. Organ. Comput. Electron. Commer. **25**(4), 379–401 (2015). https://doi.org/10.1080/10919392.2015.1089681

Lopez, F., Correa, G.: Credibilidad en Facebook entre madres seguidoras de una página sobre crianza y síndrome de down. Revista Ibérica De Sistemas e Tecnologias De Informação 92–102 (2021). https://www.proquest.com/scholarly-journals/credibilidad-en-facebook-entre-madres-seguidoras/docview/2483955613/se-2?accountid=37610

Mansour, K.B., Kooli, K., Utama, R.: Online trust antecedents and their consequences on purchase intention: an integrative approach. J. Customer Behav. **13**(1), 25–42 (2014). https://doi.org/10.1362/147539214X14024779343677

Martínez: The key figures of eCommerce in the world in 2021 (2021). https://content.blacksip.com/cifras-del-ecommerce-en-el-mundo-en-2021

Matute, P.: Utrillas: The characteristics of electronic word of mouth and its influence on online repurchase intention. Eur. J. Manag. Bus. Econ. **24**, 61–75 (2015). https://doi.org/10.1016/j.redee.2015.03.002

Muhammad, B., Zeng, J., Suad, D., Mingyue, F., Ales, T.: Understanding the effects of eWOM antecedents on online purchase intention in China. Information **12**, 1–15 (2021). https://doi.org/10.3390/info12050192

Pappas, N.: Marketing strategies, perceived risks and consumer trust in online buying behavior. J. Retail. Consum. Serv. **29**, 92–103 (2015). https://doi.org/10.1016/j.jretconser.2015.11.007

See-To, E., Ho, K.: Value co-creation and purchase intention in social netwotk sites: the role of electronic word-of-mouth and trust – a theoretical analysis. Comput. Hum. Behav. **31**, 182–189 (2013). https://doi.org/10.1016/j.chb.2013.10.013

Obaidullah, S., Shahbaz, A., Majeed, T.: Relationship between eWOM and purchase intention: moderating role of culture (evidence from university students of Pakistan). Bus. Rev. **16**(1), 101–120 (2021). https://doi.org/10.54784/1990-6587.1398

Shuaib, M., Ahma, U., Arshad, M., Ghazi, I., Krishna, A., Haroon, J.: Building electronic word of-mouth credibility through social networking sites and determining its impact on brand image and online purchase intentions in India. J. Teor. aplicación Electrón. Comer. Res. **16**, 1008–1024 (2021). https://doi.org/10.3390/jtaer16040057

Sussman, S.W., Siegal, W.S.: Informational influence in organizations: an integrated approach to knowledge adoption. Inf. Syst. Res. **14**(1), 47–65 (2003). https://doi.org/10.1287/isre.14.1.47.14767

Teng, S., Khong, K.W., Chong, A.Y.-L., Lin, B.: Examining the impacts of electronic word-of-mouth message on consumers' attitude. J. Comput. Inf. Syst. **57**(3), 238–251 (2016). https://doi.org/10.1080/08874417.2016.1184012

Truc, V., Trong, N., Viet, P.: Impact of electronic word of mouth to the purchase intention – the case of Instagram. Ind. J. Manag. Prod. **12**(4), 1019–1033 (2021). https://doi.org/10.14807/ijmp.v12i4.1336

US Food and Drug Administration: Cosmetic product category codes (2017). www.fda.gov/cosmetics/registrationprogram/paperregistration/ucm111279.htm

Zion Market Research: Global cosmetic products market will reach USD 863 billion by 2024 (2018). https://globenewswire.com/news-release/2018/06/22/1528369/0/en/Global-Cosmetic-Products-Market-Will-Reach-USD-863-Billion-by-2024-Zion-Market-Research.html

Influence of Social Identity on the Ewom of Restaurants Through a Social Network. Peru Case

Luis Jhonny Dávila Valdera[1]([envelope]) [iD], Danicsa Karina Espino Carrasco[2] [iD],
Madeleine Espino Carrasco[3] [iD], Lady Violeta Dávila Valdera[4] [iD],
Anny Katherine Dávila Valdera[5] [iD], Mayury Jackeline Espino Carrasco[3] [iD],
Royer Vasquez Cachay[3] [iD], Ricardo Rafael Díaz Calderón[2] [iD],
Ana Maria Alvites Gasco[6] [iD], Enrique Santos Nauca Torres[7] [iD],
and Edson David Valdera Benavides[4] [iD]

[1] Santo Toribio de Mogrovejo University, Chiclayo, Peru
Davalujho0215@gmail.com
[2] Cesar Vallejo University, Chulucanas, Peru
[3] Señor de Sipan University, Pimentel, Peru
[4] Pedro Ruiz Gallo National University, Lambayeque, Peru
[5] National University of San Marcos, Lima, Peru
[6] Particular de Chiclayo University, Pimentel, Peru
[7] Cesar Vallejo University, Pimentel, Peru

Abstract. The purpose of the research is to determine the influence of social identity on electronic word of mouth (eWOM) of restaurant customers on Facebook, where the model proposed by Gonzáles, Marquina & Rodríguez (2020) who study identity variables was applied. Social and eWOM, applying the instrument that is the survey to 200 people who have a Facebook account, being evaluated by a 5-point Likert scale, for which the approach is quantitative, applied type, explanatory level and non-experimental design - cross-sectional, resulting in that the social identity has a significance of 0.000, influencing the eWOM, therefore, it is concluded that customers can interact with others on Facebook, who suggest trying new things, which arouses their curiosity about other restaurants through from the comments made by users, which are similar to the experience they had after eating in a restaurant. Because customers cooperated to show that they had a successful consumption, this encourages them to eat and comment on their dining experiences.

Keywords: Social identity · eWOM · social network

1 Introduction

Social identity proposes that individuals belonging to a group express their opinions and generate comments based on their experiences of buying and using services or products, thus contributing to the generation of community knowledge and influencing consumer decisions of society or members. of the community (Kim & Kim, 2019). This definition applies both in face-to-face and electronic contexts.

C. Stephanidis et al. (Eds.): HCII 2023, CCIS 1958, pp. 285–293, 2024.
https://doi.org/10.1007/978-3-031-49215-0_34

The eWOM is positive or negative recognition made by potential, real or previous customers about a product or company, which is made available to an agglomeration of people and establishments through the Internet, being a phenomenon of constant change. The eWOM message has several forms and can be used in different marketing dynamics, for example, as part of influencer marketing (Evans et al., 2017).

According to Kim and Kim (2019), the first variable that forms social identity is self-improvement, which refers to the human need to feel good about oneself and is declared in the desire to strengthen or optimize self-concept, achieve a positive self-image and maintain self-esteem (Turel & Gil-Or, 2019). Studies on the relationship between eWOM and self-improvement find that an individual can be motivated, directly or indirectly, to comment on various consumer experiences, based on the community's recognition of the contribution that such information can make (Akpinar & Berger, 2017).

One means of communication is Facebook, which is currently a factor driving the application of social identity, for which it mentions that "friends" are the object of interactions and are considered sources of information through their activities, such as posting an opinion or upload a link However, Facebook friends differ from real life friends. While offline friends can convey varied meanings through relationships that differ in terms of intimacy and closeness, Facebook friends are based on simplified binary relationships ("Friends or not"), leading to less nuanced meanings. Therefore, the rating as a friend is low on Facebook, which makes it difficult to specify the weight of the relationship, being different from real life (Kim et al., 2020).

In the city where the research is being carried out, people have become accustomed by necessity to carrying out most activities virtually, whether it is from buying a product to using a service, such is the case in requiring the services of the restaurants, who due to the current events regarding COVID-19 have had to adapt to different changes implemented by the Peruvian government, which vary from time to time, which has allowed us to observe the increase in the use of social networks, being a concern for companies to venture into the virtual world, this generates different groups of people, who comment and provide their opinions about the shopping experience, it can also affect customer perceptions about the websites of the organizations where you are they publish information related to their services and products, managing to influence behavior and the purchase decision.

The research question is, how does social identity influence the electronic word of mouth (eWOM) of restaurant customers on Facebook, 2023?

Through the study, a model was established that allows determining the influence between the variables developed by Gonzáles, Marquina & Rodríguez (2020) who develop a model based on theories related to social identity and eWOM.

Likewise, the general objective is to determine the influence of social identity on the eWOM of restaurant customers on Facebook; Regarding the specific objective, it is: to determine the influence of the dimensions of social identity in the electronic word of mouth (eWOM) of restaurant customers on Facebook.

2 Literature Review

Regarding the background, there is Gonzáles et al. (2020) who examined how social identity affects the generation of electronic word of mouth (eWOM), developed a model that includes self-enhancement, social capital and social presence as explanatory variables of social identity, which have an effect in the generation of eWOM in social networks, at least through some channels, in relation to its constructive variables in traditional WOM, so that social capital seems to be the channel through which this effect is produced, which is why It is considered a factor that promotes the participation of people within a social context, electronic or not, through the generation of comments about their consumer experiences, which provides relevant information that can influence users on purchasing decisions. or rejection of a product or service. Similarly, Kim et al. (2020) explored the role of social identity and threats to social identity in consumer behavioral judgment and intention about electronic word of mouth (eWOM) on Facebook, found that social identity on Facebook increases perceptions utility and behavioral intention to adopt, but when a threat to social identity is posed, these positive effects are excluded. Likewise, the study revealed an opposite condition in which a threat to social identity resulting in associative responses to eWOM, when the social identity is perceived as impenetrable (vs. penetrable), the threats that are traced to the social identity increase. The perceived usefulness and the intention of adoption in the eWOM.

Furthermore, Ruiz et al. (2018) provided a deeper understanding of the role of social influences in positive eWOM behavior, in their results they found that interaction with other members of the online community (social presence) is the primary predictor of PeWOM (positive eWOM)., in addition, social identity is a mediator between social presence and PeWOM, with interpersonal influence having a significant role as a moderating variable; on the other hand, the greater the impact of interpersonal influence, the stronger the relationship between the variables social presence and PeWOM. Likewise, Jacobsen & Ganim (2017) studied the impact of social identity on social commerce for the millennial buyer, the authors inquired about social networks by Millennials on three digital platforms: Facebook, Twitter and Pinterest, the Results show that millennials preferred to make use of the identity-shaping aspects of social media and commerce, on the other hand, platforms allow for greater identity formation to increase the likelihood that millennials not only use the platform, but also make purchases through them.

Therefore, Saleem, & Ellahi (2017) investigated the outcome of electronic word of mouth on the purchase intention of Facebook users, the findings affirm that eWOM is an effective component that influences the purchase intention of Facebook brands. Fashion, in addition, the findings confirm the role of homophily, expertise, reliability, informative influence and participation in haute couture as main components that influence eWOM. Finally, Li et al. (2017) proposes an integrated framework on the effect of eWOM, with the result that characteristics, communicators and other factors influence the effect of eWOM; eWOM features include source, volume, and valence; eWOM communicators refer to the sender, the receiver and the relationship between them.

Social identity theory suggests that an individual's beliefs, attitudes, and social behaviors evolve as one becomes a member of a group and interacts with intragroup members. The main idea of social identity theory is that individuals originate a part of their self-concept from certain social groups to which they belong, for example, this theory explains how subjects describe themselves in terms of identities. Shared social networks (McGowan et al., 2017).

Social networks offer users a space in which they can share many experiences with products or services (Chang, 2015). Therefore, it is sensible to reason that social networks have a role in building a consumer's identity, articulating self-assessment and generating social capital through shared experiences in said forums (Cui et al., 2019). However, the fact that these comments are transmitted remotely, that they are disseminated differently and regardless of physical proximity, gives distinctive characteristics to social networks.

According to Kim & Kim (2019), the first dimension that forms social identity is self-improvement. Which refers to the human insufficiency of feeling satisfied with oneself (Goris, 2014), and is declared in the claim to fortify or optimize self-concept, achieve a positive self-image and preserve self-esteem (Turel & Gil-Or, 2019).

The second dimension that forms social identity is social capital, Lin (2003) defines it as the resources introduced into social networks that are accessed and used by actors for their actions. When it comes to marketing, social capital is valuable in studies of customer behavior, particularly in terms of the research that this variable can provide to social media through user feedback on product purchases or purchases. Brand experiences (Filieri, 2015).

The third and last dimension to consider is social presence. Borgman (2006) asserts that social presence is the degree to which a medium allows establishing interpersonal contacts and is closely linked to intimacy and immediacy. In the social media environment, social presence is the degree to which a person is perceived as close.

In eWOM, advances in IT (information technology) and the emergence of online networking spaces have profoundly transformed the representation in which information is exchanged, transcending the usual WOM restrictions (Shin, 2007). Today, the consumer can share their experiences related to the product on the Internet through email, chat rooms, bulletin boards, fan clubs, forums, brands and user groups (Wu, 2013).

The relationship of social identity and eWOM, data that the effects of social identity are related to the interactions of users of social networks (Ruiz et al., 2018). From a practical point of view, it is valuable to understand and evaluate the role of self-improvement, social capital and social presence (Setenay & Kara, 2015) in the eWOM generation process. Despite the similarities between the physical and electronic contexts in which WGOM and eWOM messages are generated, each context has particularities.

3   Materials Y Methods

The research has a quantitative approach, because the survey and questionnaire were used as a technique and tool respectively. It is of an applied type, since it sought to apply or use the knowledge obtained such as social identity and eWOM. Likewise, it is of an explanatory level, because it goes beyond describing the knowledge or phenomena linked to each other, responding to the causes of events of a physical and social nature. The design is non-experimental, because there was no manipulation of variables, and it is cross-sectional, because the research was carried out in a determined time. The population was made up of people from the city under study, who have their Facebook account, between 20 and 50 years old, men and women, thus being an intentional sample, where the survey was applied to 200 people.

Regarding the instrument, use was made of the one proposed by Gonzáles, Marquina & Rodríguez (2020) who study the variables social identity and eWOM, applying a 5-point Likert-type scale. Regarding the collection procedure, the survey was carried out via Facebook, the questionnaire application period was approximately two weeks, the process was carried out through a link that redirected to the Google Form website, where the questionnaire was filled out.. Regarding the processing plan, the information was ordered in Excel, then transferred to the IBM SPSS version 25 statistical program, in which Cronbach's alpha (reliability) was analyzed, as well as factorial analysis of both variables and for the influence of the variables. Linear regression was done.

4 Results and Discussion

Sociodemographic Data
It was determined that 102 people are between the ages of 20 and 29, who make more use of social networks, on the other hand, 62 people are between the ages of 30 and 39, and finally 36 people are between the ages of 40 and 50 years.

Regarding the determination of the influence of social identity dimensions on electronic word of mouth (eWOM) of restaurant customers on Facebook, it is necessary to (Table 1):

Table 1. Summary of the model of the dimensions of social identity in the eWOM

Model	R	R^2	R^2 tight	Standard error of the estimate
1	,794[a]	,638	,635	2,814

[a] Predictors: (Constant), Social face-to-face, Self-improvement, Social capital

The adjusted R^2 is 0.635, which means that the proportion of data it is possible to predict the dimensions of social identity in the eWOM, being 63.5%, which is relatively high (Table 2).

Table 2. Influence of social identity dimensions on the eWOM

Modelo		Non-standardized coefficient		Standardized coefficient	t	Sig.
		B	Desv. Error	Beta		
1	(Constante)	6,841	1,355		5,018	,000
	Self-improvement	,186	,080	,117	2,138	,028
	Social capital	,411	,044	,528	7,806	,000
	Social face-to-face	,501	,117	,218	3,979	,000

[a] Dependent variable: eWOM

It is seen that the self-improvement dimension has a significance of 0.028, social capital 0.000 and social presence 0.000, considering that the P value $< = 0.05$, the three dimensions meet this condition, therefore, there is an influence of each dimension on the eWOM.

The influence of the social identity dimensions in the eWOM is due to the fact that allowing customers to interact on Facebook with strangers who share their interest in discovering restaurants gives them a sense of belonging to a virtual community where they interact by commenting on their experiences. The client feels good when he comments on the success he had when consuming in a restaurant, that is, explaining the great consumption experience of her. Despite the above, customers believe that physical contact occurs as a result of frequent Facebook conversations about restaurants; these results, when compared with what was found by Saleem, & Ellahi (2017), confirm the reliability and informative influence. Are main components that influence the eWOM, in addition, Ruiz et al. (2018) indicate that the interaction with other members of the online community (social presence) is the main predictor of positive eWOM, therefore, social identity is a mediator between social presence and positive eWOM, therefore, the influence interpersonal has a significant role as a moderating variable; on the other hand, the greater the impact of interpersonal influence, the stronger the relationship between the variables social presence and positive eWOM, with these results it can be inferred that self-improvement, social capital and social presence influence eWOM positively., this adds value for other people and has a direct impact on the experience that the consumer wants to have because when using a good product or receiving a good service, people mention it directly on their social network Facebook.

Finally, in determining the influence of social identity on electronic word of mouth (eWOM) of restaurant customers on Facebook, it is necessary to (Table 3):

Table 3. Summary of the social identity model in eWOM

Model	R	R^2	R^2 tight	Standard error of the estimate
1	,787[a]	,629	,625	2,855

[a] Predictors: (Constant), Social identity

The adjusted R^2 is 0.625, which means that the proportion of data it is possible to predict the dimensions of social identity in the eWOM, being 62.5%, which is relatively high.T (Table 4).

It is visualized that social identity has a significance of 0.000, considering that the P value $<= 0.05$ of the three dimensions meets this condition, therefore, there is an influence of each dimension on the eWOM.

The influence of social identity on eWOM is due to the fact that the comments made are comparable to the experiences of customers in restaurants, allowing interaction with other people on Facebook who advise trying new things and arouse interest in learning about other restaurants, therefore, the cooperation of the clients shows that they make a successful consumption, these results that when compared with what was found by Gonzáles et al. (2020), found that social identity (social presence) has an effect on the

Table 4. Influence of social identity on eWOM

Model		Non-standardized coefficient		Standardized coefficient	t	Sig.
		B	Desv. Error	Beta		
1	(Constant)	7,225	1,353		5,305	,000
	Social identity	,368	,015	,778	18,823	,000

[a] Dependent variable: eWOM

generation of eWOM in social networks, with social capital being the channel through which this effect is produced. Similarly, Kim et al. (2020) detail that the social identity that develops on Facebook increases perceptions of usefulness and behavioral intention, but when a threat to social identity is posed, these positive effects are excluded, but give associative responses to eWOM, with based on these results, it can be inferred that the majority of respondents reported having similar experiences at the restaurants they visited, which is based on positive reviews that directly encourage customers to frequent these businesses on a regular basis.

5 Conclusions

The influence of social identity on electronic word of mouth (eWOM) is significant, because many people communicate through social networks, which allows users to post comments similar to the experience they had in a restaurant. This interaction with other users on Facebook results in your recommendations, which encourage customers to make a successful purchase.

Finally, there is a significant influence of social identity dimensions on electronic word of mouth (eWOM), because user comments demonstrate their successful consumption and positive comments result in close interaction with the user. Facebook users who have preferences in the restaurant industry can connect with other users by connecting as consumers.

The research makes a contribution by giving information that is generalized through a social network and the background of the tools that are developed within a social network such as Facebook, about its true use through social identity, which will lead to taking awareness about the decisions when generating comments that is helpful for any organization since Facebook is currently the most popular social tool, which is no stranger to any organization.

References

Akpinar, E., Berger, J.: Valuable virality. J. Mark. Res. **54**(2), 318–330 (2017). https://doi.org/10.1509/jmr.13.0350

Borgman, C.: What can studies of e-learning teach us about collaboration in e-research? Some findings from digital library studies. Comput. Support. Coop. Work **15**(2), 359–83 (2006). https://escholarship.org/content/qt6cj1756r/qt6cj1756r_noSplash_d1a0252 52c6b380dcf4d77ec2e674812.pdf

292   L. J. Dávila Valdera et al.

Cui, H., Zhao, T., Smyczek, S., Sheng, Y., Ming, X., Yang, X.: Dual path effects of self-worth on status consumption: evidence from Chinese consumers. Asia Pac. J. Mark. Logistics 32(7), 1431–1450 (2019). https://doi.org/10.1108/APJML-06-2019-0364

Chang, C.: Self-construal and Facebook activities: Exploring differences in social interaction orientation. Comput. Hum. Behav. 53, 91–101 (2015). https://doi.org/10.1016/j.chb.2015.06.049

Evans, N.J., Phua, J., Lim, J., Jun, H.: Disclosing Instagram influencer advertising: the effects of disclosure language on advertising recognition, attitudes, and behavioral intent. J. Interact. Advert. 17(2), 138–149 (2017). https://doi.org/10.1080/15252019.2017.1366885

Filieri, R.: What makes online reviews helpful? A diagnosticity-adoption framework to explain informational and normative influences in e-WOM. J. Bus. Res. 68(6), 1261–1270 (2015). https://doi.org/10.1016/j.jbusres.2014.11.006

Gonzáles, F., Marquina, P., Rodríguez, J.: Effect of social identity on the generation of electronic word-of-mouth (eWOM) on Facebook. Cogent Bus. Manage. 7, 1–15 (2020). https://doi.org/10.1080/23311975.2020.1738201

Goris, J.: Self-appraisals in Mexico. Int. J. Commer. Manage. 24(2), 152–166 (2014). https://ur.booksc.org/book/64319072/9f8cd4

Jacobsen, S., Barnes, N.G.: On being social: how social identity impacts social commerce for the millennial shopper. Int. J. Manage. Sci. Bus. Adm. 3(4), 38–45 (2017). https://doi.org/10.18775/ijmsba.1849-5664-5419.2014.34.1005

Kim, Y., Parkt, Y., Lee, Y., Park, K.: Do we always adopt Facebook friends' eWOM postings? the role of social identity and threat. Int. J. Advertising 37(1), 86–104 (2020). http://kiwanpark.snu.ac.kr/pdf/IJA-2018.pdf

Kim, B., Kim, Y.: Growing as social beings: how social media usage for college sports is associated with college's students group identity and collective self-esteem. Comput. Hum. Behav. 97, 241–249 (2019). https://doi.org/10.1016/j.chb.2019.03.016

Lin, N.: Social capital: a theory of social structure and action. Camb. Univ. Press (2003). https://doi.org/10.1017/CBO9780511815447

Lin, C., Wu, Y., Chen, J., others:. Electronic word-of-mouth: the moderating roles of product involvement and brand image. Diversity, technology, and innovation for operational competitiveness. In: Proceedings of the 2013 International Conference on Technology Innovation and Industrial Management, vol. 3, pp. 29–47. ToKnowPress (2013). https://www.semanticscholar.org/paper/Electronic-Word-of-Mouth%3A-The-Moderating-Roles-of-Lin-Wu/6b631579b03573c87d7afb61bfb17f03262bb295

Li, J., Xue, W., Yang, F., Li, Y.: An integrated research framework for effect of EWOM. J. Syst. Sci. Inf. 5(4), 343–355 (2017)

McGowan, M., Shiu, E., Hassan, L.: The influence of social identity on value perceptions and intention. J. Consum. Behav. 16(3), 242–253 (2017). https://doi.org/10.1002/cb.1627

Ruiz, C., Bigne, E., Sanz, S., Tronch, J.: Does social climate influence positive eWOM? a studyof heavy-users of online communities. Bus. Res. Q. 79, 1–13 (2018). https://doi.org/10.1016/j.brq.2017.12.001

Saleem, A, Ellahi, A.: Influence of electronic word of mouth on purchase intention of fashion products in social networking websites. Pak. J. Commer. Soc. Sci. 11(2), 597–622 (2017). https://www.econstor.eu/handle/10419/188307

Setenay, K., Kara, A.: Online word-of-mouth communication on social networking sites. Int. J. Commer. Manage. 25, 2–20 (2015). https://pennstate.pure.elsevier.com/en/publications/online-word-of-mouth-communication-on-social-networking-sites-an-

Shin, K.: Factors influencing source credibility of consumer reviews: apparel online shopping (2007). http://ir.library.oregonstate.edu/jspui/handle/1957/4370

Turel, O., Gil, O.: To share or not to share? The role of false Facebook self, sex and narcissism in reposting self-image enhancing products. Personality Individ. Differ. **151**, 49–60 (2019). https://doi.org/10.1016/j.paid.2019.109506

Wu, M.: Relationships among source credibility of electronic word of mouth, perceived risk, and consumer behavior on consumer generated media (2013). http://scholarworks.umass.edu/theses

Comparing Samsung and Apple Top-End Mobile Cameras by Using NR-IQA Metrics

Anderson V. C. de Oliveira$^{(\boxtimes)}$, Sergio C. Tamayo , and Rafael N. Cunha

Sidia Instituto de Ciencia E Tecnologia - Sidia Amazon Innovation - SW Solutions,
Av. Torquato Tapajos 6770, Novo Israel 69039-125, Manaus, Brazil
{anderson.oliveira,sergio.tamayo,rafael.cunha}@sidia.com
http://www.sidia.com

Abstract. In this work, we compare the picture quality provided by two popular smartphone brands: Samsung and Apple. We use the top-end model of both brands in 2022: Galaxy S22 Ultra for Samsung and iPhone 13 Pro for Apple, and we built a dataset consisting of seven different environments. For each of these environments, we captured pictures with both devices under the same conditions in two camera categories: first, using the device's native camera and then using the camera provided by the Instagram App. Since these pictures are in a compressed form, and therefore there is no reference image to compare them to, we use "No-Reference Image Quality Assessment" (NR-IQA) metrics to provide values to measure the quality of its pictures. Experimental results with some of the most used NR-IQA metrics show that Samsung device has best images for most of the environments when using the device's native camera, but Apple provides best results for the Instagram App.

Keywords: Smartphones · Photo quality · Samsung · iPhone · NR-IQA

1 Introduction

Photography is one of the most common hobbies in the world. The use of photography by ordinary people through smartphones has become increasingly popular. With the advancement of smartphone technology, the quality of the cameras built into these devices has improved significantly, allowing anyone to easily capture and share great and professional-looking photographs, even people who lacked experience in that field [4]. In addition, photo editing applications available on smartphones allow users to enhance their images, add filters, and share instantly on social networks and other online platforms. Therefore, the quality of the pictures provided by these devices is one of the main issues taken into account when the user chooses a smartphone to buy [7].

According to datareportal.com, Instagram is the fourth-largest social media platform in the world, with about 1.6 billion active users until April 2023, behind

Supported by Sidia Instituto de Ciência e Tecnologia.

of Facebook, YouTube and WhatsApp [1]. However, it is the most popular platform for sharing photos and videos, according to the same portal, with about 95 million photos and videos posted each day. Initially, Instagram was developed exclusively for iOS devices, i.e. to be used on iPhones. It was released in October 2010 and was only available for iPhone users. The developers wanted to take advantage of the features and growing market of iOS devices. However, after its initial success on iOS, Instagram has expanded its support to other platforms. In April 2012, Instagram released an Android version, opening up the app to an even larger user base, and it also offers a web version for access through internet browsers [2]. In both versions, iOS and Android, the Instagram application has a camera button to allow the user to capture a photo and share it without the need to open another capture application. However, the photo obtained within the Instagram application is different from the one obtained when using the native camera. Therefore, we investigated the quality of the photos in these two scenarios.

Section 2 describes the dataset that we built to compare the devices. Section 3 briefly covers which metric to use in order to measure the image quality. We present the experimental results in Sect. 4 and the conclusions in Sect. 5.

2 Building the Dataset

In order to compare the pictures provided by these two popular smartphone brands, we built a dataset according to the structure shown in Fig. 1. I.e., for both devices, we use two camera settings: the native camera provided by the device itself and the one provided by the Instagram application, but without using any specific filter. For both native and Instagram cameras, we collect photos under the same conditions in seven different environments, ranging from common situations of users. They are shown in Fig. 2: outdoors, indoor, against the light, color contrast, night, landscape, and selfie (in this one, we pixelate the face here for privacy purposes).

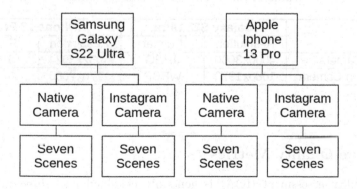

Fig. 1. Dataset structure.

Fig. 2. Scenes in the dataset.

We use the maximum resolution for both devices. Table 1 shows the characteristics of the images obtained using the native camera and the Instagram camera. Note that iPhone has a higher resolution for both cameras, and most scenarios show the images in JPEG format, except for the Galaxy's Instagram camera, which is presented in WEBP format. Theoretically, both the resolution and the format itself do not determine whether the image quality is better or worse in the tests carried out in this work.

Table 1. Characteristics of dataset images.

	Galaxy S22 Ultra		iPhone 13 Pro	
	Resolution	Format	Resolution	Format
Native Camera	4000x3000	JPEG	4032x3024	JPEG
Instagram Camera	1080x1920	WEBP	1170x2080	JPEG

3   Image Quality Metrics

Image quality assessment (IQA) is generally classified into three categories, depending on the existence of the original image: Full-reference methods (FR-IQA) compares a distorted version of an image to an original version. It often used to compare compression algorithms by measuring how far its compressed image does it look like the original. Commonly used FR-IQA metrics are PSNR and SSIM [3]. Reduced-reference methods (RR-IQA) require only partial information about the reference image. Some examples of this approach include the reduced reference variants of SSIM (MS-SSIM) [8] and Reduced Reference Entropic Differencing (RRED) [6]. No-reference (or blind) methods operate solely on the distorted image, and this is the case of our application in this work. A common way to measure it is through subjective tests, where images with the same content (but technically different from each other) are shown to some people, and they are asked to classify them on a scale. There are recommendations for carrying out subjective tests, and sometimes it is inconvenient to gather people and set up a suitable environment to perform these tests. However, there are also some algorithms that evaluate it based on human visual perception. Some of the main algorithms are BRISQUE [5] and ILNIQE [9].

4 Experimental Results

Once the pictures provided by the smartphones are in compressed form (jpeg or webp), then there is no reference image to compare them to, hence we use the third category in Sect. 3, called No-reference image quality assessment NR-IQA. Many algorithms are proposed for measuring the quality of the image, based on the subjective perception of a human observer. In our experiments, we used two popular NR-IQA techniques: BRISQUE [5] and ILNIQE [9]. As many of the IQA techniques run from trained models, note that results from the same technique can differ depending on the trained model used to score the images. In this work, we use the Brisque method available in the Python package "image-quality 1.2.7". For ILNIQE we use the Matlab implementation available in [10], both with their pre-trained models that we do not interfere with and they are available to everyone. The results are shown in the Tables 2 and 3.

Table 2. BRISQUE results for the seven scenes.

Scenes	BRISQUE			
	Native Camera		Instagram Camera	
	Galaxy	iPhone	Galaxy	iPhone
Outdoors	**42.001**	43.458	55.228	**33.918**
Indoor	**16.996**	26.719	46.727	**5.118**
Ag. Light	**10.387**	12.795	42.340	**13.086**
Color Cont.	18.293	**16.305**	29.911	**24.088**
Night	**17.260**	26.767	26.187	**10.543**
Landscape	**15.922**	20.796	13.957	**9.148**
Selfie	16.172	**15.500**	6.874	**6.091**

Numerical results for both algorithms range from 0 to 100, and the result is better as smaller the value is. Bold values show the best result between the two devices for each test scenario. Then we observed that the Galaxy S22 Ultra has the best results for most of the scenes when using the native camera, except for "color contrast" and "selfie". That behavior occurs for both algorithms, BRISQE and ILNIQE. However, for Instagram camera, Apple iPhone 13 Pro has the best results for all scenes when measured with BRISQE and most of the scenes (except for "color contrast" and "landscape") by measured with ILNIQE.

Table 3. ILNIQE results for the seven scenes.

| Scenes | ILNIQE | | | |
| | Native Camera | | Instagram Camera | |
	Galaxy	iPhone	Galaxy	iPhone
Outdoors	**23.644**	27.913	25.007	**22.037**
Indoor	**24.722**	27.310	24.057	**21.377**
Ag. Light	**26.303**	29.997	24.978	**22.844**
Color Cont.	19.244	**18.748**	**18.589**	21.258
Night	**18.827**	25.451	21.053	**20.953**
Landscape	**18.587**	19.899	**21.333**	22.144
Selfie	23.476	**23.179**	22.108	**18.341**

5 Conclusions

Image quality provided by the camera is one of the main factors taken into account when an user decides to choose a brand of smartphone. Many YouTubers and digital influencers have used iPhones for years, believing that this device provides the best image quality, which leads their followers to buy this device as well. However, this is because their judgments often correspond to the use of photos within the Instagram application, which is different for iOS and Android. Using the NR-IQA metrics cited in this work, our results with the top-end models of Samsung and Apple in 2022 showed that the Galaxy S22 Ultra is better than the iPhone 13 Pro when using the native camera, which could mean that the Instagram team somehow disadvantages Samsung in its app.

However, we must consider that there are other NR-IQA methods, and many of them are based on pre-trained models. Therefore, depending on the images used in these trainings and their settings, the results may differ when obtaining a score for an image in the test stage.

Acknowledgment. This work was presented as part of the results from Harp Plataform 2.0 Project, carried out by Sidia Instituto de Ciência e Tecnologia in partnership with Samsung Eletrônica da Amazônia LTDA, according to IT Law n.8387/91 and article 39 from Decree 10.521/2020.

References

1. DataReportal: Global social media statistics. https://datareportal.com/social-media-users. Accessed May 2 2023
2. Eldridge, A.: Instagram. Encyclopedia britannica. (2023). https://www.britannica.com/topic/Instagram Accessed May 25 2023
3. Horé, A., Ziou, D.: Image quality metrics: Psnr vs. ssim. In: 2010 20th International Conference on Pattern Recognition, pp. 2366–2369 (2010). https://doi.org/10.1109/ICPR.2010.579
4. Kiniulis, K.: 12 Mobile photography statistics and how it's changing our world (2022). https://www.eksposure.com/mobile-photography-statistics. Accessed Apr 17 2023
5. Mittal, A., Moorthy, A.K., Bovik, A.C.: No-reference image quality assessment in the spatial domain. IEEE Trans. Image Process. 21(12), 4695–4708 (2012). https://doi.org/10.1109/TIP.2012.2214050
6. Soundararajan, R., Bovik, A.C.: Rred indices: reduced reference entropic differencing for image quality assessment. IEEE Trans. Image Process. 21(2), 517–526 (2012). https://doi.org/10.1109/TIP.2011.2166082
7. Twenefour, F.: Major determinants that influence the choice of brand of mobile phone. Open J. Stat. 07, 663–675 (2017). https://doi.org/10.4236/ojs.2017.74046
8. Wang, Z., Simoncelli, E., Bovik, A.: Multiscale structural similarity for image quality assessment. In: The Thrity-Seventh Asilomar Conference on Signals, Systems and Computers, 2003. vol. 2, pp. 1398–1402 Vol. 2 (2003). https://doi.org/10.1109/ACSSC.2003.1292216
9. Zhang, L., Zhang, L., Bovik, A.C.: A feature-enriched completely blind image quality evaluator. IEEE Trans. Image Process. 24(8), 2579–2591 (2015). https://doi.org/10.1109/TIP.2015.2426416
10. Zhang, L., Zhang, L., Bovik, A.: A Feature-Enriched completely blind image quality evaluator (2014). https://web.comp.polyu.edu.hk/cslzhang/IQA/ILNIQE/ILNIQE.htm, Method webpage. Accessed Mar 5 2023

A Signature Information Generation Method for Judging the Illegality of Cloud-Based Webtoons

Seyoung Jang[1] , Injae Yoo[1] , Jaechung Lee[2] , Byeongchan Park[1] ,
Seok-Yoon Kim[1] , and Youngmo Kim[1(✉)]

[1] Soongsil University, Seoul 06978, Republic of Korea
seyjang216@soongsil.ac.kr, halo8024@beyondtech.co.kr, {ksy,
ymkim828}@ssu.ac.kr
[2] Beyondtech Inc., Seoul 08503, Republic of Korea
jclee@beyondtech.co.kr

Abstract. Recently, platforms that service digital contents such as movies, dramas, and webtoons are switching from downloading methods to streaming methods, and illegal content servicing methods are also changing from downloading to streaming. These streaming-based copyright infringement crimes avoid the blocking and investigation by law enforcement agencies through methods such as using overseas servers or disguising the IP of operating servers using cloud services, etc., which requires an appropriate measures to respond to them. In this paper, we propose a signature information generation method through which the illegality of distributed digital contents can be quickly checked. Using this method, there is an advantage in quickly finding illegally distributed digital contents based on a cloud server, which can prompt to block illegal distribution sites.

Keywords: Content Delivery Network (CDN) · Signatures · Metadata · Illegal Contents · Webtoons

1 Introduction

1.1 A Subsection Sample

Due to the recent spread of K-contents, webtoon platforms such as Kakao and Naver are expected to grow in size as webtoon platforms and their intellectual properties grow globally [1]. However, copyright infringement on webtoons is also increasing in proportion to their size [2]. If you look at illegal webtoon sites infringing copyright, their server may be located overseas or their IPs are disguised using cloud services (e.g. GCP, Azure, AWS, etc.) to avoid blocking and investigations [3, 4]. In order to block such illegal sites, it is difficult to respond using the conventional method in which the copyright infringement of the contents is checked by a person after the content list of the site is checked and the contents are downloaded [5, 6]. In this paper, we propose a method of generating signature information to build a signature DB that can quickly determine

C. Stephanidis et al. (Eds.): HCII 2023, CCIS 1958, pp. 300–309, 2024.
https://doi.org/10.1007/978-3-031-49215-0_36

whether webtoons are illegally distributed in a cloud environment. The structure of this paper is as follows. Section 2 describes text-based similarity test and text similarity as related researches. Section 3 describes the signature information generation method for judging cloud-based illegal distribution webtoons proposed in this paper. In Sect. 4, the experiments and results are reviewed, and the conclusion is given in Sect. 5.

2 Related Research

2.1 Text-Based Similarity Test

Text classification is a method of using natural language processing technology to classify a specific text to which category it belongs to among several categories set by humans. Text-based similarity test methods can be divided into text classification through supervised learning and text classification through unsupervised learning [7]. Text classification methods through supervised learning include naive Bayes classification, support vector machine, neural network classification, new classification, logistic classification, and random forest classification, etc. [8]. Unlike supervised learning, the test classification method through unsupervised learning is a process of learning by dividing each data by finding the characteristics of the data and creating appropriate categories because labels do not exist, and the typical K-means clustering method is to vectorize each sentence and express it on the coordinate axis to classify it into clusters, as shown in (Fig. 1).

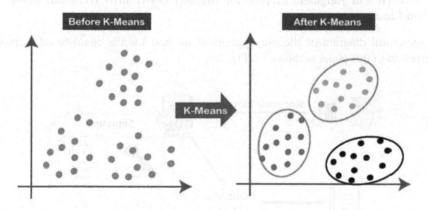

Fig. 1. K-Means Clustering

2.2 SIFT Algorithm

SIFT is an algorithm that extracts feature points that are not affected by image size and rotation. The basic principle is to extract SIFT features from two different images and then match the feature points that are most similar to each other to find the corresponding part in the two images. It also calculates values containing direction and size information that can explain the points for each feature are calculated at that point, after finding image features at various scales. After comparing the distance between the feature of the query image and the feature of the target image calculated by this method, matching is performed, and then the matched points are accurately matched by distinguishing inliers and outliers using hough transform. Finally, Least mean square is used to verify whether the matching is correct.

2.3 AKAZE Algorithm

The AKAZE algorithm uses a non-linear filter to remove noise and emphasizes the edge area, thereby guaranteeing the recognition performance of the KAZE algorithm that creates scale-space and speeding up the algorithm. The reason why AKAZE uses a nonlinear filter is that in the spatial domain, the average filter damages the high-frequency components of the image to cause a blurring phenomenon, and the median filter shows excellent noise removal characteristics, but causes visual errors in the image. Applying a nonlinear filter for such excellent noise removal is to enhance the algorithm calculation speed by emphasizing the edge area.

3 Generation of Signature Information to Judge Whether a Webtoon is Illegal or Not

3.1 Overview of Judgment Method for Illegally Distributed Webtoons Based on Cloud

The structural diagram of illegality judgment method for the cloud-based webtoon distribution in this paper is shown in (Fig. 2).

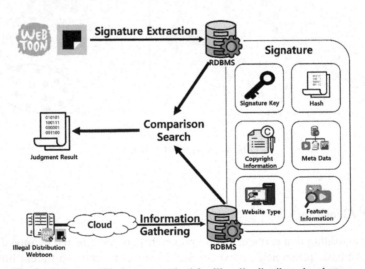

Fig. 2. Structure of judgment method for illegally distributed webtoons

The illegality judgement method for cloud-based webtoons consists of three steps, and in the first step, the original webtoon signature DB is built. Second, signatures are extracted by collecting illegally distributed webtoons serviced in the cloud. Finally, it is compared with the original dataset.

3.2 Webtoon Signature Information Extraction Method

In order to judge the illegality of cloud-based webtoon distribution, signature information must be created, and the signature information is created using webtoon hash, signature key, metadata, copyright information, cloud-based illegal site information, and feature information, which are built into a DB. The structural diagram of the webtoon signature information generation method is shown in (Fig. 3), which proceeds in 4 steps.

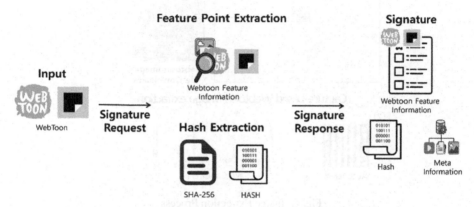

Fig. 3. Structural diagram of webtoon signature extraction method

The first frame creation step for webtoon image collection creates a standard frame for recognizing variously transformed webtoon images from the original. There are two creation methods: a download-based creation method that downloads the webtoon image from the webtoon page and a capture-based creation method that automatically adjusts the scrolling of HTML and captures the screen when the webtoon image cannot be downloaded, as shown in (Fig. 4).

The second step is the pre-processing step webtoon images. This process is for robustness and pre-processing of signature information. There are three preprocessing methods: ROI (Region of Interest) extraction method, TEXT extraction method using OCR technology, and Random ROI extraction and segmentation method. The ROI extraction method is the process of creating the webtoon in cut units, since there is a problem of inserting blanks outside the cut and unnecessary content when creating an image based on capture, as shown in (Fig. 5).

The third webtoon content signature extraction step extract the webtoon's copyright information, HASH information, and metadata, and the extraction method is as follows. Webtoon copyright information is automatically collected by crawling the copyright information provided by the platform and included in the signature. An example of the collected information is shown in Table 1.

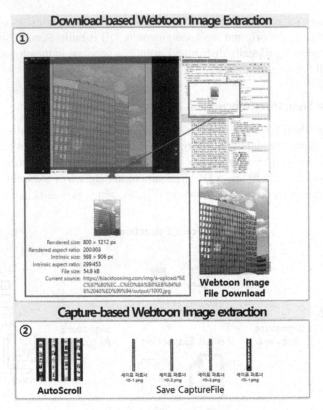

Fig. 4. Image Extraction Process

The HASH extraction method is extracted using MD5 and SHA-1, and an example of the extracted value is shown in (Fig. 6).

The items to be included in the signature among the extracted webtoon metadata are shown in Table 2, and finally, this signature information is made into a DB and indexed on the server.

4   Experimentation and Validation

In order to verify the signature information generation method for judging the illegal distribution of cloud-based webtoons proposed in this paper, an experimental environment such as Table 3 has been established.

Transformation was applied to the original dataset for the comparative verification process. The transformation items are shown in Table 4, and the data set was built and experimented with logo insertion, compression, brightness conversion, aspect ratio transformation, image format, translation, image segmentation, cut transformation, and recognition units.

Figure 7 shows the signature information verification process created to determine the illegal distribution of cloud-based webtoons.

Fig. 5. Image Extraction Process

Table 1. Webtoon Copyright Information

copyright information	Note
genre	The genre of the webtoon currently being serviced
title	The title of the webtoon currently being serviced
copyright holder	Copyright holder of the webtoon
Rating	Webtoon availability level
summary	Synopsis of the webtoon currently in service
completion	Whether or not the webtoon is complete
general meeting	Total number of episodes of webtoon (only when completed)
service platform	Platform name currently in service
Serial start date	Webtoon's first serial start date

- Step 1: Hash Comparison Search
- Step 2: Copyright information Comparison Search
- Step 3: Metadata Comparison Search
- Step 4: Site Type Comparison Search
- Step 5: Feature Information Comparison Search

Fig. 6. An Example of Extracted HASH value

Table 2. Webtoon Metadata Information

meta information	Note
resolution	Image size (width, height)
file name	name of content file
file type	file format
Size	Image Size (Byte)

Table 3. Experimental Environment

	Note
CPU	Intel Core i9 12900K
GPU	NVIDIA Geforce RTX 4090
RAM	32 GB
OS	Windows 10

The comparison and verification step proceeds, and if a similarity is found in any step, it is judged to be illegally distributed webtoon content, and the judgment process is shown in (Fig. 8).

In order to verify the signature information generated to determine the illegal distribution of cloud-based webtoons proposed in this paper, a total of 1000 data sets of 100 each with modifications to the original data were prepared, as shown in Table 4. The experimental method for verifying illegal webtoon signature information is as follows, and the experimental results are shown in Table 5.

- Recognition rate
  · Test method: Recognition rate test for 1,000 datasets
  · Result calculation method: $\sum$recognized, misrecognized, non-recognized case / $\sum$total test cases * 100
- Recognition speed
  · Test method: The time required for the recognition value to be returned from the search comparison server to the feature point client after searching for the feature point with the information generated during the recognition rate test.
  · Result calculation method: $\sum$content extraction and search comparison speed (in seconds) / $\sum$number of content extraction and search comparison cases

Table 4. Data Set

Item		Note
Original		100(EA)
Transformation	Insert logo	100(EA)
	compression	100(EA)
	brightness conversion	100(EA)
	aspect ratio transformation	100(EA)
	image format	100(EA)
	translation	100(EA)
	image segmentation	100(EA)
	cut deformation	100(EA)
	recognition unit	100(EA)
Total		1,000(EA)

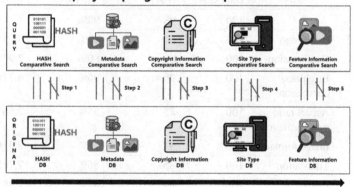

Fig. 7. Signature Comparison and Verification Process

As a result of the experiment, the recognition rate and recognition speed have been calculated for each variant item, and the average recognition rate turns out to be 89.20% and the recognition speed is 7.625 s.

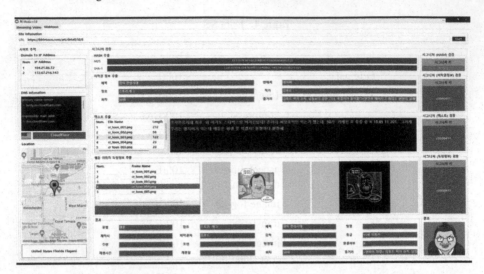

Fig. 8. Webtoon Signature DB Comparison and Verification Process

Table 5. Webtoon verification test results

Item		Original Data (EA)	Recognition (EA)	Recognition rate (%)	Recognition speed (sec)
Original Data		100	98	98%	7.593
Transformed data	Insert logo	100	88	88%	8.395
	Compression	100	80	80%	7.908
	Brightness conversion	100	96	96%	6.776
	Aspect ratio transformation	100	85	85%	7.567
	Image format	100	91	91%	7.326
	Translation	100	86	86%	7.782
	Image segmentation	100	81	81%	7.985
	Cut deformation	100	91	91%	6.685
	Recognition unit	100	96	96%	8.241
Total		1000	892	89.20%	7.625

5 Conclusion

In this paper, we proposed a method of creating a signature so that illegal distribution webtoons can be judged based on a cloud storage device that has been recently done. As elements for constructing a signature, webtoon metadata information, copyright information, HASH information, and feature information were proposed, and a method for extracting the information was proposed. In addition, a method of constructing a signature DB to use the signature index in Elasticsearch was proposed. In the experiment and verification, the signature was extracted for each element, and the recognition rate of 89% and the recognition speed of the webtoon were confirmed at 7.6 s. If the proposed method is used, it is expected that a new copyright ecosystem will be formed in the future where stakeholders in webtoon distribution and service can control themselves. Since the original work will be transformed and distributed in various forms in the future, robustness research on feature points that are resistant to deformation will be additionally needed.

Acknowledgment. This research project supported by Ministry of Culture, Sport and Tourism (MCST) and Korea Creative Content agency (KOCCA) in 2022 (R2022020109).

References

1. Park, J.J.: The power of K-content', exports increased by 13.9%. Electronic Newspaper (2022). https://www.etnews.com/20220614000187
2. Yoon, S.: What torrent do 20-year-olds think? Copyright Protection Reporters (2019). https://m.blog.naver.com/kcopastory/221661228331
3. Kim, M.D., Lee, K.L.: Review on the legality of acquiring digital evidence in cloud storage. Contemp. Rev. Crim. Law (CRCL.PS) **72**, 91–124 (2021)
4. Taylor, M., Haggerty, J., Gresty, D., Hegarty, R.: Digital evidence in cloud computing systems. Comput. Law Secur. Rev. **26**, 304–308 (2010). https://doi.org/10.1016/j.clsr.2010.03.002
5. Choung, W., Kim, Y.D.: A study on the search and seizure of user information in cloud computing service. Lawyers Assoc. J. **70**(3), 155–189 (2021)
6. Lee, W.S.: A study on the collection of digital evidences in cloud computing environment. Contemp. Rev. Crim. Law (38), 174–217 (2013)
7. Herbert, B., Andreas, E., Tinne, T., Luc, G.: SURF (speed-up robust features). Comput. Vis. Image Underst. **110**, 346–359 (2008)
8. Tareen, S.A.K., Saleem, Z.: A comparative analysis of SIFT, SURF, KAZE, AKAZE, ORB, and BRISK. In: 2018 International Conference on Computing, Mathematics and Engineering Technologies (iCoMET) (2018)

Sustainable Food Design: A Four-Dimensional Transformation of Theory and Methodology Towards Post Carbon Era

Siyang Jing(✉)

Central Academy of Fine Arts, Beijing Wangjing 100102, People's Republic of China
jingsiyang@cafa.edu.cn

Abstract. Food design is an emerging field of research in the past decade, with interdisciplinary attributes that integrate culture, ecology, health, and society. Especially in the post-epidemic and post-carbon context, the importance of food design as a pathway to sustainable development has been gradually highlighted. By summarizing the food design research from the perspectives of eating, cooking, experience design of food, as well as ecology, agriculture, and system design of food, the article defines the research scope of sustainable food design. Based on this, the author proposes a four-dimensional transformation theory of food design in the post-carbon context and analyzes how to translate strategy into action with case studies. The four-dimensional transformation are *from Human-Centered to Life-Centered, from Object-Centered to Hyper-object Centered, from Experience-Economy to Post-Carbon Economy, from design for consumption to design for Crisis*. In this way, the article builds a new framework and guideline for sustainable food design and propose strategies to deal with the crisis of the times.

Keywords: Sustainable Food Design · method transformation · Crisis · Post-epidemic Era · post-carbon era

1 Introduction

Threatened by multiple risks such as climate change, epidemic, natural resource degradation, trade frictions and regional conflicts, the current global agriculture system is developing in an unsustainable way. Thus the situation of global food security and nutrition is facing unprecedented challenges. Food is an important link among people, nature and society. Sustainable food design is an *open complex giant system* [1] involving agriculture, ecology, industry, consumption, poverty alleviation, community and other issues. Although contemporary food design just rose 20 years ago, multiple research directions have been developed so far, such as small-scale design with perspectives centered on *eating* from diet, cooking, to experience design, as well as large-scale design with perspectives centered on *production*, from ecology, agriculture, and systems design.

However, it is important to realize that food design is not new as the object of the study, but rather the link the food design made, leading to a re-examination of resources, industries, and consumption. The article focuses on food design as a response to crisis, with proposing four kinds of transformation of food design thinking: (1) shifting *from Human-Centered to Life-Centered*, (2) *from Object-Centered to Hyper-object Centered*, (3) *from Experience-Economy to Post-Carbon Economy*, (4) *from design for consumption to design for Crisis*. The following questions are addressed: How to use food to design inter-species relationships? How to reduce the carbon footprint of food consumption? How to use food waste? How to produce food in extreme climate conditions? How can food security and nutrition be addressed? What are the possibilities for future food design? As the exhibition *Edible Futures* suggested that "Changing the world through food," the article aims to provoke rethinking the value of food design with the suggestion of design solution to cope with crises in this era.

2 Research Scope of Sustainable Food Design

2.1 Food Experience Design and Food System Design

Analyzed from existing research, scholars are in the initial stage of research on food ecology and system design. Contemporary food design began around 2010 [2] and is mainly divided into small-scale design of diet, cooking and experience, and large-scale design of ecology, agriculture and systems. In China, food design research mostly revolves around food and culture. According to Linghao Zhang, food design carries aesthetics, memory, cultural meaning and values, including the perception of the naturalness of ingredients, the interaction and activities between people and food, dining and packaging design, etc. He emphasized that designers should provide new solutions for the future food system, considering experience, technology, convenience, democratic participation, social responsibility, and social education [3]. Songfei He from Beijing Institute of Fashion Technology focused on food design for rural revitalization [4]. The research of Fang Hu from China Academy of Arts focuses on the perceptual system of taste and the reconstruction of food culture, culinary experience and story-telling space [5]. Crisis and Ecology Design at Central Academy of Fine Arts focuses on food and body, culture and identity, food systems and ecology, as well as productive space in the city. Ting Liang from Hong Kong Polytechnic University, reflects on food production and consumption services in a sustainable design context [6] (Figs. 1 and 2).

In western countries, food design focuses more on eating experience and ecosystem innovation. Francesca Zampollo proposes the connotation of food design thinking: eating design, food product design, Design with food, food space design, food service design, critical food design, food system design and sustainable food design [7]. While the design approaches of Marije Vogelzang and Martí Guixé combines the methodogy within practices. Vogelzang develops sensory, natural, cultural, social, technological, psychological, scientific, and action dimensions of food design. Guixé works on topics such as the ecology, policy, science, eating rituals and habits, as well as food waste of food [8]. The research of Harvard University School of Design focuses on the intersection of food and ecology, public health, agricultural systems, and landscape design. The University of Copenhagen Sustainability Science Center focuses on how food systems can become more sustainable, including four strategies: subtle improvements, massive changes, waste reduction, and smart diet.

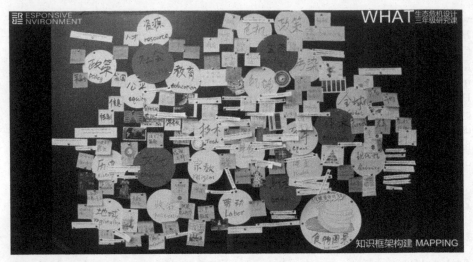

Fig. 1. The Framework of knowledges in the course of the vision of Food, School of Design, Central Academy of Fine Arts, China

Fig. 2. Part of the Student works in the course of Food Geology, School of Design, Central Academy of Fine Arts, China

In summary, the study of the entire food system, including growing, harvesting, processing, packaging, transportation, marketing, consumption, distribution, and disposal as an interacting system has not yet been proposed.

2.2   The Research Scope of Sustainable Food Design

Sustainable food design must be beneficial for food systems. The *2022 China and Global Food Policy report* points out that "agri-food systems" are an important foundation for achieving the goals of national nutrition, food security, ecological civilization, common prosperity, and "carbon peaking and carbon neutrality goals". Agri-food systems contains agricultural products and food from agriculture, forestry, pastoralism, fisheries, industry, and services, involving factors and their interactions across the entire chain of inputs, production, storage, transportation, processing, marketing, consumption, disposal, as well as the broader economic, social, and natural environments in which they are embedded" [9]. The complexity of the food topic determines that its study is trans-disciplinary, trans-historical, trans-cultural, and trans-industrial. For a long time, food design related topics have not been adequately viewed and studied in a systematic way. The concept and approach of food systems, with its importance for sustainable development, have only gradually received attention in recent years. Its complexity often involves phenomena which seemingly irreverent with food but in fact play an important role in the food system.

The transformation of technology and societal demands have led to sustainable food design that goes beyond the traditional discipline-based design of objects, brands, products, services, and spaces to a more intertwined mesh of ecological and health-based ecosystem design. The article defines sustainable food design as a system and future-oriented design that uses food design as a tool for human health and ecological sustainability, with proposing the four-dimensional transformation of sustainable food design toward carbon neutrality (Table 1).

Table 1. The research perspectives of food design in China and the World.

Category	Representative Scholar	Institute	Key Words
Eating, Cooking and Experience Design of Food	Marije Vogelzang;	Food Non Food Program, Design Academy Eindhoven, Netherland;	Eating designer, Sensory, natural, cultural, social, technological, psychological, scientific
	Martí Guixé;	Scuola Politecnica di Design, Italy;	Making food more humane and interactive; Food ecology, food policy, food science, eating rituals, eating habits, and food waste
	Francesca Zampollo		Food Design Thinking, Food Product Design, Design with Food, Food Space Design, Design for Food, Eating Design, Food Service Design, Critical Food Design, Food System Design, Sustainable Food Design

(continued)

Table 1. (*continued*)

Category	Representative Scholar	Institute	Key Words
	Linghao Zhang	Jiangnan University, China;	Aesthetics, memory, cultural meaning, values, perception of the naturalness of ingredients, interaction and activity between people and food, dining and packaging design elements
	Songfei He	Beijing Institute of Fashion Technology, China;	Food and Food Nourishment in the Chinese Cultural Context
	Fang Hu	China Academy of Art, China;	Experimental Art and Design of Food
	Wen Liang	Academe Arts and Design, Tsinghua University, China;	Food, Space and Narrative
Ecology, Agriculture and Systems Design of Food	Montserrat Bonvehi Rosich	Harvard Graduate School of Design, Course: The Landscape We Eat	The relationship between food systems and their landscape, climate, infrastructure, time and culture
		Harvard Graduate School of Design, Course: The Desert We Eat	the relationship among agricultural water, dryland diet, ecological activities, and cultural practices
	Gary Adamkiewicz	Harvard Graduate School of Public Health, Course: From Farm to Fork: Why What You Eat Matters	The study of nutrition, agricultural and environmental sciences, occupational and human health, economics and ethics to select the healthiest food for people and the planet and create it with the right tools and technology

(*continued*)

Table 1. (*continued*)

Category	Representative Scholar	Institute	Key Words
		Copenhagen University, Sustainability Science Centre, Cousre: Transformation of the Global Food System	How food systems can become more sustainable, small improvements, big changes, waste reduction, smart eating
	Ting Liang	Asian Style Design Research Laboratory, School of Design, The Hong Kong Polytechnic University	The innovative design of food is transformed from the five senses and the Eastern philosophy of life to a complex social system composed of a new economy (development, service systems, business innovation, poverty alleviation, etc.), a new society (sustainability, socialization, empowerment, health, etc.), and a new technology (manufacturing, distribution, handling, customization, etc.)
	Siyang Jing	Central Academy of Fine Arts, Direction of Design for Crisis and Ecology, China; Course: Climate Currency-The vision of Food	Food and the Body, Culture and Identity, Food Systems and Ecology, Food and the City, Design and Empowerment
		Course: Food Geology-from Cell to Metaverse	The spatial and geographic development, production, consumption and distribution of food, from molecular synthesis technology at the XS scale to planetary food strategies at the XL scale

3   From Human-Centered to Life-Centered Sustainable Food Design

3.1   Community of Life

The Community of Life refers to the empowerment of animals, plants and even microorganisms in food, as to advocate the bio-diversity and to fight against extinction, namely the "interspecies" responsibility of design, as mentioned by the curator Paola Antonelli [10].

For animal rights, Siegfried Gideon's book *Mechanization Takes Command* traces the mechanization of slaughterhouses, including devices for catching and hanging pigs, "thousand-knife" cutting machines, and design for other horrific assembly line [11]. Design works of Lala Tam "How to consume Romie18" exposed the opacity of the food production system. Through the perspective of Romie18, a cow adopted by the designer, the work follows the whole process of food related to this cow. By understanding this, the project hopes to improve people's attitude towards food. Thus, consumer choose their food types and improving the alienated relationship between humans, nature and animals.

In terms of bio-diversity, the diversity of dietary species not only ensures human health but also guarantees the stability of the entire ecosystem. However, there were once more than 6,000 species of plants eaten by humans, but today only nine commonly used. In response to this question, Chaoqun Li's work "Endless Nature: Designing for Diversity" designed new species possibilities for future wheat through style GAN techniques based on the evolutionary decomposition of large numbers of wheat and rice samples from around the world throughout history (Fig. 3).

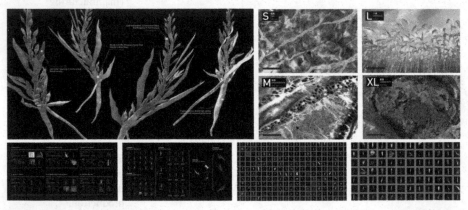

Fig. 3. Student work: Endless Nature, Chaoqun Li, in the course of the Vision of Food, School of De-sign, Central Academy of Fine Arts, China. Instructor: Siyang Jing

In the fight against species extinction, Matilda Boelhauer's fake flower is designed to help insects reproduce again by increasing the number of flowers in cities. In the last 27 years, the insect population has decreased by 75\%. The lack of habitat is one of the main reasons. To restore the food chain, designer ensured insect pollination habitat, protecting the necessary conditions for fruit growth.

3.2 Cross Integration Between Multiple Species

Focusing on a broader range of living organisms becomes one of the sustainable ways to ensure human welfare. William Myers, author of book *Biodesign* predicts that "synthetic biology and the availability of tools for genetic engineering like crispr/cas9 multiply the possible benefits of harnessing nature, much like html standards helped lay the groundwork for the web" [12]. For example, synthetic biology can help designers synthesize artificial meat to replace beef, extract edible proteins from soil molds, or grow cheese from human bacteria. Oron Catts explored the use of tissue engineering to create test-tube meat. Modern Meadow studio use sugar-fed genetically modified yeast to produce collagen, and biological tissue engineering to generate meat for in vitro applications. The Next Nature Network presents a menu of future diets, including friendly foie gras with no real goose, knitted steaks skewered with extra-long cultured tissue, and in vitro-grown meat ice cream, as well as transparent sashimi, synthetic raw fish without the blood vessels, nerves, or organs of real fish.

4 From Object-Centered to Hyper-Object Centered Sustainable Food Design

4.1 Globality and Locality

Timothy Morton coined the term "hyperobjects" to refer to the large-scale distribution of things in time and space, so that they transcend localization [13]. Morton considers a pen to be as complex as climate change, both being hyperobjects. In the case of McDonald's, for example, the flooding of the Canadian port of Vancouver triggered a "French fry panic" at McDonald's in Japan. The reason is that the potato supplier of McDonald's fries comes from North America. In the design "Culture Sample", Xiaoji Zhou traces the history of the ingredients of scrambled eggs with tomatoes, revealing the 7,000-year history behind this simplest dish, which spans four continents. Bjorn Steinar Blumenstein's artwork "Banana Story" traces the global circulation of bananas to highlight the issues raised by the demand for non-seasonal and everyday commodities, to reflect on the origins of food. The artist creates a "passport" for the banana and follows it from Ecuador to Iceland: 12,534 km in 30 days on a cargo ship, passing through 33 different hands to an Icelandic supermarket, yet a third of it ends up in the trash.

4.2 Colonialism and Class Conflict

Thomas Sankara said: "Look at your plate when you eat. All this imported rice, corn, millet, is imperialism" [14]. Kara Walker's "A Subtlety, or the Marvelous Sugar Baby" is a giant sculpture made of sugar that responds to the painful labor, oppression, race, and other power issues behind the abandoned sugar factories in which it was made. On the other hand, differences in food production, distribution, and consumption are combined with various socio-economic structures, resulting in "haute cuisine" or "common cooking" [15]. Amanda Huynh's work Diasporic Dumplings was designed to achieve human equality and resource efficiency. Thus, the kitchen is removed from the house and each community has its own dumpling, made from local materials. The shape of the dumplings is symbolic, conveying messages about politics and resistance to oppressive government.

5   From Experience-Economy to Post-Carbon Economy Sustainable Food Design

5.1   Carbon Emissions

According to a study in *Nature*, food systems account for approximately one-third of global anthropogenic greenhouse gas emissions. Of these, the largest contribution comes from agriculture and land use (71%), with the rest coming from supply chain activities: retail, transportation, consumption, fuel production, waste management, industrial processing, and packaging [16]. Therefore, reducing carbon emissions in food design has significant benefits for global carbon emissions.

Firstly, reducing carbon emissions in food production. The carbon footprint of the livestock industry is several times larger than that of other industries. Thus "alternative proteins" are a trend for the future. The beef industry research project of the author revealed the staggering land consumption and water footprint of beef production, leading to a proposal to integrate Pennsylvania's beef farm resources and to design farm resources in an overlapping and innovative way to minimize the ecological footprint of the farm (Fig. 4). Zhao and Lin's "Equivalent Exchange - Ecological Footprint of Fish" project uses Larimichthys crocea, the most commonly eaten fish in Chinese family, as the subject of their research, reflecting the overfishing and the use of "garbage fish" (juvenile fish) to feed commercial fish. This shows that consumption-driven fishing has a huge impact on the global ecology.

Fig. 4. The Meat industry Study, Siyang Jing

Secondly, controlling carbon emissions in food transportation. The MIT Media Lab has developed the "Transformative Appetite" project, which is a study of the architecture of pasta that can be flattened inside the package and expanded into various forms when exposed to water, thereby reducing packaging space, improving efficiency and reducing carbon emissions during transportation. Some restaurants have marked the food miles in their dishes directly on the plates of food, making consumers reflect on the unnoticed carbon emissions of their daily diet and thus be selective in their consumption.

Thirdly, improving the efficiency of food production. MIT Media Lab's Open agriculture project has designed small, high-tech, soil-free growing *computers*. Owners of food computers will be able to share data with each other about the perfect combination of light, water, nutrient, and temperature levels, creating an open-source framework for high-tech indoor agriculture that produces the best tasting food with the least amount of resources.

5.2 Food Waste

The exhibition "Waste age: what can design do" proposes that the Earth's waste is divided into peak-waste and post-waste. Post-waste mainly refers to materials that can be recycled such as mycelium, rice husks, fish farming and agricultural waste. Food waste basically falls into this category. GroCycle's urban mushroom farm project investigates how impossible waste can be turned into edible products through composting, for example, using discarded coffee grounds to make oyster mushrooms. The "Reinventing Food Waste" project by Siyuan Liu counts and sorts the food waste produced by a family of three in a week and provides a guide to making homemade bioplastics. Daily Dump, a company founded by Poonam Bir Kasturi, has designed an odorless home composter to clean up the entire country of India by making the disposal of food waste a part of every family's social responsibility.

6 From Design for Consumption to Design for Crisis

6.1 Extreme Climate and Food Crisis

Since the Covid-19, the world's hungry population has grown again. Poverty, unequal distribution of resources, conflict, climate change, and severe malnutrition are the main causes of this phenomenon. How do you feed a population that is exploding, with limited food, and deeply affected by climate change? Songye Tan's work "ALGAE+: Algae as a Hunger Mitigation Method" attempts to mitigate acute hunger events due to climate, conflict, natural disasters, etc. by using algae as a nutritional supplement and combining it with local food to increase regional resilience to acute hunger events (Fig. 5). Ecologic Studio and Hyunseok An are also experimenting with DIY cultivation of algae at home to provide their own nutrition for everyday use. In extreme drought conditions, designers have also experimented with resilient solutions. Drawing inspiration from the Cape Town drought period when taps were regularly turned off to conserve water, Shakira Jassat attempted to harvest her own water for tea from steamy winter morning showers and frosty dew.

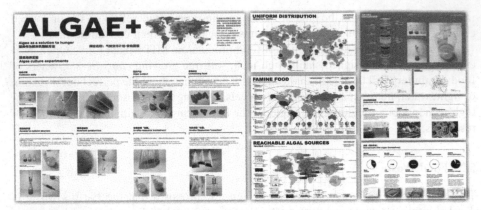

Fig. 5. Student work: Algae+, Songye Tan, in the course of the Vision of Food, School of Design, Central Academy of Fine Arts, China. Instructor: Siyang Jing

6.2 Food Safety and Nutrition

Measuring What Matters in Agriculture and Food Systems, published by the United Nations Environment Programme, states that "Our diets are now a major burden of disease, with more than 650 million people suffering from obesity and over 2 billion affected by nutritional disorders." On the one hand, the misuse of agrochemicals and GMOs since the 1950s has led to a loss of soil fertility and nutritional homogeneity of food. The work "counter meal" by Adriana David conveys the problems of food security, soil fertility and extreme poverty of farmers brought about by the agricultural revolution of that period. On the other hand, consumers don't need to take in extra nutrients. Marije Vogelzang's work Volumes is designed to control overeating by enhancing the feeling of satiety during eating.

6.3 Future Food

In the future, as technology advances and the environment deteriorate, will we develop new ways to consume essential nutrients? Paul Gong's "Human Coyote" project uses synthetic biology to create new bacteria and modify their digestive systems with novel tools so that future humans can digest scavenging food like coyotes. This is a response to the serious food waste or food shortage situation. Space 10's book "future food today" integrates the design practices of future food, from "gutless hot dogs" and "seaweed chips" to "bug burgers" and "miniature green popsicles," and how techniques for using alternative ingredients for culinary innovation (Table 2).

Table 2. The Four-dimensional transformation of food design.

Transformation	Keywords before	vs. Keywords after	Sub-Category	Case Study
From Human-Centered to Life-Centered	Humanism, user-friendly,	Animal, Plants, bacterials, micro-organism ect, inter-species,	The living community	Romie 18, Lala Tam; Endless Nature, Chaoqun Li; Insectology: Food for Buzz, Matilda Boelhauer
			Cross-border integration between multiple species	Oran Catts, Victimless leather; biofabrication, Modern Meadow; Future Food, Next Nature Network;
From Object-Centered to Hyper-object Centered	Individual, local, object, independent	Connected, inter-influential, global, interlocking, chain, loop, causal influence	Global and local	Banana story, Bjorn Steinar Blumenstein; The sample of culture, Xiaoji Zhou;
			Colonialism and class conflict	A Subtlety, or the Marvelous Sugar Baby,Kara Walker; Diasporic Dumplings, Amanda Huynh;
From Experience-Ecology to Post-Carbon Economy	Experience, enjoyment, Novelty, fun	Carbon footprint, ecology, sustainable, carbon control, carbon neutral	Carbon Emission	The Meat Industry Study, Siyang Jing; Equivalence - The Ecological Footprint of Fish Chow and Lin; Transformative Appetite, MIT Media lab; Open agriculture, MIT Media lab

(*continued*)

Table 2. (*continued*)

Transformation	Keywords before	vs. Keywords after	Sub-Category	Case Study
			The waste of food	Daily Dump, Poonam Bir Kasturi; GroCycle;
From design for consumption to design for Crisis	Econonmy, promotion, decoration, selling, branding	Problems, crisis, Prevention, future prediciton, resources redline	Extreme weather and food crisis	ALGAE+, Songye Tan; Algae DIY, Ecologic Studio; Hyunseok An; Tea Drop, Shakira Jassat;
			Food security and Food nutrient	counter meal, Adriana David; Volumes, Marije Vogelzang;
			Future Food	Human Coyote, Paul Gong; future food today, space10;

7 Conclusion

In the context of the global economic downturn following the epidemic, it is more important to focus on design responses at the level of the food crisis, both in terms of individual experience and sensory design around food itself, and in terms of collective ecological and systemic design on a larger scale and across domains. Indeed, food design has received multidisciplinary attention and serves as a key to understanding world systems. The article proposes a sustainable food design paradigm that is de-anthropocentric, de-consumption-centric, de-object-centric, and de-consumption-centric, and instead emphasizes system-oriented, crisis-oriented, and life-well-being-oriented design. The article hopes to expand the network of peers through the exploration of food research, influence public food consumption behavior, and finally establish food values in the post-carbon era.

References

1. Bruce, M.: The organization and performance of the U.S. food system. Proc. Natl. Acad. Sci. USA **79**(2), 59–65 (1985)
2. Margolin, V., Wang, Y.: Design studies and food studies: parallels and intersections. Zhuangshi **2013**(02), 54–63 (2013)

3. Zhang, L., Guo, W.: Study of the teaching mode of integrative design and the project practice of the course on food culture. Zhuangshi **2007**(11), 92–94 (2017)

4. Yang, M., He, S.: Food transmission phenomenon research based on food design field of vision-take social platforms as an example. Design **34**(17), 36–38 (2021)

5. Fang, H.: Systematic food-centered design conceives the idea of future lifestyle. Zhuangshi **2021**(03), 48–60 (2021)

6. Liang, T., Dong, H.: Chinese economy that consumes less: a sustainable design case to remodel the consumption of transportation and food. Zhuangshi **2009**(06), 64–72 (2009)

7. Zampollo, F.: Food design thinking DIY: the creative process to design food products, food services, food events, and dishes. Independently Published (2021)

8. Guixé, M., Rofes, O.: FAQ Food Design. Medium. https://medium.com/@CorrainiEd/faq-food-design-45af95c1c237. Accessed 18 May 2022

9. Institute of Global Affairs Economics and Policy: China Agricultural University, 2022 China and Global Food Policy Report (2022)

10. Antonelli, P., Tannir, A.: Broken Nature: Design Takes on Human Survival. Rizzoli Electa, New York (2019)

11. Giedion, S.: Mechanization Takes Command: A Contribution to Anonymous History. Oxford University Press, Oxford (1948)

12. Myers, W.: Bio Design: Nature + Science + Creativity. The Musuem of Modern Art, New York (2018)

13. Morton, T.: Hyperobjects: Philosophy and Ecology after the End of the World (Posthumanities). University of Minnesota Press, Minneapolis (2013)

14. Collingham, L.: The Hungry Empire: How Britain's Quest for Food Shaped the Modern World. Vintage Digital (2017)

15. Goody, J.: Cooking, Cuisine and Class: A Study in Comparative Sociology (Themes in the Social Sciences). Cambridge University Press, Cambridge (1982)

16. Crippa, M., Solazzo, E., Guizzardi, D., et al.: Food systems are responsible for a third of global anthropogenic GHG emissions. Nat Food **2**, 198–209 (2021)

AmI Garden: An Intelligent Greenhouse for the Implementation of Precision Agriculture Practices

George Kapnas[1], Maria Doxastaki[1], Manousos Bouloukakis[1], Christos Stratakis[1], Nikolaos Menelaos Stivaktakis[1], Theodoros Evdaimon[1], Maria Korozi[1], Asterios Leonidis[1], George Paparoulis[1], Margherita Antona[1], and Constantine Stephanidis[1,2(✉)]

[1] Foundation for Research and Technology - Hellas (FORTH), Institute of Computer Science, Vassilika Vouton, N. Plastira 100, 70013 Heraklion, Crete, Greece
{gkapnas,mdoxasta,mboulou,stratak,nstivaktak,evdemon,korozi,
leonidis,groulis,antona,cs}@ics.forth.gr
[2] Department of Computer Science, University of Crete, P.O. Box 2208, 71409 Heraklion, Crete, Greece

Abstract. This paper introduces the concept of an intelligent greenhouse and intelligent seedbed as innovative solutions to enhance precision agriculture in small-scale cultivation settings. The core motivation behind this project lies in the need to improve cultivation practices, by reducing resource input and adopting an overall more efficient approach, while also making the system accessible both locally as well as remotely, through a variety of interfaces, to different stakeholders. While smart agriculture solutions already exist for large-scale farming, this paper has its main focus on the specific context of greenhouse cultivation in relatively smaller, scattered plots, as commonly found in Crete; the proposed intelligent greenhouse and seedbed aim to provide automated monitoring, customized cultivation support, and accessible information to various stakeholders, regardless of their level of expertise or professional involvement in farming. Despite some technical challenges, initial tests with both systems yielded promising results, helping to effectively monitor and manage the cultivation process; furthermore, users with varying levels of agricultural knowledge found the system generally easy to control. Some of the challenges faced include maintaining sub-system reliability, interference from external factors, as well as sensor limitations.

Keywords: intelligent greenhouse · precision agriculture · pervasive interfaces · ambient intelligence

1 Introduction

Since its dawn approximately 10,000 years ago, agriculture has been the nurturing force that drives humanity forward. The increase in productivity over the ages [1], and the substantial improvement afforded by the industrial revolution and more current advancements (e.g. mechanisation, controlled irrigation, fertilisers and pesticides, etc.) [2], have

C. Stephanidis et al. (Eds.): HCII 2023, CCIS 1958, pp. 324–330, 2024.
https://doi.org/10.1007/978-3-031-49215-0_38

been further augmented in the past few years with the development and integration of electronics, IoT, as well as other relevant systems, which provide us with unparalleled abilities to monitor, control, and overall optimise the cultivation process. As the expanding global population and the threat of climate change make the demand for increased food production and food security ever more pressing, even more efficient cultivation methods are urgently required, in order to sustainably obtain optimal yields from the same cultivation area, while minimising resource waste, as well as pollutants [3]. In order to help achieve those goals, we wish to follow a user-centric approach [4], implementing modern technologies. Our aim is to enable more efficient, assisted and automated cultivation practices, while also providing stakeholders with easy access to relevant information and action options, regardless of platform or physical proximity to the cultivated areas. Our particular focus is one of the main cultivation methods in the island of Crete, where greenhouses are widely deployed for the cultivation of early vegetables and other crops.

2   Current Developments, Challenges, and Proposition

As we are currently living in the era of the Digital Revolution, the concept of Smart Agriculture has been gaining increasing traction, with significant advancements taking place in several relevant fields. The ability to monitor environmental conditions, have access to weather prediction models and automate cultivating tasks has meanwhile been complemented, among other things, by remote sensing and control capabilities and the introduction of robots and autonomous vehicles. These latest achievements have already contributed towards significantly improving overall crop productivity by providing farmers with higher levels of information, while at the same time reducing the amount of required man-hours, as well as the intensity of physical labour.

However, most currently provided solutions are geared toward industrial-scale cultivation, and therefore a relatively narrow band of parameter variability, both in terms of available infrastructure and cultivation models, as well as stakeholder expertise. Our proposition is geared mostly, albeit not exclusively, towards smaller-scale cultivation conditions, and aims to include stakeholders of varying knowledge levels and abilities, from the hobby- or first-time farmer, to the experienced agronomist who tends several cultivations.

The proposed intelligent greenhouse and seedbed will provide information as well as access to functions that will enable better control of the cultivation process, from the first instance of planting the seed, up to the moment of crop harvest. We aim to pursue a human-centred design approach in order to make the provided information, and smart agriculture in general, more easily accessible to individuals, regardless of their expertise or level of involvement in farming.

3   Design and Implementation

We based our methodology on the Design Thinking Process, which is a human-centred, iterative methodology used to better understand user requirements, challenge pre-existing assumptions, clearly define the problems presented, and create solutions that can be then tested [5, 6].

We initially investigated the relevant literature and available offerings in the field of Smart Agriculture and examined both the common, as well as the differing aspects of those approaches, compared to the one we wished to pursue. In order to better visualise our goals, we created scenarios relating to different stakeholders, with each persona corresponding to a potential user of the system with a different skillset. The initial scenarios have been developed for the following conceived personas:

- the amateur, small-scale hobby farmer, with little to no knowledge on the subject of farming;
- the skilled professional farmer, for whom farming is a major occupation; and
- the expert agronomist who assists and advises different clients of varying ability in their endeavours.

The development of the scenarios was enhanced with information provided after collaborating with actual individuals in positions similar to the ones we envisioned. This collaboration also helped set clearer goals and provide more realistic solutions, discarding suggestions that were deemed to be impractical or overly contrived.

3.1 Intelligent Greenhouse

A small (ca. $25m^2$), experimental/testbed greenhouse system has been built with a galvanised steel frame, covered with sheets of translucent polycarbonate; water and electricity connections are provided, as is access to the internet, both wired and wireless. The greenhouse is equipped with a broad range of actuators, motors, and sensors, utilising various communication standards. Commercially available items have been complemented with devices built in-house (i.a. a fruit weight sensor), where it was felt that a custom-made approach would be more efficient for the cultivation conditions that we aimed to replicate. The sensors can provide round-the-clock access to information on environmental conditions, both outside the greenhouse (e.g. air temperature, humidity, wind direction and intensity, potential rainfall, solar/UV radiation, etc.) as well as inside it (e.g. air temperature, humidity, soil temperature and moisture, soil mineral content). Various Actuators allow for the selective activation and deactivation of environmental control systems, such as zone-specific irrigation and lighting for accelerated growth, a fog/misting installation, an air circulation fan, and a motorised window. Additional sensors provide information with regard to operational and performance aspects of the system, such as the amount of consumed water, the solar/battery charge status of systems with such a capability, and the timestamp of each performed action, from irrigation to opening or closing the window.

3.2 AmI Seedbed

The AmI seedbed has been developed to enable the planting and growing of seedlings from scratch, under controlled conditions. It aims to automate several aspects of the seeding and initial growing process, while also providing rich, accessible information to allow for quick and effective decision making.

Seed starting trays are positioned at fixed locations on a base that has been custom built from galvanised mild steel square tubing and sheet metal, for longevity and cost efficiency. The seedbed operates a Cartesian coordinate robotic arm in a frame made of aluminium rail frame profiles, screwed together with 3D-printed connecting plates; the architecture is open-source based, with in-house modifications and additions. The robotic arm carries custom-made attachments for seeding and irrigation. The planting nozzle connects via tubing to a suction pump and allows for the automated planting of seeds, which have been manually placed beforehand in a receptacle, next to the trays of pots filled with soil substrate. The adjacent attachment carried by the same arm is connected to a small, submerged water pump and provides precision, automated watering, either on schedule, or upon command. Finally, the arm also carries a small camera with LED light for image capturing, allowing for the regular visual inspection of individual plant development. Grow-light bulbs have been installed perimetrically and can be operated to promote plant growth [7]. A combination of Raspberry Pi- and Arduino-based microcontrollers provides access and control to all subsystems.

3.3 Interfaces and Control

The developed system offers real-time monitoring and control of the greenhouse and the seedbed, through and extensive network of sensors, actuators and other I/O devices, both on-site, as well as remotely. One of the core propositions of the system is its ability to offer different control interfaces, in order to best suit a user's needs at any given time. This currently includes interfaces designed for remote control via PC or portable devices (a tablet or smartphone), with plans to expand to other technology-enabled devices - mainly smart home appliances, such as TVs and refrigerators. Interfaces for personal and portable computing devices have been implemented using current web technologies; unified control of the variety of utilised hardware sensors, actuators, and other I/O devices has been made possible through the in-house development of middleware implementing a custom, expandable API. Both the greenhouse as well as the seedbed can be controlled remotely from most web-enabled computing interfaces; a prototype system of dedicated devices is also being developed for on-site control of the Intelligent Greenhouse (Fig. 1).

Fig. 1. The components of the AmI Garden approach.

Data provided and collected by the system's peripherals are stored in a relational database; the amount of information made available to each individual can depend on their level of involvement and expertise, in order to provide an optimised user experience and not overwhelm them with what could potentially become disorienting information overload [8]. The system can be adjusted to the requirements of each stakeholder, e.g. taking more initiative and automating its responses to changes in climatic conditions without requiring confirmation, if the individual lacks the necessary depth of knowledge, or simply the time to invest themselves in managing the situation. Assistive information can be provided for a variety of pre-defined plants; based on what is being grown, the stage of the cultivation process, and the environmental conditions, the system can provide suggestions that rely on pre-existing knowledge, helping the user make informed decisions. Suggestions can be made on matters such as the distance required between plants when transferring them from the nursery to the greenhouse, irrigation and fertilisation tactics, and parameter manipulation (e.g. temperature and humidity), in order to create and maintain ideal growing conditions. Based on available data, predictions can also be made regarding the anticipated height of the plants, their expected development curve and the optimal harvest time. The scenarios can be implemented by the stakeholders as they see fit, and can also be enriched with additional information obtained from every new cultivation cycle instance.

4 Results and Challenges

Among the main plant selection criteria for our implementation have been the importance of the plant types to the local agricultural industry in general, and their relevance to greenhouse cultivation practices in particular. So far, tests have mainly been conducted with the small-scale cultivation of plants from the Cucurbitaceae and Solanaceae families. The system has been used by individuals of differing knowledge levels in the field of agriculture, from relative novice to expert. Growing conditions have deliberately been varied on occasion, in order to investigate the limits of what could be considered optimal conditions, while economising on resources (mainly water and fertiliser) whenever possible. Initial tests indicate that plant growth as well as crop yields in the greenhouse remain fairly good, even in instances where resources are used relatively sparingly compared to what constitutes common practice. Results in the seedbed also appear to be positive, as the robotic arm performs its tasks with good precision. Perhaps even more encouragingly, users found all systems to be easy to monitor and control, regardless of their skill level; slight usability issues revolved around the manual entry of data that cannot yet be automatically logged by the system itself, such as fruit weight.

Essentially, most challenges faced concerned practical, rather than User eXperience (UX) related difficulties, as real-life conditions proved to be somewhat unforgiving. Something that occurred in more instances than initially anticipated concerned the reliability of some sub-systems and their sensors, even when they were primarily designed for field use. Regular maintenance was required in order to clear obstructions and debris, or to mitigate naturally occurring wear in some systems; this interfered with the goal of remote management, as it made the presence of a knowledgeable human actor necessary more often than desired. Dust, water hardness, and even flora (weeds) and fauna (e.g.

arachnids and rodents) interfered with the reliability of systems such as the weather station and the misting system. High heat, humidity, and UV radiation, also took their toll, resulting in a shortened life expectancy for some devices. Furthermore, some sensors could not always provide adequately accurate results in the conditions given, providing little granularity; as a result, the measurements obtained from such sensors did not always allow for the extraction of data with a high degree of confidence.

Some slight issues also presented themselves at the computing level, as some integrated modules reached their limits when faced with the task of managing an increasingly large number of data entries. This has been mitigated by reducing the amount of data to be handled per instance, and is not considered serious, as upgrading most of the necessary hardware is relatively trivial.

5 Conclusions and Future Work

Despite the technical difficulties, the results of both the seedbed and the greenhouse are deemed to be positive, with a promising outlook. Even taking into account the challenges faced with obtaining entirely reliable data, the system has generally functioned within the anticipated parameters. It provided users with the information and tools required to be able to monitor and manage the system from practically any location with access to internet, using any available interface. It also enabled them to fully automate any repetitive tasks, as well as perform any additional ones whenever necessary. Overall, the system was able to increase the ease with which improved, or optimal growing conditions could be achieved and maintained. From a technical aspect, and excluding the need to overcome some peripheral technical challenges, it is desirable to streamline the system's overall architecture, in order achieve better affordability, and to reduce the system's overall energy consumption, so as to make it less reliant on external power sources.

Our main future goals include the more extensive and systematic use of the system by a larger number of users with varying knowledge backgrounds, in order to gain more insight on any potential usability issues that could arise in different usage scenarios, as well as obtain more data on cultivation methods. Cultivation advice offered to users will be enriched based on such data, accumulated from successfully completed cycles. Additionally, Machine Learning algorithms can be integrated in cultivation and disease recognition strategies, enhancing user response, particularly in critical or time-sensitive situations. Finally, the UI design is currently being adapted in order to provide a unified design language between device interfaces, while the addition of more smart appliances and technologically enhanced Intelligent Home devices is also envisaged.

References

1. Watson, A.M.: The Arab agricultural revolution and its diffusion, 700–1100. J. Econ. Hist. **34**(1), 8–35 (1974)
2. Pingali, P.L.: Green revolution: impacts, limits, and the path ahead. Proc. Natl. Acad. Sci. **109**(31), 12302–12308 (2012)

3. McBratney, A., et al.: Future directions of precision agriculture. Precision Agric. **6**(1), 7–23 (2005)
4. Stephanidis, C., Antona, M., Ntoa, S.: Human factors in ambient intelligence environments. In: Handbook of Human Factors and Ergonomics, 5th edn, pp. 1354–1373 (2012)
5. Plattner, H., Meinel, C., Weinberg, U.: Design-Thinking. Springer, Heidelberg (2009)
6. What is Design Thinking? I IxDF - Interaction Design Foundation. https://www.interaction-design.org/literature/topics/design-thinking
7. Ibaraki, Y.: Lighting Efficiency in Plant Production under Artificial Lighting and Plant Growth Modeling for Evaluating the Lighting Efficiency. LED Lighting for Urban Agriculture, pp. 150–161 (2016)
8. Roetzel, P.G.: Information overload in the information age: a review of the literature from business administration, business psychology, and related disciplines with a bibliometric approach and framework development. Bus. Res. **12**(2), 479–522 (2018). https://doi.org/10.1007/s40685-018-0069-z

Digital Government Integrating System Combining the Data Complexity

Aulia Nur Kasiwi[1,2]([✉]), Dyah Mutiarin[2]([✉]), Wahyudi Kumorotomo[1],
Achmad Nurmandi[2], and Agustiyara[3]

[1] Department of Management and Public Policy, Universitas Gadjah Mada, Yogyakarta,
Indonesia
`aulianurkasiwi@mail.ugm.ac.id`
[2] Doctoral Program of Government Affairs and Administration, Universitas Muhammadiyah
Yogyakarta, Kasihan, Indonesia
`dyahmutiarin@umy.ac.id`
[3] Doctoral School of Environmental Science, ELTE Eötvös Loránd University, Budapest,
Hungary

Abstract. Government applications and technologies enabled by cloud computing, mobile computing, and the Internet of Things have resulted in an increase in the volume of data that must be processed, stored, and transferred. The complexity of data centers can be difficult to comprehend, but comprehension is critical to their success. The investigation employs a qualitative approach, with graphs and tables visualized using the NVivo software tool, to detect the reconfiguration of each government actor involved in the implementation of the Electronic-Based Government System. To achieve an integrated and comprehensive Electronic-Based Government System (SPBE), Central Agencies and Local Governments must work together closely. Cloud computing enables data center infrastructure to be supplied in an adaptable, load-sensitive, and integrated manner.

Keywords: Digital Government · Integrating System · Data Complexion

1 Introduction

Digital government integrating system is a technology that combines the data complexity of various government agencies and departments into a single platform. This system helps to streamline government operations, increase efficiency, and improve service delivery to citizens [1]. The integration of data from various government agencies and departments can be a complex process. Each agency and department has its own data management system, which makes it difficult to share information across different platforms [2]. However, with digital government integrating systems, data can be easily shared and accessed by authorized personnel from various government agencies and departments. The benefits of digital government integrating systems are numerous. First, it helps to reduce duplication of efforts and resources [3]. When data is integrated, there is no need for multiple agencies to collect the same information. This saves time, effort,

C. Stephanidis et al. (Eds.): HCII 2023, CCIS 1958, pp. 331–338, 2024.
https://doi.org/10.1007/978-3-031-49215-0_39

and resources, which can be redirected towards other important tasks. Second, digital government integrating systems help to improve service delivery to citizens. When data is integrated, government agencies can provide more accurate and timely information to citizens [4, 5]. This helps citizens to make informed decisions and access government services more easily. Third, digital government integrating systems help to increase transparency and accountability in government operations. When data is integrated, it becomes easier to track government activities and monitor performance. This helps to ensure that government agencies are accountable to citizens and are delivering services efficiently and effectively [6, 7].

2 Basic Theory

Digital Governance Phenomenology. Digital governance phenomenology is a theoretical framework that examines the lived experiences and subjective perceptions of individuals and groups regarding digital governance practices [8]. Digital governance phenomenology is understanding the social issue, cultural issue, and impacting the political contexts in which the state implement the digital governance, as well as the ways in which technology shapes and is shaped by these contexts [9].

The theory of digital governance phenomenology suggests that effective digital governance requires a deep understanding of the needs, values, and perspectives of different stakeholders, including citizens, policymakers, and technology providers [10]. It also emphasizes the importance of transparency, accountability, and participation in digital governance processes, as well as the need to address power imbalances and inequalities that may arise in these processes. Overall, the theory of digital governance phenomenology highlights the complex and dynamic nature of digital governance, and the importance of taking a holistic and context-sensitive approach to understanding and improving it [11].

Governance Data Complexion. The data complexion theory of governance is a theory which argues that available data and information influences government decision making. This theory emphasizes the significance of incorporating data and information into the decision-making process in order to attain the intended outcomes. According to this theory, accurate and trustworthy data and information can help the government make effective decisions. In this situation, the government must collect, manage, and analyze data using a dependable and efficient information system [12]. The data complexion theory of governance also emphasizes the significance of openness and responsibility in decision-making. In this instance, the government must ensure that the decision-making data and information are accessible to the public and can be accounted for. By applying the theory of data complexion of governance, the government can enhance its decision-making effectiveness and efficiency [13]. Moreover, this theory can aid the government in overcoming complex and diverse problems and challenges in governance.

3 Methodology

This research is using qualitative approach that work on phenomenological of digital government integrating system in combining data complexity. Which this research explaining the country that maintenance their work on integrating system in the digital government. Content analysis is a qualitative method that involves analyzing written or visual materials (such as social media posts or government documents) to identify themes or patterns.

4   Result and Analysis

In general, digital government systems can be divided into two groups based on how they connect with their customers and what kind of services they can provide [14]. Intranets are used to support intragovernmental procedures, public accessibility in mutually networking that is functioning the interaction between the government, private, and society. Today's externalizing digital government systems exhibit four fundamental Web architecture types, each of which corresponds to one of four service levels [15]:

a) Externalization of Level 1 Services Level one services present information about a specific government agency or function through unidirectional communication.
b) Outsourcing Services at Level 2. Level two services offer fundamental two-way communication, which is typically used for simple data collection duties, such as registering comments with government authorities.
c) Outsourcing Services at Level 3. In this level expand into level two services which facilitating the completion of complex transactions, such as connecting between intra governance process and procedures.
d) Outsourcing Services at Level 4. At this part of level, means that the characterized creation of government are improve the integrating government services between each governance.

Internal digital government systems comprise a huge diversity of technologies, including those that serve services that are typical of large organizations, such as financial management, document processing, and communications. While this is the case, these technologies are all part of the same ecosystem. These systems can be broken down into two primary categories [15]:

a. To begin, there are integrative and communicative systems. These are systems that assist in the integration and collaboration of various agencies.
b. The second component is the domain-specific processing and knowledge management systems, which are subdivided into the data processing interpretation and geographical pictures from government surveys, the latter of which are included as survey data and social data enforcement.

As shown in Fig. 1 the countries that is qualified and applying for digital governance data complexion are United States, India, China, United Kingdom, Australia, Germany, Canada, Netherlands, Russian Federation, Spain. The things are coming is India is shown as the country that implement the digital governance system, but as known that India still weak in public service, as the quality of public service in community is still weak not only for the system, but also the human behaviors. It is essential to the growth and development of digital government that semantic data modeling be improved, document connection management be made more effective, and data access and retrieval technologies be made more complex [16]. The overarching objective is to provide digital government services

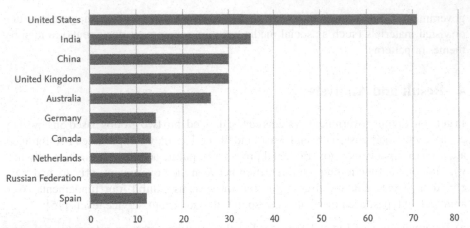

Fig. 1. Countries Classification for Digital Government System Literature. Source: Scopus Database 2023

that do not simply conform to a read-only paradigm of interactions between citizens, government officials, and government information sources. Instead, the objective is to make it possible for a more interactive, process-oriented dissemination and viewing of government information. This will be achieved through reaching the overriding objective of offering digital government services that adhere to the paradigm of read-only access [17]. The amount of data that governments collect is staggering, and a fraction of this data might be made available to consumers and authorities through the use of digital government services [18]. Significant technological obstacles have always been there when it comes to providing efficient access to massive information collections for a large number of consumers. Nevertheless, providing individuals and government employees with access to government information entails meeting a specific set of criteria (or desired functionality), which we will define in more detail below [18].

a) Document Transfer; Many digital government systems are, in essence, document transfer applications that require the downloading or uploading of government forms, reports, or other types of data. As more people obtain documents and submit forms to government institutions, competition for shared resources will increase, and efficient and scalable document management will become crucial. These methods are applicable to digital government, but document downloading and uploading present unique challenges in digital government. Government agencies are progressively making their documents available for download via the Internet [19]. Many government documents, such as pending legislation, tax codes, and related collections of regulations or laws, are vast in comparison to the content managed by most other types of Web sites. Data management services within digital government systems must support both the automatic generation of digests of multiple documents and the user's ability to select sections of monolithic documents that will then be automatically extracted and downloaded for more efficient downloading and use of such documents.

b) In the context of database systems, an ontology is a compilation of information that defines the semantics and structure of the data maintained within a particular application domain. The administration of multiple application domains within an organization frequently results in demands for their integration, thereby necessitating the integration of their respective ontologies [20]. There may be many such application domains and ontologies within a government, making their integration more difficult than other ontology integration initiatives. These information spaces are also likely to be administratively and geographically dispersed, further complicating the management issue. Government information is accessible in a variety of formats. Therefore, citizens and authorities must be able to query a wide variety of data types, including the full text of documents, geographic data, images, and audio. In addition, query methods for various data types must facilitate users with differing levels of expertise.

c) Geographic Data; Many government agencies have documents with implicit geographic connections. Even though these connections are essential for comprehension, they are frequently not reflected explicitly in these papers, and many documents are not geo-indexed. The application of geo-correlated indexing to government documents may facilitate users' comprehension of laws, rules, and other types of information [21]. For instance, a person unfamiliar with a particular political districting system may commence their search for information about a particular issue by submitting a query pertaining to geographical entities with which they are familiar (Fig. 2).

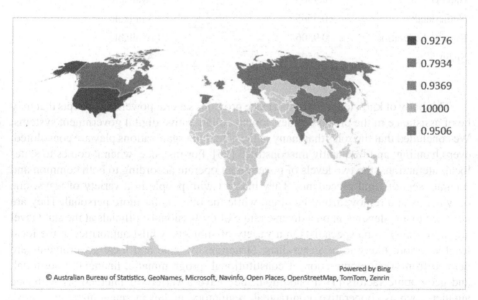

Fig. 2. Digital Governance Index in Global 2023

Significant developments in public expectations and technology for the delivery of services over the course of the past decade have made it possible for the government to provide services that are easier to comprehend, more easily available, and more cost-effective [22]. In order to turn the promise into a reality, program managers and system designers are finding that they need to be well-versed in both technological ways of collaboration and traditional methods of working alone [23]. Information systems that are coordinated and collaborative hold the promise of integrated services for the general public as well as simpler procedures for the government, but the likelihood of their realization is low. The functionality of these vital systems is the focus of significant research efforts by a variety of national governments and professional organizations several projects involving collaborative information systems, each of which will be briefly detailed (Table 1).

Table 1. National Data Integrating System

Country	Digital Government Index	National Data Centre
United States	0.9276	Available
India	0.7934	Available
China	0.7934	Available
United Kingdom	0.9369	Available
Australia	10000	Available
Germany	0.9506	Available
Canada	0.9506	Available
Netherlands	0.9506	Available
Russian Federation	0.9506	Available
Spain	0.9506	Available

This body of knowledge and experience provides several powerful concepts that may be of assistance in the process of developing collaborative digital government systems. We concluded that the roles that many of the actors in organizations play are convoluted, ever-changing, and frequently misconstrued [25]. For instance, when it comes to state-local interactions, the two levels of government operate according to both common and separate sets of legal precedents. They interact with people in a variety of ways, one of which is at a remove from the other, while the other is far more personal. They are attracted to and dependent on a diverse range of professionals: officials at the state level are more likely to be specialists in a variety of subjects, whilst authorities at the local level are more likely to be generalists. Structures of state and local governments are derived from a conglomeration of constitutional, programmatic, financial, traditional, and geographic factors [1]. In addition, they have a variety of interactions with one another, such as cooperative, contractual, regulatory, and even antagonistic ones [26]. Other aspects that differentiate the public and private sectors include the obligations that come with each, as well as the interactions that exist between them. The lack of a profit incentive, which is such a significant factor in business, is present in the government; the methods of staff recruitment and performance awards are very different from one another [8].

5   Conclusion

Digital government integrating systems are an important tool for improving government operations and service delivery. By combining the data complexity of various government agencies and departments into a single platform, digital government integrating systems help to streamline operations, increase efficiency, and improve service delivery to citizens. As such, governments should invest in these systems to improve their operations and better serve their citizens. Digital government systems can be categorized into two groups based on their customer-service capabilities. Intranets support intragovernmental procedures, public network access facilitates government-citizen interactions, and extranets facilitate interactions between the government and nongovernmental organizations. Externalizing digital government systems have four fundamental Web architecture types, each corresponding to one of four service levels: externalization of Level 1 Services, outsourcing Services at Level 2, outsourcing Services at Level 3, and outsourcing Services at Level 4. Internal digital government systems encompass a vast array of technologies, including those that perform functions typical of large businesses, such as financial management, document processing, and communications.

References

1. Dunleavy, P., Margetts, H., Bastow, S., Tinkler, J.: New public management is dead - long live digital-era governance. J. Public Adm. Res. Theory **16**(3), 467–494 (2006). https://doi.org/10.1093/jopart/mui057
2. Margetts, H., Dunleavy, P.: The second wave of digital-era governance: a Quasi-paradigm for government on the web. Philos. Trans. R. Soc. A Math. Phys. Eng. Sci. **371**, 20120382 (1987). https://doi.org/10.1098/rsta.2012.0382
3. Erkut, B.: From digital government to digital governance: are we there yet? Sustainability **12**(3), 1–13 (2020). https://doi.org/10.3390/su12030860
4. Pearce, G., Gaffney, T.: Digital governance. ISACA J. **4**, 19–27 (2020). https://doi.org/10.5860/choice.48.04.627
5. Filgueiras, F., Almeida, V.: Governance for Digital Technologies. Governance for the Digital World, no. Culkin 1967, pp. 75–104 (2021). https://doi.org/10.1007/978-3-030-55248-0_4
6. Welchman, L.: The Basics of Digital Governance. Managing Chaos. Digital Governance by Design, p. 248 (2015). http://rosenfeldmedia.com/books/managing-chaos/
7. Dunleavy, P., Margetts, H.: Design Principles for Essentially Digital Governance. Annual Meeting of the American Political Science Association, pp. 3–6 (2015)
8. Chullachakkawat, C.: Data Governance and Digital Government Development. School of Administrative Studies Academic (2020)
9. Kennedy, J.F., Fountain, J.E.: Information, Institutions and Governance: Advancing a Basic Social Science Research Program for Digital Government (2003)
10. Bekker, M.J.: Digital governance in support of infrastructure asset management Digital Governance In Support Of Infrastructure Asset Management Thinus Bekker (2016)
11. Dunleavy, P.: Governance and state organization in the digital era. The Oxford Handbook of Information and Communication Technologies, no. January 2009 (2009). https://doi.org/10.1093/oxfordhb/9780199548798.003.0017
12. Fernández-Cerero, D., Varela-Vaca, Á.J., Fernández-Montes, A., Gómez-López, M.T., Alvárez-Bermejo, J.A.: Measuring data-centre workflows complexity through process mining: the Google cluster case. J. Supercomput. **76**(4), 2449–2478 (2020). https://doi.org/10.1007/s11227-019-02996-2

13. Sun, L., Zhang, H., Fang, C.: Data security governance in the era of big data: status, challenges, and prospects. Data Sci. Manag. **2**(June), 41–44 (2021). https://doi.org/10.1016/j.dsm.2021. 06.001

14. Ubaldi, B.: The OECD Digital Government Policy Framework: Six dimensions of a Digital Government. OECD Public Governance Policy Papers, no. 2, pp. 1–40 (2020)

15. Phillips, T., et al.: Digital technology governance: developing countries' priorities and concerns Digital Pathways Paper Series (2020)

16. Gao, X.: Networked co-production of 311 services: investigating the use of Twitter in five U.S. cities. Int. J. Public Adm. **41**(9), 712–724 (2018). https://doi.org/10.1080/01900692. 2017.1298126

17. Al-Sai, Z.A., Abualigah, L.M.: Big data and e-government: a review. In: ICIT 2017 - 8th International Conference on Information Technology, Proceedings, pp. 580–587 (2017). https:// doi.org/10.1109/ICITECH.2017.8080062

18. Manoharan, A.P., Zheng, Y., Melitski, J.: Global comparative municipal e-governance: factors and trends. Int. Rev. Public Adm. **22**(1), 14–31 (2017). https://doi.org/10.1080/12294659. 2017.1292031

19. Ounifi, H.-A., Ouhimmou, M., Paquet, M.: Data centre localization for Internet services (2015)

20. Zheng, L., Zhang, H., Han, W., Zhou, X.: Technologies, applications, and governance in the internet of things. In: Proceedings of the Internet of Things-Global Technological and Societal Trends, pp. 141–175 (2011). http://books.google.com/books?hl=en&lr=&id=Eug-Rvs lW30C&oi=fnd&pg=PA143&dq=Technologies,+Applications,+and+Governance+in+the+ Internet+of+Things&ots=3Sy6ECmAEt&sig=NsG7DZSc2Uq_SmQhSXB10-89kQU%5Cn http://books.google.com/books?hl=en&lr=&id=Eug-RvslW30C&oi=fn

21. Sicari, S., Rizzardi, A., Cappiello, C., Miorandi, D., Coen-Porisini, A.: Toward data governance in the internet of things. Stud. Comput. Intell. **715**, 59–74 (2018). https://doi.org/10. 1007/978-3-319-58190-3_4

22. Sandoval-Almazán, R., Luna-Reyes, L.F., Luna-Reyes, D.E., Gil-Garcia, J.R., Puron-Cid, G., Picazo-Vela, S.: Conceptualizing and preplanning for a digital government project, vol. 16 (2017). https://doi.org/10.1007/978-3-319-60348-3_3

23. Clarke, A.: The evolving role of non-state actors in digital era government. SSRN Electron. J. **430**, 1–27 (2018). https://doi.org/10.2139/ssrn.3268084

24. Clarke, A.: Digital government units: what are they, and what do they mean for digital era public management renewal? Int. Public Manag. J. **23**(3), 358–379 (2020). https://doi.org/10. 1080/10967494.2019.1686447

25. Malhotra, C., Anand, R., Soni, V.: Creating public services 4.0: sustainable digital architecture for public services in India. Indian J. Public Adm. **66**(3), 327–342 (2020). https://doi.org/10. 1177/0019556120957421

26. Lambiase, J.J.: Searching for city hall, digital democracy, and public-making rhetoric: U.S. municipal websites and citizen engagement. J. Public Interest Commun. **2**(1), 85 (2018). https://doi.org/10.32473/jpic.v2.i1.p85

How Wish Created a Compelling Discovery Based Shopping Experience

Jonas Kong[1]([⊠]) and Pranav Nair[2]

[1] Contextlogic/Wish, San Francisco, CA 94112, USA
jonas.kong@gmail.com
[2] HubSpot Inc., Cambridge, MA 02141, USA

Abstract. Wish is an online shopping platform that differs by offering a "discovery based" shopping experience. The majority of the transactions on Wish originate without a search query, which is different from most ecommerce platforms as they are search focused. Through insights gathered via qualitative and quantitative research conducted with Wish buyers, the authors summarize in this paper four main factors that influenced Wish users to embrace the discovery based shopping experience on Wish - mobile optimization, gamified deals, personalized content, and unique inventory.

Keywords: Ecommerce · Discovery based shopping experience · Personalization

1 Wish as an Online Shopping App

Headquartered in the US and with its app first launched in 2011, Wish is an online ecommerce marketplace that allows third party sellers to list their products to sell to consumers world wide. In a few years time, Wish has achieved global success as an ecommerce platform. In 2017, Wish was the most downloaded e-commerce application in US. [4] Following the next year, Wish became the most-downloaded e-commerce app worldwide [5]. Then in 2019, Wish was the third-biggest e-commerce marketplace in the United States by sales [6]. From 2015 to 2020, the number of online shoppers who visited Wish increased steadily. The average Monthly Active Users (MAU), a benchmark for determining growth performance of a platform, reached as high as 107 million users for 2020.

While on the app, users were highly engaged with the platform. Data showed that during the months of April to September 2020, on average each active Wish user spent at a minimum 9 min per day on the app and viewed more than 500+ distinct products on a daily basis [4]. Furthermore, data shared in the Wish annual report to investors showed that over 70% of its transactions did not start with a search query, meaning that users embarked on a "discovery based" shopping journey by browsing the homepage of the Wish app for products to eventually make a purchase.

C. Stephanidis et al. (Eds.): HCII 2023, CCIS 1958, pp. 339–345, 2024.
https://doi.org/10.1007/978-3-031-49215-0_40

2 Factors that Attract Online Shoppers to Browse Wish

How was Wish able to achieve such a high engagement rate? Why do online shoppers shop on Wish? What triggered them to shop and purchase without initializing a search query? To help Wish to create an even better shopping experience, the user research team at Wish conducted qualitative research with more than 50 active Wish users across several remote user interviews and usability studies to identify the drivers and appeals of Wish. Wish users with various shopping experiences on Wish (loyal buyers, new buyers, recent buyers, reactivated buyers) were recruited for these studies. They were asked to share their most recent shopping experience on Wish, discuss why they decided to look for the items, and describe their perceived value of Wish compared to competitors.

After interviewing Wish users and observing how they shop on Wish, several themes became clear as factors that make Wish unique and appealing as an ecommerce platform to browse and purchase: 1) mobile optimization, 2) gamified deals, 3) personalized content, and 4) unique inventory.

2.1 Optimized Mobile Shopping Experience

The Wish ecommerce mobile platform was first created to provide a "discovery based" shopping experience, which means users can passively browse to find products that they might not have even thought to look for before, without having to type in a search term. This was in response to how users tend to interact with mobile phones on a small touch screen and could only use a tiny virtual keyword, which makes typing search queries to be much more tedious. Therefore, offering a discovery based shopping experience on the phone would help users to locate products faster and with greater ease by not having to type in search terms. The other rationale is that most existing ecommerce platforms at that time focused mostly on a search based shopping experience - an estimated 66% of all internet shopping searches start on Amazon [5]. In order to stand out among the competition, Wish wanted to take this approach to carve a niche in the ecommerce market space.

A key feature that Wish utilizes to support discovery based shopping is the "main feed". It is located on the homepage of the Wish app showing images of products for sale that users can scroll through endlessly. The main feed is distinguished by showing enlarged product images. By maximizing and emphasizing the product images, it allows users to focus on the photo to be able to quickly scan across the page and optimize the discovery of items of interest.

The layout and format of the main feed on Wish resembles a social media feed, such as Facebook or Instagram, where posts and images appear as an endless page for users to scroll. A lot of users visited the app after seeing Wish ads posted on social media, and therefore they are used to consuming information and content through a feed.

This was evident during user research sessions with Wish users, where they were often observed to compulsively scroll the page as soon as they opened it, being fully absorbed in scanning the feed to the point where they were too preoccupied to immediately respond to questions asked by the moderator, illustrating the level of "obsession" that online shoppers had with the Wish app. However, the feed is just the medium where

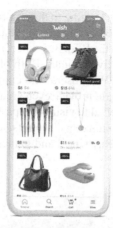

Fig. 1. The main feed on Wish

items and content are shown in the app. What captivates users to keep scrolling has to do with what is offered in the feed as explained in the subsequent sections.

2.2 Offer Incredible Discounts Strengthened by Gamification

Wish buyers indicated via surveys that the top reason they purchased on Wish was because of the low prices. Wish, being an ecommerce marketplace platform, allows third party merchants who are manufacturers and distributors in different countries to sell directly to customers all over the world. This effectively cuts down on additional markup shoppers have to pay when buying domestically from a reseller who imports the goods.

The app appeals to shoppers who are especially interested in finding deals. When Wish users were asked what they think of Wish, most mentioned the low prices which is what Wish is well known for due to the fact Wish features products with significant percent off discounts in its online ad campaigns that appeared on social media feeds and Google search results. In the app, users can find lots of items with prices that are surprisingly low, for instance a pair of headphones for $5 as shown in Fig. 1 above. It was also common to find products that were advertised as "Free", where interested buyers only have to pay for the shipping cost. Users often come to Wish looking for free or extremely low priced items that are dispersed throughout their home feed. Those who enjoy browsing online to find deals are especially attracted to visit Wish regularly hoping to scroll through and find a "treasure".

In addition to offering products at lower price points, Wish also offers incremental discounts to help further build up savings. For example, Wish has an Instant Buy offer that shows up when users are looking at the product detail page. It provides an additional discount that activates when users add the item to the cart within a very small time limit. Because this offer would show up randomly, it generates a sense of gamification that motivates users to keep scrolling and adding items of interest to get the extra savings.

Wish offers additional gamified programs to incentivize users to come back to visit. Daily Login Bonus is a program where each day upon login, users can collect a stamp.

After users collect seven stamps by logging to the app for seven days, they earn a digital discount coupon that can be applied to a future purchase on Wish. Another is the Blitz Buy program, where users can spin the Blitz Buy wheel to unlock additional discounts for a set of products that are valid for five minutes. Both of these programs offer incentives that attract a significant portion of Wish users who enjoy seeking deals to come back to earn more savings that could add up to provide even greater discounts. During interviews, users revealed that they felt compelled to visit Wish partially because of these programs. For users who are interested in maximizing discounts, it became a habit for them to open up the Wish app to spin the Blitz Buy wheel and gather further discounts with coupons from Daily Login Bonus (Fig. 2).

Fig. 2. Left: Instant Offer as a form of gamified deals. Right: the Blitz Buy wheel

2.3 Leveraging Analytics Data to Drive Personalization and Targeted Ads

Personalized shopping experiences attract customers. Existing third party research data shows that 63% of smartphone users are more likely to purchase from companies whose mobile apps offer recommendations on products relevant to them. And 58% of smartphone users feel more favorable toward companies whose apps remember who they are and their past behavior [6]. Customers are more interested in things that are relevant to them.

One of the main ways Wish created a discovery based shopping experience was to leverage user browsing and search behavior data to determine their interest and intent. Based on the types of products that users clicked on to review, as well as keyword searches they conducted, the Wish app referenced these sources of metadata to serve as signals to indicate their shopping interest. The platform then showed a heavily personalized feed of products directly related to the user's recent interests similar to social media feeds as seen in Instagram or Pinterest.

This form of personalization was one of the key reasons we observed loyal Wish users frequently browsing the home feed of the app over using search. Because of Wish's personalization algorithm, users were treated to a home feed that presented items both directly related to their prior search as well as new finds that were directly related to their interests. Often these products were things that they didn't even know existed.

For example, if a user searched for car storage containers, the algorithm would surface additional car storage solutions based on the initial query which might result in the user finding a product that better suits their personal needs (Fig. 3).

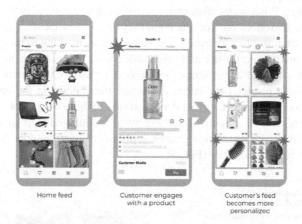

Home feed   Customer engages with a product   Customer's feed becomes more personalized

Fig. 3. Explanation of the personalized feed on Wish

From user interviews, Wish users described shopping on Wish similar to "diving into rabbit holes" based on their mood at any given moment. Unlike a traditional e-commerce platform such as Amazon where the user enters knowing exactly what they want, most users entered Wish with no clear objective in mind and the main feed inspired users to dive into a specific category or product of interest. Wish allows for this in two very unique ways - first, as soon as a user taps on a product tile, they are taken to a product page which also holds a Related tab (feed). The rabbit hole discovery would kickstart once they navigated to this related products feed to find identical or similar products of interest. An alternate approach was observed wherein, once the user finds an interesting product on their home feed, they would immediately search for it. This search query would be referenced the next time a user refreshed their home feed to show them new and interesting products based on their search behavior. This sort of rabbit hole discovery based shopping experience is why Wish became a popular app to frequent as it combined the feed-freshness of social media with unique and interesting products that attracted online shoppers.

Users often describe this as "treasure hunting" on Wish, in which they enjoy the thrill of diving into different rabbit holes and discovering unique products to purchase for themselves or as gifts for others. This sense of mystery and whimsy is what Wish aims to keep as its primary focus as it seeks to differentiate itself from its competitors.

2.4 Engage and Entertain Online Shoppers with Unique Inventory

Wish has garnered a reputation as a platform that offers unique and interesting products that consumers could not find elsewhere. Surveys conducted with Wish buyers showed that "unique" and "fun" were among the top attributes that they associated with the Wish brand. From interviews, buyers mentioned that they turn to Wish for things that they did not think their local retail stores or domestic shopping apps would offer. Merchants in different countries can offer products that are neither easily accessible nor available to consumers in other parts of the world.

While browsing Wish, users often came across such novel items in the feed. Whether they were delighted to check out a product that they never knew existed, curious to further understand a familiar product, or even surprised to see a shocking item, users would tap on the photo to investigate further and often share with others for them to see. Higher click through rates meant that particular item would get more exposure in the main feed. This triggers Wish's backend algorithm to feature these items in the online Wish ads posted in social media channels, further driving traffic to these unique, obscure, quirky or shocking products on Wish. Seeing higher exposure encouraged merchants to offer even more similar products with attention grabbing photos to continue feeding the platform with unique and quirky inventory (Fig. 4).

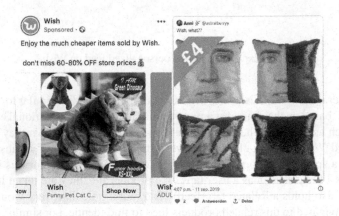

Fig. 4. Unique and eccentric items featured in Wish online ads

The interest for unique, fun and eccentric inventory is strong as it attracts online shoppers to come to Wish. Wish is a source of entertainment especially for those who are curious about new and novel things. They want to see what interesting products they might encounter, especially during "micro moments", or time of the day where they can spare a few minutes of their busy life such as waiting in line or decompressing for the day before bedtime, to browse Wish on their phone.

3 Personalized Shopping Experience Inspires Discovery

The best way to describe Wish is like a store of unique wares you might encounter in a marketplace or a mall with a highly personable store owner. Ever since your first visit, the owner pays keen attention to the items you looked at and recommend the same or similar items to you during your subsequent visits. They greet you by your name, and remember your prior conversations before proceeding to show new inventory. This type of personalized shopping experience is what attracts shoppers to frequent the same store again. The engagement feels personable and friendly yet not so transactional. Wish aims to create a similar experience in the digital realm by offering a highly personalized shopping experience for unique and low priced inventory, indexing on a discovery-first shopping approach to get users addicted to the browsing experience.

That said, having a discovery based shopping experience does not mean that only a browsing experience is sufficient for users to shop. Search is equally important as users often want to find something specific. Our research with discovery based shoppers highlighted search patterns adopted by users that lead to new product discovery. It would typically involve users searching for broad terms (like categories) as opposed to very specific products, then using the Sort and Filter features to find unique products that match what they are looking for. Similarly, even when users come to Wish intending to browse the feed, in the back of their mind they likely still have certain types of product categories that they are interested in or not at all. Providing features that support refinement of the feed is critical to help users find what they are looking for.

The key to offering a discovery based shopping experience is inspiration. When users come to Wish to browse, they need to be inspired by the products to spark interest in making a purchase, to explore related items and embark on a shopping journey. Having a personalized feed showing relevant products combined with offering attractive deals and an interesting inventory generates inspiration for users when shopping. Though we are far from having perfected the discovery based shopping experience, as there is much to be learned on how to maintain the long term interest of shoppers that will require future research and experimentation to understand.

References

1. Online Shopping Statistics: Ecommerce Trends for 2023. https://www.tidio.com/blog/online-shopping-statistics. Accessed 30 Jan 2023
2. Is Shopping Online Really Cheaper? https://www.thebalancemoney.com/is-shopping-online-really-cheaper-939778
3. How many people shop online? https://www.oberlo.com/statistics/how-many-people-shop-online
4. Wish Earnings Call 2020 Presntation. https://ir.wish.com/static-files/37b3007e-0656-45e2-a126-311309491d9b. Accessed 12 May 2019
5. Amazon Statistics You Should Know in 2022. https://www.junglescout.com/blog/amazon-statistics/. Accessed 29 Mar 2022
6. App Personalization. https://www.businessofapps.com/marketplace/app-engagement/research/app-personalization. Accessed 23 Feb 2023
7. ContextLogic Inc., Form 10-K (2020)

Technology Acceptance Model for Enhanced Shopping Experience Through Online Recommendation Agent

Dária Lališová[✉], Justina Karpavičė, and Torben Tambo

Aarhus University, 7400 Herning, Denmark
daria.lalisova@gmail.com, justina@btech.au.dk

Abstract. Nowadays, a company's website has become one of the typical touch-points of interaction enabling customers to gain more valuable knowledge about the provided products and services. However, websites tend to contain an abundant amount of information that might overwhelm customers and disturb their willingness to purchase. One of the solutions to facilitate the search process on the website is an Online Recommendation Agent (RA). As a result, this study employs user usability testing and the technology acceptance model (TAM) to investigate the user perception and acceptance of the online RA for enhanced product search on the Danish manufacturing company's webpage. The study results present factors influencing consumers' intention to adopt online RA, and challenges the company has to tackle for successful integration of the product finder to grant customers a better tailored and consistent shopping experience.

Keywords: TAM · Online Recommendation Agents · Shopping Experience

1 Introduction

Over the past years, customers' purchasing habits have shifted from brick-and-mortar stores to shopping online [1]. Since the era of the Internet has altered how companies promote their products and services, businesses are increasingly incorporating digital strategies and tools into their portfolio to upgrade their customers' shopping experiences. Companies that strive to adopt new technologies have a greater possibility of delivering unique experiences for their customers [2]. A company's website became one of the typical interaction touchpoints enabling customers to gain more valuable knowledge about the provided products and services. However, websites tend to contain an abundant amount of information that might overwhelm customers and disturb their willingness to purchase the product or service [3].

One of the solutions to facilitate the search process on the website is an online Recommendation Agent (RA) [4]. It is expected to act as a virtual product advisor that suggests products to consumers based on their responses to a few questions. It enables users to identify the products of interest more swiftly and precisely, reducing the aggravation occurring when the product search is filled with information overload [3]. Online

RAs benefit organizations as well by providing instant access to prospective customers, increasing the market share, creating cost-efficient interactions, and becoming one more valuable source of data collection [5].

Consequently, this research investigates a Danish manufacturing company's decision to implement the online RA, called Product Finder (PF), into their home web page to guide homeowners regarding product selection. However, despite the potential advantages of online RA technology, it is an entirely new way for the company to interact with their customers, and therefore, the implementation of online RA may encounter various issues in homeowners' acceptance. Before launching the designed virtual product advisor, the company wishes to explore customer perception and behavior toward the ICT system. Technology Acceptance Model (TAM) has been extensively used to test how the system's design features impact user acceptance aiming to reduce the risk of resistance or rejection [6]. As a result, this research aims to investigate factors influencing consumers' perception and intention to adopt online RA for enhanced product search.

2   Research Model and Hypotheses

2.1   Technology Acceptance Model

Reference [7] presented the Technology Acceptance Model, which proposed that the perceived ease of use and perceived usefulness are the most significant variables in determining the success of the adoption of the information system. TAM is a broadly accepted and validated theoretical model that is being used to examine an individual's propensity to adopt new technology [8]. This model aims to investigate the influence of external factors on internal beliefs in relation to technology acceptance [9]. Furthermore, TAM hypothesizes that an individual's attitude affects behavioral intention, and the intention impacts actual behavior [7]. The person's belief that a particular action would have a favorable outcome leads to a greater intention to act.

Throughout the years, the original TAM model from [7] has been subject to several expansions that pursued to improve its predictive power by adding new external variables [10]. Reference [11] presented TAM2 with the appended variable of perceived enjoyment, whereas later [12] developed TAM3 by adding trust and perceived risk of technology. These expansions demonstrate the TAM model's flexibility to adjust in regard to technology development [13]. As a result, this study proposes an extended TAM model for a thorough investigation of users' acceptance of the developed online RA system embedded in the company's content page for homeowners.

2.2   Research Hypotheses

In order to develop an extended TAM model for investigating the acceptance of online RA, ten research papers were thoroughly examined and summarized in Table 1. Overall, 64 constructs from the primary studies were gathered and classified into 26 variables. Figure 1 demonstrates the diffusion of classified variables investigated in at least two research papers.

Table 1. A summary of ten investigated research papers.

Reference	Context	Model	Variables
[14]	Online RA	Trust-TAM	Trust (Competence, Benevolence, Integrity), PU, PEoU, Intention
[15]	Chatbot	Expectation-confirmation Model, TAM, ISS	PU, PEoU, Perceived Enjoyment, Service Quality, Information Quality, Satisfaction, Need for interaction, Continuance Intention
[16]	Financial Robo-advisors	UTAUT	Tendency to rely on Robo-advisors, Effort Expectancy, Performance Expectancy, Facilitating Conditions, Social Influence, Trust, Perceived financial knowledge, Intention
[17]	Chatbot	TAM, Diffusion of Innovation	Price Consciousness, Perceived Risk, Personal Innovativeness, Perceived Enjoyment, Trust, PEoU, PU, Intention to use, Attitude
[18]	Online RA	Trust-TAM	Trust, Perceived reduction of information asymmetry, PU, PEoU, Satisfaction
[19]	Chatbots	Uses and gratifications theory, TAM	Perceived Enjoyment, Immature Technology, Convenience, Pass Time, Authenticity of Conversation, Privacy Concerns, Behavioral intention, PEoU, PU
[20]	Shopping assistant	Persuasion and social role theory	Personalization, Social Role, Product Involvement, Attitude

(continued)

Table 1. (*continued*)

Reference	Context	Model	Variables
[21]	Chatbots	A combination of TRA and ISS models	System Quality, Information Quality, Service Quality, App Satisfaction, Personalization, Purchase Intentions
[22]	Online RA	User Satisfaction and TA	Cognition-based Trust, Affect-based Trust, Perceived Enjoyment, PU
[23]	Online RA	TAM, TRA	Trust (Competence and Integrity), Explanation of reasoning (Availability and Mode), Perceived Personalization, Intention to Adopt

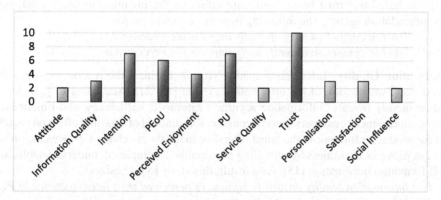

Fig. 1. Diffusion of variables in the investigated literature

Behavioral Intention to Adopt. According to the Theory of Reasoned Action, individuals' performance of a specific behavior is postulated by their behavioral intention [21]. When people tend to be interested in something, they tend to demonstrate a certain behavior, thereby, the intention to use will influence the actual use of IS [3]. For instance, a study by [21] concluded that users who are satisfied with a mobile app are more likely to use it in the long-term.

Perceived Usefulness. Perceived Usefulness (PU) is considered one of the most impactful variables in the adoption of a new IS [24]. Dutot [13] refers to PU as "the degree to which an individual believes that using a particular information technology will enhance his own performance". PU represents the idea that a specific information technology can be helpful for someone to achieve a particular outcome [24]. Consequently, TAM proposes that perceived usefulness is the main determinant of behavioral intention to use the IS [7]:

> *H1: PU positively influences users' behavioral intention to use PF.*

Perceived Ease of Use. The design of IS must address the expected target audience's cognitive skills and capabilities [24]. Reference [7] defines PEoU as "the degree to which a person believes that using a particular system would be free of effort". As a result, simple and intuitive interaction adaptable to individual's inherent capacity to complete the task would positively affect the intention to use the technology [2]. Furthermore, the IS literature also claims a positive relationship between perceived ease of use and perceived usefulness [18]. Therefore, the following hypotheses are formulated:

> *H2: PEoU positively influences users' behavioral intention to use a PF.*
>
> *H3: PEoU positively influences the perceived usefulness of a PF.*

Competence (Trust). Businesses have placed significant prominence on creating trust-based consumer-brand relationships [13]. Author of [13] defines trust as "the individual's intention to act in a certain way and reflects the security that one party has in the other one". Research performed by [14, 18, 22] claims that there is a positive correlation between trust and perceived usefulness. Moreover, studies by references [16] and [23] concluded that trust has a significant effect on the intention to adopt intelligent recommendation agents. The following hypotheses are proposed:

> *H4: Trust in competence significantly impacts the intention to use the PF.*
>
> *H5: Trust in competence significantly impacts the Perceived usefulness of PF.*

Information Quality. Information quality (IQ) as intrinsic motivation measures the success and satisfaction of the information system [15, 21]. According to [25], information quality reveals "information accuracy, relevance, sufficiency, and timeliness". Furthermore, since consumers spend a considerable amount of time and effect on searching for product information, the latest offers, or manuals via chatbot e-services, online RA can prove its usefulness by providing personalized, completed, understandable, and well-formatted information [15]. As a result, this study hypothesizes:

> *H6: Information quality positively influences perceived trust in competence of PF.*
>
> *H7: Information quality positively influences the perceived usefulness of PF.*

Perceived Enjoyment and Satisfaction. The perceived enjoyment and satisfaction (PES) may be characterized as the amount to which the action of using a technology is regarded to be pleasant in its own right and satisfies the user [15]. Prior studies have demonstrated that a person's intention to use technology is directly related to how much they enjoy and are satisfied with it [17, 19]. The hypothesis is the following:

> *H8: PES positively influences users' behavioral intention to use PF.*

3 Methodology

The study utilizes user usability testing and the technology acceptance model (TAM) to investigate the user perception and acceptance of the online RA, and identify challenges and obstacles. The research is based on the mixed-method approach, and the experiment process is divided into three stages. First, participants were asked to familiarize themselves with the product finder tool by interacting with it to accomplish a particular task. After the interaction, participants were asked to answer an online questionnaire to evaluate their experience with an online RA based on the developed extended TAM model. The questionnaire was composed of seven sub-sections, with the first exclusively focusing on demographic characteristics. The other six put emphasis on the main variables of the extended TAM model. Overall, 29 questions were asked, including 25 about the variables and 4 for demographics (see Table 2). The measures used in the questionnaire were based on the investigated literature and were selected due to confirmed reliability and validity. The primary studies, which the measures were adopted from, are provided in Table 2. All items were measured using a 7-point Likert scale varying from -3 (completely disagree) to 3 (completely agree), and closed-ended questions were used. Finally, the semi-structured interviews were conducted with respective representatives from the company after completing the questionnaire, allowing participants to comment on their evaluation freely. Questions were designed to examine the strengths and weaknesses of the product finder thoroughly.

The empirical data was obtained over the course of two weeks, starting from the 8th of December 2022. During this period, data was collected from 29 participants. Random purposive sampling method has been used in this study to purposefully select the target population via social networks [26].

The sample included the almost equivalent percentage of females and males, 52% and 48%, respectively. More than half of the participants (55%) were between 18 to 30 years, followed by 17% of 31–45 years, and 28% 46–60 years. Although the sample size is moderate, research has indicated that using the rule of 10 ± 2 is sufficient to discover 80% of usability problems [27]. Furthermore, authors in [28] indicated that at least 20 participants are enough if the usability testing includes a quantitative method.

A two-step approach to analyzing the empirical data collected from the questionnaire was utilized. First, the measurement model was examined using descriptive statistics, including Mean and Standard Deviation (SD) values. To test convergent validity, Cronbach's α has been calculated, which indicates the item's statistical significance if it is 0.7 or higher [29]. Second, the structural model was examined by assessing the p-values, path coefficients (β), and determination coefficients (R2) between constructs.

4   Results

Based on the statistical analysis findings, the measurement model's validity and reliability are well established. Regarding the structural relationships between variables, all the hypotheses are accepted based on calculated values of selected coefficients.

According to the questionnaire results (Fig. 2), information quality (β = 0.97), trust in competence (β = 0.99), and perceived ease of use (β = 0.84) significantly influences the perceived usefulness of the online RA. First, when designing the product finder, developers must ensure that sufficient, up-to-date, precise, and reliable data is presented to the user. However, only 64.29% of participants found the information reliable. The rating could be explained by the deficiency in providing information about the product at the end of the search, which increases the uncertainty of the validation of the final

Table 2. A summary of ten investigated research papers.

Variables and questionnaire items	Mean	SD	CA
Perceived Usefulness (Adopted from [14])			0.892
Product Finder enables me to decide which solution is suitable for my problem more quickly	1.52	1.21	
Product Finder improved the search quality previously performed to select a suitable product for my home	1.31	1.14	
Using Product Finder enhanced the effectiveness of finding suitable solutions	1.52	1.18	
Perceived Ease of Use (Adopted from [14])			0.754
My interaction with the Product Finder is clear and understandable	1.69	1.17	
It is easy to make Product Finder to do what I want	1.55	1.35	
It was easy to find a solution and compare it with other pumps that provides	1.41	1.12	
I have the knowledge to use the Product Finder	1.34	1.59	
Everyone can easily navigate and use Product Finder	1.59	1.45	
Competence (Trust) (Adopted from [23])			0.903
Product Finder provides the expertise that helps me to choose a solution for my "problem"	1.24	1.30	
Product Finder is like a real expert in assessing what type of solution is suitable for my home	0.90	1.32	
Product Finder can understand my needs and preferences and recommend a suitable solution	1.48	1.30	
Product Finder considers my needs and all the crucial attributes when selecting the pump	0.97	1.40	
Product Finder provides me with relevant information/ knowledge about pumps	1.59	1.32	
Information Quality (Adopted from [15])			0.876
Product Finder provides sufficient information	1.38	1.12	
The information in Product Finder is clear	1.34	1.26	
The information in Product Finder is accurate	1.55	1.06	
Information in Product Finder is up to date	1.69	1.11	
Information in Product Finder is reliable	1.14	1.09	
Perceived Enjoyment and Satisfaction (Adopted from [15])			0.861

(continued)

Table 2. (*continued*)

Variables and questionnaire items	Mean	SD	CA
I found it easy to share information by e-mail	1.07	1.53	
I am completely satisfied with Product Finder	0.62	1.92	
Using Product Finder increases the quality of my selection	1.31	1.44	
Overall, I find Product Finder interesting	1.52	1.66	
Intention to Adopt (Adopted from [14] and [23])			0.891
I would be willing to use Product Finder in the future to help me with my decision on which solution to buy	1.86	1.16	
I am willing to let Product Finder assist me in deciding what product to buy	1.72	1.07	
I would recommend others to use Product Finder	1.66	1.17	

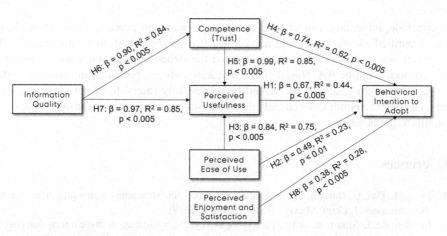

Fig. 2. Proposed research model and the evaluation of structural relationships

recommendation. Furthermore, the system that provides data to the product finder lacks consistency and integrity, leading to out-of-date and inaccurate information. There is also a deficiency in further actions and obtaining more comprehensive information about the suggested product, such as technical characteristics or how to install it.

Second, it is essential to design an online RA that can accomplish the required tasks in order to increase trust in the IS [23]. Based on the results, participants believe that product finder can only help to some degree. There is a wide range of occurring problems with the product that the online RA did not take into consideration. Likewise, participants emphasized a limited number of options and product attributes to choose from when searching for the best product. Furthermore, even though the online RA is expected to provide three comparable results of the best products fitting the search criteria, some participants received only one or two options due to the system's inconsistency.

Third, the perceived ease of use can be enhanced by creating simple and intuitive interactions with the IS adapted to the consumer's cognitive capabilities to complete the task. 85.71% of respondents consider their interaction with the product finder clear, understandable, and easily navigable.

In terms of behavioral intention to adopt the online RA, the most impactful variables are trust in competence ($\beta = 0.74$) and perceived usefulness ($\beta = 0.67$). 81.48% of respondents agreed to some degree that the product finder helped them decide which product solution would be the most suitable for their house, improved the search quality, and enhanced the overall efficiency of the search process.

However, the perceived enjoyment and satisfaction ($\beta = 0.38$) have the slightest effect on an individual's behavioral intention to use the product finder. Most respondents found it challenging to save and/or share the search results with others that highly influenced their level of satisfaction with the online RA.

5 Conclusion

To conclude, information quality, trust in competence, and perceived ease of use have been identified as the most significant constructs of the adoption of the online RA. Moreover, the results of this study identified the issues that influence the customers' decision to use online RA. Based on the research findings, potential adjustments to the online RA system could be performed to successfully integrate the product finder to grant customers a better tailored and consistent shopping experience and create multiple benefits to the business.

References

1. Devi, M., Das, L., Baruah, M.: Inclination towards online shopping - a changing trend among the consumers. J. Econ. Manag. Trade. **25**, 1–11 (2019)
2. Lydekaityte, J.: Smart interactive packaging as a cyber-physical agent in the interaction design theory: a novel user interface. In: Lamas, D., Loizides, F., Nacke, L., Petrie, H., Winckler, M., Zaphiris, P. (eds.) Human-Computer Interaction – INTERACT 2019, pp. 687–695. Springer International Publishing, Cham (2019). https://doi.org/10.1007/978-3-030-29381-9_41
3. Chen, Y.C., Shang, R.-A., Kao, C.Y.: The effects of information overload on consumers' subjective state towards buying decision in the internet shopping environment. Electron. Commer. Res. Appl. **8**(1), 48–58 (2009)
4. Xu, D.J., Benbasat, I., Cenfetelli, R.T.: A two-stage model of generating product advice: proposing and testing the complementarity principle. J. Manag. Inf. Syst. **34**(3), 826–862 (2017)
5. Guo, Y., Yin, C., Li, M., Ren, X., Liu, P.: Mobile e-commerce recommendation system based on multi-source information fusion for sustainable e-business. Sustainability **10**(1), 1–13 (2018)
6. Rostam, N.A., Zulkiffli, N.F., Ghazali, N.H., Malim, N.H.A.H., Singh, M.M., Husin, M.H.: The acceptance study of NFC technology: a survey of models and user acceptance. In: ISTMET, pp. 53–57. IEEE (2015)

7. Davis, F.D.: Perceived usefulness, perceived ease of use, and user acceptance of information technology. MIS Q. **13**(3), 319–340 (1989)
8. Shankar, V., et al.: How technology is changing retail. J. Retail. **97**(1), 13–27 (2021)
9. Museli, A., Jafari Navimipour, N.: A model for examining the factors impacting the near field communication technology adoption in the organizations. Kybernetes **47**(7), 1378–1400 (2018)
10. Brooksbank, R., Scott, J.M., Fullerton, S.: In-store surveillance technologies: what drives their acceptability among consumers? Int. Rev. Retail, Distrib. and Consum. Res. **32**(5), 508–531 (2022)
11. Davis, F.D., Richard P.B., Warshaw, P.R.: Extrinsic and intrinsic motivation to use computers in the workplace 1. J. Appl. Soc. Psychol. **22**(14), 1111–1132 (1992)
12. Venkatesh, V., Bala, H.: Technology acceptance model 3 and a research agenda on interventions. Decis. Sci. **39**(2), 273–315 (2008)
13. Dutot, V.: Factors influencing near field communication (NFC) adoption: an extended TAM approach. J. High Technol. Manage. Res. **26**(1), 45–57 (2015)
14. Benbasat, I., Wang, W.: Trust in and adoption of online recommendation agents. J. Assoc. Inf. Syst. **6**(3), 72–101 (2005)
15. Ashfaq, M., Yun, J., Yu, S., Loureiro, S.M.C.: I, chatbot: modeling the determinants of users' satisfaction and continuance intention of AI-powered service agents. Telem. Inform. **54**, 1–17 (2020)
16. Gan, L.Y., Khan, M.T.I., Liew, T.W.: Understanding consumer's adoption of financial Robo-advisors at the outbreak of the COVID -19 crisis in Malaysia. Finan. Plan. Rev. **4**(3), 1–18 (2021)
17. Kasilingam, D.L.: Understanding the attitude and intention to use smartphone chatbots for shopping. Technol. Soc. **62**, 1–15 (2020)
18. Pedeliento, G., Andreini, D., Bergamaschi, M., Klobas, J.E.: Trust, information asymmetry and professional service online referral agents. J. Serv. Theory Pract. **27**(6), 1081–1104 (2017)
19. Rese, A., Ganster, L., Baier, D.: Chatbots in retailers' customer communication: how to measure their acceptance? J. Retail. Consum. Serv. **56**, 1–14 (2020)
20. Rhee, C.E., Choi, J.: Effects of personalization and social role in voice shopping: an experimental study on product recommendation by a conversational voice agent. Comp. Human Behav. **109**, 1–11 (2020)
21. Trivedi, J.: Examining the customer experience of using banking chatbots and its impact on brand love: the moderating role of perceived risk. J. Int. Commer. **18**(1), 91–111 (2019)
22. Wang, W., Qiu, L., Kim, D., Benbasat, I.: Effects of rational and social appeals of online recommendation agents on cognition- and affect-based trust. Decis. Support. Syst. **86**, 48–60 (2016)
23. Zhang, J., Curley, S.P.: Exploring explanation effects on consumers' trust in online recommender agents. Int. J. Hum-Comput. Int. **34**(5), 421–432 (2018)
24. Liébana-Cabanillas, F., Ramos de Luna, I., Montoro-Ríos, F.J.: User behaviour in QR mobile payment system: the QR payment acceptance model. Technol. Anal. Strateg. Manage. **27**(9), 1031–1049 (2015)
25. Gao, L., Waechter, K.A., Bai, X.: Understanding consumers' continuance intention towards mobile purchase: a theoretical framework and empirical study–a case of China. Comput. Human Behav. **53**, 249–262 (2015)
26. Tashakkori, A., Teddlie, C.: Issues and dilemmas in teaching research methods courses in social and behavioural sciences: US perspective. Int. J. Soc. Res. Method. **6**(1), 61–77 (2003)
27. Hwang, W., Salvendy, G.: Number of people required for usability evaluation: the 10±2 rule. Commun. ACM **53**(5), 130–133 (2010)

28. Nielsen, J.: How many test users in a usability study? Tersedia (2012)
29. Han, H., Park, A., Chung, N., Lee, K.J.: A near field communication adoption and its impact on expo visitors' behavior. Int. J. Inf. Man. **36**(6), 1328–1339 (2016)

Study on the Cover of WeChat Red Envelope from the Perspective of brand Communication

Ouyang Li[(✉)] [iD] and Yonglin Zhu [iD]

Guangzhou Academy of Fine Arts, Guangzhou, Guangdong, China
619044205@qq.com

Abstract. In the digital economy, companies increasingly shift from physical to online marketing, leveraging the ability to transcend geographical boundaries and rapidly disseminate brand information. As a powerful online communication platform with a vast user base, WeChat plays a crucial role in mobile payment, information transfer, and emotional communication through Wechat Red Packets. When consumers engage with Wechat red envelope covers, they undergo five stages of attention, interest, search, action, and sharing, enabling the secondary communication of brand information. This study analyzes the communication influence mechanism of brand information in Wechat red envelope covers using the AISAS model. It also identifies factors influencing consumers' willingness to use Wechat red envelope covers through a survey, establishes a model for understanding these factors, and examines their impact on users' behavior from a brand communication perspective. Hypotheses are proposed based on the model and tested using PLS 3.0 software. The findings highlight the significant and positive influence of entertainment experience, effort expectation, social influence, convenience, intention to use, and user behavior on the information experience. Wechat red envelope covers hold substantial business value as a marketing method. Leveraging the festive season as a marketing hotspot and consistently conveying the brand message while sending and receiving Wechat red envelope covers will enhance brand awareness and influence.

Keywords: Brand communication · Wechat red envelope cover · The UTAUT model

1 Introduction

In the era of social media, people are inseparable from social platforms and software. WeChat red envelopes are a product of the rapid digital economy and technology development. They have a broad user base and possess both social and economic value. WeChat red envelopes have continuously evolved from a simple function of distributing money to allowing businesses or individuals to send and use customized red envelope covers, creating new avenues for brand promotion and marketing. On the one hand, the gifting nature of WeChat red envelopes inherits the cultural essence of traditional Chinese red envelopes, facilitating the spread of brand information within the users' social interactions [1]. On the other hand, using WeChat red envelopes for holiday marketing makes the marketing purpose more subtle and easily accepted by users, achieving the desired effect of brand promotion. At the same time, using WeChat red envelope covers can bring value to users in terms of personalization, emotional expression, social interaction, identity, and entertainment. Therefore, this article explores whether and how businesses can utilize WeChat red envelopes as a medium to promote brand information, providing valuable insights for brand communication.

2 Theoretical Basis and Literature Review

Existing research mainly focuses on the impact factors of enterprise marketing through WeChat red envelopes, such as information experience, entertainment experience, and the role of users in WeChat red envelope marketing, as well as the economic effects.

Firstly, through WeChat red envelope marketing, enterprises achieve integration between physical and virtual realms, online and offline, thereby increasing consumer engagement and stimulating consumption growth [2]. With the rise of digital media, people's consumption patterns and behaviors have changed. People seek information through the internet, and combining WeChat red envelopes with physical marketing activities can yield better results. Secondly, WeChat red envelope marketing offers a covert approach, leveraging cultural and social elements. Audiences typically don't perceive the commercial intent explicitly or view it as conventional advertising. This indirect method tends to resonate more with consumers compared to explicit ads. With their social nature, online red envelopes swiftly spread brand information, effectively achieving brand marketing objectives. Zhang and Liu (2016) found that the pleasure aspect of online red envelopes stimulates communication among people, fostering strong interpersonal connections. It not only satisfies socialization needs but also continuously generates consumer interest in the product [3]. Thirdly, WeChat red envelope marketing offers entertainment value, attracting consumers to engage in secondary sharing of WeChat red envelopes. The high social engagement of WeChat red envelopes fulfills social needs, while the amusement and novelty of WeChat red envelope covers cater to users' desire for entertainment and experience. Research conducted by He Linling (2016) indicates that WeChat red envelopes integrate traditional folk culture with internet-based financial payments, embodying the demand for entertaining experiences and enhancing user emotional interactions [4].

Existing research primarily focuses on brand marketing methods and discussions on the transmission of brand information from the enterprise to individuals. Although literature on brand dissemination through WeChat red envelopes explores the influential role of individual and social factors, these factors undergo significant changes in the evolving online ecosystem. To address development and practical needs, this study aims to deconstruct the topic by examining platform features and marketer characteristics. Additionally, existing research predominantly analyzes the significance and characteristics of WeChat red envelope marketing, but lacks empirical analysis of users' individual cognition in WeChat red envelope marketing. Therefore, this study attempts to construct an influencing factor model for brand dissemination through WeChat red envelope covers from the perspective of WeChat red envelope users. By employing a questionnaire survey, it will thoroughly investigate the impact mechanism of brand dissemination on the WeChat red envelope platform, providing marketing insights and recommendations for brand communication in WeChat red envelopes.

3 Mechanisms of Brand Dissemination in WeChat Red Envelopes

3.1 The WeChat Red Envelope Cover: A New Format for Marketing Strategies

WeChat introduced the customized feature for WeChat Red Envelope covers at the end of 2020, which received a strong response and became one of the hottest online activities during the Spring Festival. WeChat stated in the '2022 Tiger Spring Festival Data Report' that since introducing the WeChat Red Envelope cover feature, it has been widely embraced by businesses and users. 380 million people have used WeChat Red Envelope covers, with the overall number of red envelopes sent and received with covers exceeding 5 billion [5]. As user engagement with WeChat Red Envelopes continues to increase, numerous companies and researchers have discovered that WeChat Red Envelopes can serve as a new path for brand marketing.

In the past, the AIDMA marketing model explained consumer behavior in traditional offline marketing, focusing on attention, interest, desire, impression, and action. However, with the rise of WeChat red envelope marketing, traditional methods still need to meet consumers' diverse and personalized demands. In WeChat red envelope marketing, brand communication channels differ significantly, capturing consumer attention through the gift of red envelope covers. Consumer interest is piqued by the brand information conveyed through these covers, shifting away from traditional advertisements.

Therefore, more than the AIDMA marketing rule is needed to analyze consumer shopping behavior comprehensively. The AISAS model proposed by Dentsu is more effective in explaining customer behavior in brand marketing through social media. This study will explore the connection between the stages of the AISAS model and the process of using WeChat red envelope covers. The AISAS marketing theory consists of five steps, which can be divided into two processes. The first two stages align with the AIDMA model and belong to the consumer's cognitive process, while the last three stages pertain to consumer behavioral interaction [6]. The first two processes will have an impact on each behavior in the following three processes, ultimately resulting in the content generated from search to sharing being repeatedly processed and disseminated, and then forming the content in the first two processes again, creating a closed loop. In using WeChat red envelope covers as a medium for brand communication, the AISAS marketing theory is integrated throughout the process of utilizing WeChat red envelope covers for marketing activities (as shown in Fig. 1). WeChat red envelope covers possess strong social attributes, low marketing costs, and a wide reach, which has led many brands to leverage them for brand marketing campaigns. Brands introduce their brand information to consumers through WeChat red envelope covers, and then consumers actively distribute red envelopes using the covers, facilitating the secondary dissemination of brand information. This measure greatly enhances brand awareness and promotes the spread of product information. Starting with the definition of WeChat red envelope covers, this article analyzes their functions and characteristics and further explores their role in brand marketing.

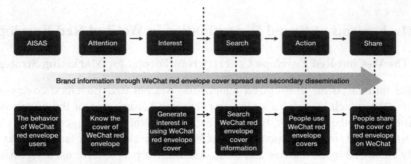

Fig. 1. The dissemination channels of brand information in WeChat red envelope covers, Image source: Created by the author.

3.2 Empirical Research Design on WeChat Red Envelopes from the Perspective of Brand Communication

In the era of Internet prevalence, social media has provided convenience for brand marketing. Combining the AISAS marketing theory analysis can offer insights into the factors influencing brand marketing through the WeChat red envelope covers. WeChat red envelopes are a form of information technology. This study analyzes the factors influencing audience attention to brands when using WeChat red envelopes. Therefore, based on integrating the User Acceptance and Use of Technology (UTAUT) model [7], a model of factors influencing the use of WeChat red envelope covers is constructed (as shown in Fig. 2).

In the model, Entertainment Experience represents the process of users experiencing entertainment when using WeChat Red Packet covers [8]. Effort Expectancy refers to the convenience and ease of understanding the usage rules when using WeChat Red Packet covers [9]. Social Influence examines whether the extensive promotion of WeChat Red Packet covers and the usage by others influence users' willingness to use them. Facilitating Condition refers to the perceived support of existing technology and devices in using the system, including the technical and objective conditions required when using WeChat Red Packet covers [10]. Usage Intention refers to users' predicted likelihood or willingness to use WeChat Red Packet covers in a specific future time, including the possibility of recommending it to others [11]. User Behavior is the action taken by individuals based on their intention, which involves the stages from motivation to execution [12], explicitly referring to users' specific behavior of using WeChat Red Packet covers within a particular period. In the era of social media, it is crucial for businesses to communicate timely relevant information about their products or brands to facilitate knowledge sharing among users [13]. Information Experience refers to the perceived usefulness and value of the information content that users feel while receiving and sharing content using WeChat Red Packet covers. Therefore, whether users can

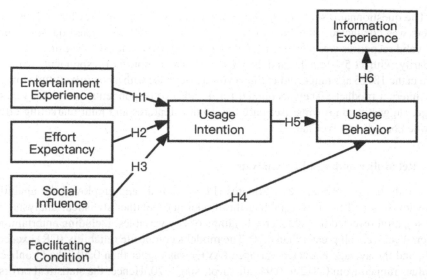

Fig. 2. The model of factors influencing the usage behavior of WeChat red envelope covers, Image source: Created by the author.

have an impression of the brand information on WeChat Red Packet covers becomes a critical factor in the study. Based on the comprehensive analysis, this article proposes six hypotheses.

H1: Entertainment Experience positively influences users' intention to use WeChat red envelope covers.

H2: Effort Expectancy positively influences users' intention to use WeChat red envelope covers.

H3: Social Influence positively influences users' intention to use WeChat red envelope covers.

H4: Facilitating Condition positively influences users' behavior of using WeChat red envelopes.

H5: Intention to use WeChat red envelope covers positively influences users' behavior toward using WeChat red envelopes.

H6: Users' behavior of using WeChat red envelope covers positively influences the information experience of WeChat red envelopes.

4 Study Design

4.1 Questionnaire Design and Data Collection

In social media marketing, a certain amount of reference data has been established, providing a basis for the quantitative analysis of the factors influencing the usage behavior of WeChat red envelopes from a brand communication perspective. Therefore, the "scale + structural equation" method can be adopted for the research.

The questionnaire study on factors influencing the usage of WeChat red envelope covers was conducted from June to July 2022. Out of 269 distributed questionnaires, 207 valid responses were received (76.95%). The analysis showed a significant gender disparity, with 71.5% females and 28.1% males. The majority of respondents (61.84%) were in the 18–25 age range, indicating a young user base with a positive attitude towards new internet products. They accounted for 44.44% of respondents over three years of usage, suggesting a growing user base due to new features and joint marketing efforts between brands and WeChat.

4.2 Reliability and Validity Analysis

This study utilized Partial Least Squares (PLS) analysis and employed the analytical software Smart PLS 3.0 to establish the model and conduct statistical analysis. The investigation revealed that the factor loadings of key variables, including entertainment experience, were all greater than 0.70. The model's composite reliability (CR) exceeded 0.70, and the average extracted variance (AVE) was higher than 0.50. The Cronbach's α values ranged from 0.812 to 0.94, all-surpassing 0.70. Hence, the statistical errors of the sample data were within an acceptable range, indicating good sample reliability.

This study utilized 207 samples and performed 5000 bootstrapping iterations using PLS analysis to establish the model. The results revealed that the path coefficients of the six hypothesis relationships (H1 to H6) were 0.301, 0.245, 0.348, 0.21, 0.645, and 0.446, all of which were statistically significant, indicating that all six hypotheses were supported. Among them, usage intention (UI) emerged as the most influential factor in the usage of WeChat red envelope covers, indicating users' willingness to continue using and recommending the covers. Usage behavior (UB) followed, suggesting that users' usage of WeChat red envelope covers influenced their information experience (IE). Entertainment experience (EE), effort expectancy (EE), and social influence (SI)

Table 1. Model path coefficients and hypothesis verification

Hypothetical		Normalized coefficients	P	Conclusion
H1	Entertainment Experience → Usage Intention	0.301	0.001*	Support
H2	Effort Expectancy → Usage Intention	0.245	0.000*	Support
H3	Social Influence → Usage Intention	0.348	0.000*	Support
H4	Facilitating Condition → User Behavior	0.21	0.001*	Support
H5	Usage Intention → User Behavior	0.645	0.000*	Support
H6	User Behavior → Information Experience	0.446	0.000*	Support

had significant positive effects on usage intention (UI) with factor loadings of 0.301, 0.245, and 0.348, respectively. This indicates that the level of interest, perceived ease of use, and social influence of others using WeChat red envelope covers have important impacts on users' choices. Finally, convenience conditions (FC) had a factor loading of 0.21 on usage behavior, indicating that objective factors such as the convenience of obtaining the red envelope covers affected users' decisions when using WeChat red envelope covers (Table 1).

5   Research Conclusions

This study examines the effectiveness of brand marketing using WeChat red envelope covers and investigates the factors that influence user behavior. By integrating the AISAS marketing theory and the UTAUT model, a model is developed, and a small-scale survey is conducted to analyze the factors that impact usage and validate the effectiveness of this strategy.

The research findings highlight vital factors influencing the usage of WeChat red envelope covers, including entertainment experience, effort expectancy, social influence, convenience conditions, usage intention, usage behavior, and information experience. Specifically, the study shows that these factors impact users' behavior in using WeChat red envelopes and influence their information experience with the brand on the covers. Incorporating entertainment and brand elements enhances the appeal of WeChat red envelopes, attracting more users to participate in their usage.

Based on the AISAS marketing theory, brand owners associate brand information with WeChat red envelope covers, which users continuously send and receive, leading to the secondary spread of brand information. The usage behavior of WeChat red envelope covers significantly impacts the information experience. Moreover, the practice of sending WeChat red envelopes aligns with traditional Chinese culture and festivals. With a large user base, using red envelope covers for brand marketing proves cost-effective and reaches a wide audience, offering significant commercial value.

In conclusion, WeChat red envelopes have emerged as a cost-effective and highly effective method of brand marketing in the evolving landscape of internet technology and digital marketing. WeChat red envelope covers are instrumental in brand communication. To adapt to the current economic climate, businesses can leverage social media marketing trends and utilize tools like WeChat red envelope covers to spread brand information and impact consumers effectively.

Acknowledgments. We want to express our gratitude for the support from the characteristic innovation project of general universities in Guangdong Province, Research on Green Gift Packaging Design Based on Lingnan Festival Culture (2022WTSCX049), and the Graduate Education Project Cultural Elements and Design Creative Education (6040122027SFJD) and research on Innovative Design of Traditional Festival Products in the Greater Bay Area (No.: 20XSB07) of Guangzhou Academy of Fine Arts.

References

1. Yang, Y.: Social marketing in cultural context: a case study of the WeChat red envelope battle. Youth Journal. **593**(9), 85–86 (2022)
2. Sun, T., Wang, Q.: Reflections on social media WeChat red envelope marketing. Publ. Wide Angle **12**, 59–61 (2016)
3. Zhang, Y., Liang, G.: The impact of product attributes on interpersonal interaction and intentional loyalty: a study on online red envelopes. Enterp. Econ. **03**, 79–82 (2016)
4. He, L.: The cultural and entertainment forms of WeChat red envelopes and their business operation modes exploration. Media **22**, 70–72 (2016)
5. WeChat Pai: Spring Festival of the Year of the Tiger: Over 5 billion WeChat Red Envelopes Sent and Received with Covers. WeChat (2022)
6. Wang, J.: Research on social media marketing based on the AISAS model - a case study of Xiaomi's online marketing. Bus. Era **34**, 83–84 (2014)
7. Venkatesh, M., Davis, D.: User acceptance of information technology: toward a unified view. MIS Q. **27**(3), 425 (2003). https://doi.org/10.2307/30036540
8. Cao, F., Na, C.: Entertainment experience: innovation in brand marketing communication. Sales Market. (Manage. Edn.) **05**, 87–89 (2011)
9. Liang, T., Liu, S.: Research on users' intention to use tourism information service platforms based on UTAUT model. Inf. Sci. **02**, 162–168+176 (2022)
10. Gan, C., Song, C.: Empirical analysis of the adoption intention of mobile libraries based on TAM. Libr. Inf. Sci. **03**, 66–71 (2015)
11. Teo, T., Zhou, M.: Explaining the intention to use technology among university students: a structural equation modeling approach. J. Comput. Higher Educ. **26**(2), 124–142 (2014). https://doi.org/10.1007/s12528-014-9080-3
12. Su, T.: A Study on the Factors Influencing the Behavioral Intention of Generation Z Users in Mobile Short Video Apps. Jinan University (2018)
13. Huang, M., Liao, J., Nan, Z.: Can community experience enhance consumer brand loyalty? A study on the role and influence mechanism of different experience components. Nankai Bus. Rev. **18**(03), 151–160 (2015)

Video Analytics in Business Marketing for Shopping Malls in Ecuador

Lizzie Pazmiño-Guevara[1]([✉]) [ID], Jorge Álvarez-Tello[4] [ID],
Mercedes Galarraga-Carvajal[1] [ID], César Pazmiño-Guevara[3] [ID],
and Alisson Maldonado-Pazmiño[2] [ID]

[1] Facultad de Administración y Negocios, Universidad Indoamérica, Machala y Sabanilla,
Quito, Ecuador
{lizziepazminio,mercedesgalarraga}@uti.edu.ec
[2] Facultad de Ingeniería, Pontificia Universidad Católica, Av. 12 de octubre, Quito, Ecuador
avmaldonado@puce.edu.ec
[3] Facultad de Ingeniería y Ciencias Aplicadas, Universidad Central del Ecuador, Ciudadela
Universitaria, Quito, Ecuador
cmpazminog@uce.edu.ec
[4] Escuela Superior de Ingeniería, Tecnología y Diseño, Universidad Internacional de la Rioja
(UNIR), Logroño, Spain

Abstract. Introduction: Video analytics has become an important tool for improving business performance, personnel management, and security in different environments, including shopping centres. However, its use also poses a threat to users' privacy. Aim: In this context the aim of the article is to determine the architecture of video analytics in shopping malls as a business marketing strategy and the vulnerability of users' privacy. Method: A descriptive methodology with a qualitative approach was used to design a prototype focused on the optimisation of customer business processes and decision making in shopping centres in Ecuador, from problem identification and information requirements management to prototype design, implementation, and training of the model with accurate data. Results: The technological solution is based on the OMIA platform, which generates relevant Key Performance Index (KPI) based on the automatic processing of images from video surveillance systems. Conclusion: It is important that the implementation of the model is trained, supervised, optimised, and regulated to guarantee the privacy and security of information and users under the Organic Law on Data Protection in Ecuador.

Keywords: video analytics · identity vulnerability · cybersecurity · marketing · user privacy

1 Introduction

Video analytics has become an essential tool in the field of business marketing, helping companies to improve business performance and enabling them to implement more efficient strategies for security and personnel management. However, the use of these

C. Stephanidis et al. (Eds.): HCII 2023, CCIS 1958, pp. 365–371, 2024.
https://doi.org/10.1007/978-3-031-49215-0_43

technologies poses a threat to people's right to privacy. In particular, the implementation of video analytics in shopping centres has generated controversy, as it is considered a risk to users' privacy. Although this system contributes to security and theft prevention, it is also susceptible to cyber-attacks by third parties. It is therefore essential to promote the ethical and responsible use of video analytics, so that they can provide more secure technological solutions that respect people's rights. Despite the risks it presents, video analytics has reached a higher level in the use of a standard surveillance system and has become a main tool for corporate marketing, allowing the design of strategies that captivate the customer.

Consequently, video analytics has become a valuable tool in crime prevention and detection, with multiple successful applications in specific sectors such as traffic control, people counting and number plate reading. Thanks to the integration of artificial intelligence algorithms, it is now possible to identify suspicious behaviour and criminal patterns in real time, allowing authorities to respond more efficiently and effectively to risky situations. However, as technology advances, video analytics is becoming more accurate in identifying situations that affect security [1]. In this regard, studies on video analytics have shown that it is an increasingly used tool to help business owners make informed decisions on product layout, point-of-sale advertising and people flow management. The identification of people in video surveillance systems is one of the previous research topics that has improved the efficiency of video analytics. One approach presented has shown a discriminative learning algorithm that handles uncertainties in pairwise constraints, minimising the exposure of people's identities [2]. Another relevant issue is privacy in the distribution of audio and video content. They present an identity-based rights management system to solve privacy issues and allow the device to verify the user's right of access in a secure way [3]. The problem of security and privacy in traditional video surveillance systems has also been a previous research concern. A mechanism called SePriS uses smart contracts [4], blockchain and advanced encryption to share surveillance video securely and privately between authorised nodes and law enforcement entities. Furthermore, a normative UI-REF ethno-methodological framework has been presented to support the design and implementation of privacy-preserving filtering techniques for video surveillance [5]. The use of various web platforms and mobile applications to improve education is another topic of previous research [6]. Garaizar & Guanaga highlight the potential of HTML5 APIs to enhance education in mobile environments and address the privacy risks associated with this new era of multimodal learning analytics [7]. Finally, a user study investigating which pixel operations are suitable for protecting the privacy of individuals in video data, without compromising the human operator's ability to recognise people's activities, concludes that it is possible to preserve the usefulness of video data without sacrificing privacy by properly anonymising the data [8]. There are various didactic methodologies for training in video analytics, considering the ethical and privacy aspects of users, using project-based learning and cooperative learning [9], providing skills in critical analysis, teamwork, problem solving, fostering creativity and innovation in the design of techno-logical solutions [10]. Nowadays, video surveillance systems have been very important in reducing crime to a great extent and new forms of security have been adopted. In addition, their implementation in the marketing of premises has also generated a great impact with the combination of video analytics integrated into video surveillance systems by identifying and tracking the analysis of CCTV graphics, providing the possibility to obtain valuable records of user behaviours [11], enabling shopping centres to improve the way their premises are managed and distributed.

Video analytics has become an important tool for improving business performance and implementing more efficient strategies in personnel and security management. This technology is also used in shopping malls as a fundamental tool, but at the same time it poses a threat to users' privacy. The objective of this scientific paper is to determine the architecture for video analytics in shopping malls in Ecuador as a business marketing strategy and to maintain the security of user privacy.

2 Method

This is a descriptive study that aims to detail the different uses of video analytics in public spaces, specifically in shopping centres. In addition, the study variables are presented, which include both business marketing benefits and security for user privacy. The research has a qualitative approach, through techniques such as content analysis, documentary analysis and interviews, relevant information was collected to understand the advantages of video analytics in shopping malls and the main vulnerabilities in terms of user privacy.

The methodology proposed for the development of a video analytics control prototype with Artificial Intelligence (AI) is based on a series of generic steps that seek to obtain an optimal result in the process. First, the discovery and prioritisation of the problems to be solved is proposed. Then, we move on to design, where an initial mapping is carried out to define the tasks and people in charge. The next stage is modelling, in which a traffic analysis is created to establish patterns and behaviours of the people in the process. This is followed by the implementation of the model and the learning stage, which consists of training the AI algorithm. Supervision is essential for the correct monitoring and analysis of the process indicators, identifying opportunities for improvement in the optimisation stage, adjustments are made to improve the process and the results obtained (see Fig. 1). Information requirements management is the first fundamental step in making data-driven decisions. This process starts with the identification of the need by gathering additional information for decision making. Once this need is established, information is gathered, and terms of reference (TOR) are generated and approved by the corporation. If the TORs do not meet expectations, the design analysis continues, and the project is reconsidered. If the TORs are approved, they are sent to local providers to request the required information, such as the number of people entering per gate, gender of people, age range and frequency of entry.

This process is repeated until the information requirements necessary for decision making are met, which can be seen in the discovery phase (see Fig. 1). The design phase (see Fig. 1), in which, once the objectives and goals have been established, the design of the prototype is carried out, which will allow a concrete visualisation of what the final project will look like. Then, a detailed analysis of the design is carried out, with the aim of approving it and, if it meets the requirements, the prototype is developed. Subsequently, improvements are made prior to testing and quality control, which will ensure that the

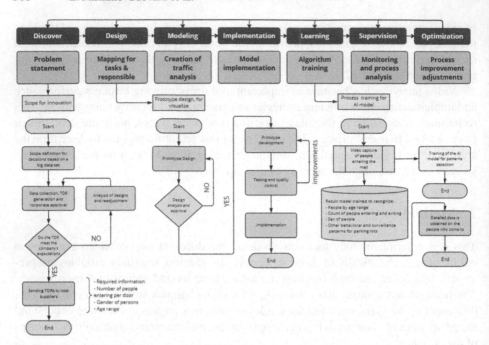

Fig. 1. A figure caption of the method for the development of video analytics control prototype in shopping centres in Ecuador. Source: elaborated by the authors.

project meets the necessary standards. Finally, we proceed with the implementation and the end of the project, thus ending the design stage and initiating the next phase of the process. For the training of the IA model, two methodologies are proposed: project-based learning and cooperative learning. In the former, a project is proposed for the design of a video surveillance system integrated with video analysis, while in the latter, working groups are formed to analyse and discuss the different aspects of the technology and its impact on the context. Once the model is implemented, as can be seen in the learning phase, it is trained (see Fig. 1), with data from people entering for 3 months to improve accuracy. With around 50,000 records, the model achieves a certainty of 90%, with a tolerance margin of 10%. The information is stored in a Data Warehouse and a dashboard is created with Power BI, for socialisation and decision making regarding the location of premises and contracts, based on the information generated. A well-trained model and accurate data are crucial to make the right decisions in the Monitoring and Optimisation Phase of the proposed methodology.

3 Results

The proposed solution includes three stages: the definition of corporate objectives, the collection of information and the technological solution in a platform that generates relevant KPIs based on the automatic processing of images from video surveillance systems. It can measure various behaviours such as micro-segmentation for marketing activities, customer experience, traffic statistics and crowd detection (see Fig. 2). The seven shopping centres they operate are equipped with more than 400 video surveillance cameras, which generates a large amount of data that, if processed correctly, can generate KPIs to improve business processes and results. For the development of the model, the existing infrastructure related to analog camera that are currently used for the surveillance of the mall, improving the system with digital cameras for data acquisition, these are hosted on a server, from where the intelligent analysis process will be performed for the construction of the scorecard and the corresponding decision making. The basic architecture model for implementing the solution includes servers for processing and storage, network infrastructure, cameras, and analytical applications. The number of cameras required for each centre varies by location and purpose, such as number plate recognition, customer tracking and traffic flow monitoring. Depending on the number of signals needing processing and the bandwidth available at each location, one or more servers may be needed to process the data.

Based on the results, it is possible to highlight the great usefulness of video analytics in two major segments of interest, security, and marketing, in both of which video analytics offers the possibility of obtaining records of people's behaviour, which are valuable depending on their purpose and scope of application.

Table 1. Expected results of the pilot proposal.

N°	Results	Description
1	Detailed knowledge of traffic patterns	Make informed decisions on store placement and resource allocation
2	Improved customer experience customer experience	Making shops and services more attractive to each age range and gender and making informed decisions about the placement of services
3	Increased efficiency of the company	Determine which areas of the mall need more attention and resources at specific times and allocate more staff and resources to improve service at those times
4	Increased security in the shopping centre	Identify suspicious traffic patterns and reinforce safety in areas where accidents occur and take measures to prevent future accidents

User behaviour stands out as the fundamental basis of video analytics systems, based on algorithms to verify autonomously and in real time what is happening in each environment. People's privacy is frequently violated; however, it is evident that, in shopping centres, information security is highly controlled, under Ecuador's Organic Law on Data Protection [12].

Detailed understanding of traffic patterns improves customer experience, increases business efficiency, and enhances security (see Table 1).

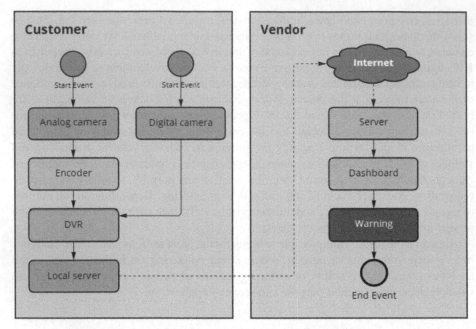

Fig. 2. Prototype architecture model. Source: developed by the authors.

4 Conclusion

It is evident that the theoretical foundations of video analytics state that it has a wide variety of applications in the business field of marketing, based on the analysis of behaviours and patterns, among the main ones are facial recognition, age and gender identification and people counting, information that is monitored to subsequently obtain strategic points of entry and exit of customers in shopping centres, this being just one of the examples seen in this study. The proposed implementation of video analytics in shopping malls is a promising solution to improve business processes and results. It is an effective way to measure customer and employee behaviour and improve security measures. The implementation of the pilot project is an excellent way to test the feasibility of the solution and mitigate any potential risks before full-scale implementation. In view of the above the study provides a solid basis for research in this field, the authors have addressed important issues around privacy and security in video surveillance, as well as the identification of individuals in surveillance systems and the proper anonymization of video data to protect the privacy of individuals. This area of research can be of great importance for the use of video analytics in business marketing in shopping centres in Ecuador and could be a useful basis for future studies in this field.

Finally, video analytics applied to business marketing in shopping centres plays an important role in implementing strategies to improve user experience and decision making. The correct selection of algorithms and the use of small data sets for the development of the prototype must be considered to adjust the visualization of results with the application of business intelligence at the same time. It is also perceived that there is a certain rejection to the use of these technologies, due to the lack of knowledge and the belief that users' privacy can be violated, which is why the responsible companies are constantly working with ethics and professionalism to mitigate any vulnerability to their clients.

Acknowledgements. We are grateful for the openness and collaboration of the companies managing the shopping centres for the publication of this manuscript.

References

1. Fernández, S., Narváez R.: Descripción y aplicaciones de la analítica de video. Universidad Tecnológica de Bolívar. Cartagena D.T. y C. (2012)
2. Chang, Y., et al.: People identification with limited labels in privacy-protected video. In: IEEE International Conference on Multimedia and Expo. vol. 2006, pp. 1005–1008. Canada (2006)
3. Conrado, C., et al.: Privacy in an identity-based DRM system. In: ACM Proceedings of the 14th International Workshop on Database and Expert Systems Applications (DEXA2003), pp. 389–395. IEEE Computer Society (2003)
4. Fitwi, A., Chen, Y.: Secure and privacy-preserving stored surveillance video sharing atop permissioned blockchain. In: Proceedings - International Conference on Computer Communications and Networks. IEEE (2021)
5. Badii, A., et al.: Holistic evaluation framework for video privacy filtering technologies. Signal Image Int. J. **4**(6), 1–20 (2013)
6. Almaraz, F., et al.: Análisis de la transformación digital de las Instituciones de Educación Superior. Un marco de referencia teórico. Revista de Educación Mediática y TIC. **6**(1), 181–202 (2017)
7. Garaizar, P., Guenaga M.: A multimodal learning analytics view of HTML5 APIs: technical benefits and privacy risks. In: ACM International Conference Proceeding Series, pp. 275–281. (2014)
8. Birnstill, P., et al.: A user study on anonymization techniques for smart video surveillance. In: AVSS. 12th IEEE International Conference on Advanced Video and Signal Based Surveillance (2015)
9. Bará, J., Domingo, J., Valero M.: Técnicas de Aprendizaje Cooperativo y Aprendizaje Basado en Proyectos. 1era ed. UPC, Zaragoza (2011)
10. Fortea, M.: Metodologías didácticas para la enseñanza/aprendizaje de competencias, 2da edn. Universitat Jaume I, España (2019)
11. García S., Zamora, N.: Estado actual de los sistemas de seguridad y monitoreo basado en la tecnología CCTV con video analítica para uso residencial y comercial en la ciudad de Guayaquil. Propuesta de una guía para vinculación. Universidad Católica de Santiago de Guayaquil, Ecuador (2019)
12. Enríquez, A.: Paradigmas de la protección de datos personales en Ecuador. Análisis del proyecto de Ley Orgánica de Protección a los Derechos a la Intimidad y Privacidad sobre los Datos Personales. Revista de Derecho **27**, 1–19 (2017)

Designing Scalable Manufacturing Methods for Integrated E-Textile Technologies

Sarah A. S. Pichon[1], Melissa E. van Schaik[1], Marina Toeters[2],
Eliza Bottenberg[1(✉)], Jolien J. J. T. Hermans[3], and Javier Ferreira Gonzalez[1]

[1] Saxion University of Applied Sciences, Van Galenstraat 19,
7511 JL Enschede, The Netherlands
{s.a.s.pichon,E.Bottenberg}@saxion.nl
[2] Eindhoven University of Technology, Den Dolech 2,
5612 AZ Eindhoven, The Netherlands
[3] Research Group Applied Natural Sciences, Fontys University of Applied Sciences,
De Rondom 1, 5612 AP Eindhoven, The Netherlands

Abstract. E-textiles involve seamlessly embedding electronic components into fabric, enabling textiles to sense, react, and communicate with the environment. However, the development of embedded textiles requires collaboration across multidisciplinary research fields. This study aims to address the need for large-scale textile-electronic research and development methods that can be applied in the textile industry. By bridging the gap between industries, this research aims to facilitate the creation of innovative e-textiles by showing the potential of technical embroidery, lamination, conductive screen-printing and modular, flexible electronic components through the showcase of four demonstrators.

Keywords: e-textile design · large-scale production · technical embroidery · lamination · conductive screen-printing

1 Introduction

E-textiles are fabrics with embedded electronics to sense, react and communicate with the environment [5]. This can include passive electronics such as wires or conductive yarn and more advanced electronics like solar cells, enabling the seamless integration of sensors, cables microcontrollers and actuators [11]. By integrating electronics directly into textiles, e-textiles offer a wide range of possibilities for wearable technology, communication, safety and beyond [10]. However, integrating hard electronic components directly into textiles is challenging and calls for textile-electronics innovations regarding manufacturing methods and electronics [1]. Next to that, it also requires the expertise and collaboration of multidisciplinary research fields, bringing experts together from different

Supported by Sia Raak Pro project.

industries such as textile designers, engineers, textile producers, software and hardware developers. Yet, this collaboration is often challenging among industrial companies, or they individually lack expertise to develop such an innovative e-textile, and particularly, to implement it in their current industrial production process. This study therefore focuses on the development of e-textiles for large-scale surface that can be implemented in current industrial processes. For this study, thirteen textile and electronics companies, spanning the entire value chain, collaborate to develop the route to 'e-textiles'. To showcase the textile-electronic solutions, four demonstrators are developed with integrated use cases.

2   Methodology

This study follows applied research in combination with the V-model, a widely used tool for systems engineering [14], and agile project management [7]. Agile as a structure is used by software developers and is briefly mentioned in research as a way to increase output and improve motivation. It keeps focusing on specific aspects and realizing each component while interacting with the other components. Development is based on three stages: proof of principles, prototypes and demonstrators, which are evaluated by companies and developers using user and functional requirements. Proof of principles are developed to test the feasibility of all techniques; prototypes are developed to evaluate the combination of various techniques; and demonstrators are developed as the "end product" aimed at TRL level 5.

3   Results

Four demonstrators have been designed and created to showcase embedded textile opportunities for large-scale production with confining business cases.

4   Anti-theft System

To protect trucks from theft, intrusion, and vandalism, an intelligent anti-theft system is developed that can detect where the tarpaulin has been cut. The innovation consists of an embroidered conductive grid (see Fig. 1), which is implemented in the tarpaulin on a textile level. The intelligent tarpaulin protects the cargo by sending a signal to the truck driver and emergency services once the tarpaulin is cut. The PVC coating protects the cargo from (heavy) weather influences and can therefore be used in different weather circumstances.

4.1   Materials

Technical embroidery was investigated as it allows for more complex e-textile designs to be integrated with a conventional embroidery machine. Silver-coated polyamide and polyester hybrid thread (120) from Silver-Tech was used to create

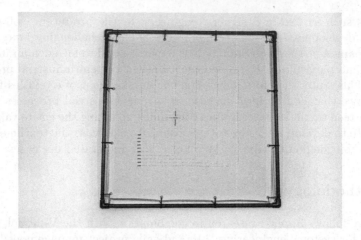

Fig. 1. Prototype of anti-theft system.

the conductive tracks. A current source with a current sensor (INA219AIDCNR) is used to measure breakage in the grid, in combination with I2C to communicate. The embroidery process was accomplished with a JCZA 0109-550 embroidery machine (F-head and W-head) [2], with DBX K5 round point with small ball needles. Technical embroidery requires only one extra processing step before coating the woven fabric with Polyvinyl chloride (PVC). This provides good chemical resistance to protect the load and the conductive track [13].

To connect electronics with textiles, a small flexible interposer PCB (13,41 cm × 2,11 cm) was designed. The flexible substrate consists of two layers with a surface finish made from immersion gold (ENIG) and finished copper (0.5 oz Cu 18 um) on the top layer, the layer that will be laminated. Along the edge, there are in total ten contact areas for the textile interconnection. The material used to manufacture the PCB is Polyimide SF305C Flex with a high temperature resistance up to 388 °C. Thermoplastic elastomer adhesives (TPU) are used as a bonding material for the flexible PCB due to their promising characteristics and compatibility with MCA-bonding. The liquid BEMICOLL MPR waterborne polyurethane adhesive was used, which has excellent running properties and results in a fine coating picture.

4.2   Methods

A square-shaped embroidery grid was made using the EPCwin7 embroidery software (ZSK Stickmaschinesn GmbH), creating a 4 × 4 grid of conductive and non-conductive polyester thread. The software enables adaptability to new grid sizes [12]. All the rows are connected to one flexible PCB at the top. The plus line (red) consists of both a conductive upper (needle 5) and conductive bottom bobbin thread, connecting the entire grid. When a conductive track is used on both the top spool and the bobbin, the resistance decreases due to an increase in contact points [8]. This means that only a conductive thread is used on the bottom for the horizontal tracks (blue) and a non-conductive thread for the upper spool. Another needle (needle 4) is activated within the software.

After that, an automatic stop is programmed into the design to change the bottom bobbin thread from conductive to non-conductive, meaning the vertical tracks (green) are embroidered with a non-conductive bottom thread and a conductive upper thread (needle 5). Lastly, conductive rectangular-shaped connectors are embroidered on the grid to the flexible PCB through non-conductive adhesive bonding (NCA).

After the embroidery process is completed, the PCB is laminated at 150° for 15 s under a pressure of 0.5–2.0 bar using the bonding machine calortrans-heatpress-3838ii. Using NCA thermoplastic bonding makes the connection resistant to temperature and humidity cycling because it forms a layer of isolation. Thermoplastic can remelt, which is an advantage for repairable and reusable components. It is widely used for textile lamination and coating due its high flexibility [4]. It is demonstrated to work with 1.27 mm pitch components and provides a reliable contact resistance, therefore increasing electrical connection reliability. Die bonder machines can be used for large scale and high accuracy bonding [4], or they can be applied by means of rotary screen technology, full surface coating, knife coating, or reverse roll coating.

5   LED Curtain

In current areas or events where it is often dark, such as in cinemas, theaters, or concert halls - emergency instructions are static and non-intuitive whereby comprehension of the location can be hard due to the thick smoke. When fire occurs in an unfamiliar area, due to thick smoke and short circuits, the comprehension of the location becomes hard. This concept implements lighting in curtains on a textile level, that provide dynamic emergency instructions. The curtains create an intuitive fading direction to a secure location. It can be applied everywhere on large indoor surfaces. The curtains can be rented for specific occasions or placed permanently positioned in desired areas. The customer can select the color of the curtain or LEDs and put them elegantly in various interior designs.

5.1   Materials

Silver-coated polyamide continuous filament (100 and 150) from Silver-tech+ was used to create the conductive tracks and to attach electronic components. The prototype is embroidered with the JCZA 0109-550 embroidery machine. This method was chosen as embedding electronics through embroidery can be accomplished later in the product development stage, allowing for flexibility in the manufacturing process [8]. Moreover, this technique is compatible with almost all textiles and looks and feels like textile [4]. Micro-circuit boards were mounted on rolls onto a traditional sequin carrier, the left Functional Sequin Device (FSD). The FSD consists of a sequin feed mechanism for feeding a sequin strip towards the programmed position and a sequin-cutting cutter located in the predetermined cutting position [2]. The white ⌀ 7 mm LED from Imbue with form factor 0805 was used (3,2 V at 20 mA).

5.2   Methods

An arrow shaped embroidery circuit has been designed by using the EPCwin7 embroidery software, in which each row was connecting 17 LEDs in series. The software enables adaptability to new designs [12]. All the rows are connected to one flexible PCB at the top, without any sharp corners. The mounted LEDs are first embroidered by using polyester yarn for fixation, followed by conductive yarn as an interconnection technique (Fig. 2).

Fig. 2. Development of embroidery circuit with mounted LEDs.

This e-textile process does not require post-process soldering or additional conductive epoxies, which greatly reduces the risk of human error, the amount of labor required, and reduces mechanical strains on the connectors which decreases mechanical fatigue-based failure [2]. This makes the connection precise, reliable, fully automatic, and fast. Lastly, the conductive track and LED are covered with 100% polyester thread to isolate the circuit and for aesthetics, creating a multilayered structure.

6   Smart Shelter Tent

Shelter tents often lack the ability to provide protection, sufficient ventilation, and energy facilities. To improve this, a new design for a shelter tent is created. The material of the tent has flame-retardant properties, is water resistant, and is still breathable. The integrated flexible solar panels provide energy to charge your phone, but also to charge the combination detector, which detects carbon dioxide and carbon monoxide. In addition, a panic button is integrated into the tent design to alert emergency services in case of an immediate danger.

6.1   Materials

Laminated triangular organic photovoltaics (OPVs) from Armor Group were used to create the flexible light-trapping design. Using these OPVs offers highly aesthetic, customizable, and unlimited design freedom. Solar energy conversion is a major renewable energy technology, and OPVs embedded textile solar energy conversion method is promising due to its scalability, flexibility, transparency, lightweight, ultra-thinness and low cost [6]. In addition, the OPVs are designed from organic polymers using a very energy-efficient process, creating a film with a low carbon footprint. Hardware was developed to convert the energy generated by the solar panels into energy that can be stored in batteries and to use this stored energy for actuation and charging. The hardware of this prototype consists of mostly off-the-shelf components to speed up the development of the prototype and make it easily implementable. The system consists of two main components: the MPPT LiPo charger and the power converter MT360, which is connected to the output connector. The charger is connected to the solar panels and the battery and uses a manual maximum power-point tracking system to get the most power out of the solar panels.

Fig. 3. Attachment of modular LEDs on a laminated grid.

6.2   Methods

A triangular-shaped module, consisting of nine big triangles (173 × 173 × 173 cm) and ten small triangles (73 × 73 × 73 cm), was designed, produced, and laminated. After this process, the Shieldex fabric was laser cut into a hexagon-shaped grid design. The width of the power rails is 1,2 cm and the tracks are 0,7 cm, with a distance of 0,3 cm in-between (see Fig. 3). This makes it an easy process where the functional electronic patterns can be easily and rapidly changed, and manufacturing of bespoke or mass-produced designs can be done with a good reproducibility rate [12], meaning only one extra processing step is needed before sewing together the entire tent. Depending on the design and pattern of the tent, the embedded electronics can be adjusted accordingly. On this laminated grid, the 3D-printed modular connectors and LEDs can be pick and placed. These modular connectors are 3D printed and overmolded. This prototype brings together state-of-the-art technological advancements and textile integration methods in the field of photovoltaic-thermoelectric energy harvesters and modular connectors, with overarching relevance for the development of self-empowered electronics for large textile surface area applications.

7   Heated Roller Blind

In single-glazed homes, resident comfort is often low due to heat loss and poor insulation. A roller blind with heating capabilities is developed to reduce the feeling of cold. The roller blind heats up once the touch sensor is touched. It can be turned off similarly. Different heating states can additionally be chosen. This way, it can be used for various purposes: partly heated, completely heated or not heated to e.g. provide shading.

7.1   Method

Recent innovations in the field of printed electronics for heating solutions highlight the potential for screen-printing for e-textiles [3,9]. On top of that, screen printing allows for a great degree of flexibility in the design. Designs are created digitally and thereafter transferred to a screen by lithography methods. Furthermore, techniques like screen printing are additive manufacturing techniques. In comparison to traditional ways of producing electronics, which is done by etching away parts of a copper layer, this process produces much less waste since only the needed amount of material is applied.

8   Discussion

Four prototypes with integrated business cases relating to the interests of the partners were created to demonstrate textile-electronics advancements. Conductive grids were developed using technical embroidery for mounting LEDs and connecting flexible PCBs for different functionalities. Flexible integrated solar panels and modular LEDs were additionally developed. Finally, screen printing silver and carbon tracks was used to create heating elements and a touch sensor for activation.

As an applied research method is partly followed, the results should be treated as preliminary but lay the groundwork for future analysis. Despite these limitations, the findings of this study contribute to the understanding of seamlessly integrating e-textiles for large-scale surfaces and provide practical insights that can guide future research and industry practices.

9 Conclusion

This study shows the potential of technical embroidery, conductive screen-printing, lamination and modular, flexbile electronic components to be integrated into industrial processes for large-scale surfaces. During the study, multiple textile and electronic companies collaborated to develop promising e-textile solutions. To showcase the textile innovations, four demonstrators were developed with an integrated use case.

Funding. Hitex Sia Raak Pro 03.001.

References

1. Du, K., Lin, R., Yin, L., Ho, J.S., Wang, J., Lim, C.T.: Electronic textiles for energy, sensing, and communication. iScience **25**(5), 104174 (2022). https://doi.org/10.1016/j.isci.2022.104174
2. GmbH, Z.S.: The ZSK Technical Embroidery Systems Magazine, p. 1–24 (2020)
3. Gozutok, Z., Agırbas, O., Bahtiyari, M.I., Ozdemir, A.: Low-voltage textile-based wearable heater systems fabricated by printing reactive silver inks. Sens. Actuators A **322**, 112610 (2021). https://doi.org/10.1016/j.sna.2021.112610
4. Linz, T., Simon, E., Walter, H.: Fundamental analysis of embroidered contacts for electronics in textiles. In: 3rd Electronics System Integration Technology Conference ESTC. IEEE, September 2010. https://doi.org/10.1109/estc.2010.5642823
5. Nayak, R., Wang, L., Padhye, R.: Electronic textiles for military personnel. In: Electronic Textiles, pp. 239–256. Elsevier (2015). https://doi.org/10.1016/b978-0-08-100201-8.00012-6
6. Park, Y., et al.: Flexible, light trapping substrates for organic photovoltaics. Appl. Phys. Lett. **109**(9) (2016). https://doi.org/10.1063/1.4962206
7. Pirro, L.: How agile project management can work for your research. Nature (2019). https://doi.org/10.1038/d41586-019-01184-9
8. Ruppert-Stroescu, M., Balasubramanian, M.: Effects of stitch classes on the electrical properties of conductive threads. Text. Res. J. **88**(21), 2454–2463 (2017). https://doi.org/10.1177/0040517517725116
9. Saito, M., Kanai, E., Fujita, H., Aso, T., Matsutani, N., Fujie, T.: Flexible induction heater based on the polymeric thin film for local thermotherapy. Adv. Func. Mater. **31**(32), 2102444 (2021). https://doi.org/10.1002/adfm.202102444
10. Scott, R.A.: Textiles for Protection. Elsevier (2005)
11. Stegmaier, T.: Recent advances in textile manufacturing technology. Glob. Text. Clothing Ind., 113–130 (2012). https://doi.org/10.1533/9780857095626.113
12. Tao, X.: Smart Fibres, Fabrics and Clothing. CRC Press (2008)
13. Tsolis, A., Whittow, W., Alexandridis, A., Vardaxoglou, J.: Embroidery and related manufacturing techniques for wearable antennas: challenges and opportunities. Electronics **3**(2), 314–338 (2014). https://doi.org/10.3390/electronics3020314
14. Weilkiens, T., Lamm, J.G., Roth, S., Walker, M.: Model-Based System Architecture. Wiley (2015). https://doi.org/10.1002/9781119051930

Identification of Consumer Factors that Influence Purchase Intention in Online C2C Second-Hand Transactions

Peihan Wen(✉) ⑩, Lizhu Tao, and Qian Zhang

Chongqing University, Chongqing 400044, People's Republic of China
wen@cqu.edu.cn

Abstract. Despite the increasing popularity of the online Customer-to-Customer (C2C) second-hand market, factors that affect consumers' willingness to engaged in online C2C second-hand transactions are not fully investigated. Therefore, we take an approach to identify the factors influencing consumers' intention to purchase on C2C second-hand platforms in China, verifying the applicability of existing achievements in China's second-hand trading context and exploring new factors based on the characteristics of C2C second-hand transactions. Based on the literature review and characteristics of C2C second-hand transactions, eight consumer factors were introduced into the research model: disposition to trust, familiarity with buying, familiarity with selling, frugality, environmentalism, dematerialism, fashion consciousness and hygiene consciousness. Among them, *familiarity with selling* and *hygiene consciousness* are new research variables that never appeared in previous studies. A questionnaire containing 38 questions with 10 constructs and demographic data was designed and distributed to 425 participants, where 377 valid responses were finally obtained. The results provided evidence that consumers' familiarity with buying, frugality, dematerialize, fashion consciousness and hygiene consciousness all significantly affected their intentions to purchase in C2C second-hand transactions. Also consumers' familiarity with selling and disposition to trust had positive impacts on purchase intention through the mediation effect of trust. Another important finding revealed that the impact of environmentalism on second-hand purchase intention was not significant, showing a difference in the role of environmentalism in China and developed countries. The findings provided insight into marketing and design strategies for C2C second-hand platforms to promote C2C second-hand consumption.

Keywords: Purchase Intention · Second-Hand Consumption · Consumer Factors · C2C E-Commerce

1 Introduction

With the rapid changes in fashion and the reduction of production costs, global commodity consumption has increased significantly in the past few decades, resulting in a phenomenal increase in the amount of wastes and a negative environmental consequence [1]. The emergence of second-hand transactions provides a solution to this problem. It offers great opportunities for both buyers and sellers to reduce unsustainable resource consumption and gain economic benefits. Buyers are able to spend less money on products, and sellers are able to sell idle items for economic benefits conveniently.

Despite the fact that the C2C second-hand market flourishes in recent years and still has huge development potential, empirical researches on consumers behaviour on C2C second-hand transactions is still limited [2]. Most of the existing results are based on the research scenarios of Western developed countries [4], that is to say, the applicability of these factors in developing countries needs to be tested. In China, the factors driving second-hand consumption might be different, as second-hand consumption is an activity closely related to consumers' cultural customs and consumption orientations. Therefore, this study conducts empirical research to identify the consumer factors influencing consumers' purchase intentions in online C2C second-hand transactions, verifying the applicability of existing achievements in China's second-hand trading context and exploring new factors based on the characteristics of C2C second-hand transactions.

2 Hypotheses and Model

Consumers' purchase intention is the probability of choosing a certain commodity under the influence of various factors, and is an important predictor of purchase behaviour [7]. Perceived ease of use [8, 9], information quality [10, 11], third-party guarantees [12], privacy assurances and security features [10, 13] have been identified as the most critical website factors to develop purchase intention in e-commerce. In 2018, Swapana and Padmavathy found that prices, product brands, and website quality all had an impact on consumers' repurchase intentions through the intermediary role of satisfaction in B2C second-hand shopping [14]. Disposition to trust has been widely studied and was proved to influence purchase intention positively through trust [15]. Familiarity has been identified as an crucial consumer factor that influences purchase in e-commerce [15, 16]. Familiarity in previous studied generally refers to familiarity with platform, which is sweeping and fuzzy. In C2C second-hand transactions, users play two roles of both seller and consumer, so it is necessary to consider both familiarity with buying and with selling. In second-hand consumption, consumers' fashion consciousness [4], frugality [5], environmentalism [6], dematerialism [3] have been proved to significant affect their intentions to purchase second-hand goods.

2.1 Research Hypotheses

Considering that second-hand consumption is an activity closely related to consumers' personal characteristics, this study investigates the impact of consumer factors on purchase intention. Based on the literature review and characteristics of C2C second-hand transactions, eight consumer factors related to C2C second-hand consumption were introduced, where familiarity with selling and hygiene consciousness are new research variables proposed based on the characteristics of C2C second-hand transactions.

Disposition to trust is the tendency to have faith in the honesty and reliability of other entities, which is not influenced by continuous interactions [17]. Mayer et al. first investigated the relationship between consumers' disposition to trust and online trust, and find that disposition to trust was positively related to consumers' initial trust [18]. Thus, we hypothesized that:

H1: Disposition to trust positively influences the trust towards platform.

Familiarity refers to the extent of which the consumer is familiar with other objects, which often depends on the previous interaction with the objects and their own relevant experience [19]. Current researches on familiarity usually only measures the consumer's familiarity with buying. In the C2C second-hand transactions, many consumers have also become commodity suppliers, that is to say, users of C2C second-hand trading platforms are both online shopping consumers and commodity sellers. Therefore, in addition to familiarity with buying, familiarity with selling should also be considered in C2C second-hand transactions. Also previous research has proved that familiarity not only affects trust, but also directly influences consumers' willingness to engaged in transactions. We postulated the following hypothesis:

H2a: Familiarity with buying positively influences the trust towards platform.
H2b: Familiarity with selling positively influences the trust towards platform.
H3a: Familiarity with buying positively influences purchase intention.
H3b: Familiarity with selling positively influences purchase intention.

Frugality was defined by Lastovicka et al. as a mode of consumption, representing the extent to which consumers were restricted in obtaining and making full use of economic commodities to achieve long-term goals []. In second-hand transactions, the relationship between frugality and purchase behaviour is usually different from first-hand shopping. Cervellon et al. validated that frugality could directly drive second-hand consumption [10]. Therefore, we hypothesized that:

H4: Frugality positively influences purchase intention.

Environmentalism. The prevalence of low-carbon environmental protection concepts is one of the important factors driving the phenomenal growth of second-hand market. Some scholars have confirmed through empirical studies that the second-hand consumption is driven by consumers' awareness of the ecological environment. We postulated the following hypothesis:

H5: Environmentalism positively influences purchase intention.

Dematerialism. Materialism was defined as the importance of material possessions in achieving a person's life goal [20]. Roux and Guiot found that dematerialistic consumers were more willing to buy second-hand goods than materialistic consumers [3]. Thus, we hypothesized that:

H6: Dematerialism positively influences purchase intention.

Fashion consciousness was defied as the consumer's tendency to keep up-to-date with styles [21]. Usually, consumers with low fashion consciousness are prone to buy second-hand goods since second-hand goods are mostly outdated, and consumers will pay more attention to the use value of second-hand products [5]. Thus, we hypothesized that:

H7: Fashion consciousness negatively influences purchase intention.

Hygiene Consciousness. In C2C second-hand transactions, individual sellers directly sell second-hand goods directly to consumers, eliminating platform audits, so it is difficult to guarantee the cleanliness, which many consumers are concerned about. Therefore, we hypothesized that:

H8: Hygiene consciousness negatively influences purchase intention.

Trust Towards Platform. Trust has been proved to be a crucial factor determining the long-term success of C2C transactions. When it comes to C2C second-hand transactions, there are few reviews of sellers and commodities that consumers can refer to, and consumers will pay more attention to the reputation of the platform. On this basis, we postulated the following hypothesis:

H9: Trust towards platform positively influences the purchase intention.

2.2 Research Model

Based on the above hypotheses, we build the research model as shown in Fig. 1.

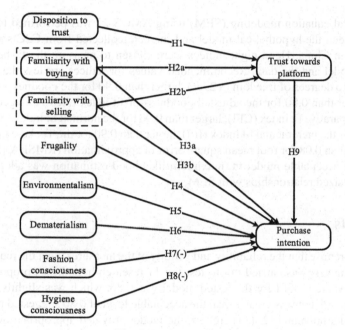

Fig. 1. Research model

3 Research Methodology

This research employs a survey methodology to collect primary data for empirical analysis. The sample is made up of a selection of people who had used at least one C2C second-hand transaction platform. We distributed 486 questionnaires and 425 participants who were involved in second-hand transactions before completed the full survey.

Then, 48 of the 425 participants were dropped who were found to be dishonest in the survey, and 377 valid responses were finally obtained. The sample consisted of 197 (52.3%) males and 180 (47.7%) females valid participants. There were 45.6% participants aged under 25, 42.2% participants aged from 25–35 and 12.2% participants aged over 35.

Convergent validity refers to the degree to which one or more observed variables can measure the corresponding unobserved variable because they share variance. Here, the commonly used method of evaluating convergent validity were adopted, which contains three criteria, namely item reliability, composite reliability (CR) and the average variance extracted (AVE) of each construct. The item reliability is considered acceptable if each item has a factor loading larger 0.50. The CR of every construct needs to be above the satisfactory value of 0.8. The AVE indicates how much variance captured by the construct is shared among other variables, and is considered acceptable if it has a value above 0.50. Discriminant validity refers to the degree to which a construct differs from other constructs, and is acceptable if a construct' square root of the AVE is greater than its correlations with other constructs. Reliability is assessed by Cronbach' alpha value, and is considered good if the Cronbach' alpha value of a given construct is larger than 0.70.

Structural equation modeling (SEM) using AMOS 22 was performed to calculate the fit between the hypothetical model and the data collected from C2C second-hand consumers in China. Here, eight indices were chosen to measure the fit between the research model and the data. Recommended values for indices are less than 3 for the ratio of $\chi 2$ to degrees of freedom ($\chi 2$ /df), larger than 0.90 for the goodness-of-fit index (GFI), larger than 0.80 for the adjusted goodness-of-fit index (AGFI), larger than 0.90 for the comparative fit index (CFI), larger than 0.90 for the normed fit index (NFI), larger than 0.90 for the incremental fit index (IFI), larger than 0.90 for the Tuckere Lewis index (TLI), less than 0.08 for root mean square error of approximation (RMSEA)[59,60]. On the basis of acceptable model fit, maximum likelihood estimation was adopted to test the hypothesized relationships with SEM.

4   Results

Under the premise that the reliability and validity of the measures meet the requirements, the SEM analysis was carried out to test the 11 research hypotheses proposed in this paper. The value of GFI for the tested model was 0.86, which was slightly below the 0.90 benchmark, but was greater than the acceptable level of 0.80 suggested by Etezadi-Amoli and Farhoomand [22]. Therefore, the model provided appropriate overall fit to the data.

Table 1 presents the summary of the path coeefficients (β) of all the hypotheses and the corresponding significance. As shown, only H3b ($t = -0.397$; $p = 0.691$) and H5 ($t = -0.095$; $p = 0.925$) were not significant, indicating that FamSe and Env didn't directly influence Pur. H1 ($\beta = 0.574$; $t = 10.021$; $p < 0.001$), H2a ($\beta = 0.199$; $t = 3.148$; $p = 0.002$) and H2b ($\beta = 0.182$; $t = 4.072$; $p < 0.001$) was reported to be significant, reflecting that DisTr, FamBu and FamSe positively affected Tru. FamBu ($\beta = 0.084$; $t = 2.13$; $p = 0.033$), Fru ($\beta = 0.205$; $t = 3.719$; $p < 0.001$), Mat ($\beta = 0.224$; $t = 5.982$; $p < 0.001$), Fas ($\beta = -0.314$; $t = -10.754$; $p < 0.001$), Hyg ($\beta = -0.308$; $t = -10.11$; p

< 0.001) and Tru (β = 0.183; t = 5.820; p < 0.001) were found to significantly predict Pur.

Table 1 Results of hypothesis testing

	Hypothesis	Path coefficient	t	P	Supported?
H1	DisTr → Tru	0.574	10.021	0.000	Yes
H2a	FamBu → Tru	0.199	3.148	0.002	Yes
H2b	FamSe → Tru	0.182	4.072	0.000	Yes
H3a	FamBu → Pur	0.084	2.13	0.033	Yes
H3b	FamSe → Pur	−0.01	−0.397	0.691	No
H4	Fru → Pur	0.205	3.719	0.000	Yes
H5	Env → Pur	−0.003	−0.095	0.925	No
H6	Mat → Pur	0.224	5.982	0.000	Yes
H7	Fas → Pur	−0.314	−10.754	0.000	Yes
H8	Hyg → Pur	−0.308	−10.11	0.000	Yes
H9	Tru → Pur	0.183	5.820	0.000	Yes

After deleting H3b and H5 which were found not significant, a modified estimated model was conducted again. The results are shown in Fig. 2. The coefficients of determination (R2) were 0.47 (trust towards platform) and 0.85 (purchase intention), indicating strong explanations of the variance that the model provided.

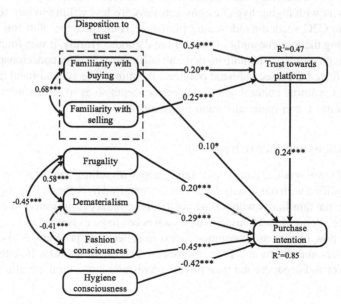

Fig. 2. The results of tested model with significant path coefficients. **p < 0.01; ***p < 0.001.

5   Implications and Conclusion

The results showed that consumers' disposition to trust, familiarity with buying and selling had positive influences on their trust towards platform. In addition, it was found that familiarity with buying had a direct influence on purchase intention. Frugality, dematerialism, fashion consciousness and hygiene consciousness were found to significantly influence purchase intention in C2C second-hand transactions. Specifically, as consumers' frugality increased, dematerialism increased, fashion consciousness decreased and hygiene consciousness decreased, their intentions would increase. The results suggested that hygiene consciousness exerted a negative effect on purchase intention. Surprisingly, environmentalism didn't influence purchase intention directly, which is different from many research results in developed countries [5, 6], indicating a cross-cultural difference.

5.1   Practical Implications

Theoretically, this study contributes in two ways. Firstly, this paper validated the cross-cultural differences in factors affecting second-hand consumption, such as the influence of environmentalism. Secondly, this paper supplemented factors influencing C2C second-hand consumption by adding "familiarity with selling" and "hygiene awareness" based on the characteristics of C2C second-hand transactions.

From a practical perspective, the study provides a reference for improving consumers' purchase intentions. Firstly, companies could improve consumers' purchase intentions by increasing their familiarity both with buying and selling. Meanwhile, the familiarity was found to be affected through non-socially interactions, which suggested that the second-hand platforms should be designed with a consistent architecture and interface style as commonly used online trading platforms. Secondly, this study shows that consumers with higher hygiene consciousness are less willing to buy second-hand goods on the C2C second-hand trading platform. Therefore, the platform could consider including the hygiene audit of second-hand goods. Thirdly, it was found that consumers' frugality, environmentalism, dematerialism, and fashion consciousness all significantly affected C2C second-hand purchase intention. The second-hand trading platforms should promote cultural and consumer concepts so as to attract more frugalists, environmentalists, non-materialists and pragmatists.

5.2   Limitations and Future Research

The effect of the new added antecedent "familiarity with selling" on behavioral intentions cannot be clarified with our results due to the unsupported hypothesis H3b. In this regard, it is possible that familiarity with selling positively influences consumers intention to sell in online C2C second-hand transactions, which needs to be examined in future research. In addition, how to increase consumers' trust in sellers and products is also important for both sellers and platforms. Thus, future research could identify the antecedents of trust in sellers and products and their effects on distinct behavioral intentions.

References

1. Birtwistle, G., Moore, C.: Fashion clothing – where does it all end up? Int. J. Retail Distrib. Manage. **35**(3), 210–216 (2007)
2. Parguel, B., Lunardo, R., Benoit-Moreau, F.: Sustainability of the sharing economy in question: when second-hand peer-to-peer platforms stimulate indulgent consumption. Technol. Forecast. Soc. Chang. **125**, 48–57 (2017)
3. Roux, D., Guiot, D.: Measuring second-hand shopping motives, antecedents and consequences. Recherche et Appl. Market. (English Edn.) **23**(4), 63–91 (2008)
4. Ferraro, C., Sands, S., Brace-Govan, J.: The role of fashionability in second-hand shopping motivations. J. Retail. Consum. Serv. **32**, 262–268 (2016)
5. Cervellon, M.-C., Carey, L., Harms, T.: Something old, something used: Determinants of women's purchase of vintage fashion vs second-hand fashion. Int. J. Retail Distrib. Manage. **40**(12), 956–974 (2012)
6. Yan, R.N., Bae, S.Y., Xu, H.M.: Second-hand clothing shopping among college students: the role of psychographic characteristics. Young Consum. **16**, 85–98 (2015)
7. Burke, J.J., Hatfield, J.L., Klein, R.R., et al.: Accumulation of heat-shock proteins in field-grown cotton. Plant Physiol. **78**(2), 394–398 (1985)
8. Chau, P.Y.K., Hu, P.J.H., Lee, B.L.P., et al.: Examining customers' trust in online vendors and their dropout decisions: an empirical study. Electron. Commer. Res. Appl. **6**(2), 171–182 (2007)
9. Gregg, D.G., Walczak, S.: The relationship between website quality, trust and price premiums at online auctions. Electron. Commer. Res. **10**(1), 1–25 (2010)
10. Chen, D.Y., Lai, F.J., Lin, Z.X.: A trust model for online peer-to-peer lending: a lender's perspective. Inf. Technol. Manage. **15**(4), 239–254 (2014)
11. Gao, W., Li, X.: Building presence in an online shopping website: the role of website quality. Behav. Inf. Technol. **38**(1), 28–41 (2019)
12. Jones, K., Leonard, L.N.K.: Factors influencing buyer's trust in consumer-to-consumer E Commmerce. J. Comput. Inf. Syst. **54**(4), 71–79 (2014)
13. Bart, Y., Shankar, V., Sultan, F., et al.: Are the drivers and role of online trust the same for all Web sites and consumers? A large-scale exploratory empirical study. J. Mark. **69**(4), 133–152 (2005)
14. Swapana, M., Padmavathy, C.: Relationships among dimensions of online second-hand shopping, satisfaction, and repurchase intention. Int. J. E-Bus. Res. **14**(1), 89–102 (2018)
15. Gefen, D.: E-commerce: the role of familiarity and trust. Omega-Int. J. Manage. Sci. **28**(6), 725–737 (2000)
16. Mittendorf, C.: Collaborative consumption: the role of familiarity and trust among Millennials. J. Consum. Mark. **35**(4), 377–391 (2018)
17. Kim, D.J., Ferrin, D.L., Rao, H.R.: A trust-based consumer decision-making model in electronic commerce: the role of trust, perceived risk, and their antecedents. Decis. Support Syst. **44**(2), 544–564 (2008)
18. Mayer, R.C., Davis, J.H., Schoorman, F.D.: An integrative model of organizational trust. Acad. Manag. Rev. **20**(3), 709–734 (1995)
19. Komiak, S.Y.X., Benbasat, I.: The effects of personalization and familiarity on trust and adoption of recommendation agents. MIS Q. **30**(4), 941–960 (2006)
20. Richins, M.L.: The material values scale: measurement properties and development of a short form. J. Consum. Res. **31**(1), 209–219 (2004)
21. Sproles, G.B., Kendall, E.L.: A methodology for profiling consumers decision-making styles. J. Consum. Aff. **20**(2), 267–279 (1986)
22. Etezadi-Amoli, J., Farhoomand, A.F.: A structural model of end user computing satisfaction and user performance. Inf. Manage. **30**(2), 65–73 (1996)

Sustainable Hybrid of Agriculture and Urban Ecology Base on Web 3.0 Technology

Yuqi Zhang and Yiyuan Huang[✉]

Beijing Institute of Graphic Communication, Daxing District, 1 Xinghua Street (Section 2), Beijing, China
yiyuan.huang@bigc.edu.cn

Abstract. This paper addresses the global issues of food scarcity and ecological imbalances, resulting in hunger, malnutrition, and health complications. To foster sustainable development and harmonize human-ecological balance, an interdisciplinary approach utilizing web3.0 technology is adopted to promote the integration of agriculture and urban environments. The research explores the web3.0 technology to select crops and plans manual work by utilizing the internet of things and blockchain. This facilitates real-time monitoring and recording of environmental, climate, and soil information, allowing for the selection of suitable crops in specific areas, improving agricultural efficiency, and ensuring food safety. The study also investigates the destination of agricultural products, selling them directly to the public using web3.0 technology to provide green ecological food while ensuring the income source of low-income farmers. This strategy promotes economic growth and achieves a virtuous circle of economy and ecology. In addition, the study explores the recycling of agricultural plants, aiming to identify the most optimal recycling program through the utilization of web3.0 technology. By implementing this approach, we can facilitate the sustainable development of agriculture and rural areas while mitigating the impact on the environment. At last, a sustainability model based on trust mechanisms, cooperation and benefit mechanisms, and coordination mechanisms is developed, mobilizing multiple sectors to ensure sustainable integration of Web3.0 agriculture and ecological systems for economic growth and ecological balance. To effectively address the food and ecological crisis, the study puts forward a web3.0 technology-assisted sustainability model and multi-participation sustainability model based on web3.0 technology, which can promote the benign interaction between cities and agriculture and build a more beautiful and livable city, and im-prove food security and environmental preservation.

Keywords: Web3.0 · Sustainable development of agricultural economy · Eco-City

1 Introduction

Food security is crucial for maintaining national and regional social stability. In fact, the 2022 Global Food Crisis Report predicts that nearly 200 million people worldwide will face severe food shortages in 2021. However, there is little room for the growth of world

C. Stephanidis et al. (Eds.): HCII 2023, CCIS 1958, pp. 388–394, 2024.
https://doi.org/10.1007/978-3-031-49215-0_46

grain output, and the supply of cultivated land and its sustainable utilization restrict grain production [1]. At the same time, the development of agricultural technology is very slow, and the process of urbanization is developing rapidly, and farmers' production capacity cannot keep up, resulting in low agricultural production efficiency and low farmers' income [2]. Moreover, the influx of farmers into cities has worsened population expansion while also creating many challenges for urban residents. Furthermore, the traditional agricultural management model is often insufficient to keep pace with the evolving demands of today's urbanization processes.

Based on the combination of small-scale agriculture and cities, this paper discusses how to use Web0 technology to establish a multi-field and multi-participation sustainability model to achieve sustainable development. By analyzing the existing data and projects, this paper explores the rationality and feasibility behind the model, and then constructs a sustainable model that can be "linked". This paper will demonstrate with practical examples to provide reference for exploring the sustainability model.

To achieve integration between agriculture and cities, we can enhance the technical level of agriculture, improve farmers' living standards, restructure agricultural production, and establish agricultural technical service networks. Additionally, we can leverage the city's resource advantages to improve the agricultural production and management environment, promoting sustainable agricultural development while enabling cities to obtain resources like organic products and raw materials. By pursuing mutually beneficial outcomes, we can realize innovative integration between agriculture and cities that enable sustainable development. Ultimately, we hope this paper will offer new ideas and directions for achieving this goal.

2 Small-Scale Agriculture and Urban Integration

The integration of small-scale agriculture with cities is an innovative approach to achieving sustainable agricultural production amidst urbanization. It leverages technology, capital, and human resources to complement traditional agricultural practices and foster innovation in agricultural production. By addressing food safety and environmental challenges caused by urbanization [3], this approach can accelerate the modernization of agriculture while promoting sustainable development.

Traditional agriculture leads to land over-reclamation, water pollution and ecosystem destruction. However, with the support of modern technology, the concept of urban agriculture is moving towards the context of "sustainable development" [4]. Urban green infrastructure and agricultural cities based on agricultural production can improve urban environment and build ecological cities.

Small-scale agriculture has diversified in functional value, production types. Integration with the city has led to various business models such as roof agriculture, balcony agriculture, vertical farming, and community agricultural parks. This has also expanded the area of cultivated land and increased grain output.

A new agricultural model combining small-scale peasant agriculture with cities shows modernization based on people-oriented needs [5]. The model takes urban residents as the main consumers and employs small-scale, scientific, standardized, and diversified management methods. This approach helps address the employment problem of farmers and low-income people, providing them with employment opportunities and promoting social equity.

3   Web3.0 Technology-Assisted Sustainability Model

With the increasing importance of sustainable development in the global society, Web3.0 technology, as a new digital technology, has become one of the important tools to achieve the goal of sustainability. Therefore, Web3.0 technology has been widely used in agriculture, environmental protection, energy and other fields, and has played an important role in achieving sustainable development [6]. In this study, a web3.0 technology-aided sustainable development model is proposed to promote the benign interaction between cities and agriculture and realize sustainable development (see Fig. 1).

In the field of agriculture, the advantages of Web3.0 technology have been fully reflected. By establishing a decentralized trust mechanism, we can effectively coordinate and manage the activities of all participants in agricultural production involving planting, breeding and circulation. In order to achieve this goal, regional management agencies can be established in a unified way, responsible for coordinating and managing farmers, distributors and consumers in all aspects, and ensuring information sharing and transparency among them.

The application of artificial intelligence technology in agriculture can not only realize intelligent division of labor and resource optimization, but also help to realize more refined agricultural management [7]. In agricultural production, different crops need different growth conditions and management methods, and by using artificial intelligence technology, the environmental conditions and resources of each planting site can be analyzed and evaluated, so as to formulate the optimal planting scheme and management strategy. For example, by using artificial intelligence algorithm to analyze and predict the data of soil, meteorology and other factors, it can provide farmers with suggestions on the best planting time, variety selection, fertilizer and irrigation amount. At the same time, based on big data and cloud computing technology, data from different farms can also be integrated and compared, so as to provide farmers with more comprehensive and accurate agricultural management suggestions. In addition, artificial intelligence technology can also help achieve a more effective regulatory system. By using the camera, agricultural activities can be monitored in real time, and possible problems can be found and dealt with. At the same time, natural language processing technology is used to provide farmers with guidance on production technology and management, and improve the quality and yield of crops.

Web3.0 technology can bring innovative multi-party sales channels for agricultural production and consumption. By collecting agricultural products information and establishing a unified platform for sales, the quality monitoring and tracking of agricultural products can be realized, and the safety and traceability of agricultural products can be improved. People can buy safe and green food on the platform, which can not only meet their green needs, but also support the production of local farmers. After the purchase is completed, the platform can use smart contract technology and blockchain technology to realize real-time tracking and management of order status. At the same time, the

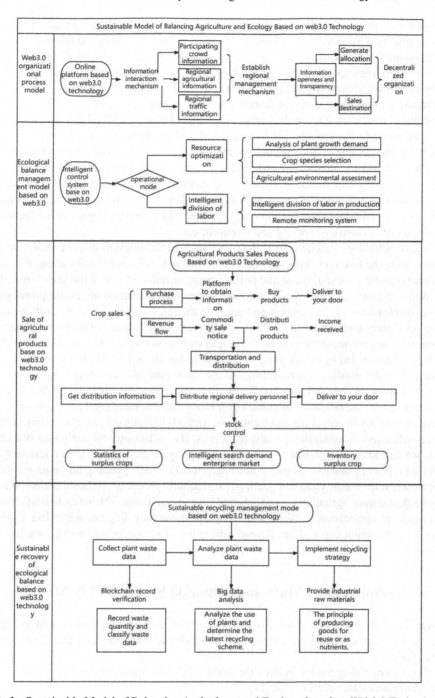

Fig.1. Sustainable Model of Balancing Agriculture and Ecology based on Web3.0 Technology.

platform can also uniformly plan regional delivery to improve delivery efficiency and service quality. This direct sales model based on Web3.0 technology can not only reduce intermediate links and reduce the cost of agricultural products, but also improve consumers' shopping experience and trust. In addition, the platform finally counts the data of the remaining vegetables and fruits of the day, and sells them again in the companies and manufacturers that search for demand, which can also maximize the utilization and recycling of resources. This multi-party sales channel based on Web3.0 technology can not only promote the virtuous circle of agricultural production and consumption, but also bring more value to society and environment. By establishing a unified platform for sales, the quality monitoring and tracking of agricultural products can be realized, and the shopping experience and trust of consumers can be improved; At the same time, it can also maximize the utilization and recycling of resources, promote a virtuous cycle of agricultural production and consumption, and achieve the goal of sustainable development of economy, society and environment.

Web0 technology can help to collect and analyze the relevant data of waste, so as to determine the best recycling scheme [8]. In this way, reasonable utilization of waste resources can be achieved, waste and pollution can be reduced, and at the same time, the environment can be protected and sustainable eco-city construction can be promoted. Using Web0 technology to collect and analyze the relevant data of waste garbage can more accurately understand the output, components and sources of different types of waste, so as to determine the best recovery and treatment scheme. For example, organic waste can be recycled by composting or anaerobic digestion; For electronic waste, it can be reused by dismantling and recycling. At the same time, the recycling scheme can be continuously optimized and improved by monitoring and evaluating the recycling effect, so as to improve the resource utilization efficiency and environmental protection effect. In addition to waste recycling and treatment, Web3.0 technology can also promote the better utilization of agricultural plant resources. By collecting and analyzing relevant data, we can know the planting situation, growth cycle and quality characteristics of different types of plant resources, so as to determine the best planting and management scheme and improve the yield and quality of agricultural products. At the same time, it can also track and trace agricultural products and improve consumers' trust and satisfaction. In a word, the application of Web0 technology in waste recycling and agricultural plant resources utilization can realize rational utilization of resources and reduce waste and pollution.

4   Multi-domain and Multi-participation Sustainability Model

Under the Web 3.0 environment, trust mechanism, cooperation and benefit mechanism and linkage coordination mechanism can mobilize multi-domain and multi-party participation.

The sustainability model ensures the sustainable integration of Web 3.0 technology agriculture and urban ecology (see Fig. 2).

Policies supporting Web 3.0 can accelerate the technology's adoption and popularization in agriculture and environmental management. Enterprises and institutions can

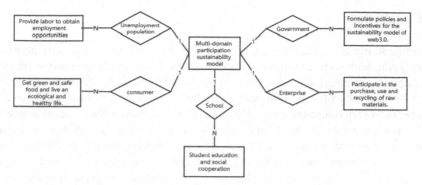

Fig. 2. Multi-Domain and multi-Participation Sustainability Model.

be encouraged to innovate and research using Web 3.0 technology, speeding up its commercialization and widespread use. Policy support can also promote coordinated development between urban and rural areas, achieving sustainable integration of agriculture and environment while implementing sustainable development principles.

Unemployed urban residents can participate in the sustainable integration of Web 3.0 technology in agriculture and environmental management, which provides employment opportunities and income sources. Web 3.0 technology offers a business model and platform for these individuals to engage in agriculture and environmental work while accessing information on local production and labor demand. With web3.0 technology-based distribution management, unemployed individuals have the opportunity to join agricultural production acquisition programs.

Web 3.0 technology-based sustainable agriculture and environmental management can produce safer, healthier, and higher quality agricultural and ecological products. This encourages consumers to consider the source, production process, ecological benefits, and social responsibility of products, promoting more rational and sustainable consumption behavior. Additionally, this approach promotes exchange and cooperation between urban and rural areas by establishing an integrated urban-rural ecosystem.

Incorporating Web 3.0 technology-based sustainable agriculture and environmental management in schools can foster students' understanding and practice of sustainable development, cultivating their environmental awareness and innovation skills. By participating in local agricultural production or environmental services, students can explore the concept of sustainability through practical activities, stimulating their innovative thinking and practical skills. This approach also promotes collaboration between schools and social organizations.

It is an active way for enterprises to recover and reuse resources by applying the recovered resources to agricultural production or urban construction, which is helpful to promote the development of closed-loop circular economy in the market.

5 Conclusion

According to our research, a sustainable model combining small-scale agriculture and urban system with web 3.0 technology are introduced. Meanwhile, we also established a multi-party participation sustainability model based on web3.0. Those models demonstrate the feasibility of web3.0 in promoting the cooperation and sustainable development between agriculture and cities, and how web3.0 technology can be used to promote agricultural sustainability development. The study highlights the importance of multisectoral involvement for small-scale agriculture and urban integration, which requires support from governments, businesses, and social organizations to form a complete sustainable ecosystem. We also provide innovative solutions for promoting sustainable development and calls for further improvement and involvement from various sectors for greater progress.

Acknowledgments. This research is supported by Beijing Institute of Graphic Communication: the Beijing Association of Higher Education Project in 2022 (No. 22150223016) and the program of The Characteristic Talent Training and Innovation Practice Of "ZhiXing" (No. 22150323004).

References

1. Grassini, P., Eskridge, K.M., Cassman, K.: Distinguishing between yield advances and yield plateaus in historical crop production trends. Nat. Commun. 4(1), 1–11 (2013)
2. Chu, M.: The dynamic mechanism and practice path of complete urbanization. Urban Probl. 10, 39–45 (2019)
3. Zhou, D., Yang, H.: Theoretical research and practice of urban agriculture. China Rural Surv. 4, 60–67 (1997)
4. Coles, R., Costa, S.: Food growing in the city: exploring the productive urban landscape as a new paradigm for inclusive approaches to the design and planning of future urban open spaces. Landsc. Urban Plan. 170, 1–5 (2018)
5. Feng, L., Zhang, W.: Analysis of Xi Jinping's modernization exposition of harmonious coexistence between man and nature. Res. Marxist Theory 4(04), 72–82 (2018)
6. Xiong, H., Zhang, C., Li, Y.: Research on the construction of personal knowledge management platform based on Web 3.0. Libr. Inf. Work. 54(18), 95–99 (2018)
7. Yang, X.: OPAC conception based on Web3.0. J. Acad. Libr. 28(6), 98–101 (2010)
8. Jiao, Y., Yuan, J.: Research on personalized service of digital library based on scenario model. J. Libr. Sci. China 6, 58–63 (2008)

HCI in Mobility and Aviation

The Real Sorting Hat – Identifying Driving and Scanning Strategies in Urban Intersections with Cluster Analysis

Bianca Biebl[(✉)] and Klaus Bengler

Chair of Ergonomics, Technical University of Munich, Boltzmannstraße 15, 85748 Garching, Germany
Bianca.Biebl@tum.de

Abstract. Identifying individual driving strategies often relies on theoretical task models, arbitrary group divisions, or somewhat untransparent evaluations by instructors. We propose using cluster analysis as an exploratory, data-driven approach to categorize drivers based on their driving and scanning behavior. Therefore, we analyzed a combination of variables regarding longitudinal vehicle guidance, lateral vehicle guidance, and gaze behavior when approaching an intersection. Data stemmed from a driving simulator study including drivers with normal vision, simulated, and pathological visual field loss. They performed 32 intersections that varied concerning complexity and the availability of an auditory scanning assistant. The total sample comprised 2145 data points. K-means on two dimensions of a prior Principal Component Analysis yielded the best results with two clusters that can be interpreted as *high acter* and *low acter*, referring to the extent and earliness of gaze shifts as well as the duration of the intersection approach. These two strategy clusters were rated based on performance criteria to check the effectiveness of these strategies for the different driver groups and situations. While high acters were more frequent under complex conditions, this strategy failed more frequently in these cases. Future developments for this promising approach to cluster strategies in driving-related areas are discussed.

Keywords: K-means · Driving Strategy · Visual Field Loss

1 Theoretical Background

The ability to classify and rate driving and scanning strategies is an important goal for developing efficient driver assistance systems that can recognize and predict inefficient strategies and avoid hazardous situations in time. Action sequences are often characterized by a theoretical succession of phases with individual tasks and goals [1, 2]. Other models propose a causal tree structure to describe the different behavioral paths that lead to an accident [3]. While such theoretical models help to define the driving task, they do not allow for an in-depth numerical differentiation between the behaviors and strategies of individual drivers. Many research areas focus on identifying and explaining differences between driver groups regarding their driving and scanning strategies, e.g.,

C. Stephanidis et al. (Eds.): HCII 2023, CCIS 1958, pp. 397–404, 2024.
https://doi.org/10.1007/978-3-031-49215-0_47

considering the effect of age, experience, culture, or gender [4, 5]. One area with a particular interest in the identification of patterns both between and within driver groups is the understanding and licensing of impaired drivers. For example, different approaches have been used to identify so-called high-performing and low-performing drivers among persons with visual impairments to characterize their ability to compensate for their deficits. The median-split method [6, 7] divides the sample into two equally sized subgroups based on a singular criteria (top and bottom half represent high-performers and low-performers respectively). Evaluations by driving examiners use real-time or video-based ratings [8–11]. In both cases, the subgroups are characterized by comparing driving or scanning parameters after the categorization. It must, however, be noted that these approaches often use arbitrary or untransparent criteria to divide the sample. They also only allow a differentiation into two groups, which might not represent the potential multitude of existing compensatory strategies. Moreover, we propose that identifying (compensatory) behavior should not be performed after subdividing the group. Instead, the complex behavior structures should be the informing criterion to divide the sample into subgroups according to their strategies or performances.

2 Objective and Methods

We aimed to derive a novel approach to classify, describe, and rate all naturally occurring driving and scanning strategies with a data-driven exploratory approach. Therefore, we performed cluster analyses on longitudinal vehicle guidance, lateral vehicle guidance, head and eye movements when approaching an intersection where participants had to yield to crossing traffic. In total, 106 participants with 99 viable data sets performed four drives in a static driving simulator, each consisting of eight intersections where the participants had to turn left among crossing traffic. The drives differed in the complexity of the intersection (high vs. low; via an increase of the traffic density, the number of pedestrians, and the visual clutter in the environment) and the existence of a simple scanning reminder device that issued a warning if no large gaze was made to the participants' blind side during the intersection approach phase (with vs. without the assistant). These manipulations were part of another research question that is not elaborated further here. A total of 2145 intersections could be analyzed, performed by drivers with pathological visual field loss (VFL; $n = 182$), with simulated VFL using the gaze-contingency paradigm presented in Biebl et al. [12] ($n = 1004$), and with normal vision ($n = 959$). All analyses were performed using RStudio version 4.2.2.

3 Procedure and Results

3.1 Variable Selection and Principal Component Analysis

The term *strategy* can refer to numerous aspects of the primary, secondary, or tertiary driving task regarding the existence of actions, their timing, duration, order, or magnitude. Focusing on behaviors that can compensate for visual deficits, we only regarded variables that can be assumed to counteract the adverse effects of partial blindness in driving. Literature search on relevant variables and extensive considerations yielded a set of variables that should give a lean but comprehensive representation of the driving and scanning characteristics. It comprised longitudinal vehicle guidance (represented by the duration of the intersection approach phase), lateral vehicle guidance (represented by the mean offset from the central lane position), and scanning (i.e., *how often, how long, how early,* and *how* drivers scanned *where* and *how far*). The latter was represented by the number, mean duration, and timing (seconds until arriving at the intersection) of gaze scans to near (defined as $\pm 5°$ until $\pm 45°$) and far regions (defined as above $\pm 45°$, cut-off indicates the minimum gaze shift to fixate a hazardous crossing vehicle with the same speed and distance to the intersection) in the left and right periphery respectively as well as the mean offset between the eye and head position. These variables can be found in similar forms dispersed among previous research works and publications (for reviews, see for example [13, 14]). It must be noted that due to the individual driving strategies, we found a great number of outliers in some variables, especially those considering the timing. While outliers are fundamentally subpar for many clustering approaches due to their definitional dissimilarity from the majority of the sample, they are typical for this field of research and should, therefore, not be dismissed. In the final set of starting variables, we found some correlations that must be regarded as high, according to Cohen [15]. Those concerned the covariance between the duration metrics (length of the approach phase; mean duration of scans) and the covariance between the mean duration of scans in different areas of interest. The following iterative process also aimed to optimize the input variables by comparing clustering results (see Sect. 3.2). To reduce the potential overlap of variances in each iteration and to better understand the structure of variable connections, we performed Principal Component Analysis (PCA) on the input variables in each iteration. PCA is used to find latent constructs underlying a set of variables and to make a weighted allocation of the examined variables to these constructs. We performed principal component analysis on the scaled and normalized input variables (function *prcomp* in the package *stats*), visualized the results and the quality (functions using *fviz_* in the package *factoextra*) and chose the optimal number of dimensions based on the Kaiser Criterion (eigenvalue > 1) (function *get_eig* in the package *factoextra*) and Horn's Parallel Analysis with scree plot (function *paran* in the package *paran*). If a number of dimensions narrowly missed the threshold but yielded a considerable benefit regarding the explained variance, we also performed the further clustering steps with this number of dimensions to avoid overinterpreting the somewhat arbitrary thresholds in these exploratory analyses. We could check which variables loaded on each dimension using the function *fviz_cotnrib* (in the package *factoextra*). To ensure that the PCA did not lead to a distorted image or unduly reduction of variance, we additionally performed the further clustering procedure on the scaled variables without PCA.

3.2 Selection of Cluster Algorithm

Using either the results of the PCA or the scaled raw variables as input variables, we performed a cluster analysis to identify distinct patterns. In the past decades, a multitude of algorithms to perform clustering have been developed. The most frequently used approaches can be divided into hierarchical, partition-based, density-based, model-based, and fuzzy clustering algorithms [16], all of which provide different strengths and weaknesses for different research questions. In driving-related research, we found that all methods have been used in the past. For example, Hiroguchi et al. [15] used Markov Cluster Algorithms to extract characteristic eye gaze patterns among AOIs in train conductors. Clustering has often been used to identify groups with different objective or subjective risk levels, which has been done with fuzzy clustering [17] or k-means [18]. K-means has often been used to investigate individuals' driving styles [19]. Hill et al. [20] used k-means to categorize subjects into one of four categories regarding the aggressiveness of their lane change behavior. K-means is one of the most common types of partitional clustering that allocates data points to a prespecified number of clusters by minimizing the distance from the data points to the cluster's mean or so-called centroid. Hierarchical clustering is often used as a prequel to k-means clustering for identifying the appropriate cluster number and/or the initialization of the centroids [21]. We identified k-means as an appropriate approach for our use case since it allows the straightforward interpretation of the clusters and the allocation of each data point to only one cluster and requires few prior assumptions about the data while also being appropriate for larger samples [19]. It must, however, be noted that different use cases or data types might require another approach. One issue of our data was mentioned above and concerned the number of outliers. Since k-means is – as the name states – based on means, it lacks robustness against outlier-prone data. To account for that, we performed the Partitioning Around Medoids (PAM) algorithm in addition to k-means clustering, which uses medoids instead of centroids and is more robust against outliers [22].

3.3 Performing the Cluster Analysis

Before running either the k-means or PAM algorithm, we used the *fviz_nbclust* function in the *factoextra* package to derive the optimal number of clusters via silhouette plot, gap statistic, and elbow plot. A dendrogram gave additional input from the hierarchical cluster analysis. If the combination of these four metrics yielded two potential cluster numbers, clustering was performed with both separately. The cluster analyses were performed with the *eclust* function from the *factoextra* package. The quality of the cluster results was then evaluated and compared by visualizing the silhouette score (function *fviz_silhouette* in the package *factoextra*), calculating the average silhouette width, and looking at the explained variance by viewing the sums of squares.

3.4 Iterative Procedure

The described process was repeated and compared multiple times to decipher a) the optimal set of input variables, b) either using scaled raw values or the optimal number of dimensions from the PCA, and c) to identify the best number of clusters using the d) ideal clustering algorithm. This was an iterative process where we identified the best combination per set of variables and then used these results to refine the set of variables. The PCA, descriptive analyses, and theoretical considerations were used for this refinement of variables and exploratory changes in the depth or informativeness of the parameters.

3.5 Result

The optimal clustering algorithm proved to be k-means on two dimensions (dimension A: duration of approach, seconds to the intersection at first gaze movement towards left and right respectively; dimension B: mean duration of gaze movements to the left and right respectively, number of gaze movements to the left; not included in these dimensions is the number of gaze movements to the right). The iterative process showed that the differentiation of the areas of interest into near and far did not add informative value to clustering. The dissociation between eye and head movements and the lateral offset from the central lane position showed small variances within our sample. In most cases, they were also excluded from the relevant PCA dimensions, so they did not benefit the clustering algorithm. The two dimensions explained 69.42% of the sample's variance. With a Hopkins score of 0.98, we can assume that they have a high clustering tendency. The two clusters using k-means provided a mean silhouette score of 0.44. The silhouette score ranges from 1 to -1 with high values indicating a better cluster fit [23]. While there are no clear thresholds, the acquired value presents a moderate goodness of fit. The explained variance of 42.87% supports this interpretation.

Table 1. Distribution of the two strategy clusters among subject groups and situations.

	Path. VFL	Normal	Sim. VFL	With Assistant	Without Assistant	Simple Intersec.	Complex Intersec.
High acter	34.07% ($n = 62$)	19.71% ($n = 189$)	25.90% ($n = 260$)	24.41% ($n = 258$)	23.25% ($n = 253$)	18.61% ($n = 220$)	30.22% ($n = 291$)
Low acter	65.93% ($n = 120$)	80.29% ($n = 770$)	74.10% ($n = 744$)	75.59% ($n = 799$)	76.75% ($n = 835$)	81.39% ($n = 962$)	69.78% ($n = 672$)

Cluster 1 showed a longer duration of the intersection approach phase and a greater number, duration, and earlier timing of gaze movements compared to cluster 2 and can therefore be regarded as more ample anticipatory scanning ("high acters"). Table 1 shows that behavior described as high acting was generally apparent in much fewer cases. Compared to normal-sighted drivers, it was more often evident in drivers with vision loss, especially pathological vision loss. It can also be seen that the respective frequency of high and low acters was consistent with and without the assistive device. However, participants tended to show the high acter strategy more frequently in complex compared to simple intersections.

In conclusion, the cluster analysis revealed two driving strategies in all subject groups and situations. It could however be the case that a driver with VFL and a driver without VFL exhibited the same strategy, but that would not lead to the same performance or only under certain situational conditions because of the differences in their visual abilities. The second step of our analysis focused on rating the identified strategies to get a clearer picture of how drivers with VFL compensate for their deficits. This was done by checking if the participants crashed into crossing traffic, if the latter had to reduce speed to avoid a crash, or if the overall duration of the waiting period before entering the intersection was too high. The latter indicates getting stuck in the intersection, negatively affecting traffic flow and safety. Following Jenjiwattanakul [24] and Cooper and Zheng [25], we set 30 s as a threshold. It should be noted that due to theoretical considerations of the minimal required gaze shift at intersections, some cluster 1 cases (40 of originally 511; 7.83%) were resorted for this step: Cases in which participants did not make at least one gaze shift of at least 45° to the left and right side prior to entering the intersection were manually recoded to be identified as the low acter cluster 2. This allows enrichment of the exploratory data-driven procedure with theoretical cut-off criteria. As shown in Fig. 1, being classified as high acter did not lead to a greater chance of being rated as a high performer. On the contrary, among drivers with pathological VFL, those who scanned extensively were more likely to be unsafe than safe. The same was true for high acters in complex intersections.

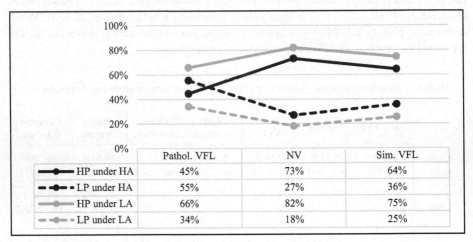

	Pathol. VFL	NV	Sim. VFL
HP under HA	45%	73%	64%
LP under HA	55%	27%	36%
HP under LA	66%	82%	75%
LP under LA	34%	18%	25%

Fig. 1. Conditional probabilities of drivers with high (HP, $n = 1603$) or low performance (LP, $n = 542$) among behavior classified as high acter (HA, $n = 471$) and low acter (LA, $n = 1674$).

4   Discussion

We found that cluster analysis can serve as a valuable tool to classify, interpret and rate driving and scanning strategies under varying conditions. Therefore, the described procedure provides a valuable method to categorize drivers' behavior and its effectiveness. Especially in the research area of impaired driving, in which the dissociation between high and low compensators is often desired but holds methodological limitations, this paper provides a new, exploratory, and data-driven approach. This led us to the surprising finding that extensive and early scanning with low speed during the intersection approach was related to lower safety for drivers with pathological VFL. This is most likely mediated by the tendency of more challenged drivers to execute a more cautious strategy.

It must, however, be noted that the results from the cluster analysis are highly dependent on the chosen variables and clustering algorithm. Our clustering results provided sound yet not excellent goodness of fit. This might have been due to the underlying data structure, where PCA could only represent a proportion of the total variance, and outliers aggravated clustering. Furthermore, it must be assumed that the scanning and driving variables share some variance and cannot be regarded as entirely independent parameters. Future research should therefore revisit the clustering process and compare further clustering algorithms. It might also be helpful to perform individual cluster analyses on specific user groups to rule out that large groups overshadow different behavior in small subgroups. Especially in time-critical driving data, the usage of time series might provide additional value.

Acknowledgement. This work was supported by the Deutsche Forschungsgemeinschaft (DFG) under grant no. BE4532/15–1.

References

1. Plavsic, M.: Analysis and Modeling of Driver Behavior for Assistance Systems at Road Intersections [Dissertation]. Technical University of Munich, Munich (2010)
2. Richard, C.M., Campbell, J.L., Brown, J.L.: Task analysis of intersection driving scenarios: Information processing bottlenecks: No. FHWA-HRT-06–033 (2006)
3. Biebl, B., Kacianka, S., Unni, A., Trende, A., Rieger, J.W., Lüdtke, A., et al.: A causal model of intersection-related collisions for drivers with and without visual field loss. In: Stephanidis, C., (eds). HCI International 2021 - Late Breaking Papers: HCI Applications in Health, Transport, and Industry. Cham: Springer International Publishing, pp. 219–234 (2021). https://doi.org/10.1007/978-3-030-90966-6_16
4. Bauer, M.J., Adler, G., Kuskowski, M.A., Rottunda, S.: The influence of age and gender on the driving patterns of older adults. J. Women Aging **15**, 3–16 (2003). https://doi.org/10.1300/J074v15n04_02
5. Son, J., Reimer, B., Mehler, B., Pohlmeyer, A.E., Godfrey, K.M., Orszulak, J., et al.: Age and cross-cultural comparison of drivers' cognitive workload and performance in simulated urban driving, pp. 1976–3832 (2010). https://doi.org/10.1007/s12239-010-0065-6
6. Hardiess, G., Papageorgiou, E., Schiefer, U., Mallot, H.A.: Functional compensation of visual field deficits in hemianopic patients under the influence of different task demands. Vision. Res. **50**, 1158–1172 (2010). https://doi.org/10.1016/j.visres.2010.04.004
7. Papageorgiou, E., Hardiess, G., Mallot, H.A., Schiefer, U.: Gaze patterns predicting successful collision avoidance in patients with homonymous visual field defects. Vision. Res. **65**, 25–37 (2012). https://doi.org/10.1016/j.visres.2012.06.004
8. Kasneci, E., et al.: Driving with binocular visual field loss? A study on a supervised on-road parcours with simultaneous eye and head tracking. PLoS ONE **9**, e87470 (2014). https://doi.org/10.1371/journal.pone.0087470
9. Tant, M., Cornelissen, F.W., Kooijman, A.C., Brouwer, W.H.: Hemianopic visual field defects elicit hemianopic scanning. Vision. Res. **42**, 1339–1348 (2002). https://doi.org/10.1016/s0042-6989(02)00044-5
10. Coeckelbergh, T.R.M., Brouwer, W.H., Cornelissen, F.W., van Wolffelaar, P., Kooijman, A.C.: The effect of visual field defects on driving performance: a driving simulator study. Arch. Ophthalmol. **120**, 1509–1516 (2002). https://doi.org/10.1001/archopht.120.11.1509

11. Kübler, T.C., Kasneci, E., Rosenstiel, W., Aehling, K., Heister, M., Nagel, K., et al.: Driving with homonymous visual field defects: driving performance and compensatory gaze movements. J. Eye Mov. Res. **8**(5), 1–11 (2015). https://doi.org/10.16910/jemr.8.5.5

12. Biebl, B., Arcidiacono, E., Kacianka, S., Rieger, J.W., Bengler, K.: Opportunities and limitations of a gaze-contingent display to simulate visual field loss in driving simulator studies. Front. Neuroergonomics **3**, 916169 (2022). https://doi.org/10.3389/fnrgo.2022.916169

13. Bowers, A.R.: Driving with homonymous visual field loss: a review of the literature. Clin. Exp. Optom. **99**, 402–418 (2016). https://doi.org/10.1111/cxo.12425

14. Patterson, G., Howard, C., Hepworth, L., Rowe, F.: The impact of visual field loss on driving skills: a systematic narrative review. Br. Ir. Orthopt. J. **15**, 53–63 (2019). https://doi.org/10.22599/bioj.129

15. Cohen, J.: Statistical power analysis for the behavioral sciences: Academic Press (2013)

16. Wang, X., Wang, H.: Driving behavior clustering for hazardous material transportation based on genetic fuzzy C-means algorithm. IEEE Access **8**, 11289–11296 (2020). https://doi.org/10.1109/ACCESS.2020.2964648

17. Ni, D., Guo, F., Zhou, Y., Shi, C.: Determination of risk perception of drivers using fuzzy-clustering analysis for road safety. IEEE Access **8**, 125501–125512 (2020). https://doi.org/10.1109/ACCESS.2020.3007151

18. Zheng, Y., Wang, J., Li, X., Yu, C., Kodaka, K., Li, K.: Driving risk assessment using cluster analysis based on naturalistic driving data. In: IEEE, pp. 2584–2589

19. de Zepeda, M.V.N., Meng, F., Su, J., Zeng, X.-J., Wang, Q.: Dynamic clustering analysis for driving styles identification. Eng. Appl. Artif. Intell. **97**, 104096 (2021). https://doi.org/10.1016/j.engappai.2020.104096

20. Hill, C., Elefteriadou, L., Kondyli, A.: Exploratory analysis of lane changing on freeways based on driver behavior. J. Transp. Eng. **141**, 4014090 (2015). https://doi.org/10.1061/(ASCE)TE.1943-5436.0000758

21. Shirmohammadi, H., Hadadi, F., Saeedian, M.: Clustering analysis of drivers based on behavioral characteristics regarding road safety. Int. J. Civ. Eng. **17**, 1327–1340 (2019). https://doi.org/10.1007/s40999-018-00390-2

22. Chen, K.-T., Chen, H.-Y.W.: Driving style clustering using naturalistic driving data. Transp. Res. Rec. **2673**, 176–88 (2019). https://doi.org/10.1177/0361198119845360

23. Belyadi, H., Haghighat, A.: Machine Learning Guide for Oil and Gas Using Python: A Step-by-Step Breakdown with Data, Algorithms, Codes, and Applications: Gulf Professional Publishing (2021)

24. Jenjiwattanakul, T., Sano, K.: Effect of waiting time on the gap acceptance behavior of u-turning vehicles at midblock median openings. In: Eastern Asia Society for Transportation Studies, p. 314. https://doi.org/10.11175/eastpro.2011.0.314.0

25. Cooper, P.J., Zheng, Y.: Turning gap acceptance decision-making: the impact of driver distraction. J. Safety Res. **33**, 321–335 (2002). https://doi.org/10.1016/S0022-4375(02)00029-4

A Follow-Up to an Age-Friendly Protocol to Support Investigations of Autonomous Driving Disengagement on Driver Safety: Results and Recommendations

Kirsten Brightman[1]([✉]) [iD], Kathleen Van Benthem[1] [iD], Chris Herdman[1] [iD],
Bruce Wallace[2,3,4] [iD], Aidan Lochbihler[2,3] [iD], Will Sloan[2,3] [iD],
Frank Knoefel[2,3,4,5,6] [iD], and Shawn Marshall[4,5,6] [iD]

[1] Advanced Cognitive Engineering Laboratory, Faculty of Arts and Social Sciences, Carleton University, Ottawa, ON K1S 5B6, Canada
kirstenbrightman@cmail.carleton.ca
[2] Department of Systems and Computer Engineering, Faculty of Engineering and Design, Carleton University, Ottawa, ON K1S 5B6, Canada
[3] AGE-WELLNIH-SAM, Ottawa, ON K1N5C8, Canada
[4] Bruyère Research Institute, Ottawa, ON K1N 5C8, Canada
[5] Faculty of Medicine, University of Ottawa, Ottawa, ON K18L6, Canada
[6] Bruyère Continuing Care, Ottawa, ON K1N 5C8, Canada

Abstract. Driving cessation in old age is linked to negative mental and physical health outcomes. Autonomous vehicles offer an opportunity to maintain independence and mobility for older adults. However, vehicle automation can compromise driver engagement, posing risks to drivers and the public. The concern is particularly significant for older and novice drivers who are already overrepresented in accident statistics. Driving simulators provide a safe environment to evaluate performance and assess driver skills and engagement. This study employed a specialized protocol to accommodate older drivers and minimize the adverse effects of simulated driving. The complete number of participants included older (n = 13) and novice drivers (n = 9), who underwent manual and semi-autonomous driving simulations. Results included positive impacts of the simulator modifications with only two dropouts (both from the older group) resulting in a total dropout rate of 9% (15% of older drivers). Driver engagement varied between driving conditions, with superior performance in responding to surprise events during manual driving condition.

Keywords: Driving simulation · Simulator Sickness · Aging Drivers

1 Introduction

The advent of vehicle automation offers several potential benefits for vulnerable driver groups (e.g., aging and novice drivers) such as enhanced safety and accident mitigation as well as continued independence and mobility. However, there are concerns regarding the effect of automation on driver engagement. Research has shown that vehicle

© The Author(s), under exclusive license to Springer Nature Switzerland AG 2024
C. Stephanidis et al. (Eds.): HCII 2023, CCIS 1958, pp. 405–412, 2024.
https://doi.org/10.1007/978-3-031-49215-0_48

automation can negatively impact driver attention, vigilance, and overall engagement in the driving task [5, 14]. The challenges associated with autonomous driving are particularly concerning considering that drivers must remain available and prepared to regain vehicle control when necessary. Understanding the potential impacts of vehicle automation on driver engagement, particularly for at-risk populations is crucial for developing appropriate strategies to mitigate traffic risks and ensure the safe integration of vehicle technology.

This research aimed to identify how vehicle automation impacts relevant cognitive faculties, such as engagement, situation awareness, mental workload, and prospective memory among two at-risk populations; novice and older drivers. Novice drivers face risks due to inexperience and can struggle to recognize risks when driving [12]. Older drivers can suffer from skill decline due to aging, increasing their risk for driving accidents and injuries [8].

As part of the present research agenda, a driving simulator study was conducted to assess drivers' performance under manual and autonomous driving conditions [2]. Driving simulators are valuable tools for road safety research as they allow for the recreation of difficult or dangerous scenarios under safe and controlled conditions. Unfortunately, the utility of driving simulators is limited by negative autonomic symptoms that can result from these virtual environments, known as simulator sickness. There are multiple factors that have been shown to influence simulator sickness such as individual characteristics (e.g., age, gender, susceptibility to motion sickness), the simulator itself (e.g., display field-of-view, fidelity, content), and the simulated task (e.g., duration of exposure, amount of virtual movement). Previous research has shown that older individuals are more susceptible to simulator sickness [3] resulting in high study dropout rates. In a large virtual driving study (N = 118) Park [15] reported a dropout rate of 37% due to simulator sickness for participants over the age of 70. The dropout rate for older individuals was 2.5 times higher than that of younger participants. Other studies using driving simulators have reported dropout rates exceeding 25% for older participants [10, 11]. The present research employed an age-friendly protocol to minimize simulator sickness and study dropouts, particularly among participants over the age of 65.

2 Methodology

2.1 Participants

Twenty-two drivers were recruited to participate in a two-part driving study. Two older participants were unable to complete the study in full, thus the final sample nineteen individuals (novice driver = 9, older drivers = 11). The novice driver group included 5 males and 4 females, ages 19–37 years (M = 25.2, SD = 6.61). Novice drivers held a driver's license for 1–6 years (M = 3.11, SD = 1.83). The older drivers group comprised 7 males and 4 females, ages 67–84 years (M = 74.8, SD = 5.42) who had held a driver's license for 46–66 years (M = 55.33, SD = 6.00).

2.2 Apparatus

Simulated driving took place in a custom static driving simulator (Fig. 1). The setup included three 27-in LCD screens with an embedded rear-view mirror and side mirror.

To minimize simulator sickness, adaptations were made. Increased realism and optic flow have been demonstrated to negatively impact simulator sickness [6], as such this study employed a flat display configuration rather than curved or side displays. The area surrounding the simulator was covered by black fabric. Scenarios were designed to feature minimal roadside objects. Simulation exposure was reduced to approximately 30 min total with breaks provided in between scenarios. This approach is supported by empirical evidence highlighting the relationship between prolonged simulation exposure and increase severity of simulator sickness symptoms [7, 9, 13]. Finally, a speed governor was used to limit the maximum speed to 50 km/h [1]. Table 1 summarizes the adaptations of the age-friendly display.

Table 1. Adaptions of Age-Friendly Display

Factors Influencing Simulator Sickness	Age-Friendly Accommodations
Optic Flow	Flat display, minimal peripheral objects in scene, covering around simulator area, speed governor
Time	Two sessions, short scenarios, frequent breaks
Monitoring	Use of symptom scales after each exposure to identify any changes in negative symptoms

Using the York Technologies driving simulation environment, four comparable 3–4 km long routes (approximately eight minutes in length) were constructed. The simulator was equipped with brake and accelerator pedals alone with a Logitech steering wheel with signal controls and other experimental buttons. Participants sat in an adjustable bucket-style driver's seat. The seat height was adjustable to ensure participants were optimally positioned to reduce the need for visual accommodation.

Fig. 1. Driving Simulator Components

2.3 Procedure

The driving simulator study had two sessions, with similar procedures. In session one, participants drove the driving simulator using in manual mode (i.e. fully responsible for all driving tasks and vehicle control actions). In session two, autonomous vehicle features were engaged, and participants were responsible for monitoring the autonomous driving system's performance (AV mode) and intervening only when necessary. The autonomous vehicle system controlled all vehicle actions but did not respond to unexpected (surprise) events. Sessions one and two were separated by a period of at least 6 days. Cognitive factors that reflect important driver tasks, such as situation awareness and prospective memory, were measured in each session.

Before each session, participants had a short practice drive and received information about the driving environment and vehicle controls. They also completed an initial simulator sickness questionnaire to obtain a baseline. Participants were instructed to follow all typical traffic and speed laws, with a posted speed limit of 30 km/h enforced by a speed governor to prevent speeds exceeding 50 km/h.

2.4 Independent Measures

The first independent measure was the driver group: novice and older drivers. While the primary purpose of the research did not specifically include hypotheses about the performance of one group versus another, each subsample of drivers had particular recruitment methods and concerns regarding safety. The novice group inclusion criteria were such that only drivers with 6 or fewer years of licensed driving experience were included. The older driver group consisted of drivers aged 65 years or older. During recruitment participants were excluded from the study if they did not meet these criteria, or if they had a history of motion or simulator sickness. The second independent measure is the repeated measure of driving mode: manual or AV mode.

2.5 Dependent Variables

In both sessions, a surprise hazard was presented during one driving scenario. The sudden appearance of an object from the periphery was determined to be a useful event in terms of representing an index of driver engagement. In session one (manual driving) a large traffic cone appeared in the center of the road. In session two (autonomous mode) a ball crossed the vehicle's path. Participants had to take manual control of the vehicle and stop to avoid a collision. A researcher scored participants' responses from 0–3 by using video replay.

Simulator sickness was assessed with two items measuring participants' queasiness and dizziness. Participants rated the severity of each symptom (queasiness and dizziness) on a 6-point Likert scale. Total simulator sickness scores for manual and autonomous driving were calculated by summing the questionnaire scores. Higher scores indicate more severe sickness.

To assess situation awareness (SA) participants map identified their estimated end location on a map of the driving environment. A score of zero to five was awarded based on the accuracy of the indicated endpoint. A higher score indicates greater situation awareness.

Participants received an environmental prospective memory (PM) cue before each scenario (e.g., roadside buildings) and had to press a button the steering wheel in response. A performance score was calculated by summing the number of correct responses. A higher total PM performance score indicates better PM.

Mental workload demand for each driving scenario was assessed using a subset of items from the NASA Task Load Index (TLX) Questionnaire. Participants rated their score on a 10-point Likert-like scale. Higher scores reflect a greater subjective mental workload.

3 Results

3.1 Driver Engagement

On average participants performed significantly better ($p > .001$) on the cone surprise scenario during manual driving ($M = 2.85$, $SD = .489$, $Min = 0$, $Max = 3$) compared to the ball scenario during AV mode ($M = 1.55$, $SD = 0.826$, $Min = 0$, $Max = 3$). Older drivers scored an average of 3 on the surprise event during manual driving and 1.73 on the surprise event during AV mode. Novice drivers scored an average of 2.67 on the surprise event during manual driving and 1.33 on the surprise event during AV mode.

3.2 Simulator Sickness

Reported simulator sickness symptoms were overall very low and did not significantly differ ($p = 0.159$) between manual and autonomous driving conditions. Table 2 below summarizes simulator sickness scores by driver group and driving condition. Although, two of the thirteen older drivers (15%) who were recruited to take part in the study did not complete the study in full due to simulator sickness.

Table 2. Simulator Sickness Score by Driver Group and Driving Condition

Driving Condition	Novice Drivers		Older Drivers		Total	
	M	SD	M	SD	M	SD
Manual	10.00	3.64	9.73	2.00	9.85	2.78
Autonomous	10.44	5.27	8.18	0.40	9.20	3.62

3.3 Cognitive Measures

There were no significant main or interaction effects of driving condition or age on situation awareness or prospective memory. The average self-reported mental workload was significantly greater ($p < .001$) for manual ($M = 95.95$, $SD = 24.10$) compared to autonomous ($M = 59.95$, $SD = 31.75$) driving conditions. Table 3 below summarizes findings for each cognitive measure by driver group and driving condition.

Table 3. Cognitive Results by Driver Group and Driving Condition

Dependent Variable	Driving Condition	Novice Drivers		Older Drivers		Total	
		M	SD	M	SD	M	SD
Situation Awareness	Manual	8.56	4.77	5.36	4.08	6.80	4.58
	Autonomous	8.56	7.03	6.91	3.59	7.65	5.32
Prospective Memory	Manual	16.33	2.16	16.88	2.15	16.67	1.59
	Autonomous	16.33	2.26	18.00	1.32	17.35	1.46
Mental Workload	Manual	97.00	20.80	95.01	64.09	95.95	24.10
	Autonomous	54.89	31.75	64.09	32.65	59.95	31.75

4 Discussion

The simulation protocol permitted the exploration of surprise events in both manual and autonomous driving conditions. The cone surprise (manual mode) was determined to be fairly simple to manage, and the task suffered from ceiling effects, where most participants (and all older drivers) responded with the highest score. The ball surprise (autonomous mode) was more difficult to manage and most participants did not avoid contacting the ball.

The two participants who dropped out due to simulator sickness were both older drivers, reflecting trends reported in previous research. However, the results of this study revealed lower dropouts due to simulator sickness compared to other research [10, 11, 15] indicating the effectiveness of the age-friendly display. It cannot be determined which specific elements of the age-friendly display were most influential. Future research should investigate specific adaptations to displays and protocols more closely. It is possible that certain adaptations, such as reduced realism, may have implications for participants perceptions of authenticity and immersion in driving simulators, which could conceivably influence engagement and responses to simulated events.

There were no significant main or interaction effects of driving condition or age group on situation awareness or prospective memory. Although older drivers did perform somewhat less accurately on the SA task, particularly in manual mode. Both novice and older drivers found manual driving significantly more mentally demanding than autonomous driving. The finding that autonomous driving reduces mental workload for drivers is in line with previous research using Level 2 vehicle autonomation [4]. Underload during autonomous driving may have influenced why many drivers were unable to successfully reclaim vehicle control and avoid the ball hazard.

5 Conclusion

To ensure the safe integration of vehicle technology and mitigate traffic safety risks, it is essential to understand the impact of vehicle automation on driver engagement, especially among at-risk populations such as novice and older drivers. By examining the effects of vehicle automation on driver cognition this research aimed to inform the development of appropriate strategies to mitigate risk and promote the safe and integration of vehicle technology for these vulnerable driver groups. The present work found that simulated vehicle automation reduced mental workload for both novice and older drivers. However, it was observed that drivers' performance declined when they encountered a surprise event in autonomous mode compared to manual driving.

This research employed driving simulation technology to investigate the effects of vehicle automation in a safe and controlled environment. Novice and aging drivers face unique challenges while driving and it is crucial to include these driver groups in research aimed at making driving safer and more accommodating for their specific needs. Consequently, it is highly important that simulator sickness among older participants be addressed so that they may participate in driving simulation research. The present work demonstrated potential benefits of tailored preventative measures in minimizing simulator sickness and reducing study dropouts. By combating simulator sickness through proactive measures, researchers can attempt to maintain an immersive and pleasant experience for participants and ensure older adults are not deterred from participating in research.

Acknowledgment. The work was supported by the Transport Canada Enhanced Road Safety Transfer Payment Program (ERSTPP). This work was also supported in part by the AGE-WELL NCE Inc. And the AGE-WELL National Innovation Hub Program. F. Knoefel acknowledges funding for the University of Ottawa Brain and Mind – Bruyère Research Institute Chair in Primary Health Care Dementia Research.

References

1. Almallah, M., Hussain, Q., Reinolsmann, N., Alhajyaseen, W.K.M.: Driving simulation sickness and the sense of presence: Correlation and contributing factors. Transport. Res. F: Traffic Psychol. Behav. **78**, 180–193 (2021). https://doi.org/10.1016/j.trf.2021.02.005
2. Brightman, K., et al.: Age-friendly protocol to support investigations of autonomous driving disengagement on driver Safety. In: Stephanidis, C., Antona, M., Ntoa, S. (eds.) HCI International 2022 Posters: 24th International Conference on Human-Computer Interaction, HCII 2022, Virtual Event, June 26 – July 1, 2022, Proceedings, Part IV, pp. 147–154. Springer International Publishing, Cham (2022). https://doi.org/10.1007/978-3-031-06394-7_21
3. Brooks, J.O., et al.: Simulator sickness during driving simulation studies. Accid. Anal. Prev. **42**(3), 788–796 (2010). https://doi.org/10.1016/j.aap.2009.04.013
4. Chen, W., Sawaragi, T., Horiguchi, Y.: Measurement of driver's mental workload in partial autonomous driving. IFAC-PapersOnLine **52**(19), 347–352 (2019). https://doi.org/10.1016/j.ifacol.2019.12.083
5. Cunningham, M.L., Regan, M.A.: Driver distraction and inattention in the realm of automated driving. IET Intel. Transport Syst. **12**(6), 407–413 (2018). https://doi.org/10.1049/iet-its.2017.0232
6. Davis, S., Nesbitt, K., Nalivaiko, E.: Comparing the onset of cybersickness using the Oculus Rift and two virtual roller coasters. Undefined (2015). https://www.semanticscholar.org/paper/Comparing-the-onset-of-cybersickness-using-the-Rift-Davis-Nesbitt/7300bdd5ad6abd25b6c6e9b5484e423f410a8630
7. Dużmańska, N., Strojny, P., Strojny, A.: Can simulator sickness be avoided? A review on temporal aspects of simulator sickness. Front. Psychol. **9**, 2132 (2018). https://www.frontiersin.org/article/10.3389/fpsyg.2018.02132

8. Edwards, J., Lunsman, M., Perkins, M., Rebok, G., Roth, D.: Driving cessation and health trajectories in older adults. J. Gerontol. B Psychol. Sci. Soc. Sci. **64**(12), 1290–1295 (2009)
9. Kennedy, R.S., Stanney, K.M., Dunlap, W.P.: Duration and exposure to virtual environments: sickness curves during and across sessions. Presence: Teleoperators Virtual Environ. **9**(5), 463–472 (2000). https://doi.org/10.1162/105474600566952
10. Keshavarz, B., Ramkhalawansingh, R., Haycock, B., Shahab, S., Campos, J.L.: Comparing simulator sickness in younger and older adults during simulated driving under different multisensory conditions. Transport. Res. F: Traffic Psychol. Behav. **54**, 47–62 (2018). https://doi.org/10.1016/j.trf.2018.01.007
11. Matas, N.A., Nettelbeck, T., Burns, N.R.: Dropout during a driving simulator study: a survival analysis. J. Safety Res. **55**, 159–169 (2015). https://doi.org/10.1016/j.jsr.2015.08.004
12. McKnight, A.J., McKnight, A.S.: Young novice drivers: careless or clueless? Accid. Anal. Prev. **35**(6), 921–925 (2003). https://doi.org/10.1016/S0001-4575(02)00100-8
13. Min, B.-C., Chung, S.-C., Min, Y.-K., Sakamoto, K.: Psychophysiological evaluation of simulator sickness evoked by a graphic simulator. Appl. Ergon. **35**(6), 549–556 (2004). https://doi.org/10.1016/j.apergo.2004.06.002
14. National Highway Traffic Safety Administration. Highway Accident Report: Collision Between a Car Operating With Automated Vehicle Control Systems and a Tractor-Semitrailer Truck Near Williston, Florida, May 7, 2016 (NTSB/HAR-17/02) (2017). https://trid.trb.org/view/1485316
15. Park, G.D., Allen, R.W., Fiorentino, D., Rosenthal, T.J., Cook, M.L.: Simulator sickness scores according to symptom susceptibility, age, and gender for an older driver assessment study. Proc. Hum. Factors Ergon. Soc. Ann. Meet. **50**(26), 2702–2706 (2006). https://doi.org/10.1177/154193120605002607

Designing a Hazard Taxonomy: A Key Step in Studying the Risk Perception of Aviation Maintenance Mechanics

Raphaël Chirac[1]([⊠]), Herimanana Zafiharimalala[1], Arturo Martinez-Gracida[2], Franck Cazaurang[3], and Jean-Marc Andre[3]

[1] Human Design Group, Toulouse, France
{raphael.chirac,herimanana.zafiharimalala}@humandesign.group
[2] Airbus SAS - IIOM Aircraft Maintenance Operations, Blagnac, France
arturo.martinez-gracida@airbus.com
[3] UMR CNRS 5218 Laboratoire, IMS - Intégration du Matériau au Système, Université de Bordeaux, Bordeaux, France
franck.cazaurang@u-bordeaux.fr, jean-marc.andre@ensc.fr

Abstract. As part of our research on the perception of risk by aircraft mechanics, our objective is to evaluate how they perceive risk when exposed to different types of hazards. For this purpose, we chose to construct a taxonomy of hazards which will allows us to: 1) Meet the requirements of the International Civil Aviation Organization (ICAO), which mentions the importance of identifying hazards before assessing risks [1]. This step is also crucial to address risk perception [2]. 2) Be able to study the impact of a hazard category on mechanics' risk perception.

First, two concepts must be distinguished: hazard and risk. Risk refers mainly to the probability and severity of consequences [3]. Hazard is a subjective property of an object or situation [4]. A hazard becomes a risk for the person who is exposed to it [5]. In our study, we consider the hazard as: "Anything that can injure the mechanic and/or damage the aircraft and is a result of the design of the aircraft, the GSEs and tools". This in order to be able, based on a literature review, to list the hazards, to select those that meet the definition, and finally to classify the hazards into categories and create a taxonomy.

Keywords: Aircraft maintenance · Hazard · Taxonomy

1 Hazard in Aircraft Maintenance

Before talking about risk, it is important to understand what is hazard and to make a distinction between the two concepts (hazard and risk) to avoid confusion. Hazard is a widely used concept that can be defined as a threat to those exposed to it [6]. It is an inherent characteristic of an object or situation [7] and exists independently of any interaction. Risk, on the other hand, refers to an uncertain event [8] that is directly related to the occurrence of negative consequences and the associated severity [3]. The distinction between hazard and risk can be explained by a cause-and-effect relationship.

© The Author(s), under exclusive license to Springer Nature Switzerland AG 2024
C. Stephanidis et al. (Eds.): HCII 2023, CCIS 1958, pp. 413–421, 2024.
https://doi.org/10.1007/978-3-031-49215-0_49

Specifically, there is a continuous shift from hazard to risk and both boundaries are difficult to identify. In other words, hazard is an intrinsic characteristic of an object, a situation that becomes a risk to the person through exposure to the hazard [5]. For example, fuel is a hazard because it has the characteristic of being "flammable". When a person is exposed to fuel, it becomes a risk because of the probability of a fire starting and the associated severity.

In aeronautics, a hazard is anything that can cause an incident or accident during flight operations [1]. In other words, a hazard is anything that can impact the airworthiness of the aircraft, which mainly concerns safety during flight operations [9, 10]. Zhang, Sun, Chen & Rong [11] indicate that regulatory agencies such as the Federal Aviation Agency (FAA) or the Civil Aviation Administration of China (CAAC) do not provide a clear and precise taxonomy of hazards. In the second edition of the Safety Management Manual (SMM), they present a breakdown into three categories: natural hazards, technical hazards, and economic hazards. However, the content of these three categories focuses on the consequences and not on the hazards. Thus, the authors propose a two-level classification: The first level represents the category in which the hazards can be grouped. For example, all the hazards that will be related to the "procedure". The second level allows to create subcategories, for example "Safety policy", "Procedure" and "Standard" in the "Procedure" category. The taxonomy presented by the authors allows to obtain a first vision of the categories of hazards to consider for the aeronautical domain in general.

Before discussing hazards in aviation maintenance, let's look at what exists in the literature. For example, Chen, Golparvar-Fard & Kleiner [12] provide a summary table of the types of hazards associated with energy sources in the construction field. This classification can help in the identification of hazards in aviation maintenance. For example, mechanics are exposed to chemicals under pressure. The aircraft is also composed of electrical components, and may emit radiation, sound or high temperatures. Basu [13] proposes a list of the most common hazards, the category to which they belong and the effects/impacts that correspond to the potential consequences. This allows a more precise representation with, for example, an "electrical" dimension composed of the hazards "potential energy release, arc, electric shock" where Chen, Golparvar-Fard & Kleiner [12] speak only of "electrical" hazards. Rausand & Haugen [14] also propose a categorization of the various hazards which allows other hazards such as "sharp edges" to be highlighted. It should be noted that the authors place certain specific categories such as "noise risks" on the same level as more global categories such as "organizational risks". We can also cite the list established by the Institut National de Recherche et de Sécurité (INRS) which provides examples of hazards such as "gases under pressure", "flammable liquids" and a categorization corresponding to "physical hazards", "health hazards" and "environmental hazards" [7]. However, some hazards refer more to consequences such as "eye injury".

In aeronautical maintenance, from our knowledge, few literatures deal with the hazards related to this field and propose a taxonomy. The most developed literature identified is that of Necula & Zaharia [15] who propose a classification into four categories of hazards: "the individual level", "the maintenance task level", "the environmental level" and "the organizational level". For each category, the authors establish a list of hazards to be considered. Nevertheless, even if the proposed classification is interesting because it seems to consider a more elaborate and broad representation of hazards in the field of aeronautical maintenance, some hazards cited by Yazgan, Ozkan & Ulutas [16] such as the presence of pneumatic and vibrating tools, and the presence of dust are absent. Yiannakides & Sergiou p70 [17] also propose a list of the most common hazards in aeronautical maintenance considering both the impact on health and safety and the airworthiness of the aircraft. These include "Electrical sources", "Flammable materials", "Slippery floor", "Working at height", "Confined space", "Inappropriate or lack of light", "Environmental climate", "Vibrating tools", "Heavy objects", "Noise", "Moving vehicle", "Dangerous area of the aircraft", "Damage caused by foreign objects".

The literature search provides a relevant basis for the creation of a taxonomy. Nevertheless, there are many hazards that can fluctuate depending on the location of the maintenance, the organizational and cultural context, etc. Thus, it will be necessary to specify the definition of the hazard in order to meet the needs of the study which is the creation of a taxonomy sufficiently representative of the maintenance activity. The definition will have to consider the hazard from the point of view of the mechanic and underline the impact of the design of the aircraft, Ground Support Equipment (GSE) and tools on the maintenance activity.

2   Methodology

The first step is to establish a hazard definition that must consider: 1) The potential impacts on both the health and safety of the mechanics and the airworthiness of the aircraft; and 2) The hazard resulting from a decision in the design of the aircraft, GSE, and tools. The next step is to develop a list of hazards that meet the definition. Specifically, to be selected, the hazards had to answer "yes" to the following question: "Does this hazard come from a design office decision?". After selecting the hazards, the objective is to gather them and create categories. To do this, many iterations were performed, and five versions of the taxonomy were created before reaching a satisfactory result. These iterations consisted in the setting up of working sessions allowing, based on the literature, to adjust the taxonomy as the reflections progressed. In order to judge the completeness of our work, we considered the following points: 1) All the hazards present meet the definition; 2) We are no longer able to identify new hazards that meet the definition; 3) All the hazards are linked to one and only one category. In addition, we relied on the recommendations provided by Szopinski [18] who states that it is important to: 1) define the scope of the taxonomy evaluation by knowing why/for whom it is designed and what is going to be evaluated; 2) to be able to assess its level of completeness in the field of study, having defined the framework of the taxonomy content for example; 3) to evaluate the taxonomy on 5 criteria which are " being concise (e.g., taxonomy has seven plus/minus two dimensions), robust (e.g., when it can differentiate among objects), comprehensive (e.g., when all relevant objects can be described), extendible (e.g., when new dimensions or characteristics can be added), and/or explanatory (e.g., when it can explain objects)".

3   Results

3.1   Hazard Definition in Aircraft Maintenance

Defining the hazard allows us to establish a study framework with the aim of creating a taxonomy representative of the aviation maintenance activity. Thus, considering the hazard from the point of view of the mechanic implies considering the impact on both the health and safety of professionals and the airworthiness of the aircraft. Furthermore, we wish to focus our research on hazards that are derived from the design of aircraft, GSE and tools for two reasons: 1) Hazards derived from design do not vary or vary only slightly depending on the location of the maintenance. Indeed, a toxic product, a protruding edge or a moving part will always be so, regardless of the country or structure in which the maintenance is performed. 2) Mechanics are exposed to hazards that are the result of decisions made during the design phase of the element with which they interact and/or are in contact during their activity. For this, we choose to consider only hazards as "Anything that can injure the mechanic and/or damage the aircraft and is a result of the design of the aircraft, the GSEs and tools".

3.2   Hazards Selection

Thirty-three (33) hazards were identified as meeting the full definition. Of these hazards, 32 have an impact on the health and safety of the mechanics and 26 hazards have an impact on the airworthiness of the aircraft. In order to clarify each hazard, we have added a column entitled "Definitions" (Table 1).

Table 1. Extract from the hazard selection table (6 examples among 33 identified)

Hazard	Definition	Impact on Health & Safety?	Impact on Airworthiness Safety?	Is coming from a design office decision?
Unbalanced aircraft	Aircraft mass balance is not distributed as required	yes	yes	yes
Slippery floor, hole presence, not smooth floor	Floor characteristics of the aircraft	yes	no	yes
Hermetic/confined area	All areas which can host someone but only punctually and without enough air renewal	yes	yes	yes

(continued)

Table 1. (*continued*)

Hazard	Definition	Impact on Health & Safety?	Impact on Airworthiness Safety?	Is coming from a design office decision?
Electrostatically charge	Anything that can be electrostatically charged	yes	yes	yes
Bad Visual/Physical accessibility	Any configuration which is not (or is not easily) accessible visually and/or physically	yes	yes	yes
Sharp	Anything sharp	yes	yes	yes

Nevertheless, there are some hazards that we wish to consider in our study although they do not directly meet the definition of hazard that we have established. Indeed, the hazards "wind", "ambient humidity" and "ambient temperature" are related to weather conditions and do not come from a decision during the design of the aircraft. However, because they are the subject of warnings and/or cautions in the work cards, this means that they have been identified as hazards by the design office. Thus, because they were identified as a potential threat to the aircraft and/or mechanics during the design phase, we decided to include them in our hazard taxonomy.

3.3 Hazards Taxonomy

Our taxonomy is divided into four categories, "Structure," "System," "Chemical," and "Environment" (Table 2). "Structure" and "System" represent hazards that are intrinsic characteristics of the aircraft structure or system, tools, and GSE. They correspond to the breakdown that can be found in the chapters of ATA 100 (document written by A4A for Airlines For America). Hazards arising from structural features of the aircraft such as protruding edges, large objects, etc. are considered structural elements. Hazards arising from hydraulic and electrical systems on the aircraft, such as pressurized liquids, are included in the "System characteristics" category.

Chemicals are a separate category of aviation maintenance activities and are not only included in aircraft systems. Indeed, "consumables" are also present in containers, tools, GSE before being disposed on or in systems. The "environment" category allows for the inclusion of all hazards that are not an intrinsic characteristic of the aircraft, GSE, tools. This category represents all environmental hazards that have been identified by the design office and are subject to warnings and cautions.

Let us take up the criteria listed by Szopinski [18] to evaluate our taxonomy. According to the author, the taxonomy should be concise and consist of only seven plus or minus two dimensions. Our taxonomy is composed of four dimensions which is below the minimum proposed by the author. Nevertheless, the author does not mention the reason for this number. Thus, from our point of view, the limit defined by Szopinski [18] will not

Table 2. Taxonomy of hazards in aviation maintenance

Categories	Hazards
Structural characteristics	Unbalanced aircraft
	Slippery floor, hole presence, not smooth floor
	Hermetic/confined area
	Electrostatically charged
	Bad Visual/Physical accessibility
	Height
	Electrostatically charged
	Height
	Sharp
	Mobile
	Protruding edge
	mobile/rotating part
	Voluminous
	Small
	Heavy
System characteristics	Poor artificial lighting
	Strong artificial lighting
	different configuration system
	high voltage with continuous courant
	Under pressure liquid/air
	Operating temperature system, air, liquid
	Noise
	Radiation
	Vibration
	Magnetic field
Chemical product characteristics	Toxic liquid/solid/gas
	Oxiding liquid/solid/gas
	Flammable liquid/solid/gas
	Corrosive liquid
	Explosive liquid/solid/gas
	Radioactive liquid/solid/gas
Environment characteristics	Winds

(*continued*)

Table 2. (*continued*)

Categories	Hazards
	Overcrowd
	Local humidity
	Local temperature

impact the applicability and quality of the proposed taxonomy. The taxonomy appears to us to be robust because it allows us to differentiate the categories between them. The completeness of the taxonomy is ensured by describing each dimension and defining each factor. The taxonomy can be extended if needed and other hazards can be added. Finally, the categories appear sufficiently affording to explain their content.

4 Discussion

The identification and realization of a taxonomy of hazards in aviation maintenance is a complex task, especially because many hazards fluctuate during the maintenance activity depending on different parameters: the location of the maintenance organization, national regulations, company culture, individuals, etc. Nevertheless, some hazards may be common to all maintenance organizations because they originate from the characteristics of the aircraft, GSE or the tools. Moreover, the consideration of these hazards allows to put forward the impact of the design offices, and thus the design, on the maintenance activity. Indeed, during the design phase of the aircraft in particular, engineers rely themselves on ergonomic standards to consider the impact of a design on the activity and more precisely on the health and safety of mechanics. Concerning the airworthiness of the aircraft, the engineers also consider standards that allow them to meet the requirements of the CS-25 written by the EASA [19]. This regulation mentions all the points that an aircraft must meet in order to be airworthy when it leaves the factory. Thus, the two notions of safety (health and safety and airworthiness safety) are supposed to be considered during the design phase. However, from our knowledge, there is no study that allows us to identify the way in which mechanics perceive the risks for the two notions of safety when exposed to hazards that have been created or identified during the design phase. In this sense, we have chosen to consider hazards that are not the direct result of a design decision, for example "wind", "local humidity" and "local temperature".

The hazards included in the taxonomy had to meet the definition chosen is "Anything that can injure the mechanic and/or damage the aircraft and is derived from the design of the aircraft, GSE and tools". This allowed us to narrow the scope of the study and to have a criterion evaluating the level of completeness of the taxonomy [18]. Nevertheless, the definition we propose does not consider the diversity of hazards faced by mechanics as Necula & Zaharia [15] have done. This choice allows us to focus the study on the hazards resulting from a decision of the design office and to measure the impact on the mechanics' perception of risks. Moreover, in order to evaluate the impact of the type of hazard on the perception of risk, it is important to focus on hazards that are present regardless of the social, environmental, or individual context. Indeed, these dimensions will be considered as factors that have an influence on risk perception. In order to verify the completeness of the taxonomy, a validation step with mechanics and engineers will be performed.

The results indicate that the consequences related to the exposure to a design-related hazard have a greater impact on the health and safety of mechanics (32 hazards are concerned) than on the airworthiness of the aircraft (26 hazards are concerned). The reason could be because we consider mainly hazards resulting from the design and which are therefore intrinsic characteristics of the aircraft, the GSE and the tools. Indeed, we may think that elements being characteristics of the aircraft cannot damage it because it is designed to work with it. For example, chemicals that could cause damage are contained in appropriate systems designed to resist possible leakage and protect the aircraft. However, not all parts of the aircraft have these specific protections and can be damaged if they encounter the hazardous materials. The differentiation of the two levels of safety at this stage is crucial because it allows to obtain a first vision of the distribution of the dangers according to their impact.

The creation of the hazard taxonomy is the first step before assessing the risk perception of mechanics. Our constraint is to create a taxonomy that can be understood and used by both mechanics and engineers, which can represent a real challenge. For this, we have chosen to create categories by ATA because these are groupings known by both populations. For example, the term "Structure" and "System" are supposed to be sufficiently affording for mechanics and engineers. Nevertheless, since the categorization is based on our own mental representation, it will be necessary to verify the validity of our work with mechanics and engineers.

5 Conclusion

The taxonomy that we present here is the result of a collaborative and iterative work that led us to propose a version that we consider sufficiently complete and mature. Nevertheless, it is now necessary to test the usability by engineers and mechanics and the applicability of the taxonomy to the domain of aeronautical maintenance [18]. Moreover, it is necessary to verify that the taxonomy is exhaustive and representative of the hazards to which mechanics are exposed. To do this, a validation step will be carried out with mechanics and engineers in the design office.

References

1. ICAO. Safety Management Manual (2018)
2. Pandit, B., Albert, A., Patil, Y., Al-Bayati, A.J.: Impact of safety climate on hazard recognition and safety risk perception. Saf. Sci. **113**, 44–53 (2019). https://doi.org/10.1016/j.ssci.2018.11.020
3. Nyre, Å.A., Jaatun, M.G.: Seeking risks: towards a quantitative risk perception measure. In: Cuzzocrea, A., Kittl, C., Simos, D.E., Weippl, E., Lida, X. (eds.) Availability, Reliability, and Security in Information Systems and HCI, pp. 256–271. Springer Berlin Heidelberg, Berlin, Heidelberg (2013). https://doi.org/10.1007/978-3-642-40511-2_18

4. Różycki, M.: Paradigms of Risk, Hazards and Danger. In: Perspectives on Risk, Assessment and Management Paradigms (2019). https://doi.org/10.5772/intechopen.80822
5. Wilson, R.S., Zwickle, A., Walpole, H.: Developing a broadly applicable measure of risk perception. Risk Anal. **39**(4), 777–791 (2019). https://doi.org/10.1111/risa.13207
6. Slovic, P., Fischhoff, B., Lichenstein, S.: Characterizing Perceived Risk. ERN: Uncertainty & Risk Modeling (1985)
7. Évaluation des risques professionnels. Évaluation des risques professionnels - Démarches deprévention -INRS (2022). https://www.inrs.fr/demarche/evaluation-risques-professio nnels/ce-qu-il-faut-retenir.html
8. Aven, T.: Risk assessment and risk management: review of recent advances on their foundation. Eur. J. Oper. Res. **253**(1), 1–13 (2016). https://doi.org/10.1016/j.ejor.2015.12.023
9. EASA: Part-M maintenance: continuing airworthiness requirements. Part M Generall Course **2042**, 1–193 (2009)
10. EASA. User Guide Foreign Part 145 approvals User Guide for Maintenance Organisation Exposition (2020)
11. Zhang, Y., Sun, Y., Chen, Y., Rong, M.: Hazards taxonomy and identification methods in civil aviation risk management. In: Yamamoto, S. (ed.) Human Interface and the Management of Information: Supporting Learning, Decision-Making and Collaboration: 19th International Conference, HCI International 2017, Vancouver, BC, Canada, July 9–14, 2017, Proceedings, Part II, pp. 288–301. Springer International Publishing, Cham (2017). https://doi.org/10.1007/978-3-319-58524-6_24
12. Chen, A., Golparvar-Fard, M., Kleiner, B.: Design and development of SAVES: a construction safety training augmented virtuality environment for hazard recognition and severity identi-fication. In: Computing in Civil Engineering - Proceedings of the 2013 ASCE International Workshop on Computing in Civil Engineering (2013). https://doi.org/10.1061/978078441302 9.105
13. Basu, S.: Qualitative hazard analysis. In: Plant Hazard Analysis and Safety Instrumentation Systems (2017). https://doi.org/10.1016/b978-0-12-803763-8.00003-0
14. Rausand, M., Haugen, S.: Risk Assessment: Theory, Methods, and Applications. Wiley (2020)
15. Necula, F., Zaharia, S.-E.: Capturing hazards and eradicating human errors in aircraft main-tenance. Rev. Air Force Acad. **13**(3), 155–160 (2015). https://doi.org/10.19062/1842-9238.2015.13.3.27
16. Yazgan, E., Ozkan, N.F., Ulutas, B.H.: A questionnaire-based musculoskeletal disorder assess-ment for aircraft maintenance technicians. Aircr. Eng. Aerosp. Technol. **94**(2), 240–247 (2022). https://doi.org/10.1108/AEAT-03-2021-0076
17. Yiannakides, D., Sergiou, C.: Human Factors in Aircraft Maintenance (1re éd.). CRC Press (2019)
18. Szopinski, D., Schoormann, T., Kundisch, D.: Criteria as a prelude for guiding taxonomy evaluation. In: Proceedings of the 53rd Hawaii International Conference on System Sciences, Ed. (2020)
19. EASA. CS-25_Amdt 3_19.09.07_Consolidated version (2007)

HMI Interfaces of Unmanned Automated Taxi Services: What Is Essential Information?

Bogyu Choi[1] , Wonjun Seo[1] , and Ji Hyun Yang[2](✉)

[1] Graduate School of Automotive Engineering, Kookmin University, Seoul 02707, Republic of Korea
[2] Department of Automotive Engineering, Kookmin University, Seoul 02707, Republic of Korea
yangjh@kookmin.ac.kr

Abstract. At SAE Level 4, the Automated Driving System (ADS) handles all driving tasks, including emergencies, within a defined Operational Design Domain. This shift in driving responsibility has enabled the development of Unmanned Automated Taxi (UAT) services that can operate without a human driver. Since UAT services rely on system-user interactions, the role of the Human-Machine Interface (HMI) is crucial to improve the user experience. Therefore, this study aims to derive the mobile phone HMI (Human-Machine Interaction) interface for improving the UAT user experience by creating use cases in UAT services and proposing mobile phone User Interface (UI) examples. First, we created the user interaction use cases in the seven stages of the UAT service user journey (Lim and Hwangbo, 2021). And we categorized the information that can be provided in each use case based on the In-Vehicle-Information (IVI) classification criteria (Choi, 2017). A UAT mobile phone UI example was designed using the classified information. These use cases and UI examples can be utilized for future HMI interface research to improve UAT user reliability and satisfaction. In future studies, we plan to evaluate the effectiveness of the proposed UI using vehicle simulator-based experiments.

Keywords: User Journey · User Interface · Unmanned Automated Taxi

1 Introduction

1.1 Automated Driving Technology and Unmanned Taxi Service

SAE Level 4 ADS (Automated Driving System) is capable of handling various driving tasks, including emergencies, within the designated ODD (Operational Design Domain) [1] (Table 1). This signifies that a human driver is no longer required for vehicles equipped with Level 4 ADS. This shift in driving dynamics has paved the way for the emergence of Unmanned Automated Taxi (UAT) services that can operate autonomously, without the need for a human driver.

The UATs currently being tested in service include Waymo One by Waymo, IONIQ5 Robotaxi by Motional, and the automated driving taxi by Zoox. Waymo One offers an automated taxi service in Phoenix, San Francisco, and LA. Level 4 automated driving,

© The Author(s), under exclusive license to Springer Nature Switzerland AG 2024
C. Stephanidis et al. (Eds.): HCII 2023, CCIS 1958, pp. 422–430, 2024.
https://doi.org/10.1007/978-3-031-49215-0_50

Table 1. Comparison of ADS-human roles for each level of SAE automated driving

Category		Automated Driving		
		level 3	level 4	level 5
Name		Conditionally Automated Driving	Highly Automated Driving	Fully Automated Driving
DDT	Human	Should be prepared to takeover driving at the request of ADS	No need to operate DDT within limited ODD	ADS operates the entire DDT and DDT fallback within unlimited ODD
	ADS	Operate the entire DDT within limited ODD		
DDT Fallback	Human	Fallback-ready user drives the vehicle during fallback	No need to operate DDT fallback	
	ADS	When DDT fallback is required, user with a request to intervene, and then take over control at the appropriate time	ADS operates fallback and achieves MRC	
ODD		limited		unlimited

which responds to all kinds of situations, is possible in the service areas [2]. When unanticipated operations or conditions occur during driving, Waymo One attempts to respond. When it is difficult for the system to respond on its own, it was designed to avoid accidents through remote control by a human driver [3]. Motional is preparing to commercialize an UAT service based on IONIQ5 made by Hyundai [4]. IONIQ5 Robotaxi can also perform all kinds of driving tasks in the service area without a human driver. In unusual situations during driving, it stops in a safe area or can connect to the remote vehicle assistance [5]. Zoox is also being tested as a commuter shuttle for Zoox executives in Poster City, California [6]. The Zoox Robotaxis, built without pedals or driving wheels, do not need the intervention by passengers on all situations occurring during driving. When the Robotaxis encounter uncertain or unknown situations, they come to a safe stop [7].

1.2 UAT and User Experiences

In a UAT service, there is no human driver present in the vehicle to interact with the passenger. Consequently, the role of system-user interaction becomes crucial as the user engages with the UAT through communication with the system. For example, Waymo One service application was designed in such a way that the user can experience seamlessly through the application the entire process of the service. Especially, the UI was designed in order for users to make emergency calls using their mobile phones or to send messages in a situation when help is needed [2].

Due to the lack of general guidelines in HMI designs, however, companies provide different UIs. The UI designs, that are not standardized, make it difficult for users to understand the intentions of UIs, interfere with users in understanding how the system works and how to operate the system. Such designs become the factors hindering the users' experience [8]. In this study, therefore, the optimum HMI interface is derived in order to improve the service use experience of UAT service, and mobile phone UI guidelines are presented to standardize UAT services.

2   Derivation of UAT Service Use Case

2.1   Analysis of Manned Taxi User Journey– Uber

What Is Uber?. Uber is a taxi calling service available in seventy countries in the world [9]. Uber changed the taxi industry by making it possible to call a taxi to any desired location on a mobile application. Because the service use can be done with application, Uber has a user journey like the UAT service in terms of the system-user interaction.

User Journey of Uber. Uber presents the method of using its application by dividing it into five stages, and users can use all services through the mobile application [10].

(1) A Rider Opens the App. The user begins by opening the Uber app and entering their desired destination. Following that, the user has the option to select various preferences such as vehicle type, fare, and more.

(2) The Rider is Matched with a Driver. When a car is dispatched according to the options the user selected, the user waits for the vehicle at the departure point, and the dispatched driver moves to the departure point.

(3) The Driver Picks Up the Rider. When the driver arrives at the location of the user, the user identifies the called taxi. After identification, the user gets on the taxi. The driver also identifies the user based on the information provided by the application and starts driving.

(4) The Driver Takes the Rider to the Destination. While the driver is driving, the user gets on the taxi, and is provided with a moving service to the destination.

(5) The Driver and Rider Leave Ratings and Reviews. When the vehicle arrives at the destination, the user can evaluate the service as soon as he/she gets off the vehicle.

2.2   Six Stages of the UAT User Journey (Lim and Hwangbo, 2021)

Kim et al. (2019) made up five stages of UAT user journey: (1) calling a taxi, (2) pick up, (3) travelling, (4) drop off, and (5) arranging for the next service [11]. Lim and Hwangbo (2021) classified the five stages [11] into five normal phases and included system abnormalities as an additional unexpected failure case [12] (Fig. 1).

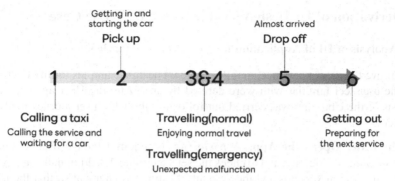

Fig. 1. Six Stage of UAT service user journey (Data derived from Lim and Hwangbo. AHFE 2021; 275; 977. [11])

2.3   Derivation of UAT User-System Interaction Use Case

Because this study focuses on the UAT service, use cases were derived using the six stages of UAT service user journey [12] to explain the scenarios generated.

(1) Calling a Taxi. The user carries out first the process of opening the UAT service app and inputting the destination. Through inputting the destination, the user checks the driving route from the departure point to the destination, the estimated travel time, and the estimated amount of payment and payment method. At this moment, identification of the taxi is made between the system and the user in the case of UAT, unlike the case of manned taxi.

(2) Pick Up. After the user gets on the taxi through the process of identifying the taxi, the UAT service should allow the user to use the process of starting the vehicle. Especially, because there is no driver, a process to check if the seatbelt is worn and fastened is needed before departure. The UAT can start driving the vehicle once the seatbelt is checked, or the user can ask the UAT to drive the vehicle after wearing the seatbelt.

(3) Travelling (Normal). The user begins to experience driving without the duty of driving once the vehicle starts moving. Thus, the user can engage in various activities other than driving. At this time, the user can watch videos or listen to music on the mobile phone. If the user wants, he/she can also use the UAT service application.

(4) Travelling (in Emergency). When the UAT encounters an abnormal situation during driving, the UAT takes appropriate. Thus, because the user does not have to take any actions on the abnormal situation, he/she can engage in various activities as in a general driving situation.

(5) Drop Off. The user prepares to get off the vehicle as the vehicle approaches the destination. During this process, the user may try to unfasten the seat belt or end the contents that he/she watched or listened to.

(6) Getting Off. When the vehicle arrives at the destination, the user removes the seat belt and gets off the vehicle. The user may evaluate the use of the service for this time. If the user leaves an item in the vehicle, the user can find the lost item in the application.

3   Derivation of UI Design Examples for UAT Use Case

3.1   Analysis of UI of Application for Manned Taxi Service

To improve the user experience, mobile phone UI design examples for the UAT service that the user feel familiar with were derived by analyzing the Uber app [9, 11]. The analysis of the Uber app was carried out following the Uber user journey analyzed in Chapter 2.

(1) The Rider Opens the App. A navigation is required for the user to select the departure point, destination and to check the selected route. In addition, the app provides the information on vehicles and the amount of estimated payment so that the user can select the options.

(2) The Rider is Matched with a Driver. When dispatching is completed according to the options that the user selected, the user can check in the application the information on the vehicle and the driver. In case the user wants, a button is activated so that the user can call or send messages to the driver.

(3) The Driver Picks Up the Rider. As the driver arrives at the location of the user, the Uber application provides a notification of the expected arrival. Also provided are the current location of the vehicle and the expected driving time to the departure point.

(4) The Driver Takes the Rider to the Destination. While the driver is driving the vehicle, the user is provided with the current location of the vehicle, ongoing route, and the expected arrival time in the application.

(5) The Rider Leave Ratings and Reviews. When the vehicle arrives at the destination, the user can leave a review on the driving and evaluate the service upon getting off the vehicle.

3.2   Structuring the Information Provided for UI Design

Norman's Principle for Visibility. The visibility principle dictates that when information is provided to the user using a limited screen, caution should be exercised not to provide unnecessary information that can confuse the user [13]. This study proposes a UI design that provides information according to the Norman's visibility principle.

In-Vehicle-Information (IVI) Classification Criteria (Choi, 2017). Choi (2017) classified the information in the vehicle according to its functions, which are related or not related to driving [8] (Table 2). The information was structured by the classification method by Choi (2017) to select the information to be provided to the users in the vehicle who do not drive.

3.3   UI Design Examples for Each UAT Service Use Case

In this study, mobile phone UI design examples were derived by selecting the major information to be provided in each use case on the basis of the expected actions that

Table 2. Classification of information factors according to the functions of information (Data from Choi. 2017;45. [8])

Category	Information factors
Driving information	Information that changes as the car is driven through the car's ECU Speedometer, Tachometer, Fuel gauge, Trip distance, Drivable distance, Gear position etc
Vehicle Warning information	Information provided when a hardware or software failure, shortage, anomaly, or error occurs while the vehicle is in motion Seat belt warning light, Airbag warning light, Engine warning light, Oil pressure gauge, Battery ampere meter, Break system malfunction warning sign, Emergency warning signal light, Fuel gauge, etc
Comfortability information	Information about the various add-ons that help you drive Headlight, High Beam, Parking Lamps, Rear Fog Lamp, Turn Signal, Air-conditioning, Seat adjustment, Door adjustment, etc
Pleasure information	Information about features that don't directly affect driving but are used for driving pleasure Navigation, Telephone, Radio, AUX, CD, USB, DVD, Internet connection, etc

users carry out. Use cases, information to be provided, and the purposes of provision are organized in Fig. 2.

The major information selected in Fig. 2 was visualized as the UI design examples according to the user journey in Fig. 3. For visualization, the arrangement of information and the size of areas where the information is arranged were decided by referring to the UI design of Uber mobile application. A separate start ride button was provided in order for the user to be able to engage in driving in Pick up stage in Fig. 3. The manned taxi scenario, in which start driving can be decided through the communication with the driver, was implemented also in the UAT service. Thus, the user can experience more subjectively by allowing the user to start driving when he/she wants after wearing the seat belt.

Calling a taxi - User selects departure point, destination, vehicle type, and payment method		
Classification	Driving information	Pleasure information
Information provided	Trip distance, driving time	Navigation, Taxi/payment info
Purpose of provision	Notify the driving information to be provided	Select service options
Pick up - User wears safety belt and select 'start driving		
Classification	Driving information	Pleasure information	Comfortability information
Information provided	Driving distance/time/speed, gear position	Navigation	Air-conditioning/seat adjustment buttons, safety belt status
Purpose of provision	Notify the current driving information	Notify the current driving information	Maintain safety while driving and operate the devices in the vehicle
Traveling(normal) - User is engaged in free activities		
Classification	Driving information	Pleasure information	Comfortability information
Information provided	Driving distance/time/speed, gear position	Go to Navigation	Air-conditioning/seat adjustment buttons, safety belt status
Purpose of provision	Notify the current driving information	Select to confirm the current driving information	Maintain safety while driving and operate the devices in the vehicle
Traveling(emergency) - User is engaged in free activities as in general driving situations		
Classification	Vehicle Warning information	Pleasure information
Information provided	Warning information	Provide information on unnormal situation occurred while driving
Purpose of provision	Call	Request for help in an emergency
Drop off - User ends the activities during driving and prepares to get off the vehicle		
Classification	Driving information	Pleasure information	Comfortability information
Information provided	Driving distance/time/speed, gear position	Navigation, summary of journey	Air-conditioning/seat adjustment buttons, safety belt status
Purpose of provision	Notify the current driving information	Notify the current driving information and the provided driven information	Maintain safety while driving and operate the devices in the vehicle
Getting out - User gets off the vehicle and evaluate the service use		
Classification	Pleasure information	
Information provided	Rating journey, lost and found	
Purpose of provision	Evaluate the driving provided	

Fig. 2. Provided information for each use case

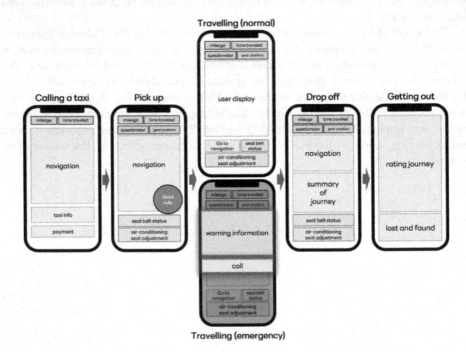

Fig. 3. Mobile phone UI design examples for each user journey

4   Discussions and Conclusion

In this study, in order to improve the user experience of the UAT service, mobile phone UI designs were presented to provide necessary information. In Chapter 2, six use cases in the UAT service were derived by analyzing both manned taxi and UAT user journey. In Chapter 3, the information that users need in the six use cases was sorted out, and mobile phone UI design examples were specified and proposed. The system-user interaction use cases derived in this study could be utilized to improve the service on the user side in UAT service. In addition, the mobile phone UI examples proposed in this study could be used in the studies of HMI interface in future and be expected to contribute to increase the service reliability and the degree of satisfaction of the UAT service users.

This study is meaningful in proposing a basis for new service design in that mobile phone UI design examples were derived for improving the user experience of the UAT service. However, the result for the mobile app UI design came from the analysis of the UI of Uber only. Thus, the basis including the cases of various service apps could not be proposed. Moreover, because this study was conducted based on literature studies, there is a limitation that the usability was not verified by the actual users. Therefore, in future studies, standardized UI design directions will be proposed by analyzing various taxi call service apps. The UI design derived from the simulator-based experiment will be evaluated from the viewpoints of users.

Acknowledgment. This study was supported by the Technology Innovation Program (20018101, development on Automated driving with perceptual prediction based on T-Car/vehicle parts to intelligent control/system integration for assessment), funded by the Ministry of Trade, Industry & Energy (MOTIE, Korea), Basic Science Research Program of the National Research Foundation of Korea (No. 2021R1A2C1005433), and BK21 program through the National Research Foundation of Korea (NRF), funded by the Ministry of Education (5199990814084) and the Korea Institute for Advancement of Technology (KIAT) grant funded by the Korea Government (MOTIE) (P0017120, Competency Development Program for Industry Specialist). The authors thank Sara Hong, Changsu Kim for supporting manuscript editing.

References

1. SAE On-road Automated Vehicle Standards Committee: Taxonomy and Definitions for Terms Related to On-road Motor Vehicle Automated Driving Systems (2021)
2. Waymo Homepage. https://waymo.com/waymo-one/. Accessed 16 Jul 2023
3. California Department of Motor Vehicles.: Disengagement Reports (2021)
4. Motional Homepage. https://motional.com/news/motionals-ceo-2023-going-driverless-and-staying-motivated-after-20-years. Accessed 15 Jul 2023
5. Motional Homepage. https://motional.com/news/driverlessed-chapter-6-during-your-ioniq-5-robotaxi-ride. Accessed 15 Jul 2023
6. Zoox Homepage. https://zoox.com/press/. Accessed 15 Jul 2023
7. Zoox: SAFETY INNOVATION AT ZOOX: Setting the Bar for Safety in Autonomous Mobility (2018)
8. Choi, B.: A Research of Information Structure and Information Layout in Vehicle Display based on Information Property (doctoral dissertation). The Graduate School Ewha Womans University, Seoul (2017)

9. Uber Homepage. https://www.uber.com/kr/en/about/?uclick_id=55337eb1-18e5-499f-8fa5-9843d0e815c1. Accessed 16 Jul 2023

10. Uber Homepage. https://www.uber.com/kr/en/about/how-does-uber-work/?uclick_id=553 37eb1-18e5-499f-8fa5-9843d0e815c1. Accessed 15 Jul 2023

11. Kim, S., Chang, J., Kim, J., Kang, N.: Autonomous taxi service design and user experience. Int. J. Hum. –Comput. Interact. **36**(5), 429–448 (2019)

12. Lim, D., Hwangbo, H.: UX design for holistic user journey of future robotaxi. In: Ahram, T.Z., Falcão, C.S. (eds.) AHFE 2021. LNNS, vol. 275, pp. 976–984. Springer, Cham (2021). https://doi.org/10.1007/978-3-030-80091-8_116

13. Educative homepage. https://www.educative.io/answers/what-are-normans-design-princi ples. Accessed 16 Jul 2023

Exploring the Driver's Mental Control Model: Concepts and Insights

Sara Hong[1] and Ji Hyun Yang[2]

[1] Graduate School of Automotive Engineering, Kookmin University, Seoul 02707, Republic of Korea
[2] Department of Automotive Engineering, Kookmin University, Seoul 02707, Republic of Korea
yangjh@kookmin.ac.kr

Abstract. This study aims to develop a comprehensive model that accurately represents the perceptual system of drivers and provides insights into their behavior. Existing models, namely the Skill-Rule-Knowledge model and the dynamic driving task model, were integrated. This integrated model successfully elucidates the sequential processes involved in sensation reception, recognition, judgment, and control. Furthermore, the study investigates the drivers' behavior during takeover situations. Specifically, the model's sequence was determined by considering two distinct scenarios: unplanned operational design domain (ODD) exit resulting from automated driving system (ADS) failure and planned ODD exit during highway driving. Empirical data was gathered using a simulator with 36 participants in the ADS failure situation and 40 participants in the highway exit situation. Two takeover situations were compared based on drivers' perception time and perception-reaction time. The results revealed that both the perception time and perception-reaction time were significantly longer in the highway exit situation compared to the ADS failure situation. These findings have important implications for understanding the differences in drivers' cognitive processes and reaction times in varying driving contexts. It is worth noting that this model will undergo further refinement, validation, and application to other features of ADS or different driving scenarios in future research.

Keywords: Driver Model · Driver Behavior · Takeover

1 Introduction

While driving, drivers make decisions and select strategies for various situations, such as maintaining and changing lanes, or responding to hazardous situations. A human model could be a useful tool for explaining the perception and decision-making processes of drivers. Wickens (1974) compared the perception process with the process of computer information processing [1]. Thereafter, studies to express the mentality or behavior of humans quantitatively have been conducted [e.g., 2–4]. The studies were applied in driving contexts since, and a model explaining hierarchically the driving tasks was developed [5]. The driver model, that can explain the behavior of drivers, was used to

© The Author(s), under exclusive license to Springer Nature Switzerland AG 2024
C. Stephanidis et al. (Eds.): HCII 2023, CCIS 1958, pp. 431–437, 2024.
https://doi.org/10.1007/978-3-031-49215-0_51

analyze the safety of car systems [6, 7]. With the recent development of automated driving systems (ADS) technology, the roles of the vehicle and the driver are constantly changing. For the safety analysis of automated vehicle, Monkhouse et al. (2020) explained adaptive cruise control, lane centering, and traffic jam assist functions using a conceptual driver model [8]. Not only such a taxonomy, but also the studies explaining the interaction between drivers and vehicles as a control model were conducted [9, 10]. There are models explaining the motion sickness symptoms as well [11, 12]. Although the models were developed to explain the behavior of drivers, many studies were limited to only conceptual studies. Further, because the role of human drivers changes as technologies like automated driving develop, follow-up studies like development and verification of models, that can explain the changing roles, are needed. Therefore, the aim of this study is to model the perception system of drivers and to explain their behavior. Section 2 explains the steps of developing a model for the perception system. Section 3 explains the steps for drivers to take over from automated driving to manual driving utilizing the model described in Sect. 2. Section 3 also compares the driver behavior in the takeover situation using the human-in-the-loop experimental data. Section 4 discusses the result of data analysis, the limitations of this study, and future studies.

2   Development of Perception System Model

2.1   Skill-Rule-Knowledge Model (Rasmussen, 1983)

Skill-Rule-Knowledge model, as a model started from the symbolism in philosophy, classified tasks as Skill (S), Rule (R), Knowledge (K) depending on the level of human consciousness. The lowest level of consciousness is involved in the skill-based behavior which has the characteristics of smooth, automated, highly integrated patterns. Some degree of consciousness or attention is necessary in the rule-based behavior in that workers have know-how and knowledge to solve problems as in familiar situations. Workers' full consciousness and training are required in the knowledge-based behavior in which there is no known solution as in unfamiliar situations. The S-R-K model has an advantage of explaining the process of perception and decision hierarchically, but it has a limitation in that it is not specifically designed for driving context (Table 1).

2.2   Dynamic Driving Task Model (SAE J3016, 2021)

SAE J3016 (2021) shows a schematic of driving tasks in Dynamic Driving Task (DDT) model [13]. This model was modified from Michon's task model which hierarchized the driving tasks into strategic, tactical, and operational tasks [5]. In this study, the model was named as DDT model. The DDT model can explain the vehicle control process starting from planning destination. The strategic task involves the process of planning destinations and waypoints, the tactical task involves the process of planning and execution of driving events/objects, avoidance and expedited route following, and the operational task involves lateral and longitudinal motion control (Table 1).

Table 1. S-R-K model and DDT model

S-R-K model		DDT model	
Classification	Description	Classification	Description
Goal	Task objectives	Strategic	Destination and waypoint planning
Knowledge	Unfamiliar tasks Conscious control Needs training	Tactical	Planning and execution for event/object, avoidance and expedited route following
Rule	Familiar tasks. Conscious control. Needs know-how		
Skill	Automated tasks No need for conscious control	Operational	Lateral and longitudinal motion control

2.3 Model Integration

In this study, the S-R-K model [5], in which tasks are defined hierarchically, and the DDT model [13] related to driving tasks are integrated (Table 1, Fig. 1). The rule and knowledge-based behavior was compared with the tactical task in this study. This approach is different from the studies of Hale et al. (1990) and Negash and Yang (2023) that compared skill and operational, rule and tactical, and knowledge and strategic tasks [14, 15]. The reason for the difference is as follows. As the level of automation increases, the frequency for drivers (passengers in Level 4 or above) to conduct tactical tasks decreases. However, drivers can judge the next task using the information provided by the vehicle and from the external driving situations in the event which the drivers experience for the first time in automated vehicles.

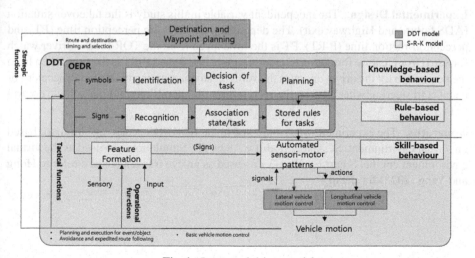

Fig. 1. Integrated driver model

3 Application to Driving Situations and Analysis

3.1 Application to Driving Situations

In this study, the process of takeover from the Level 3 automated driving mode to the manual driving mode is explained through the model in Fig. 1. This process was assumed as the rule-based behavior because the volunteers learn the take-over method during practice driving in the experiment. The model corrected by reflecting the above situation is shown in Fig. 2.

ADS Failure (Unplanned ODD Exit). This is an unplanned takeover situation because of ADS failure [16]. When ADS requests the driver to drive himself through the takeover request warning (TOR warning), the driver forms the features of the TOR warning (feature formation). Then, the driver recognizes the TOR (recognition), associates with the driving task (association task), and decides on the takeover method using his knowhow (stored rules for tasks). After that, the driver controls the lateral/longitudinal vehicle motion through his automated sensori-motor patterns, changes to the manual driving mode, keeps the lane, and continues driving.

Highway Exit (Planned ODD Exit). This ADS is a planned takeover situation asking the driver to takeover fifteen seconds before exiting a highway [16, 17]. As in the ADS failure, the driver conducts the feature formation-association tasks. Then, in the stored rules for tasks, the driver is involved in destination and waypoint planning because the driver already knows the route that he has to drive manually after the takeover as a planned ODD exit. This point is different from the ADS failure in which the control is transferred without any destination. After that, the driver changes to manual driving through the automated sensori-motor patterns, changes to the right lane, and exit the highway.

3.2 Experimental Design and Data Collection

Experimental Design. The independent variable in this study is the takeover situation (ADS failure and Highway exit). The dependent variables are perception time (PT) and perception-rection time (P-RT). PT is the time taken from the TOR till the driver watch forward (from feature formation to recognition in Fig. 2) and P-RT is the time taken from the perception till the driver operates the vehicle (any one among brake pedal, accelerator pedal, and steering wheel) (from the recognition till lateral/longitudinal vehicle control in Fig. 2).

Apparatus. The experiment was conducted in the KMU-DS, a driving simulator based on virtual environment. SCANeR studio v.1.8 by AV Simulation was used as the virtual environment engine. Smart Eye Pro-3 was used as an eye tracker. (Please refer to Hong and Yang (2022) for detail.)

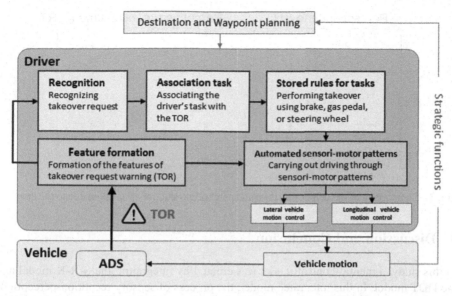

Fig. 2. Driver mental-control model for takeover situation

Volunteers. The volunteer drivers are adults with at least one year experience of driving. The numbers of participants are 36 for the ADS failure situation (22 males and 14 females) and 40 for the highway exit situation (20 males and 20 females). The average age of the participants was 40.9 years (SD = 11.3 years) for the ADS failure situation and 40.2 years for the highway exit situation (SD = 11.2 years). The data collection was approved by the institutional review board (KMU-201803-HR-174).

3.3 Result

PT and P-RT according to the takeover situation were analyzed using independent t-test. The statistical analysis showed that there was a statistically significant difference in PT according to the takeover situation ($t(553) = -5.083$, $p < 0.001$). PT (M = 0.92 s, SD = 0.59 s) in the ADS failure was faster than PT (M = 1.20 s, SD = 0.66 s) in the highway exit. In the same manner, there was statistically significant difference P-RT according to the takeover ($t(551.793) = -5.085$, $p < 0.001$). P-RT (M = 1.53 s, SD = 1.11 s) in the ADS failure was faster than that (M = 2.04 s, SD = 1.23 s) in the highway exit (Fig. 3).

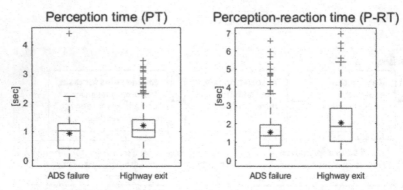

Fig. 3. Comparison of the perception time and perception-reaction time taken due to the takeover

4 Discussion and Conclusion

In this study, a mental-control model was created by integrating the S-R-K model and the DDT model. In this integrated model, the process of sensory reception-perception-decision-control can be explained hierarchically. Two kinds of takeover situations were applied for model validation. The behavior of drivers during the takeover was explained using the model through data analysis. The result showed that the PT and P-RT of the drivers were shorter in the ADS failure situation. In other words, the drivers perceived faster the TOR warning in the ADS failure situation, and the time taken till operating the vehicle was shorter. It seems because drivers might have felt the situation to maintain the lane without any destination more urgent. Conversely, the reactions of drivers were slower in the planned ODD exit. This seems because the destination and waypoint were involved in the process of deciding to takeover, and because additional operations like turning on turn signals for lane change and checking side mirrors were conducted.

However, there are the following limitations in this study. First, the takeover task was assumed as the rule-based behavior only. Nonetheless, in case that the drivers do not have any driving experiences, it could be the knowledge-based behavior which needs training. Second, although one participant in the experiment experienced eight kinds of multimodal TOR warnings, the effect of TOR warnings was not taken into account. But Hong et al. (2022) showed that there was no difference in the perception time according to TOR warnings in urgent situations like ADS failure [18]. On the other hand, the use of haptic seat induced the fast perception of drivers in the high-way exit situation. Along with this, the use of the A-pillar LED light and the haptic seat induced the drivers to operate the vehicle fast in both situations. This result can be extended to explain the behavior of drivers when the TOR warnings were provided as an input using the driver mental-control model.

This study explains only the takeover situations in Level 3 automated driving. In the future, other features or situations in automated driving can be applied to the created model. The evaluation of the model is also needed. This study is expected in the future to be applied to the analysis of driver behavior patterns and user evaluations.

Acknowledgment. This study was supported by the Basic Science Research Program of the National Research Foundation of Korea (2021R1A2C1005433), and BK21 program through the National Research Foundation of Korea (NRF), funded by the Ministry of Education (5199990814084) and the Korea Institute for Advancement of Technology (KIAT) grant funded by the Korea Government (MOTIE) (P0017120, Competency Development Program for Industry Specialist).

References

1. Wickens, C.D.: Temporal limits of human information processing: a developmental study. Psychol. Bull. **81**(11), 739 (1974)
2. Wilde, G.J.: The theory of risk homeostasis: implications for safety and health. Risk Anal. **2**(4), 209–225 (1982)
3. Rasmussen, J.: Skills, rules, and knowledge; signals, signs, and symbols, and other distinctions in human performance models. IEEE Trans. Syst. Man Cybern. **3**, 257–266 (1983)
4. Reason, J.: Human Error. Cambridge University Press, Cambridge (1990)
5. Michon, J.A.: A critical view of driver behavior models: what do we know, what should we do?. Hum. Behav. Traffic Saf. 485–524 (1985)
6. Leveson, N., Daouk, M., Dulac, N., Marais, K.: Applying STAMP in accident analysis. In: NASA Conference Publication, pp. 177–198. NASA, Virginia (2003)
7. Abdulkhaleq, A., Wagner, S., Leveson, N.: A comprehensive safety engineering approach for software-intensive systems based on STPA. Procedia Eng. **128**, 2–11 (2015)
8. Monkhouse, H.E., Habli, I., McDermid, J.: An enhanced vehicle control model for assessing highly automated driving safety. Reliab. Eng. Syst. Saf. **202**, 107061 (2020)
9. Pauwelussen, J.: Essentials of Vehicle Dynamics. Butterworth-Heinemann, Oxford (2014)
10. Zhao, Y., Pano, B., Chevrel, P., Claveau, F., Mars, F.: Driver model validation through interaction with varying levels of haptic guidance. In: 2020 IEEE International Conference on Systems, Man, and Cybernetics (SMC), pp. 2284-2290. IEEE, Toronto (2020)
11. Oman, C.M.: Motion sickness: a synthesis and evaluation of the sensory conflict theory. Can. J. Physiol. Pharmacol. **68**(2), 294–303 (1990)
12. Irmak, T., Pool, D.M., Happee, R.: Objective and subjective responses to motion sickness: the group and the individual. Exp. Brain Res. **239**, 515–531 (2021)
13. SAE On-road Automated Vehicle Standards Committee: Taxonomy and Definitions for Terms Related to On-road Motor Vehicle Automated Driving Systems (2021)
14. Hale, A.R., Stoop, J., Hommels, J.: Human error models as predictors of accident scenarios for designers in road transport systems. Ergonomics **33**(10–11), 1377–1387 (1990)
15. Negash, N.M., Yang, J.: Driver behavior modeling towards autonomous vehicles: Comprehensive Review. IEEE Access **11**, 22788–22821 (2023)
16. Hong, S., Yang, J.: Effect of multimodal takeover request issued through A-pillar LED light, earcon, speech message, and haptic seat in conditionally automated driving. Transp. Res. F: Traffic Psychol. Behav. **89**, 488–500 (2022)
17. Yun, H., Yang, J.: Multimodal warning design for take-over request in conditionally automated driving. Eur. Transp. Res. Rev. **12**, 1–11 (2020)
18. Hong, S., Maeng, J., Kim, H.J., Yang, J.: Development of warning methods for planned and unplanned takeover requests in a simulated automated driving vehicle. In: Proceedings of the 14th International Conference on Automotive User Interfaces and Interactive Vehicular Applications, pp. 65–74. ACM, Seoul (2022)

Evaluation of ATCO Situational Awareness in a Flow-Centric Air Traffic Environment Using SAGAT

Kiranraj Pushparaj[(✉)] [iD], Ahmad Sufian Bin Jumad, Duy Vu-Tran[iD],
Koji Tominaga[iD], and Sameer Alam[iD]

Air Traffic Management Research Institute, Nanyang Technological University,
Singapore, Singapore
kiranraj.pushparaj@ntu.edu.sg

Abstract. With current airspace infrastructure being stretched to their limits by the increase in demand for air traffic, Flow Centric Operations (FCO) have been touted to be a possible solution to efficiently manage airspace capacity to support more traffic. However, the novelty of such a concept (assigning flights to Air Traffic Controllers (ATCOs) based on traffic flows) necessitates human factors evaluation in this environment. Particularly, ATCO situational awareness rose to the forefront as a crucial human factor in this arena due to the difference in mental models adopted in this concept. Three fundamental traffic flows, with varying levels of complexity, as determined by a subject matter expert were evaluated for ATCO Situational Awareness. The behavioral results obtained using SAGAT revealed that Situational Awareness for more complex flows were higher, even though participants self-indicated that their situational awareness was lower during the complex flows. This mismatch could be a result of paradoxical complacency during less complex flows, and increased focus during the more complex flows.

Keywords: Flow Centric Operations · Situational Awareness · Air Traffic Management

1 Introduction

Presently, provision of air traffic control (ATC) in en-route airspaces is often organised by dividing the volume of airspace into area control centre (ACC) sectors. In each of ACC sectors, up to two air traffic control officers (ATCOs) may be deployed to deliver necessary ATC tasks. The ACC sectors are usually of fixed nature (except airspace organisation concepts such as Dynamic Airspace Configuration in Europe [9] which collapses and merges sector blocks, sub-unit airspaces, depending on the demand and flow patterns on a sub-daily basis). Although this 'sector-based' paradigm of ATC provision in en-route airspace has proven functional for several decades, the en-route ACC sectors are limited to operational capacity (for example entry counts for a given unit time slot) due to geometric, navigational, surveillance and communication constraints [11].

The Flight Centric Operations or Sector-less Operations [1,4] were conceptualised to overcome the spatial capacity constraints of the sector-based paradigm. In Flight Centric settings, the responsibility of ATC provision are organised by assigning the incoming flights to ATCOs irrespective of the physical location and by retaining the flight-specific ATCO assignment throughout the course of the en-route transit. Anticipated benefits include possible increase in total service capacity. However, the concept still requires research and development, especially in the evaluation of several safety related factors (such as alteration to ATCO's mental model [2] as well as airspace organisation approaches for a highly spatially and temporarily dynamic assignment of area of responsibility to an ATCO [6]).

However, there are also some concerns with this operational setting, largely in part to the departure from conventional Air Traffic Control (ATC), where an Air Traffic Controller (ATCO) adopts responsibility for a single geographical sector with established airways. When considering the fundamental responsibilities of an ATCO regardless of airspace orientation, it is evident that maintaining situational awareness, which is the use of a mental picture (mental model) that is generated from the data conveyed to ATCOs, to manage air traffic safely and efficiently, is crucial in every single ATCO task [12].

The Flow Centric Operations (FCO) concept [7,8] expands on the Flight Centric Operations concept. The FCO concept aims to overcome some of the operational challenges to Flight Centric Operations by determining controller assignments by grouping of flights by considering trajectory similarity and complexity. The approach builds on several other operational concepts in complexity studies and dynamic density and flow characterisation [3,14]. In its logic, by grouping flights by similarity in trajectory, the Flow-Centric concept aims to reduce complexity in traffic and reduce the need for ATCO-to-ATCO coordination [7,10]. In terms of concept maturity, the first human-in-the-loop study focusing on qualitative feedback for identifying its key characteristics was only recently conducted [8]. The results of the study suggested that both crossing and merging flows were operationally feasible in an FCO environment. However, human factors studies with a more quantitative approach is necessary for a more comprehensive evaluation of the FCO concept.

Previous human-in-the-loop experiments have also been conducted on Flight Centric Operations, which showed that ATCOs could effectively monitor up to six individual aircraft in different locations under Flight Centric airspace concepts, which are the predecessor to FCO concepts, eliminate sector boundaries but do not organize flights into flows that are central to Flow Centric concepts, but they struggled to maintain situational awareness of the broader traffic situation in a larger area, making it more difficult to manage potential conflicts [2].

2   Problem Formulation

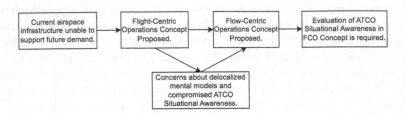

Fig. 1. Research Problem Formulation

Novel airspace concepts are required to manage the anticipated increase in future air traffic demand. While Flight Centric operations showed some promise previously, the delocalized mental models in that concept yielded some concerns. FCO may prove to address this limitation by grouping the aircraft by flows and thus enhancing the global situational awareness of ATCOs by resulting in a singular localized mental model, similar to conventional sectored airspace. As such, an investigation on ATCO situational awareness under FCO needs to be carried out. The formulation of this research problem can be seen in Fig. 1.

3   Methodology

As such, a pilot study designed to evaluate ATCO situational awareness during FCO was developed. Three different fundamental types of flows, based on input from a subject matter expert who had professional ATC experience, were devised, with each type of flow being tested separately in individual simulations in a high fidelity NLR Air Traffic Control Research Simulator (NARSIM) located in Air Traffic Management Research Institute, Nanyang Technological University, Singapore.

Ethics approval for this study was obtained from Nanyang Technological University Institutional Review Board (IRB-2023-276). A total of 4 participants, consisting of 2 professional ATCOs, and 2 novice ATCOs, who have had no professional experience, were recruited for this pilot study. Prior to the beginning of the study, participants were afforded a familiarization run to ensure they are comfortable operating in a flow-centric environment. Subsequently, the 3-simulation experiment began, with the first run involving the management of 2 merging flows, prior to transfer to another air navigation service provider. The second run involved the management of a flow, which crossed with another flow, which was under the management of a pseudo-controller, who was the subject matter expert involved in this study. The third run combined both of the previous concepts together, where a merged flow subsequently crossed with another flow, with the secondary flows being managed by the pseudo-controller.

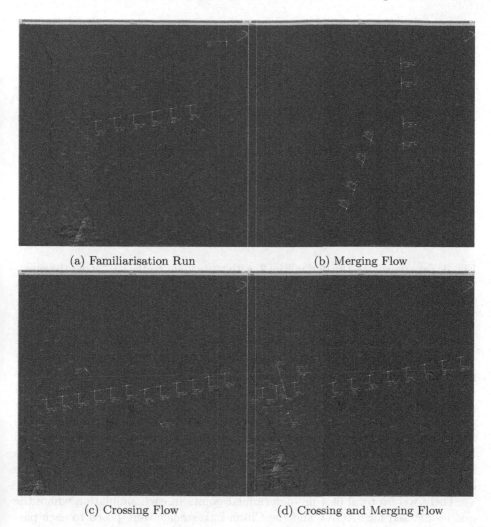

(a) Familiarisation Run   (b) Merging Flow

(c) Crossing Flow   (d) Crossing and Merging Flow

Fig. 2. Simulation runs during experiment. 2a: Familiarisation run for participants to be more comfortable in FCO environment, 2b: Run 1 with the Merging Flow, 2c: Run 2 with the Crossing Flow, and 2d: Run 3 with both Crossing and Merging Flow

These runs, which were arranged in increasing order of difficulty, as deemed by a subject matter expert, were designed to test limited but fundamental tasks in the context of flow-centric airspace, since the purpose was that of a pilot study. The designed flows, as well as the flow utilized for the familiarization run can be seen in Fig. 2, while the experimental setup can be seen in Fig. 3.

There were two different metrics of Situational Awareness used in this study. Situational Awareness Global Assessment Technique (SAGAT) has been demonstrated to be a sensitive and minimally intrusive technique to evaluate situational awareness, particularly in dynamic environments such as ATC [5]. This was

Fig. 3. Experimental setup during Run 2, with participant on the left, under the supervision of Subject Matter Expert, who also served as Pseudopilot during the experiment, on the right.

achieved by freezing simulations before the SAGAT queries are posed to participants. The simulation screen was turned off during this "freeze", to ensure that participants were giving answers based only on current situational awareness. As such, SAGAT was adopted as a behavioral measure of situational awareness, with a 10-point China Lakes Scale for Situational Awareness providing a secondary source of questionnaire data for comparison. The time taken to respond to the SAGAT queries, as well as the accuracy levels of the responses were recorded. Due to the study being an exploratory pilot study, more advanced measures such as eye tracking and neuroimaging were not utilized. However, they can be considered for future studies that are more sophisticated.

There were a total of 4 pre-determined points in each simulation where the queries devised for SAGAT and the China Lakes Scale were posed to each participant, with 3 questions addressing each of the 3 different levels of situational awareness (Level 1: Perception of data; Level 2: Comprehension of meaning; Level 3: Projection of near future) [13]. As such, a total of 10 questions (1 Question from China Lakes Scale and 9 Questions from SAGAT) were posed to the participants during each freeze. The freeze points were determined by the subject matter expert with each point corresponding to moments in the simulation where situational awareness needed to be optimal, such as just before and after the flows merged and/or crossed. The specific timestamps of each freeze can be seen in Table 1. The total length of each simulation varied due to different ATC strategies employed by each participant. Overall, a total of 36 queries from SAGAT and 4 questions from the China Lakes Scale for Situational Awareness were posed for each run. The queries were also developed in consultation with the aforementioned subject matter expert, utilizing the Goal Directed Task Analysis approach recommended by [5].

Table 1. Timestamp of each pre-determined freeze for each run based on Subject Matter Expert recommendation, in minutes.

Run	Timestamp/(mm:ss)			
	Freeze 1	Freeze 2	Freeze 3	Freeze 4
Familiarization	8:00	NA	NA	NA
Run 1	1:00	5:00	10:00	18:00
Run 2	2:00	8:00	11:00	24:00
Run 3	0:40	7:15	12:45	20:00

4 Results and Discussion

A visualization of the results from the China Lakes Scale for Situational Awareness revealed expected results, with decreased Situational Awareness for more complex flow settings, as can be seen from Fig. 4a, where the self reported scores for Situational Awareness are visibly lower. Greater interactions between the aircraft in different flows will naturally drain cognitive resources and cause a strain on Situational Awareness. However, these results are based solely on self-reported levels of Situational Awareness. Further analysis of the SAGAT results were required to corroborate these findings.

Accuracy levels for SAGAT queries ranged from 33% to 100% for all participants throughout all runs. Surprisingly however, the best performance, in terms of accuracy in answering SAGAT queries occurred during Run 2, followed by Run 3, then Run 1, as can be seen from Fig. 4b, whereas the expectation was that accuracy levels will decrease with each simulation run. This was unexpected due to the fact that the merging flows in Run 1 were deemed to be the least challenging. Taken in context with the data outlining the time taken for participants to answer their queries, which had a range of 1.03 s to 41.96 s, Run 1 was again the most challenging for the participants to maintain Situational Awareness. Participants answered most quickly for Run 3, which was the most demanding flow, whereas the expectation was that time to answer will increase with each simulation run.

One possible explanation for these results could be that of complacency. Participants were aware that the simulations were in increasing level of difficulty, as evidenced by their China Lake Scores. However, it could be the same awareness that could have encouraged them to focus more on the challenging simulations, which yielded improved Situational Awareness behavior for Runs 2 and 3. Run 1 may have been deemed to be easy and may have resulted in increased complacency, which led to poorer performance for SAGAT queries.

This paradox needs to be examined further in future studies. Furthermore, methods to mitigate this behavior needs to be explored, as ATC is a dynamic environment, where unexpected events such as weather can cause sudden changes, which can only be managed safely and efficiently if ATCOs are able to maintain their Situational Awareness. More complex experimental tasks in more sophisticated experimental designs with more participants are crucial in ensuring comprehensive human factors evaluation of FCO.

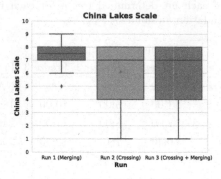

(a) China Lakes Scale

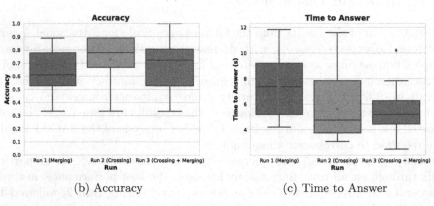

(b) Accuracy   (c) Time to Answer

Fig. 4. Questionnaire and Behavioral Data Visualization; 4a: China Lakes Scale for Situational Awareness Results, 4b: Accuracy Levels for SAGAT Queries, and 4c: Time to Answer SAGAT Queries.

Acknowledgement. This research is supported by the National Research Foundation, Singapore under the Aviation Transformation Programme and by the Civil Aviation Authority of Singapore (CAAS) and Nanyang Technological University, Singapore under their collaboration in the Air Traffic Management Research Institute. Any opinions, findings and conclusions or recommendations expressed in this material are those of the author(s) and do not reflect the views of the National Research Foundation, Singapore and the Civil Aviation Authority of Singapore. We would also like to thank Mr Dennis Ng for his timely technical support with the NARSIM simulator, which proved crucial to the expedient and smooth completion of this study.

References

1. Birkmeier, B., Korn, B., Kügler, D.: Sectorless ATM and advanced SESAR concepts: complement not contradiction. In: 29th Digital Avionics Systems Conference (2010)
2. Birkmeier, B., Korn, B., Flemisch, F.O.: First findings on the controller's mental model in sectorless air traffic management. In: 2011 IEEE/AIAA 30th Digital Avionics Systems Conference, pp. 6C1-1. IEEE (2011)
3. Delahaye, D., García, A., Lavandier, J., Chaimatanan, S., Soler, M.: Air traffic complexity map based on linear dynamical systems. Aerospace 9(5) (2022). https://doi.org/10.3390/aerospace9050230. https://www.mdpi.com/2226-4310/9/5/230
4. Duong, V.N., Gawinowski, G., Nicolaon, J.P., Simith, D.: Sector-less air traffic management. In: 4th USA/Europe Air Traffic Management R&D Seminar (2001)
5. Endsley, M.R.: A systematic review and meta-analysis of direct objective measures of situation awareness: a comparison of SAGAT and SPAM. Hum. Factors 63(1), 124–150 (2021)
6. Gerdes, I., Temme, A., Schultz, M.: Dynamic airspace sectorisation for flight-centric operations. Transp. Res. Part C Emerg. Technol. 95, 460–480 (2018). https://doi.org/10.1016/j.trc.2018.07.032
7. Gerdes, I., Temme, A., Schultz, M.: From free-route air traffic to an adapted dynamic main-flow system. Transp. Res. Part C Emerg. Technol. 115, 102633 (2020). https://doi.org/10.1016/j.trc.2020.102633
8. bin Jumad, A.S., Tominaga, K., Chua, X.Y., Itoh, E., Schultz, M., Duong, V.N.: Flow-centric air traffic control: human in the loop simulation experiment. In: Accepted and to be Presented at 42nd Digital Avionics Systems Conference (2023)
9. Lema-Esposto, M.F., Amaro-Carmona, M., Valle-Fernández, N., Iglesias-Martínez, E., Fabio-Bracero, A.: Optimal dynamic airspace configuration (DAC) based on state-task networks (STN). In: 11th SESAR Innovation Days (2021)
10. Ma, C., Alam, S., Cai, Q., Delahaye, D.: Air traffic flow prediction using transformer neural networks for flow-centric airspace. In: 12th SESAR Innovation Days (SIDs 2022) (2022)
11. Martins, A.P.G., Finck, T., Mollwitz, V., Kling, F., Rohács, D.: Feasibility study of flight centric mode of operations - a human performance approach. In: 9th SESAR Innovation Days (2019)
12. Papenfuss, A., Capiot, K., Korn, B.: We need to talk about this! Assessing information needs for collaboration in a sectorless working environment. In: 2021 IEEE/AIAA 40th Digital Avionics Systems Conference (DASC), pp. 1–8. IEEE (2021)
13. Salmon, P.M., et al.: Measuring situation awareness in complex systems: comparison of measures study. Int. J. Ind. Ergon. 39(3), 490–500 (2009)
14. Sridhar, B., Sheth, K.S., Grabbe, S.: Airspace complexity and its application in air traffic management. In: 2nd USA/Europe Air Traffic Management R&D Seminar, pp. 1–6. Federal Aviation Administration Washington, DC (1998)

Case Studies in HCI

Ergonomic Risk Exposure Groups:
An Experience of a Mining Company in Brazil

Simony Andrade[✉]

Global Corporate Ergonomist, Charlotte, USA
tandradesimony1@gmail.com

Abstract. The nature of ergonomics performs a unique role in protecting human health and preventing health risks. Improvements in productivity indices in the systems can be seen, resulting in better work conditions for people employed in production and services systems. To manage the processes of Ergonomics seeking to continuously adapt the working conditions to the psycho-physiological characteristics of the workers, by means of techniques, methods, and process controls, becomes the problematic adduced in this work, when there is no data to facilitate integration to the other processes of the company. The purpose of this descriptive study aims to demonstrate how the formation of homogeneous groups for ergonomics keeps the process dynamic through the generation of data that allows easy integration with other areas. This integration makes it possible to support the operational areas in risk management and consequently in the prevention of occupational diseases, reduction of absenteeism and incidents, providing improvements in the environment aiming at comfort, increased productivity, and better quality of life.

Keywords: Ergonomics · Ergonomic data · Ergonomics hazards

1 Introduction

Since applied ergonomic principles have been recognized as a saving method for decreasing MSDs [3], it is necessary to perform research to develop approaches to solve problems at work, thereby increasing productivity. Effective execution of ergonomic programs can increase ergonomic awareness. Some research results show that distributing ergonomic knowledge among staff leads results in a better execution of production service programs. Studies of their application in industrial settings have been performed [1–3], but the reality is that industrial corporations often develop their own internal methods for evaluation or use a national provision as pass-fail criteria. Consequently, research articles that address corporate internal or national standard ergonomics evaluation procedures are few and far between [10].

The prevention of work-related injuries and other health problems drew much attention in the 19th century and flourished in the 20th century. This was driven by scientific medicine, public health development, and advancing technologies such as safety engineering, occupational hygiene, and ergonomics (Santana, 2006). Ergonomics is an interdisciplinary applied science. It concentrates on the optimization and improvement of the human–machine-environment system. The ergonomics research aims to make workers more efficient, safer, and more comfortable. In the construction industry, occupational injuries and accidents caused by poor ergonomics were common, leading to human casualties, disrupting the construction process, increasing project costs, and adversely affecting productivity and reputation.

According to Straker (1990), ergonomic interventions developed by participatory work teams may result in significant impact, but the efforts of the work teams may not continue unless the work teams are part of a process integrated with management systems and supported with written policies, procedures, and responsibilities.

Despite the numerous reports of ergonomics programs in a variety of industries, no examples of implementing an ergonomics program in the mining industry have been reported. Mining environments pose challenges to implementing ergonomics processes and demonstrating effectiveness not found in other industries. Unlike manufacturing facilities, mining environments are constantly changing and can be considered very dynamic work environments (Steiner et al., 1999; Scharf et al., 2001).

This qualitative description, which was conducted in different levels of the company developed a comprehensive strategy to facilitate the integration of ergonomics into a mining company. The objective of this study is to demonstrate the program process in an industry with dynamic work conditions and environments and demonstrate how the formation of homogeneous groups for ergonomics keeps the process dynamic through allowing effective integration with other areas.

2   The Corporate Program Stages

The company where this program was implemented operates in fourteen Brazilian states and on five continents and has about two thousand kilometers of railroad network and nine port terminals of its own. In addition to operating logistics services. These are large numbers that create complexity in bringing an ergonomics program that is adapted to different businesses and countries.

The Program aims to support operations in preventing occupational diseases, reducing absenteeism and work accidents, providing improvements in the environment for comfort, increased productivity, and a better quality of life. The basic premises are described, and the local programs follow the corporate program according to its specifics. So, each operational area/unit needs to implement the corporate procedure of the company following the minimum stages described below:

2.1   Planning

The objective of this step is structuring the Process in the site/operational area. Each area needs to perform a self-diagnosis of Ergonomics management based to identify the status of the unit/site with the main requirements of the global procedure, understand the business characteristics to stablish the local Ergonomics Program. Other point is to define the ergonomic organizational structure of the unity (Involved professionals and the Committee), define the roles and responsibilities to all involved and the documentation standards to be used.

2.2 Leadership Involvement

Develop leadership awareness-raising actions, to inform about the impact of their decisions on the health and safety of employees and on the objectives is crucial to support the program. Formalize the process to ensure the necessary resources and commitment of leadership. The leader must ensure the participation of Ergonomists and professionals responsible for Ergonomics in the process of the management of change, in compliance with the Guidelines and systems of the company.

2.3 Management of Change and Risk Management

Establish and implement practices of systematic identification and assessment of ergonomic hazards following the risk matrix adopted considering Ergonomic Risk Exposure Groups. Using the methodology "see and act" to implement control measures in less complex situations. Insert the vision/approach to human factors in the change management process (technical, administrative, or organizational) needs to be part of the local program.

2.4 Legal Requirements

It's necessary to Identify legal and regulatory Ergonomics requirements applicable to the business and country and verify the compliance to the identified requirements.

2.5 Planning of the Process Actions

Prioritize actions in accordance with the level of risk mapped, using the risk matrix as reference is another part of the process. A schedule of actions (based on the previous steps, setting necessary resources, priorities, deadlines, and responsibilities) needs to be stablished and validated. Indicators needs to be monitored at the operational leadership routine, considering high and very high-risk scenarios for the Ergonomic Risk Exposure Groups.

2.6 Implementation and Control

Training and Qualification. The area defines the specific training needs regarding Ergonomics/human factors) and identify educational initiatives that are related to Ergonomics/human factors (e.g., behavioral development, leader's academy, risk management, incident analysis, etc.).

Communication and Consultation. It's a requirement of this stage to develop a communication tool for the employees to report any complain or deviation related to Ergonomics issues, with the objective to identify and immediately treat these issues.

Operational Control. Define the process efficiency indicators and related costs to ergonomic hazards to raise awareness to their financial impact and calculate the investment return time of the control measures to be adopted. Implement the defined control measures prioritizing them according to the level of risk Ergonomic exposed group. Another objective of this element is to Identify critical items from the ergonomic point of view and establish minimum requirements to acquisition/purchases.

Processes, Machinery, and Installations Projects. It's a requirement to include professionals responsible for Ergonomics in multidisciplinary teams of change management process whenever occurs projects of implementation/acquisition or change in facilities, equipment, or processes; Identify ergonomic risk situations in installations and processes projects, in the task planning and work organization, and implement control measures from the conception stage.

2.7   Monitoring, Critical Analysis and Learning

Incidents Analysis and Management. It's a requirement to insert the vision/approach of human and organizational factors in the incident management process and the analysis methods used. Monitor the results of incident analysis to assess whether the contributing factors related to human and organizational factors are properly identified.

Monitoring and Critical Analysis. Periodically the units need to monitor the indicators defined in the planning stage, perform a critical analysis of the process with an annual minimum frequency, or whenever significant changes occur in the installations, processes or work organizational take place, to evaluate its the effectiveness and the efficiency of the program. Identify major issues and opportunities to improve the process. Discuss these opportunities to implement and optimize the process.

3   The Ergonomic Risk Management by Exposure Groups

To make this process run more efficiently the risk mapping process takes place by homogeneous exposure group. The Ergonomic Risk Exposure Group is the group of workers exposed to ergonomic risk hazards in a similar circumstance, so that the evaluation of any of its hazards offers useful data to estimate the risks of the other members.

The Group formation process is initiated in risk anticipation and confirmed during recognition of the hazard and, after qualitative and quantitative assessments.

These groups are obtained through the analysis of the basic characterization documents and professional judgment, following the parameters and sequence presented (Fig. 1):

The process for the basic characterization of ergonomic risks includes the phases of Anticipation, Recognition, and Qualitative Evaluation, in which the professionals technically responsible for ergonomics contribute to the planning, design, and evaluation of tasks, workstations, products, environments, and systems to make them compatible with people's needs, abilities, psychophysiological characteristics, and limitations (Fig. 2).

The creation of the ergonomic risk exposure group is the key to accelerate the risk mitigation and elimination process, since when a new position is created in the company it already needs to be inserted in an exposure group or a new exposure group needs to be created to admit this new position. So, control measures can already be implemented in this phase according to the risk category of the qualitative assessment applying the ergonomic risk matrix.

The generation of indicators after this flow allows the area to recognize and prioritize actions for scenarios classified as high and very high risk. Furthermore, the scope is

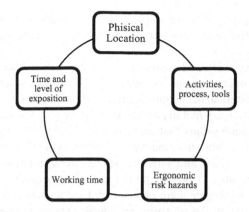

Fig. 1. Data to generate ergonomic risk exposure groups.

Fig. 2. Ergonomic risk management flow.

facilitated by the visibility of areas that have good indicators and that can share good practices. Monitoring the indicators is part of the leadership's routine, and the leaders need to know the risks in his area (including high and very high ergonomic risk scenarios) as part of the routine management of the company's production system.

4 Discussions

Ergonomics is mainly associated with the workers well-being, being most often housed within the Occupational Safety and Health (OSH) department, therefore managers tend to inadvertently restrict its scope of intervention to OSH hazards, instead of benefiting from its help to organizational effectiveness, business performance or costs. In fact, the value of Ergonomics is beyond health and safety since Ergonomics can add value to a company' business strategy to reach the ultimate business goal of profit, or intermediate business goals related to profit drivers like cost minimization, productivity, quality, delivery reliability, responsiveness to customer demands, or flexibility [16]. Therefore, it is necessary a paradigm shift, which requires a re-positioning from a primary health ergonomics approach to a more business-oriented ergonomics approach [16]. The integration of Ergonomics data in companies' production system matches this paradigm.

The approach of focus on anticipating the actions before undesirable events happen effectively promotes a culture of prevention. Besides the health and safety areas, the company is benefited from the principles of resilience because of the promotion of learning and the ability to see opportunities amid problems [3]. Some advantages can be highlighted when applying these principles, mainly because it enables the development of capabilities for setting and monitoring of the system by the ergonomics management [4].

Ergonomics management, which has a macro approach and seeks to understand the human-organization interaction and its complexity [11, 12], must act proactively, and not only based on past historical occupational injuries. It is essential to know the ergonomic risks to encourage decision-making at an assertive way when dealing with them, or even, to anticipate future events that bring potential risks [13]. The knowledge of the risk enables its identification, information, priority ranking with the purpose of taking actions on the vulnerabilities, and anticipating dangerous situations [14, 15].

Risk anticipation aims to predict potential risks to workers' health and take the necessary measures to mitigate them before they have a chance to happen. In practice, risk anticipation begins in the planning and design stages through, for example, the selection of less aggressive technologies and the early inclusion of control measures.

5 Conclusions

The purpose of this descriptive study aims to describes the process of ergonomic management in a qualitative approach, demonstrating how the formation of homogeneous groups for ergonomics keeps the process dynamic through the generation of data that allows easy integration with other areas. This integration makes it possible to support the operational areas in risk management and consequently in the prevention of occupational diseases, reduction of absenteeism and incidents, providing improvements in the environment aiming at comfort, increased productivity, and better quality of life. Furthermore, the provided overview may be subjective to the author's knowledge and the parameter results may be chosen to be analyzed in the future. Overall, the results of this study can benefit scholars and practitioners in identifying areas of practice associated with risk assessment and possible integrations with other areas.

References

1. Leigh, J.P., Markowitz, S.B., Fahs, M., Shin, C., Landrigan, P.J.: Occupational injury and illness in the United States: estimates of costs, morbidity, and mortality. Arch. Internal Med. 157(14), 1557–1568 (1997)
2. Pransky, G., et al.: Outcomes in work-related upper extremity and low back injuries: results of a retrospective study. Am. J. Ind. Med. 37(4), 400–409 (2000)
3. Hendrick, H.W.: Good Ergonomics is Good Economics. Human Factors and Ergonomics Society, Santa Monica (1996)
4. Dempsey, P.G.: Effectiveness of ergonomics interventions to prevent musculoskeletal disorders: Beware of what you ask. Int. J. Ind. Ergon. 37, 169–173 (2007)
5. Koukoulaki, T.: New trends in work environment – New effects on safety. Safety Science xxx (2009)
6. Shaliza, A.M., Kamaruddin, S., Zalinda, O., Mohzani, M.: The effect of ergonomics applications in work system on mental health of visual display terminal workers. Eur. J. Sci. Res. 31(3): 341–354 (2009). ISSN 1450–216X

7. Jan Dul, W., Neumann, P.: Ergonomics contributions to company strategies. Appl. Ergon. **40**, 745–752 (2009)

8. Steiner, L.J., Cornelius, K.M., Turin, F.C.: Predicting system interactions in the design process. Am. J. Ind. Med. **36**, 58–60 (1999)

9. James, P., Turin, F.C.: Partnering for successful ergonomics: a study of musculoskeletal disorders in mining. Min. Eng. **56**(11), 39–44 (2004)

10. Straker, L.M.: Work-associated back problems: collaborative solutions. J. Soc. Occup. Med. **40**, 75–79 (1990)

11. Hendrick, H.W.: Applying ergonomics to systems: some documented "lessons learned." Appl. Ergon. **39**(4), 418–426 (2008)

12. Karsh, B., Waterson, P., Holden, R.J.: Crossing levels in systems ergonomics: a framework to support 'mesoergonomic'inquiry. Appl. Ergon. (2013)

13. Hollnagel, E.: From protection to resilience: changing views on how to achieve safety. In: Proceedings of the 8th International Symposium of the Australian Aviation Psychology Association (2008)

14. Amalberti, R. Da gestão dos erros à gestão dos riscos. In: Falzon, P. (ed.) Ergonomia, pp. 235–248. Editora Blucher, São Paulo (2007)

15. Rozlina, M.S., et al.: Perceptions of ergonomics importance at workplace and safety culture amongst safety & health (SH) practitioners in Malaysia. In: Proceedings of the World Congress on Engineering (2012)

16. Dul, J., Neumann, W.: Ergonomics contributions to company strategies. Appl. Ergon. **40**, 745–752 (2009)

How Anonymous Are Your Anonymized Data? The AnyMApp Case Study

Ana Ferreira[1]([⊠]) [iD], Francisco Bischoff[1] [iD], Rute Almeida[1,2] [iD],
Luís Nogueira-Silva[2,3] [iD], Ricardo Cruz-Correia[1] [iD], and Joana Muchagata[1] [iD]

[1] CINTESIS@RISE, FMUP-MEDCIDS, Porto, Portugal
{amlaf,rutealmeida,rcorreia}@med.up.pt, franzbischoff@gmail.com,
joanamuchagata@gmail.com
[2] PaCeIT- Patient Centered Innovation and Technologies, CINTESIS, FMUP-MEDCIDS, Porto,
Portugal
luisnogueirasilva@gmail.com
[3] Centro Hospitalar e Universitário São João - Internal Medicine Department, Porto, Portugal

Abstract. Privacy is a Fundamental Human Right and data anonymization is
an essential process that aims to render data unidentifiable, therefore, private.
The aim of this work is to test the anonymity of the first data collected via
AnyMApp, a platform to anonymously perform online usability tests. Due to time
and resource constraints, the authors opted to identify open-source free tools,
which were evaluated recently for their usability and functionalities. Even being
a highly ranked anonymization tool (ARX), the use of this tool in our data setting was not straightforward and required guidance from tutorials. In the end, it
was not possible to run any of the anonymization models available in ARX in
our dataset because there were no quasi-identifier attributes within the collected
data. There were sensitive data collected though, with medical diagnosis information, but not able to cause privacy concerns when added with all the other
non-identifiable and non-sensitive attributes. Despite our results for this use-case,
we will keep verifying/anonymizing collected data from AnyMApp because we
will have different use-cases and health-related data that can be more complex and
comprise quasi-identifiers and sensitive attributes that we nee to guarantee that are
anonymized.

Keywords: Anonymization tools · health data anonymization · mobile
applications · online usability · privacy

1 Introduction

Health data privacy is a critical research subject [1]. On the one hand, the access to health
data collected in surveys and used in analysis can mean an improvement of the health
care service quality and outcomes; on the other hand, these are personal and sensitive
data that need protection [2–4]. One way to achieve this is by anonymizing those data
with techniques that can preserve their privacy [2, 4].

© The Author(s), under exclusive license to Springer Nature Switzerland AG 2024
C. Stephanidis et al. (Eds.): HCII 2023, CCIS 1958, pp. 456–463, 2024.
https://doi.org/10.1007/978-3-031-49215-0_54

However, selecting the best tools can be challenging because data anonymization is a complex process that requires technical skills and an understanding of privacy requirements to select the most adequate techniques and settings to provide the best anonymization results. This may also depend on the specific purposes of each research project and type of collected data [2, 5].

This work aims to provide an analysis of open-access health data anonymization tools, analyse them and identify which can be used to test anonymity of data collected with the AnyMApp framework [6].

2 Background

2.1 AnyMApp and Use-Case

AnyMApp is an exploratory project (duration 18 months) aiming to build a digital twin framework to anonymously simulate and analyse online interactions and usability between humans and mobile applications (fictitious or existing) [6]. The AnyMApp framework allies mock-up interfaces with anonymous data from the users, e.g., demographic, interactional and opinions regarding those interactions (see Fig. 1). This helps AnyMApp testing parameters other than usability related aspects, as it opens the possibility to easily and anonymously study other behavioural and interactional variables, still difficult to study with current solutions, e.g., personality and/or victimization traits or even mental, cognitive and even ageing related issues [7, 8].

Fig. 1. AnyMApp architecture. Interactional data from both mock-ups and interfaces that request demographic and other opinions/preferences from users (top) are collected for analysis (bottom).

Data to be tested for their anonymization properties was collected via AnyMApp framework, which simulates, as its first use-case, the Inspirers-HTN mobile application (app) [9]. This app supports patients' self-monitoring and management of hypertension (see Fig. 2).

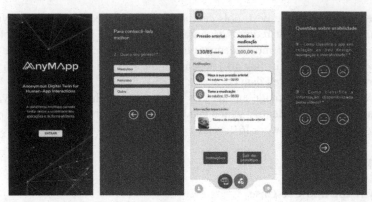

Fig. 2. Screenshots of the AnyMApp framework simulating some Inspirers-HTN functionalities.

2.2 Anonymization Tools

According to GDPR [10], anonymous data are "information which does not relate to an identified or identifiable natural person or to personal data rendered anonymous in such a manner that the data subject is not or no longer identifiable". The re-identification likelihood is the probability in a given dataset of re-identifying an individual, by turning anonymised data back into personal data through the use of data matching, triangulation or similar techniques.

Although, as already mentioned, we do not collect identifiable data within the AnyMApp platform, for each use-case, gathered data will be different and adaptable to the scenario at hand. It will give a greater sense of trust in the anonymization of the platform if we still test, with existing, current and evaluated tools, data anonymization, each time we produce a new use-case.

It is also important to assert if the tools can verify data as it is, collected from AnyMApp, as the goal is not to anonymize data but to test if what are being collected have a high degree of anonymity. We want to make sure that privacy is implemented by design and by default, together with the data minimization principle. If there is no need to collect identifiable data then we need to make sure this is so, for all use-cases.

3   Testing Anonymization in AnyMApp

3.1   Collected Data

Data collected via AnyMApp framework and tested within the selected anonymization tools comprise: a) participants' demographics such as gender, age group (18–34; 35–59; more than 60), education and current activity; b) interactional data from the mock-ups, the browser or device being use to perform the test; and c) satisfaction and feedback data from participants regarding the use-case, diagnosis of hypertension, if they have medical care or how frequently they use mHealth. Data are stored in a.CSV or.txt format, depending on the format that the anonymization tool is able to import.

For the INSPIRERS-HTN use-case tests within the AnyMApp framework a convenience sample of 25 adults was recruited from CINTESIS personnel. The goal was to perform the first tests of both the AnyMApp platform and the app.

3.2 Selection Criteria and Testing

Due to time constraints we opted to search for recent revision works on open-source anonymization tools that could suggest which ones could be used in our scenario. With this in mind, we selected all the tools that were reviewed in [2], and installed them in order to find the quicker/easier ones to use and test our sample with.

Table 1 presents the list of anonymization tools from [2] and summarizes authors' experience while installing, configuring and understanding what functionalities those tools comprise.

Table 1. Anonymization tools and associated analysis.

Anonym. Tools	Install/Config.	Test
ARX	Easy; Ready to import from.csv, excel, relation DB files, and many others	Anonymization features, models and risk analysis are available; Need support to interpret results
Amnesia	Online demo; Ready to import.txt format	Similar to ARX but requires data to be organized in txt format and does not include risk analysis
sdcMicro	Required R installation and specific knowledge	Not possible to install/configure and test in such short period of time
μ-ANT	Run from shell	Similar to ARX but requires knowledge of the necessary commands, java installation and does not include risk analysis
Anonimatron	Run from shell	Similar to μ-ANT

While we were installing and configuring the selected anonymization tools, we realized that one of them needed some more time and expertise to configure, install and use. SdcMicro requires R, so due to time constraints we opted to exclude it from the test. The other four tools are very similar in the functionalities they provide. The main difference is that two of them run via command line, in a console, while the other two provide a graphical interface, but they are all quite easy to install.

However, none of the tools can simply test anonymization on a data sample but use specific anonymization and privacy models to perform the anonymization and only then, make a comparison of the sample before and after anonymization.

Nevertheless, after our assessment of the anonymization tools, we chose the ARX tool to test the anonymization as it provides risk analysis and does not require additional software. To use the ARX anonymization tool we need to input the type of data for analysis, what types of methods to use, and other configurations.

We imported the .CSV file with an extract of the use-case logs (500 records) from March 2023. Once we imported the data file we selected and described the attributes to include in the test in terms of type of attribute (string, integer, etc.) and sensitivity/identifiability (e.g., non-sensitive; sensitive; quasi-identifier, identifier) (see Fig. 3).

jsonPayload....	jsonPayload....	jsonPayload....	jsonPayload....	receiveTime...	timestamp
avancar_btn		Page 9	1679046687...	2023-03-17...	2023-03-17...
apps_mhealt...		Page 9	1679046684...	2023-03-17...	2023-03-17...
avancar_btn		Page 7	1679046626...	2023-03-17...	2023-03-17...
hipertensao_...		Page 7	1679046625...	2023-03-17...	2023-03-17...
avancar_btn		Page 7	1679046622...	2023-03-17...	2023-03-17...
avancar_btn		Page 6	1679046608...	2023-03-17...	2023-03-17...
profissao	rrrr	Page 6	1679046608...	2023-03-17...	2023-03-17...
avancar_btn		Page 5	1679046604...	2023-03-17...	2023-03-17...
ensino_supe...		Page 5	1679046603...	2023-03-17...	2023-03-17...
avancar_btn		Page 4	1679046601...	2023-03-17...	2023-03-17...
feminino		Page 4	1679046600...	2023-03-17...	2023-03-17...
avancar_btn		Page 3	1679046598...	2023-03-17...	2023-03-17...
entre_35_59_...		Page 3	1679046597...	2023-03-17...	2023-03-17...
iniciar_btn		Page 2	1679046593...	2023-03-17...	2023-03-17...
entrar_quest...		Page 1	1679046591...	2023-03-17...	2023-03-17...
video_medir...		Page 12	1678474649...	2023-03-10...	2023-03-10...
video_escol...		Page 12	1678474642...	2023-03-10...	2023-03-10...

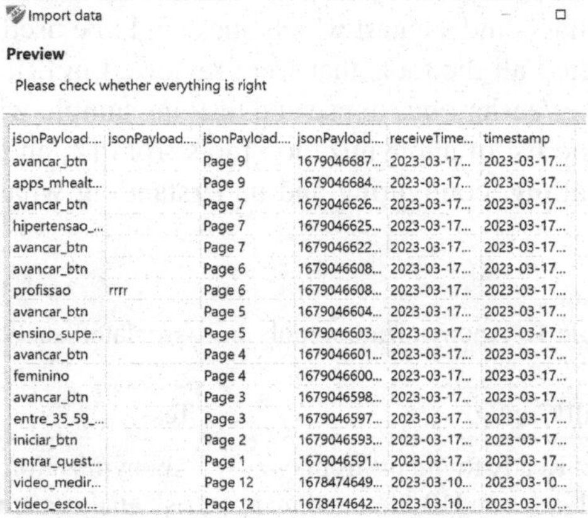

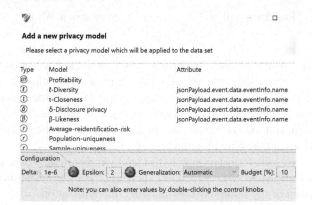

Fig. 3. Screenshot of the description of the attributes in.CSV (ARX tool).

The sample included mostly one attribute that could be sensitive, as it could integrate data regarding hypertension diagnosis, all the other attributes were non-sensitive. No "quasi-identifier" attributes were identified. Next, we defined hierarchies for those attributes, which mainly included the definition of categorical or numerical variables and subsets. A list of anonymization models is available and we selected privacy models that can assess sensitive attributes, as suggested by the tool (see Fig. 4).

Fig. 4. Setting the privacy anonymization models.

3.3 Results

After all the settings we verified that it was not possible to run the anonymization process unless we specified one attribute that was a quasi-identifier (see Fig. 5).

In our case, we did not have any attribute that was a quasi-identifier, so we could not make the tool run for this specific use-case data. In a way, this confirms one of the main premises of the AnyMApp project and platform: to collect anonymous data that cannot be identifiable, in order to have high confidence that online participants maintain their anonymity and privacy.

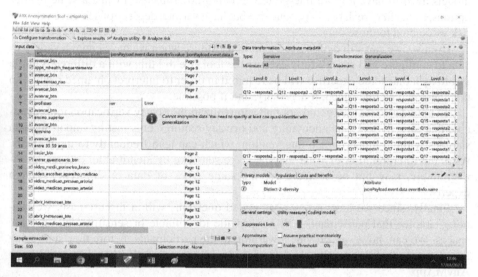

Fig. 5. Error message when we try to run the ARX tool with one sensitive attribute and no "quasi-identifier" or "identifier" attributes.

4 Discussion

Anonymization tools are not straightforward to use and need a lot of intervention from the user, including some previous knowledge or expertise in order to configure the parameters adequately and to choose the anonymity model accordingly.

Considering time and expertise constraints, we opted to consider some of the recent analyzed anonymization tools to identify which was the easiest and quicker to give us anonymization results for our data - ARX. Even so, in order to start working with the tool, although assessed as one of the best from a usability perspective, we still needed to search for tutorials to perform the first anonymity test. Thus, our study confirms the difficulties that are also presented in [2].

For each different field/parameter, we needed to define types of attributes, and to have some confidence in the choices that we made. As there is commonly a pre-defined scale (e.g., non-sensitive, sensitive, quasi-identifier, identifier), the classification of some attributes can be easily defined, for instance, email address could be classified as an "identifier". For other attributes, this classification may be less obvious. For example, if the IP address that is sent from the browser from where a user is accessing the online AnyMApp platform were registered, would this be classified as a "quasi-identifier"?

In our use-case, the process was more straightforward because the data sample was very simple and with no "identifier" or "quasi-identifier" attributes. This also impaired the anonymization process to run. There was an error because none of the listed anonymization models could be executed without one of the attributes being identified as a "quasi-identifier". Due to this result, the authors consider that such tools and models need to have a more fine-grained configuration instead of just a scale of four options, as healthcare data can be sensitive but have various degrees of sensitiveness and risk associated to those data.

Even so, we can still devise a moment in the future when we have enough variety of data to configure and successfully execute the tool (we did this with a different sample just to try), that some expertise will be required in order to interpret obtained results, so that these can be fine-tuned, if necessary, and if possible.

To notice also that we could not find anonymization/privacy verification tools available that directly test data anonymity and privacy requirements just by importing data samples without much human intervention, which can lead frequently to input errors. Also, the interpretation of what may be more sensitive or identifiable, or even quasi-identifiable, may not be standard for the same types of data or different research experts.

Finally, since we have a few open-ended questions within the use-case, we cannot guarantee that participants will not provide identifiable or sensitive data in those spaces. We can, however, provide a warning to the participants, before they start using the platform, that no identifiable data should ever be provided, when interacting with AnyMApp.

5   Conclusions

Performing tests with an open-source anonymization tool within AnyMApp was not possible due to the "non-identifiable" characteristics of the attributes.

Although it was not possible to reach our initial goal, this also shows that data collected for this specific use-case are not "fit" for anonymization for lack of varied and more "risky" attributes. The AnyMApp platform needs to guarantee that this is so at all times, so this study does not exclude future tests for other use-cases where data may be more complex, sensitive and quasi-identifiable.

In the end, the more we anonymize and test data anonymity with updated/revised tools, the highest is the probability that those data stay anonymous.

Acknowledgements. This work is financed by project AnyMApp - Anonymous Digital Twin for Human-App Interactions (EXPL/CCI-COM/0052/2021) (FCT – Fundação para a Ciência e Tecnologia).

References

1. Valli Kumari, V., Varma, N.S., Sri Krishna, A., Ramana, K.V., Raju, K.V.S.V.N.: Checking anonymity levels for anonymized data. In: Natarajan, R., Ojo, A. (eds.) ICDCIT 2011. LNCS, vol. 6536, pp. 278–289. Springer, Heidelberg (2011). https://doi.org/10.1007/978-3-642-19056-8_21

2. Vovk, O., Piho, G., Ross, P.: Evaluation of anonymization tools for health data. In: Bellatreche, L., Chernishev, G., Corral, A., Ouchani, S., Vain, J. (eds.) MEDI 2021. CCIS, vol. 1481, pp. 302–313. Springer, Cham (2021). https://doi.org/10.1007/978-3-030-87657-9_23

3. Pinnmaneni, N., Dodda, S., Muvva, S.C.: Anonymization and pseudo-anonymization for E-health care (2021)

4. Li, X.-B., Qin, J.: Anonymizing and sharing medical text records. Inf. Syst. Res. **28**(2), 332–352 (2017)

5. Pawar, A., Ahirrao, S., Churi, P.P.: Anonymization techniques for protecting privacy: a survey. In: 2018 IEEE Punecon (2018)

6. Ferreira, A., Chilro, R., Cruz-Correia, R.: AnyMApp framework: anonymous digital twin human-app interactions. In: HCI International 2022 - Late Breaking Papers. Design, User Experience and Interaction. Springer, Cham (2022). https://doi.org/10.1007/978-3-031-17615-9_15

7. Donker, T., Petrie, K., Proudfoot, J., Clarke, J., Birch, M.R., Christensen, H.: Smartphones forsmarter delivery of mental health programs: a systematic review. J. Med. Internet Res. **15**(11), e247 (2013). https://doi.org/10.2196/jmir.2791.PMID:24240579;PMCID:PMC3841358

8. Gordon, M.L., Gatys, L., Guestrin, C., Bigham, J.P., Trister, A., Patel, K.: App usage predicts cognitive ability in older adults. In: Proceedings of the 2019 CHI Conference on Human Factors in Computing Systems (CHI 2019), vol. 168, PP. 1–12. Association for Computing Machinery, New York (2019). https://doi.org/10.1145/3290605.3300398

9. Nogueira-Silva, L., et al.: Development of a mobile health app for the management of hypertension, including treatment adherence assessment, using image detection technology – inspirers-HTN. J. Hypertens. **39**, e380 (2021)

10. General Data Protection Regulation (EU) 2016/679 of the European Parliament and of the Council L 119. Official Journal of the European Union

Toxic Behavior and Tilt as Predictors of Mental Toughness in League of Legends Players of Argentina

Pablo Christian González Caino[1,2]($\boxtimes$) and Santiago Resett[1,2]

[1] Universidad Argentina de la Empresa, Buenos Aires, Argentina
pablo.cg.caino@hotmail.com
[2] Consejo Nacional de Investigaciones Científicas y Técnicas, Buenos Aires, Argentina

1 Introduction

Esports scene has grown globally in recent years, captivating millions of people (Marques 2019). Within South America, the latest data shows Argentina as the third most important country in the Latin American esports market, behind only Mexico and Brazil (Gala 2019). Being competitive in nature, esports can cause various negative emotions, such as frustration and sadness (Smith et al. 2019). One of the common phenomena related to this is Tilt, which is defined as a deviation from the typical way of playing in cognitive ability and self-control (Laakasuo et al. 2014). Its origins date back to pinball machines, where a player, out of frustration, would strike the machine, causing it to go into 'tilt' mode and cease to function correctly (Duncan 2015). Now, in the esports world, it refers to a loss of emotional control that impacts all game skills, such as reaction time and decision-making, and could lead to aversive behaviors during the game.

Different studies have shown that toxic behavior, characterized by anger and frustration, is expressed when players attribute performance problems to their teammates (Adinolf and Turkay 2018). This behavior negatively impacts communication within the game and contributes to a general negative atmosphere within the team (Kordyaka et al. 2019). Previous studies have also found that toxic behavior affects teammates more than opponents, influencing the emotional state of other players and potentially causing them to become toxic as well (Neto et al. 2017). Moreover, these behaviors also impact the well-being of players, leading to decreased enjoyment and retention of the game (Beres et al. 2021).

On the opposite end is mental toughness, which refers to an individual's ability to maintain high levels of subjective and objective performance despite challenges and stressors (Gucciardi et al. 2015). In the context of esports, mental toughness has been found to be closely related to high performance (González Caino 2020), and its study has gained significance in recent years (Poulus et al. 2020; González Caino 2020). It is important to be able to measure these phenomena within the context of esports, as factors like tilt and toxic behavior hinder a player's normal development in the game and can lead to them quitting (Kou and Gui 2020). The present study aims to examine the correlation and prediction of mental toughness based on tilt levels and toxic behavior in League of Legends.

C. Stephanidis et al. (Eds.): HCII 2023, CCIS 1958, pp. 464–468, 2024.
https://doi.org/10.1007/978-3-031-49215-0_55

2 Method

Participants. The sample for this study consisted of 1,210 League of Legends players, with 97% of them being male. The participants had a mean age of 21 years (SD = 4.06). They reported playing the game an average of 4.98 days per week (SD = 1.17), spending an average of 4.46 h per day playing (SD = 2.78). The majority of participants (70%) played the most during the night, followed by the afternoon (25%).

Measures

Sociodemographic Questionnaire: This assessed participants' gender, age, and other relevant information about their League of Legends usage habits.

Mental Toughness Index (MTI; Gucciardi et al. 2015): This measure evaluated levels of mental toughness, with higher scores indicating a greater presence of this trait. It utilized a unifactorial structure and a 7-point Likert scale (ranging from 1 - never to 7 - always). The Cronbach's alpha coefficient for this study was .87.

Toxic Behavior (TB; Kordyaka et al. 2019): This measure assessed toxic behavior within a League of Legends game, with higher scores indicating a greater presence of this negative behavior. It employed a unifactorial structure and a 5-point Likert scale (ranging from 1 - totally disagreed to 5 - totally agreed). The Cronbach's alpha coefficient for this study was .77.

Online Poker Tilt Scale (OPTS; Moreau et al. 2017): This scale measured the loss of control and deviation from strategy exhibited by players at cognitive, behavioral, and emotional levels. The structure consisted of three factors, and a 5-point Likert scale (ranging from 1 - totally disagreed to 5 - totally agreed) was used. The Cronbach's alpha coefficients for this study were .85 for the behavioral factor, .76 for the emotional factor, and .63 for the cognitive factor.

Data Recollection and Analysis. Data was collected through an online battery of questionnaires. Participants were recruited from various League of Legends-related social network groups, ensuring their confidentiality and anonymity throughout the study. The purpose of the study was clearly explained as being purely academic. Individuals who played for professional teams were excluded from the study, following the guidelines outlined by González Caino (2020).

Descriptive statistics, inferential analyses, and structural equation modeling were conducted using SPSS version 28 and AMOS version 20.

3 Results

Results showed a negative relationship between mental toughness and all Tilt dimensions, being the highest with emotional tilt ($r = -.280$, $p < .001$), as well as with toxic behavior ($r = -.122$, $p < .001$), which correlated positively with all dimensions of tilt. To analyze the effects of Tilt and toxic behavior on mental toughness, a structural equation model was performed. Figure 1 shows the proposed model with Tilt and toxic behavior as observable variables and mental toughness as an endogenous variable. An acceptable fit was found (CFI = .98, TLI = .95, RMSEA = .09; $x^2(4)$ = 43.188, p < .001). Table 1 shows the predictors produced by the model, where a direct effect of tilt on toxic behavior and mental toughness was found, but not of toxic behavior on the latter.

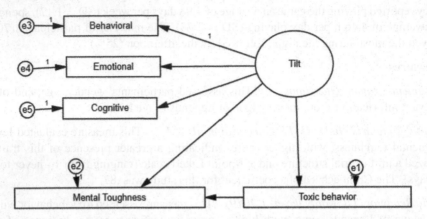

Fig. 1. Hybrid model with tilt and toxic behavior as observable variables and mental toughness as an endogenous variable.

Table 1. Predictors of the hybrid model with tilt and behavior as observable variables and mental toughness as endogenous variable

Predictors	
Tilt—>Toxic behavior	.569**
Tilt—>Behavioral tilt	1.00
Tilt—>Emotional tilt	.806**
Tilt—>Cognitive Tilt	.447**
Tilt—>Mental toughness	−.489**
Toxic behavior—>Mental toughness	−.006

*p < .05; ** p < .001

4   Discussion

The main objective of the present study was to analyze the correlations between tilt, toxic behavior, and mental toughness in the context of esports. The results revealed a negative correlation between both aversive behavior and mental toughness, but only tilt had a direct impact on mental toughness. This suggests that difficulties in emotional control have a stronger impact on performance than toxic behavior. Similar to traditional sports (Mohebi et al. 2017; Mutz and Clough 2017), emotional regulation plays a crucial role in esports performance. Situations within the game that cause frustration, such as losing a buff to another player, trolling behaviors, or errors in game performance, can lead to a decrease in mental toughness and performance. Studies in League of Legends have found that players manage their own emotions, as well as those of their opponents and teammates (Kou and Gui 2020). Therefore, when tilt occurs, it disrupts this emotional management, leading to difficulties in winning the game.

Furthermore, the results indicated that tilt is a strong predictor of toxic behaviors. The loss of emotional regulation during tilt may increase these kinds of behaviors, including trolling, flaming, or other aversive behaviors within the game (Lapolla 2020; Hilvert-Bruce and Neil 2020). These behaviors directly impact mental toughness and performance on both team and individual levels (Monge and O'Brien 2021), as they serve as a means of relieving the frustration experienced during tilt.

In conclusion, in-game frustration can lead to a breakdown in emotional control, which in turn impacts mental toughness and results in a decrease in team and individual performance. These behaviors may also have a contagious effect on other team players, accelerating the decline in performance and ultimately leading to a loss in the game. Future studies should explore other aversive behaviors, such as trolling, cyberbullying, or flaming in the esports context, and evaluate their impact on team performance and individual mental toughness. This knowledge can then be used to develop interventions aimed at preventing these aversive behaviors and enhancing mental toughness in esports players.

References

Adinolf, S., Turkay, S.: Toxic behaviors in Esports games: player perceptions and coping strategies. In: Proceedings of the 2018 Annual Symposium on Computer-Human Interaction in Play Companion Extended Abstracts, pp. 365–372 (2018). https://doi.org/10.1145/3270316.327 1545

Beres, N.A., Frommel, J., Reid, E., Mandryk, R.L., Klarkowski, M.: Don't you know that you're toxic: normalization of toxicity in online gaming. In: Proceedings of the 2021 CHI Conference on Human Factors in Computing Systems, pp. 1–15 (2021)

Duncan, A.M.: Gambling with the Myth of the American Dream. Routledge, Abingdon (2015)

Gala, R.: Mapa de la Industria Cultural de Videojuegos en Argentina: un estado de situación. Electron. J. SADIO (EJS) 18(2), 103–118 (2019)

González Caino, P.C.: Predicción de los estados de Flow según la personalidad en jugadores amateurs de deportes electrónicos. Acta Psiquiatr. Psicol. Am. Lat. 66(1), 32–38 (2020)

Gucciardi, D.F., Hanton, S., Gordon, S., Mallett, C.J., Temby, P.: The concept of mental toughness: tests of dimensionality, nomological network, and traitness. J. Pers. 83(1), 26–44 (2015). https://doi.org/10.1111/jopy.12079

Hilvert-Bruce, Z., Neill, J.T.: I'm just trolling: the role of normative beliefs in aggressive behaviour in online gaming. Comput. Hum. Behav. 102, 303–311 (2020). https://doi.org/10.1016/j.chb.2019.09.003

Kordyaka, B., Klesel, M., Jahn, K.: Perpetrators in league of legends: scale development and validation of toxic behavior. In: Proceedings of the 52nd Hawaii International Conference on System Sciences, Hawaii, pp. 2486–2495 (2019). https://doi.org/10.24251/hicss.2019.299

Kou, Y., Gui, X.: Emotion regulation in eSports gaming: a qualitative study of league of legends. In: Proceedings of the ACM on Human-Computer Interaction, vol. 4, no. CSCW2, pp. 1–25 (2020). https://doi.org/10.1145/3415229

Laakasuo, M., Palomäki, J., Salmela, M.: Experienced poker players are emotionally stable. Cyberpsychol. Behav. Soc. Netw. **17**(10), 668–671 (2014). https://doi.org/10.1089/cyber.2014. 0147

Lapolla, M.: Tackling Toxicity: Identifying and Addressing Toxic Behavior in Online Video Games (2020)

Marques, N.: The role of breakthrough technologies in the growth of esports. IEEE Pot. **38**(3), 24–26 (2019). https://doi.org/10.1109/mpot.2019.2893754

Mohebi, M., Zarei, S., Sohbatiha, M.: The relationship between Emotion regulation strategies and mental toughness in elite taekwondo athletes. Sport Psychol. Stud. **6**(21), 29–42 (2017)

Monge, C.K., O'Brien, T.C.: Effects of individual toxic behavior on team performance in League of Legends. Media Psychol. **25**(1), 82–105 (2022)

Moreau, A., Delieuvin, J., Chabrol, H., Chauchard, E.: Online Poker Tilt Scale (OPTS): creation and validation of a tilt assessment in a French population. Int. Gambl. Stud. **17**(2), 205–218 (2017). https://doi.org/10.1080/14459795.2017.1321680

Mutz, J., Clough, P., Papageorgiou, K.A.: Do individual differences in emotion regulation mediate the relationship between mental toughness and symptoms of depression? J. Individ. Diff. (2017)

Neto, J.A., Yokoyama, K.M., Becker, K.: Studying toxic behavior influence and player chat in an online video game. In: Proceedings of the International Conference on Web Intelligence, pp. 26–33 (2017). https://doi.org/10.1145/3106426.3106452

Poulus, D., Coulter, T.J., Trotter, M.G., Polman, R.: Stress and coping in esports and the influence of mental toughness. Front. Psychol. **11**, 628 (2020). https://doi.org/10.3389/fpsyg.2020.00628

Smith, M.J., Birch, P.D., Bright, D.: Identifying stressors and coping strategies of elite esports competitors. Int. J. Gaming Comput.-Mediat. Simul. (IJGCMS) **11**(2), 22–39 (2019)

Furry - Design of Augmented Reality Blind Box

Winchy Wenqi Jia and Mickey Mengting Zhang[✉]

Macau University of Science and Technology, Macau, China
mtzhang@must.edu.mo

Abstract. Furry fandom becomes an influential sub-culture in social media among the young generation. More and more people love anthropomorphic animal characters and like to engage in magical thinking, the fantasy activities like a furry animal. However, the furry content or activities are mainly based offline, on the website, or scatter on social media. It is hard to find a mobile-based platform for furry fans to create, share, and exchange. In addition, the blind box industry develops quickly, which grabs the imagination of young consumers and raises incredible social excitement. However, the physical version of the blind box has various limitations, such as delivery, space occupation, expense, etc. Inspired by the needs of furry fans and the concept of a blind box, we develop a platform named 'FURRY' - a creative, fantasy, and interactive platform for the creation, sharing, and monetization of the animal-themed virtual blind box based on augmented reality technology and social media. Users can collect random parts of a virtual animal from the blind box and wear them to become an anthropomorphic animal character they prefer. In this paper, the whole structure of the platform is discussed. The four sections of FURRY including obtaining, playing, building fursona, and mine are introduced in detail. Then the markerless AR applied in the project is discussed. Two stages preprocessing and real-time processing are introduced to create an interactive user experience. The results of the present research are expected to help vitalize and expand the practice of AR-based culture content.

Keywords: Blind Box · Augmented Reality · Furry Fandom

1 Introduction

1.1 Blind Box Strategy

The blind box concept first originated in Japan in the 1980s with the "Fukubukuro" [1], which means "lucky bag" or "fortune bag" as a marketing strategy. Goods are wrapped randomly in one bag at a lower price than usual, while people do not know exactly what they buy before they purchase. Many merchants use the lucky bag as a way to clean up storage, as they mix unpopular products with hot ones in one bag. The products inside of a box can be a doll, a book, a video game, and so on. The "lucky bag" is the early form of blind box, which continues to evolve rapidly grow in China since 2019. A series of products, usually a doll, with specific features like facial expressions, clothes, or decoration are sold in terms of the blind boxes [2]. Consumers that purchase the blind box know which product line the product belongs to, but do not know the exact product they purchase in advance. In order to collect the whole series, a consumer usually needs to purchase more times than ordinary times. Since some hidden figures are very popular and rare, and the probability of getting them is extremely low, many people are willing to pay exponential prices for them. For example, the price of a popular blind box toy from POP Mart brand grew 39 times, from 59 RMB to 2,350 RMB. The revenue of POP Mart increased from 2,513.5 million RMB in 2020 to 4,490.7 million RMB in 2021, representing a year-on-year increase of 78.7% [5]. The market size of the blind box in China is about to exceed 47.8 billion CYN by 2022 [6]. This has also led to the development of a secondary market for trading products from the blind box (e.g., Idle Fish). In 2019, approximately 300,000 blind box players successfully traded on Idle Fish throughout the year. The intentional reduction of production, limited selling, and hunger marketing strategy, together with the exchange community stimulate a strong purchasing desire of consumers and the prosperity of the industry [4].

1.2 Augmented Reality Technology

Although the blind box industry develops at a tremendous speed, the products sold are still in terms of physical form rather than virtual form. We consider integrating the concept of the blind box together with augmented reality (AR) technology. AR technology combines virtual information with the real world, which users can rely on it to enhance their perception of the real world [30]. Its principle is to apply computer-generated virtual information, such as text, images, 3D models, music, video, etc. to the real world after simulation [31]. In this way, the two kinds of information complement each other, thus achieving the enhancement of the real world. Mobile phones have become increasingly capable of interactive 3D graphics, which increases the application of AR technology in fields like tourism, archaeology, art, commerce, industrial manufacturing and restoration, education, emergency management, entertainment and leisure, medical treatment, and so on. From its technical means and expressions, AR technology can be divided in to at least two categories: Vision-based AR and Laser Beam Scanning AR (LBS) AR. The first is based on computer vision, while the second is based on geographic location information [34]. Most mobile phones on the market are already equipped with AR function. In the project of FURRY, the Vision-based AR is applied based on the smart phone's camera, processor, and display to recognize and augment what the camera sees.

1.3 Furry Fandom

The furry fandom is a subculture interested in anthropomorphic animal characters [13–15]. Examples of anthropomorphic attributes include animal figures that exhibit human intelligence and facial expressions, speaking, walking on two legs, and wearing clothes. Furry fans, or "furries," are defined by their interest in anthropomorphism - the ascription of human traits to animals [22]. Furries build community to create share and gather at furry conventions [16, 17]. While the literature has illustrated the varieties of human-animal relationships, much of the research has treated the human-animal connection as one-dimensional. Furry fandom treats animals in a different way. They admire and learn from animals and build a spiritual connection with them [18]. A person can identify himself/herself as a furry animal-fursona, and engage in magical thinking, fantasy experiences, or fantasy activities [19]. The fursona is idealized and represent who they want to be. They feel the animal circle is a more comfortable place, because their public identity is set and constrained, while the fursona can protect them to be themselves [20]. The fursona that these furries craft requires a great deal of time and energy [21]. Furries perceive the furry fandom to be distinct from other fan groups [24] and the extent to which they feel they belong to the furry fandom strongly predicts their identification with the fandom. However, currently most of the furry groups are offline community, website-based ones or scattered on social media (Fig. 1). There is great potential to create a mobile-based furry community for people like furry culture.

Fig. 1. Furry fan in social media

2   Design Solution of Furry

Based on the evaluation above, we initiate a project named FURRY - a creative, fantasy, and cozy platform for people who like furry culture. The platform enables users to create, exchange, and trade virtual random parts (RP) inspired by the image of cute animals like ears, clothes, limb, head, or accessories. These RPs are in the form of blind boxes, which are created by artists, designers, or from IP, or general users. After collecting it, a user can wear it in the digital world supported by AR technology. When users are moving on the screen, the wearable RP will move accordingly in real-time, producing an interactive experience. With wearable RP, users can create and share interesting content, like stickers, photos or short videos. The platform helps people that like furry culture to express themselves (e.g., interests, personality, lifestyle); build up the social relationship; and sense the feeling of connection, love, and self-accomplishment.

2.1   Get Section of FURRY

Users can go to the 'free' section, to download the RP blind box without cost. The free RP are basic furry parts, which enable users to try. Some of them are already embedded in the system. As soon as a user launch FURRY, they can find them. Others can be downloaded immediately. Users can purchase the RP blind box from their favorite collections in the 'market' section. Users can check information on the whole collections already offered on the platform, the latest ones, and the 'coming soon' RP. The RP sold can be created by artists, designers, famous IPs, or anyone. Detailed information about the RP and the creators is provided, together with NFT information. In addition, users can exchange for limited edition RP with points collected from online tasks, activities, communities, or purchases. Users can also share, exchange, or sell RP they do not want in the 'community' section. Information about the furry fandom, new IP on the market, popular creators will also be displayed in this section. Users can make collecting plans according to their interests and the new trend (Fig. 2).

Fig. 2. Design Strategy of FURRY

2.2 Play Section of FURRY

After collecting an RP, a user can 'wear' it on his/her face to see the effect. They can take photos or videos with it, then download and store them, or share them with friends. They can also make static or dynamic furry stickers, save or share with friends. Users can build and choose to demonstrate their own digital museum with the RP collection they gathered. All of the RPs collected can be displayed in the section of 'achievement', users can see the progress of the collection to know which parts they still need to assemble a whole furry figure. Other furries can also view the 'achievement' of the user, which may attract attention, and traffic and bring a sense of accomplishment and fulfillment.

In the project of FURRY, we use Marker-less AR technology. When users turn on the function, they can select the RP in their 'achievement' and see themselves wearing RP on the screen. When they are moving on the screen, like shaking or turning their head, the RP will move accordingly, producing an interactive experience. Generally, there are two stages to achieve this model-based object recognition and creation of augmented reality via computer vision: pre-processing and real-time processing [41]. In the pre-processing stage, a user's facial features and the RP features are extracted. Then a correspondence between facial features and RP features is found. After that, the system determines the pose of RP from correspondence. The structure from motion (SfM) method is used to reconstruct a user's 3D facial model with photographs taken from multiple viewpoints. The position and orientation data of a user's face from all viewpoints are stored in a database. Second, the coordinates of RP that should be augmented are defined relative to coordinates of the user's face model reconstructed by SfM and are stored in a database. Finally, key points and features of each photograph used for the SfM are extracted and saved in a text file (Fig. 3).

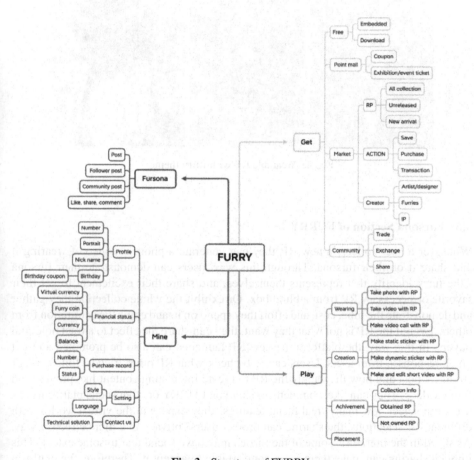

Fig. 3. Structure of FURRY

In the real-time processing stage, first, the files created in the pre-processing stage are imported. Second, features of the live video images of users are extracted using algorithms like Speeded-Up Robust Features (SURF) in real-time, and extracted features of users' live video images are compared with features of stored images in the database [42].

Finally, the 3D RP is precisely rendered in an AR display using position and orientation data of the camera and by finding the most similar image in the database. Motion vectors are calculated using optical flow for tracking. Then, by using internal parameters, the position of points on the screen, and the world coordinates of their corresponding points, the system calculate external parameters. For comparing key features between live video images of a user and all stored images in the database, approximate nearest neighbor search by Locality Sensitive Hashing (LSH) algorithm is also applied [43] (Fig. 4).

Fig. 4. Wearable RP with furry theme

2.3   Fursona Section of FURRY

Whenever a user collects a new RP, they can generate a photo or video of wearing it and share it on their fursona. Through this way, users can demonstrate their fursona - the furry identity that represents themselves, and share their excitement to get their favorite or necessary RP from a blind box. Or exhibit the whole collection they gather and demonstrate the time, cost, and effort they spend on it, and enjoy the admiration from others. Even if the RP is not what they want, they can share the effect to attract potential buyers. In this way, the platform the new RP launched can also be promoted and get quick responses from users. Users can also check what RP other friends, followers, or strangers post and how they apply the RP to create interesting content like pranks, and funny videos. They can like, comment, or share on FURRY or other social platforms. As users can select how many 'real facial features' they expose in the virtual worlds with different RP selections, the sharing can protect users' privacy in a more effective way. As stated in the literature, some of the furries may have social fear to some extent. This implicit sharing can make them more comfortable to accept it. Therefore, the platform has a social function, which allows users to easily trigger a conversation with people who have similar interests and creates a sense of belonging and social recognition. We intend to create a cozy, cute, and inclusive atmosphere. Furries are likely to identify themselves with other members of the fan community. The community is based on fandom and fanship. Fandom relates to fursona, which identifies a person primarily within the fan community. The sense of identity gained from being a part of the community is an important motivator for a user's participation. While fanship identifies primarily with the figure/item of fan interest. It also helps to build up the relationship between fans.

2.4   Mine Section of FURRY

Users in the section of mine can edit and display their 'profile' with member number, portrait, nick name, birthday and other information. They can check their financial account status in 'financial service' section, to see the balance of virtual currency, furry coins, currency, coupon, points and other information. Users can also see the purchase RP status. They can setup the style, language and other information on the 'mine' page. They can also contact with the FURRY team through the 'contact us' function.

References

1. Yu, S.: Blind Box, the Latest Trend Taking Over China by Storm. Pingwest (2019). https://en.pingwest.com/a/3720#:~:text=The%20idea%20of%20blind%20box,"for tune%20bag"%20in%20Japanese. Accessed 28 Dec 2021
2. Huidobro Giménez, C.: Normalizing sustainable consumption: how marketing is used to fight food waste. a case study with too good to go, the movement that fights food waste across Europe. Master's Thesis, Lund University, Lund, Sweden (2019)
3. Zhao, R., Xu, J.: New marketing inspired by blind box. In: 2021 4th International Conference on Humanities Education and Social Sciences (ICHESS 2021), pp. 1673–1676. Atlantis Press (2021)
4. Gao, J., Chen, R.: Understanding consumer behaviors of Generation Z under China's blind box economy: case company: POP MART (2022)
5. Among them, one of the most sought-after blind boxes from POP MART grew 39 times in price, with an original price of 59 CNY selling for 2,350 CNY
6. Securities Times. Chinese Academy of Social Sciences(2021,)
7. Released a report on the market development of trendy games: the scale is https://baijiahao. baidu.com/s?id=1720033572506757950&wfr=spider&for=pc
8. Jabr, F.: How the Brain Gets Addicted to Gambling. Scientific American, a division of Nature America, Inc. (2013)
9. Arain, M., et al.: Maturation of the adolescent brain. Neuropsychiatr. Dis. Treat. **9**, 449–461 (2013). https://doi.org/10.2147/NDT.S39776
10. Zhang, Z.: Research on blind box and its marketing strategy. In: 2021 International Conference on Economic Development and Business Culture (ICEDBC 2021), pp. 115–118. Atlantis Press (2021)
11. Zendle, D.: Links between problem gambling and spending on booster packs in collectible card games: a conceptual replication of research on loot boxes (2019). https://doi.org/10. 31234/osf.io/ps54r
12. Walker, M.B.: Irrational thinking among slot machine players. J. Gambl. Stud. **8**(3), 245–261 (1992)
13. Gupta, A., Eilert, M., Gentry, J.W.: Can I surprise myself? a conceptual framework of surprise self-gifting among consumers. J. Retail. Consum. Serv. **54**, 101712 (2020)
14. Staeger, R.: Invasion of the Furries. The Wayne Suburban (2001). Accessed 20 May 2009
15. Matthews, D.: 9 questions about furries you were too embarrassed to ask. Vox. Archived from the original on July 29, 2016 (2015). Accessed 07 Aug 2016
16. Aaron, M.: More than just a pretty face: unmasking furry fandom. Psychol. Today (2017)

17. Kurutz, D.R.: It's a furry weekend in Pittsburgh. Pittsburgh Tribune-Review. Archived from the original on March 3, 2016 (2006). Accessed 30 June 2006

18. Hsu, K.J., Bailey, J.M.: The "Furry" phenomenon: characterizing sexual orientation, sexual motivation, and erotic target identity inversions in male furries. Arch. Sex. Behav. **48**(5), 1349–1369 (2019). https://doi.org/10.1007/s10508-018-1303-7

19. Gerbasi, K., et al.: Furries from A to Z (anthropomorphism to zoomorphism). Soc. Anim. **16**, 197–222 (2008)

20. See Furry Fiesta 2012 and International Online Survey III; Furry Fiesta 2012 and International Online Survey III

21. 驳静 路雅. 逃離內捲、治愈社恐: 迷戀"毛毛"的獸世界小孩. 三聯生活周刊 (2021). Accessed 30 Aug 2022

22. Reysen, S., Plante, C.N., Roberts, S.E., Gerbasi, K.C.: My animal self: the importance of preserving fantasy-themed identity uniqueness. Identity **20**(1), 1–8 (2020)

23. Gerbasi, K.C., et al.: Furries from A to Z (anthropomorphism to zoomorphism). Soc. Anim. **16**, 197–222 (2008)

24. Reysen, S., Plante, C.N., Roberts, S.E., Gerbasi, K.C.: Social identity perspective of the furry fandom. Manuscript submitted for publication (2015)

25. Plante, C.N., Roberts, S.E., Snider, J.S., Schroy, C., Reysen, S., Gerbasi, K.: "More than skin-deep": biological essentialism in response to a distinctiveness threat in a stigmatized fan community. Brit. J. Social Psychol. **54**, 359–370 (2015)

26. Reysen, S., Shaw, J.: Sport fan as the default fan: why nonsport fans are stigmatized. Phoenix Pap. **2**, 234–252 (2015)

27. Reysen, S., Plante, C.N., Roberts, S.E., Gerbasi, K.C.: Optimal distinctiveness and identification with the furry fandom. Curr. Psychol. **35**(4), 638–642 (2016)

28. Schroy, C., Plante, C., Reysen, S., Roberts, S., Gerbasi, K.: Different motivations as predictors of psychological connection to fan interest and fan groups in anime, furry, and fantasy sport fandoms. Phoenix Pap. **2**, 148–167 (2016)

29. International Furry Survey: Summer (2011). https://furscience.com/research-findings/app endix-1-previous-research/international-summer-2011

30. Caudell, T.: AR at Boeing (1990). Accessed 10 July 2002. https://www.idemployee.id.tue.nl/ gwmrauterberg/presentations/hci-history/sld096.htm

31. Chen, Y., Wang, Q., Chen, H., Song, X., Tang, H., Tian, M.: An overview of augmented reality technology. J. Phys: Conf. Ser. **1237**, 022082 (2019). https://doi.org/10.1088/1742-6596/1237/2/022082

32. Tianyu, H., et al.: Overview of augmented reality technology. Comput. Knowl. Technol. **34**, 194–196 (2017). (in Chinese)

33. Robinett, W.: Synthetic experience: a proposed taxonomy. Pres. Teleoper. Virt. Environ. **1**(2), 229–247 (1992)

34. Lee, C., et al.: Indoor positioning system based on incident angles of infrared emitters. In: 30th Annual Conference of IEEE Industrial Electronics Society, 2004. IECON 2004, vol. 3, pp. 2218–2222. IEEE (2004)

35. https://www.qualcomm.com/news/onq/2011/02/vision-based-augmented-reality

36. Bachmann, D., Weichert, F., Rinkenauer, G.: Review of three-dimensional human-computer interaction with focus on the leap motion controller. Sensors **18**(7), 2194 (2018). https://doi. org/10.3390/s18072194

37. Lepetit, V., Fua, P.: Monocular model-based 3d tracking of rigid objects: a survey. Found. Trends® Comput. Graph. Vision **1**(1), 1–89 (2005)

38. Feng, C., Kamat, V.R.: Augmented reality markers as spatial indices for indoor mobile AECFM applications. In: Proceedings of 12th International Conference on Construction Applications of Virtual Reality (CONVR 2012), pp. 235–24 (2012)

39. Behzadan, A.H.: ARVISCOPE: georeferenced visualization of dynamic construction processes in three-dimensional outdoor augmented reality. Doctoral dissertation, University of Michigan (2008)
40. Kubac, L., Kebo, V., Benes, F., Stasa, P.: RFID and augmented reality. In: Proceedings of the 14th International Carpathian Control Conference (ICCC) (2013)
41. Gerstweiler, G., Vonach, E., Kaufmann, H.: HyMoTrack: a mobile AR navigation system for complex indoor environments. Sensors **16**(1), 17 (2015)
42. Lutfi, A., Putra, F.P., Prayitno, E.: Multi Marker Augmented Reality sebagai Media Edukasi Bahaya Merokok. In: Seminar Nasional Industri Dan Teknologi (SNIT), Politeknik Negeri Bengkalis, pp. 247–255 (2016)
43. Bay, H., Ess, A., Tuytelaars, T., Van Gool, L.: Speeded-up robust features (SURF). Comput. Vis. Image Underst. **110**(3), 346–359 (2008)

Evaluation of Emotional Changes Caused by Wearing Gothic Lolita Using Physiological Sensors

Linze Jing, Chen Feng, Yanzhi Li, and Midori Sugaya(✉)

Shibaura Institute of Technology, Koto-ku, Tokyo 135-8548, Japan
{ma22056,i042370,nb22509,doly}@shibaura-it.ac.jp

Abstract. Goth is a music-based subculture that has a dark worldview and has influenced fashion, fiction, and art. In Japan, the Goth subculture was merged with Lolita clothing to create Gothic Lolita, which has been popular for over 20 years. Although previous research has shown that wearing Gothic Lolita can have positive emotional effects on the wearers. However, these studies mainly rely on questionnaires and interviews, which can be influenced by various factors such as the possibility of mixing the intentions of participants into the results. To address this issue, we applied a method that applied EEG signals and HRV indexes to evaluate the emotions of the participants. Since the Gothic Lolita is the darkest style within Lolita clothing, in this study, we did a preliminary experiment to collect physiological information while wearing Lolita clothing. We applied time-series analysis to collected data. As the result, the collected EEG signals and HRV indexes were more positive when wearing Lolita clothing than when wearing ordinary clothing. Both questionnaires and physiological information evaluations showed that wearing Lolita clothing increased the participants' arousal, valence, and dominance.

Keywords: Gothic Lolita · Physiological Sensors · Emotion Evaluation

1 Introduction

Goth is a music-based subculture that has a dark worldview that exists in fashion, fiction, and art [1]. After the Goth subculture spread to Japan, it was combined with Lolita clothing to produce Gothic Lolita [2]. And Gothic Lolita has been for at least 20 years [3]. However, the psychology-related studies on Gothic Lolita are not sufficient. Tokuyama conducted a psychology study by using questionnaires and interviews and the results indicated that Gothic Lolita could give wearers the emotion of being "protected" and bring positive emotional effects [4]. The methods used in the above previous studies were questionnaires and interviews. Although questionnaires are the most common form of emotion evaluation, they suffer from such demerits as linguistic ambiguity and the possibility of mixing the intentions of participants into the results [5]. To better evaluate participants' emotions while wearing Gothic Lolita, we adopted Ikeda's [6] method of estimating emotion. which uses physiological information such as EEG signals and

C. Stephanidis et al. (Eds.): HCII 2023, CCIS 1958, pp. 478–484, 2024.
https://doi.org/10.1007/978-3-031-49215-0_57

heart rate variability (HRV) indexes to infer the participants' emotions. Ikeda's method can obtain emotional data without participants' subjective thinking. To obtain a more accurate evaluation of the emotion of Gothic Lolita wearers, a method combining both questionnaires and physiological information evaluations was utilized. Because Gothic Lolita is the darkest style within Lolita clothing [3], Before using Gothic Lolita for the experiment, we conducted a preliminary experiment using Lolita clothing to evaluate the emotion of the participant wearing Lolita clothing. The data collected from the preliminary experiment with Lolita clothing was subjected to time-series analysis, and the results of the preliminary experiment were obtained. From these results, it was observed that the EEG signals and HRV indexes collected from the participant were more positive when wearing Lolita clothing than when wearing ordinary clothing. The results of both questionnaires and physiological information evaluations revealed that wearing Lolita clothing led to an increase in participants' arousal, valence, and dominance.

2 Literature Survey

In Tokuyama's [4] study, Gothic Lolita wearers were asked to fill out a questionnaire and be interviewed for one hour. Tokuyama asked the wearers to use their own words to describe their emotions while wearing Gothic Lolita. The results of Tokuyama's study showed that Gothic Lolita can bring confidence to wearers. However, the method used by Tokuyama is inevitably subject to certain drawbacks, such as linguistic ambiguity and the potential for participants' intentions to affect the results.

Ikeda [6] proposed a method for evaluating emotion using a simple EEG sensor and a pulse sensor. He established a correspondence between the psychological Russell's circle model [7] and physiological indexes. The y-axis (arousal index) in the circle model is represented by the EEG signal. The x-axis (valence index) in the circle model is represented by the HRV index detected. This method can obtain the nonconscious emotion of the participant objectively. However, this model cannot evaluate the confidence of the participant.

Meanwhile, the psychological model PAD [8], based on the original 2D model, adds the dominance index. A higher value of the dominance index that the participant is confident [9]. Because we need to evaluate the confidence emotions of the participant, we choose the PAD model. Liu [10] combined dominance index and EEG signals so that dominance indexes could be quantified using β/α from the prefrontal lobes of the brain.

In this study, the above three indexes will be used to evaluate emotions.

3 Method

3.1 Emotion Estimation with Physiological Information

In this study, a simple EEG sensor was used to collect EEG signals. The values of attention-meditation represent the arousal index. Attention represents a state of focused thinking, while Meditation indicates a relaxed yet conscious state. So, attention-meditation can be used as an index of arousal. In this study, the higher the arousal index, the more focused the participants' attention.

The value of β/α of the prefrontal lobe of the brain represents the dominance index. In this study, the higher the dominance index, the more confident the participants were.

Also, the HRV index was collected using a pulse sensor, and the value of pNN50 represented the valence index. pNN50 is an index of the magnitude of fluctuation in the R-R interval (RRI), which represents the time interval of HRV, and a higher value is considered to indicate parasympathetic dominance. Therefore, a lower value of pNN50 indicates sympathetic dominance and a state of tension, while a higher value indicates parasympathetic dominance and a state of relaxation. In this study, the higher the valence index, the more enjoyment experienced by the participants.

3.2 Questionnaire

To evaluate emotions, Margaret M. Bradley proposed a subjective questionnaire which is the Self-Assessment Manikin (SAM) [11]. SAM questionnaire contains three indexes of valence-Arousal-Dominance. SAM questionnaire is not related to language. It can reduce the influence of linguistic ambiguity.

In this study, the results of the SAM questionnaire were used as a supplement and comparison to the method of using physiological information emotional evaluation results.

4 Purpose and proposal

In this study, we aim to provide a more accurate emotional evaluation of participants who wear Lolita clothing. Both methods were used to evaluate the participants' emotions while wearing Lolita clothing. We used a simple EEG sensor to collect EEG signals and a pulse sensor to collect the HRV indexes. The results of the EEG signal and HRV were used to classify three indexes arousal, valence, and dominance. And we also used the SAM questionnaire. The results of these methods were combined to obtain the results of evaluating the emotions of Lolita clothing wearers.

5 Experiment

We conducted a preliminary experiment to evaluate the emotion of the Lolita clothing wearer.

First, the participant was asked to wear two sensors, a simple EEG sensor, and a pulse sensor. Then, the participant was asked to stand in front of a full-length mirror wearing different clothes and view themselves in the mirror. The appearance seen in the mirror was used as the stimulus for this experiment, and the data of EEG signal and HRV indexes were collected. The participant stands in front of a full-length mirror covered with white fabric and looks at the white fabric for two minutes. Then, the white
We conducted a preliminary experiment to evaluate the emotion of the Lolita clothing wearer.

First, the participant was asked to wear two sensors, a simple EEG sensor, and a pulse sensor. Then, the participant was asked to stand in front of a full-length mirror wearing different clothes and view themselves in the mirror. The appearance seen in the mirror was used as the stimulus for this experiment, and the data of EEG signal and HRV indexes were collected. The participant stands in front of a full-length mirror covered with white fabric and looks at the white fabric for two minutes. Then, the white fabric is removed from the mirror and the participant is asked to look at her reflection in the mirror for 2 min. Finally, we used the SAM questionnaire to obtain subjective data (Fig. 1).

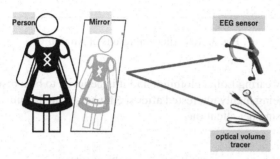

Fig. 1. The preliminary experiment

6 Results

The results of the preliminary experiment are as follows:

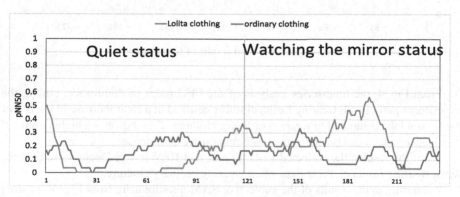

Fig. 2. Experimental results of Valence

Figure 2, the time-series analysis of the HRV index of valence. Compared to wearing ordinary clothing, wearing Lolita clothing resulted in a higher pNN50 value, indicating increased enjoyment while wearing Gothic Lolita clothing.

Figure 3, the time-series analysis of the EEG index of arousal. Attention-Meditation during Lolita clothing wearing is higher compared to wearing ordinary clothing, indicating higher arousal. In particular, the arousal during the first half of the experiment

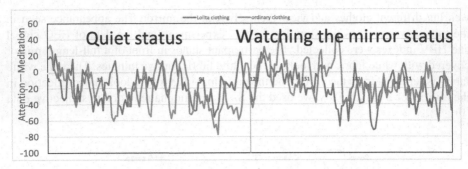

Fig. 3. Experimental results of Arousal

was higher when wearing Lolita clothing, and it is believed to be a result of the experiment participant being highly interested after seeing herself in the mirror wearing Lolita clothing and focusing her attention.

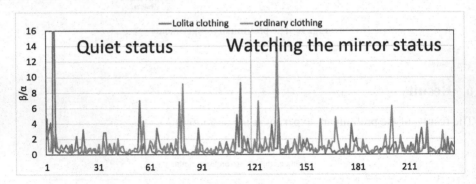

Fig. 4. Experimental results of Dominance

From Fig. 4, the time-series analysis of the EEG index of dominance, among the experiment participant, wearing Lolita clothing resulted in a clear increase in the β/α of the frontal lobe compared to wearing ordinary clothing. This indicates a higher value of dominance, which can be interpreted as having more confidence.

From the results, the collected EEG signals and HRV indexes were more positive when wearing Lolita clothing than when wearing ordinary clothing.

According to the results of the subjective SAM questionnaire from Fig. 5, wearing Lolita clothing was perceived to result in higher arousal, indicating higher levels of concentration, compared to wearing ordinary clothing. The valence level was also higher, and the participant was found to be clearly experiencing more enjoyment when wearing Lolita clothing compared to ordinary clothing. Furthermore, the value of dominance was higher, and the participant was found to have more confidence when wearing Lolita clothing.

The SAM questionnaire also gave a positive result.

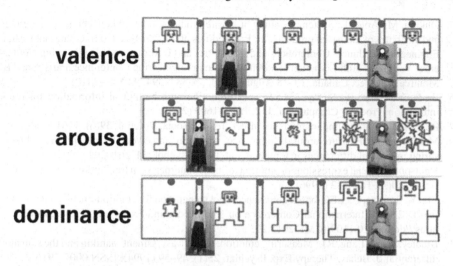

Fig. 5. Experimental results of SAM questionnaire

The results of the questionnaire and physiological information evaluations corroborated with each other, indicating that wearing Lolita clothing could increase the enjoyment and confidence of the participant.

7 Conclusion

In this study, a method combining questionnaire, and physiological information evaluations were applied to evaluate the emotions of Lolita clothing wearers. In the preliminary experiment, the results of the questionnaire and physiological information evaluations of emotions corroborated each other, demonstrating the validity of this method. Additional experiments will be conducted in this study for more detailed data analysis for the evaluation of emotions.

In future studies, we will focus on Gothic Lolita, the darkest style within Lolita clothing. We plan to conduct the next experiment using Gothic Lolita as the experimental clothing. We will increase the number of participants to 30 or more to enhance the persuasiveness of the results.

References

1. Newman, S.: The evolution of the perceptions of the goth subculture. Evolution **4**, 26–2018 (2018)
2. Winge, T.: Undressing and dressing loli: a search for the identity of the Japanese Lolita. Mechademia **3**(1), 47–63 (2008)
3. Carriger, M.: "Maiden's Armor": global gothic lolita fashion communities and technologies of girly counter identity. Theatr. Surv. **60**(1), 122–146 (2019)
4. Tomoe, T.: Clinical psychological potential of gothic lolita. Res. Rep. Fac. Clin. Psychol. **7**, 71–84 (2015)

5. Ohkura, M., Aoto, T.: Systematic study of kawaii products: relation between kawaii feelings and attributes of industrial products. In: Proceedings of the ASME 2010 International Design Engineering Technical Conferences and Computers and Information in Engineering Conference. Volume 3: 30th Computers and Information in Engineering Conference, Parts A and B. Montreal, Quebec, Canada, 15–18 August 2010. pp. 587–594. ASME (2010)

6. Ikeda, Y., Horie, R., Sugaya, M.: Estimate emotion with biological information for robot interaction. Procedia Comput. Sci. **112**, 1589–1600 (2017)

7. Russell, J.A.: A circumplex model of affect. J. Pers. Social Psychol. **39**(6), 1161 (1980)

8. Mehrabian, A.: Pleasure-arousal-dominance: a general framework for describing and measuring individual differences in temperament. Curr. Psychol. **14**, 261–292 (1996)

9. Knutson, B.: Facial expressions of emotion influence interpersonal trait inferences. J. Nonverb. Behav. **20**(3), 165–182 (1996)

10. Liu, Y., Sourina, O.: EEG-based dominance level recognition for emotion-enabled interaction. In: 2012 IEEE International Conference on Multimedia and Expo, pp. 1039–1044 (2012). https://doi.org/10.1109/ICME.2012.20.

11. Bradley, M.M., Lang, P.J.: Measuring emotion: the self-assessment manikin and the semantic differential. J. Behav. Therapy Exp. Psychiat. **25**(1), 49–59 (1994). ISSN 0005-7916

A Study of the Comparative Evaluation System of the Lower-Limb Exoskeleton

Yong-Ku Kong[1], Sang-Soo Park[1], Jin-Woo Shim[1], Dae-Min Kim[2], Heung-Youl Kim[3], and Hyun-Ho Shim[1(✉)]

[1] Department of Industrial Engineering, Sungkyunkwan University, Seoul, Korea
shim2906@naver.com
[2] Department of ICT Convergence Engineering, Dongseo University, Busan, Korea
[3] Physical Education Center, Nanzan University, Nagoya, Japan

Abstract. The aim of this study is to develop a comparative evaluation system of the lower-limb exoskeletons. First, the comparative evaluation factors were classified into five categories: *ease of wearing, safety, sense of wearing, effectiveness*, and *ease of use*, based on the characteristics of the lower-limb exoskeletons. Then, a total of 15 questions were designed for 20 participants who had no experience with musculoskeletal disorders in this study. All participants tested the three lower-limb exoskeletons (CEX, Archelis, and Chairless Chair) and scored their subjective ratings on an 11-point scale. The results showed that the CEX was rated the highest for *ease of wearing* and *effectiveness*, whereas Archelis received the highest score for *safety* and *ease of use*. Based on the results, it was noted that the back support of the lower-limb exoskeletons should be removed, and the knee angle should be adjustable for various ranges to fit the users. In addition, exoskeleton developers would be better focused on *ease of wearing* and *ease of use* to improve the lower-limb exoskeleton. Based on this study, it is expected to be used as important and fundamental data for users' requirements for more convenient and safer exoskeletons' design.

Keywords: lower-limb exoskeleton · Work-related musculoskeletal disorder (WMSDs) · Comparative evaluation · CEX · Chairless Chair · Archelis

1 Introduction

Work-related musculoskeletal disorders (WMSDs) cause chronic damage to muscles, bones, and joints due to accumulated workload, which restricts working and daily life by reducing strength and range of motion [1]. Work-related musculoskeletal disorders that caused pain in various body parts, such as the lumbar, neck, and shoulder, occurred in many fields of industries, such as manufacturing, agriculture, construction, and transportation [2]. Among them, in the case of agriculture, awkward postures such as squatting, knee flexion, back flexion, and stretching arms far away frequently appeared, which caused pain in the lumbar, leg, and knee [3].

An exoskeleton that supports motion and posture has recently been attracted worldwide to prevent work-related musculoskeletal disorders [4, 5]. The exoskeleton was

C. Stephanidis et al. (Eds.): HCII 2023, CCIS 1958, pp. 485–492, 2024.
https://doi.org/10.1007/978-3-031-49215-0_58

classified into three types: upper-limb exoskeleton, lower-limb exoskeleton, and lumbar exoskeleton, according to supporting body parts. The upper-limb exoskeleton prevented shoulder lifting posture at high working point, the lower-limb exoskeleton prevented knee and lumbar flexion posture and helped both standing and sitting working when performing standing working, the lumbar exoskeleton supported lumbar when performing heavyweight work [4, 6, 7]. Among them, the lower-limb exoskeleton could be adjusted the sitting angle and didn't require a separate space, which could reduce the risk of lower-limb musculoskeletal disorders in various industries such as manufacturing and agriculture.

There were various studies to verify the effectiveness of the lower-limb exoskeleton. Pillai et al. [8] showed that the muscle amplitude of the rectus femoris decreased when performing a kneeling posture with the exoskeleton. Luger et al. [7] also showed that the muscle amplitude of the calf decreased when working with the lower-limb exoskeleton. In addition, when the sitting angle was higher, the amplitude of the erect spinae decreased. However, those studies focused on biomechanical factors such as muscle amplitude and the angle of body segments. Then, the studies on the usability of lower-limb exoskeleton were insufficient.

Therefore, the aim of this study was to evaluate the lower-limb exoskeleton in terms of usability.

2   Methods

2.1   Factors and Detailed Questions for Evaluation of Lower-Limb Exoskeleton

Since the lower-limb exoskeleton was worn and used on the body, it is in direct contact with the body, so there should be no inconvenience when wearing it and balanced for use. In addition, it should be easy to attach and detach without difficulty. Based on those characteristics, evaluation factors were defined as 'ease of wearing', 'safety', 'sense of wearing', 'effectiveness', and 'ease of use', and three detailed questions were composed in each factor.

2.2   Experimental Tasks for Lower-Exoskeleton Evaluation

It would be appropriate for the user to perform specific experimental tasks and evaluate the exoskeletons rather than simply wearing it and using it freely to evaluate the exoskeleton using detailed questions. Therefore, the experimental tasks consisted of a total of five tasks as follows:

The first task was size adjustment and wear. The participants had information on how to adjust the size and wear the exoskeleton, then performed himself. The second task was the acquisition and application of the method of use. The participants got information on how to use the exoskeleton, such as sitting down and adjusting the knee angle, then using it freely in various environments. The third task was TUG (Timed Get Up and Go Test) & picking up & passing stairs and obstacles. The participants started sitting on the lower-limb exoskeleton, picked up the object on the floor, walked 3m to the return point by crossing the stairs placed at the middle site from the start point to the return point, turned around the return point, walked back to start point with crossing the obstacle located on the middle site from the return point to the start point, and sat down. The fourth task was to conduct a task simulation. The participants detach the Styrofoam ball by moving to the side. The fifth task was to detach and arrange the exoskeleton. The participants got information on how to detach and arrange the exoskeleton, then performed himself. The participants were asked to score detailed questions related to each task after performing the tasks (Table 1).

Table 1. Evaluation factors for exoskeleton & detailed questions

Evaluation factors for Exoskeleton	Detailed question
Ease of wearing	Can it be worn quickly and easily? (Task1)
	Can it be taken off quickly and easily? (Task5)
	Is it easy and convenient to adjust the size according to the user's body size? (Task1)
Safety	Is it easy to balance when sitting with wearing an exoskeleton? (Task2)
	Are the straps, belts, etc. sticking out when worn safely and without being caught in the working environment? (Task2)
	Can it be used safely on soft-condition floors? (Task2)
Sense of wearing	Is it comfortable without the pressure on your hips, thighs, and calves when wearing an exoskeleton? (Task2)
	Is it comfortable without the pressure on other parts (lumbar, shoulder, foot, etc.) when wearing an exoskeleton? (Task2)
	Is the weight of the exoskeleton light when worn? (Task2)
Effectiveness	Is it easy at working at calf height (20-50cm) with wearing an exoskeleton? (Task4)
	Is it easy at working at knee height (50-80cm) with wearing an exoskeleton? (Task4)
	Is it easy to carry out the work by continuously changing the height of the work with wearing an exoskeleton? (Task4)
Ease of use	Is it convenient to rest (in the sitting posture) with wearing an exoskeleton? (Task3)
	Is it easy to pick up items that fell on the floor with wearing an exoskeleton? (Task3)
	Is it convenient to carry around after taking the exoskeleton off? (Task5)

2.3 Lower-Limb Exoskeleton Used in the Experiment

This study used three kinds of lower-limb exoskeletons (CEX, Hyundai; Chairless chair, Noonee; Archelis, Archelis) to conduct an evaluation. The CEX could be adjusted in three steps of knee flexion angle, 55°, 70°, and 85°, respectively. The Chairless chair could be freely adjusted in the range of 100°–156°, and the Archelis could be adjusted at 140°, allowing the users to sit obliquely.

2.4 Experimental Protocol

This study was conducted on 20 healthy adults (12 males and eight females) who had no experience with musculoskeletal disorders. The basic information for participants was as follows (Table 2).

Table 2. Information of participants

	Male	Female
Age	24.9(1.9) yrs	23.1(1.3) yrs
Height	173.1(4.9) cm	165.1(4.3) cm
Weight	70.9(10.9) kg	54.9(4.6) kg

Each participant conducted five tasks with three kinds of lower-limb exoskeleton, respectively. Then, participants recorded their satisfaction scores for detailed questions on an 11-point scale. The order of using the exoskeleton was configured randomly.

2.5 Statistical Analysis

The ANOVA analysis was performed using SPSS 20 (SPSS Inc., Chicago, Illinois, USA), and post-analysis was performed through the Tukey test for significant variables.

3 Results

3.1 Evaluation of Exoskeletons for the Five Tasks

The results of task 1 (size adjustment and wearing) showed that CEX had a significantly higher score, whereas Archelis showed low scores. Those of task 2 (acquisition and application of the method of use) showed that Archelis scored significantly higher score, and CEX also scored higher score in the other evaluations. When conducting task 3 (TUG & picking up & passing stairs and obstacles), Archelis scored significantly higher, whereas CEX scored a lower score. Finally, the results of task 4 (task simulation) and task 5 (detach and arrange the exoskeleton) showed that CEX and Archelis scored significantly higher scores.

3.2 Scoring of the Exoskeletons for Evaluation Factors

The scores on the evaluation factors had significant differences according to the types of exoskeletons. CEX scored significantly higher in 'ease of wearing' and 'effectiveness' due to simple and easy to attach and detach and easy to adjust the knee angles. CEX showed a high score for 'ease of use' due to a simple structure (Table 3). Archelis scored significantly higher in 'safety' because it had the best finish. Archelis also had high scores for 'ease of use' because it moves conveniently due to the lack of support in Fig. 1.

Table 3. Scores of the exoskeletons for the detailed questions

Evaluation factors for Exoskeleton	Detailed question	CEX	Chairless Chair	Archelis
Ease of wearing	Can it be worn quickly and easily? (Task1)	8.00^A	5.55^B	5.43^B
	Can it be taken off quickly and easily? (Task5)	8.51	7.88	7.89
	Is it easy and convenient to adjust the size according to the user's body size? (Task1)	5.37^A	5.41^A	4.07^B
Safety	Is it easy to balance when sitting with wearing an exoskeleton? (Task2)	8.25^B	6.17^A	6.68^A
	Are the straps, belts, etc. sticking out when worn safely and without being caught in the working environment? (Task2)	6.41^B	5.31^C	8.15^A
	Can it be used safely on soft-condition floors? (Task2)	5.37^B	3.96^C	7.88^A
Sense of wearing	Is it comfortable without the pressure on your hips, thighs, and calves when wearing an exoskeleton? (Task2)	5.12^B	6.68^A	6.51^A
	Is it comfortable without the pressure on other parts (lumbar, shoulder, foot, etc.) when wearing an exoskeleton? (Task2)	7.96^A	6.38^B	7.88^A

(continued)

Table 3. (*continued*)

Evaluation factors for Exoskeleton	Detailed question	CEX	Chairless Chair	Archelis
	Is the weight of the exoskeleton light when worn? (Task2)	7.92^A	7.52^A	5.19^B
Effectiveness	Is it easy at working at calf height (20-50cm) with wearing an exoskeleton? (Task4)	8.76^A	4.76^B	7.88^A
	Is it easy at working at knee height (50-80cm) with wearing an exoskeleton? (Task4)	8.31^A	6.87^B	6.80^B
	Is it easy to carry out the work by continuously changing the height of the work with wearing an exoskeleton? (Task4)	8.10^A	3.95^B	8.15^A
Ease of use	Is it convenient to rest (in the sitting posture) with wearing an exoskeleton? (Task3)	7.17^B	7.23^B	8.72^A
	Is it easy to pick up items that fell on the floor with wearing an exoskeleton? (Task3)	8.48^{AB}	7.79^B	8.73^A
	Is it convenient to carry around after taking the exoskeleton off? (Task5)	7.56^A	5.33^B	7.50^A

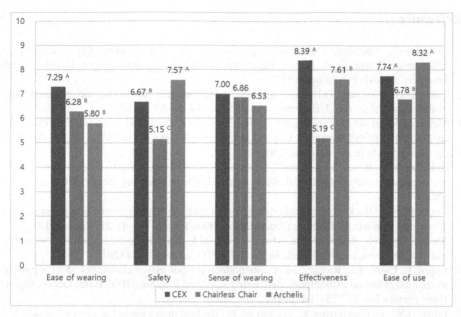

Fig. 1. Results of evaluation factors for each exoskeleton

4 Discussion

In this study, a comparative evaluation of the lower-limb exoskeleton was conducted using a questionnaire. The results showed that CEX, which had a simple structure and could adjust the knee angle appropriately for various working heights, and Archelis, which had high mobility and was excellent in the making, scored significantly higher. Those results expressed user requirements, suggesting that the user requirement should be sufficiently considered in developing an exoskeleton in the future.

The significance of this study is that the factors related to user requirements should be evaluated with quantitative evaluation using biomechanical factors such as EMG, angle of the segment, etc. For example, if the user scored a low score in the balancing part, the measurement of the lower extremity muscle amplitude could help identify the reason for the low score and conduct further research.

The limitations of this study were that there was a lack of verification of evaluation factors by experts, and laboratory-based experiments were conducted, not actual industrial fields. In the future, the evaluation factor should be verified by experts, and the evaluation should be conducted in actual industrial fields for more meaningful results.

Acknowledgments. . This work was carried out with the support of "Cooperative Research Program for Agricultural Science and Technology Development (Project No. PJ017099)" Rural Development Administration, Republic of Korea.

References

1. Cohen, A.L., Gjessing, C.C., Fine, L.J., Bernard, B.P., McGlothlin, J.D.: Elements of Ergonomics Programs: A Primer Based on Workplace Evaluations of Musculoskeletal Disorders. DIANE Publishing (1997)
2. Punnett, L., Wegman, D.H.: Work-related musculoskeletal disorders: the epidemiologic evidence and the debate. J. Electromyogr. Kinesiol. **14**, 13–23 (2004)
3. Meyers, J.M., et al.: High risk tasks for musculoskeletal disorders in agricultural field work. In: Proceeding of the Human Factors and Ergonomics Society Annual Meeting, Los Angeles, pp. 616–619. SAGE Publications (2000)
4. de Looze, M.P., Bosch, T., Krause, F., Stadler, K.S., O'sullivan, L.W.: Exoskeletons for industrial application and their potential effects on physical work load. Ergonomics **59**(5), 671–681 (2016)
5. Toxiri, S., et al.: Back-support exoskeletons for occupational use: an overview of technological advances and trends. IISE Trans. Occup. Ergon. Hum. Factors **7**(3–4), 237–249 (2019)
6. Rashedi, E., Kim, S., Nussbaum, M.A., Agnew, M.J.: Ergonomic evaluation of a wearable assistive device for overhead work. Ergonomics **57**(12), 1864–1874 (2014)
7. Luger, T., Cobb, T.J., Riegger, M.A., Steinhilber, B.: Subjective evaluation 35 of a passive lower-limb industrial exoskeleton used during simulated assembly. IISE Trans. Occup. Ergon. Hum. Factors **7**(3–4), 175–184 (2019)
8. Pillai, M.V., van Engelhoven, L., Kazerooni, H.: Evaluation of a lower leg support exoskeleton on floor and below hip height panel work. Hum. Factors **62**(3), 489–500 (2020)

A Close Observation of the Dynamic Inspiration for Interactive Jewelry

Shoupeng Li[1], Dihui Chu[1], Fangzhou Dong[2]([✉]), and Qiang Li[2]

[1] Southeast University, Nanjing, China
{220214957,220214976}@seu.edu.cn
[2] Monash University, Suzhou, China
{Fangzhou.Dong,Li.Qiang}@monash.edu

Abstract. Interactive jewelry and kinetic jewelry are emerging concepts in the field of jewelry design which overlaps with each other. However, interactive jewelry lacks specific parameters and a standard definition, which hinders early research progress and designers' idea construction. To address this challenge, based on the idea of taking ambiguity as a design strategy, the fuzzy definition boundary between kinect jewelry and interactive jewelry makes the design features of kinect jewelry have certain enlightening significance for the interactive jewelry. This paper aims to collect design pictures related to kinetic jewelry using a Python model, analyze the collected pictures, and obtain current mainstream design parameters to reference for interactive jewelry design. The data will show details such as the interaction mode, wearing part, and materials used of kinect jewelry, thus providing valuable suggestions for interactive jewelry design. Additionally, the paper considered the possibility of how to leverage ambiguity in design as a resource.

Keywords: Design Thinking · interactive jewelry · kinect jewelry · Design theory · Multidisciplinary

1 Introduction

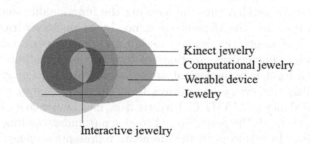

Fig. 1. An interpretation of the co-relationship among multiple jewelry concepts

C. Stephanidis et al. (Eds.): HCII 2023, CCIS 1958, pp. 493–502, 2024.
https://doi.org/10.1007/978-3-031-49215-0_59

1.1   Jewelry and Its Developing Concepts

Jewelry has been evolving and developing from traditional jewelry making to modern science and technology. The classification and frontier concepts of jewelry are constantly refined and developed. Figure 1 shows an interpretation of the co-relationship among kinetic jewelry, computational jewelry, wearable device, interactive jewelry and whole scope of jewelry, which will be referred to later in this article. At the macro level, jewelry is frequently used to describe bodily adornments [1] which express the wearers' taste and preference. Motivated by the fashion trend and curiosity, artists explore the relationship between new materials, forms and functions of jewelry [2]. Therefore, the kinetic jewelry was explored, this jewelry design creates dynamic effects through precise mechanical structure, so that jewelry is no longer a static object, but an artwork that can move [3]. Another practical exploration is wearable devices. General wearable devices usually is understood to be electronic devices that are implanted or fixed on the body, collect, process, display, and transmit information through hardware components such as sensors and displays, and can communicate with the network [4], but the nature of jewelry which needs to be worn on a certain part of the body to show aesthetics makes it also a wearable device. The field of the wearable device that overlaps with the jewelry is the kinect jewelry which includes movable parts that can produce dynamic effects as the human body moves when worn [5]. Kinetic jewelry often designed as an interactive form of art that invites the wearer to play and engage with their adornment. It can also serve a functional purpose, such as providing sensory stimulation for individuals who may fidget or need tactile feedback [2]. Their design concept is to produce more abstract dynamic effects through the mechanical structure of jewelry, like simulating petal opening and closing, notes rising and falling, etc., to attract visual attention. In the late 1950s, electronic and mechanical elements were integrated into jewelry design. Thanks to burgeoning progress and innovation of science and technology, jewelry design is developing in the direction of both beauty and function [5], completely subverting the definition of traditional jewelry [6]. An increasing number of measures and media have been developed to document human lives in virtual forms such as videos, pictures, and audio. Such rich, contextual forms of interaction can be incorporated into jewelry design through interactive jewelry, thus augmenting the functionality and practicality of jewelry. For instance, the Memento designed by Niemantsverdriet et al. serves as an exemplar of interactive jewelry design [7] - it is a personalized, interactive sound locket that evokes emotions of intimacy and sentimentality closely associated with its non-technological predecessor. From a memory-studies perspective, traditional jewelry has always functioned as a physical reminder of autobiographical memory (AM) [6]. Investigating how interactivity in jewelry can augment this role holds the potential to broaden our understanding of the underlying mechanism. In this respect, the Memento represents a remarkable instance where interactivity enhances the memorability-function within jewelry, combining interactive scenarios for recording, playback, and audio fragment browsing that are influenced by people's interactions with conventional lockets.

1.2 Design Fuzziness

The design of interactive jewelry and wearable devices lacks detailed boundary regulations. Jewelry designers tried adding chips or programming techniques during design may not be satisfactory [2]. Similarly, wearable device designers will also consider adding the aesthetic concept of jewelry designers when designing products, but the results are still criticized aesthetically [8]. Exploring product modeling design makes the two intersect to produce the concept of "interactive jewelry", but there are still few related studies. How to define the shape, color, material, function and wearing parts has become a challenge. The technologies and functions involved in interactive jewelry often extend to wearable devices such as smart watches. Some jewelry also contain interactive or dynamic elements [9]. Therefore, the differences between these fields become seriously blurred. Similar problems occur in the design of interactive jewelry too. There is rare clear reference of the category and standard of jewelry design which hinders designers' work progress. Different from the practice of eliminating ambiguity, this paper uses this fuzziness as a resource when conducting early research stage on interactive jewelry.

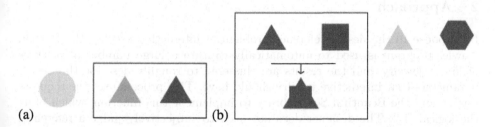

Fig. 2. Logical classification when compared with more references

There are often various contradictions and unclear boundaries in product design. [10] Designers hope that product planning is complete and visionary, and the reality is that every new iteration may bring about some adjustments. [11] The three graphics in the Fig. 2 (a) represent three product modules. If the strict classification logic is followed, the latter two can be considered to belong to the same category in terms of traits, and should be folded into a module at the level. When compared with more modules, the first two can be classified into one category according to color(b). The impact of this classification in reality is like classifying social media users according to algorithms. It may be that some users with low fitness are also labeled as a less appropriate tag because of the need to distinguish data. Users will receive advertisements and information pushed due to the influence of this tag, but the actual recommendation results may not meet the user's emotional needs. For example, too much negative news may cause the user to be depressed [12], and the user is not originally a sentimental personality. What is involved here is the concept of the so-called user psychological model.

Compared with the logic at the technical level, designers pay more attention to the user's cognition of the interface establishment, and the user's psychological cognition is often not very similar to the technical logic. Therefore, this article proposes that designers may make some logical concessions in the face of similar design ambiguity problems, not limited to the constraints of concepts so that the design of interactive jewelry can also be carried out.

1.3   Research Focus

This article researches into existing kinect jewelry design to provide design reference for interactive jewelry. The aim of the study is to provide suggestive design parameters for designers. The method used is through the fuzzy design theory, compromising on a reference for the specific definition of interactive jewelry. Instead, the study analyses the clustering results of Python for kinect jewelry, deducing the design parameters of kinect jewelry related to that of interactive jewelry. Additionally, the study discusses the helpfulness of fuzziness as an auxiliary research method for design research.

2   Approach

In response to the design reference problem of interactive jewelry, the Python crawler program is used to automatically capture a large number of pictures of kinect jewelry, and the results are clustered to roughly describe the design parameters that interactive jewelry should have. This process uses the requests library and the Beautiful Soup library to implement this function, which blurs the logical [13]. The designer does not need to subjectively judge a reference, and the result only has a difference in relevance.

The Python model collected interactive jewelry related design in the past ten years from multiple channels, including social media (such as WeChat, Facebook, Instagram, etc.), popular blogs and magazines about fashion, design and technology (such as www.klimt02.net, www.tasaki.co.uk, www.jewellerycut.com, www.londonjewelleryschool.co.uk,etc.), designer personal blogs, scholarly publications and several University Libraries. Terms used for web and academic searches include but are not limited to: movable jewelry, kinetic ring, kinetic jewelry, etc. The search ends when no new images appear. These works were classified according to attributes of different dimensions, and SPSS was used for analyzing statistical results. The analysis dimension was divided into wearing position mode of motion. The results summarize the design trend in kinetic jewelry in multiple aspects including their interactive and manufacturing characters. Clustering result of materials, interactive mode, shape and wear positions from kinetic jewelry design that has been searched. Includes the image metadata, the year of release, wearing positions.

As an innovative development direction for jewelry, both interactive jewelry and kinetic jewelry show great potential in endowing more interactive functions and meanings to traditional jewelry. While it is not uncommon for interactive jewelry to be critiqued for lack of fashion expression, kinetic jewelry tends to create desirable interactions and fashionable aesthetics. Many artists and jewelry designers have been setting foot in kinetic jewelry, deriving more and more ideas and perspectives from their own understandings [14]. Excellent artworks and extraordinary products have been made through this exploring process. This article reviews the kinetic jewelry design to gain an overall perspective of this area. The analysis revealed certain patterns and suggested future developments that can make it easier to collaborate on creating interactive and kinetic jewelry and promote their widespread usage.

3   Results

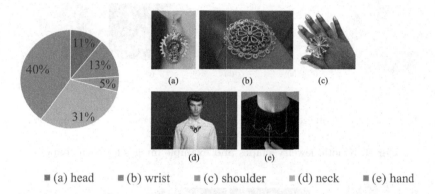

■ (a) head   ■ (b) wrist   ■ (c) shoulder   ■ (d) neck   ■ (e) hand

Fig. 3. The wearing position of kinetic jewelry and example images for each position

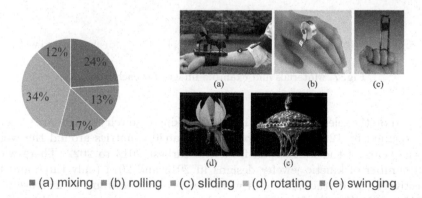

■ (a) mixing ■ (b) rolling ■ (c) sliding ■ (d) rotating ■ (e) swinging

Fig. 4. The mode of motion of kinetic jewelry and example images for each mode

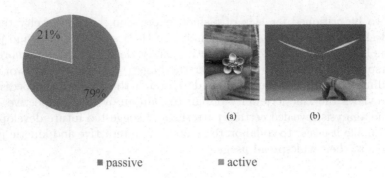

passive   active

Fig. 5. Active and passive interaction and example images

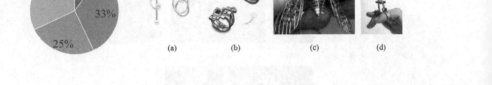

▪ (a) abstract shapes   ▪ (b) geometric shapes   ▪ (c) bionics shapes   ▪ (d) skeuimorphic shpaes

Fig. 6. Kinetic jewelry shapes and example images for each shape

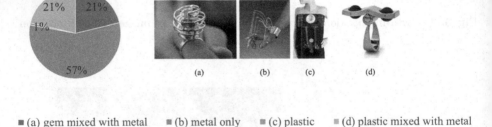

▪ (a) gem mixed with metal   ▪ (b) metal only   ▪ (c) plastic   ▪ (d) plastic mixed with metal

Fig. 7. Materials and example images for each material

Based on the selection criteria, 142 eligible kinetic jewelry images are screened out, designed by 126 designers from more than30 countries around the world, and the years of the works span from the earliest 2013 to 2022. There was a small number of kinetic jewelry designs in 2013 and 2014 (only three and five respectively), while the number of works experienced a dramatic increase of 24 in 2015 to2016 (300%). In 2020 the number reached a maximum of sixty-seven, and in 2021 there was a brief drop. Image data that met the eligibility criteria was imported into the SPSS data software for analysis. Results illustrate the wearing position of kinetic jewelry and its mode of motion show correlations between them. The analysis revealed that 64.7%, 54.5%, and 71.1% of jewelry

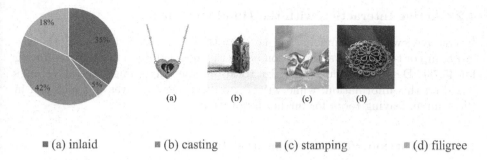

■ (a) inlaid   ■ (b) casting   ■ (c) stamping   ■ (d) filigree

Fig. 8. The manufacturing techniques and example images for each technique

utilizing rolling, sliding, and rotating as interactive modes are mostly worn on wrists, while 88.9% of jewelry that employs swinging as an interaction mode is typically worn on the neck. Among all kinetic jewelry designs, 51.4% of those worn on the neck featured a bionic shape. Skeuomorphic shaped jewelry (55.6%) was mostly designed to be worn on the hand, while facial features predominantly appeared in skeuomorphic-shaped (47.1%) jewelry. Additionally, abstract shapes constituted 60% of kinetic jewelry worn on the shoulder. Jewelry designs in geometric shapes were found to be most suitable for rotary motion (40%). Rolling and rotating motions were mainly adopted by jewelry designed in bionic (40.9%) and skeuomorphic (44.4%) shapes (Figs. 3, 4, 5, 6, 7, 8).

The analysis of wearing position shows that the neck and hand are popular areas for kinetic jewelry, with 44 pieces and 56 pieces respectively. The mode of motion can be divided into four types: rotating, sliding, swinging, and rolling. Rotating is the most common mode of motion with forty-five designs. Most kinetic jewelry designs require active interaction with the body, such as by hand touch. The shapes of kinetic jewelry include bionic and skeuomorphic shapes, geometric shapes, and abstract shapes. Metal is the most common material used in creating kinetic jewelry, comprising sixty percent of the collected works. Production techniques include stamping, filigree, inlaying, and casting. In conclusion, kinetic jewelry is a unique design that emphasizes movement, form, and function, and it offers a variety of possibilities for jewelry makers to explore.

4   Discussion

4.1   Natural Interaction with Wearing Position and Shapes

The most commonly used modeling method for necklaces is bionics, with the popular method being to imitate blooming flowers. Shapes like butterfly wings and fish bones have interactive qualities, with rotation being the most common movement (44.4%). Jewelry worn on the shoulder is usually large and abstract (60%), with different shapes having different interactive properties - beaded shapes are good for rolling/sliding, round shapes for rotation, square for opening/closing, and linear as tracks.

4.2   Active Interaction with the Hand and Fingers

Interactive jewelry is commonly worn on hands (57.1%), with rings being the easiest to flip or turn/press, and rotation being the most common motion accounting for 45.7%. Designers should prioritize rotation when designing interactive rings based on this information, while wrist/arm-driven jewelry was not included in the sample, leaving room for further innovation.

4.3   Interaction with Materials and Technics

The choice of material affects the movement of jewelry, with magnets often used for orbital motion, pearls for sliding and rolling, and composite paper/soft material with metal for swinging. Manufacturing processes play a role in realizing different types of motion, with cold links, cutting, hinges, chains, punching, riveting, and shaft connections being common methods for connecting movable jewelry.

4.4   A Compromise Strategy in Interactive Jewelry Design

The fuzzy design theory mentioned in interactive jewelry design research is only for the lack of design reference for emerging concepts, but it also needs to solve a design problem. Product design involves users ' habits and psychological needs. To a certain extent, fuzzy design is advocating universal products. Therefore, fuzzy design sometimes cannot accurately take care of users ' emotions and experiences. The concept of design cannot be a shelter to avoid thinking. Designers should avoid their own design products becoming undefined and cannot be accurately described by language. For example, the design mentioned in the article should not be questioned by jewelry designers or product designers. This design is neither jewelry nor product, but a new category between the two. Fuzzy design is only a compromise strategy when the existing logic chain is not perfect or the existing theoretical reserve is not enough to support the design problem.

5   Conclusion

This paper reviews kinetic jewelry design works from 2013 to 2022 in order to understand the interactivity and fashion expression in kinetic jewelry and provide inspirations for interactive jewelry and wearable devices. It first introduces the similarities and differences between interactive jewelry and Kinetic art and jewelry, and expounds the research objectives. Then, based on the computer network technology, the kinetic jewelry keywords were searched, and 142 jewelry samples were found. The attributes of the samples were classified and counted into seven attribute categories, and the quantitative statistical values between multiple attributes were analyzed. Finally, the results were discussed based on the multidimensional analysis chart. The results show that the interaction of kinetic jewelry with the body is often naturally linked with its shape, wearing position, and materials. One of the design strategies is to mimic the shape and movement of the creatures and items in daily life and nature. By reviewing the design of kinetic jewelry, this paper will contribute to providing a dynamic inspiration for the interactivity design of interactive jewelry and wearable devices to enhance their cultural meanings, fashion expression and aesthetics. In the design research of interactive jewelry, the fuzziness of information is used. In this paper, all pictures are summarized as related designs, only the correlation is different. Through the clustering of all the image features with high and low correlation, the proposed reference for interactive jewlery is obtained.

6   Contribution

Take fuzziness can increase the flexibility and openness of products, and show more adaptive characteristics in the face of different needs, scenarios and markets. The interactive Jewelry, kinect jewelry mentioned above blurs similar concepts when conducting research and reference, but this strategy solves the design problem well. Although there is no interactive reference directly in the example, the results of the images with the highest similarity of kinect jewelry were obtained by python model. The results about kinect jewelries' wearing position, materials choosing and motion can still be used as a reference for interactive Jewelry. Based on this, it is meaningful not to be limited to clear conceptual regularization and precision of interactive jewelry.

References

1. Unger-de Boer, M.: Sieraad in context: Een multidisciplinair kader voor de beschouwing van het sieraad [jewellery in context: a mulitidisciplinary framework to study jewellery] (2010)
2. Kao, H.L.C., et al.: Exploring interactions and perceptions of kinetic wearables. In: The 2017 Conference (2017)
3. Unger-Boer, M.D.: Sieraad in context: een multidisciplinair kader voor de beschouwing van het sieraad. Leiden University (2010)
4. Silina, Y., Haddadi, H.: New directions in jewelry: a close look at emerging trends & developments in jewelry-like wearable devices (2015)
5. Versteeg, M., Hoven, E.V.D., Hummels, C.: Interactive jewellery: a design exploration. In: The TEI 2016: Tenth International Conference (2016)
6. van den Hoven, E., Eggen, J.H.: The cue is key: design for real-life remembering. Zeitschrift Für Psychologie **222**(2) (2014)
7. Niemantsverdriet, K., Versteeg, M.: Interactive jewellery as memory cue: designing a sound locket for individual reminiscence. ACM (2016)
8. Devendorf, L., Ryokai, K., Lo, J., Howell, N., Paulos, E.: "i don't want to wear a screen": probing perceptions of and possibilities for dynamic displays on clothing. In: The 2016 CHI Conference (2016)
9. CNET: Kovert connected jewellery is high-tech and high fashion, 4 July 2014
10. Stacey, M., Eckert, C.: Against ambiguity. Comput. Support. Coop. Work **12**(2), 153–183 (2003)

11. Adegbile, A., Sarpong, D., Meissner, D.: Strategic foresight for innovation management: a review and research agenda. Int. J. Innov. Technol. Manag. (2017)
12. Aoki, P.M., Woodruff, A.: Making space for stories: ambiguity in the design of personal communication systems. In: Proceedings of the SIGCHI Conference on Human Factors in Computing Systems, pp. 181–190 (2005)
13. Haitao, W., Da, Q.I., Radio, S.S.: The role of data collection and analysis based on python in fusion media. Audio Eng. (2018)
14. Order, P.: The influence of modernism on artistic jewelry. Korean Arts Crafts **17**(1) (2014)

AnyMApp for Online Usability Testing: The Use-Case of Inspirers-HTN

Joana Muchagata[1] , Francisco Bischoff[1] , Rute Almeida[1,2] ,
Luís Nogueira-Silva[2,3] , Ricardo Cruz-Correia[1] , and Ana Ferreira[1]([✉])

[1] CINTESIS@RISE, FMUP-MEDCIDS, Porto, Portugal
Joanamuchagata@gmail.com, Franzbischoff@gmail.com, {rutealmeida,
rcorreia,amlaf}@med.up.pt
[2] PaCeIT- Patient Centered Innovation and Technologies, CINTESIS, FMUP-MEDCIDS, Porto,
Portugal
luisnogueirasilva@gmail.com
[3] Centro Hospitalar e Universitário São João - Internal Medicine Department, Porto, Portugal

Abstract. The AnyMApp platform enables the testing of mock-ups from web or
mobile applications, anonymously, and online, with the integration of three main
parts: 1) survey-like questions regarding demographics and information about the
project and use-case; 2) the mock-up interfaces of the use-case functionalities to
be tested; 3) and survey-like questions regarding satisfaction and experience. The
aim of this work is to present the preliminary results of the first use-case tested
within the AnyMApp platform. Results show that the integration of diverse data
can help define a comprehensive overview and improvement strategy for the tested
application. All participants agree the AnyMApp platform is useful and simplifies
and quickens usability testing, with bigger samples.

Keywords: Online usability · Mobile applications · User experience

1 Introduction

Successful healthcare outcomes for patients with chronic diseases greatly depend on
their adherence to the treatment plan. Mobile applications (apps) have a huge potential
to empower patients in the management of their disease, namely regarding treatment and
monitoring. Also, they may improve health literacy through the delivery of information
regarding the disease and its treatment [1]. However, many factors intervene in the
relations and interactions between humans and those apps [2–4]. Uptake and continued
use of technology highly depends on users' acceptance and the value and support they
receive from it on a daily basis. Thus, testing different parameters for those apps (e.g.,
analytics, interactions, usability, UX, etc.), is crucial to better understand critical factors
that can make it or break it, for the long-term technology adherence [5–9].

The aim of this work is to present preliminary results from a use-case tested online,
regarding those same parameters, using the AnyMApp framework [10]. The use-case
simulates the interaction of selected functionalities of the Inspirers-HTN app [11], an
app that supports daily management and self-monitoring of patients with hypertension.

© The Author(s), under exclusive license to Springer Nature Switzerland AG 2024
C. Stephanidis et al. (Eds.): HCII 2023, CCIS 1958, pp. 503–510, 2024.
https://doi.org/10.1007/978-3-031-49215-0_60

2 Background

2.1 The AnyMApp Project

AnyMApp is a project aiming to build a digital twin framework to anonymously simulate and analyse online interactions and usability between humans and apps (fictitious or existing) [10]. The AnyMApp framework allies mock-up interfaces with anonymous data from the users, e.g., demographic, interactional and opinions regarding those interactions (see Fig. 1). This helps AnyMApp testing parameters other than usability-related aspects. It opens the possibility to easily and anonymously study other behavioural/interactional variables, still difficult to study with current solutions (e.g., personality or victimization traits, cognitive or ageing related issues [7, 12]).

Fig. 1. AnyMApp framework – All interactional data (top) are collected for analysis (bottom).

2.2 The Inspirers-HTN App

The Inspirers-HTN is a mobile application to promote the adequate management of hypertension, including the measurement of adherence to treatment, self-monitoring support tools and educational contents. The app allows the patient to register their pharmacological treatment, customize alerts to take the medication and measure the blood pressure (BP). It generates reports with BP and adherence to treatment data, that can be easily shared, fostering the relationship between the patient and the health care team. Also, it includes educational material [11], consisting of a set of five animated videos related to relevant subjects in hypertension monitoring and management: 1) BP measurement technique, 2) adherence to therapy importance, 3) BP values, 4) how to measure waist circumference and 5) how to measure arm circumference. A sixth option supports the choice of a BP measuring device by linking to the STRIDE BP list of validated devices. Shortcuts for all 6 materials are available at main screen after login. The beta version of Inspirers-HTN, is currently being validated; it is available both for Android (Playstore) and iOS (by TestFlight invitation) in three languages (Portuguese, English and French). For this use-case, the AnyMApp framework was only used to examine the participants ability to access the educational contents in the Portuguese version of Inspirers-HTN.

3 Use-Case

3.1 Mockup Design

Axure was chosen as the tool to implement the app mock-ups so that html files could be easily generated and adapted to collect and register usage data [13]. The AnyMApp framework was structured into four parts: *1. Beginning*: presentation of the project, data protection and informed consent for compliance with GDPR (see Fig. 2 – left); *2. Demographics*: a section requesting some general demographic data about the participant (see Fig. 2 – middle); *3. Mock-ups*: the mock-ups of the use-case with the interfaces that simulate the selected functionalities) (see Fig. 2 – right); *4. Feedback*: from the participant regarding usability, satisfaction and assessment of acquisition of the main messages of the educational material (see Fig. 3).

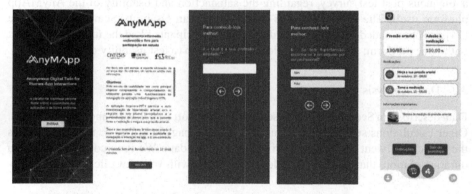

Fig. 2. Mock-up interfaces describing the project and data protection (left), requesting general demographic data from participants (middle), and app access to educational content (right).

3.2 Backend and Data Collection

Mock-ups are used almost as exported from Axure with some required adaptations. AnyMApp framework is responsible for two separate modules: *the Client*, which observes users' behaviour interacting with the mockup interface, for example, which button was pressed, at which moment and if it took longer or not to be pressed, after the previous action. All collected data are sent to the server module; *the Server*, which

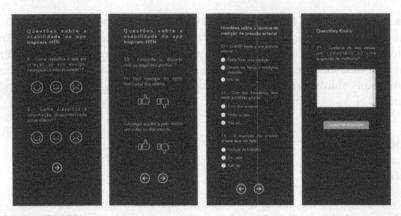

Fig. 3. Final interfaces asking participants regarding satisfaction and user experience.

receives the events generated by the client via REST, stores them in a structured/tabular way. Data are registered and exported into a.CSV file, for posterior analysis.

These data include: TIMESTAMP; EVENT (click, tap, etc.); ACTION (button clicked, data selected, etc.); DATA (selected or inserted in text box by the participant); and LOCATION (interface or page where the action was taken).

Besides all data collected within the use-case, we asked participants to answer an anonymous post-test survey, regarding the satisfaction and usability of the AnyMApp platform itself. The survey includes the SUS (System Usability Scale) questionnaire [14] and open-ended questions regarding: what participants liked the most and the least within the platform; and if they would use AnyMApp to test usability of apps and why.

3.3 Data Analysis

Data described in Sect. 3.2 are analysed using Microsoft Excel 2016 and Google Forms. Other calculations such as time spent on a specific page/interface or number of times the participant went back, were derived from these data. We ignored sessions with a duration of more than one hour and less than 5 min, with very few clicks.

3.4 Recruitment of Participants

For the first use-case tests within the AnyMApp framework, we selected a small convenience sample from CINTESIS personnel, adults who could or could not have a diagnosis of hypertension. We intended to test the platform itself as much as the specific use-case, so a short number of participants should be enough to obtain the first feedback and help us to define a larger scale study.

The link to access the AnyMApp framework and an anonymous online post-test survey were sent by email to 25 people, on the 7th March 2023. Log data were retrieved for seven days, and analysed afterwards.

4 Results

4.1 Use-Case Analysis

For this study, we only analysed data from completed sessions, that started on the first page and finished on the last, or previous to last page. In total, from 18 incomplete sessions, 12 complete sessions were analysed. Most participants, 9 on windows and 2 on Mac used a computer browser to test the use-case, while only one used a smartphone with iOS. The average number of clicks per session was 50 and the average time for session completion was around 13 min (See Table 1).

Table 1. Demographics characteristics of use-case participants.

	Participants (n = 12)
Demographic characteristics	
Female n (%)	7 (54%)
35 to 39 years old n (%)	8 (66%)
High education n (%)	10 (83%)
Use of technology	
Rare use of mobile health n (%)	8 (62%)
Frequent use of mobile health n (%)	2 (16%)
Clinical characteristics	
Do not have hypertension n (%)	7 (58%)
Have Hypertension n (%)	4 (33%)
Followed by professionals n (%)	2 (50%)

Regarding the app, and the functionality that was tested, in all twelve sessions, at least one video was selected. Five participants only saw the first video, while others, selected different videos multiple times. Still, the most selected was the first video and only one participant accessed all 6 materials available. Figure 4 shows usability and satisfaction evaluation by the participants, after interacting with the use-case.

How do you classify information in the videos?	Design, navigation and interactivity	Easy to navigate horizontal menu (access videos)
☺ 10 (83%)	☺ 7 (54%)	👍 6 (50%)
☹ 2 (16%)	☹ 5 (42%)	👎 6 (50%)

Fig. 4. Usability and design evaluation of the use-case app.

Regarding the tested knowledge from the education materials, all participants answered correctly regarding adherence to therapeutics as well as how and when to measure BP. There were however some doubts regarding the frequency of measurements (83% got it right); how to measure waist (83% got it right) and arm perimeter (75% got it right); and the normal values of BP (62% got it right). There were also a few additional comments in the final open-ended question: "the first part of the first video is too long as the main messages could have been given in the first minute"; "horizontal navigation was not easy, when trying to advance to the next video, it kept selecting the first one, maybe a vertical list would be more intuitive, or the indication that there are more videos on the right" (2 participants); and video is very clear and images complement the text well (2 participants).

4.2 Framework Analysis

Regarding the testing of the AnyMApp framework itself, seventeen participants (N = 17) filled the post-test survey, after they interacted with the AnyMApp framework.

We detected an inconsistency in the SUS, as we missed to introduce one of the questions (No. 2). So, in order to be able to still do some analysis and score, we took out the one related to it but in even number (No. 3). We analysed 8 questions, 4 odds (1, 5, 7, 9) and 4 evens (2, 4, 6, 8), with a maximum score of 32 points, which we multiplied by 3.125 to have a range between 0–100. The obtained score was: 85, 84.

All respondents found the AnyMApp platform useful to perform online usability apps testing. Figure 5 present some of the examples given by the participants to confirm this.

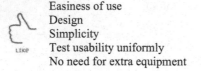

Easiness of use	Not well adapted to iPhone
Design	Instructions not well positioned
Simplicity	Difficulty to press some buttons
Test usability uniformly	Cursor has big circle
No need for extra equipment	Bigger satisfaction scale (4/5 points)

Fig. 5. Usability and design evaluation of the AnyMApp framework.

5 Discussion

Due to space limitations, we can only provide a summarized analysis of the study.

Overall, the first test of both platform and prototype went well. The average of 50 clicks per user's session seems reasonable in a prototype with 23 different pages and the need to view information outside the platform. This is corroborated by the average time of 13 min per session, which is also reasonable for the various interactions and questions that were required from the participants. Still, this analysis is only focused on the completed sessions that were performed without interruptions. This is an issue that we need to take into account with online platforms. Nevertheless, even incomplete sessions by a bigger sample can be very informative.

Answers regarding knowledge about the videos were also recorded, and although the sample was mostly highly educated, there were some doubts regarding general issues of hypertension. Still, participants were not requested to access all the videos but just browse the functionality. In future studies, we will need to decide to allow participants to test the prototype randomly, or to define a list of instructions that participants will have to follow.

In terms of design, navigability and usability, the platform and use-case were well rated. There was not a negative scoring, and this is also confirmed by the SUS score, above average (85, 84). However, a question from the SUS was lacking, which may obviously have impacted the final result; the fact that this was detected on the preliminary test will allow for timely correction. Moreover, it may not have been clear to all participants that the SUS questionnaire aimed to assess the AnyMApp platform only and not the use-case in particular. This needs to be clarified in the future.

Regarding the functionality that was tested (access to the educational videos) there is the need to improve the horizontal scroll. Most participants either did not identify that there were several videos or had difficulties scrolling left to the other available links. This functionality will need to be redesigned.

In future works, a more integrated analysis of the various types of data (demographics, usage logs and satisfaction/experience) will need to be performed. Broadening the scope to include the other functionalities of the Inspirers-HTN app, will allow to have a better assessment of the app and of the AnyMApp framework. Finally, AnyMApp will need to be tested in other use-cases and in larger samples. With the AnyMApp architecture now established, the next prototypes will be quickly adapted and tested.

6 Conclusions

The first proof of concept and associated results and feedback regarding the implementation and testing of the AnyMApp framework has showed that it is a viable tool to study the usability of other apps, motivating the authors to continue to the next stage of the project.

Acknowledgements. This work is financed by project AnyMApp - Anonymous Digital Twin for Human-App Interactions (EXPL/CCI-COM/0052/2021) (FCT – Fundação para a Ciência e Tecnologia).

References

1. Lu, C., et al.: The use of mobile health applications to improve patient experience: cross-sectional study in Chinese Public Hospitals. JMIR Mhealth Uhealth **6**(5), e126 (2018). https://doi.org/10.2196/mhealth.9145
2. Ferreira, A., Muchagata, J., Vieira-Marques, P., Abrantes, D., Teles, S.: Perceptions of security and privacy in mHealth. In: Moallem, A. (ed.) HCII 2021. LNCS, vol. 12788, pp. 297–309. Springer, Cham (2021). https://doi.org/10.1007/978-3-030-77392-2_19
3. Billmann, M., Böhm, M., Krcmar, H.: Use of workplace health promotion apps: analysis of employee log data. Health Policy Technol. **9**(3), 285–293 (2020). ISSN 2211-8837. https://doi.org/10.1016/j.hlpt.2020.06.003

4. Tian, Y., Zhou, K., Lalmas, M., Liu, Y., Pelleg, D.: Cohort modeling based app category usage prediction. In: Proceedings of the 28th ACM Conference on User Modeling, Adaptation and Personalization, UMAP 2020, pp. 248–256. Association for Computing Machinery, New York (2020). https://doi.org/10.1145/3340631.3394849

5. Sigg, S., Lagerspetz, E., Peltonen, E., Nurmi, P., Tarkoma, S.: Exploiting usage to predict instantaneous app popularity: trend filters and retention rates. ACM Trans. Web **13**(2), 1–25 (2019). https://doi.org/10.1145/3199677

6. Mennig, P., Scherr, S.A., Elberzhager, F.: Supporting rapid product changes through emotional tracking. In: 2019 IEEE/ACM 4th International Workshop on Emotion Awareness in Software Engineering (SEmotion), Montreal, QC, Canada, pp. 8–12 (2019). https://doi.org/10.1109/SEmotion.2019.00009

7. Donker, T., Petrie, K., Proudfoot, J., Clarke, J., Birch, M.-R., Christensen, H.: Smartphones for smarter delivery of mental health programs: a systematic review. J. Med. Internet Res. **15**(11), e247 (2013). https://doi.org/10.2196/jmir.2791

8. Boateng, G., Batsis, J.A., Halter, R., Kotz, D.: ActivityAware: an app for real-time daily activity level monitoring on the Amulet wrist-worn device. In: 2017 IEEE International Conference on Pervasive Computing and Communications Workshops (PerComWorkshops), Kona, HI, pp. 431–435 (2017). https://doi.org/10.1109/PERCOMW.2017.7917601

9. Van Schalkwyk, A., Grobbelaar, S., Herselman, M.E.: A scoping review of the use of data analytics for the evaluation of mHealth applications. In: 29th International Conference of the International Association for Management of Technology, Nile University, Cairo, Egypt, 13–17 September 2020 (2020)

10. Ferreira, A., Chilro, R., Cruz-Correia, R.: AnyMApp framework: anonymous digital twin human-app interactions. In: Kurosu, M., et al. (eds.) HCI International 2022 - Late Breaking Papers. Design, User Experience and Interaction: 24th International Conference on Human-Computer Interaction, HCII 2022, Virtual Event, June 26 – July 1, 2022, Proceedings, pp. 214–225. Springer, Cham (2022). https://doi.org/10.1007/978-3-031-17615-9_15

11. Nogueira-Silva, L., et al.: Development of a mobile health app for the management of hypertension, including treatment adherence assessment, using image detection technology – inspirers-htn. J. Hypertens. **39**(Suppl. 1), e380 (2021). https://doi.org/10.1097/01.hjh.0000748952.19902.f5

12. Gordon, M.L., Gatys, L., Guestrin, C., Bigham, J.P., Trister, A., Patel, K.: App usage predicts cognitive ability in older adults. In: Proceedings of the 2019 CHI Conference on Human Factors in Computing Systems, CHI 2019, vol. 168, pp. 1–12. Association for Computing Machinery, New York (2019). https://doi.org/10.1145/3290605.3300398

13. Axure RP 10: Software para criação de protótipos e especificações para sites e aplicativos. https://www.axure.com/

14. Brooke, J.: SUS: A quick and dirty usability scale. Usability Evaluation in Industry, pp. 189–194 (1995)

Electric Toothbrush Modeling Design Based on Kansei Engineering

Yan Wang and Qiuyue Jin[✉]

East China University of Science and Technology, Shanghai, China
y81210062@mail.ecust.edu.cn

Abstract. Based on the theory of Kansei Engineering, the relationship between user's perceptual elements and the design elements of electric toothbrush modeling is quantified through Kansei Engineering to provide new ideas for the innovative design of electric toothbrush. The existing products were researched based on users' perceptual elements, and representative product samples were selected to dismantle the modeling elements of electric toothbrushes through morphological analysis. Collect and establish the user's perceptual vocabulary, quantify the user's perceptual vocabulary by using the Semantic Difference method, use the Quantitation Theory Type I and SPSS software to count and analyze the correlation between the perceptual vocabulary and the modeling elements of the electric toothbrush, and derive the user's perceptual imagery preference. Summarizing the design points and proposing modeling design options of the electric toothbrushes, which makes the electric toothbrush better meet the user's emotional needs and promote the human-computer interaction between the user and the electric toothbrush product.

Keywords: Kansei Engineering · Electric Toothbrush · Modeling Design · Semantic Difference Method · Quantitation Theory Type I

1 Introduction

With the wave of consumer upgrading in China and the gradually increasing awareness of oral care among Chinese residents, electric toothbrushes have become one of the most rapidly developing small home appliance categories in China [1]. According to the market research on electric toothbrushes, we found that there is a problem of "emerging local brand products focusing on value and cost performance but lacking quality, and old brand products focusing on professional technology but lacking youthful content" [2]. The young consumers, represented by Generation Z, are emerging strongly, with a more personalized view of consumption, showing multiple characteristics such as willingness to pay for innovation and enthusiasm for experiential consumption [3]. Their individual preferences, psychological characteristics and consumer consciousness will influence the trends of product design in this era, and this group of people is gradually becoming the main target users of brands and the main consumer groups of products.

This study combines research methods of Kansei Engineering with human-computer interaction design to investigate the design of emotional interaction between users and

C. Stephanidis et al. (Eds.): HCII 2023, CCIS 1958, pp. 511–519, 2024.
https://doi.org/10.1007/978-3-031-49215-0_61

products, focusing on Generation Z users. Firstly, representative product samples and perceptual vocabulary are collected and screened, and the identified product samples are analyzed and extracted morphologically; secondly, a semantic difference scale is established to evaluate the perceptual imagery of the product, and multiple regression analysis is conducted with the help of SPSS statistical analysis software to construct a mathematical model of Quantitation Theory Type I; finally, Drawing conclusions and guiding design practice.

2   Overview of Kansei Engineering

"Kansei Engineering" is a comprehensive and interdisciplinary discipline between design, engineering, and other disciplines [4]. It uses modern computer technology to qualitatively and quantitatively analyze perceptual responses that were previously difficult to quantify, irrational, and illogical, and has been developed as a new design technology and method [5]. The purpose of "Kansei Engineering" is to study the influence of "things" on the senses of users, so that "things" can better meet the requirements of consumers for pleasure and comfort. At present, the application of Kansei Engineering in product modeling imagery involves several fields and directions, such as shape optimization, function matching and brand imagery enhancement for products such as transportation [6], clothing design [7], food packaging [8], and small home electronics [9, 10]. It mainly provides directional guidance for target product design by obtaining consumers' demands on product shape, function and emotion.

The Semantic Differential (SD) method was originally proposed by Charles Osgood in the 1950s and has since been widely used in product design, social psychology, marketing, and other fields, and has become a common research tool [11]. This method is the most simple and easy to operate, and only requires subjects to semantically evaluate their true feelings about objects and then generalize them using mathematical statistical analysis methods to complete the data quantification of users' perceptual needs [12]. By data-quantifying user perceptual needs, designers can intuitively study users' emotional tendencies and guide product design so that users can generate positive emotions when using the products.

Morphological analysis is an innovative method of using Morphology to analyze things, aiming to consider an essential element as part of a whole combination and analyze the "shape" and "state" of each essential element in detail, and is now widely used in graphic design, industrial design, etc. [13, 14]. The possible forms or solutions of each element are listed separately, and a morphological matrix is constructed to summarize the possible overall combination of solutions, and the best solution is selected by evaluating each combination of morphological solutions using demand as the evaluation criterion [15].

Quantitation Theory Type I is mainly used to explore the intrinsic relationship between the user's perceptual imagery assessment value and the modeling of a certain product, by quantifying the qualitative data and using mathematical statistical methods such as multiple linear regression analysis to establish a mathematical mapping model between the perceptual imagery assessment and the design elements, so as to project the predicted contribution of the dependent variable to the perceptual cognition, which can save the time of preliminary research and analysis and obtain the best design solutions [16, 17].

3 Research Process

3.1 Collection and Establishment of Product Samples

Through e-commerce platforms, social networks, and product manuals, 200 electric toothbrush sample images were widely collected, categorized according to the modeling features, and samples with high similarity in modeling were excluded. In order to highlight the elements of modeling features and avoid the influence of factors such as material and color, the collected samples were uniformly processed with white background and gray scale. Twenty people were invited to participate in the screening of typical samples, including 10 users and product designers each. According to the sample pictures, 60 sample pictures with a frequency of more than 50 times were screened for the first time, and the focus group research method was used in the second round, and 12 sample pictures that were more typical and representative were finally selected, see Fig. 1.

Fig. 1. Selected representative samples.

3.2 Electric Toothbrush Modeling Deconstruction and Analysis

In this study, starting from the basic concept of morphological analysis method, the 12 electric toothbrush samples collected were analyzed to obtain five modeling elements: brush head (X_1), connection (brush head to body) (X_2), body (X_3), button (X_4) and bottom (X_5) (Fig. 2). Among them, the brush head shape contains three categories: round X_{11}, oval X_{12}, rounded rectangle X_{13}; the connection between the brush head and the body includes four categories: concave X_{21}, right angle X_{22}, curved X_{23}, streamline X_{24}; the body shape contains four categories: beveled X_{31}, vertical X_{32}, outer curved X_{33}, inner curved X_{34}; the button shape contains four categories: round X_{41}, rounded rectangle X_{42}, square X_{43}, bar X_{44}; the bottom includes three categories: flat corner X_{51}, curved corner X_{52}, rounded corner X_{53}. According to the identified modeling elements of electric toothbrushes and their categories, the categories of modeling elements belonging to each experimental sample were analyzed and coded, and the samples were coded from top to bottom according to Fig. 2, and the obtained results are shown in Table 1.

3.3 Perceptual Vocabulary Collection and Establishment

In this study, we first collected perceptual word pairs that could describe electric toothbrushes from various platforms, and then obtained 30 perceptual word pairs after excluding words that were not related to electric toothbrushes or had similar word meanings by

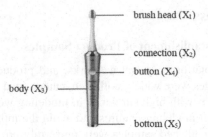

brush head (X₁)

connection (X₂)

button (X₄)

body (X₃)

bottom (X₅)

Fig. 2. Electric toothbrush modeling elements.

Table 1. Modeling elements and categories coding table.

Sample No.	Brush head (X_1)	Connection (X_2)	Body (X_3)	Button (X_4)	Bottom (X_5)
	1.round ⭕	1.concave ⌇	1.beveled ‖	1.round ⭕	1.flat corner ⊔
	2.oval ⬭	2.right angle ⌐	2.vertical ‖	2.rounded rectangle ⬭	2.curved corner ⌣
	3.rounded rectangle ▢	3.curved ⌒	3.outer curved ⟨⟩	3.square ▢	3.rounded corner ∪
		4.streamline ⁄\	4.inner curved ⁄\	4.bar ▯	
A	3	1	1	1	1
B	2	4	3	1	1
C	2	3	2	1	1
D	1	4	3	2	2
E	2	1	4	1	1
F	3	2	2	2	1
G	2	3	2	4	1
H	3	4	2	4	3
I	1	3	4	1	2
J	2	4	2	2	1
K	3	4	2	3	2
L	2	3	1	1	1

means of cluster analysis and focus groups. Since the perceptual imagery of the above screened words covers a wide range and the complexity of the semantic imagery space is too high, which will lead to an increase in the cognitive load of the subjects [18], it is necessary to 30 perceptual lexical pairs after the initial screening were subjected to the questionnaire, so that the lexical pairs with high cognitive rate could be further extracted. The main respondents of this questionnaire were design professionals and young users of Generation Z. Respondents were asked to select 6 word pairs from the 30 word pairs that they personally thought best described the electric toothbrush. After the questionnaire was distributed, the data was aggregated and ranked in descending order of the number of choices, resulting in the top 6 perceptual word pairs, which are "simple - complex (Y_1)", "rounded - rigid (Y_2)", "cute - mature (Y_3)", "personalized - general (Y_4)", " innovative - old-fashioned (Y_5)" and "delicate - rough (Y_6)".

3.4 Establishment Experiment on Perceptual Imagery Evaluation

In this study, based on the SD method, the Likert 7-level scale was used to quantify the subjects' perceptions of the morphological features of the 12 electric toothbrush samples and to establish the relationship between each electric toothbrush modeling and perceptual imagery. This questionnaire was designed using the Questionnaire Star platform and distributed mainly through major online social media platforms. As of February 24, 2023, a total of 54 questionnaires were collected, and 4 invalid questionnaires with short filling time and unclear answers were excluded, and the final number of valid questionnaires was 50, with an effective rate of 92.59%. The characteristics of the survey sample were as follows: 44.0% were male and 56.0% were female; 96.0% of the subjects were between 19 and 27 years old; 90.0% of the respondents obtained bachelor degree or above; all subjects were users of electric toothbrush products.

3.5 Construction of Mapping Model Based on Quantitation Theory Type I

According to Table 1, according to the Quantitative Class I theory, if the sample has the corresponding category modeling feature, it is assigned a value of 1, and the opposite is 0. The mean value of perceptual imagery evaluation, modeling elements and category features were coded to form the perceptual evaluation matrix of 12 electric toothbrush samples, which is shown in Table 2. Assuming the modeling element of electric toothbrush as the independent variable X and the mean value of perceptual vocabulary evaluation as the dependent variable Y, multiple linear regression analysis was conducted using SPSS 24.0 software to obtain the mapping relationship between the modeling design element and perceptual imagery. At this point, the linear mathematical model between the evaluation value of perceptual vocabulary and the modeling design elements of electric toothbrush was expressed as follows:

$$y = \lambda_{11}X_{11} + \lambda_{12}X_{12} + \lambda_{13}X_{13} + \cdots + \lambda_{ij}X_{ij} + M \tag{1}$$

Where, y represents the mean value of perceptual vocabulary evaluation; λ_{11}, $\lambda_{12}, \cdots$, λ_{ij} is the regression coefficient of the independent variable; X_{11}, $X_{12}, \cdots$, X_{ij} is the modeling design element; and M is a constant term.

3.6 Experimental Results and Analysis

The data were brought into SPSS 24.0 for multiple linear regression analysis to obtain a library of associations between modeling design elements of electric toothbrushes and perceptual imagery, see Table 3. The absolute magnitude of the standard regression coefficients in the table reflects the degree of influence of a shape category on the target perceptual imagery, and the positive or negative indicates the direction of influence on the target perceptual imagery. The vocabulary of perceptual imagery (simple, rounded, cute, individual, innovative, and delicate) is positively correlated with the regression coefficient, and the larger the absolute value of the modeling design elements, the more representative the imagery is. Different perceptual imagery is composed of different shapes to be influential respectively [15]. From this, corresponding modeling design suggestions can be inferred.

Table 2. Perceptual evaluation matrix of electric toothbrush samples.

	Mean value						Modeling elements						
							X_1			$\cdots$	X_5		
	Y_1	Y_2	Y_3	Y_4	Y_5	Y_6	X_{11}	X_{12}	X_{13}	$\cdots$	X_{51}	X_{52}	X_{53}
A	1.12	−1.24	−1.74	0.4	0.36	0.44	0	0	1	$\cdots$	1	0	0
B	1.70	1.70	0.74	0.22	−0.1	0.74	0	1	0	$\cdots$	1	0	0
C	1.02	1.34	0.78	0.88	0.92	1.18	0	1	0	$\cdots$	1	0	0
D	−0.36	0.7	−0.02	−0.20	−0.10	−0.1	1	0	0	$\cdots$	0	1	0
E	−0.4	−1.32	−1.38	1.18	0.96	1.22	0	1	0	$\cdots$	1	0	0
F	1.12	−0.88	−1.06	−0.28	−0.28	0.6	0	0	1	$\cdots$	1	0	0
G	1.16	0.82	0.08	0.68	0.62	0.54	0	1	0	$\cdots$	1	0	0
H	0.84	1.66	1.00	0.76	0.78	0.58	0	0	1	$\cdots$	0	0	1
I	−1.42	−0.16	−0.32	0.58	0.36	−0.32	1	0	0	$\cdots$	0	1	0
J	−0.48	0.36	−0.3	−0.18	−0.26	0.48	0	1	0	$\cdots$	1	0	0
K	0.24	−0.50	−0.72	−0.22	−0.40	−0.72	0	0	1	$\cdots$	0	1	0
L	−0.74	0.64	0.08	0.90	0.64	0.92	0	1	0	$\cdots$	1	0	0

4   Design Practice

This study is based on the "personalized" sensual imagery style for innovative design practice, in which Option A is the personalized style, X_{12}, X_{21}, X_{31}, X_{42}, X_{53} modeling elements are selected for combination; Option B is the popular style, X_{13}, X_{24}, X_{32}, X_{44}, X_{51} modeling elements are selected for combination. The software Rhino is used for computer 3D modeling, and Keyshot is used for material rendering, and the final effect is shown in Fig. 3. Meanwhile, the design scheme was evaluated for perceptual intention, proving the accuracy and effectiveness of perceptual engineering in the design of electric toothbrush modeling.

Table 3. The association library of modeling elements and perceptual imagery.

	X_1			X_2				X_3				X_4				X_5		
	X_{11}	X_{12}	X_{13}	X_{21}	X_{22}	X_{23}	X_{24}	X_{31}	X_{32}	X_{33}	X_{34}	X_{41}	X_{42}	X_{43}	X_{44}	X_{51}	X_{52}	X_{53}
Y_1	-0.16	-0.44	0.54	0.10	0.21	-0.25	-0.12	-0.84	0.34	1.31	-0.87	0.19	-0.74	-0.20	0.69	0.79	-0.36	-0.49
Y_2	0.17	0.08	-0.27	-0.75	-0.26	0.48	0.51	-0.31	0.39	0.83	-0.94	0.80	-0.21	-0.70	0.10	-0.45	0.17	0.08
Y_3	-0.04	0.29	-0.41	-0.63	-0.08	0.41	0.14	-0.38	0.36	0.57	-0.71	0.52	-0.13	-0.36	-0.18	-0.64	-0.04	0.29
Y_4	-0.05	0.73	-0.23	0.51	0.23	0.25	-0.55	0.23	-0.04	0.21	0.05	0.05	0.35	0.03	0.03	-0.05	0.73	-0.23
Y_5	0.06	0.54	-0.21	0.77	0.02	0.22	-0.61	0.05	0.09	0.46	-0.22	0.13	0.22	-0.05	0.09	0.06	0.54	-0.21
Y_6	-0.15	0.83	-0.27	0.92	0.22	0.08	-0.80	-0.06	0.26	0.84	-0.62	0.32	0.44	-0.06	-0.28	-0.15	0.83	-0.27

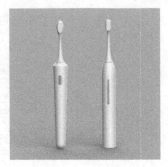

Fig. 3. Electric toothbrush modeling design practice.

5 Conclusion

Based on the concept of human-computer interaction, this study uses theories and methods related to Kansei Engineering to scientifically and effectively capture users' perceptual evaluation of electric toothbrush modeling, construct a mapping relationship between modeling features and perceptual imagery, and quantify the correlation between modeling features and perceptual imagery in the form of data, and combine the modeling with higher contribution to generate design prototypes that conform to the corresponding imagery style, so as to guide the modeling of electric toothbrush design. Practice shows that this method can clarify the design direction of product innovation, meet the emotional needs of users, and promote the human-machine interaction between users and electric toothbrush products. At the same time, the method can also be applied to other product designs with multiple combinations of styling design elements, providing guidance for the design of product style diversification.

References

1. Chen, Y., et al.: Innovative design of home water dispenser based on users' perceptual needs. Packag. Eng. **08**, 173–179+197 (2020). https://doi.org/10.19554/j.cnki.1001-3563. 2020.08.024
2. Zhang, J., Jin, X.: Product image design oriented by perceptual elements - taking smart speakers as an example. Des. Art Res. **05**, 115–120 (2019)
3. Cheng, Z., et al.: Parametric design of car wheels based on perceptual imagery. J. Mach. Des. **04**, 135–141 (2022). https://doi.org/10.13841/j.cnki.jxsj.2022.04.020
4. Wei, S., Liang, J.: Grey correlation analysis and evaluation of modified hanbok based on Kansei Engineering. Wool Text. J. **02**, 94–100 (2022). https://doi.org/10.19333/j.mfkj.202 10807307
5. Shen, Y., et al.: Candy packaging design based on Kansei Engineering. Packag. Eng. **06**, 280–285 (2020). https://doi.org/10.19554/j.cnki.1001-3563.2020.06.044
6. Liu, M., et al.: Research on product form design based on Kansei Engineering-Eye movement test of insulated water dispenser as an example. J. Shanghai Univ. Technol. **05**, 504–511 (2020). https://doi.org/10.13255/j.cnki.jusst.20191122008
7. Li, Q., Huang, L., Li, M.: Female electric toothbrush texture imagery perception and design. Packag. Eng. **08**, 108–114+136 (2022). https://doi.org/10.19554/j.cnki.1001-3563. 2022.08.014

8. Zhu, L.: Research on human-machine interface design of automotive instrumentation based on Kansei Engineering. Wuhan Textile University (2011). https://kns.cnki.net/KCMS/detail/detail.aspx?dbname=CMFD2012&filename=1011296042.nh
9. Zhang, X.: Research on the design of lamps based on Kansei Engineering. North China University of Technology (2019). https://kns.cnki.net/KCMS/detail/detail.aspx?dbname=CMFD201902&filename=1019156133.nh
10. Zhao, X., et al.: Research on the design of electric kettle shape based on Kansei Engineering. Art Des. (Theor.) **06**, 117–121 (2021). https://doi.org/10.16824/j.cnki.issn10082832.2021.06.031
11. Cong, H.: Inverse parametric modeling based on morphological analysis method. Manuf. Autom. **05**, 115–119 (2016)
12. Wang, X.: Simple intelligent water dispenser design based on morphological analysis method. Mach. Build. Autom. **03**, 140–142 (2019). https://doi.org/10.19344/j.cnki.issn1671-5276.2019.03.036
13. Wang, X., et al.: Electric mobility scooter styling design based on quantitative class I theory. Mech. Des. Manuf. **07**, 165–169 (2020). https://doi.org/10.19356/j.cnki.1001-3997.2020.07.039
14. Xu, X., et al.: Study of center control panel modeling design based on Quantitative Class I Theory. Packag. Eng. **04**, 175–181+250 (2022). https://doi.org/10.19554/j.cnki.1001-3563.2022.04.021
15. Report Network 168. https://baijiahao.baidu.com/s?id=1713403444023067715&wfr=spider&for=pc. Accessed 19 Apr 2023
16. China Research Network. https://www.chinairn.com/news/20220125/100333652.shtml. Accessed 19 Apr 2023
17. Zhao, M.: Electric toothbrushes to defend oral health, thousands of brands flocked to tap into the tens of billions of dollars market. CHINA APPLIANCE No. 20 (2021)
18. Liu, Y., Liu, L.: Study on the design of ceramic wine bottle based on Kansei Engineering. Packag. Eng.. Eng. **20**, 330–340 (2021). https://doi.org/10.19554/j.cnki.1001-3563.2021.20.039

Proposal of Kansei Support System to Choose Menu Based on a Survey at Kaiten-Sushi Restaurant

Atsuhiro Watanabe[1]([☒]) and Namgyu Kang[2]

[1] Department of System Information Science, Future University Hakodate, Hakodate, Japan
b1019084@fun.ac.jp
[2] Future University Hakodate, Hakodate, Japan

Abstract. In recent years, the development of food culture and transportation has increased our chances of meeting unknown dishes. However, it is not easy to choose these new dishes without enough information about them. Although there is much research on menu choice and new dining experiences, but only some research is based on the behavior analysis of menu choice at a restaurant. Moreover, there have yet to be approached to propose a menu choice system based on this analysis. This study aims to survey users' behavior when choosing a menu at Kaiten-Sushi restaurants and clarify users' dissatisfaction and factors to interrupt the choice of new dishes using the service blueprint method and the customer journey map method. Moreover, the proposal of a new support system to choose a menu based on the survey result is the final purpose of this research. Therefore, we visited three Kaiten-sushi restaurants in Hakodate and investigated dining experiences there. As a result, we could extract the following three points; 1) There is an active type of menu choice and a passive one at Kaiten-sushi restaurants. 2) There are different types of expressions of allergy information, easy to understand or not. 3) Different languages in the menu information depending on the restaurant. Based on these results, we proposed a new Kansei support system. The Kansei support system has two main features; 1) Allergy information for specific products is expressed on each dish information page of the system. 2) The new expression of dish information which users can be interested to learn new information about the dish.

Keywords: Behavior Analysis · Menu Choice · Kansei System

1 Introduction

In recent years, the number of people traveling between Japan and other countries has been increasing due to the development of transportation systems. According to the Japan Tourism Agency, the number of foreign visitors to Japan increased fivefold from 2011 to 2019 [1]. Due to COVID-19, 2020 and 2021 decreased significantly, but after the end, we estimate that the number of travelers to Japan will increase again. An increase in travelers has increased our chances of meeting unknown dishes. However, choosing these

C. Stephanidis et al. (Eds.): HCII 2023, CCIS 1958, pp. 520–527, 2024.
https://doi.org/10.1007/978-3-031-49215-0_62

new dishes is not easy. That means choosing these new dishes requires more information about them. For example, we often choose only familiar dishes from multiple choices on a menu. That means we lose the opportunity to encounter a variety of dishes. This study focuses on Kaiten-Sushi as a research subject. Sushi is a typical example of Japanese food culture. Therefore, Japan's Kaiten-Sushi market continues to grow. According to a survey by Teikoku Databank, the Japanese Kaiten-sushi market expanded 1.6 times from 2011 to 2021 [2]. However, in recent years, the depreciation of the yen and declining marine resources have led to an upward trend in sushi prices. Therefore, the Kaiten-Sushi market needs to create value other than price to maintain and improve user satisfaction. This background is consistent with our research.

2 Previous Studies

There is much research on menu choice. For example, Murai et al. suggested adding specific images during food choice increased users' restful feelings and preference for healthy foods [3]. Likewise, Kato et al. indicated that users' emotions change, and their food choice is affected by adding an image that differs from their image of a particular food [4]. Furthermore, Hosoya et al. suggested that the choice rate of pop-out products increased when users made menu choices, suggesting that pop-outs help choose various products [5].

There is also much research on new dining experiences. For example, Ohno created a "table-type projection mapping system" focusing on tableware and desk surfaces and attempted to visualize the effects on people's emotions and sensibilities [6]. In addition, Konishi focused on soup curry menus and investigated the relationship between the spiciness of the soup curry and its understandability, as well as the order of the ordering process. Based on the results, he proposed a new soup curry menu [7].

In conclusion, although there is much research on menu choice and new dining experiences, only some research is based on the behavior analysis of menu choice at a restaurant. Moreover, there have yet to be approached to propose a menu choice system based on this analysis.

3 Purpose

This study aims to survey users' behavior when choosing a menu at Kaiten-Sushi restaurants and clarify users' dissatisfaction and factors to interrupt the choice of new dishes using the service blueprint method and the customer journey map method. Moreover, the final purpose of this research is to propose a new support system to choose a menu based on the survey result.

4 Method

4.1 Field Survey

We conducted the field survey at two Kaiten-Sushi named Sushiro, Hamasushi, and Uobei. At each restaurant, we recorded the customer's behavior from entering the restaurant, choosing a menu item, eating, and exiting, as well as the things they touched on the electronic menu choice system (Fig. 1).

Fig. 1. Photographs recorded during the field survey

4.2   Creation of a Table of Dining Experiences

Based on the records from the field survey, we compiled a timeline of the dining experience from entry to exit on a single table. We also described what we could analyze regarding users' feelings, thoughts, and actions in the table. This is useful in determining whether the service is appropriate to the user's needs. The table also makes it easier to understand what changes have occurred to the users over time. We used Figma, a design tool for web design, graphic design, application UI design, and wireframe creation, to create the table. In addition, we referred to the service blueprint method and the customer journey map in visualizing the table.

4.3   Comparison and Analysis Using Tables

Based on the table, we compared and analyzed Sushiro, Hama-sushi, and Uobei. In the comparison, we described the number of steps to complete the menu choice on the tablet device, the mechanism, and its problems. We also described the issues we noticed things while our dining experience.

5   Results

Figures 2, 3 and 4 illustrate the created table of three Kaiten-sushi restaurants. By summarizing a series of dining experiences chronologically, we could visualize the differences in the user's burden situations during menu choice and product arrival in the dining experience at Kaiten-Sushi restaurants.

5.1   Menu Selection

Menu choice acts can be classified into two main categories: Active and Passive choice acts. Active choice act is a choice made with a decision to eat in advance. Passive choice is a choice made under the influence of an external source after the menu choice has begun (Fig. 5).

5.2   Allergy Labeling

The electronic menu choice system at Sushiro and Uobei had all information on allergies on one page of the system. However, the system at Hama Sushi displayed information on allergies for each sushi product on their page. Therefore, the electronic menu choice

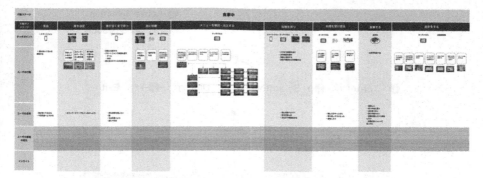

Fig. 2. Table summarizing Sushiro in chronological order

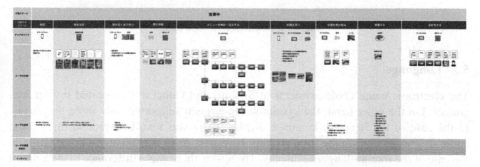

Fig. 3. Table summarizing Hamasushi in chronological order

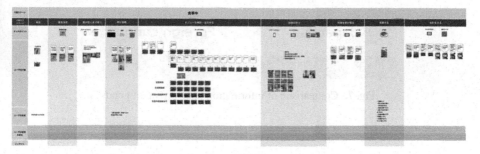

Fig. 4. Table summarizing Uobei in chronological order

system at Sushiro and Uobei had less exposure to allergy information because the information was displayed in a list. In contrast, the system at Hamasushi had multiple occasions to check the allergy information, for example, each time a product was choosed. Therefore, users are more likely to obtain information if the information is grouped by-product rather than if all the information is posted at once (Fig. 6).

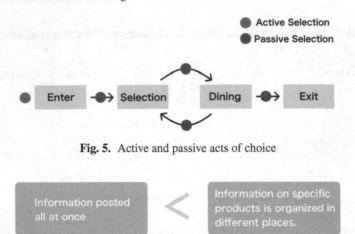

Fig. 5. Active and passive acts of choice

Fig. 6. Comparison of each store

5.3 Language

The electronic menu choice systems at Sushiro and Uobei are supported in four languages. On the other hand, the system at Hamasushi supported only three languages. In the case of the Japanese-language display, there was text, background music, and audio information when the food arrived. However, there was no audio information in the case of the foreign-language display. Therefore, there was a difference in the amount of information that could be obtained depending on the language. We hypothesized that this may have influenced the choice of a menu for an unknown dish (Fig. 7).

Fig. 7. Comparison of information upon arrival of goods

6   Discussion

Based on our analysis, we got the following three results;

1) There is an active type of menu choice and a passive one at Kaiten-sushi restaurants. Furthermore, users' passive choices are more likely to be influenced by external information, and passive choices are essential in creating a richer dining experience.

2) There are different types of expressions of allergy information on the electronic menu choice systems, easy to understand or not to depend on the restaurant. For example, users are easier to understand allergy information when it is displayed on each sushi product than when it is displayed on one page of the system.

3) Different languages in the menu information depend on the restaurant. In particular, the amount of information involved in menu choice could be higher when a customer uses the system in Japanese than in a foreign language version. So, depending on the used language, this information difference influences the act of menu choice in unknown cuisines.

Therefore, we inferred that the above factors are essential in menu choice and inhibit choice.

7 Proposal of Prototype

7.1 Proposal Concept

Our prototype of an electronic menu choice system is proposed with the following two concepts;

1) The system has allergy information for each sushi product on each product page. The allergy information is essential for choosing a menu for some customers.
2) With an attractive showing of information about the new sushi product, a customer is interested in the new sushi product, which might lead to a new menu choice. In addition, animations and images effectively convey information about the new sushi product to customers who cannot understand specific languages, such as Japanese.

Furthermore, we designed the screen so they can switch screens easily when they want to see information on other products. We post below a transition diagram of the system (Fig. 8).

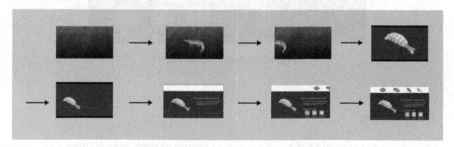

Fig. 8. The transition diagram of the system

7.2 System Features

Since the information that attracts the customer's interest is essential in choosing a new sushi product, an animation video is used in the new system. As an example, in the "Extra-large wild tiger prawn" video, the following two pieces of information were shown: "A high-class food along with lobster" and "The stripes on the rounded body resemble the wheels of a car" (Fig. 9).

Fig. 9. Information of interest to users

The experimental investigation in Sect. 3 suggested that users may be more likely to use the system if allergy information is displayed for each product rather than in a single location. Based on these results, we designed the proposed system to display allergy information for each product. When showing the information, the icons are enlarged, and the names are written in text as additional information (Fig. 10).

Fig. 10. Allergy Information

8 Conclusion

In this study, we surveyed to analyze a series of dining experiences at three Kaiten-sushi restaurants. As a result, we could extract the following three points;

1) Users' passive choices in dining experience are more likely to be influenced by external information, and passive choices are essential in creating a richer dining experience.
2) Users are easier to understand allergy information when it is displayed on each sushi product than when it is displayed on one page of the system.
3) In particular, the amount of information involved in menu choice could be higher when a customer uses the system in Japanese than in a foreign language version. So, depending on the used language, this information difference influences the act of menu choice in unknown cuisines.

Based on these results, we proposed a new Kansei support system to choice various menus with the concept of 'Getting various information with fun.'

The Kansei support system has two main features;

1) Allergy information for specific sushi products is expressed on each dish information page of the system.
2) The information is easier to understand with fun, regardless of language.

9 Outlook

We proposed a new menu choice support system in this study but have not conducted any evaluation experiments yet. We need to verify whether the proposed system leads to more new menu choices than the conventional system. Therefore, we plan to conduct an evaluation experiment, analyze the results, and continue to improve the proposed menu choi support system based on the results.

References

1. Japan Tourism Agency: Number of Foreign Visitors to Japan and Number of Japanese Departing from Japan. https://www.mlit.go.jp/kankocho/siryou/toukei/in_out.html. Accessed 9 July 2022
2. PR TIMES: Kaiten Sushi Market Booming, Corona Disaster at Record High, Major Chains Increase by 800 Restaurants in10 Years. https://prtimes.jp/main/html/rd/p/000000474.000043465.html. Accessed 10 July 2022
3. Murai, M., Kato, K., Tsuzuki, K., Kasaoka, S.: Video-induced resting emotion increases preference for healthy foods. Kita-Kanto Med. **71**(3), 169–176 (2021)
4. Kato, K., Kasaoka, S., Tsuzuki, K.: Influence of emotional state on food choice - does the evaluation of "deliciousness" depend on the emotional state? Proc. Japan. Psychol. Assoc. Conf. **78**, 2AM-2-054–2AM-2-054 (2014)
5. Hosoya, M., et al.: An investigation of the influence of pop-out on product selection behavior. Trans. Inf. Process. Soc. Japan **62**(12), 2079–2089 (2021)
6. Ohno, S.: Possibility of Expanding Food Expression Using IT - Focusing on Proposal and Application of Table-Type Projection Mapping System
7. Konishi, Y.: Analysis and Proposal of a Soup Curry Menu that Easily Conveys Spiciness

A Study on GML-Based Encryption Technology for Open-Source Software License and Service Structure Analysis in Cloud-Based Micro Service Architecture Environment

SeongCheol Yoon[1] , YongWoon Hwang[1] , Won-Bin Kim[2] ,
and Im-Yeong Lee[1(✉)]

[1] Department of Software Convergence, Soonchunhyang University, Asan 31538,
Republic of Korea
{dbstjdcjf333,hyw0123,imylee}@sch.ac.kr
[2] Lsware Inc., Seoul 08504, Republic of Korea
wbkim29@lsware.com

Abstract. Micro-service architecture (MSA) refers to a structure in which several software with different roles are bundled into one service, rather than one or a small number of software when building a service. A lot of software is used to build a service with an MSA structure, and recently, open-source software is being actively used. Open-source software is not always available free of charge as each license exists. However, since commercialized MSA-structured cloud-based software does not provide execution code to consumers, it is difficult to check whether open-source software is used without permission. Therefore, even if the licenses granted by open-source software are violated or open-source software contains potential risks, it is very difficult for consumers to identify these issues. To solve this problem, a graph modeling language (GML) can be used as a method for analyzing the structure of software operating based on the cloud MSA environment and determining the open-source license included in the software. However, since GML contains a lot of information such as software structure and information, it can be abused by analyzing the software structure when GML is leaked. To solve this problem, in this study, we conduct research on how to encrypt GML and perform analysis in the encrypted state.

Keywords: Micro-service architecture (MSA) · Graph modeling language (GML) · Open-source Software · Software License · Encryption

1 Introduction

Recently, rapidly developing ICT is bringing about changes in the development environment and method of software. In particular, as accessibility to software development increases, anyone can easily develop software, so small-scale software is being developed by individual developers, and the developed software is shared through online communities. Therefore, the overall size of the software market is growing rapidly, and the pool of reference software available to developers is also growing. The concept of open-source software that emerged in this environment is recognized and used as the same public goods that anyone can easily use. Open-source software is a type of software that can be used freely if it meets the specified license terms. Therefore, there are various forms, ranging from very small units of software modules to large-scale software contributed by numerous developers. Therefore, for developers who develop software that integrates numerous functions, it is more efficient to utilize open-source software than to directly develop small modules that play a specific role. Therefore, open-source software is used in most software development, and the role of open-source software becomes more important in the case of micro-service architecture (MSA) in which small services are linked to each other to form a system rather than one integrated service.

Open-source software means open software, just like its name. However, there is a limitation that open-source software can only be used under certain conditions. Therefore, in the process of developing or selling software that performs complex functions after development, disputes may arise due to violations of licensing policies if the open-source software used in the software does not meet the conditions set out [1–3]. To avoid this problem, it is necessary to analyze the structure of the software that has been developed to identify conflicting licenses, find alternatives, or enter into new licensing agreements. However, it is difficult to identify the inside of software that has already been developed and is packaged or provided in the form of cloud services, and it is practically impossible to provide source code to companies with analysis technology for structural analysis. Eventually, software developers sell products while hiding a list of open-source software used in the software, and even if some of the open-source software contained in the software exists, it becomes very difficult to recognize and solve the problem. Therefore, to solve this problem, this study identifies the structure of the software and organizes it in the form of Graph Modeling Language (GML) [4–6]. In addition, it proposes a method to determine whether the open-source software used and whether there is a license conflict without disclosing the source code of the software through GML [7].

2   Related Work

2.1   Micro-service Architecture (MSA)

MSA is a software system built through organic connections of numerous services in small units. A typical example is a cloud service. A cloud service is a type of software that can be accessed and used over a network, and users can only use the resources of the cloud service and receive the results back. Users do not know the structure of the software, and service providers can provide complex services in combination with different services over the network, so scalability and usability are very high. However, these advantages can lead to problems such as continuing the service without knowing the inherent vulnerability information of the open-source software or using the software without recognizing the problem of license conflicts between the open-source software. Therefore, means are needed to respond to these problems.

2.2 Graph Modeling Language (GML)

GML is a language and format in which graph structures are expressed in text form. GML can represent hierarchical structures and interrelationships that are characteristic of graphs, and can represent their structures in the form of simple text rather than graphic forms such as shapes. In this study, these features are used to express the structure of the software in the form of GML and to determine whether open-source software has a license conflict based on GML. This method enables structural analysis by a third party without disclosing the detailed code of the software. In addition, source code obfuscation is different from obfuscation because source code obfuscation is a form of securing security by disclosing source code but not easily grasping its structure, whereas the GML method of this study allows the structure to be identified without disclosing source code.

3 Proposed Method

In this chapter, the method proposed in this study is explained.

3.1 Structure of the Whole Study

The overall structure of this research team's research is shown in Fig. 1. In Fig. 1, it is largely composed of *License analysis technology*, *License Conflict Determination Technology*, and *Service Structure Determination Technology*, and various detailed technologies are located in detail. This is a diagram of the final goal of this research team, and in the current study, it is a certificate of performance for the technology indicated by the red frame in Fig. 1. A description of the technology currently under study is detailed in the next section.

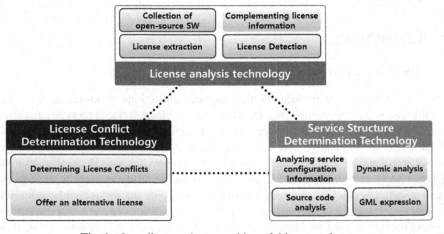

Fig. 1. Overall research composition of this research team

3.2 Open-Source Software License Clause Analysis and License Conflict Determination Logic

In order to understand the structure of open-source software and analyze license conflicts, this research is mainly conducting research on two technologies, which are as follows:

1. Open-source software structure analysis and GML expression technology
   a. Analysis of service structure information expression conditions and identification items to identify software source code service structure
   b. GML-based data (service structure) service structure information expression and identification extraction
   c. Reducing the calculation amount of GML-based license determination by reducing subgraphs unnecessary for license compatibility determination
   d. GML-based data (service structure) relationship analysis
   e. One-way GML code conversion to prevent source code recovery through reverse analysis of GML data
2. Open-source software license analysis technology
   a. Analysis of terms and conditions related to conflicts in open-source software licenses
   b. Extract feature information for each version according to the distribution license of each software
   c. Accelerated license determination
   d. Automatic analysis of software combination structure within software source code and build information-based service

The process performed through the above technology is shown in Fig. 2, and through this, the structure of the open-source software used in the software can be analyzed and license conflicts can be determined without disclosing the software source code.

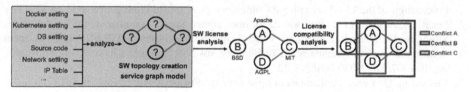

Fig. 2. Open-source Software License Conflict Analysis Process

4 Conclusion

As software development has become commonplace, it has become an era in which anyone can easily develop software. Open-source software, which emerged in this environment, made it possible for anyone to easily create new software by combining open software modules, which accelerated the creation of new open-source software. However, unlike the name of open-source software, each usage condition is presented, which is called a software license. Open-source licenses show unlimited possibilities for software that satisfies the conditions, but if not, negative results such as license disputes, disposal of developed software, and unauthorized use of open-source software may occur. In particular, MSA-based cloud services are developed using numerous open-source software, but because the internal structure cannot be grasped, license compliance of open-source software can be intentionally ignored. Can the cause of these problems is not simply because it is difficult to use open-source software under conditions. This is because it is difficult to analyze each and every license that conflicts with each other in the process of using numerous open-source software complexly, and managing them requires a long development period and high costs. Therefore, in order to solve this problem, the research team studied a method of relatively efficiently analyzing software composed of numerous open-source software such as the MSA environment. To this end, the software structure was analyzed and expressed in GML form, and the license correlation of the open-source software used was analyzed. In addition, in this process, the detailed source code of the software cannot be grasped through the GML structure, so that the source code of the developed software cannot be exposed. Based on these technologies, this study is expected to contribute to more efficient and conflict-free software development in the large-scale MSA software market that is gradually developing.

Acknowledgement. This research was supported by SW Copyright Ecosystem R&D Program through the Korea Creative Content Agency grant funded by the Ministry of Culture, Sports and Tourism in 2023 (Project Name: Development of large-scale software license verification technology by cloud service utilization and construction type, Project Number: RS-2023-00224818, Contribution Rate: 100%).

References

1. Gordon, T.F.: Analyzing open-source license compatibility issues with Carneades. In: Proceedings of the 13th International Conference on Artificial Intelligence and Law (2011)
2. Fendt, O., Jaeger, M.C.: Open source for open source license compliance. In: Bordeleau, F., Sillitti, A., Meirelles, P., Lenarduzzi, V. (eds.) Open Source Systems. OSS 2019. IFIP Advances in Information and Communication Technology, vol. 556. Springer, Cham (2019). https://doi.org/10.1007/978-3-030-20883-7_12
3. McGowan, D.: Legal implications of open-source software. U. Ill. L. Rev., p. 541 (2001)
4. Xia, Y., Glinz, M.: Rigorous EBNF-based definition for a graphic modeling language. In: 2003 Tenth Asia-Pacific Software Engineering Conference. IEEE (2003)
5. Borutzky, W.: Bond graph modeling from an object oriented modeling point of view. Simul. Pract. Theor. **7**(5–6), 439–461 (1999)
6. Miftari, B., et al.: GBOML: graph-based optimization modeling language. J. Open-Source Softw. **7**, 4158 (2022)
7. Rosen, L.: Open-Source Licensing. Software Freedom and Intellectual Property Law (2005)

Author Index

C. Stephanidis et al. (Eds.): HCII 2023, CCIS 1958, pp. 533–538, 2024.
https://doi.org/10.1007/978-3-031-49215-0

Printed in the United States
by Baker & Taylor Publisher Services